THE 12TH SS

VOLUME ONE

D0771876

0 11557 03198 0

THE 12TH SS

VOLUME ONE

The History of the Hitler Youth Panzer Division

Hubert Meyer

STACKPOLE
BOOKS

Published in 2005 by
STACKPOLE BOOKS
5067 Ritter Road
Mechanicsburg, PA 17055
www.stackpolebooks.com

www.jjfpub.mb.ca

Printed in the United States of America

10 9 8 7 6 5 4 3 2 1

FIRST EDITION

Library of Congress Cataloging-in-Publication Data

Meyer, Hubert, 1913–
    [Kriegsgeschichte der 12. SS-Panzerdivision "Hitlerjugend". English]
    The 12th SS : the history of the Hitler Youth Panzer Division / Hubert Meyer ; translated by H. Harri Henschler.— 1st ed.
      p. cm. — (Stackpole Military history series)
    Originally published in English as: The history of the 12. SS-Panzerdivision "Hitlerjugend". Winnipeg, Man. : J.J. Fedorowicz, 1994.
    Includes bibliographical references and index.
    ISBN 0-8117-3198-7
    1. Waffen-SS. SS-Panzerdivision "Hitlerjugend," 12. 2. World War, 1939–1945—Regimental histories—United States. 3. World War, 1939–1945—Tank warfare. 4. World War, 1939–1945—Campaigns—Western Front. I. Meyer, Hubert, 1913– History of the 12. SS-Panzerdivision "Hitlerjugend". II. Title. III. Series.

    D757.5612th .M4913 2005
    940.54'21422—dc22
                               2005001216

This book is dedicated to the gallant soldiers who, at one time, faced each other as enemies, and whose survivors are today's allies. The dead are entitled to our grateful remembrance.

Table of Contents

Translator's Note

A historical work of this nature brings together a variety of many voices. They range from those of the supreme commanders, the staff officers, the unit leaders, to those of the men in the Panzers. Their reporting styles extend from the methodical, impersonal, meticulous, and dry, to the direct conversational manner of describing personal involvement in action, and even every-day, mundane experiences.

It is my hope that the translation of this variety may faithfully reflect the original to the reader.

H. Harri Henschler

Foreword to original English translation first published in 1994

During the second day after their landing in Normandy, British and Canadian troops encountered the first elements of the 12. SS-Panzerdivision "Hitlerjugend" which was being brought up for the counterattack. It became apparent that the Division, ridiculed by the Allied war propaganda as the "Baby-Division", was an elite division. It inspired fear and, at the same time, admiration in its enemies. For a whole month, in bitter combat, it denied the landing force the attack objective of the first day: the city of Caen.

Throughout six weeks of fighting against a brave and vastly superior enemy, the Division blocked his breakthrough to Falaise, thus delaying the formation of the Falaise pocket, and prevented the total destruction of two German armies.

In the rearguard fighting across the Seine River and in Belgium, the Division battled US troops for the first time. After an inadequate refitting with personnel and material, it fought at the focal points of the Battle of the Bulge against American elite divisions.

In February and March 1945, the Division was at the centers of the last successful offensive battles against the Red Army in Slovakia and Hungary. Suffering grave losses, it fought its way back through Hungary and the Vienna Woods to the Soviet-American demarcation line in Lower Austria where it surrendered to American forces on 8 May 1945.

German and foreign military historians have intensively studied the "Hitlerjugend" Division, since it was constantly in action at decisive locations. However, these historians did not have adequate sources available for their studies. Of the twenty-seven war diaries kept by the Divisional staff, the regiments and the battalions, only that of one battalion for the period of one month in action has been preserved. Those of the senior commands, the corps, also no longer exist. Thus, a correct or detailed presentation of the actions of this Division was hardly possible.

After a labor of fourteen years, I was able to submit this Divisional history to the public in the German language. It was my goal to reconstruct the events down to the level of the companies and to present them objectively. To do this, I have used the war diaries, as far as they have survived, of the senior command authorities. In addition, I have made use of the war diaries of the British, Canadian and United States corps and divisions which faced the "HJ" Division. Trustworthy secondary sources were used only to a minimal extent. Furthermore, I evaluated the notes and later reports of former members of the Division and, after extensive comparisons with other data, incorporated them.

I have attempted to describe the events, some of which occurred forty-seven years ago, as they really happened, including the evaluations of the situations, the basis for the decisions, from the view of the time and not to let today's thoughts and opinions be incorporated. The magnitude of elapsed time makes this simultaneously easier and more difficult. I have used the technical language of the period, as it was also used in the preserved orders and reports. The conceptual contents equal those which were also used in the armed forces of the Allies in the west. It is in this light that the reader, who was not a soldier then, should see them. The verbatim reports on events are meant to convey to the reader the atmosphere in which these events occurred, and to relate the actions and feelings of the individual soldiers.

I have restricted myself to describing the facts. This also brought some scars to light, but the demand for truthful reporting makes this unavoidable. This is the only way in which factual understanding can be achieved. The final judgment is left to the reader.

Many surviving soldiers of this Division, of all ranks, have collaborated in producing this book. For that, I am very grateful to them. Particular thanks are due to the former soldiers and the friends in Great Britain, France, Canada, and the United States for their understanding support of my work.

After the war, I repeatedly took part in battlefield studies with British, Canadian, and United States veterans in Normandy and the Ardennes. Former enemies, who have been joined as allies for a long period of time now, met each other in a spirit of comradeship on the battlefields of the Second World War.

This encouraged me to aspire to the publication of my book in the English language. I owe a debt of gratitude to Mr. John J. Fedorowicz for having taken on this project. My thanks are also due to the translator, Mr. H. Harri Henschler, who successfully solved a difficult task with expertise and empathy.

May this book become a useful contribution to military history and, at the same time, serve the promotion of reconciliation.

Hubert Meyer
Leverkusen, Spring 1992

PART I

The Formation of the Division and Its Preparation for Action

CHAPTER 00.1
The Plan for the Formation of the Division

The first weeks of the year 1943, almost three-and-one-half years after the start of the Polish campaign from which had developed the Second World War, brought two events which had a determining influence on the further course of the war.

During the period of 14 to 26 January, US President F. D. Roosevelt and the British Prime Minister Winston Churchill, with their advisers, met in Casablanca, Morocco. They determined the future political and military strategy as it applied to the Western Allies. Above all, considerations and decisions on the "Second Front" which Stalin had demanded to relieve the Soviets, formed part of their deliberations. Even more important, and in its impact of greater consequence, was the decision, as conveyed to the world public by Roosevelt on 23 January, that the Western Allies would not agree to a truce without the 'unconditional surrender' of the Axis Powers.

After months of bloody battles, the remains of the 6. Armee, which had advanced in the course of the summer offensive of 1942 far to the east, capitulated at Stalingrad on 2 February. Ninety-one thousand men were taken prisoner. These events led to extraordinary measures on the German side which can most easily be summed up with the expression 'Total War'. It was obvious that a turn-around could only be brought about by uncommon efforts.

The formation of the 'Hitlerjugend' Division was also a part of this program. SS-Gruppenführer Gottlob Berger who, as chief of the SS-Hauptamt (SS central office), was in charge of the replacement office of the Waffen-SS, became responsible for the provision of personnel in cooperation with the supreme command of the Wehrmacht (army) and its subordinate recruiting offices. It was probably his idea to create a new division consisting exclusively of volunteers from the Hitler-jugend (Hitler youth) born in the year 1926. The division was to be a symbol of the willingness of the German youth to sacrifice itself and of its will to achieve victory. Berger initially won over the Stabsführer (chief of staff) of the Reichs-jugendführung (Reich youth directorate) Helmut Möckel for this plan.

On 10 February 1943, Adolf Hitler gave his agreement in principle. This was conveyed by the Reichsführer SS (Reich leader SS) in a letter to the Reichsjugendführer (Reich youth leader) Artur Axmann of 13 February 1943. To quote:

> I have submitted to the Führer your offer, on behalf of the youths born in 1926, to form a division of volunteers for the Waffen-SS, and of the same value as the "Leibstandarte". I have also informed him of your desire and request that this division be identified in a manner which would clearly emphasize its origins and its

simultaneous membership in the HJ. The Führer was highly pleased and has directed me to convey to you that you should immediately begin the recruiting of volunteers. Confidentially, I can inform you that the Führer, based on the reality of the situation, will likely direct that the volunteers will report without having to first go through the national labor service term.

I have reported to the Führer that all SS-Führer, who are also HJ-Führer, will be transferred into this division. I have further proposed that the name "Hitlerjugend" be conferred on the division, as well as the name "Herbert Norkus" on one of its units. The Führer has not yet made a final decision on the bestowal of the names, but he did make positive remarks.

I may now request that you discuss the details of recruiting and examination of the volunteers with SS-Gruppenführer Berger.

During a number of discussions between the Reichsjugend leadership and Gruppenführer Berger and his colleagues, the planning was decided upon and the preparatory measures agreed on. The details were described, based on preserved documents, in a dissertation by Gerhard Rempel for a doctorate in philosophy at the University of Wisconsin in 1971, with the title "The Misguided Generation: Hitler Youth and SS: 1933–1945". The author is an ethnic German, born in 1934, from the Ukraine who had relocated to the Warthegau between 1943–45, lived in West Germany from 1945 to 1949 and then emigrated to the USA. It is questionable if the few preserved documents are representative of the whole. They were judged to be so by Rempel since he had no other sources of information. It appears to be sufficient to state here only the most important points.

Berger did not involve the command office of the Waffen-SS in the initial planning since he expected to find no agreement there. The command felt that it was more sensible to replace the losses in existing divisions, or those in the process of being established, time and again and to keep them at full fighting strength rather than to set up new divisions and, additionally, keep the old ones at fighting strength.[1] The participation of the command office was essential, but by the time it became aware of the planning the basic decisions had already been made.

The plan envisioned:

1. The volunteers were to be recruited from those born during the first half of 1926. Minimum height for the infantry: 170 cm; for the communications, Panzer and motorcycle units, in exceptional cases if boys had had special training, 168 cm. (The minimum height for the sister-division Leibstandarte SS "Adolf Hitler": 180 cm). The boys had to be fit for active service and should have been, preferably, in possession of the HJ achievement badge.

2. The Reichsjugend leadership had to provide 30,000 Hitler youths from among whom those qualified would be selected by the replacement offices of the Waffen-SS. Those boys who were in vocational training had to complete it. Exceptions were possible and had to be justified by the Reichsjugend leadership. (The exemption from the national labor service was only ordered during the recruiting campaign by a Führer decree).

3. All those found to be fit for service had to serve a six-week period in a pre-military training camp.

4. The division, to be set-up, required approximately 840 Führer (leaders) and 4,000 Unterführer (non-commissioned leaders). Of these, the HJ was to provide 400 officers of the army who were serving in positions up to battalion commander, and 2,500 non-commissioned leaders.

5. The ongoing recruiting action for 35,000 replacements for the Waffen-SS was not to be influenced by the special action for the Hitlerjugend Division.[2]

The following timetable was established:

1. On 4 April 43, 2,000 HJ Führer, freed from the national labor service by a decree of the Führer, were to report at 20 pre-military training camps, together with instructors of the Waffen-SS. After four weeks of training they would be qualified to be used as assistant instructors in pre-military training camps.

2. On 1 May, 6,000 mustered and accepted volunteers born in 1926 were to report to pre-military training camps. A further 2,000 volunteers born in 1926 were to report at a special camp in St. Veith/Oberkrain for special training. The 8,000 volunteers were to be trained for six weeks until 15 June by instructors from the Waffen-SS and assistant instructors referred to under 1. above.

3. On 1 July, the 8,000 volunteers, born in 1926 and mentioned under 2. above, had to be available to report to the division under formation. The 2,000 assistant instructors born in 1925 were to report to the training institutes for non-commissioned leaders of the Waffen-SS and would be used as non—commissioned leaders after completion of the training.

4. On 1 July, a further 6,000 volunteers born in 1926 were to report to the pre-military training camps and 2,000 volunteers to the special camp in St. Veith. The Waffen-SS alone now had to provide the instructors in St. Veith. (It cannot be determined from the documents who was to take the place of the 2,000 assistant instructors born in 1925 in the other camps). The training was to be completed on 15 August.

5. On 1 September, 16,000 volunteers were to be available for training in the division, as well as the 2,000 prospective non-commissioned leaders in training at the institutes.

6. In order to fill the Führer (officer) positions, 600 HJ Führer serving in the field and reserve units of the Waffen-SS as non-commissioned Führer and men were to be pulled out and brought together for a Führer course. Those who could not pass the course would be used as non-commissioned Führer in the "HJ" Division.[3]

These proposed plans could not be realized in the expected scope and time frame. Initially there were problems in attracting enough volunteers, partly because the reasons for the recruiting drive were not immediately made public. It was believed that the populace, in memory of Langemark in 1914, would be afraid that the volunteers would be sent into battle insufficiently trained. In addition there were problems with the chambers of commerce and industry since apprentices, who would normally complete their training in autumn, were to be called up prematurely and without finishing their training. There was also resistance from the Reich education ministry against the call-up prior to completing a normal graduation from school.

Because of these particular circumstances, the adults responsible, parents and guardians, attempted to prevent the boys from volunteering. Their fathers were often in action, and the mothers refused to let their sons go without their concurrence. In some areas, the recruiting officers applied gentle pressure because of this.

The quotas prescribed to the Hitlerjugend could not be achieved in the required time frame because of these obstacles. The number of prospective non-commissioned leaders was also not reached. In addition, it proved impossible to pull the 600 prospective Führer from the troops for training in a special course for the "HJ" Division, since other new formations such as the "Hohenstaufen" and "Frundsberg" divisions also had to fill numerous Führer positions.[4] The various departments involved attempted their utmost to remove the obstacles. Short term solutions were found, but the division itself had to overcome the largest obstacles during the formation and training.

CHAPTER 00.2
Formation—Structure

In June 1943 a Führer's Order on the formation of the division was issued. It read as follows:

1. I order the formation of an SS-Division made up of Hitler youths born in the year 1926. It will be named . . .
2. The day of formation will be 1.6.1943.
3. A pre-military training period of six weeks in a HJ training camp will replace the national labor service for these boys.
4. The cadre groups to be made available to the division will be composed of 400 HJ-Führer in essential positions in the home territories

as Führer (officers) and 2,500 HJ members in essential positions as Unter-führer (noncoms). It is irrelevant if these are members of the reserves of the army, air force (ground personnel) or Waffen-SS.

The Reichsjugendführer will provide the relevant names to the OKW (supreme command of the armed forces) and the Waffen-SS respectively.

5. For reasons of effectiveness the pre-military training will take place in the area of the formation of the division. All departments of the Reich will ensure that clothing and equipment will be available on a timely basis.

6. All questions on details will be settled by the Reichsführer-SS with the supreme command of the armed forces."[1]

Based on this the command office of the Waffen-SS issued an order on the "Formation of the SS-Panzer-Grenadier—Division "Hitlerjugend". A copy of this order is contained in the Annex as Appendix 1.

Paragraph 1. of this order read:

By order of the Führer, the immediate formation of the SS-Panzer-Grenadier-Division "Hitlerjugend" is to begin at the training grounds at Beverloo (northwest of Brussels).[2]

It appears reasonable to initially have a closer look at the structure of the division. It is surprising that it was to be set up as a Panzergrenadier division. On the occasion of a visit by the Inspector General of the Panzer forces, Generaloberst (four-star general) Guderian, to the division in autumn 1943, this question was addressed by the divisional command. It was requested that a change to a Panzerdivision should be brought about so that both divisions of the I. SS-Panzerkorps (tank corps) would be structured identically and could be used in the same manner. This request was indeed granted soon after. On 30 October 1943 the command office of the Waffen-SS issued an order which contained as its most important paragraphs:

1. The Führer has ordered the implementation of the attached structure for the SS-Panzer.Gren.Div. -"Hitlerjugend" and the renaming to 12. SS-Panzer-Division "Hitlerjugend".

2. The re-structuring has to take place using existing personnel, weapons and equipment.[3]

A copy of this order with appendices is contained in the Annex as Appendix 2. The structure of a Panzerdivision differs from that of a Panzergrenadierdivision in the following important points:

Division Staff: no war correspondent platoon

Panzer regiment: no Panzerpionier (engineer) company

Panzergrenadier regiments: heavy infantry gun company instead of motorized Z, self-propelled guns; no motorcycle company with the regiment; in the Panzer-grenadier battalions, each a Panzergrenadier company with an additional platoon with two 7,5 cm and three 3,7 cm guns; and in the heavy company a Pionier platoon.

Reconnaissance unit (Aufklürungsabteilung): one armored reconnaissance company, half-tracks instead of wheeled vehicles; one motorcycle company instead of a reconnaissance company with half-tracks.

Armored assault gun unit with 45 guns instead of an assault gun unit with 40 assault guns: in the heavy unit three batteries of heavy self-propelled field howitzers instead of motorized Z.

Flak (anti-aircraft) unit: additionally one searchlight platoon

Tank destroyer unit: not applicable

Pionier battalion: bridge column K instead of B

Communications unit: Panzer communications company instead of motorized communications company.

Indeed, at the end of its formation the "Hitlerjugend" division had a structure which was different from the one ordered on 30 October. This was caused partly by changes in the official structure, partly by decisions of the divisional command on its own. The latter were not shown in the reports on the active structure which had to be submitted to the inspector general of the armored forces together with the so-called situation reports on a monthly basis. They were replaced by the structure ordered by the Führer's executive department. The official structure as of 1.6.44 can be found in the text on pages D-4 to D-6, the situation report. The real structure differed from the official in the following essential points:

Panzerregiment 12:

I. Abteilung (detachment):

No 2 cm Flak (anti-aircraft) platoon, no maintenance platoon but a repair unit (I-Staffel) in the strength of approximately one company.

II. Abteilung:

Instead of the 2 cm Flak platoon with 6 guns: 1 Panzer-Flak platoon with three 2 cm four barreled guns on Panzer IV chassis, a new and distinctive construction which became the model for the Flakpanzer "Wirbelwind" (tornado). 5 Panzer companies with 17 Pz IVs each instead of 4 companies with 22 Pz IVs each; a complete maintenance company, not 'without 2. -platoon'.

Panzerjügerabteilung 12 (tank destroyer detachment):

Initially, only two companies were equipped with the Jagdpanzer IVs (tank destroyer). The 3. company received 7,5 cm Pak 40 mot Z (anti-tank gun). At an undetermined time this company, too, received - Jagdpanzer IVs.

Panzergrenadierregiment 25:

Received an additional reconnaissance company which was structured in the same way as the motorcycle company of the Panzergrenadier-division and equipped with Volkswagen.

Numbering of the companies:

13. (heavy infantry gun) company
14. (2 cm Flak) company
15. (reconnaissance) company
16. (Pionier-engineer) company
Panzergrenadierregiment 26:
  The same as Regiment 25.
Artillerieregiment:
  The Werferabteilung 12 (mortar detachment) was carried as an independent detachment, not as IV. Abteilung of the Artillerieregiment.

The structure of the division can also be found in the list of units which
was established by the German Red Cross tracing service. It also contains the
field post numbers of all units. Appendix 3 shows this list.

In June 1943, the commander of SS-Panzergrenadier-regiment 1 of the 1.
SS-Panzerdivision Leibstandarte SS "Adolf Hitler", SS-Oberführer Fritz Witt,
holder of the Knight's Cross with Oak Leaves, was appointed as commander
of the "Hitlerjugend" division and received orders to set up the division. A
formation staff was established which initially had its offices in the barracks of
the Leibstandarte at Berlin-Lichterfelde where the Panzergrenadier Ausbil-
dungs (training) and Ersatz (reserve) battalion 1 was located since the beginning of the war.

The "LAH" division was in action at the front in Russia/Ukraine at this
time. It had taken part in the withdrawal fighting in the Charkow area and
the re-capture of the city, during which strong enemy forces were destroyed,
during the months of February and March within the framework of the
SS-Panzerkorps. The division had suffered significant losses during the
extremely heavy defensive and offensive battles. Since approximately April
1943 it was being refitted in the Charkow area and preparing for the offensive against the Russian front bulge at Bjelgorod/Kursk. In addition to the
divisional commander, and despite the losses it had suffered, the "LAH" had
to give up a number of officers, noncoms and specialists of lower rank to the
newly-established division. This was an additional blood letting. To fill the
commander posts in the "HJ", the following were transferred:
  To the division staff:
    as 1. Generalstabsoffizier (Ia) (general staff officer)
    Sturmbannführer (major) Hubert Meyer, whose last post had been
    commander of III./SS-Panzer-grenadier-regiment 1. He had been
    posted repeatedly with various units as preparation for general staff
    training since November 1941, and he took part in the 10th general
    staff course at the war academy of the Heer (army) from 15 June to
    30 September 1943. He graduated with the qualification for 1. Gen.
    St. Offz. (general staff officer) of a Panzer division;
    as 2. Generalstabsoffizier (Ib)
    Hauptsturmführer (captain) Fritz Buchsein from the divisional staff
    of "LAH";

as Divisionsadjutant (division adjutant)
Hauptsturmführer (captain) Heinrich Springer.

To Panzerregiment 12
as regimental commander
Sturmbannführer (major) Max Wünsche;
as Abteilung (detachment) commanders
Hauptsturmführer Arnold Jürgensen and
Hauptsturmführer Heinz Prinz.

To Panzergrenadierregiment 25 (previously Panzer-grenadier-regiment 1 "Hitlerjugend")
as regimental commander
Obersturmbannführer (lt. colonel) Kurt Meyer;
as battalion commander
Hauptsturmführer Hans Scappini.

To Panzergrenadierregiment 26 (previously 2 "Hitler-jugend)
as regimental commander
Obersturmbannführer (lt. colonel) Wilhelm Mohnke (from the training and reserve battalion);
as battalion commanders
Hauptsturmführer Bernhard Krause,
Sturmbannführer Bernhard Siebken and
Hauptsturmführer Gerd Bremer.

To Aufklürungsabteilung 12 (reconnaissance unit)
Hauptsturmführer Erich Olboeter.

To Artillerieregiment 12
as regimental commander
Sturmbannführer Fritz Schröder;
as detachment commanders
Hauptsturmführer Erich Urbanitz and
Hauptsturmführer Karl Bartling.

To Flakabteilung 12 (anti-aircraft detachment)
Hauptsturmführer Rudolf Fend.

To Panzerjügerabteilung 12 (tank destroyer detachment)
Hauptsturmführer Jakob Hanreich.

To the Werferabteilung (mortar detachment)
Hauptsturmführer Willy Müller.

To the Sanitütsabteilung (medical detachment)
Sturmbannführer Rolf Schulz, MD.

To the divisional supply unit
Hauptsturmführer Rolf Kolitz.

To the maintenance detachment, and at the same time division engineer (Va),
Hauptsturmführer Artur Manthey.

The first of the young volunteers arrived at Lichterfelde at the beginning of July 1943. At the end of July there were approximately 10,000 men. The situation reports from 4 October 1943 onwards indicate the following figures on required strength and shortages of personnel.

Date		Unter-führer	Führer	Men	Aux.
4.10.43	Req. Strength	768	3,957	15,122	
	Reinforcements	20	111	5,130	
	Shortfall	585	3,149	3,641	
1.11.43	Req. Strength	770	4,013	15,057	
	Reinforcements	48	1,554		
	Shortfall	539	2,943	2,556	
1.12.43	Req. Strength	728	appr. 3,923	appr. 14,802	
	Reinforcements	114	4,903		
	Shortfall	388	2,616	+2,289	
1.1.44	Req. Strength	720	3,943	14,753	1,095
	Reinforcements	33	1,073		
	Shortfall	347	2,396	+3,118	1,065
3.2.44	Req. Strength	656	3,881	14,460	1,024
	Reinforcements	31	1,515		
	Shortfall	258	2,170	494	
3.3.44	Req. Strength	624	3,878	13,643	1,024
	Reinforcements	29	1,255		
	Shortfall	194	2,008	828	
3.4.44	Req. Strength				
	Reinforcements	44	650		
	Shortfall	169	2,208	+5,718	828
1.6.44	Req. Strength	664	4,575	15,277	(1,103)
	Reinforcements	26	125	341	216
	Shortfall	144	2,192	+2,360	(887)

In May 1944, 2,055 Unterführer and men were transferred to the "LAH" division which had arrived in the former "HJ" quarters in Belgium from Russia for re-fitting. The surplus of soldiers mathematically balanced the shortfall of officers and noncoms. With a total required strength of 20,516 and a total available strength of 20,540, there was a surplus of 24.[4]

The delays in the numerical personnel build-up were also reflected in the availability of weapons, fighting vehicles, motor vehicles and equipment. Figures are available only from the situation reports from 4 October onward. For reasons of clarity, only a few items are shown here.

Date	Req. Avail.	Carbine 98k	Light Machine Guns	Panzer	Armored Pers. Carriers (SPW) and Armored Rec. Vehicles	Artillery Guns	Pak 7,5 cm (Pak 40)	Cars	Trucks
1.10.43	Req.	15,751	1,584	198	347	46	33	1,067	2,152
	Avail.	7,540	431	3	-	20	16	4	8
1.11.43	Req.	15,751	1,605	228	314	46	33	1,102	2,193
	Avail.	9,040	654	10	-	20	16	11	10
1.12.43	Req.	no	no	198	314	46	27	1,102	2,193
	Avail.	data	data	21	15	24	24	4	14
5.1.44	Req.	-	1,761	221	320	47	31	1,067	2,243
	Avail.	12,615	1,173	40	143	40	24	37	702
3.2.44	Req.	-	1,695	217	367	47	31	887	2,012
	Avail.	12.500	1,403	105	241	47	28	547	1,252
3.3.44	Req.	-	1,730	190	413	47	24	814	1,756
	Avail.	12.500	1,495	117	320	52	28	1,000	1,412
3.4.44	Req.	-	1,736	186	387	47	24	903	1,901
	Avail.	12.500	1,495	119	333	52	28	803	1,653
1.6.44	Req.	-	1,730	186	390	47	24	1,007	2,214
	Avail.	12,351	1,628	148	333	52	28	923	1,834

Regarding the number of motor vehicles, it has to be taken into account that the division was equipped with captured Italian vehicles. At the start of the invasion only a portion had been exchanged for German vehicles. Thus, as per the situation report of 1 June 1944, of 1,320 vehicles without cross-country capability, 160 were Italian vans with 420 kg payload and 128 were light trucks with only 800 to 1,000 kg payload. While 92% of the required cars were available, almost half (406) of the required cars with cross-country capability were missing. They had to be replaced with cars without cross-country capability. The situation with the trucks was even worse. The total requirement, numerically, was met at 82,8%. However, of the required number of 1,245 with cross-country capability, 1,011 were missing. Of the required number of tractors up to 5 tons, only 20.4% were available; of the tractors from 8–18 tons, 58%. Thus, there is no validity to the claim in relevant literature that the divisions of the Waffen-SS enjoyed preferential fitting with equipment.

CHAPTER 00.3
Training

Contrary to the widely-spread belief, there was no pre-military training during peace time in the Hitlerjugend (HJ). The Reichsjugendführer of the time, Baldur von Schirach, had refused it quite determinedly and put special emphasis on the artistic education of the boys and girls. The field and track sporting events which were carried out had nothing to do with military training. They were really sport activities which, of course, served to increase physical fitness and to promote personal growth. In this manner, boys grew up in the Hitler-jugend who were physically fit and vigorous, able to fit into a community willingly but without giving up their individuality. Love of the fatherland, a feeling of responsibility and a sense of duty towards the smaller or larger community were, based on their own personal experiences, self-evident to these boys. Before the war, the future Feldmarschall (field marshal) Erwin Rommel, served as liaison officer of the army to the Reichs-jugend leadership for a period of time. He judged then: "There is no trace of mindless drill. Rather too much spontaneity than too little. It is surprising that the boys then adapt to the discipline as recruits without any friction."[1]

During the war, only in 1942, was pre-military training for the 16 to 18 year old boys introduced. It was exclusively in the hands of Hitlerjugend leaders who had been wounded serving as officers and noncoms in the armed forces, and who had been assigned to the Hitlerjugend for this purpose. A former Hitlerjugend leader and Waffen-SS officer, Herbert Taege, wrote in his book "Across the Times—The Face of a Youth in Rise and Ruin" about the pre-military camps:

> The training program of the pre-military camps was restricted to 160 hours. It included firing small-caliber weapons in the frame of the historical shooting sport tradition, and training in terrain in the frame of military sports. At the end of this training the boys received the 'War Training Certificate'. It did not relieve anyone from the basic training in the armed forces.[2]

Most recruits were seventeen years old at the start of their service. The applicants who had been accepted during a second recruiting drive, those born in the second half of the year 1926, were at least sixteen and a-half years old. The four years of war had not passed by the boys without a trace. Their fathers were soldiers, many dead or missing. Their mothers were working outside the home, their teachers and Hitlerjugend leaders were, in most cases, soldiers and had been replaced insufficiently and with difficulty. The bombing raids on the residential quarters of the cities had ripped many of them from their normal environment by destroying their homes and being evacuated. In addition, many of the boys were poorly nourished and had only a limited ability to endure more strenuous physical exertions.

These unexpected circumstances required that unusual priorities had to be established. The divisional commander thus issued an order to all unit leaders. The Divisionsadjutant, Sturmbannführer Heinrich Springer, wrote about it:

> Priorities during training:
>> Priority 1: Physical Fitness
>> Priority 2: Character Development
>> Priority 3: Weapons- and Combat Training.
>
> All schedules were based on this order and Ober-führer Fritz Witt constantly carried out unannounced inspections of the units. After only a short time, the bearing and efficiency of the young soldiers proved that the divisional commander had made the right -decision.[3]

Efforts by departments at home to provide additional rations were unsuccessful. The troops were supplied with the regular provisions by the supply offices of the Heer. However, the recruits were not issued with tobacco products but received candy instead.[4]

Character development and military training were dependent on the officer and noncom instructors. In the previous chapter it was shown that throughout the training period there was a severe shortage of officers, in particular company commanders, and noncoms. This meant that young platoon leaders had to take over commanding companies and that noncoms had to take their place. The lack of noncoms, at the start of the invasion on 6 June there was still a shortage of 2,192 noncoms and a further 144 officer positions had to be filled, forced the division to establish internal noncom training courses. These courses would train volunteers born in 1926 for noncom duties and to take over noncom positions after graduating from the courses. Hauptsturmführer Bubenzer distinguished himself greatly as the officer responsible for the courses of the division. At the same time the holder of the Knight's Cross, Hauptsturmführer Wilhelm Beck of the Panzerregiment, conducted a course for officer cadets. Some information on the training can be found in the diary entries of Sturmmann (lance corporal) Elmar Lochbihler. He had been assigned to the course from the 3. Panzerkompanie of Obersturmführer Rudolf v. Ribbentrop. Here are his notes:

> 19.2.44 Travel to the course at 2./SS-Pz.Rgt. 12, at the monastery near Hasselt.
> 21.2.44 Welcome by course director Hauptsturmführer Wilhelm Beck.
> 5.3.44 Tour to Antwerp, visit to the theater "De Vogel-handelaar", afternoon get-together with HJ from Flanders.

23.3.44 Visit by Obergruppenführer (three-star general) Sepp Dietrich.

2.4.44 Visit by BDM girls (Bund Deutscher Mädschen-association of
German girls) from Antwerp. In the evening, the HJ band from
Landsberg am Lech, my home town, visits us.

4.4.44 The band from Landsberg visits us again.

7.4.44 Loading onto train in Waterscheid.

8.4.44 Arrival in Evreux, quartered in St. Michel air force barracks.

17.4.44 City tour of Paris.

19.4.44 Untersturmführer (2nd. lt.) Fritz Menzel bids us farewell.
(Fritz Menzel, born 29.5.22 in Berlin, died on 10.6.44 near Caen,
was leader of the 2. platoon during the course)

20.4.44 40 km orienteering march around Evreux with simulated
fighting, followed by a short celebration.

21.4.44 Attendance at a court martial of the I. SS-Pz.Korps in the justice building in Evreux.

23.4.44 Graduation ceremony, farewell from Hauptsturmführer
Beck.

I was promoted to corporal-officer cadet. By order from the division (Brigadeführer Witt) we cadets reported to the Junkerschule
(officer cadet school) at Tölz. As a Panzer soldier I was at the wrong
place there and was transferred to the Panzer officer cadet course in
Fallingbostel on 9.5.44.

My last unit was the staff company of SS-Panzer-Aufklürungs-
Abteilung 12 (Panzer reconnaissance detachment) "HJ" were I was,
with the rank of Untersturmführer (2nd. lt.), orderly officer with
Sturmbannführer Gerd Bremer and at the same time led the Pionier platoon.[5]

Not all officers and noncoms were immediately able to handle as difficult a task as training and molding such young recruits. In special orders,
during visits to the troops and briefings of the officers, the divisional commander issued basic instructions time and again, and made sure that they
were carried out. In addition, the divisional adjutant, Sturmbannführer
Heinrich Springer, supported the educational process through dissertations
before the officer corps.

At the same time the division attempted in any way possible to fill the
officer positions. Springer wrote about this:

At the end of 1943, after completion of basic training, the training
in the unit began. Now it became obvious that, not only were many
officer positions unmanned, but that, in particular, specialist officers
were lacking, e.g. for light and heavy infantry guns, pioneers, etc.
We made a listing of all unmanned positions and with the agree-

ment of Gruppenführer (2 star general) Berger, whose son had died in my 1. Kompanie ("LAH", the author) on 12.2.43, Oberführer Witt sent me to the Heer personnel department at Cottbus with this list. After a short time, some 20 officers arrived one after the other. They had been assigned to us. At the beginning of 1944 I traveled to Cottbus two more times, again with good success.[6]

In total, some fifty officers of the Heer were assigned to the division. They served in Heer uniform, but other than that assimilated completely into the division.

How the young volunteers experienced the start of their service with the division and the training period was described in the report of Sturmmann (lance corporal) Paul Kamberger who very likely spoke for many:

It was 1943 when I, as so many others, volunteered for service with our division. As students we had been part-time air force helpers until the long awaited order to report for duty arrived at the beginning of November. On 15.11. we had to report in Unna, Westphalia. Around midnight we left the unit and the deserted railway station in a westerly direction. Loud jubilation set in when I found that the only other passenger in the compartment was an old acquaintance from the Hitlerjugend. As it soon turned out, he was, of course, headed for the same destination. On the way the train filled up. At many stations youths of the same age got on. The well-known Persil (soap powder) box or a small suit case in their hand made it easy to guess what their destination was. Soon, small and large groups had formed and when we arrived at our destination in the morning, a great mood prevailed.

After a day and a-half, which was used to organize the groups, we set out again by train, this time with unknown destination. We were, by the way, the second contingent for the newly formed 12. SS-Panzerdivision "Hitlerjugend". After passing the German-Belgian border, the town of Turnhout turned out to be our destination station. After arriving there we marched in orderly formation to the quarters of the Aufklürungsabteilung (reconnaissance unit) which was also being set up. Soon we were standing in a square in the barracks grounds and waited for things to begin happening. And they did!

In the meantime we had assembled in detachments. Everyone had joined the bunch for the branch he wanted to get into. The various branches were unevenly popular. Well over a dozen officers began walking along our lines. They stopped in front of our group who all wanted to join the Panzers. There was a short discussion among the officers, then came the question: "Who is a student?" Ten to twelve arms flew up, step forward, and the motorcycle dispatch unit of the division was created! Mechanics completed the cadre, and from then on we formed the 1. Gruppe (group) of the I. Zug (platoon) of the 1. Kompanie.

Then began the usual basic training. Just before Christmas we were charged with the outstanding responsibility to arrange the Christmas celebrations for the company. This turned out to be such a great success that we were booked up with arranging festivities for other companies until after Christmas.

At the end of February the actual motorcycle dispatch training began. In the meantime we had been moved into the immediate vicinity of the Division command post at Zwanestrand. In the truest sense of the word we climbed onto our Italian Moto-Guzzi for the first driving practice. The drivers licenses were obtained on the road to Mol during a heavy hail shower.

The training was pushed ahead with much theoretical teaching, practical training, with emphasis on driving behavior during special situations. It was interrupted only occasionally by guard duty at the Division staff guard. The weeks flew by, and the Division was deployed to France and we were equipped with brand-new German motorbikes with side cars.[7]

The young volunteers had reported for duty in their own civilian clothes or in the HJ uniform. At the beginning there were problems with providing them with uniforms so that they showed up for duty occasionally in color-fully assembled pieces of clothing. The HJ-Führer transferred from the Heer and Luftwaffe also continued to wear their old uniforms for some time. But this, and the lack of weapons, did not prevent training from beginning immediately with great enthusiasm.

Accommodation for the troops was of great importance for the success of the training, and some information on the subject is provided here. The Belgian troop training grounds at Beverloo, seventy-two kilometers southeast of Antwerp, were the location where the Division was to be set up. Initially, the recruits for the two Panzergrenadier regiments were trained there. When the training in units began, only Panzergrenadierregiment 25 remained there. Regiment 26 was transferred to the troop training grounds at Maria-ter Heide, fifteen kilometers northeast of Antwerp. The Artillerieregiment was also located in the vicinity of the troop training grounds at Beverloo, in the area around Mol. The Aufklärungsabteilung (reconnaissance detachment) and Sanitätsabteilung (medical detachment) were stationed in Turnhout, forty-eight kilometers northeast of Antwerp. The Pionier battalion was advantageously quartered in Herentals at the Albert canal, thirty-six kilometers east of Antwerp. The supply troops had taken up quarters in the area around Geel, fifty kilometers east of Antwerp. The Panzerregiment was stationed at the French troop training grounds Mailly-le Camp, thirty-five kilometers south of Chalons-sur-Marne, approximately 250 kilometers from the divisional staff quarters in Zwanestrand near Turnhout. All of the training concentrated on the coming action in battle. Formal training was reduced to the absolute minimum. All the rest was training for fighting in terrain. The weapons drill, also, took place in the terrain.

After completion of the individual training for the volunteers who had arrived with the first contingents, the Division issued the "Ausbildungsbefehl Nr. 1" (training order no. 1) on 17.11.43. It spelled out the guidelines for the further training in groups, platoons, and company/battery. This training was to be completed at the beginning of December 1943 and confirmed by visits to the companies and batteries.

The firearms training with carbines, pistols and submachine guns, as well as on machine guns, formed a significant part of the training for battle. It, too, took part in the open terrain under simulated battle conditions. Under the guidance of the company chief, Obersturmführer Ritzert, the Aufklärungs-kompanie (reconnaissance company) of Panzergrenadier-regiment 25 established guidelines for the basic training with the rifle under battle-like conditions. These were introduced by order of the Division. They are shown as Appendix 4. The guidelines were unusual under the conditions of the time. The General der Panzertruppen West (general of the Panzer troops west), General der Panzertruppen Leo Frhr. (baron) Geyr von Schweppenburg, who was responsible for the training aspect of the Division, was very much impressed by the firearms training. He directed the interest of the inspector general of the Panzertruppen, Generaloberst (four-star general) Heinz Guderian to the training. He ordered Obersturmführer Ritzert together with a group from his company to work out firearm training directives at the school for the Panzer troops at Bergen. It was introduced into the Panzer forces. The command of the infantry decided against its introduction.

General von Geyr put great emphasis on camouflage, radio codes, secrecy, and night- and hand-to-hand combat training. These were all practiced by the Division with considerable seriousness and energy.

Hauptsturmführer Erich Olboeter, the commander of the Aufklärungsabteilung during the first half year, and later of the SPW (Schützen Panzer Wagen—armored personnel carrier) battalion, developed internal guidelines for hand-to-hand combat training. Olboeter had an area set aside in the terrain for this training where practice using live ammunition also took place.

All branches placed great value on sports. The aim was physical fitness and a loosening-up of the routine of duty. In addition to good results in the team sports there were also outstanding individual achievements. For instance, the German youth heavyweight boxing champion as of 1 April 1944, Sturmmann Gerhard Steinmetz was a member of the Pionier reconnaissance platoon of the Stabskompanie (staff company) of Panzerpionier-bataillon 12. As Harald Zimmermann reported, Gerhard Steinmetz was taken prisoner during a reconnaissance mission on 11.8.44 and was released only three years later.[8]

✠

To convey an understanding of the formation of the Division and its training in the different branches, some reports are cited here. Panzerregiment 12, which was to be set up, had an additional special task. It had to provide a Panther Abteilung (detachment) for the "LAH" division. In order to make that possible, the I. Abteilung of Panzerregiment "LAH" which had been led by Sturmbannführer Max Wünsche during the fighting for Charkow in February and March, was removed from the divisional structure of the "LAH" at the beginning of April 1943. The Panzers and trucks were handed over to the II. Abteilung. The personnel was initially moved to Berlin.

The following is taken from a report by the regimental adjutant, Hauptsturmführer Georg Isecke:

In order to have any possibility at all to train with Panzers right away, the I. Abteilung brought together 4 damaged Panzer IVs, two knocked-out Panzer IIIs and two mobile Russian T-34 tanks in the Charkow area and loaded them for transport to Berlin. The Panzer works Allkett in Berlin agreed to repair the six German Panzers and received one T-34 in return. Beginning in mid-April, the personnel of the I. Abteilung, numbering 412 officers, noncoms and men, arrived in Mailly. The additional personnel required for the formation of the Panther Abteilung "LAH", strength approximately 900, was brought in from reserve units. The training took place with the repaired Panzer IIIs and IVs. Sturmbannführer Herbert Kuhlmann took on the leadership of this Abteilung. Approximately half of the personnel of the former I. Abteilung integrated into his Abteilung, the other half formed the core of Panzerregiment 12. The Kuhlmann Abteilung was ordered to report for Panther courses at Erlangen at the end of July. There, they were equipped with Panthers and incorporated into the "LAH" division at the beginning of September 1943.

Thus, the training for the formation of Panzerregiment 12 could only begin at the end of July. The core was made up of 15 officers, 44 noncoms, and 146 men. From this, a regiment of the strength of 71 officers, 850 noncoms, and 1,380 men was to be formed.

In order to fulfill this large and extremely difficult objective, the following training plan was established:

Phase 1: Functional training

1. Training company for Panzer commanders, gunners and loaders
     Chief: Hauptsturmführer Arnold Jürgensen, future commander I. Abteilung.

2. Training company as 1. above
   Chief: Hauptsturmführer Karl-Heinz Prinz, future commander
   II. Abteilung.
3. Training company for radio operators
   Chief: Obersturmführer Schlauss, future communications officer
   of the regiment staff.
4. Training company for Panzer drivers
   Chief: Obersturmführer Samman, future technical officer for vehicles of the regiment.
5. Training company for car and truck drivers
   Chief: Untersturmführer Robert Maier, future officer in charge of
   the maintenance company of the I. Abteilung.
   Training group for medical services
   Chief: Obersturmführer Stiawa M.D.
   Training group for administrative services
   Chief: Obersturmführer Lütgert, future administrations officer of
   the regiment.

The arriving recruits were assigned to the training -companies and groups after short tests and appraisals. Most of the Panzer commanders were high school graduates born in 1925. There was no drill, except that marching to the training areas was done singing and in step. Phase 1 was completed after ten weeks with an individual appraisal of each man.

Phase 2:
   Establishing the units,
   Training in cooperating for the Panzer crews,
   Zug (platoon) training,
   Company training.

Based on the appraisals, all personnel was assigned and integrated into the lists of war strength availability and classification. In addition to the six repaired Panzers, there were ten Panzer IVs available for training at the end of November.

Until the end of the year, 600–700 members of the regiment were constantly attending courses. Panzer crews and officers worked for eight to fourteen days in the Panzer production at MAN in Nürnberg as the result of a personal initiative of Obersturm-bannführer Wünsche. Others took part in Panzer firing -training at the Putlos range, in Flak training at Schongau, in driver training at the technical institute for motor vehicle studies of the Waffen-SS in Vienna, and in training for transmission specialists at the gear manufacturing factory in Friedrichshafen.

Special attention was paid to the setting up of the repair services since it was expected that Panzer losses would not be made up by replacements for a lengthy period of time. The Panzerregiment had two repair companies, one for each Abteilung, when the Division went into action. Available, among others, were:

1 recovery platoon,
1 motor and transmission repair platoon,
1 weapons repair platoon with a twenty-ton portal crane to lift the
    Panzer turret,
1 transport staff.

The backbone of the repair establishments was made up of well-experienced reservists.[9]

In early January 1944, the Panzerregiment was moved from Mailly-le Camp into the general area of the Division and took up quarters around Hasselt, fifty-seven kilometers southeast of Antwerp, near the Beverloo troop training grounds. On 6 February, parts of the regiment conducted a field exercise which was attended by Generaloberst Guderian, General von Geyr and Obergruppenführer Sepp Dietrich. The further supply of Panzers was dependent on the results of the exercise. The high level of training found high praise and this expedited the delivery of Panthers. [10]

During the same time an exercise was conducted by I./SS-Panzergrenadierregiment 25, using live ammunition, with the participation of one battery of the Artillerieregiment and also attended by the three generals. This exercise, too, was accepted as proof for the unexpectedly high quality of training. The supreme commander in the west, Generalfeldmarschall (field marshal) Gerd von Rundstedt, attended the exercise by an armored group at the Beverloo training grounds. The exercise was conducted by the III. (armored)/SS-Panzergrenadier-regiment 26 and a number of companies of the Panzer-regiment 12. This exercise ended as convincingly as the previous ones.

The usual exercises of various kinds took place additionally, and only the ones concerning different communications practices will be mentioned here.

The training suffered, apart from the personnel problems, from the slow delivery of weapons, material and vehicles as already described in the previous chapter and, additionally, from a shortage of ammunition for practice and of fuel. For instance, only one Panzer could be driven into the terrain during firing practice near Winterslag, and it had to be used by all crews in the platoon or the company. Of course, all units of the Division made do in a similar fashion. Improvisation and self help were necessary, as reported by Obersturmführer Karl Kugler, adjutant of the III. (SPW)/Panzergrenadier Regiment 26:

The greatest lack during the training was in gasoline for the vehicles. There was not enough for the motorcycle dispatch riders. Only seldom could the SPWs (armored personnel carriers) be driven and such occasion was looked upon like a holiday by all. Mostly, one

SPW would be fueled up at the companies and it would be used in training drives by all the groups. There was only a special reserve of 3,000 liters available and it was sealed and strictly guarded.

The boys were in love with their vehicles. It happened in the 11. Kompanie that some of the boys stole some grease from a private firm to lubricate their vehicles since their company did not have any. The theft was noticed and the perpetrators were given three days confinement. As they stated, it was not the arrest which caused them the most grief but the fact that they had to give back the grease.[11]

The following extracts from the situational reports to the inspector general of the Panzer troops provide an insight into the progress of the training and of the difficulties which had to be overcome:

4.10.43 Training Situation:

All reserves which have arrived until now have received an average of six weeks of training.

Special Problems:

1. Lack of training personnel (in particular for special weapons)
2. Lack of all types of practice ammunition
3. Lack of cleaning material for weapons
4. Lack of fuel for training purposes
5. Minimal provision of medical supplies

Overall Assessment by the Division Commander:

The training and formation process greatly impaired through lack of officers and noncoms.

The available training personnel can only conditionally meet the requirements.

Some small improvement in the noncom situation has occurred, further improvement can be expected with the arrival of 200 noncom applicants (without combat experience) at the end of October.

The physical fitness of the recruits is, at this time, still below the average.

1.11.43 Training Situation:

All reserves which have arrived until now have received an average of ten weeks of basic training.

Special Problems:

1. Lack of training personnel (in particular for special weapons)
2. Lack of all types of practice ammunition, except for pistol
3. Lack of weapons cleaning material
4. Lack of fuel for training purposes
5. Minimal provision of medical supplies

Overall Assessment by the Division Commander:

The training and formation process has become even more difficult owing to the lack of officers and noncoms. The available training personnel can only conditionally meet the requirements. The level of training has been elevated through schooling.

A noticeable improvement in the noncom situation has not yet been achieved since the 200 noncom applicants (without combat experience) promised for the end of October will only arrive in mid-November.

The physical fitness of the recruits continues to be below the average.

The Division is not ready for action.

1.12.43 Training Situation:

Except for the III./SS-Pz.Gren.Rgt. 25 and the I./Pz.Art.Rgt. 12 which have been newly formed with untrained reserves, the units and detachments are in the fourteenth week of training. The group inspection of the Pz.Gren. regiments is pending.

Special Problems:

1. Lack of training personnel (in particular for special weapons)
2. Lack of all types of practice ammunition, except for pistol.

Short Assessment by the Commander:

Based on the level of training and the physical fitness of the men, born in 1926, the combat forces are only fit for defensive and security duty. They are not yet ready for attack action in unit formation.

5.1.44 Training Situation:

The majority of the Division finds itself in the eighteenth week of training. Company inspections will commence in January 1944. The III./SS-Pz.Gren.Rgt. 25 and the I./SS-Pz.Art.Rgt. 12 are in their eighth week of training.

Special Problems:

1. Lack of training personnel (in particular for special weapons)
2. Lack of light infantry gun and pistol ammunition

Level of Mobility: 19%

Fighting Fitness and Usability:

Portions of the Division (combat forces) are ready for defensive action.

3.2.44 Training Situation:

The majority of the Division finds itself in unit training.

The training on batteries could not yet begin for the I.(SF)/SS-Pz.Art.Rgt. 12 since no Panzer observation -vehicles have been supplied so far and thus there is a total lack of a communications network.

Special Problems:
1. Lack of fuel
2. Lack of practice ammunition for the Panzers and heavy weapons
3. Absence of special vehicles: a) shielded radio vehicles, b) Panzer command vehicles, c) Panzer observation vehicles for the artillery, d) tractors for the III./Pz.Art.Rgt.
4. Lack of repair installations and crew for the repair Abteilung
5. Lack of communications personnel with the artillery (communications platoon leaders and in particular communications noncoms)

Fighting Fitness:
The motorized combat forces are conditionally ready for offensive action.

The non-motorized combat forces (rail transport) are conditionally ready for defensive action.

3.3.44 Training Situation:
The Division is involved in unit training. Only limited unit training could be started with the I.(SF)/SS-Pz.Art.Rgt. 12 since no Panzer observation vehicles have so far been supplied and thus there is an absence of a communications network.

Special Problems:
1. Lack of fuel for training. (The amount requested and received for operations are the absolute minimum required)
2. Lack of Practice ammunition for Panzers and heavy infantry weapons
3. Absence of the basic operational Panzer ammunition
4. Absence of special vehicles: a) shielded radio vehicles for the division communications Abteilung, b) Panzer command vehicles, c) Panzer observation vehicles for the artillery, ammunition carriers for the I.(SF)Art.Abt., d) tractors for the III./Pz.Art.Rgt., e) tractors for the Flak Abteilung
5. Absence of repair installations and means of recovery for the Pz.Rgt.
6. Lack of communications personnel (communications platoon leaders and in particular communications noncoms) with the Art.Rgt.

Fighting Fitness:
The motorized combat forces are ready for offensive actions, the rail transport combat forces for defensive action.

3.4.44 Level of Training:

The Division finds itself in unit training with the exception of SS-Pz.Jäger-(destroyer) Abt. 12 and SS-Werfer-(mortar) Abt. 12

Special Problems:

1. Lack of fuel for training
2. Lack of special vehicles: a) Panzer command vehicles, b) Panzer observation vehicles for I.(SF)/SS-Pz.Art.Rgt. 12, c) 1 ton tractors to rebuild the 2 cm motorized Flak into 2 cm self-propelled Flak

Fighting Fitness:

The motorized parts, ready for action, are usable for offensive operations, the conditionally ready motorized parts are only conditionally ready for offensive action.

1.6.44 Level of Training:

The Division, with the exception of Pz.Jäger-Abt. 12 and the SS-Nebelwerfer-(rocket launcher) Abt. 12, finds itself in unit training.

Special Problems:

a) Shortage of 3 Panzer command vehicles (Pz.Bef.-Wagen V)
b) Shortage of recovery Panzers
c) Shortage of the required number of vehicles for the Panther Abt.
d) The I.(SF)/SS-Pz.Art.Rgt. 12 is still short 2 artillery observation Panzer IIIs
e) Lack of ammunition carriers for the I.(SF)/SS-Pz.Art.Rgt. 12
f) Lack of 1 ton tractors to rebuild the 2 cm motorized Flak into self-propelled 2 cm Flak
g) Shortage of 12 Sd.Kfz. 222 (armored cars) and 6 Sd.Kfz. 233 (armored cars) for SS-Pz.Aufkl.Abt. 12 (Panzer reconnaissance Abteilung)
h) Shortage of 11 armored personnel carriers for SS-Pz.Nachr.Abt. 12 (Panzer communications Abteilung)
i) Absence of all tractors for SS-Werfer-(mortar) Abt. 12
k) Absence of command Panzers for SS-Pz.Jäger-Abt. 12

Fighting Fitness:

The Division is ready for offensive actions.

Signed: Witt
SS-Brigadeführer and
Generalmajor of the Waffen-SS

Short Comment by the Superior Department:

The Division, with the exception of the mortar Abteilung and the Panzerjäger Abteilung, is fully fit for any action in the west.

For the general command
The chief of the general staff
Signed: Kraemer[12]

CHAPTER 00.4
Occupation Force in Flanders—Contact with the Homeland—Spiritual Orientation

With the deployment to the troop training grounds at Beverloo, the young volunteers entered an occupied country for the first time. Those in quarters at the training grounds at Leopoldsburg had little contact with the population at the beginning. The majority of the troops, however, were distributed in towns and villages and there were quartered in barracks, schools or halls. Despite the fact that free time was scarce, it offered the frequent opportunity to get to know the Flemings, their life style and way of thinking. Friendships began. It was well known that many Flemish volunteers were fighting in the ranks of the Waffen-SS at the eastern front. Thus, the members of the Division in Flanders did not feel as an occupation force but rather more like troops in an allied country.

As was the case in all other occupied countries, the Allies attempted to incite the Belgian population through propaganda against the German authorities and troops. They were not squeamish in their choice of means. While a portion of the Flemish had a friendly attitude towards the German troops and another portion was neutral in their behavior, there were also hostile families and individuals. This latter group was obviously in the minority. But it had secret connections to England and was provided from there with weapons, means of sabotage, propaganda material, and instructions for their underground missions. The observation and fight against this activity were the responsibility of the military commander for Belgium and Northern France. The units of the Division protected themselves and their installations through the required guard duty. There was occasional sabotage of vehicles or telephone lines, but it was of no consequence.

The enemy provided supplies to the underground movement by air. Parts of the Division were occasionally requested by the military authorities to take part in search actions. The Abteilung Ic (enemy information) of the

Division reported on the results of such an action on 19.9.43. The report read:

Concerning: Drop of ammunition, explosives and -weapons.

Increased nightly air activity in the area Turnhout-Gheel-Deschel was the reason for a search action for air-dropped agents or ammunition.

During the action, 48 cases of submachine guns and accompanying ammunition, parachutes and a radio were found in a wooded area north of Gheel.

As well, suspected civilians were arrested on charges of helping the enemy and unlawful carrying of weapons. The civilians were in possession of weapons, including signal pistols.

Other areas also reported drops of ammunition, explosives and weapons.

The enemy has increased his activities in this respect. At the same time, his propaganda is directed at inciting the population in the occupied territories to revolt, and to commit sabotage and assassinations with explosives.

This order is to be used to inform the troops. All guards are to be instructed to pay special attention to the surveillance of the air space."[1]

An example of the friendly attitude of the Flemings is reported by Oberscharführer Karl Friedrich Hahn of the 1. Kompanie of the SS-Panzerregiment 26, based on entries in his diary:

24.12.43 The Christmas Eve festivities, in the gathering of the company, turned out to be very enjoyable. A pro-German family in Fort Brascat had provided us with their large guest hall. I prepared the hall together with Unter-scharführers Sommer and Brandt for the celebration. We received generous gifts and returned home quite late in a special streetcar.[2]

Even more so than today, there existed a tense relationship in Belgium between the Flemish and the Walloons. The official language, which most of the Dutch speaking Flemings did not understand, was French. Through this alone, the Flemish were at a disadvantage compared to the Walloons. The German occupation administration made Dutch (Flemish) a second official and equal language. This ruling, by the way, could not be reversed after the war. Under these circumstances, the members of the Division had feelings of sympathy in particular for the Flemish and thought the Walloons would harbor less friendly feelings towards them. They were to find out differently. Oberscharführer Hahn reports:

31.3.44 Together with Untersturmführer Gross, 3 noncoms, and 35 men from our company we set out in the direction of Brussels in the evening after drill duty and inspection by Oberführer Witt. We traveled throughout the night in open vehicles and arrived in the southern Belgian industrial city of Charlerois in the morning. We provided an honor company at the returning home of the assault brigade 'Wallonien' after the break-out from the Tcherkassy encirclement. Leon Degrelle was awarded the Oak Leaves, many other members of the assault brigade received medals from the hand of Oberführer Witt. The drive, through the jubilation of the populace, took us past Waterloo to Brussels. The main street was packed with people, waving flags (the Belgian lion and the swastika), bidding a heartfelt welcome to Leon Degrelle and his assault brigade. There were scenes which indicated that the Belgians had, with us, recognized the dangers of Bolshevism and were prepared to fight on our side.[3]

While the young volunteers grew into a new community, into a completely new world and while Hitler youths turned into soldiers, the Divisional leadership and those responsible, of all ranks, contributed to ensure that the ties with home, to the homeland, were not cut but fostered instead.

On the invitation of the Divisional commander, the Reichs-jugendführer Artur Axmann visited the Division from 5 to 7 December 1943. A special order, regarding the reason for the visit and issued the day previous to the visit, stated:

The Reichsjugendführer wishes to receive an understanding of the present situation of the formation of the Division. To achieve this, it is necessary that the units not offer a wrong impression but that the real level of achievement is shown. This will allow the Reichsjugendführer to form his own impression of the spirit of the "Hitlerjugend" Division.

According to the inspection program, the Reichsjugendführer visited the following units:
Panzergrenadierregiment 25,
III. (armored)/ Regiment 26,
Flakabteilung,
Artillerieregiment (firing of a light and a heavy battery),
Communications Abteilung (instruction in theory and maintenance),
Aufklührungs (reconnaissance) Abteilung (hand-to-hand combat, training in close combat using live ammunition)
SS-Panzergrenadierregiment 26.[4]

The Reichsjugendführer was greatly impressed by what had been achieved during training. He had numerous opportunities to discuss any items which were of importance to them with both the volunteers and the instructors as well as items he wished to know more about. Thus, he took part in the evening meal of a company of the Aufklührungsabteilung, sat among the young soldiers and talked with them. He also liked to hear reports on the social and entertainment services offered to the troops, a responsibility he had taken over since mid-November. Since then, bands, musical groups and folk dancers had visited the Division. Books, magazines and useful articles for daily use had been sent and gratefully received.

Often, however, anxious thoughts of home filled the minds. Oberscharführer Hahn noted:

> 20.3.43 The daily duties take on more serious proportions, in particular they last too long. Every day and almost every night, squadrons of Anglo-American bombers fly over us on their way to Germany. It is a terrible feeling to have to watch passively as they fly undisturbed on their way to reap havoc in our homeland.[5]

Many field post letters and telegrams from home reported on the destruction caused by them. Some requests for leave, with documentation, survived and they offer an idea of the various tragic events burdening the young soldiers.

Gunner Wilhelm Schmidt, for instance, was given special leave from 4.10. to 9.10.43 because his mother had been killed in a bomb attack. On 7 December of the same year the 5. Batterie of the Artillerieregiment 12 received a telegram from a police detachment in Berlin that his parents' apartment had again been heavily hit during a bombing raid and that his father was missing since.

Gunner Otto Wezel of the same battery received a telegram on 13 November from his widowed mother, his father had died in 1933, in Metzingen, Württemberg province, that his second brother had been killed.

Gunner Ernst Pfromm, also of the 5. Batterie, received a letter on 20.11.43 from his parents in Heimboldshausen on the Werra river informing him that his brother had been killed in Russia on 30 October.

All three men requested and received home leave, eighteen days, fourteen days and eight days respectively. The surviving documents are reproduced in the Annex as Appendix 5.

Members of all other units of the Division met with similar occurrences which put a particular heavy burden on the young soldiers. These matters were discussed in closer as well as wider circles of comrades. Each one had to prepare for the possibility of receiving such notification some day. However, the consequence was not despair or fanaticism of the men, rather a determination to apply oneself in the coming combat with all one's force in order to bring about a change of fate. It was reported repeatedly by the enemy later, and even still seen in that way by the former enemies after the war, that the young soldiers of the "Hitlerjugend" Division had fought fanatically. This was attributed to the instructors' having trained the soldiers in hate and fanaticism. This was reported to have been most obvious by the fact that, even in hopeless situations, they did not surrender but fought on.

On the whole, this is certainly not correct. Without question, the terror bombing of the home land, losses in the families, the demand for an unconditional surrender from Roosevelt and Churchill reinforced the existing determination to fight, but there was no hatred because of this for the soldiers on the opposite side. The enemy, in the knowledge of his vast numerical superiority and immense quantities of materiel, fought differently from the German soldier who strove to overcome the shortages and disadvantages of his side through great personal skilled use of occasionally superior weapons and a special courage. The men were trained in that spirit. They did not receive directions on how and when they were supposed to surrender as prisoners but rather on how to fight best. The instructors attempted to develop in the men a feeling of responsibility for their weapons, equipment, their vehicles, Panzers and armored personnel carriers. Once more, Oberscharführer Hahn is cited here:

> 9.11.44 In the afternoon, a ceremony took place in the framework of the battalion which achieved its objective. Once more, we were completely enthused by our commander, our 'Papa' Krause. The men were sworn in on their weapons during a solemn ceremony. Our company provided a dignified frame to the ceremony through group recitals, songs and poetry.[6]

The divisional emblem also served the cohesiveness of the Division and the feeling of being a part of the I. SS-Panzerkorps and thus a sister division of the combat experienced "Leib-standarte". The emblem was the result of a contest begun on 10 November 1943. Franz Lang of Abteilung V (motor transport) of the division staff won first prize. All of the vehicles of the Division, from motorcycles to Panthers, received the emblem in white paint. It was affixed, for instance, to the right front fender and the left side of the rear of the trucks. The members of the Division were proud of this emblem. They were to show themselves equal to their comrades of the "Leib-standarte".[7]

The Division later received a sleeve band with the name "Hitlerjugend" as recognition for their action during the invasion battles. Until then, the members of the Division who had come from the "Leibstandarte", wore its sleeve band with the inscription "Adolf Hitler".

To Whom It May Concern:

SS-Sturmbannführer Max Wünsche, commander I./Pz.Rgt. Leib-standarte SS Adolf Hitler is under my orders to inspect the assembly facilities for the "Panther", and to make preparations to bring training personnel into the facilities.

signed: The Minister of the Reich for Armament and Munitions

CHAPTER 00.5
Strategic Considerations of the German and Allied Leaderships

The supreme command of the armed forces and the chief command offices in the west had been contemplating defenses against an invasion in the west ever since that had become a possibility. Here, only those considerations which had an influence on the decisions and subsequent developments in the fighting since the autumn of 1943 will be reported.

On 3 November 1943, the Führer directive (Führerweisung) number 51 was issued. It clarified the importance of the expected invasion and demanded the required actions to fortify the defenses from all command offices. Here, only the introductory paragraphs and the passage which applied to the "HJ" Division will be cited:

The difficult battles, high in losses, of the last two-and-one half years against bolshevism have occupied the majority of our military forces and efforts to the extreme. This was a reaction to the magnitude of the threat and the overall situation. In the meantime, the situation has changed. The danger in the east remains, but a greater one is starting to show itself in the west: the Anglo-Saxon landing! The vast-ness of the territory in the east allows major loss of ground in extreme circumstances, without fatal impact on German survival.

It is different in the west! If the enemy was successful in breaking through our defenses on a wide front, the consequences, in the short term, would be unpredictable. All indications are that the enemy, at the latest in the spring and possibly earlier, will begin an attack on the western front of Europe.

Thus, I can no longer justify weakening the west any further in favor of other locations of fighting. For this reason, I have decided to increase defensive capability in the west, in particular where we will begin the long-range battle against England. It is there that the enemy must and will attack, it is there, if all indications are not

wrong, that the decisive landing battles will be fought. Diversion and attacks to tie down our forces must be expected on the other fronts.
In this respect I order . . .
Expedited supply of weapons to the SS-Pz.Gren.Div.HJ, to the 21. Pz.Div. and . . .[1]

This indicated the general direction. Carrying out the -orders was a different story. Just how slowly the "expedited supply" really took place was shown in the previous section, "Formation".

The first requirement for an assessment of the situation in the west and for the required decisions was the determined enemy situation. It was the responsibility of the general staff of the Heer (army), department of the foreign armies in the west (FHW), to establish position and situation of the enemy from various sources. Its determination of the enemy situation was, among others, submitted to the supreme command of the armed forces (OKW)/ armed forces staff and forwarded to the subordinate commands. Based on this information the situation report, west, developed. The situation reports, west, are contained in appendices to the war diary of the supreme command of the 7 army which led the troops in northwestern France from straight east of the mouth of the Orne river to the mouth of the Loire river. The following picture on the enemy troops in Great Britain and Northern Ireland developed:

Situation report, west, number 36 of 7.10.43:
The total number of British/American units ready for action in Great Britain and Northern Ireland at present amounts to probably
40–42 infantry divisions, 4 independent (infantry) -brigades
9–10 tank divisions, 11 independent tank brigades
2–3 airborne divisions and 7 paratrooper battalions

In total, 51–54 divisions and 15 brigades. The structure of the British and Canadian infantry- and tank divisions is detailed in Appendix 7. It should be mentioned here only that, in addition to the staff, support and supply units, the British/Canadian infantry divisions consisted of three infantry brigades of three infantry battalions each.

The British/Canadian tank divisions had one tank brigade with three tank detachments and a vehicle battalion, and one infantry brigade of three infantry battalions. During action, one tank brigade was normally assigned to an infantry division for the forward lines.

Situation report, west, number 42 of 21.12.43:
The total number of British/American units ready for action in Great Britain and Northern Ireland has been increased since the end of November by a newly established English airborne division

and one American infantry (mountain infantry?) division brought in from the USA and thus amounts, at present, to probably

41–42 infantry divisions and 5 independent infantry brigades

11–12 tank divisions and 12 independent tank brigades

4 airborne divisions and 6 paratrooper battalions

(A total of 56–58 divisions and 17 brigades, the author)

The enemy situation continues to show further systematic progress of the preparations for a landing.

Situation report, west, number 47 of 25.4.44:

The total number of British/American units ready for action in Great Britain and Northern Ireland has been increased since the beginning of April by 2 American infantry divisions brought in from the USA and North Africa respectively and by 2 newly-established English tank divisions and amounts, at present, to probably

50–51 infantry divisions and 5 independent infantry brigades

7 airborne divisions and 8 paratrooper battalions

14–15 tank divisions and 13 tank brigades

(A total of 71–73 divisions and 18 brigades, Author)

The general impression that the preparations for the invasion have been mostly complete since the beginning of April has been confirmed by other indications.[2]

Finally, the situation map of the Supreme Command West of 6 June 1944, the day of the start of the invasion, showed in a table the strength of units ready for action in Great Britain/Northern Ireland:

British units:	41 infantry divs.	5 indep. inf. brigades
	5 aiborne divs.	6 paratroop batls.
	10 tank divisions	13 tank brigades
American units:	15 infantry divs.	
	2 airborne divs.	
	5 tank divisions	1 tank brigade
French units:	2 paratroop batls.	
Totals:	56 infantry divs.	5 indep. inf. divs.
	7 airborne divs.	6 paratroop batls.
	(1 airborne division being set up)	
	15 tank divisions	14 tank brigades

Underneath, a note:

Of these, operational units are 48 infantry divisions, 4 infantry brigades, 7 airborne divisions, 8 paratroop battalions, 15 tank divisions, 14 tank brigades. Strength in total is 79 units.[3]

In fact, the Allied supreme commander, General Dwight D. Eisenhower, had available on 6 June: 23 infantry divisions, 10 tank division and 4 airborne divisions, a total of 37 divisions.[4]

Thus, the German troops in the west were facing not 70, but only just over half of that number, 37, divisions apart from the existing and imaginary independent brigades.

The wrong picture of the enemy was the foundation of all operational decisions on the German side. Certain mistakes must always be expected; with the terrific scale of faulty estimating, all decisions which were based on logical considerations had to be wrong from the beginning. It is then necessary to explore the causes.

The book "The Struggle for Europe" by Chester Wilmot, London, September 1951, issued in German under the title "Der Kampf um Europa", Frankfurt a.M./Berlin 1954, informed a wider public for the first time about these facts and their probable causes. In the book it is said that the office 'foreign armies west' set up approximately 30 'invented' British and American divisions. Wilmot cited as the source "File on Colonel M.", British Army of the Rhine Intelligence Review, 4 March 1946.(5) The mentioned "Colonel M." was the Major (major) in the Generalstab (general staff), later Oberstleutnant i.G. (lt. colonel in the general staff), Roger Michael. He had been posted to the office of foreign armies west after graduating from the military academy of the Heer (army) at the end of May 1942. There he had become a specialist on the British army. His superior officer was Major i.G. Staubwasser, the chief of the office foreign armies west was Oberst i.G. (colonel) Freiherr von Roenne. On 1.1.44, Staubwasser was assigned as Ic (enemy intelligence) to the staff of the Heeresgruppe B (Rommel) (army group B). His successor in the office foreign armies west was Michael. In a report given by Michael during questioning by British secret service officers after being taken prisoner he said, according to the "Intelligence Review":

Towards the end of 1943 my chief and I were called to the Heer (army) command staff at least once per month for briefings. We were always amazed by the illogical under-estimation of the Anglo/American forces and by the equally illogical over-estimation of the potential of the defending German forces in France, Norway and the Balkans. Units were constantly deployed to different theatres of war. Based on this, my chief approved an increase in the number of British divisions in our estimates to counterbalance the much too optimistic tendency of the Heer command staff.

Our estimates were some 20 divisions too high (8 infantry divisions, named after shires or regions, 4 or 5 infantry- or partly armored divisions with numbers from 900 up, 5 Canadian divisions, 7 or 8 tank divisions and 3 or 4 divisions in the Mediterranean theater of war. I cannot remember details without reference to the brochure "The British Army in War" which I issued at the beginning of the year . . .

As sources to predict the Anglo/American attack from Great Britain I had the usual intercepted radio messages and statements by prisoners in Italy. Particularly valuable were messages sent through the Royal Air Force network, especially when they provided information on the four Allied Armies already in action. Radio messages from the convoys en route from North America were also useful. Our infiltration of the French resistance movement also provided us with some very valuable indications and clues.

The invasion itself confirmed our picture of the enemy.[6]

Whatever the reasons for the deliberate falsification of the picture of the enemy may have been—Major Michael was reported by David Irving to have been seen in a US Army uniform after the war before he disappeared behind

the Iron Curtain[7]—this conduct was unjustifiable and unworthy of German general staff officers. It was the mission of the office of foreign armies west to establish the most reliable picture of the enemy possible. The opportunities to do this were, without question, limited. However, when questionable methods were used, the officers of the general staff in the office of foreign armies west, who were not part of the deception, should have so informed the authorities who had to make basic and grave decisions based on this picture. This was obviously not the case. (One should imagine how the actions of a reconnaissance platoon would be judged which, having heard a metallic rattle somewhere, would then report having observed the deployment of twenty-six tanks.) If, however, as Michael said, his and von Roenne's

Prize-winning design for the divisional insignia, by SS Rottenführer Fritz Lang, Div. HQ Staff, Battalion V.

BERLIN W 8, DEN 28.3.43
REICHSKANZLEI

DER FÜHRER UND KANZLER DES DEUTSCHEN REICHES

ADJUTANTUR

B e s c h e i n i g u n g.

   SS – Sturmbannführer Max Wünsche, Kdr.
1./ Pz. Rgt. Leibstandarte SS Adolf Hitler, ist
von mir beauftragt, sich die Fertigungsstätten
der " Panther " anzusehen, und Vorbereitungen
zur Kommandierung des Ausbildungspersonals in
die Werke zu treffen.

                    Der Reichsminister für
            Bewaffnung und Munition.

behavior was a part of the "fight against the intrigues by Himmler and Kaltenbrunner" who had the intention "to ensure that the SS controlled all of the counter-intelligence", then it is quite outrageous. Not only were the chief of the general staff of the Heer, the chief of the armed forces command staff and the chief of the supreme command of the armed forces deceived, who were supposedly being helped, but also the whole of the leadership, and uncounted soldiers paid for it with their blood.

It is striking that the falsification of the enemy situation by the office of the foreign armies west, and in particular the reasons for it, are hardly being mentioned or examined in German war historical literature. A thorough examination appears necessary.

Which of our own forces were facing the enemy ready to land on the continent? Only the territories of Holland, Belgium and France will be examined here. On 6 June 1944 the supreme commander, west, commanded:

33 immobile, dug-in, divisions in positions to defend the coast,
13 infantry divisions (mobile),
2 paratrooper divisions,
6 Panzer divisions.

Together with the reserves of the supreme command of the armed forces of four Panzer and Panzergrenadier divisions; this was a total of fifty-eight divisions. If the difficulties of transporting troops and materiel across a 160 kilometer wide channel, Portsmouth-Arromanches, are considered alone with respect to the technical effort and the weather, the relationship of forces was not unfavorable for the German side. The enemy could land a first wave of six to seven divisions simultaneously. It would take weeks to land all thirty-seven divisions, and this did not only depend on the shipping capacity and the weather, but also on the development of the situation in the landing area. This favorable relationship could only be assumed, however, if the defenders had a relative certainty of where the landing would take place. This was not the case, at least not initially. Consequently, the forces had to be distributed through all of the western area. This changed the relationship of the forces in the planned landing sector in favor of the enemy. There is no intention to describe here the last phase of the decision making at the various commands regarding the probable Allied landing sector. That will be done later. However, since issuance of the Führer directive number 51 of 3.11.43, new points of main effort had been determined which were supposed to ease operational considerations. For that reason, it is being examined here.

The Führer directive number 51a of 27.12.43 stated, among others:

Since the front of the AOK 15 (Armee-Ober-Kommando: army supreme command) and the right flank of the AOK 7 (Contentin peninsula) are particularly threatened, the body of the available forces must be concentrated behind these fronts.[9]

With this, Denmark as well as the southern, southwestern and western coasts of France were dropped from further considerations. Full attention was then to be directed to the sector of the Channel coast from Holland to the mouth of the Loire.

Directive 51 stated unequivocally that the planned invasion in the west would be of life-threatening importance. The objective of the defensive fighting in the west could thus not be to repel the landing, it would then soon be repeated in a different area, but to inflict a heavy, if not decisive, defeat on the enemy. Only a clear defeat, which would negate for a long time another landing attempt by strong forces, could free German divisions in the west for the east and win time for the long-range battle of the retaliatory weapons. It was basically this set of problems which caused the opposing interpretations by those responsible.

Feldmarschall Rommel had the mission to smash the expected invasion. He interpreted it to mean that the main front line was at the beach, that it had to be held, and to be re-established immediately after clearing up of eventual breakthroughs. He concentrated all his efforts on making the coastal defenses as impregnable as possible. His forceful efforts brought about the installation, improvement and strengthening of obstacles in the water ahead of the beach, concrete reinforced positions for the coastal artillery and anti-tank guns, fortified field positions for the infantry, mine fields and bogus mine fields against tanks and infantry, and finally of obstacles against airborne troops, the so-called Rommel asparagus. Throughout, the Feldmarschall showed an extraordinary inventiveness. Not all sectors of the coast from Holland to the mouth of the Loire could be equally fortified in the time available and also because of the amount of material required. In this respect it was of the greatest importance to accurately predict the landing sector of the enemy.

Feldmarschall Rommel proceeded on the assumption that it would not be possible to drive an enemy back into the sea in a counterattack once he had gained a firm foothold. Thus he wanted to have all available reserves, including the Panzer divisions, deployed immediately behind the coastal defenses, and under his command, so that he could counterattack the landed enemy within a short period of time and destroy him. As long as the landing sector of the enemy was not known with a high degree of probability, however, this assumption required that the Panzer divisions be lined up 'like a string of pearls' behind the coast from Holland to the base of the Contentin peninsula and Brittany.

The supreme commander of the Panzergruppe Command West, General von Geyr, used this quotation to define the concept of Feldmarschall Rommel regarding the deployment of the Panzer divisions to the leadership of the "HJ" Division. He stated his conviction that a landing by the enemy could not be prevented. Thus, the Panzer divisions should be held back as operational reserves and positioned in a way that they could be quickly thrown into critical hot spots. Despite the enemy air superiority he thought it possible that the Panzer divisions, split apart in depth and width, could be moved at night in particular. Once the points of main force had been identified, he wanted to attack the enemy who had broken through with the Panzer divisions outside the range of the ship's artillery. He hoped, thanks to the mobile fighting tactics of the German Panzer troops, to be able to destroy the enemy.

In addition to the landing by sea, General von Geyr expected a simultaneous air landing of great dimension. He was not thinking of just a tactical operation but of a decisive air drop. He considered it necessary to first attack an operational airborne enemy, dropped far from the coastline, with the concentrated Panzer units, he said to 'pounce on them", and destroy them. Only then would he move against the enemy landed by sea. Based on this concept of his, the Panzer divisions would be in concentrated readiness in the woods north of Paris. The exact positions are not shown in the surviving documents. In his book "The Defense against the Invasion, the Concept of the Supreme Commander West 1940–1944" (Freiburg i.Br., 1979), Hans Wegmüller has studied the concepts of the main participants in depth, using the surviving documents, and related them impartially. The know-ledge from surviving participants has not been incorporated. The opinion cited above had been repeatedly stated by Gene-ral von Geyr to the leadership of the "HJ" Division. It was the basis of a communications situation exercise in early 1944 northeast of Paris and of a war game conducted soon there-after in Paris in which the ranking officers of the general staff of the Panzer divisions in the west took part. Generaloberst (4 star general) Guderian was a guest at the war game. The author participated in both, he well remembers this set of objectives and the basics established by General von Geyr.

This theme was also examined in a study by the General for the US Historical Division titled "The History of the Panzergruppe West". There he stated that he was certain that large airborne units would play a considerable role. In preparation for the defense against their action, an extensive war game had taken place in Paris in September 1943. It had been assumed that the opposite side would deploy eight Anglo-American airborne divisions. In accordance with the plan, the body of the airborne troops were to be used in an operational manner.

The memory of the author was confirmed by a letter to him from the General of 20.2.71. In it he wrote concerning this question:

> The reason for my Panzer-airborne mentality was twofold. A former orderly officer of mine worked in the intelligence center of Von Rundstedt. He had been with me when I was the Ic and intelligence officer for half a year with Heeresgruppe Albrecht from the front at Verdun to the Swiss border in 1917–18. He provided me with excellent English press material through Portugal. From that I knew who

was behind the strengthening of the English airborne troops, an outstanding personality whom I knew extremely well. During my time he was with the Grenadier Guards. I also knew that the British had conducted a very successful airborne operation in southeast Asia recently. I had never estimated the units available in England to be as strong as seven divisions (as had the office for foreign armies west, the author). If the British had mounted an operational airborne action with some four divisions, the flow of oil and other supplies to the Panzer divisions at the coast would have been cut off immediately.

I did not only, or even overwhelmingly, expect an airborne enemy. The only considerations we had left were those for our well-trained Panzer divisions. They were, on purely leadership-technical grounds, superior to the US divisions and, with the exception of the 7. English Division (desert rats), to the Anglo-Saxons.

On the subject of the differences of opinion between Feldmarschall Rommel and General von Guderian, this same letter states:

The disagreement between Rommel and myself centered mostly on the fact that I, supported by Guderian and in retrospect by many smart thinkers who were there, wanted to hold back the Panzer divisions in the vast woodlands north of Paris. This would keep them out of range of the Anglo-Saxon ship's artillery and protect them from the twentyfold air superiority in fighter aircraft and would allow them to counter attack a night or dusk air drop. This would have averted almost any impact by the Allied navy or air force. In realization of the situation, Guderian tried one more time to change Rommel's mind. I had been allowed by von Rundstedt to travel to Berchtesgaden and do a briefing there on the situation. I met only with Jodl whom I knew very well. Sitting at a round table, I showed him that, in accordance with the present planning, all forces from Holland to Italy were lined up at the edge of this table rather than in the center. Was this still the German Strategy? After my return the most senseless of all decisions was made. Half of the Panzer divisions were given to Rommel, the other half were held back.[11]

Generaloberst Guderian informed General von Geyr in a letter after the war on his discussions on the matter in the Führer headquarters:

Through the situation briefings for Hitler I became informed in March 1944 of the distribution of the motorized reserves at the invasion front in France, in particular of the deployment of the reserves of the Heeresgruppe (army group) Rommel so close to the Atlantic line of fortifications. It was my opinion that this robbed the reserves of their mobility. This would negate the only possibility of rapidly meeting a successful landing with battle-ready units. Thus, I used one of my regular briefings for Hitler on Panzer matters to bring up the unfortunate utilization of the Panzer units at the Atlantic front and to ask Hitler to intervene.

Hitler replied that he did not want to make a decision which contradicted Rommel's opinions without a verification on the spot. He ordered me to visit Rommel during my up-coming tour of inspection to France and to discuss the question with him. He would then make a decision based on my report.

With this order, accompanied by yourself and Woell-warth, I went to la Roche Guyon to see Rommel. This was on approximately 20 April 1944. During my visit I asked Rommel why he had deployed the motorized forces so close to the coast that they would, in case of an invasion elsewhere, sit immobile and would have to arrive too late. Rommel answered with a long dissertation on his ideas which culminated in, firstly, that the invasion could not come elsewhere but only between Schelde and Somme because this was the shortest distance between England and the continent and, secondly, that any movement by motorized forces, even at night, was impossible. This was one of the main experiences made in Africa. Despite the arguments made by you and myself, Rommel would not change this opinion. I was never close to sharing Rommel's opinion.

After this discussion there was, as I remember, a briefing with Rundstedt who shared our opinion on the deployment and utilization of the motorized reserve but had been unable, so far, to convince the armed forces command staff.

After returning to the Führer headquarters at the beginning of May, I reported to Hitler on the process of these briefings in France and requested again that he direct Rommel to deploy and use the motorized units differently. Hitler answered me at the time: 'I do not wish to oppose the judgment of the commanding field marshal on the spot and will thus refrain from interfering.'

Above all, history must not be twisted to the greater glory of Rommel.

Signed Guderian.[12]

It was the responsibility of the Supreme Commander West, Feldmarschall von Rundstedt, to direct the fighting in the west. He demanded on one hand, as stated in basic order number 37 of the Supreme Commander West of 27.2.44: ". . . to smash the attacking enemy in the water even well before reaching the main line of battle, the coast, and force him to turn back . . ."[13] On the other hand, he realized that his troops were not sufficient to be equally strong in all threatened sectors of the coast. For this reason, he strove to establish and maintain an operational reserve which would enable him to reinforce the troops in the eventual landing sector of the enemy, in case the landing was successful. He certainly considered the possibilities that the enemy landing from the sea would be able to break through the coastal defensive positions and also to conduct larger aerial landings. A strong operational reserve seemed to be a requirement to him in both cases.[14]

Feldmarschall Rommel was unable to get his opinions accepted by Feldmarschall von Rundstedt and so succeeded in getting a Führer decision in April. It stated that Adolf Hitler would decide the point in time when a portion or all of the motorized units in the west would be attached to the Heeresgruppe B (Rommel). Until then they would be under the command of the Supreme Commander West.[15] The Supreme Commander West let himself finally be convinced by Feldmarschall Rommel to tactically assign to him the 2., the 21., and 116. Panzerdivisions after approval by the supreme command. The only battle-ready divisions then available to the Supreme Commander West in the northern sector were the general command I.SS-Panzerkorps with its corps troops, the 12.SS-Panzerdivision "HJ", and the Panzer-Lehr-Division (Panzer- training division). They were declared to be reserves of the supreme command of the armed forces.[16] The 1.SS-Panzerdivision "LAH" was in Belgium for refitting, the 17.SS-Panzergrenadierdivision "G.v.B." (Götz von Berlichingen) was being assembled south of the Loire river. Both were not yet ready for action.

As well as an assessment of the enemy forces and a basic concept for the defense against the invasion, the question the sector in which the landing was expected played a decisive role. In directive 51 of 3.11.43, the Pas de Calais, from where the long-range war against England was planned to begin, was still mentioned. Directive 51a of 27.12.43 had already inclu-ded the Cotentin peninsula in Normandy. Heeresgruppe B (Rommel), however, was still convinced that the enemy landing was to be expected in the sector between Dunkirk and Dieppe. The weekly report of the Heeresgruppe for the period 28.5-3.6.44 defies any attempts to falsify this fact.

Generalmajor (one-star general) of the Bundeswehr a.D. (armed forces of the Federal Republic of Germany, rtd.) Heinz Guderian, a son of Generaloberst Guderian of the Second World War, has examined all available sources on the pre-invasion history and questioned many witnesses of the time in order to clarify this question. The results were published in concentrated form in the magazine "Europüische Wehrkunde" (European defense science), issue 2/80:

> The reinforcing of defenses in Normandy was brought about almost exclusively by Hitler as clearly shown in the daily orders. Hitler's pressure began at the latest at the end of February/beginning of March 1944. He quite correctly judged the intentions of the Anglo-

Americans, namely that they needed a large harbor and would choose one of the two peninsulas, Cotentin in Normandy or Brittany with Cherbourg and Brest harbors. Either one could be relatively easily cut off. On 5.3. he demanded a map of Cotentin peninsula with exact markings of the forces and defenses, and a study on providing of reserves. The inclusion of the 352. Infanterie-Division in the coastal defense and its reinforcement by the 77. Infanterie-Division near Caen can be traced to Hitler's insistence. At the end of April-beginning of May, Hitler increased his influence towards strengthening the forces in Normandy and Brittany. The general command of the II. Fallschirm-Korps (paratroop corps) and the 5. Fallschirm-Division (paratroop division) were moved to Brittany where their task was to defend against air landings together with the 3. Fallschirm-Division which was deployed there. The 21. Panzerdivision was deployed in the Caen area. The 77. Infanterie-Division, deployed there, was added to the coastal defenses at the western base of the Cotentin peninsula. Hitler sent the 91. Luftlande-Division (air landing) and Fallschirmjäger-(paratroop) Regiment 6 to the Cotentin peninsula. The staffs in the west pleaded to move the division not there but to southern Brittany.

They accepted Hitler's concerns only hesitatingly. The Supreme Commander West reported on 7.5.: "With this, the measures by the Supreme Command West to reinforce Normandy from its own forces have been exhausted, until a possible later deployment of OKW (supreme command of the armed forces) reserves. For the near future, these forces are considered to be sufficient."[17]

Feldmarschall Rommel used any opportunity to have the Panzer divisions of the OKW reserves assigned to him. On 2. May 1944 the OKW had once more given its opinion on the probable landing sector:

Even if the majority of all reports speak of an enemy landing between Calais and Le Havre, one must expect, and this is also the opinion of the Führer, above all, the establishment of beachheads in Brittany and on the Cherbourg peninsula, involving 6 to 8 enemy airborne divisions. However, there we are not as strong as in the 15. Armee sector. . . . The Führer demands . . . a report on the planned measures for the reinforcement of defensive forces against enemy air landing on the Cherbourg peninsula and in Brittany.[18]

Heeresgruppe B reported on this subject:

The additional reinforcement of the peninsula requested by the Führer is possible if the OKW reserves general command I. SS-Panzerkorps, Panzer-Lehr-Division (training), 12. SS-Panzerdivision, or parts of theses divisions, are brought in and attached if necessary. Also, parts of the Flak (anti-aircraft) corps, at least one regiment, should be attached to the II. Fallschirmjäger (paratroop) Korps.[19]

The Supreme Commander West reacted to this as follows:

As much as I can appreciate the proposal to bring the OKW reserves into the area under discussion as purely local reinforcements of the line between Normandy and Brittany, I consider it my duty to point out that the last and best mobile units would already be committed to a certain extent even before the fighting begins.[20]

The OKW declined Feldmarschall Rommel's proposal.[21]

On 10 May, during a tour of inspection in the region of the LXXXIV. A.K., the supreme commander of the 7. Armee, Generaloberst Dollmann, met with Feldmarschall Rommel who told him that the Führer judged the situation so, ". . . that the English intend a minor solution at Cotentin with the aim of Cherbourg in order to achieve an initial success." For the Cotentin case, ". . . the Heeresgruppe planned to bring in as further reinforcements the 12. SS-Pz.Div., Nebelwerfer (rocket launcher) Brigade . . ."[22]

The Feldmarschall had still not accepted that the "HJ" Division belonged to the OKW reserve and that he had no jurisdiction over it.

A file note on a commanders' briefing at the Supreme Command West on 26.4.44 indicates how the prospects of defending against the invasion were judged. The chief of staff of the Supreme Command West, Generalleutnant (two-star general) Blumentritt stated to the assembled chiefs of the general staffs of the subordinate command offices, of Luftflotte 3 (air fleet), and the admiralty staff of Kriegsmarinegruppe (navy group) West, as well as members of his own staff:

. . . that everything possible had been done for the defensive effort at the coast, and that the enemy, despite all of his air and materiel superiority was in for a tough fight, which the Supreme Commander West looked forward to with confidence.[23]

During this briefing, a new authority structure in the region of the Supreme Command West was given out by order of the OKW. The Supreme Command West became a pure command staff, no longer joint with Heeresgruppe D. The 1. and the 19. Armee, as well as the front along the Pyrenees front were assigned to Heeresgruppe G, previously H.Gr.D. (Heeresgruppe D). Generaloberst Blaskowitz became its supreme commander, it was assigned to the Supreme Command West. The 15. and the 7. Armee were then assigned to Heeresgruppe B of Feldmarschall Rommel in all aspects, not only the tactical ones.

The opposite side was well informed on the extent of the German defensive preparations through its almost unimpeded aerial reconnaissance and through reports from its extensive network of agents in the area occupied by German troops. In addition, German radio messages could be decoded within a short time period, one to five days. The German side believed that, using the coding system "Enigma" and additional safeguards, as well as code names, the enemy was unable to decipher coded radio messages. The enemy owed important intelligence information to this fact, but of course only to the extent that radio was used to transmit orders from the commands, and not teletype, telephones with scrambler systems, or the dispatch vehicle. (Directive number 51: "Command matter, only through officer").

The landing operation near Dieppe in 1942 had cost the attackers heavy losses. The Canadians lost 3,369 men, among them 907 killed, while total German losses were less than 600.[24] The English thus regarded the dangers of a landing in the area of the "Atlantikwall" (Atlantic fortifications) as considerably higher than did the Americans. It was on their urging that simultaneous landing operations in Northern France (OVERLORD) and Southern France (ANVIL) had initially been planned to splinter the German forces.

The lack of required landing ships forced a delay of a few weeks on ANVIL in order to bring a portion of the landing ships used in Northern France to the Mediterranean.

The following objective had been established for OVERLORD:

> To prepare and conduct an operation, using the military forces deployed and fitted in the United Kingdom and with 1 May as day X, to establish a base on the continent from where further offensive operations can be developed. The base must include harbor facilities which are suitable for shipping supplies for a force of 26 to 30 divisions, and would further enable this force to be reinforced by 3 to 5 divisions and auxiliary units per month from the United States and elsewhere.[25]

Since the landing fleet and the landed forces would have to be supported by fighter units which had to start initially from British airfields, only the coast between Vlissingen and Cherbourg could be considered for the main landing. Dieppe had shown how difficult and time-consuming it was to take a strongly fortified harbor which had to be made usable afterwards. That is why troops and supplies had to be landed on a suitable beach for weeks. From the Allied viewpoint, only the Pas de Calais between Dunkirk and the mouth of the Somme river, and western Normandy between Caen and the Cotentin peninsula could be considered.

A landing at the Pas de Calais was tempting, from there it was the shortest distance to Germany, in particular to the Ruhr valley. It was also the shortest distance for the transport fleet and the fighter aircraft. However, significant portions of the flying units deployed for the defense of the Reich could be brought into this area. In addition, the strongest fortifications had been built in this sector, the majority of these are still there today. At the time, railway guns were added to the bunkered long-range batteries. It was considered necessary to include the harbors of Antwerp or Le Havre. This would have meant too large an extension of the beachhead, and, besides, Ant-werp could only be reached after overcoming numerous water obstacles.

Much spoke in favor of western Normandy: The bay of the Seine river was protected from storms by the Cotentin peninsula, there were sufficient wide, flat landing beaches, the territory inland was mostly unsuitable for Panzer attacks, the Carpiquet airfield already existed in the Caen area and the terrain was suitable for building further airfields. The German Luftwaffe would have to be deployed a long distance from the terrain of the Reich. The drawbacks of greater distance of the beachhead from the Reich territory and from England seemed to play a comparatively smaller role.

In order to expedite the capture of Cherbourg, the initial plan which envisaged only a landing in the Caen/mouth of the Vire river sector was expanded, and another landing on the east coast of the Cotentin was included. The capacity of the landing ships, which was initially thought to be required, was found to be insufficient on closer scrutiny to transport five divisions simultaneously, which was thought to be necessary to form the beachheads. It was sufficient for only three divisions. Also, General Montgomery considered it imperative to subsequently transport a further two divisions in landing ships. The air transport capacity was only sufficient for two airborne brigades while two to three airborne divisions appeared to be necessary. In order to procure the necessary additional transport capacity, extra time was needed and day X was moved from 1 May to the beginning of June.

The Allies expected the following deployment of forces on both sides:

Time	Allies	Germans 1
X + 10 days	18 divisions	25 divisions
X + 20 days	24 divisions	30 divisions
X + 35 days	30 divisions	37.5 divisions[26]

"Basic Conception of the Army Plan"[27] shows the planned time progress of the "OVERLORD" operation.

In order to delay the German deployment, some preconditions and special measures appeared necessary. In particular, simultaneous strong pressure by the Allies on the German fronts in Russia and Italy had to prevent the removal of reinforcements from there to France. Stalin had promised in Teheran a simultaneous offensive and, because of this, pushed for an early determination of the date for the landing in France. Also, the concentration of the forces deployed in France itself at the Normandy front had to be prevented. To achieve this, the threat of a landing in Southern France had to be maintained. As a special measure, a large fake operation for the Pas de Calais was planned and executed. It was given the code name "Fortitude".

Only the most important measures employed will be listed here. The Allied air force concentrated its attacks on targets north and northeast of the Seine river, in this area it conducted twice as many reconnaissance flights as to the west of the river. A fake headquarters of superior Allied command authority was established in southeastern England, storage depots and roads to the loading facilities were built, false fronts were set up, and agents were sent phoney radio messages on the assembly of an army group Patton in southeastern England. In addition, there was misleading radio traffic. For instance, Montgomery's radio messages from his headquarters in Portsmouth were carried to Kent and sent out by radio from there. These activities were observed by the German side and seen as confirmation of the falsified picture of the enemy from the office of foreign armies west. Field marshals von Rundstedt and Rommel, and in particular their Ic (intelligence) officers but also their chiefs of staff, Generalleutnants Blumentritt and Speidel, believed their own judgment that the invasion would take place at the Pas de Calais, confirmed. The OKW accepted at least the danger of a second landing at the Pas de Calais after an initial one in Normandy as certain. What other purpose could the thirty-three operational divisions, invented by Oberst i.G. von Roenne and Major i.G. Michael, possibly serve?

Adolf Hitler was the only one in the supreme command to recognize the deception. He said to Generaloberst Jodl on 6 April 1944:

> This whole activity of the English strikes me as theater. These new reports on blockade measures they take, the defensive measures, and so on, one does not normally do that when such an action is planned. I cannot help but feel that all it turns out to be in the end is shameless play-acting.[28]

Finally, some words on the structure of the commands on both sides need to be added. General Dwight D. Eisenhower was the supreme commander of all invasion forces, his deputy was Air Chief Marshal Sir Arthur Tedder. General Bernard L. Montgomery initially commanded the land forces which were gathered in the 21st Army Group, under Eisenhower. Supreme commander of the Allied fleet was Admiral Sir Bertram Ramsay, supreme commander of the Allied air forces was Air Chief Marshal Sir Trafford Leigh-Mallory.

During the landing phase, Montgomery commanded the 1st Canadian Army, the 2nd British Army and the 1st US Army. Its commander, Lieutenant General Omar N. Bradley was scheduled to become the supreme commander of the 12th Army Group as soon as the 3rd US Army under General Patton entered the action. General Eisenhower would then command both army groups. The bomber command operated independently under the general operational direction of Eisenhower. When comparing this to the German command structure it is striking that General Eisenhower, in addition to the land forces, commanded the navy and tactical air forces which were part of his mission while Generalfeldmarschall von Rundstedt could not issue orders to the navy and air forces. They were commanded by the supreme commanders of the Kriegsmarine and the Luftwaffe respectively. This was unquestionably a drawback for the German side which was partly caused by a lack of forces which often had to be deployed from one front to another in order to exert maximum efforts. Since Germany had the advantage of the inner lines, the disadvantages should have been equal, but only as long as there were no emergency situations on different fronts at the same time. On the Allied side, which fought in a number of theaters of war, far apart, and had to use the slower sea transport to their most distant lines, it was essential and imperative to concentrate the command of all branches of the forces in a theater of war under one supreme commander.

Experience only would show if the disadvantages of the command on the German side would be overcome by good collaboration between the staffs of the Supreme Commander West and Heeresgruppe B with the Kriegsmarinegruppe (navy group) Command West of Admiral Krancke and the Luftflotte 3 of Generalfeldmarschall Sperrle. In order to improve cooperation with the Kriegsmarine, Vizeadmiral (vice admiral) Ruge had been assigned to the staff of Feldmarschall Rommel.

CHAPTER 00.6
Redeployment from Flanders to Normandy in April 1944

A new phase for the "HJ" Division began in April 1944, it was redeployed to Normandy. The threat of the encirclement of the 1. Panzerarmee at the southern Russian front between the Bug and Dnjepr rivers forced the OKW to move the II. SS-Panzerkorps with the newly created SS-Panzerdivisions "Hohen-staufen" (9.) and "Frundsberg" (10.) in fast transport to the eastern front. The "Hitlerjugend" Division was to take over the vacant quarters of the "Frundsberg" Division between the lower Seine and Orne rivers. During the last days of March, the Ia and a small staff drove to Normandy, as an advance party, to make contact and explore. The Ib of the "Frundsberg" Division showed them its previous divisional staff headquarters near Lisieux. The Ia was surprised to learn that the division had been deployed close to the coast. This was in drastic contrast to the opinions of the general of the Panzer troops, west, who was still in charge of the "HJ" Division's training. So the Ia drove immediately to the headquarters of General Geyr von Schweppenburg in Paris and reported to his chief of staff, Generalmajor Ritter and Edler von Dawans which area had been assigned to the Division. The general thought this decision indefensible. He promised to discuss this with the Supreme Command West and predicted a decision within a short period of time since the first parts of the Division could arrive as soon as within two days. The following day, already, the Division was assigned an area further south: Nogent le Roi-Houdan-Pacy sur Eure-Louviers-Elbeuf-Bernay-Vimoutiers-Sees-Mortagne. The Panzerregiment was deployed to the northeastern part: Elbeuf-le Neubourg-Louviers in order to be close to the Seine river crossings. At the time, General Geyr von Schweppenburg, as well as the Supreme Command West and Heeresgruppe B, still regarded the landing of the enemy north of the Seine as most probable. For the same reason, the Pionierbataillon was deployed on both sides of the Eure river from Pacy to Autheuil while the Flak-Abteilung was deployed in the vicinity of the Dreux airfield for its defense.

Panzergrenadierregiment 26 was assigned the area around Houdan in order to be close, in particular with its armored battalion (III./26), to the Panzerregiment. Panzergrenadierregiment 25 was deployed in the western section of the area Bernay-Orbec-Vimoutiers-Sees for possible action in a westerly direction.

The artillery regiment was approximately in the middle near Damville, the reconnaissance Abteilung was deployed in the area around Rugles, the communications Abteilung at Verneuil and Brézolles. The Panzerjäger Abteilung was located in the area near Nogent-le-Roi, and the Werfer Abteilung in the area of Mantes, later in the area Dreux-Nonancourt. The supply troops were moved into the area around Mortagne in the south and the divisional staff headquarters was established in Acon, seven kilometers west of Nonancourt (Appendix 9).

Beginning on 1 April the Division was transported by rail from Belgium to Normandy. The 4./Flak Abteilung 12, for instance, took the following route: on 10 April, march from quarters in Oolen to Mol, there loading and start of rail transport via Mecheln, Gent, Arras, Amiens, Abancourt (fourteen kilometers south of Aumale), Sommery (seven kilometers west of Forges-les Eaux), Darnétal (six kilometers east of Rouen), Sotteville (four kilometers south of Rouen), Oissel (eleven kilometers south of Rouen), Glos (four kilometers south of Montfort-sur-Risle), Brionne, Beaumont-le-Roger (fourteen kilometers southeast of Brionne), Conches, Evreux. Arrival and unloading was at Ivry-la-Bataille in the evening of 11.4. On 12.4. continued march to

Garnay (four kilometers south of Dreux). The battery set up camp there, moved the guns into position around the Dreux airfield, and dug the vehicles with great difficulty into the rocky ground.[1]

CHAPTER 00.7
Reconnaissance—Plans for Deployment—Readiness

Discussions by the Ia with the chief of staff of the general of the Panzer troops, west, had confirmed the conjecture that the "HJ" Division had been moved close to its expected area of action. The Allied landing had to be expected at any time.

While the troops were getting to know their new quarters, the divisional commander and the Ia explored the terrain and informed themselves about the prepared measures for the defense along the coast in the sector from the mouth of the Seine to Bayeux. Initially, they visited the general command of the LXXXIV. A.K. in St. Lô. The commanding general, general of the artillery Erich Marcks, briefed them on the situation in his sector. It extended from Merville-Franceville-Plage just east of the mouth of the Orne river along the coast of Normandy to the mouth of the Vire river, and along the east, north and west coast of the Cotentin to Avranches. General Marcks considered two possibilities for the imminent Allied landing:

1. Landing between Orne and Vire and on the east coast of the Cotentin with Paris as the objective of the operation,
2. A major landing in another sector and simultaneous smaller landings in sectors of his corps on the east and west coast of the Cotentin in order to capture the harbor of Cherbourg.[1]

The 716. and 352. Infanteriedivisions were deployed in the sector between Merville and the mouth of the Vire river. The 716. Inf. Div. was a so-called 'static' division, immobile and weak in numbers. Its mission was the defense of the coastal sector between Merville and Asnelles-sur-Mer (eleven kilometers northeast of Bayeux). The 352. Inf. Div. was deployed in the adjoining sector on the left which extended to the mouth of the Vire. This division was structured as a regular infantry division. It contained core personnel which had fought in the east and of reserves newly brought-in during the course of refitting in the west. It had been moved into this sector only at the beginning of March on the urging of Adolf Hitler. Until then, the 716. Inf. Div. had to defend this sector in addition to its own. The 77. Inf. Div. was deployed in the area around Caen at the time as reserve. It was replaced at the end of April by the 21. Panzerdivision. The major effort in building defensive installation had initially been directed to the northern part of the eastern coast of the Cotentin and to the beaches of the port-town of Cherbourg. The strengthening of positions in the sector between Merville and the mouth of the Vire had only begun later. The defensive positions and bases there were mostly not reinforced yet, the artillery bunkers were still under construction. Great effort was directed to the construction of obstacles against airborne troops, the so-called "Rommel asparagus", and of obstacles in the water before the beaches.

General Marcks expected the first landing to be successful. He was unsure if it was possible to drive back the enemy with his own forces. He was dependent on the provision of further forces and expected that the "HJ" Division would be assigned to him. The general was certain that the Allied landing would take place in June.[2]

Brigadeführer (one-star general) Witt and Sturmbannführer (major) Meyer were greatly impressed by General Marcks who had lost a leg during the campaign in the east. His judgment of the situation was convincing. The briefing on preparations for the defense made them anxious. In order to gather a personal impression they drove to the Channel coast. They found that the positions of the 716. Inf. Div. consisted of a line of bases and defensive positions along the beach, spaced 800–1,200 meters apart. Behind it were only a few anti-tank weapons and the artillery of the division was deployed almost completely in unprotected firing positions. Some artillery bunkers were under construction, e.g. near Mont Fleury, six kilometers east of Arromanches. The artillery of the defenders was unprotected from an aerial bomb attack and subsequent bombardment by ship's artillery from the sea. Once it had been knocked out, the same fate awaited the positions of the infantry. It was surprising and alarming that many French civilians, some of them taking part in the construction of the fortifications, were moving about freely through the positions. The doors were wide open to espionage. It was shown later how justified these misgivings really were. Adjoining the sector of the 716. Inf. Div. to the right, was the 711. Inf. Div., also a 'static' division. It belonged to the LXXXI. A.K. which had its staff headquarters in Rouen. The line between the 711. and the 716. Inf. Div. was at the same time the line between the 15. and the 7. Armee. In the sector of the 711. Inf. Div., on Mont Canisy hill near Deauville, bunkers for a heavy battery were under construction. The 112 meter high hill controlled a significant part of the Seine estuary. It was hoped that the battery would be operational in time. Other than that, the defensive preparations were the same as in the sector of the 716. Inf. Div.

Brigadeführer Witt and his Ia became convinced that the enemy would be successful in a landing operation due to his superiority in materiel and the insufficient reinforcement of the German defensive positions, their lack of depth and weak numbers. It would be even more easily achieved if the attack from the sea was coupled with an aerial landing in the rear of the coastal positions. The area around Caen was particularly suitable for this. The Carpiquet airfield had to be a tempting target for the enemy. The terrain north and northwest of Caen was the best suited for tanks in the sector of the 716. Inf. Div. Concentrated action by Allied tank units had to be expected there as well as actions by German Panzer divisions in the counterattack. The area around Caen would likely become a center of the fighting after a landing on the Normandy coast.

The general of the Panzer troops, west, issued a directive to the "HJ" Division to prepare three plans of advance into action in case of an Allied landing:

1. Crossing the Seine between Paris and Rouen for action between the Somme and Seine rivers,
2. Deployment for action between the mouths of the Seine and Orne rivers,
3. Deployment for action in the area northwest and west of Caen.

After exploring the roads and bridges, the staff of the Divisional staff prepared plans for advance A, B and C. In order to break up the Division in width and depth, four marching routes for each were envisaged. One of the four roads was to be used by the tracked vehicles, i.e. the Panzerregiment, the Schützenpanzer (APC) battalion (III./26), and the I. Artillerieabteilung (self-propelled). Panzergrenadier regiments 25 and 26 (without III. battalion), with an attached artillery detachment each, and the other units of the Division would march on the other three roads. The march routes were located in four separate areas of movement so that a detour was possible without impeding the neighbor convoys. The units received the required orders and maps for each of the three plans. The maps showed the areas of movement, points of departure, destinations points, feeder routes and the march routes. Towns which could not be driven through were also indicated. The map for the III. Artillerieabteilung of march plan C has survived. Departure point for the Abteilung was Gacé, the feeder route joined the marching route at Vimoutiers. It led from there via Courcy-Rouvres-Grainville Langannerie-Barbery-Brieux (crossing of the Orne) to Tournay-sur-Odon (twenty kilometers west of Caen).

The plans for the deployment were submitted to the general of the Panzer troops, west. He requested a further plan soon thereafter for a deployment in the area of the mouth of the Loire river. This plan was also developed. It can no longer be established which superior command offices were informed by the general of the Panzer troops, west, but it can be expected that the Supreme Command West and the supreme command of the Heeresgruppe B received these documents. One of these two supreme commands had probably issued directives to prepare the plans for deployment.

In order to be able to alert the troops immediately in case of a landing by the Allies, the Division command did not want to wait for the orders from the superior command office. It was agreed that the 711. Inf. Div. would immediately report any relevant sightings. To ensure rapid transmission, the telephone company of the communications Abteilung 12 established a direct connection to the neighboring Heer switchboards through the French postal telephone network and set up a switchboard of its own in the post office at Verneuil.[3]

The Ia and the 01, Obersturmführer (1st. lt.) Meitzel, established contacts with the long range reconnaissance squadron of the Luftwaffe based in Evreux in order to secure additional information. They learned from its commander, Oberstleutnant (lieutenant colonel) von Riebesel, that his crews in their Me 110s had been almost completely unsuccessful for weeks in intruding into English airspace. This prevented any new information on the status of the preparations by the Allies for the invasion from becoming available. The long range reconnaissance crews judged the extraordinary increase in enemy defenses to be a sign of the impending landing operation. Oberstleutnant von Riebesel promised to advise the staff of the "HJ" Division of any new developments.

As soon as they had taken up their new quarters, all units of the Division continued their interrupted training. The emphasis was on the training in units, but it was hampered by the shortage of fuel. The lively Allied air activity forced the training to take place during dusk and night hours. Such training was conducted on three days of each week. Another day was set aside for training exclusively in fighting airborne enemy forces after a landing. Frequent practice alarms increased the speed of combat readiness of the troops. Because of the expected landing from the air, the troops had set up their camp for defense on all sides. Sturmmann Hans Lierk of the escort company of the Division reported:

> We were working hard on setting up the all-round defenses of the Divisional command post. As the Pak (anti-tank) platoon, we were assigned the sector to the left of the road to Nonancourt. The farms were called le Mesnil. In a depression in the terrain we dug a position. I well remember these days when we had to get up at 02.00 hours because of the heat. Apart from taking turns at the anti-aircraft machine gun, we had 'a very easy job' during the day.[4]

The vehicles, even the Panzers, were dug in to protect them from bomb splinters and on-board weapons. The best possible camouflage was provided.

After completion of the unit training, the various courses continued. Under the direction of Hauptsturmführer Wilhelm Beck, chief of the 2. Panzerkompanie and a holder of the Knight's Cross, an officer cadet course was held in Elbeuf. On 1 and 15 May, a total of fifty-eight noncoms and men who had successfully completed the course, were assigned to the officer training schools. In Château Condé, noncom training courses continued, directed by Hauptsturmführer Bubenzer. Sturmmann Jochen Leykauff of the Aufklärungsabteilung of SS-Panzergrenadierregiment 25 reported:

> The Divisional commander inspected the course. Early in the morning we left for combat training with live ammunition. Our platoon deployed from a village towards cardboard cut-out soldiers to the left of a heavy machine gun position whose firing range restricted our attack sector on the right. Bullets were just whistling past us. We crawled into firing range of the cardboard soldiers and fired on them with all we had. This exercise was applauded by Divisional commander Witt who had just been promoted to Brigade-führer (one-star general). After that, our platoon sat with mixed feelings before the sand box which was set up in a building next to the castle; we were supposed to demonstrate our tactical knowledge to the commander. Witt himself, while his calmness and relaxed behavior set us at ease, picked one of the course participants by putting a kindly hand on the shoulder of our comrade during his briefing of the situation. Witt explained the mission to him and suggested our comrade think about the best tactical approach outside in the open for five minutes. It worked out well. Contact was quickly established and we answered without hesitation and in an acceptable manner.
>
> In the afternoon the commander invited the whole course for coffee and cakes. We sat in a mixed row, the commander, instructors and students in a ground-level hall of the castle. During those days I saw my Divisional commander for the last time.[5]

The Flakabteilung was moved from the area around Dreux in mid-May. It was deployed to secure bridges across the Seine River. The 1. and the 3. Batterie (8.8 cm Flak) took up positions in Elbeuf, the 2. (8.8 cm Flak) and the 4. (3.7 cm Flak) took up positions first at Pont-de-l'Arche, then near Gaillon. The 14. (Flak-) Kompanie of Panzergrenadierregiment 26, under the command of the Flakabteilung, also took up position near Gaillon. Until the start of the invasion the Abteilung shot down four or five Allied four-engined bombers, but it could not prevent the destruction of the bridges.[6] The Abteilung lost three men dead and two wounded.[7]

In May the Division turned over its surplus of 2,042 men and an additional 13 officers to the "LAH" Division which had returned from Russia and was being refitted in Belgium. It had been quartered in the same area which the "HJ" Division had left at the beginning of April. The men left the circle of comrades with whom they had grown together for three-quarters of a year with heavy hearts. On paper the Division, with a requirement for 20,516 officers, noncoms and men, had a surplus of 24 men. However, since the previously mentioned 58 officer cadets had been assigned to the schools, there existed an unimportant shortage of 34 men. The missing weapons and vehicles arrived at the Division during April and May. The missing "Panthers" arrived only during the first days of June. The Panzerjägerabteilung still did not have command Panzers, the Werfer Abteilung had no tractors at all. Thus, both Abteilungen were not ready for action and they could not even conduct unit training. Missing, in addition, were some command Panzers, recovery Panzers, reconnaissance Panzers for the Artillerieregiment, ammunition carriers for the I. Artillerie-abteilung, armored reconnaissance vehicles for the Aufklärungsabteilung, APCs for the communications Abteilung and light tractors for the 2-cm Flak. The Division was reported "ready for offensive action" on 1 June 1944. The general command of the I. SS-Panzerkorps stated in its comments on the report from the Division:

> The Division, with the exception of the Werferabteilung and the Panzerjägerabteilung, is fully ready for any action in the west.[8]

The leadership and troops fully realized that difficult and, at the same time, decisive battles lay ahead. After nine months of intensive combat training they trusted their own abilities. All in all, they were well equipped and armed. They were looking at the coming action with confidence. Sturmmann Jochen Leykauff, a volunteer born in 1926, wrote down his thoughts and feelings which moved him just before the start of the invasion battle. He probably spoke for many others:

> Everyone was waiting for the attack across the Channel. We were fully aware that decisive battles were approaching. Our first action lay ahead. We were looking forward to it.
>
> The Allies planned to take apart the "baby milk division", as they called us. But we were not afraid. Sometimes we even got carried away a bit, and big-headed. After the intensive training on our weapons we felt sure we could take the heat. It had been said that the enemy would be physically superior to us. Well, we knew that we were quick, agile and confident. We trusted our officers and noncoms who had been hardened in battle. We had known them since the beginning of the training. During combat training with live ammunition we had enjoyed seeing them in the mud together with us, with steel helmet and submachine gun.
>
> We were afraid that the bomber squadrons which droned overhead day after day would soon also drop their loads on us. I had noted down for my father how I wanted to be mentioned in the newspaper. I was often on edge without discernible reason. During my time off I tried to be alone, walked in the spring woods, took in many sights. My confidence remained high.[9]

Summer 1943. Volunteers for the "Hitlerjugend" Division at the training camp in Wildflecken/Rhön.

They are trained by Hitler Youth leaders, Waffen-SS NCOs, and NCO candidates.

Summer 1943. Rifle firing training at the camp in Wildflecken/Rhön.

Final parade.

Recruits arrive at the Reconnaissance Battalion in Turnhout, Belgium, on 30 September 1943.

A company marching to field training. The commanding officer is an Army (Heer) officer assigned to the division.

Winter 1943–44. Divisional Security Company—panzer-grenadiers with 2-cm Flak—practices street fighting in Turnhout, Belgium.

Oud Turnhout, Belgium, Autumn 1943. A 2-cm Flak platoon of Divisional Security Company marches, singing, to a field exercise. Because of the lack of fuel, the guns are drawn by the men.

Winter 1943–44. The first motorcycles for the motorcycle messenger section of the Divisional Headquarters. The motorcycles here are Italian "Moto-Guzzi" models.

Turnhout-Zwanestrand, Belgium, Winter 1943–44. SS-Mann Gert Rittner of the motorcycle messenger section of the Divisional Headquarters with his sidecar motorcycle, a BMW-R12 (20PS/750 ccm).

Belgium, Autumn 1943. "Chicken" Section of the 11th Company of SS Panzergrenadier-regiment 26 in front of the living quarters in the Beverloo training area.

Oolen, Belgium, 9 April 1944. The signals staff of the 4th Battery of SS Flak Battalion 12 with their improvised, converted Italian vehicles.

Signals soldiers of SS Flak Battalion 12 with a backpack radio transmitter b/f during a signals exercise on 24 April 1944 in Garney, Normandy.

Damville, May 1944. Burial of two motorcycle messengers of the flak platoon of SS Panzerartillerieregiment 12, who were involved in a fatal accident at Castle Coulonges.

Summer 1943. 2nd Company of SS Panzerregiment 12 marches, singing, on the way to their training at the military camp at Mailly le Camp, France. That was their only formal training.

Summer 1943. SS Panzerregiment 12, training with the Panzer IV in Mailly le Camp. Tank crew members Hartmann, Buntrock, and Vogel.

Panzer IV No. 636 with loader Sturmmann Georg Fugunt and radio operator (in front) Sturmann Erich Moro.

Winter 1943–44. March exercise of SS Panzerregiment 12 in the Ostend area. The first panzer of 6th Company is driven by Unterscharführer Heinz Berner, commander of the maintenance section.

Beek on the Albert Canal, Belgium, Spring 1944. 4th (heavy) Company, SS Panzergrenadierregiment 26. Company commander: Untersturmführer Alois Hartung.

10 November 1943 to 2 January 1944. Training course for the signals men of SS Flak Battalion 12, at SS Signals Battalion 12 in Turnhout.

Panzer IV during a firing exercise. The commander of 1st Battalion, Sturmbannführer Jürgensen, is standing next to the panzer.

Winter 1943–44. Panther of 3rd Company of SS Panzerregiment 12 on a firing exercise at Beverloo, Belgium.

Recruits of Panzer Reconnaissance Battalion 12 are sworn in on 22 January 1944 in Turnhout.

23 December 1943. New vehicles arrive at SS Panzer Reconnaissance Battalion 12 in Turnhout. On the left is Staff Sergeant Rasmussen.

Parts of SS Panzer-regiment 12 on exercise on 6 February 1944 in the training area at Beverloo, Belgium. In the turret is Obersturmbann-führer Max Wünsche. In front of the Panther, from left: General Frhr. Geyr v. Schweppen-burg, Colonel General Guderian, Oberführer Fritz Kraemer, and Oberführer Fritz Witt.

The Inspector General of the Panzer Troops, Colonel General Heinz Guderian and the Chief of Staff of 1st SS Panzer Corps, Oberführer Fritz Kraemer.

Sturmbannführer Fritz Buchsein, GSO 2.

Evreux, 20 April 1944. Hauptsturmführer Wilhelm Beck, leader of the officer candidates course, distributes prizes to the winners in a multidisciplinary military sports competition. Beck was killed in action on 10 June 1944 near la Caine.

Oud Turnhout, Belgium, Autumn 1943. From the left: Untersturmführer Günther Doldi, intelligence officer, and Untersturmführer Hausrath, orderly officer No. 4. Hausrath was killed in action, together with Brigadeführer Fritz Witt, on 14 June 1944 at the divisional command post in Caen/Venoix.

Spring 1944. Introduction of officers to the Supreme Commander of Heeresgruppe D and Supreme Commander West, Generalfeldmarschall von Rundstedt, on the occasion of an exercise in the west. Generalmajor der Waffen-SS Fritz Witt, GFM von Rundstedt, the IIa Hauptsturmführer Fritz Buchsein, the Ia Sturmbannführer Hubert Meyer, the commander of I. Abteilung of SS-Panzerregiment 12 Sturmbannführer Arnold Jürgensen.

Normandy, Spring 1944. An Obersturmführer briefs the Division Commander, Generalmajor der Waffen-SS Fritz Witt, during an exercise. On the left: Ia, Sturmbannführer Hubert Meyer.

The exercise is observed from a gun tractor by (from the right): the Field Marshall, Sturmbannführer Hubert Meyer, Obergruppenführer Sepp Dietrich, Oberführer Fritz Witt, and Standartenführer Kurt Meyer.

SS Panzerregiment 12 on parade. Here several Panzer IVs of 2nd Battalion.

Spring 1944. 1st Company of Panzer Reconnaissance Battalion 12. In the middle of the first row, from left to right: Staff Sergeant Rasmussen, Obersturmführer Peter Hansmann, Untersturmführer Theo Flanderka. The crews of the armoured cars wore black, the motorcyclists wore grey.

March 1944. Members of the first course for officer candidates of the Division visit the young men and girls of the Flemish Youth Organization in Antwerp.

14 March 1944. The return home of SS Sturmbrigade Wallonien after breaking out of the Cauldron of Cherkassey, Ukraine. A march past in Charleroi in front of Sturmbannführer Leon Degrelle.

The Sturmbrigade on its march from Charleroi to Brussels.

Guard duty.

Normandy, 1 May 1944. 3rd Company of SS Panzerregiment 12. First row, in the middle, from left: Untersturmführer Jungblut, Staff Sergeant Post, Obersturmführer Rudolf v. Ribbentrop, Oberjunker Alban, Oberjunker Bogensberger, and Obersturmführer Stagge.

Members of the Kraderkungs-Zug (motorcycle reconnaissance Zug) of SS Panzerregiment 12. Rear center: Oberscharführer Harry Wontorra.

Aquigny, near Louviers, May 1944. Unterscharführer Harry Wontorra, leader of the motorcycle reconnaissance Zug of SS Panzerregiment 12, with some of his men in an amphibious vehicle. From the left, standing: Schmieder, Kaiser; sitting: Heinz Krohn, Günter Kleist, Harry Wontorra, Kurt Schoppe, ?.

Normandy, May 1944. Visiting a training course for NCOs. From left to right: Hauptsturmführer Bubenzer (course leader), Brigadeführer Fritz Witt, Sturmbannführer Hubert Meyer (GSO I), Hauptsturmführer Siegfried Rothemund (divisional adjutant), and Hauptsturmführer Wilhelm Beck (SS Pz.Regt. 12).

Waiting for Reichsjugendführer Artur Axmann in front of Castle Broglie, Normandy. From left to right: Oberführer Fritz Witt, Hauptsturmführer Albert Schuch (divisional HQ commander) Obergruppenführer Sepp Dietrich (GOC 1st SS Panzer Corps), Sturmbannführer Hubert Meyer (GSO I), and Obersturmbannführer Max Wünsche (commander, SS Panzerregiment 12).

Spring 1944. Reichsjugendführer (Reich Youth Leader) Artur Axmann and Oberführer Fritz Witt.

Generalmajor der Waffen-SS Fritz Witt on his last birthday on 27 May 1944 in Tillières-sur-Avre.

Normandy, 1944. The Commander General of I. SS-Panzerkorps, General der Waffen-SS Sepp Dietrich, and the Commander of "HJ" Division, Generalmajor der Waffen-SS Fritz Witt.

Dietrich and Witt. The photo was a gift from Dietrich to the killed general's son, Peter, with a dedication on the reverse.

Lunch on the go. Note the combination spoon-fork cutlery.

The Division during the Defensive Battles against the Allied Invasion in Normandy

CHAPTER 0.1
The Last Preparations and Decisions

During the summer of 1944, the Western Allies used double daylight saving time, based on western European time. The Germans used simple daylight saving time, based on central European time. Western European time is one hour behind central European time. 14.00 hours at double summer time west equals 12.00 hours western European time. 14.00 hours German summer time equals 13.00 central European time and 12.00 west European time. So the German and Allied times in the documents coincide, but they are two hours ahead of the standard time of the area of battle, the west European time. All times are given as they are in the original documents since they do coincide, which is the important consideration in this context.

The directive No. 51a from the supreme command of the armed forces (OKW)/armed forces staff of 27.12.1943 stated, among others:

> The concentration of enemy forces in southern England is almost completed. It can be expected that it will be complete by mid-February. From mid-February onwards, the start of the major enemy landing can be expected at any time.

In reality, the Allies were not yet ready at that time. Only on 18 May did its supreme command establish 5 June as the probable date.

Certain meteorological data played a decisive role in determining the start of the landing. The landing by sea had to take place during daylight so that the planned coastal sectors and points of orientation could be recognized by the landing craft, the ship's artillery and the air force. The bombers required one hour of daylight for their attack in preparation of the sea landing. The first waves of the landing troops were originally scheduled to land with the high tide which occurred at dawn. The second wave had to land before dark with the next high tide. After the coastal defense had been reinforced by the obstructions ahead of the beaches on the orders of Feldmarschall Rommel, the Allies decided to land the first wave three hours before high tide, outside of the obstructions. These were to be removed by special teams in order to allow further unloading close to the beaches.

Tactical air landings were planned to precede the sea landings. The transport aircraft with the paratroopers and the gliders with the airborne troops had to fly in undetected during the dark and then drop the troops by moonlight. That meant that the full moon had to rise around midnight during the night of the landing.

These conditions could be expected on the east coast of the Cotentin, where the Americans were to land, on 5 June. Namely, half tide forty minutes before there was enough light to fire, and a full moon rising late on 4 June.

Certain meteorological conditions were also required for a possible landing: On the day of the landing and for the following three days, the wind could not be stronger than force 4, the cloud base had to be around 1,000 m, the cloud coverage could not exceed 5/10, and a visibility of 3 nautical miles was necessary. The final decision on the day of the landing could thus be made only a few days prior, when the meteorological developments could be forecast.

Such considerations also formed the basis of planning at Supreme Command West and Heeresgruppe Rommel. The Kriegsmarine (navy) group command west had spotted a landing exercise by the Allies on the northern coast of the Channel. The sea landing had taken place two hours after low tide and during a full moon. This report indicated to the Supreme Command West and the Heeresgruppe B the possibility that the sea landing would not take place during high tide. An entry in the war diary of the Heeresgruppe B on 3 June 1944 stated:

> . . . available reports indicate possible use of the time of low tide for an enemy landing. Obstructions ahead of the beaches are to be moved forward again during the spring low tide. Details are contained in order H.Gr. Ia No. 2363/44 geh. (secret) of 2.6. to the armies and the W.B. Ndl.[1]

The landing had initially been expected at the beginning of May, then on 18 May. In the monthly report of the Heeresgruppe B for the period 21-27 May 1944 it is stated, among others:

> Strongly increased enemy air activity. However, this is not to be judged as the last phase of preparations for the invasion.

The following weekly report for the period from 18 May to 3 June said on the subject:

> Systematic continuation and increase of enemy air attacks and increased mining of our harbors using improved mines indicate elevated readiness for enemy air drops. The concentration of air attacks on the coastal positions between Dunkirk and Dieppe and the Seine-Oise bridges confirm the expected main location of a major landing and the possibility of cutting the connection with Flanders and the rear . . . Since 1.6. there has been an increase in the numbers of messages to the French resistance organizations in enemy radio broadcasts. Based on experience so far, they cannot be used to confirm the imminent start of the invasion.[2]

It must be remembered that this report assumed the probable landing sector to be the coast between Dunkirk and Dieppe. It is surprising that the bombardment of the battery "Riva Bella" at the mouth of the Orne river during the night from 28 to 29 May, and of the battery at Longues, north of Bayeux, on 3 June, were not mentioned in this context.

That the Pas de Calais had really been assumed to be the landing sector was confirmed by the tide tables for the time period in question. The following times for the morning high tides and morning low tides were given in the 'Annuaire Ports de France 1944' for 5, 12, and 15 June:

	St. Mâlo	Cherbourg	Ouistreham	Le Havre	Dieppe	Cayeux-sur-Mer (Somme estuary)
5 June						
morning low	11.47	01.10	03.13	03.24	04.03	04.12
morning high	04.57	06.47	08.26	08.05	09.44	09.53
5 June	**Boulogne**	**Dunkirk**				
morning low	04.54	05.12				
morning high	10.05	10.54				
12 June						
morning low	04.17	06.13	08.18	09.19		
morning high	09.52	11.52	00.45	02.23		
12 June						
morning low	09.56	10.19				
morning high	02.42	03.29				
15 June						
morning low	07.25	09.36	11.28			
morning high	00.33	02.39	05.31	04.24	05.26	05.39
15 June						
morning low	00.28	00.45				
morning high	05.52	06.53				

The times are "temps universel" = western European time.

The times given in the following table are based on the times above, and are 'Allied double summer time' = 'single German summer time' (see introductory remark) and the times for the morning low tide plus two hours. The data for Ouistreham and Cayeux-sur-Mer are actual data calculated by the 'Service Hydrographique et Océanographique de la Marine' in Brest.[2a]

	St. Mâlo	Cherbourg	Ouistreham	Le Havre	Dieppe	Cayeux-sur-Mer (Somme estuary)
5 June						
morning low +2	15.47	05.10	07.13	07.24	08.03	08.12
morning high	06.57	08.47	10.26	10.05	11.44	11.53
5 June	**Boulogne**	**Dunkirk**				
morning low +2	08.54	09.12				
morning high	12.05	12.54				
12 June						
morning low +2	08.17	10.13	12.18	13.19		
morning high	11.52	13.52	02.45	04.23		
12 June						
morning low +2	13.56	14.19				
morning high	04.42	05.29				
15 June						
morning low +2	11.25	13.36	15.28			
morning high	02.33	04.39	06.24	07.26	07.39	
15 June						
morning low +2	04.28	04.45				
morning high	07.52	08.53				

These tables clearly show that Heeresgruppe B could not expect a sea landing on 5 June in the coastal sector between Dieppe and Dunkirk either at morning high tide or 2 hours after morning low tide. The times were at least some three to six hours after first light at which the start of the landing could be expected. The morning high tide, during which a landing was still considered most likely, occurred in this sector at approximately that time of day between 12 and 15 June.

This judgment of enemy intentions regarding timing led to a number of grave decisions. On 4 June Feldmarschall Rommel, together with his Ia, Oberst i.G. von Tempelhoff, traveled to Germany after having handed over command to Feld-marschall von Rundstedt, during his absence, on 3 June. He wanted to be in Herrlingen near Ulm for his wife's birthday on 6 June. Thereafter he would try to set up a meeting with Adolf Hitler at Obersalzberg to clarify a number of important questions. The commander of the Kriegsmarine (navy) group command west, Admiral Krancke, informed the Supreme Command West that the ships on guard duty along the coast could not leave their bases due to heavy seas. He set out for an inspection tour to

Bordeaux on 5 June.[3] Generaloberst (four-star general) Dollmann, the supreme commander of the 7. Armee, scheduled a planning exercise for 6 June. It would take place at Rennes, Brittany, and all the divisional commanders of his Armee would participate. Generalleutnant Hellmich, commander of the 243. Infanteriedivision (west coast Cotentin), Generalleutnant von Schlieben, commander of the 709. Infanteriedivision (Cherbourg and east coast Cotentin) and Generalleutnant Falley, commander of the 91. (airborne) Luftlandedivision (central Cotentin) departed in the evening of 5 June for Rennes. These decisions were supposedly made easier by the forecast of a period of bad weather for early June. The reports by the liaison meteorologist at the Supreme Command West, Regierungsrat (senior administrative official) Dr. Müller, did not confirm such claims, just the opposite.

On 3 June, one day prior to Feldmarschall Rommel's departure for Ulm, he reported at 05.00 hours:

General weather situation:
Rising pressure in southern England and northern France/Belgium has pushed the ridge of low pressure stretching from Russia westward to the mid-Atlantic northward. It will thus influence only the northern and eastern sections of the area of the Supreme Command West through occasional extensive cloud cover and light scattered rain. The remaining larger area of the Supreme Command West will remain, under the influence of the high pressure to the west, generally free of disturbances . . .
Forecast until tomorrow, 4.6.1944, evening: No significant change in the present weather situation is foreseen. France will be generally without disturbances, clearing during the night and sunny to cloudy during the day. The remaining sectors of the Supreme Command West will be cloudier in the north and east, with scattered rain. Moderate winds from western and northern directions. Localized morning fog, but generally good visibility. temperatures during the night around 10 degrees C, during the day 15 to 20.
Predictions regarding enemy air activity until evening today: Departures from the English bases without interference by weather, air activity in the area of the Supreme Command West will be possible without significant problems, except to the north and east where increasing cloudiness will interfere.[4a]

On the same day, the "Weather forecast regarding enemy action during the night of 3.6 to 4.6.1944" were issued. It stated:

1) Air force: Departure from English bases without weather problems, air activity in most of the area of the Supreme Command West will be possible without interference by weather conditions.

2) Navy: In the Hoofden (most southerly part of the North Sea) and
the eastern section of the Channel, moderate to strong westerly
to northwesterly winds approximately strength 2–4, occasionally
5. Wave height 2–3. Mostly good visibility, local morning fog. In
the western Channel and the Bay of Biscay weak to moderate
northerly winds, strength 1–3, occasionally to 4. Wave height 2–3.
Mostly good visibility, locally reduced by morning fog . . .[4b]

The weather report of 4 June predicted a change to a more unstable
weather situation. The report of 05.00 hours stated, among others:

General weather situation:
   The low pressure area south of Ireland has strengthened significantly during the last 24 hours. It will extend further to the south
and erode the small high pressure ridge which stretches from the
Azores across the Bay of Biscay to the Alps. Southern England as
well as the northern section of the Supreme Command West can
expect a transition to an unstable weather situation for the next
days.
   Forecast until today 24.00 hours: In the area south and west of
the Seine generally clear, to the north increasing, and mostly high,
cloudiness. Weak to moderate westerly winds. Mostly good visibility.
Temperatures climbing to 20 to 25 degrees C during the day . . .[4c]

The weather forecast regarding enemy actions for the night of 4.6 to
5.6.1944 stated:

1) Air force: Departures from the English bases will at times or in
places be impeded by a relatively small area of bad weather, but
will generally be without major problems. Air activity in the
region of the Supreme Command West will generally take place
without problems. Later, especially in the north, increasing
cloudiness will slightly interfere.
2) Navy: In the Hoofden and in the Channel mostly fresh southwesterly winds, in the Hoofden strength 4–6, occasionally 7. Wave
height in the Channel 3–4, in the Hoofden occasionally to 5.
Mostly good visibility, in the Hoofden later reduced by rain . . .[4d]

The reports for the day of the invasion and the previous night stated,
among others:

Weather situation as of 5.6.1944, 0500 hours:
   General weather situation: As expected, the strong central low
pressure area between Iceland and Scotland has greatly eroded the

BASIC CONCEPTION OF THE ARMY PLAN

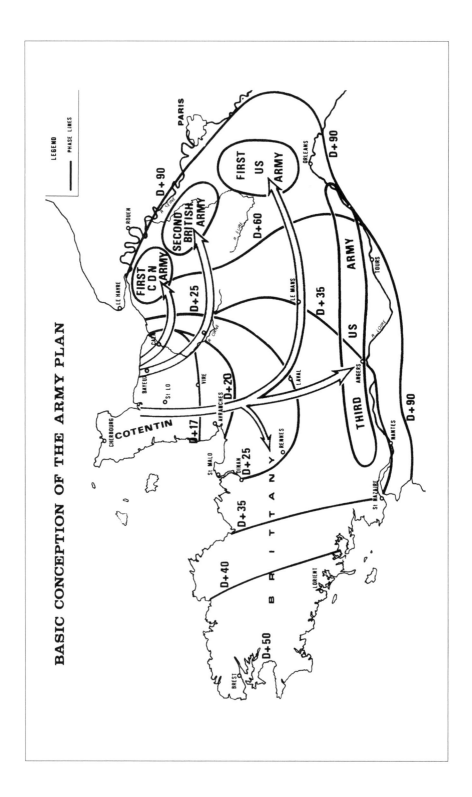

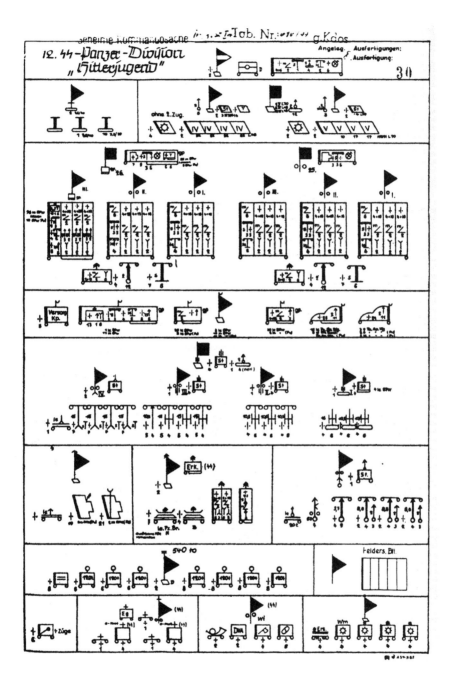

Report of establishment strength from 1 June 1944

Meldung vom _____ 1944   **Verband:** 12.SS-Pz. Div. "H.J."
                                      Unterstellungsverhältnis: _____

1. Personelle Lage am Stichtag der Meldung:

a) Personal:

	Soll	Fehl
Offiziere	664	144
Uffz.	4 575	2 192
Mannsch.	15 277	+2 360
Hiwi	(1 103)	(887)
Insgesamt	20 516	+ 24

c) in der Berichtszeit eingetroffener Ersatz:

	Ersatz	Genesene
Offiziere	26	-
Uffz. und Mannsch.	125 / + 216 Hiwi	-
	341	

b) Verluste und sonstige Abgänge in der Berichtszeit vom _____ bis _____

	tot	verw.	verm.	krank	sonst.
Offiziere	1	-	-	-	13
Uffz. und Mannsch.	20	11	-	25	2042
Insgesamt	21	11	-	25	2055

d) über 1 Jahr nicht beurlaubt:

insgesamt: **181** Köpfe **0,9** % d. Iststärke

davon:	12 - 78 Monate	19 - 24 Monate	über 24 Monate
	170	8	3

Platzkarten im Berichts-monat zugewiesen _____

2. Materielle Lage:

		Gepanzerte Fahrzeuge						Kraftfahrzeuge				
	Stu. Gesch.	III	IV	V	VI	Schtz.Pz. Pz.Sp. Art.Pz.B. (o.Pz.Fu.Wg)	Pak Sf.	Kräder Ketten	m.angetr. Bwg	sonst.	Pkw gel.	Pkw o
Soll (Zahlen)	-	4	101	81	-	390	45	132		671	908	99
einsatzbereit zahlenm.	-	2	91	48	-	306	12	2	(22)	(692) 670	474	265
einsatzbereit in % des Solls	-	50	90	59,2	-	78,4	26,6	1,5		103,1 / 99,8	52,2	267
in kurzfristiger Instandsetzung (bis 3 Wochen) zahlenm.	-	-	7	2	-	27	1	-	-	128	31	153
in % des Solls	-	-	6,9	2,3	-	6,9	2,2	-	-	19	3,5	154,5

	noch Kraftfahrzeuge				Ketten-Fahrzeuge		Waffen			
	Lkw Maultiere	gel.	o	Tonnage	Zgkw. *)	RSO **)	s Pak	Art.- Gesch.	MG. ( )	sonstige Waffen
Soll (Zahlen)	50	1245	969	935	201 / 112	-	24	47	1750 (1308)	27 1.I.G. / 38 2cmFl.
einsatzbereit zahlenm.	-	232	1320+)	604	39 / 63	-	28	50	1530 (1243)	88 / 42
einsatzbereit in % des Solls	-	18,6	136	64,5	19,4 / 56,2	-	116	106	(94) / 89 / 744	110%
in kurzfristiger Instandsetzung (bis 3 Wochen) zahlenm.	-	8	274	-	2 / 2	-	-	2	90	2 2cmFl.
in % des Solls	-	0,6	28,2	-	0,9 / 1,7	-	-	4,2	5,2	5,2%

++ K.K.St.1 (Nr 79c)

*) Zgkw. mit 1-5t, **) Zgkw. mit 8-18t
( ) davon MG.42

3. ~~Pferdefehlstellen~~

+) davon 160 Lieferwagen m. je 420 kg Nutzlast und 128 le. Lkw mit je 800 - 1000 kg Nutzlast.

Equipment report from 1 June 1944

4. Kurzes Werturteil des Kommandeurs:

1. Ausbildungsstand:

   Die Division außer ᛋᛋ-Pz. Jäger-Abt.12 und ᛋᛋ-Nebelwerfer-Abt.12 befindet sich in der Verbandsausbildung.

2. Besondere Schwierigkeiten:

   a) Fehl von 3 Pz. Bef.-Wagen V,
   b) Fehl an Bergepanzern,
   c) Fehl der sollmäßigen Kfz.-Ausstattung der Panther-Abt.,
   d) Der I.(Sf.)/ᛋᛋ-Pz. Art.Rgt.12 fehlen noch 2 Art. Beob.-Panzer (III)
   e) Mangel an Mun.-Trägern für I.(Sf.)/ᛋᛋ-Pz. Art.Rgt.12,
   f) Mangel an 1 t - Zugmaschinen zum Umbau der 2 cm Flak (mot-Z) in 2 cm Flak (Sf.),
   g) Fehl von 12 Sd.-Kfz. 222 und 6 Sd.-Kfz. 233 bei ᛋᛋ-Pz.Aufkl.Abt.
   h) Fehl von 11 SPW bei ᛋᛋ-Pz. Nachr.-Abt. 12,
   i) Fehl sämtlicher Zugmittel für ᛋᛋ-Werfer-Abt. 12,
   k) Fehl der Befehlspanzer für ᛋᛋ-Pz. Jäger-Abt. 12.

3. Einsatzbereitschaft:

   Die Division ist für Angriffsaufgaben einsatzbereit.

ᛋᛋ-Brigadeführer und
Generalmajor der Waffen-ᛋᛋ

Anmerkung zur "Personellen Lage":

58 Unterführer und Mannschaften sind seit 1.5., bzw. 15.5. zu den Junkerschulen kommandiert. Ihre Versetzung wurde bisher nicht verfügt.

5. Kurze Stellungnahme der vorgesetzten Dienststelle:

Division ist mit Ausnahme der Werferabteilung und der Panzer-Jäger-Abteilung im Westen für jede Aufgabe voll einsatzbereit.

Für das Generalkommando
Der Chef des Generalstabes

Report on establishment of SS Pz.Jäger Abt. 12 and SS Nebelwerfer Abt. 12

ridge of high pressure over western Europe. This has opened the way to the associated disturbances to cross into western Europe.

The first area of bad weather, a cold front, will cross through the region of the Supreme Command West during the day. Behind it, the clouds will break up, with embedded areas of showers. It can be expected that further disturbances will form on the western and southern edge of the central low . . .

Forecast until tomorrow evening, 6.6.1944: Moderate to fresh westerly to northwesterly winds. Areas of clearing during the night. During the day, mostly changing cloudiness, occasional rain showers, in particular during the afternoon. Some local clearing will occur. Temperatures during the night around 10 degrees C, during the day 15–20. Mostly good visibility, occasionally reduced by showers or morning fog.

Forecast regarding enemy air activity for this evening: Departures from the English bases, especially for smaller squadrons, will be without problems. Action by large squadrons will probably be impeded by bands of showers and heavy clouds. Air activity in the region of the Supreme Command West in southern France will be without problems. In the other regions, an area of bad weather with heavy clouds and rain will interfere. The clouds will break up later from the west and somewhat more favorably flying conditions will set in.[4e]

During the same day of 5 June, at 17.50 hours, Dr. Müller issued another weather forecast regarding enemy actions during the night of 5.6. to 6.6.44. It read as follows:

1) Air force: Departures from English bases will be generally without major problems, only heavy cloudiness in the east will interfere there. Air activity in the region of the Supreme Command West will be possible generally without problems due to the breaking up of the cloud cover and local clearing, except in southern and southeastern France where an area of bad weather will interfere, and in Holland where a heavy cloud cover is expected.

2) Navy: In the Hoofden and the Channel, fresh southwesterly to westerly winds, strength 3–5, in places to 6, decreasing towards morning. Wave height 3–4, occasionally 5, also decreasing towards morning. Mostly good visibility . . ., along the west coast of Brittany wave height up to 4, caused by Atlantic wave activity. Apart from some morning fog, generally good visibility. The Mediterranean coast . . .

3) High tide: 1. From Le Havre (22.20h) via Ijmuiden (04.15h) to south of Den Helder (approximately 07.30). 2. From the Spanish

border (04.45h) via Brest (05.30h) to St. Mâlo (07.40h). Moon
light throughout the night, one day before full moon. First light
on 6.6.: 05.21h.[4f]

These weather reports and forecasts for the 3 to 6 June were sent to,
among others, the chief of the general staff of the Supreme Command West
as well as to the Ia and Ic of his staff, the liaison command of the Luftwaffe
and the liaison officer of the Kriegsmarine. The reports indicated clearly that
an invasion from the air and also by sea would be possible during the night
from 5 to 6 June, and again on 6 June. Despite this, the troops were not put
on alert nor were Feldmarschall Rommel, Admiral Krancke, and the division
commanders on their way to Rennes, called back. Such behavior could only
be explained if one assumed that the Supreme Commander West and his
staff, as well as Feldmarschall Rommel and his chief of staff, Generalleutnant
Speidel, had been of the firm conviction that the invasion would come at the
Pas de Calais, and that the meteorological conditions such as tides and hours
of moon light for that sector of the coast would be completely unsuitable. If
a major landing in Normandy between the mouth of the Seine and the
Cotentin had been seriously considered, it would have been clear that 5–6
June was a possible date for it. Then, the supreme commander of the Heeresgruppe would not have been allowed to travel home, nor would the supreme
commander of the 7. Armee have ordered his divisional commanders to a
planning exercise in Rennes so that they were up to 180 kilometers away
from their command posts.

Another very clear indication of the impending start of the invasion
existed. In the weekly report of the Heeresgruppe Rommel, for the period 28
May to 3 June, there had been mention of increased message traffic on Allied
radio to the French resistance organizations. However, it was not judged to
be an indication of the impending invasion. German counter-intelligence
had learned, quite some time previously, that the French resistance movement would be informed through the British radio station BBC of the date
the invasion would start. There would be a special coded message for each
resistance group. It would be sent in two parts. Transmitting of the first part
meant that the invasion would begin in two weeks, of the second part that
the invasion would begin within 48 hours. The BBC transmitted 125 messages containing the first parts on 1 June. German counter-intelligence monitoring recognized them and found at the same time that the coded messages
for some of the groups were missing. The enemy obviously assumed that
these had been infiltrated by the counter-intelligence. It was fairly certain
that this was not an attempt to mislead. So the invasion had to start within
the next 14 days. It was also illuminating that the groups addressed were
located in Brittany, Normandy and in the area of Lille/Amiens. The central
point was obviously in the west. Oberstleutnant (lieutenant colonel) Reile
reported his most important findings to the Supreme Command West and

the supreme intelligence office of the Reich (Reichssicherheitshauptamt) which passed on the information to the supreme command of the armed forces (OKW). The OKW relayed the information to the general staff of the Heer, office of the foreign armies, west, with the advice that the invasion was to be expected before 15 June. This office, whose strange behavior was already outlined earlier, did nothing. The responsible office Ic of the staff of the Supreme Command West, informed by Oberstleutnant Reile, either did not relay the report, or take the report seriously as proven by the weekly report of the Heeresgruppe.

A radio monitor of the 15. Armee intercepted the second half of a coded message for a resistance group at 22.15 hours on 5 June. It consisted of one stanza of a poem by Verlaine which read, translated: "The long sobbing of the violins in autumn, it wounds my heart with its monotonous melancholy." The Ic of the 15. Armee relayed the information that the start of the invasion had to be expected within 48 hours to the Ic of the Heeresgruppe Rommel, Oberstleutnant i.G. Staubwasser. He, in turn, reported to the chief of staff, Generalleutnant Speidel and was directed to request advice from the staff of the Supreme Command West. According to his account, he was given direction from the Supreme Command West, not to alert the 7. Armee. The 15. Armee had issued an alert on its own. There is no record of these discussions in the war diary of the Heeresgruppe. The staff of Oberstleutnant Reile had also heard the BBC transmission, and the staff of the Supreme Command West had been informed. Its Ia, Oberst i.G. Zimmermann sent an urgent message to the subordinate command offices. In it he said that messages, known since 1943 to indicate the impending start of the invasion, had been sent by English radio to the resistance movement. He said further: "Although it is not to be assumed that the invasion itself will be announced by radio, it must be expected that the sabotage plans of the communications and traffic networks prepared for the case of an invasion, and under certain circumstances also resistance actions, are set in motion by these messages. It is the judgment of the Ic of the Supreme Command West that an invasion at this time is not very probable."[5] With this assessment of the situation it is surprising that Generalleutnant Speidel did not recommend to the Supreme Command West to cancel the alert for the 15. Armee, and that the Supreme Command West did not do so on its own. The only rational explanation can be that the BBC message was judged skeptically, but that the increased readiness of the 15. Armee was left at that level since the invasion was basically expected for its sector, between Dunkirk and Dieppe, but not in Normandy. (see weekly report of the Heeresgruppe B for the period 28 May to 3 June). Without question, the large-scale fake operations, in particular "Operation Fortitude", confirmed the assessment of the Supreme Command West and the Heeresgruppe B, but they should not have carried decisive weight.

Neither the 7. Armee nor the "Hitlerjugend Division", part of the OKW reserves and assigned to the general of the Panzer troops, west, were alerted.

Despite all this, the Division had prepared itself for the imminent invasion for quite some time. In the Panzerregiment, for instance, this took on the following form according to a report of the then-chief of the 8. Kompanie, Hans Siegel:

> Bomber squadrons were flying overhead every night and none of us knew whether paratroopers would not suddenly drop from the bomb bays and come floating down on us. Max Wünsche had prepared for this eventuality by ordering absolute quiet and camouflage during the day, the village offering a peaceful appearance and the soldiers were sleeping, armed. During the nights, everyone was up and about. The crews were ready for action right next to their Panzers and extra live ammunition was ready to be issued. It was practically an alert situation, each in his position or immediate vicinity, ready for instant action. This began some four weeks before the start of the invasion.[6]

Sturmmann Willy Schnittfinke of the 5. Panzerkompanie reported on the matter from his notes: "31.5 . . . because of the duty during the previous night, we had the day off. Another order arrived during the afternoon: for the near future only reduced activity and duty."[7]

A communications exercise began on 3 June and ran through the night to 4 June. The then-Untersturmführer Willi Kändler, assigned by the Panzerregiment to the divisional staff as liaison officer, wrote:

> In the late evening of 4 June the O1 of the Division handed me an urgent order which I had to take to one of the units in the exercise during the same evening. Obersturmführer Menzel informed me verbally of the content of the written order: The exercise was to be terminated immediately since the Allied landing was imminent.

Obersturmführer Rudolf von Ribbentrop, son of the Reich foreign minister, was taking part in the radio communications exercise as a referee. During the drive back he was wounded by a low level air attack. A member of the German embassy in Paris visited him the following day, 5 June. Ribbentrop reported:

> . . . he told me that, according to the latest report, the invasion would commence on 5 June, a Monday. When he said good bye on Monday, 5 June, I said to him: 'well, another false alarm' and he replied dryly: 'the 5th is not quite over yet.'[8]

Until then the lack of fuel had made joint exercises by Panzers and Panzergrenadiers almost impossible. However, new fuel supplies had just arrived and such joint exercises were ordered for the beginning of June. For this reason, parts of the I. Panzerabteilung deployed to the area of Panzergrenadierregiment 26, parts of the II. Panzerabteilung into the area of Panzergrenadierregiment 25. The troops were equipped for combat and carried their first issue of live ammunition.[9]

On the opposite side, where the questions of action had to be answered, even more grave decisions had to be made than those at the German high commands. On 25 May, General Eisenhower had once more confirmed 5 June as "D-Day". The heavy units of the Allied war fleet which would take part in the invasion left their harbors in Scotland and Northern Ireland on 2 June. The navy received orders to prepare for the departure of the landing fleet in the evening of 3 June. The weather reports provided on 3 June were so unfavorable that it was decided during the early morning of 4 June to postpone "D-Day" by at least twenty-four hours. At that time, a portion of the American landing fleet which would land its soldiers first, had already left its harbors. Heavy seas forced the ships to turn back and seek shelter in the harbors. Since they could not remain at sea for days without refueling, the choice was to either start the invasion on 6 June or delay it by two weeks. However, the orders had been issued and thus the landing areas were known. It would have been very difficult to maintain secrecy for that length of time. During the night of 4 to 5 June the Allied supreme command was briefed once more by its meteorologists. They predicted that an approaching front of fine weather would likely dominate until late morning or afternoon of 6 June. The cloud cover would be 3/10 or less, the cloud base 700 to 1,000 meters, wind force at the landing coast 4 to 5, but probably 3. The visibility would be good. General Eisenhower ordered the start of the invasion for 6 June. The landing of the Americans would begin at 06.30 hours, that of the British and Canadians from 07.25 to 07.45 hours.[10]

The course of events on the opposite side is described using the war diary of the 6th Battalion The Durham Light Infantry. This battalion which belonged to the 151st Brigade of the 50th (Northumberland) Infantry Division, was one of the opponents of SS-Panzeraufklärungsabteilung 12 (Panzer reconnaissance Abteilung). The commander of the battalion was Lieutenant Colonel A. E. Green. His troops were assembled, before embarkation, in Nightingale Wood, Romsey, Hants (Camp C.17).

> 3 June, 09.00. Field service of the battalion (C to E) in the NAAFI tent (Navy Army Air Force Institute)
>
> 13.30. Main body of the battalion departs camp C.17 and embarks on LCI (landing craft infantry) at Southampton Water. The Prime Minister and Field Marshal Smuts (W. Churchill and the Prime Minister of South Africa) were at the pier during embarkation. The Prime Minister shook hands with the commander and wished the

battalion "god speed". The landing craft was anchored at Southampton Water for the rest of the day.

4 June. In the course of the day the battalion received information that "D-Day" had been postponed by 24 hours. During the day, the 'loads' of two landing craft visited the transit camp in the morning, those of two others in the afternoon.It had been set up by loading control in sheds on the pier. The men could properly wash there and received hot food. The camp offered facilities for writing, entertainment, NAAFI-organized games and offered all ranks a chance to stretch their legs after the cramped conditions of the landing craft.

5 June. The landing craft are still in Southampton Water. The transit camp was again visited during the morning and afternoon. The commander, Lieutenant Colonel A. E. Green, suffered a malaria attack and had to leave ship to go to a hospital. Major G. L. Wood, his deputy, took over command of the battalion. The landing craft set out during the night 5 to 6 June.[11]

The invasion fleet of almost 6,500 ships, among them 6 battle ships, 23 cruisers and 104 destroyers, was on its way to the Normandy coast.[12]

CHAPTER 0.2
The Landing

The plan of the Allies intended the landing of two armies under the supreme command of General Bernard L. Montgomery: The First US Army under General Omar N. Bradley and the Second British Army under General Mike Dempsey. The Americans were scheduled to land the VII US Corps at the southeast coast of the Cotentin at the landing beach UTAH, and the V US Corps east of the mouth of the Vire river at the OMAHA landing beach. The defense of their western flank was the responsibility of the 82nd and 101st Airborne Divisions. The British and Canadians had determined three landing sectors to establish the eastern beachhead from Arromanches (nine kilometers northeast of Bayeux) to the mouth of the Orne river near Ouistreham. They were, from west to east: the GOLD sector, from Arromanches to La Riviere, for the XXX British Corps, the JUNO and SWORD sectors, east of La Riviere to Ouistreham, for the I British Corps. The dividing line between JUNO and GOLD ran near Luc-sur-Mer. The 50th (Northumbrian) Infantry Division with the 8th Armoured Brigade were scheduled as the first wave for GOLD, the 7th Armoured Division and the 49th (West Riding) infantry Division as the second wave. The JUNO sector was set aside for for the 3rd Canadian Infantry Division and the 2nd Canadian Armoured Brigade as the first wave, and the 4th Special Brigade as the second wave. The 3rd British Infantry Division together with 27th Armoured Brigade would form the first wave for the SWORD sector, followed by the 1st Special Brigade, the 51st (Highland) Infantry Division and the 4th Armoured Brigade as the second wave. A prior landing from the air by the 6th Airborne Division between the Orne and the mouth of the Dives river, north of a line Colombelles-Troarn, had been ordered to secure the eastern flank of the beachhead.

It was the objective of the landing operation to establish two beachheads in Normandy on the first day: an American one at the base of the Cotentin on its east coast, and an American-British-Canadian one from the mouth of the Vire near Isigny via Bayeux, Caen to Cabourg at the mouth of the Dives. These beachheads would be enlarged during the following days particularly towards the northwest, west and south. It was planned that on day D+9 a line Caen-Villers Bocage-Caumont-St. Lô-La Haye du Portbail, on the west coast of the Cotentin, would be reached. This would secure the planned artificial harbors near Vierville-sur-Mer and Arromanches from the impact of the German artillery. The Allies expected that the counterattack by the German Panzerdivisions would be directed towards the Caen area. That area would therefore be defended with all available force.

In this framework, the mission of the 6th Airborne Division was to, above all, capture intact the bridges across the Orne river and the Orne canal near Bénouville, nine kilometers northeast of Caen. However, the bridges across the Dives river near Troarn, Bures and Robehomme as well as the road bridge near Varaville were to be destroyed in order to hamper a counterattack from that direction. It had also been ordered to wipe out the fortified battery at Merville, consisting of four guns, located two kilometers south of the coast near the mouth of the Orne river. After that, the division was to occupy the area between the Orne and Dives rivers north of the line Troarn-Colombelles and to delay any advance of enemy on the beachhead.

Around midnight of 5 June the Allies dropped life-sized dolls with parachutes. They were rigged with explosives which were to go off after landing to simulate combat noise. The intent was to divert attention from the real landing zones.

Shortly after midnight the first paratroopers of the 101st and the 82nd US Airborne Divisions jumped into the Cotentin. At 00.15 hours of 6 June, the first gliders of the 6th (British) Airborne Division were released. The mission of the 6th Airborne was to take the Orne bridges. They glided from an altitude of 1,500 meters down to 300 meters and then dove towards their targets. They succeeded in taking both bridges intact and to overpower their defenders. The bridges had been prepared to be blown up, but the explosives were not in place. That was supposed to be done when the invasion alarm was issued, but that had not been given by Heeresgruppe B for the 7. Armee.[1]

After this successful surprise attack, the jump zones for the 3rd and 5th Parachute Brigades were marked. These brigades jumped at 00.50 hours. A strong wind blew the paratroopers a considerable distance to the east and dispersed them, making it difficult for them to meet up. Hundreds of paratroopers landed in the area flooded by the Dives river and in the trees of the Bois de Bavent. One of the objectives of the 5th Brigade was to clear a landing area for a formation of transport gliders which were scheduled to land at 03.30 hours to deliver primarily anti-tank guns, Jeeps and other heavy equipment. The landing of the main body of the 6th Airlanding Brigade was scheduled for 6 June at 21.00 hours.[2]

Brigadeführer Fritz Witt, commander of the "HJ" Division, his first general staff officer and some members of the division staff were sitting by the fireplace in the house of the commander in the evening of 5 June in Tillières-sur-Avre, ten kilometers east of Verneuil-sur-Avre. Around midnight the duty officer at Division staff headquarters at Acon, two kilometers east of Tillières, called on the telephone. He relayed a report from the field headquarters of a Luftwaffe unit. It said that uniformed straw dolls had been dropped by parachute in the vicinity of airfields and that enemy paratroopers had jumped behind the coastal sector. Air traffic control had reported brisk enemy air activity. The Division inquired at the 711. Infanteriedivision which defended the coastal sector from the mouth of the Seine to just east of the mouth of the Orne, and at the 21. Panzerdivision. The 711. Inf.-Div. confirmed the drop of uniformed straw dolls, but not that of paratroopers. They reported the sea was silent, the weather was stormy, it was raining occasionally. The 21. Panzerdivision had no reports on enemy activity. The reports were discussed in detail by the fireplace. The consensus was that the enemy was attempting to determine what the German reactions in case of an air landing would be. Finally, they all went to bed, except for the commander who stayed up. A little later he woke up his Ia: "Meyer, the invasion has started in earnest!" It was approximately 01.30 hours on 6 June. The Ia got up immediately, put on his clothes and rushed to the telephone to get more details and contact the I. SS-Panzer-korps. The 711. Inf.-Div. reported that paratroopers in still unknown strength had indeed landed in the western sector of the division. The 21. Panzerdivision had received reports that enemy paratroopers had been sighted in the area of Troarn.

The I. SS-Panzerkorps had not received any orders or reports. At approximately 02.30 hours the Division, on its own, alerted its units. Unterscharführer August Zinßmeister, sergeant in charge of a reconnaissance platoon in the 1. Panzerspäh (Panzer reconnaissance) company of the Aufklärungsabteilung, noted in his diary:

> 6.6.1944. Tuesday, 03.00 hours. Alert. The Anglo—Americans have landed! Code word 'Blücher'! At 04.15 hours the Panzers are rolling to the Abteilung command post.

Hauptsturmführer Gerd Freiherr (baron) von Reitzenstein, of the staff of the Aufklärungsabteilung, noted:

> 6 June 1944. Alert of all units at approximately 02.00 hours. Immediate readiness to move out must be established. It was still dark when the AA (Aufklärungsabteilung = reconnaissance Abteilung) pulled forward to the Division departure point. At approximately 04.00 hours the vehi-cles take position near the crossroads, with anti-aircraft protection.

The diary of the Division escort company indicates the time of the alert as 03.00 hours.[3]

Sturmmann Oswald Beck of the communications platoon of Regiment 26 describes the alert as follows:

> We telephone operators had undergone tough training by Unterscharführer (sergeant) Kleff. During the recent past there had been many night exercises. I was the driver of Uscha. Kleff, and he always told me in advance when a night exercise was planned. I told my comrades and, after the evening bunk inspection, they all dressed again and went to sleep in combat uniform. So it was no wonder that the communications group was always first to be ready to march when there was a night exercise for the APCs. During the night of 5 to 6 June, Unterscharführer Kleff burst into our room: 'Let's go, boys, get out! The Tommies have landed!' Was this another night exercise and Kleff had not warned us? One of us suddenly said: 'Kleff is not wearing his uniform, just a track suit. Is this for real? I can't believe it, they would not dare.' Everything went as practiced, the APCs were loaded in no time, and we sat and waited. It had never taken this long until the order to start out came. The communicator on duty came over to us after he was relieved and confirmed that the English and Americans had landed. We had everything ready and could have departed at 03.00 hours. But we were sent back to our quarters and stretched out on our beds, ready to go. Those who could, slept. The others were talking quietly. When the morning light came, we were all sitting on top of the APCs and expected that we would soon start out.[4]

At approximately 04.00 hours all units of the Division were sitting ready in their alarm positions. Panzergrenadier-regiment 25 began reconnaissance operations on its own in the Caen area. The Division reported the alert to the Korps but could not get any orders there since none had arrived from the Panzergruppe.

The entries in the war diaries of the Supreme Command West, of Heeres-gruppe B, of 7. Armee and of the Kriegsmarinegruppe Command West indi-cate when the respective command offices received what reports on which enemy actions, which decisions were made based on this, and which orders were issued. The entries are suitable to correct a number of incorrect descrip-tions in war historical publications which are widely circulated.

The units of the 716. and the 711. Infanteriedivisions and of the 21. Panzerdivision, the latter without orders from above, in position near the bridges of Bénouville and east of the Orne river began the attack on the enemy who had landed there. In his in-depth examination, Generalleutnant Richter, commander of the 716. Infanteriedivision, reported later that the artillery commander had been given the order to begin firing as planned on the expected landing areas through the use of the code word 'Hansa' at 01.45 hours. The fire was to be directed by air surveillance located in the rear and motorized artillery observers. At 2 A.M. he had ordered 21. Pz.-Div. to attack the enemy with the whole division and, together with units of 716. Infanteriedivision, to clear out the area east of the Orne river.[5] But since 21. Panzerdivision was a Heeresgruppe reserve, Generalleutnant Richter could not issue any orders to it. They would not have been accepted or carried out. So this is probably an error. Only those units of the 21. Panzerdivision posi-tioned in the sectors of his Division near the front were tactically subordi-nated to him with the start of the landing. They were the only ones he could issue orders to, which is what happened. The entries in the war diary of the Heeresgruppe, show that the Heeresgruppe, as the command office for the 21. Panzer-division, had not issued any combat orders by 04.30 hours and wanted to wait even longer.

Werner Kortenhaus has determined the following facts concerning the 21. Panzerdivision. They differ, at times, from those quoted by the divisional commander, Generalmajor Feuchtinger, from memory in his study right after the end of the war:

> 00.30 hours: First report on enemy paratroopers in the Troarn area from 5./Panzergrenadierregiment 125 to the regimental com-mand post 125 in Vimont. The company was surprised during a night exercise when it carried only blank cartridges. The report was passed on to the divisional staff headquarters in St. Pierre-sur-Dives.
>
> 00.35 hours: Highest level of alert ordered for the division.
>
> 00.30 to 01.30 hours: Reports received on landings of paratroop-ers from the 7./125 in the vicinity of Ranville and from the 6./125 in the area north of Sannerville, near Touffreville and Escoville. First combat actions.
>
> 02.45 hours: The first prisoners were brought in, some with their parachutes still attached, by the II./125. It was determined that they were members of the British 6th Airborne Division.

03.10 hours: The 8. (heavy)/ Panzergrenadierregiment 192 of
the 21. Panzerdivision under the command of Grenadierregiment
736 of the 716. Inf.-Div. started the attack on the enemy bridgehead
across the Orne river and the Orne canal near Bénouville. Its
advance reached Biéville at 04.00 hours.[6]

During these battles for the air landing zones, the landing fleet was
approaching the coasts of Calvados and the Cotentin. Allied bomber
squadrons had attacked the coastal batteries in Normandy from the mouth
of the Seine to St. Marcouf on the east coast of the Cotentin at 01.30 hours.
Each of the eight batteries was attacked by at least 100 heavy bombers which
dropped 500–600 tons of bombs on each target. The impact on the mostly
bunkered guns was surprisingly minimal. The battleships and cruisers
opened fire on the German front lines at 05.00 hours, in particular on the
coastal batteries which fired back. After an exchange of fire, which lasted for
hours in many cases, the ships' superior artillery prevailed.

The landing from the sea by the Allied invasion troops began at approximately 06.30 hours. The DD tanks (duplex drive, tracks and propeller) were
first to roll off the landing craft. These were Sherman tanks which had a har-
monica-like superstructure of heavy tarpaulin which allowed them to wade
through deep water. They were followed by landing craft carrying self-propelled artillery. Behind these were landing craft with engineers whose mission it was to remove the obstacles ahead of the beaches, clear mines, and
neutralize defensive positions. The next wave was the landing craft with the
assault companies and after them those with the reserve companies of the
forward infantry battalions. Behind them came boats with rocket launchers
and landing craft carrying the reserve battalions of the infantry brigades
which were to attack first. They were followed by landing craft with anti-tank
guns and self-propelled artillery guns. The landing craft were accompanied
by destroyers and cruisers on the flanks. The destroyers, together with the
self-propelled artillery on the landing craft, attacked targets on the beach,
the cruisers attacked those inland. The landing troops of the 50th Infantry
Division encountered an effective defense by 352. Infanteriedivision near le
Hamel and could only advance very slowly. The 69th Infantry Brigade faced
tenacious resistance near La Rivière although the town was completely
destroyed. To the east, the positions of an east European battalion were
quickly over-run.

The 3rd Canadian Infantry Division of the I. Corps could only begin to
land at approximately 07.30 hours, two hours after sun rise, because of the
cliffs ahead of the beach and the high tide coming in later. The resistance in
some of the front positions could be overcome quickly, but the Canadians
were engaged in heavy combat near Bernières. After maximum bombardment of the German coastal batteries and infantry positions by warships and
bombers, the assault battalions of the 3rd British Infantry Division went

ashore at 07.30 hours. By 09.30 hours they had taken Hermanville, two kilometers inland, and dug in for the defense. By late morning the two British and Canadian divisions had established a firm foothold on land. They were able to break through the German coastal lines in a number of places.

In the UTAH landing sector on the east coast of the Cotentin, the American air and sea landing forces had also been able, in cooperation, to establish a small beachhead. They had taken a narrow strip of beach in the OMAHA sector, with heavy losses, but were bogged down in the face of the mined and heavily defended cliffs.[7]

Further developments depended on how quickly local reserves or additional reinforcements could start counterattacks. The race between the landing operations and the German counter measures is reflected in reports, situation assessments, decisions and orders of the German high and supreme command offices.

Some of the most important dates and times which form the total picture are again highlighted here:

1. On 6 June, at 00.15 hours, the air landing of the British northeast of Caen and of the Americans on the Cotentin began.

2. The AOK 7 (Armee supreme command) reported the start of the air landing to Heeresgruppe B. It viewed this, "differing from the opinion of Heeresgruppe B and the Supreme Command West", as the start of a large-scale enemy operation.

3. At 05.30 the Supreme Command West stated to Heeresgruppe B that the width of the sector in which the air landings had taken place indicated that this "was not an action of only local importance".

4. After the Kriegsmarinegruppe Command West reported that German torpedo boats had engaged 6 battleships and 15–20 enemy destroyers at sea west of Le Havre, the Supreme Commander West determined, at 06.24, that the invasion had begun. He requested from the OKW (supreme command of the armed forces) the release of the OKW reserves. On his own responsibility and without awaiting the approval of the OKW, he already assigned the 12. SS-Panzer-division to Heeresgruppe B at 05.00 hours. Proposed advanced assembly area was Bernay-Lisieux-Vimoutiers.

5. At 05.30 hours AOK reported to Heeresgruppe B that it was quiet to the north of the Seine, and at 09.25 hours, that in the sector of the Armee no sea landings had taken place.

6. Heeresgruppe B assigned the 21. Panzerdivision to the 7. Armee at 06.15 hours (the war diary of the 7. Armee, section 'telephone calls', gives this time as 06.45 hours) in order to eradicate airborne enemy forces east of the Orne river.

7. The sea landing by the Americans began at 06.30 hours.

8. At 10.20 hours the chief of staff of Heeresgruppe B informed the chief of the operations section of the OKW/command staff of the

armed forces on the situation: "Assessment of the situation by the Heeresgruppe (not only by the chief of its staff, author): A large-scale enemy operation against Normandy is likely. Measures by the Heeres-gruppe: assigning the 21.Pz.Div. to the 7. Armee. 116.Pz.Div. deploys into the area northwest of Rouen (on the right of the Seine, author). Re-deployment of the 12.Pz.Div. is suggested."

9. At 10.00 hours the OKW refused to release the 12. SS Panzerdivision but approved its advance. At 14.15 hours the Supreme Command West again -requested the release of the division from the OKW for a joint counterattack with the 21. Panzerdivision. The 12. SS-Panzerdi-vision and the Panzer-Lehr- -Division were released at 14.30 hours, soon after the general command I. SS-Panzerkorps and the -required corps troops were released. At 15.00 hours the order arrived at the 7. Armee that both these Panzerdivisions were attached to the Armee. It ordered the deployment of the "HJ" Division into the area on both sides of Evrecy (twenty-six kilometers southwest of Caen), in order to link up to the west of the Orne river with the 21. Panzerdivision to eradicate the enemy forces landed there. The Panzer Lehr Division was ordered to initially secure the area of Flers-Vire (approximately fifty kilometers southwest of Caen).

10. The chief of staff of Heeresgruppe B reported to the chief of the operational section in the OKW at 17.10 hours that his overall judg-ment was that of a "large-scale enemy operation, an even larger oper-ation cannot be ruled out."

Based on the reports from the 15. and the 7. Armee, it should have been clear to Heeresgruppe B at 09.25 hours at the latest, that the invasion had begun and that it was taking place in the sector from the mouth of the Dives—southeast coast of the Cotentin to east of Montebourg, and not at the Pas de Calais or on both sides of the mouth of the Somme river. However, as late as 17.10 hours, Gener-alleutnant Speidel, chief of staff, declared to the OKW that in his opinion a much larger enemy operation could not be ruled out. He defined the landing in Normandy as a "large-scale" enemy operation, and not the invasion.

Based on the available reports, in particular from the Kriegsmarine, the Supreme Commander West had drawn the conclusion already at 06.24 hours that the invasion had started. He emphatically used this important word 'invasion'.

As early as 04.45 hours the Supreme Commander West had requested the release of the OKW reserves (the "HJ" Division and the Panzer Lehr Divi-sion) from the OKW, "to be prepared for any eventuality". The release was only granted after repeated telephone and teletype requests at 14.30 hours. This is seen as a grave, even crucial, omission by the OKW. In the serious war historical literature, the reason for this is repeatedly given that Feldmarschall

Keitel and Generaloberst Jodl had not dared to have Hitler woken up and requested a decision from him. This is not factual as is shown in a statement from the then-Hauptsturmführer Otto Günsche. It reads:

> Since March 1944 I was the "Personal Adjutant of the Führer. I took part, among other duties, in the situation briefings in the FHQ (Führer headquarters) and was a member of the inner circle of the Führer.
>
> The FHQ was located at that time, June 1944, at the Berghof on the Obersalzberg mountain. The chief OKW (Keitel) and the chief WFST (Jodl) had their headquarters in Berchtesgaden.
>
> There was a basic standing order from the Führer to his adjutants and his servant which he had also issued in my presence to Keitel, to Jodl, and to the chief of the general staff, Generaloberst Zeitzler, to wake him at any time if the situation required this. I remember his words: 'I prefer to be woken up 100 times for unimportant reasons to not being awoken the one time when an important measure or decision depends on it'.
>
> In my experience and recollection, the course of the night of 5 to 6 June 1944 developed as follows. The Führer said good-night to his guests and assistants at approximately 02.00 hours and withdrew to his private quarters. In the early morning hours of 6 June, Jodl demanded by telephone to speak to the chief adjutant of the Führer, Generalleutnant Schmundt. He reported air and sea landings at the Cotentin peninsula. Schmundt immediately woke up Linge and requested urgently to speak to the Führer. Linge woke up the Führer who subsequently spoke to Schmundt.
>
> Contrary to his normal routine, the Führer entered the great hall of the Berghof already at 8 A.M. He looked animated and alert. Only a few minutes later, Keitel and Jodl arrived and were received by the Führer with the words: 'Gentlemen, this is the invasion. I have said all along that that is where it would come.'[8]

The question arises why the release of the OKW reserves did not take place. It can be accepted as a basic principle that the last operative reserves must only be sent into action when the situation has been sufficiently clarified and all other reserves are already in action, and it has become obvious that they are not sufficient. So it must be examined how Heeresgruppe B and the Supreme Command West judged the situation and how they deployed their reserves. As late as 17.10 hours Heeresgruppe B judged that a further 'larger-scale" enemy operation was possible. The Supreme Command West did not contradict this. Was it not natural that the OKW did not want to release its last reserves during the morning when the situation at the Heeresgruppe had not been sufficiently clarified? And what about the reserves of Heeresgruppe B? It had only assigned the 21. Panzerdivision to the 7. Armee at 06.15 hours with the mission of eliminating the airborne enemy troops east of the Orne river. Generalleutnant Speidel had advised the OKW/armed forces command staff of this at 10.20 hours by telephone. He further informed them that he had ordered the 116. Panzerdivision (part of the Heeresgruppe reserves) to deploy in the area northwest of Rouen. It was thus not deployed to the landing area in Normandy, neither was the 2. Panzerdivision, the third part of the Heeresgruppe reserves, in position north of the Somme river. Instead, Generalleutnant Speidel had "encouraged the deployment of the 12. SS-Pz.Div." In this context it must be emphasized that the 116. Panzerdivision had not yet been completely refitted. A deployment could only have the rationale of bringing the division closer to an expected combat area. In the same manner, the Heeresgruppe could have started the 116. Pz.Div. on the march to Normandy. The only reason that these two Panzerdivisions were not deployed to Normandy and sent into action there by the Heeresgruppe could have been that Generalleutnant Speidel expected a further large-scale landing in the sector between the mouths of the Seine and Somme rivers, or on both sides of the mouth of the Somme, in the immediate future and wanted to have these divisions available there. Political reasons have also been mentioned, in the first few years after the war by General-leutnant Speidel himself. David Irving examined this question in his biography of Rommel. The retired Generalmajor Heinz Guderian, at the time the Ia of the 116. Panzerdivision, will certainly contribute authentic material on the subject in the war history of that division. With regard to the level of battle readiness of the 116. Panzerdivision, it must not be forgotten that the "HJ" Division was also not completely fitted. The Panzerjägerabteilung (tank destroyer) did not have any tank destroyers and the mortar Abteilung did not have tractors for its guns. Both Abteilungen could only be brought into action weeks after the invasion had begun.

The OKW finally gave in to the urging of General-feld-marschall von Rundstedt and released its reserves at 14.30 hours instead of demanding that the 2. and the 116. Panzerdivisions go into action in Normandy. This can probably be traced to the negative development of the situation in Normandy. The two Panzerdivisions of the OKW reserves were deployed closer to the invasion area than the Heeresgruppe reserves which were not yet in action. The demand of General-feldmarschall Rommel to have the Panzerdivisions lined up like a string of pearls behind the coastal divisions proved to be inexpedient.

At this point, a few words must be said regarding the decisions by the Supreme Commander West. During the absence of the supreme commander of Heeresgruppe B, General-feldmarschall Rommel, Generalfeldmarschall von Rundstedt acted in his behalf. Obviously, he had given the chief of staff, Generalleutnant Speidel, a free hand and allowed that the OKW was directly kept informed by Heeresgruppe B which certainly did not contribute to a clear assessment of the situation. It is also surprising that the Supreme Command West agreed to the request of Heeresgruppe B at 05.45 hours to move the 12. SS-Panzerdivision forward into the lines on both sides of Lisieux. It ordered only at 11.50 hours that the division had to also be prepared to be shifted in a westerly direction. This indicates that the Supreme Commander West was still in doubt at that time whether the landing in Normandy would be expanded further east, at least to the mouth of the Seine river. The only reasonable explanation for the air landing between the Orne river and the flooded valley of the Dives river, and the blowing-up of the bridges across the Dives, could be that the sea landing had to be expected west of the mouth of the Orne river and later, that it would not be expanded to the east.

CHAPTER 0.3
The Deployment

While the "HJ" Division was being alerted, and while the units assembled at their alarm positions and rolled towards the departure points, Heeresgruppe B relayed a message from the 15. Armee to the Supreme Command West at 02.30 hours. It stated that paratroopers had landed in the sector of the 711. Infanteriedivision. The noise of battle could be heard at its divisional command post in Château le Quesnay, directly north of Glanville and nine kilometers west of Pont-l'Evêque. No details were known. The Armee requested reconnaissance from the 12. SS-Panzerdivision. The Supreme Command West agreed and issued the following order to Panzergruppe West:

> The 12. SS-Panzerdivision, without diminishing its role as OKW reserve, will immediately commence reconnaissance in the direction of the 711. Inf.-Div., establish and maintain contact with the 711. Inf.-Div., and watch in its own sector for a possible landing by air.[1]

Ten minutes later, orders for increased march readiness were issued to Panzergruppe Command West, the 12. SS-Panzerdivision, the Panzer-Lehr-Division, and the 17. SS-Panzer-grenadier-division "Götz von Berlichingen". The Division relayed the order to reconnoiter, after it had been received from Panzergruppe West, to the Aufklärungsabteilung.

The chief of the Panzerspähkompanie (armored car company) of the Aufklärungsabteilung, Obersturmführer (1st lt.) Peter Hansmann reported:

> It was past midnight, 02.30 hours. The phone in the guard room rang. The adjutant, Obersturmführer Buchheim gave the code word

for the alert at the start of the invasion and asked that the company chief come to the telephone to speak to the commander, Sturmbannführer (major) Gerd Bremer.

Seconds later, my noncom in charge, Hannes Rasmussen was shaking me by the shoulders, shouting: 'Obersturmführer, the invasion has started. This is not an exercise but the real thing. The commander is on the telephone and waiting for you.' I jumped off my bed and stood by the open window. From the outside I could only hear the company alarm bell and the humming of the bomber squadrons which had been flying overhead for days in uninterrupted streams towards our supply routes and our home towns. Other than that, it was quiet. The first of our Panzer drivers were already running in their underwear to their vehicles to start them. While I was jumping down the stairs to the guard room, my thoughts were swinging back and forth between 'practice alert exercise' and 'are they really coming?' But there was my commander on the telephone, repeating the alert code word. He ordered me to report to him in thirty minutes with ten armored reconnaissance vehicles and two squads of motorcycle riflemen. The rest of the company was to make ready to move out and remain on call in their quarters.

It did not take fifteen minutes before the noncom in charge reported the crews, as well as the officers of the platoons and the scout parties, ready for action. They were standing in a semicircle as I briefed them on the situation, spoke about the seriousness and the importance of our action: 'As Panzer scouts we must be quick but also circumspect, we must see everything but not be seen, if possible. We must report to our commander where and how the enemy is located. Our light machine guns are primarily for defense, and remember, if you use them, you are also spotted. And, you are not sitting in a Tiger! Keep a particularly close watch on the road surfaces to spot mines set by partisans on whom we can count today in increased numbers!'

March sequence: 1 squad motorcycle riflemen, 8-wheeler and 4-wheeler alternating, distance 50 meters, 1 squad of motorcycle riflemen as rear guard.

Destination: the Abteilung command post.

I was standing in the turret of the first 8-wheeled armored car and ordered: 'Panzer, march! 40 kilometers per hour'. The night was pleasantly cool and medium bright. The moon could occasionally be seen shining pale through breaks in the fog and clouds. We had a visibility of 50 to 100 meters, and were driving with camouflage headlights. After only a few kilometers, it felt like one of the many practice alarms of the previous weeks. The few houses along the village road were unlit, people were still asleep, and there was no sign of the predicted French partisans.

After fifteen minutes we pulled up to the reinforced Ab-teilung command post and I reported, together with the platoon and scout group leaders, to the commander, Sturm-bannführer Bremer.

We immediately received information on reports of enemy landings by air in the coastal area and to the rear of our fortified positions, from the areas to the west of the mouth of the Seine to Carentan. 'Since these reports are still imprecise and contain sometimes contradictory statements, I want you to find out what is happening in the coastal sectors north of us, from the mouth of the Seine to Bayeux. I want to know what enemy troops have landed, what they have been able to achieve and what further intentions can be made out.

I will split you into four scouting parties, from east to west:

1. party: Untersturmführer (2nd lieutenant) Kudoke. Route of march via Bernay, Lieurey into the Pont l'Evêque area including the coastal sector Villers-sur-Mer—Deauville to Honfleur.
2. party: Unterscharführer (sergeant) Zinßmeister. Route of march: Lisieux, Branville, coastal sector: Houlgate—Dives—Cabourg and east of the mouth of the Orne river.
3. party: Unterscharführer Fingerhut. Caen area and west of the mouth of the Orne river-Riva-Bella and the coastal sector up to St. Aubin.
4. party: Obersturmführer (1st lieutenant) Hansmann. Bayeux area and the eastern coastal sector to Courseulles.
5. party to remain at Abteilung command post.

Report your position in case of contact with the enemy and when you have reached your objectives. Avoid fighting if possible. Bring back any prisoners immediately.'

We received the communications codes and checked our radios.

The scouting parties departed at 4 o'clock.

My party consisted of an 8-wheeled armored car with its commander Hans Krapf and the 8-wheeler with Heinz Dahmann. Both were experienced Panzer reconnaissance leaders who had learned their trade in Russia. I quickly briefed my men on our destination and mission and ordered them to keep an eye on each other during the drive. It had become a little lighter and the visibility was now more than 100 m. Since our destination was about eighty kilometers away, I chose the fastest route via Broglie, Lisieux to Caen. The knowledge of the roads and towns we had built up during the exercises and practice reconnaissance drives of the previous months was now helpful. After one hour we drove through Lisieux. There, we already saw the occasional pedestrian, workers and farmers begin-

ning their day, as on any other day before. Some of the windows in
the houses were lit. Motorcycle dispatch riders and VW-Kübel (jeep-
type vehicle) were driving in the opposite direction. An army guard
stood in front of a house and saluted. A group of soldiers was standing at the bridge across the Touques river. The sergeant replied to
my questions that they were at an increased level of alert, but that,
other than the constant bomber squadrons, nothing had happened
in the west. Since we had another sixty kilometers to our destination,
and the coast was approximately forty kilometers to the north, we
took the major highway to Caen. The visibility had improved and
soon the sun would come through the fog and the clouds. My eyes
were watering from the cold wet morning fog. We were now meeting
considerably more Wehrmacht vehicles, so the road had to be open.
We soon reached Caen. At the entrance to the town there was hectic
movement by vehicles of all types. Wehrmacht platoons had taken
up positions. A lieutenant asked where we had come from and
whether we had encountered any enemy troops. He was willing to
take me to his superior officer who was located a few streets to the
north. At the same time he drew our attention to the noise of fighting. He reported that enemy paratroopers had attacked the Orne
bridges approximately ten kilometers to the north and that fighting
was going on. Now I understood the hectic activity in the streets and
the massing of infantry at the edge of town. They were Panzergrenadiers of the 21. Pz.-Div. A captain of this company asked where
we had come from and informed me that strong British airborne
units had landed on both sides of the Orne river. The bridges were
probably in enemy hands, since there was no longer a telephone
connection with Ranville. The sound of fighting, which could clearly
be heard, came from there. Even as we were talking, fighter-bombers
attacked and fired randomly into the city. French civilians were leaving their houses in panic and rushing out of the town. When I
returned to my men, Unterscharführer Fingerhut had also arrived. I
briefed him on what I had just learned and recommended close contact with the security forces of the 21. Pz.-Div., the 716. Inf.-Div. and
the local command post. Also, extreme caution during the further
advance to the north. Our radio operator Siemers sent my coded situation report to the Abteilung.

    We drove right through the center of town to the west exit where
we found the same situation. The roads were almost clogged, mostly
by Flak soldiers with and without vehicles. A heavy cloud of smoke
was drifting to the southeast, likely a successful fighter-bomber
action. If I had wished for more light, even sunshine before, I was
now hoping for more fog which was drifting in from the coast to the
right of the road. I was glad that the straight road to Bayeux was

lined by trees and that most villages along the road were surrounded by wooded areas. Twenty more kilometers and we would
reach our destination. With the heavy opposite traffic, no Tommy
could have landed here yet. This meant we could speed up. Panzer,
march, 80! The first houses of the town were along the road, civilians were running. Older soldiers who could have been our fathers
were standing at the garden fences, talking with the civilians. The
closer we came to the center of town, the larger grew the crowd of
people. There were supply vehicles, VW-Kübels, motorcycles, uniforms of all the different services, only the Kriegsmarine was missing. A platoon of military police was trying to establish some order. I
tried in vain to get to the town commander. Then I heard that
artillery had already fired into Bayeux. Well, if fighter-bombers
showed up here, that would really mean trouble. A sergeant told me
that heavy fighting was going on in the bay of Arromanches and the
English were being landed at the coast by hundreds of ships. Judg-
ing by the noise of the battle there had to be heavy action under
way, one could clearly hear the hammering of the artillery. We had
to see that! Not only airborne landings, but also landings by sea! I
informed Unterscharführer Dahmann that we would avoid the road
from now on and only drive cross country under cover. To the north
of the exit from town the terrain was rising slowly, covered by farms
and pastures. As we were observing and taking turns being in the
lead on the drive towards the small village of St. Sulpice we could
see to the left, in the direction of the coast near Tracy, columns of
dirt rising and houses burning. I could not yet see the ocean. We
had to drive another 1,000 meters before we reached the highest
spot in the terrain. Continuing at walking speed, hugging walls of
rocks and hedges, we reached the heights, approximately fifty
meters, of Magny-en-Bessin. There we found a farm with trees and a
barn. From here we had a view all across the bay of Arromanches.
The armored cars remained on the rear slope. Thanks to the good
camouflage which Hans Krapf and Heinz Dahmann had attached at
the exit from Bayeux, looking just like big bushes, we could observe
the unknown, the improbable, the really unimaginable spectacle.
What was this large gray mass spreading out in front of us? I had to
make sure once more: There, to the left, to the west, was the steep
shore of the bay of Arromanches. The heaviest artillery fire was concentrated there. Columns of dirt, as big as house, rose into the air
and then collapsed. To the east stretched an endless dark-gray mass,
the sea. Even the horizon seemed endless, just a little lighter than
the ocean. I was looking through my binoculars, now recognizing
the individual outlines of ships. Next to each other, behind, right to
the horizon were ships,—ships, masts, ships' bridges. At irregular

intervals, flashes were constantly coming from various spots. Ship's artillery! A dark-gray sea stretched between the beach and the armada of ships out there. White lines were racing at us through these dark masses of water from the endless line of ships deployed from the steep shores of Arromanches to the horizon east of the mouth of the Orne.

These were fast boats with high, white, foamy bow waves, landing craft which then spit out brown clumps of soldiers at the beach. I could see white columns of water rising in the landing area. Those were probably our coastal batteries. Then I could clearly hear the muzzle fire from German MG 42s. At least our coastal defenses had not been completely overrun. Unterscharführer Dahmann drew my attention to the brown figures who were slowly moving through the dunes. They were wearing flat steel helmets, so they were Brits. In groups, platoon strength, even whole companies they were advancing slowly through the dunes towards us, seemingly without finding any resistance. They were still about 3,000 meters away, could be seen only with the binoculars. Some houses were burning in Arromanches. The smoke was drifting across to us, sometimes covering all of the bay from our view. Then I spotted tanks, 1,2,3—a whole pack, strange forms. They came out of the bay, drove up the coastal road towards us, then swung east and zigzagged through the dunes without stopping to fire. They were probably crushing some individual pockets of resistance. Then I could clearly make out the large scoops on the front of the tanks. Did they want to build a coastal road right away or dig out mines? Without pause, more and more tanks appeared directly from the sea. Was this possible? First, we could occasionally see their cupolas, then they rose from the waves like dinosaurs. And no one seemed to interfere with them. Was there no 8.8 Flak? Well no, the fighter-bombers were attacking the back slopes of the steep coast without hindrance. They dropped their rocket bombs into the concrete walls of the fortifications. I took another look at our lightly armored reconnaissance vehicles. Were they sufficiently camouflaged? If they spotted us, we had had it. Even our Tigers were helpless against these 'meatflies'.

But now it was time to quickly send off a report. The Division must immediately be warned of what was happening here! This was the invasion, there was no question. There were almost more ships than water. But who would believe it if he did not see it for himself.

We had to take a sober count. Where were we? '7.45 hours, bay of Arromanches. Our own position is three kilometers south of Magny. (Then I counted the ships between two lines in the binoculars, approximately 50 times 8 = 400) More than 400 ships with a wall of tethered balloons above along the whole coastal strip of thirty kilometers length to the mouth of the Orne in the east. The British are constantly landing troops and heavy equipment without hindrance. We have spotted eleven heavy tanks. The coastal defenses have been eliminated and overrun. Infantry of battalion strength is moving south towards Bayeux. Enemy ship's artillery is firing on Bayeux and the approaches. Fighter-bombers are attacking pockets of resistance in the cliffs.

We will continue reconnaissance in the direction of Creully . . . Out.'

While I walked a few hundred meters east in the direction of Ryes with Hans Krapf in order to get a view of the northeastern coastal area from an elevated spot, Hans Dahmann at his gun gave us cover. From this point we could also observe the previously hidden field of view northeastward to the coast. We found the same picture every-where: troops were constantly brought to shore from the endless row of ships to the east. The strip of beach here was somewhat wider and the Brits had to cover quite a distance in the water. The beach was full of Tommies who were moving only very slowly towards the dunes. Where on earth was our own artillery? This would make a promising target, if only there was a mortar company here. Further east there was a lot of smoke at the beach, apparently there was some resistance left. But there, too, the large caliber ship's artillery was digging through the land back of the beach. We walked back to our armored cars and I inquired whether my message had been acknowledged yet. The radio operator answered in the negative and called again. The British advance groups were not far from the coastal road. They were forming up and I was contemplating if and how we could cut off an advance group or a scouting party, and grab them. Into the middle of these thoughts dropped a bad surprise from the sky. Suddenly, the ground around us was shaking, almost without warning. There had only been the slurping sound dropping bombs make, but we had not noticed any aircraft. Then it came to me, this was ship's artillery. There were immense explosions, whole mountains of dirt were hurled into the air and came crashing down in a radius of a few hundred meters. We were pressed flat to the ground, wishing to be back in our steel hulls which would at least protect us from shrapnel. But the side hatches were closed. I lifted myself up a bit and knocked against the armor plate. I yelled, but the gunner, driver and radio operator did not understand that we wanted to get in from below rather than through the turret. We had exited through it, but the waves of pressure from the explosions would blow us away up there. Then, finally, it worked out. The 8-wheeler was waving back and forth, chunks of earth were crashing onto the armor. As long as we could still hear that, everything was all right, we would not hear a direct hit at all. I was trying to figure out how we had been spotted. We were well camouflaged, a long distance away. Even the advancing Tommies at two kilometers away could hardly have spotted us. If so, the tanks would have fired on us directly. Had someone from the farm close-by given us away? But that would have meant directing the fireworks on themselves. I pressed my forehead to the narrow viewing slits. There was no movement on the farm. Its roof looked strange, there was hardly a tile left on the rafters. Then everything quietened down again except for the distant noise of battle at the coast. The cows which had previously been grazing quietly and individually close by were now crowded into a far corner. Maybe we had been too obvious in our black uniforms? I took off my black Panzer tunic right away and planned to go outside only in the brown shirt. After we got back we would all slip on our camouflage jackets and tighten the tunics with the belts. That way we would also not get snagged by bolts, levers and locks inside the Panzer. Everything had now become a question of practicality. We could not count on surprising anyone at this spot, so we went to scout along the ridge to the east. We would travel exclusively in the terrain, avoiding all paths and the ridge road, since they were all dominated by enemy artillery. If only we had an 8.8 cm gun together with our 2 cm machine gun, we could have knocked out the tanks from here with a surprise fire attack. Thereafter, a quick change of position and into hiding, since no Panzer could hold its own against the long arm and range of the ship's guns.

Together with the fresh smell of the green and succulent pastures, the smoke and powder vapors were drifting up from Arromanches and rolled in wide waves across this high plain. We welcomed the cover they brought, but the attacking Tommies were probably thinking the same.

As we could observe from here, each soldier had to first go through the water before reaching the beach. And that through the wind today, almost a storm, which was whipping the seas down there. On top of that, there were the waves caused by the fast landing craft. That was certainly not a leisurely walk and now I understood why the Tommies were moving forward so slowly and sluggishly. Only the vehicles, large and small tracked ones, trucks and Jeeps, were racing back and forth. They were attacking the town with machine gun fire from the rear.

By now, the bunkers seemed to have been put out of action by the firing war ships in our field of vision. We could no longer spot any muzzle fire. If these positions could still fight, the Tommies could not be running and driving around directly below them, they would all be dead. There was almost no hope for a relief reserve from Bayeux, located only some 4 kilometers behind us. Those we had seen there were mostly members of the national labor service and administrators. I remembered with great alarm that our Division was still 100 kilometers away. It would probably take two days before it could get into action here. But the 21. Pz.-Div. should be able to join the action here. Who knew what the picture was like by now in Caen, Cabourg, Houlgate or Deauville? Those were the areas of action closer to us.

During these thoughts the radio operator handed me the confirmation of the message I had sent. There was no new orders or information on our other scouting parties, only one from Unterscharführer Fingerhut that he had captured paratroopers and already brought them back.

We left our positions one at a time and drove along pasture fences and hedges east of Ryes and Bazenville in the direction of Creully. Enemy artillery was firing on Creully and had set houses on fire. I made a number of observation stops and determined that we could observe the wide sandy beach west of Courseulles quite well, off and on, despite the hazy weather and the clouds of smoke along the coastal road. Along the whole twenty-kilometer wide coast, the bright wavy lines of the fast landing craft were constantly racing towards the beach. Hundreds of these boats were sitting in the shallow water, unloading. Vehicles dove into the sea and waded to shore. Our own artillery had to be in position in Creully, hammering this section of the coast. Impacts of explosions in the water and on the beach showed results. The beach was strewn with a lot of equipment and the Tommies were trying to reach the first houses by the beach quickly. Around some of the houses, masses of men in company strength had assembled. The front had to hold here. But, tanks were already rolling on the coastal road. The short silhouette of the Shermans gave them away as enemy tanks. Heavy enemy artillery was thoroughly plowing the terrain to the rear, the roads which led along this ridge to Caen. And then, there were the fighter-bombers. Despite the low cloud base, they appeared at lightning speed and fired into Creully from the south. We could only scurry from cover to cover, always prepared to find an enemy scouting party in the field of fire of our gun.

Despite the noise of our own engine I could hear the loud hum of an aircraft. It had to be directly above us in the clouds. What would happen next? Maybe they wanted to eliminate the resistance and the battery position near Creully. I was already searching for cover under the wall of a house in the village ahead of us when I saw the explosions. Distance twenty kilometers to the southeast, that could only be Caen. The black column of smoke was growing ever larger, lit by flames. Then we could also hear the boom of the explosions! What a terrible spectacle, what a drama when one thought of the many people in this town. Only hours ago we drove through it, or was it days ago? During these few short hours, in the face of this immense steamroller of destruction coming at us from the north, at sea, in the air and on land, I wanted to shout at all the generals right up to Adolf Hitler: 'Over here, quickly, before it is too late! Whoever can still fight, come here! The fastest, most powerful divisions, send them here! The Luftwaffe . . . where is it? Bring it in! The Navy . . . where is it? It must get here!'

In these few hours I had observed the wave of ten thousand soldiers already rolled ashore. With every new second, more ships came in with soldiers, unloading them like ants. After only a short pause to catch their breath, they trampled our thin lines of defense.

Back to the Division! I had to report to the commander himself. Otherwise, no one would believe this. And whoever doubted it afterwards would have to see it for himself. In a few hours, however, they would not be able to stand in this spot. British tanks would be milling about here. It was 11.00 hours. We would send one more report on the sector up to Cabourg in the northeast which I could overlook. Everywhere in the whole coastal sector from the bay of Arromanches in the west, across the mouth of the Orne river to the east, ships of all types were landing troops and firing on the coastal areas.

Heavy fighting was taking place along the coastal road Courseulles-St. Aubin-Luc—Lion. I by-passed Caen to the south.[1a]

The leader of the second scouting party, Unterscharführer August Zinßmeister noted in his diary:

I had received my orders at 04.00 hours and set out with my scouting party via Laigle, St. Gauburge, Gacé, Livarot, and past Lisieux to the bases at the Channel coast and to Houlgate (at the mouth of the Dives river, approximately 20 kilometers east of the mouth of the Orne river. Author). At sea, I recognized 60 landing ships, among them cruisers, which were firing on the fortifications built into the mountain near Houlgate and the city itself. Most of the roads had been destroyed by bombs. Initially, the Jäger group and I went on foot, then I pulled the vehicles into the city behind us. The ship's artillery destroyed our way out. We drove cross-country back to the ridge and found ourselves suddenly in the midst of Ami-(American) paratroopers. (A mistake, they were British. Author). Bergmüller shot one of them before he could get me. We took another one prisoner, and fired on others from the road. We radioed the Division and established contact with the 711. Wehrmachtsdivision.[2]

At 05.00 hours, the 15. Armee reported to the Heeresgruppe that enemy air landings in the Houlgate area were continuing. It requested the release of the "HJ" Division in order to push with it quickly into the landed enemy troops. No sea landings had been reported from this sector. One half hour later, the Armee again requested that the Division be sent into action quickly. However, Generalleutnant Speidel wanted to first discuss the matter with the chief of staff of the Supreme Command West. Ten minutes later, the chief of the 7. Armee, Generalmajor Pemsel, reported that the situation east of the Orne river had apparently been cleared up, but that the enemy was still holding the Bridge at Bernville (read Bénouville). Immediately after this conversation, Generalleutnant Speidel spoke with the chief of the Supreme Command West, General of the infantry Günther Blumentritt, by telephone. He advised him of the latest reports from the 15. and the 7. Armee and reported that the Heeresgruppe planned to deploy the "HJ" Division in the line on both sides of Lisieux as soon as it had been released. Between 05.00 hours and 05.20 hours, the Supreme Commander West had reached the decision to attach the "HJ" Division to Heeresgruppe West, without having received approval of the OKW. He ordered the deployment of the Division in the sector of the 711. Inf.-Div. so that imme-diate action against the landed enemy would be possible. The area of Bernay-Lisieux-Vimoutiers was chosen. The order to deploy the "HJ" Division in this area was issued by the Heeresgruppe to Panzergruppe West at 05.50 hours. The Division was to establish immediate contact with the general command LXXXI A.K. in Rouen and with the 711. Infanteriedivision in le Quesnay, and report its assembly.

At 05.20 hours, already, the Supreme Command West had authorized the Panzergruppe, at its request, to prepare Flakabteilung 12. and 14. (Fla)/26 to join up with the Division. They had been deployed to provide air defense at the Seine crossings near Elbeuf and Gaillon. Soon after this order arrived at the Division, the order to deploy into the previously mentioned areas was received. This would have been between 06.30 and 07.00 hours. The order had a shocking impact. The Division had already deployed its most forward units, namely the whole of the Panzerregiment, north of the line Bernay-Lisieux. In accordance with the order of the Heeresgruppe, it had to march initially to the southwest and then to the north, northwest or possibly even northeast, for action in the sector of the 711. Inf.-Div., a time consuming detour. In addition, the Division had prepared deployment plan B in case of action between the mouths of the Seine and Orne rivers. It envisaged four routes of advance which had been scouted, also with regard to the width and stability of the bridges. This deployment plan was not used. Rather, the Division was only to bring forward its rear units and assemble in an area of only twenty-five kilometers width and twenty-five kilometers depth.

From this assembly area, only two good roads, not four, led in the direction of the coast. The crossroads at Lisieux were particularly threatened by enemy air attacks because of its location in a deep gully. The Division was convinced that this plan could not expedite action at the coast, rather it would slow it down considerably.

Although the Division was not tactically attached to the general command, the Ia immediately telephoned the chief of the staff of the I. Panzerkorps, Brigadeführer Fritz Kraemer, and made him aware of the concerns of the Division. All efforts by the chief were to no avail, the order had to be carried out without changes. It remains an open question whether the Heeresgruppe acted in ignorance of the prepared and officially submitted deployment plans or whether it took advantage of the situation to bring the Division into the area which it had been destined for in April when it was deployed from Belgium.

An order for the march into the new assembly area was prepared immediately and carried to the regiments and self-contained battalions/Abteilungen by orderly officers. The war diary of the I./ SS-Panzergrenadierregiment 25 indicates that the battalion received the alarm at 03.00 hours, and the code word "Blücher" at 05.55 hours. It had been ready to march since 06.00 hours. (The code word "Blücher indicated that the units had to be deployed, ready to march, within one-and-one half hours at the designated departure points.) The battalion commenced its march along the designated route in deployment plan "Z" (deployment B) at 10.00 hours after receiving the order by radio from the regiment.[3]

The Flakabteilung received the order to depart for the assembly area at 08.00 hours, together with instructions to take up air defense positions around Lisieux. The 2. and 4. batteries (8.8 cm and 3.7 cm Flak, respectively) had first to be taken across the river by ferries near Les Andelys. They marched separately. The other regiments and battalions/Abteilungen also set out between ten and eleven o'clock, no exact information can be offered on them. The Division command post remained initially in Acon since telephone connections existed there. A reporting post was set up in Lisieux.

It has already been mentioned that the commander of Panzergrenadierregiment 25, Standartenführer Kurt Meyer, had begun independent reconnaissance action in the Caen area immediately after the alarm. The report of one of the leaders of the scouting parties is inserted here, despite the fact that it is occasionally in advance of the developments. Unterscharführer Peter Hederich reports:

I am leading the scouting party in the direction of the coast via Troarn. We are supposed to establish contact with the 21 Panzerdivision of the Heer and, at the same time, scout in the direction of landed enemy paratroopers in the area. We set out with motorcycles, a communications car and an armored car with a 2 cm gun. It turns into a drive through no-man's land, past wooded areas in which enemy paratroopers are reported. Since our main objective is to reach and secure the bridge across the Dives river behind Troarn, we drive like crazy. Also, to get away from the damned fighter-bombers which were chasing us. I have the two heavy side car motor-cycles with the mounted machine guns at the point. They are very maneuverable and have considerable fire power. Then follows my Schwimmwagen (amphibious car) with the radio in it and behind me is the motorcycle dispatch rider. The armored car with the 2 cm gun is at the rear. It provides fire cover to the lighter vehicles ahead and is not in danger of driving onto a mine first or of facing the bar-rel of an anti-tank gun.

So we reach, chased by fighter-bombers but unharmed, the bridge across the Dives behind Troarn. There we find an infantry scouting party in platoon strength, led by a lieutenant. They were made mobile by use of bicycles. Smaller groups which have been sent to the surrounding towns are returning with wounded and dead. They have been fired on from ambush in the towns. It is use-less for them to scout any further. As infantry, they are not suffi-ciently armed to offer effective opposition to the Maquis (French underground) or the hidden enemy paratroopers.

Since we have reached our objective unharmed, I now drive with my whole party into these towns but return without any results, we do not find a human soul. At a crossroads we encounter the com-mand post of a Panzergrenadierbataillon of the 21. Panzerdivision. Contact is made and reported to my regiment by radio. The scout-ing party is called back since its mission has been accomplished. As we are driving back to Troarn, we are in for an unpleasant surprise. Enemy transport gliders have landed in the pastures to the right and left of the road despite the "Rommel asparagus" and the boys aim their infantry fire on us. However, after our 2 cm gun hammers explosive shells among them and sets the gliders, which are used for cover, on fire with incendiary grenades, the brothers from the other side withdraw into the near-by woods. From there, their fire can no longer harm us. So we drive on. Our next surprise is the bridge across the Dives. It is no longer there. The fighter-bombers have done their work. The infantry platoon is seeking cover, completely bewildered, in the ditch. It is their first acquaintance with the fighter-bombers and they have suffered terrible losses. They had crawled under the bridge during the fighter-bomber attack without considering that these aircraft can also offer rockets and bombs.

We are cut off from the way back. The Schwimmwagen is the only one in my party which can swim and cross the Dives without a bridge. The motorcycles can get across using a near-by wooden dam, but not the armored car with the 2 cm gun. We have to stay together, there is no question of separating since it cannot be predicted when engineers will repair the bridge. This means looking for another route for all of us. This is found after some searching on the map in the form of a railroad embankment which takes us to a road leading to Caen and back to our bunch.

I will not forget this drive along the railroad embankment as long as I live. After only a short time we have written ourselves off, whether to heaven or hell, I do not know. We just wanted to get away from this damned railroad embankment. Like a target on a shooting range we move high above the terrain. And that at a snail's pace, since the rail ties and the tracks are gone, only the deep ruts in the loose rocks remain. This is tough on us all, but it is not all. We still have to drive along an extensive wooded area from where we are getting infantry fire. This means every time, down from the motorcycles and out of the Schwimm-wagen, taking cover behind the armored car, and firing from all barrels. Only when the 2 cm gun hammers the edge of the woods are we getting peace and can go on. And finally, just before dusk, two fighter-bombers show up. Now it seems to be over since they are flying along both sides of the embankment and we do not have any other cover. Only the devil or well-aimed fire can save us now. I jump into the open armored car to share my thoughts with my men in a few seconds and to encourage them. I believe that I need courage more than anyone. Previously, scouting had been fun, as playing cowboys and indians is for children. But then it had become deadly serious. The machine gunners jump behind the armored car and lift their guns. The unbalanced chase can begin. Of course, we are thinking of ourselves as the hunters and not as the rabbits, although we feel a little more like the latter. My gunner has the strict order not to let the fighter-bombers out of his cross hairs. That is not too difficult since they are flying so close that they almost touch. As soon as the first one begins its dive, pushes its nose down, all of us will aim everything our barrels can spit out just ahead of it. The seconds turn into eternity. Finally, one of them, I think it is the guy on the right, does us the favor. We immediately start shouting, yelling, since he plunges into the ground next to the embankment and breaks into pieces. We probably managed direct hits on the poor guy over there. We do not notice the howling and whistling of the bullet salvo from the other fighter-bomber. In our giddiness, we first think that we are blown to bits. The second fighter-bomber either has no bombs or rockets on board, or he is so shocked about the fate of his comrade that he pulls up and disappears into the dusk at the horizon. There is no movement from the near-by edge of the woods either. We waste no

time to get going as quickly as is possible on this damned embankment. I no longer know how often we bailed out, except for the
driver of the armored vehicle, to pry the rocks from the tires of the
vehicle with our hands. It is slowly turning dark, only the occasional
signal rocket rises from the edge of the woods. It turns into a ghostly
drive since we are not safe from an infantry attack by the paratroopers hidden there. Finally, after a period of time which seems to last
forever, the embankment swings to the south. Soon, we are on the
road and drive, with our headlights almost completely shielded, in
the direction of Troarn-Caen.[3a]

The weather before noon was still favorable for the march. The clouds
were hanging low, it was very windy, and rain fell on and off. In the afternoon, from about 18.00 hours on, the sun came out and sunshine alternated
with fast moving clouds.[4]

During the morning, the Supreme Commander West became convinced
that the sea landing would be limited to the strip of beach west of the mouth
of the Orne river. Only there had the enemy landed by sea so far. In addition, the 15. Armee had reported to the Heeresgruppe at 10.20 hours, it had
relayed the report to the Supreme Commander West at 11.00 hours, that the
airborne enemy in battalion strength had been wiped out to the rear of the
711. Inf.-Div. and that 40 prisoners had been taken. Based on this, the
Supreme Commander West ordered, probably through Panzergruppe West,
"that the 12. SS-Panzerdivision was to prepare to be shifted in a westerly
direction". He informed the Heeresgruppe of this at 11.50 hours. The Division was unable to do anything in accordance with the intent of the order at
this time since all the units were still on the march to the assembly areas.
The Supreme Commander West informed the Heeresgruppe at 14.32 hours
that the OKW had released the "HJ" Division for action to the 7. Armee. It
had to still be determined which command would directly lead the Division.
Soon after, the Heeresgruppe was also informed that the Panzer-Lehr-Division had equally been released by the OKW, and that the Supreme Command West recommended deployment in the Flers area. At 15.07 hours, the
Supreme Commander West advised the Heeresgruppe that the general command of the I.SS-Panzerkorps and the required corps manpower had been
released to lead the two Panzerdivisions. The Heeresgruppe informed the 7.
Armee. Its war diary shows the following entry at 15.00 hours:

The 12. SS-Pz.-Div. and the Pz. Lehr-Div. are attached to the AOK
with immediate effect for action against the bridgehead in the sector of the 716. Inf.-Div. The AOK issues the following order through
the Panzergruppe Command West:
  1) "The 12. SS-Pz.-Div. deploys immediately northward to a line
     Alencon (outside)—Carrouges (inclusive)—Flers (outside) in

the area on both sides of Evrecy (8.5 kilometers southwest of Caen, Author) and is initially attached to the LXXXIV A.K. Its mission is to drive the enemy who has broken through, adjacent to the 21. Pz.-Div. on the west, back into the sea and destroy him.

2) The Pz.Lehr-Div. deploys immediately south of the stated line and initially captures the area Flers-Vire [approximately fifty kilometers southwest of Caen]."

After the AOK had been informed that the general command of the I. SS-Panzerkorps with all its corps troops had been attached to it, it advised their commander, Brigadeführer Kraemer of the AOK's intentions. It was planned to attach the 21. Panzerdivision, the 12. Panzer-division, the Panzer-Lehr-Division and the 716. Infanteriedivision to the I. SS-Panzerkorps and to "bring them together in the right sector of the LXXXIV A.K. (Armee Korps)."[5]

The order from Panzergruppe West to turn the Division towards the area of Caen, arrived at the divisional command post at approximately 17.00 hours. Parts of the Division had reached their assembly areas in the meantime. The I./25 had reached St. Pierre-des-Ifs, six kilometers southwest of Lisieux, around 13.00 hours and taken up positions on both sides of the road. The baggage trains and rear guard of the Bataillon assembled at a base set up in Vimoutiers.[6] Since the bulk of the Division was still on the march, the previous marching arrangements had to be maintained. The Division did not even have a rough idea of the situation in the Caen area. It only knew that the enemy had landed airborne troops east of the Orne river and west of the mouth of the Orne in a broad front from the sea. Thus, no other preparations could be made except reconnaissance in the new assembly area and from there towards the coast. The arrangement of the regiments and battalions along the route of advance required that, in the new assembly area, Panzergrenadierregiment 26 together with the I. Panzer-abteilung had to take up positions to the right, and Panzergrenadierregiment 25 together with the II. Panzerabteilung, to the left. Two companies each from both Panzerabteilungen, with half of their Panzers, had been at the two Panzergrenadier regiments for joint exercises at the time of the alarm. For the continued march into the area southwest of Caen, the routes of "Deployment Plan C" could generally be used. The Division issued the respective orders by radio, and in written format by orderly officers or dispatch riders, to the regiments and the independent battalions and Abteilungen.

The war diary of I./25 noted:

17.40 hours. After receiving verbal regimental order, the battalion set out from St. Pierre-des-Ifs along march route 'Blue', situation 'C'. Route via St. Pierre-sur-Dives to Missy [fifteen kilometers southwest of Caen]. After St. Pierre-sur-Dives, constant attacks by low-level aircraft with on-board weapons, and by fighter-bombers on the marching columns. The battalion and the attached weapons suffered their first losses and breakdowns. Hauptsturmführer (captain) Peinemann was wounded in the left leg by shrapnel, Untersturmführer (2nd lieutenant) Gschaider took over 3. company.[7]

The divisional commander, Brigadeführer Witt, drove ahead of the divisional staff for a briefing on the situation at the command post of the 21. Panzerdivision at St. Pierre-sur-Dives. The operations group of the divisional staff, together with the Divisional escort company, left Acon at 18.00 hours. Their destination was les Moutiers-en-Cinglais, located seventeen kilometers southwest of Caen, at the southern edge of the Forêt de Grimbosq. Passing through St. Pierre-sur-Dives, the Ia received a briefing on the situation, at the rear command post of the 21. Panzerdivision in the late hours of the evening. He reached the prepared divisional command post at les Moutiers, with the operations group and the escort company, during the night.

The OKW had ordered during the afternoon: ". . . care has to be taken that all planned movements will take place under cover of the bad weather situation." This directive was passed on to the Heeresgruppe by the Supreme Command West at 16.50 hours. One hour later, the poor weather had passed through, the sun had occasionally come out, and the clouds were breaking up more and more. The supreme commander of Panzergruppe West, General of the Panzer troops Freiherr (baron) Geyr von Schweppenburg, had requested from the Supreme Command West, in the early afternoon, that the Panzerdivisions should assemble only from 20.00 hours onwards, to avoid attacks from the air. Generalleutnant Speidel was of the opposite opinion and demanded immediate assembly, as ordered. The Panzergruppe then reported to the Heeresgruppe that the Panzer-Lehr-Division had assembled along three roads at 19.00 hours.[8]

The march of the "HJ" Division, in particular from the early afternoon on, was being delayed by more and more frequent fighter-bomber attacks. The columns had to stop and take cover when attacks threatened, except to fire at the attackers with 2 cm Flak, machine guns, and hand weapons. Afterwards, the vehicles pulled out from their cover, the troops mounted again. Damaged or destroyed vehicles had to be moved from the roads, the wounded had to be looked after, and the dead had to be handed over to the services to the rear. A member of the I. Zug (platoon) of the 13. Kompanie of the Regiment 25, Sturmmann (lance corporal) Martin Besel, reports:

During our march to the assembly we were attacked by fighter-bombers. In the course of this, our regimental commander 'Panzermeyer' was extremely lucky to jump from his vehicle just in time. He got away to the left as a bomb exploded to the right and completely destroyed his vehicle. The attack was meant for a bridge which, thank God, remained intact.[9]

Sturmmann Hellmuth Pock of the Panzerregiment reports on his experiences during the alarm, while waiting for marching orders, and on the march. Many other members of the Division experienced these decisive hours in a similar manner. He writes:

Our dream of the exercise, which featured chicken and broiled potatoes, is now over, at least for the near future. In and around our quarters, lively activity has begun. The soldiers are, once again, busy with the never-ending preparations of supplies and equipment, while officers and dispatch riders arrive constantly. Every time one or more of our officers arrive, there is a loud hurrah among them. Some embrace and slap each other's shoulders. Others rip their caps from their heads and throw them high into the air. There is a mood of exuberance which also begins to grip us. It cannot be explained, it is just there and being felt. Then, engine noise in the air, and here they come already. The officers holler 'Cover!' and everyone tries to find some as quickly as possible, and to become as close to being invisible as one can. As I look up I recognize the Balken cross on the fuselage and the wings of the aircraft. Those are ours, our Me 109s, thirty to forty of them, which roar above us at low altitude. We have jumped from cover and wave anything we can move at our pilots. 'Hurrah', 'Heil', 'Bravo' and whatever other shouts of enthusiasm one can think of, are being yelled at the fighter aircraft. We wonder if they can see us. Yes! They fly a loop, rock their wings in greeting, and roar across our heads. They are flying so low that we can distinctly make out the pilots in their cockpits. That is something which makes our soldiers' hearts glad, a picture of might and strength, of force ready for action, and of determination. There is enthusiasm everywhere. 'We'll show the Tommies', and similar lines dominate our -conversation.

The order to get ready is issued and we walk to the vehicles. The drivers check their engines once more to make sure everything is all right. This is more a reaction to the stress rather than a technical necessity. We are waiting for the order to mount. Our gear has long been stowed and in our opinion there is no need to stay here any longer. Time is running out. We are worried that we will be too late, too late for heavy fighting ahead of us. The tension of the men is obvious to all. Even those among us who are known for their humor cannot overcome the tension with their jokes. After that first rush of enthusiasm, we have now been gripped by a certain apprehension of the unknown. We all know that having to wait is the worst the troops could face. We would prefer to get going right away. 'Well, I wonder if they are about to start, or if they don't need us anymore', says one of our comrades standing around. We try to calm our nerves by smoking, but the expected result does not happen today. We know what is at stake, and it is only normal that we feel the developments are too slow in moving ahead.

Finally, the order comes: 'Mount! Let's go!' After many hours of driving on dusty roads, we run into a traffic stoppage at a crossroads. We meet other units of our division. They are mostly engineers. Their vehicles are perfectly camouflaged, they appear to be moving bushes, the faces of the men are covered with dust from the long drive. They are very young faces under the steel helmets, led by officers who look daring and almost as young. They pass us, having priority, without pause, vehicle after vehicle, unstoppable. Armored personnel carriers, radio vehicles, tractors with mounted infantry, anti-tank guns, motorcycle gunners and dispatch riders, command vehicles, and many others. Everything is fully motorized. As far as the eye can see, and wherever there is a path a vehicle can drive on, units are moving in the direction of the coast. Such a massing of troops is something new for me. In addition, the weather is beautiful and, strangely, there is not an enemy aircraft in the sky. We assume that our fighter aircraft have looked after that. There can be no question, victory is ours! 'Good luck, comrades!', we shout at those passing us. 'The same to you', they answer. We can continue our drive, the other units have passed the crossroads area.

This was still in the morning and before noon. The situation changed completely with improving visibility. Sturmmann Hellmuth Pock continues:

At a rise in the road we re-establish contact again with our company. A motorcycle dispatch rider has arrived. We learn that the company is also on the march here. We also hear of the first losses. The provisions vehicle was knocked out by strafers, the driver and his mate were killed.

We keep going. The number of our vehicles knocked out by the enemy keeps growing. They are sitting where they were hit, burnt out, with the typically rusty-red color. One can only guess what most of this equipment used to be, the result of terrible explosions. Grenades are scattered about, shells, all types of ammunition, among them, dead soldiers. Without doubt, a supply column was hit here. Next to one of the large bomb craters sits a knocked-out armored personnel carrier. The hatch at the rear of the vehicle is open, the legs and lower body of a soldier are sticking out. It looks as if the man is kneeling. As we drive by slowly I see that the upper body is completely burnt. Maybe, a merciful bullet killed him before this.

The march during the day becomes more and more dangerous. The pastures and fields are plowed by bomb craters and we start to slowly wonder why we still have not arrived. We realize more and more that the enemy, as far as materiel is concerned, does not seem to be inferior to us. Yet the march continues without halt.

As we are driving through a small town I see the soldiers on the vehicles ahead of us jumping off very suddenly and seeking cover. Just as I want to ask what is happening, I can see it for myself. Enemy fighter-bombers are attacking us. As we had been taught, I take my carbine, load it, and follow the daring flight of the fighters from under my cover. Now they have disappeared into the sun, we cannot spot them anymore. But then, with the engine howling and at high speed, the first one comes racing at us. 'Brrt, drrt, brrt', the salvo bangs into the road. Low-level attack! Just as we have been drilled, I lead the aircraft with my carbine and fire. In the meantime, my comrades around me have also opened fire on the attacking fighters. 'These damned dogs don't notice anything at all', one of them next to me curses. And he seems to be right with his opinion. Despite the fact that our fire is fairly accurate, we do not manage to shoot down even one. We cannot even spot a trail of smoke. After a few moments of contemplation we arrive at the conviction that we are fairly harmless to enemy aircraft with our trusty 98 K carbines. This realization does not create any joy at all, we are used to seeing positive results from our actions, or at least we expect these. The initial frequent mounting and dismounting has become more rare. A few hours ago we still dismounted when any aircraft came into suspicious proximity. Now we remain mounted and jump off only when we think we are spotted, but then at lightning speed.

In a small village, really just a few houses, another halt is ordered. The fighter-bombers are again raking the roads. We are fairly well covered and camouflaged behind the houses. We wait under an archway until the fireworks are over. Some vehicles must have been caught outside the town by the aircraft which dive constantly, and badly aimed salvos slap into the walls next to us and into the street.[10]

Initially, both the leadership and the troops were under the impression that the fighter-bomber attacks had caused severe losses of men and extensive damage to materiel. In reality, the losses, even if painful, and the damage to vehicles and weapons, were not very severe. Here are some examples. The escort company of the Division did not have any dead or wounded during the march on 6 June from 18.00 hours into the night. The company lost:

6 vehicles from the Schützenzug (gunner platoon),
1 vehicle from the Flakzug (anti-aircraft platoon),
2 vehicles from the infantry gun platoon,
2 vehicles from the motorcycle gunner platoon,
5 vehicles from the baggage train.

The majority of these vehicles became inoperable due to technical problems which could be repaired again.[11]

The war diary of the I./25 reports on losses and damage on 6 June:

dead: 1 noncom, 3 men,
wounded: 1 officer, 1 noncom, 10 men, of which remained with the
    unit 1 officer and 2 men,
missing: 1 man.
(The losses of the attached platoons are contained in these figures).
Losses of vehicles, weapons and equipment:
2 Kompanie:
    1 medium all-terrain truck through low-level attack,
    3 heavy trucks badly damaged,
    1 signal pistol, 5 rifles, original supply of flares, anti-tank mines
    and a supply of maps.
3 Kompanie:
    1 Kfz 1 (Volkswagen) total, aircraft attack,
    2 other vehicles badly damaged.
4 Kompanie:
    1 Pak 40 (anti-tank gun) and its vehicle, total, through fighter-
    bomber attack, 1 rifle.
Ammunition used:
    2,000 rounds SS (infantry ammunition for machine guns and
    rifles).[12]

The bridge engineers column B, led by Untersturmführer Hans Richter, was attacked by fighter-bombers in the area of Evreux. During this attack all of the pontoons and most of the vehicles were destroyed.[13]

The losses of soldiers to the Division on 6 June amounted to:
22 dead, of which were 3 noncoms and 19 men.
60 wounded, of which were 2 officers, 10 noncoms and 48 men.
Missing: 1 man.
A total of 83 casualties.[14]

As a result of the deployment into the assembly area Bernay-Lisieux-Vimoutiers and of the later re-direction into the area southwest of Caen, of the delays due to fighter-bomber attacks which required increased distance between vehicles, only parts of the Division reached the assembly area southwest of Caen on 6 June. The I. Bataillon of Panzer-grenadierregiment 25 arrived at Missy, fifteen kilometers southwest of Caen on the road from Caen to Villers-Bocage, in the late evening. It set up camp in a forest southeast of the village, and marched on foot to take up position at the railroad line northwest of Noyers, 1.5 kilometers northwest of Missy at 23.00 hours. A reconnaissance group, led by Untersturmführer (2nd lieutenant) Exner, advanced to Tilly-sur-Seulles, eight kilometers northwest of Missy.[15] The other two battalions of Regiment 25, the regimental staff and the regimental companies, would also have reached their assembly areas at approximately the same time. There are no confirmed reports on this. The II. Panzerabteilung and the III. Artillerieabteilung also arrived in the area southwest of Caen during the course of the night 6–7 June. The batteries marched with the battalions with which they were to cooperate: the 7. Batterie with the I./25, the 8. Batterie with the II./25, the 9. Batterie with the III./25, the Abteilung staff and the 10. Batterie between the 2. and 3. marching group, the Abteilung commander and adjutant with the staff of Regiment 25.[16]

Regiment 26 and the I. Panzerabteilung, the Pionier-bataillon, the I. and II. Artillerieabteilung, and the Flak-abteilung deployed near Lisieux, were still far behind.

To judge the time required for the deployment of the Division under 'normal' circumstances, the routes of the march and distances are important. The plans for the deployment did not survive. Only the map of the III. (heavy) Artillerieabteilung for the deployment plan "C" and used during the fighting, is available in the German Federal archives/military archives. The 10. Batterie of this Abteilung, until the start of the invasion deployed at Moulins-la-Marche (twenty kilometers southeast of Gacé), had to reach from there the assembly point at Vimoutiers via St. Gauburge and Gacé. This meant that it had to cover thirty-nine road kilometers to Vimoutiers. From there, the route of advance led in a northwesterly direction via Jort (twenty kilometers northeast of Falaise), where the Dives river was crossed, via Rouvres, Estrées, Grainville—Langannerie, St. Germain-le Vasson, Barbéry, les Moutiers-en-Cinglais, Brieux (where the Orne river was crossed), la Caine, Banneville to Villedon on the Odon river. From the gathering point, this was a distance of about seventy kilometers. From the previous deployment area to the assembly area twenty kilometers southwest of Caen, the total marching distance was 110 kilometers. The I./25, in whose movement area the III. Artillerieabteilung marched from Vimoutiers onwards, had to cover seventy kilometers from there to Villedon. The 5. Kompanie of the Panzerregiment, stationed at la Vallée (eight kilometers southeast of Elbeuf) until the invasion, had to cover 125 kilometers via le Neubourg, Lisieux, Vimont, St. André-sur-Orne to the Odon river. The 2. Pionierkompanie had a total marching distance of 142 kilometers from Pacy-sur-Eure via Evreux, la Neuville, Lisieux, Vimont, St. André to Verson.

The I./26, one of the units with the longest march to the assembly area, had to cover 190 kilometers from Houdan via Dreux, Damville, Broglie, Orbec, St. Pierre-sur-Dives, St. Sylvain, Amayé-sur-Orne to Fontaine-Etoupefour. This distance is based on the shortest route north of the movement area of the I./25 and the III./AR, the effective route is not known.

Based on the consideration that one battalion had 100 vehicles which would travel at a distance of 100 meters between vehicles, as ordered, and at thirty kilometers per hour, the I./25 required 140 minutes for seventy kilometers plus twenty minutes for the length of the column of ten kilometers, for a total of 160 minutes. When one assumes two stops of twenty minutes each, the battalion would need 200 minutes, or three hours and twenty minutes, for the march alone, without any threat from the air. If the I./25 had set out on 6 June at 11.00 hours as per deployment plan "C", it could have assembled at 14.20 hours near Villedon on the Odon river. If one uses as a base the effective time and distance required for the march into the Lisieux area, we arrive at the following result: the distance of fifty kilometers from Chambois (where the most distant 1. Kompanie was stationed)-Vimoutiers-St. Pierre-des-Ifs (six kilometers southwest of Lisieux) in three hours means a marching speed of seventeen kilometers per hour. If we assume twenty minutes to arrange the vehicles in the assembly area, we arrive at an average marching speed of twenty kilometers per hour. Thus, the battalion would have required three-and-one-half hours of marching time for the seventy kilometers to Villedon on the Odon river. If the twenty minutes to arrange the vehicles of the last company are added, the I./25 could have assembled on 6 June 1944 at 15.00 hours at the Odon river if it had left at 11.00 hours. The II. Bataillon had to cover an extra twenty-four kilometers from Nonant-le-Pin (twelve kilometers southwest of Gacé) via Trun. The III. Bataillon had approximately the same distance from Orbec as the I. Bataillon, the regimental staff at Gacé had an additional eighteen kilometers to Vimoutiers. Based on this, the whole regiment could have assembled at the Odon river at 16.00 hours. A total marching distance of 125 kilometers is assumed for the most distant, the II. A reduced result must be assumed since technical stops were necessary. One can use an average marching speed of fifteen kilometers per hour. The Abteilung would thus have needed eight hours and twenty minutes, for the march and a further twenty minutes to arrange for the last company. This means that it would have joined the assembly at the Odon river as the last unit of the Panzerregiment at 19.40 hours.

One can assume a greater distance of 190 kilometers and an average marching speed of twenty kilometers per hour for Regiment 26. Thus, it would have assembled at 21.00 hours at the Odon river. But one must take into consideration that, between 18.00 and 21.00 hours (sunset 21.48 hours) when the cloud cover broke up, the march would have been significantly delayed by fighter-bomber attacks. The war diary of I./25 notes that it set out from St. Pierre-des-Ifs on the march into the area southwest of Caen and that it had been under constant fighter-bomber attacks from St. Pierre-sur-Dives (twenty-two kilometers from St. Pierre-des-Ifs) onwards. That would have been from 19.00 hours on. The Bataillon required for the marching distance of seventy-one kilometers four hours and twenty minutes. This indicates an average marching speed of seventeen kilometers per hour. It can be assumed that Regiment 26 had a reduced marching speed, by three kilometers per hour for three hours, meaning a total reduced marching effort of nine kilometers and a delay of approximately one hour. The same would be true for the II. Panzerabteilung. Thus, Regiment 26 could have arrived in the assembly area southwest of Caen at 22.00 hours, the Panzerregiment at 20.40.

We can base our calculations on the assumption that Regiment 25 set out for the area southwest of Caen at 11.00 hours in accordance with deployment plan "C" once the situation had been sufficiently clarified. It had been reinforced by the III. Artillerieabteilung and two Panzer IV companies with half of their Panzers. These units had been there on exercises. Thus, Regiment 25 could have started an attack on the bridgehead no later than 18.00 hours on 6 June, i.e. two hours after assembling at the Odon river. An attack of the whole Division could have begun, in this case after careful reconnaissance and from a readiness area further north, in the early morning hours of 7 June at around 5 A.M.

The First Battle for Caen from 6 to 10 June 1944

CHAPTER 1.01

Developments within the Bridgehead on Both Sides of the Mouth of the Orne River on 6 June 1944

The 12. SS-Panzerdivision "Hitlerjugend" marched initially into the area around Lisieux and then to the area southwest of Caen during the course of 6 June. At the same time, decisive developments were taking place at the coast of Normandy where the Allies had landed and in the two air landing zones. Only the course of the battles in the British-Canadian landing zone, in particular in the Caen area, will be examined here in broad outlines.

Units of Panzergrenadierregiment 125 of the 21. Panzer-division, which were stationed in the vicinity of the air landing zone of the 6th Airborne Division northeast of Caen, had, as already mentioned, attacked the British paratroopers and airborne landing units without orders from above. At 04.30 hours, the 7. Armee had requested action by the 21. Panzer-division east of the Orne river from Heeresgruppe B. General-leutnant Speidel decided, however, that such action was not immediately required.[1] Parts of the II. Bataillon of Panzergrenadierregiment 192 of this Division had advanced, as ordered by Feldmarschall Rommel, already at the beginning of May into the area Anisy-Villons-Cairon-Buron-la Bijude (some eight kilometers northwest of Caen). They were ordered by the 716. Infanteriedivision at 03.10 hours, under the command of Grenadierregiment 736, to commence an attack on the enemy bridgehead near Bénouville. They had been able to push into the town, but the determined resistance by the British paratroopers prevented them from reaching the bridges across the Orne canal and the Orne river. This would have required support by Panzers. The Panzerregiment of the 21. Panzer-division was ready to march at that time with the I. Abteilung in an

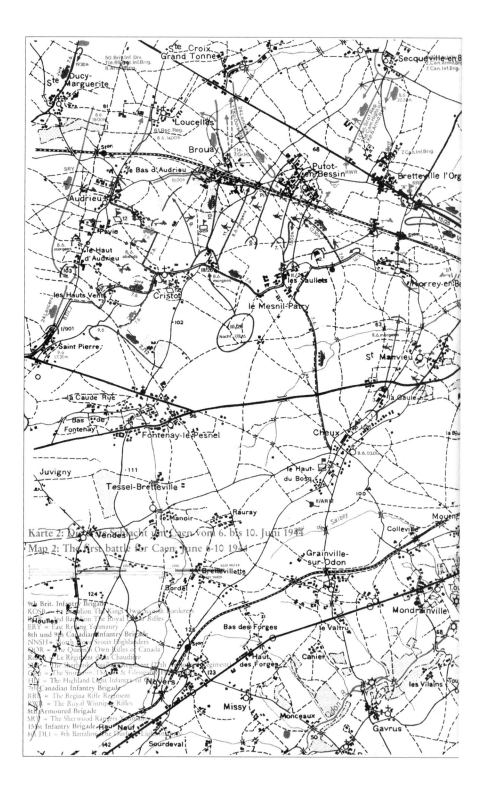

Karte 2: Die erste Schlacht um Caen vom 6. bis 10. Juni 1944
Map 2: The first battle for Caen, June 6-10 1944

9th Brit. Infantry Brigade
KOSB = 1st Battalion The King's Own Scottish Borderers
RHoulles 2nd Battalion The Royal Ulster Rifles
ERY = East Riding Yeomanry
8th und 9th Canadian Infantry Brigade
NNSH = North Nova Scotia Highlanders
QOR = The Queen's Own Rifles of Canada
RdlC = Le Régiment de la Chaudière
SrdH = The Sherbrooke Fusiliers Regiment (27th Armoured Regiment)
SD&G = The Stormont, Dundas & Glengarry Highlanders
HLI = The Highland Light Infantry of Canada
7th Canadian Infantry Brigade
RRR = The Regina Rifle Regiment
RWR = The Royal Winnipeg Rifles
8th Armoured Brigade
SRY = The Sherwood Rangers Yeomanry
151st Infantry Brigade
8th DLI = 8th Battalion The Durham Light Infantry

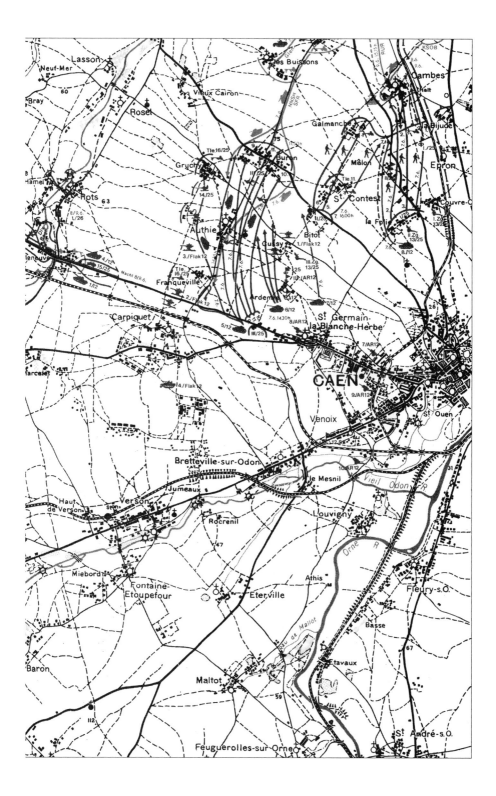

area some ten kilometers northeast of Falaise and with the II. Abteilung in the area near Fresné-la-Mère, five kilometers east of Falaise. The Division was still without combat orders from the Heeresgruppe.[2] Only at 06.15 was it attached to the 7. Armee, when the 7. Armee had reported that the enemy had opened fire from the sea on the coastal defense line at the mouth of the Orne river and near Asnelles (eleven kilometers northeast of Bayeux).

The 7. Armee attached the 21. Panzerdivision to the LXXXIV A.K. at 07.00 hours with the mission to destroy the airborne enemy east of the Orne river. At that time, the landings from the sea in the British-Canadian sector had not yet begun. However, they could be predicted since fire on the coastal defense positions from the sea had already been reported. The Armee obviously calculated that it would be possible to neutralize the airborne enemy east of the Orne river before the landings from the sea began. However, at 09.25 hours already, it became obvious that this decision had been a mistake. General Marcks, the commanding general of the LXXXIV. A.K. requested the attachment of the "HJ" Division for action west of Caen against the enemy who had been landed by sea, since the 21. Panzerdivision would be needed as a 'mobile reserve' to the right of the Orne river. A good hour later, at 10.35 hours, he advised the Armee that he wanted to send the 21. Panzerdivision into action west of the Orne river because of the changed situation. Since the Division was far to the rear at the time, a re-routing would still have been possible.[3]

This change in the mission of the 21. Pz.Div. had a very negative impact. The Assault Gun Abteilung 200 was, at this time, marching through Caen on its way to support the 8./Panzergrenadierregiment 192 which was stuck near -Bénouville. Since the Panzerregiment was now ordered to attack to the west of the Orne river, the Division wanted to add another armored unit to its Panzergrenadierregiment 125. It was in battle against paratroopers and airborne troops east of the Orne river. The Assault Gun Abteilung 200 was ordered to turn back and deploy through Caen to the east shore of the Orne river. It was needed at Bénouville. The 21. Pz. Div. was split into two parts: Panzergrenadierregiment 125, without I. Bataillon, and the Assault Gun Abteilung 200 were tied down in battle with paratroop and airborne units to the right of the Orne river, the bulk of the Division was supposed to attack west of the Orne. Parts of it had already been in battle for hours. The 8. Kompanie of Panzergrenadierregiment 192 was fighting near Bénouville. The I. Abteilung of Panzerartillerie-regiment 155 was in a fire fight from positions in the area of Mathieu. It had suffered significant losses through air attacks and fire from the sea. Heeres-Flakabteilung 305, together with the Flak command Caen, was in action to the northeast of the city. Finally, Panzerjägerabteilung 200 with twentyfour 8.8 cm guns was in position in the area northwest and west of the city.[4] Massive action by the whole Division in a narrow area was thus no longer possible. But the loss of time, too, caused by the change in mission, had to have a negative impact.

While the bulk of the Division was on the march into the area north of Caen, the enemy had already been able to break through the coastal defenses in a number of spots and pushed his attack further inland. The Canadians who had landed near Courseulles advanced southward for approximately three kilometers during the morning. The units which had landed after the assault battalions were able to assemble only slowly on the narrow beach for a further advance. Immediately to the east, another Canadian brigade had taken Bernières after heavy fighting until 12.30 hours. The following brigade could start out towards the south only at 15.00 hours because of the crowding at the beaches. The German batteries, mostly in open firing positions, could have caused havoc here, but they had already been put out of action by aerial bombardment and shelling from the sea.

The 3rd British Infantry Division had captured Hermanville at 09.30 hours. The 8.8 cm Pak of Panzerjägerabteilung 200, in position on a hill near Périers, had successfully fought back a tank attack from Hermanville so that the British infantry had reverted to defense there. To the east, a bitter battle for valiantly defended positions had only been decided through the action of a commando of the 1st Special Services Brigade from Ouistreham. There, too, congestion had considerably delayed the advance, in particular as German artillery was able to fire on the beaches occasionally, with significant effect. Shortly after 13.00 hours, parts of the 185th Infantry Brigade set out on foot along the road to Caen, which was their mission objective. The tanks which were supposed to carry them were still stuck in the traffic jam at the beaches.

The Canadians had been able to take St. Aubin on their left flank. Further to the east, the strong points in Langrune-sur-Mer were holding out. Since the right, westerly, flank of the 3rd British Infantry Division had been unable to capture Lion-sur-Mer, a link-up between the two divisions of the I Corps was not established. Between them was an open gap of five kilometers width which offered good prospects for a counterattack.

The troops of the 21. Pz.Div. scheduled for action west of the Orne had to cross the river at Caen. The city had been bombarded by heavy Allied bomber squadrons. The streets were partly blocked by rubble, clouds of smoke wafted through the town. The bulk of the troops crossed the Orne river by the street bridge along Route Nationale No. 158. Parts of Panzerregiment 22 used the bridge near Colombelles, 4.5 kilometers to the northeast. Two Kampfgruppen (battle groups) were formed. The "Gepanzerte Gruppe (armored group) Oppeln" under the command of the commander of Panzerregiment 22, Oberst (col.) von Oppeln, consisted of I./Panzerregiment 22 (without 4. Kompanie); II./Panzerregiment 22 (with only approximately 5 Panzer IVs per company); I.(armored)/Panzergrenadierregiment 125 (without 1 Kompanie); 1.(armored)/Panzerpionierbataillon 220; and III./Panzer-artillerieregiment 155. It deployed in the area west of Hérouville and west of Point 23 (approximately one kilometer north of Calix). Its attack objective was the coast between the mouth of the Orne and the eastern edge of Lion-sur-Mer.

"Kampfgruppe (Panzergrenadierregiment 192) Rauch", consisting of Panzergrenadierregiment 192 (without II. Bataillon); 2./Panzerpionier-bataillon 220; and II./Panzerartillerieregiment 155 was commanded by the commander of Panzergrenadierregiment 192, Oberst Rauch. It deployed in the area around St. Contest. Its objective was the coast near Lion-sur-Mer.

"Kampfgruppe von Luck" was deployed east of the Orne. It was made up of 4./Panzerregiment 22; Panzergrenadierregiment 125 (without I. Batail-lon); Panzeraufklärungsabteilung 21 (Panzer reconnaissance); and Stur-mgeschützabteilung 200 (assault gun Abteilung). This Kampfgruppe was commanded by Major von Luck.

Kampfgruppen "Oppeln" and "Rauch" were ready to attack at 16.00 hours. Some units, in particular the Panzer-regiment, were still on the march or had been taken out of action during the march. Eight Typhoons, for instance, had attacked the column of the Panzerregiment at the edge of Caen and damaged six Panzers.

At approximately 16.20 hours, Kampfgruppen "Oppeln" and "Rauch" began the attack. When the first Panzer IVs rolled out of the wooded terrain near Lebisey to advance to the north, they received fire from British tanks in the Biéville area which had been captured by the British.

Four Panzer IVs were knocked out. The attack was broken off. However, the I. Abteilung of Major von Gottberg managed to advance further west via Epron and Cambes into the area of Mathieu. There it received heavy fire from British anti-tank guns and from tanks in the hills near Périers which had been taken by the British in the meantime. After six Panzer IVs had been knocked out and one British seventeen-pound anti-tank gun had been destroyed, Major von Gottberg tried, swinging even further to the left, to capture the hills near Périers. In the vicinity of Mathieu he again received heavy fire from tanks and anti-tank guns and lost three Panzer IVs. The attack was broken off.

It is surprising that the hills near Périers had been occupied by British tanks and anti-tank guns. During the morning, 8.8 cm Pak and infantry of the 21. Panzerdivision had still successfully fought off an attack from Her-manville from those same hills. Since the positions on these hills were of sig-nificant importance, the development of the situation there must be explored in some detail.

In accordance with the position map of 716. Infanterie-division, the staff of Panzerjägerabteilung 200 of 21. Panzer-division was located in St. Pierre, to the west of Fontenay- le-Pesnel (17.5 kilometers west of Caen), before the start of the invasion. At the same time, the 1. Kompanie was located near St. Croix (7.5 kilometers northeast of St. Pierre), the 2. Kompanie north of Mes-nil Patry (thirteen kilometers west-northwest of Caen) and the 3. Kompanie near Camilly (eleven kilometers northwest of Caen). Only the 5. Kompanie of Sturmgeschützabteilung 200 (assault guns) is shown in the vicinity of the hills near Périers, namely in Cambes (4.5 kilometers southwest of Périers).

Generalleutnant Richter, commander of the 716. Infanterie-division stated in his study that he ordered Panzerjäger-abteilung 200 in the early morning hours of 6 June between 6 and 7 A.M. "to depart the area Brécy-Basly-Camilly [seventeen kilometers west, six kilometers northwest, and ten kilometers west of Périers] to the north and make contact with the II./726 which was in urgent need of armor-piercing weapons." For unknown reasons the Abteilung only departed at around 11 A.M. and encountered enemy tanks already at the Seulles valley. It knocked out several tanks there, but did not reach the II./726 which then bled to death further north.[5] Generalmajor Feuchtinger, commander of the 21. Panzerdivision wrote in his study that a company of Panzerjägerabteilung 200 was sent out at 08.05 hours to engage enemy tanks near Asnelles (approximately three kilometers east of Arromanches on the beach). Soon after, the bulk of the Abteilung had been brought up. It encountered enemy tanks in the Seulles valley at 11.00 hours. According to Werner Kortenhaus, the whole Abteilung with the exception of three Pak 8.8 cm, which remained in position near Périers, had been drawn off to the west.[6]

The development of the fighting for the important hills of Périers on the German side can, because of the contradictory and incomplete information, no longer be stated with certainty. It is only certain that they were not held by sufficiently strong anti-tank and infantry forces during the decisive hours. Thus, they were lost before the counterattack by "Gepanzerte Gruppe Oppeln" reached them in the afternoon. This counter attack was fought off, three Panzer IVs were lost.

"Kampfgruppe Rauch", attacking further to the left was able to make good headway. It pushed exactly into the gap between the 3rd British and the 3rd Canadian Infantry Division. During the further advance, the III./Grenadierregiment 736 with the 15 cm self-propelled batterie "Graf Waldersee" joined this attack from the area north of Plumetot. This Kampfgruppe had already reached the beach near Lion-sur-Mer during a counterattack before noon, but had to withdraw when it was attacked on the flank and in the rear. Around 19.00 hours the reinforced Kampfgruppe Rauch reached the beach near Luc-sur-Mer where a few German strongpoints had withstood all attacks so far. The Kampfgruppe prepared to advance further along the coast and to cut off the English, who were advancing to the south, from their supply bases. Then an event occurred which brought about a decisive turn-around.[7]

Around 21.00 hours a large number of enemy aircraft approached from the Channel. Approximately 250 aircraft with transport gliders in tow, and with fighter protection, brought the 6th Airlanding Brigade to reinforce the bridgehead east of the Orne river. No German aircraft threatened them. The Flak, if it had not already been overcome, was only of minor effectiveness since it was constantly being attacked by fighter-bomber squadrons. The fleet of aircraft continued unimpeded. The transport gliders disengaged and landed in the planned landing zone east of the Orne river. At the same time, supply containers on parachutes were dropped. Some of them landed to the west of the Orne. The 21. Panzerdivision developed the impression that the enemy, at least some of them, were landing to the rear of the attacking Kampfgruppen "Rauch" and "Oppeln". The "Rauch" Kampfgruppe broke off its attack. A British attack with tanks from the Cresserons area threatened its rear. Faced with this seemingly hopeless and threatening situation, Oberst Rauch decided to withdraw initially to Anguerny and later, on the order of the LXXXIV. Korps, to the area of Epron. All the wounded and the prisoners were taken along. The 1. Kompanie of Panzergrenadier-regiment 192 had come across the radar station near Dourvres-la Délivrande during its withdrawal. It had been reinforced as a major strong point and so far withstood all attacks. The Kompanie was incorporated into its defense as welcome reinforcements.

The "Oppeln" Kampfgruppe also withdrew approximately to its starting positions. It established contact with the "Rauch" Kampfgruppe to its right. The remaining Panzers, except for the 4. Kompanie in action to the right of the Orne, were distributed along the sector from the Orne to Epron and dug in. This was done because of the lack of sufficient anti-tank guns. The 8./Panzergrenadierregiment 192, battling the constantly increasing numbers of paratroopers near Bénouville and almost encircled, also had to withdraw to the south. It took up defensive positions at the southern edge of Blainville. It established contact with "Kampfgruppe von Luck" across the Orne river. Only dispersed units of the 716. Inf.Div., together with the "Graf Waldersee" battery and parts of the II./736 were available for the defense of Epron to the west.[8]

By dusk, the enemy had managed to form two landing zones in the area north and northwest of Caen, but had not been able to link them up. The front line of the westerly one ran at midnight of 6 June from Arromanches via Sommervieux (4.5 kilometers northeast of Bayeux)-Vaux sur Seulles-Creully-west of Pierrepont-Cainet-south of la Fresne Camilly-south of Fontaine Henry-west of Basly-west of Colomby-northeast edge of Villons les Buissons-Anisy-northeast of Anguerny-east edge of Basly-half way to Bény/ Douvres-from there in a northeasterly direction to the beach between St. Aubin-sur-Mer and Langrune-sur-Mer. Inside this beachhead were the 50th (Northumbrian) Infantry Division with the 8th Armoured Brigade and the 3rd Canadian Infantry Division with the 2nd Armoured Brigade.[9]

The front line of the easterly beachhead extended from the eastern edge of Lion-sur-Mer to the west of Hermanville, via the hills east of Périers,

west of Biéville and south of Blainville to the Orne river. There, the airlanding zone connected. Its front positions were located from south of Ranville-
south of Hérouville-the western edge of the Bois de Bavent-crossroads west of
le Prieure-Bréville to the Orne river near Sallenelles. However, these positions were not fully connected. They were a defensive front based on individual strongpoints.[10]

The weak forces of "Kampfgruppe von Luck" had been unable to push
back the lines of the beachhead. They had only managed to cut it off to the
south. However, it had not been the mission of the 6th Airborne Division to
expand its beachhead during the first day. The forces of the 21. Pz.Div.
which were in action to the left of the Orne river had been able to stop the
attack of the British on the right from Biéville on Caen, four kilometers from
the northern edge of the city. This, despite the failure of the attack by the
"Gepanzerte Gruppe Oppeln". To the west of the road Caen-Luc sur Mer a
dangerous gap had remained. Luckily, it coincided with the gap between the
two beachheads. The important airfield of Carpiquet to the west of Caen was
practically undefended. Only dispersed units of the 716. Inf.Div. and a small
Kampfgruppe from the 21. Pz.Div. with a few 8.8 cm Paks faced the Canadians, who were some six kilometers from the edge of Caen, from there to the
area northeast of Bayeux.

Under the existing circumstances, an enemy landing in the sector of the
716. Inf.Div. could not be prevented. A list of the most important shortcom-
ings includes, without order of priority: a lack of advance warning; an
absence of sea mine barriers; an absence of obstructions ahead of the beach
outside of the low tide water line; and the loss of most of the artillery
through barrages from warships and air attacks before and after the start of
the landing. This was caused mainly by insufficiently reinforced firing positions. The lack of prime movers made it impossible to change positions rapidly, there were insufficient communications connections between observer
positions and the firing positions; the insufficient numerical strength of the
716. Inf.Div. (7,771 men) made a defense from the rear, and in the right sector to the rear, only possible in a limited manner; the attachment of two
unreliable Eastern battalions; insufficient anti-tank forces close to the beach
against the first wave of landing enemy tanks.

The lack of sea and air reconnaissance and the non-arrival of Kriegsmarine (navy) fighting units, apart from a single attack by speedboats, and of
appreciable fighter and dive-bomber units, need hardly be mentioned in this
context. Had they been available in sufficient force, the invasion would not
have taken place.

It had not been possible during the first day to restrict the beachheads
or to break them up. This, despite the actions by the operative reserves, and
although the 21. Panzerdivision was in close vicinity to the beachhead as
Heeresgruppen reserve. Among other reasons, some tactical decisions can

be listed as causes for this. Even the deployment of the 21. Pz.Div. by the Heeresgruppe on 6 June proved to be impractical. Since the most advanced units of the II./Panzergrenadierregiment 125 and the II./Panzergrenadier-regiment 192 were located only ten kilometers and seven kilometers respec-tively from the beach, it was unavoidable that they would become involved in local actions immediately after an enemy landing. The same was true for the I./Panzerartillerieregiment 155 and Panzerjägerabteilung 200. Both had to go into action separately, which they did, under the command of the 716. Inf.Div. However, attaching Heeresflakabteilung 305 to the Flak Command Caen appears reasonable. It was necessary, in any case, to defend the road junction and the river crossing at Caen as effectively as possible against air attacks. On top of that, an enemy landing on both sides of the Orne river would lead to a splitting of the Division. The most advanced units of the 21. Pz.Div. were located partly to the right, partly to the left and north of the river crossing at Caen. A joint action was thus impossible from the begin-ning.

The late release of the 21. Pz.Div. by Heeresgruppe B and the subse-quent contradictory orders prevented early action by the still available units. In addition, the absence of the commander of the 21. Panzerdivision, Gen-eralmajor Feuchtinger and of his first general staff officer, for non-official reasons, and their late return to the Division caused lost time (Generalmajor Feuchtinger reported to the 7. Armee for the first time only at 05.20 hours by telephone). It is not known if there was any reconnaissance by Panzer-aufklärungsabteilung 21 in the area north of Caen. In any case, the Division did not know at the start of the attack that there existed a gap, inviting a counterattack, between the two beachheads, or where it was. Otherwise, it would surely not have deployed two separate Kampfgruppen but rather con-centrated all available forces under its direct command. Such an attack would have had an excellent chance of success.

In the previous chapter it was stated that the "Hitlerjugend" Division with Panzergrenadierregiment 25, two half companies of Panzer IVs, and the III. Artillerieabteilung could have been ready to attack west of Caen on 6 June at 18.00 hours. This, even if it had started out only at 11.00 hours in accordance with the prepared "Deployment C". One could imagine the results if this Kampfgruppe, made up of the concentrated 21. Pz.Div. (without II./125), had pushed into the still open gap, and if Panzergrenadierregiment 26, as well as the I. Panzerabteilung and the I. and II. Artillerieabteilung, had fol-lowed during the night. These contemplations have no other reason but to show that in the existing framework, and without assuming ideal conditions, there was a real possibility to contain the landings in the British sector along the coast. At the same time, this would have created a favorable starting posi-tion to smash, initially, the two British-Canadian beachheads. Even the air-landing bridgehead could then not have been held by the enemy. It must be stated at the same time, that errors in judgment and wrong decisions on various levels prevented this.

The first day of the invasion battles showed with frightening clarity that not only the fighting troops were taking part, but that the civilian population in the invasion area was not spared either. This population was exposed not so much to the action by the land forces, but rather to the Allied air force. The civilian population was evacuated as far away as possible to areas to the rear from actions by the ground forces, but the air force caught up with them during their escape, and even in their shelters. Caen, as one of the hot spots, was a victim of heavy air attacks even during the day of the landing. Just how the start of the invasion affected the population in the vicinity of Caen, and in the city itself, was recorded by Monsieur P. At the time, he lived in Verson, seven kilometers southwest of the city, and attended secondary school in Caen. He wrote:

> Around midnight of the night of 6 June an air-raid warning woke up the whole family. The sky looked like a beehive, large squadrons of aircraft flew overhead. The Flak at the Carpiquet airfield spit out its deadly shells. Without pause, the tracer bullets traveled along their bright paths. Steel was hitting the roofs. Suddenly, in the light of the Flak search-lights, I spotted a "Liberator" being hit. It was on course to Verson, dropping paratroopers. In the morning we found a number of man-size dummies filled with explosives hanging in the trees near the church. Around 5 A.M. I discussed the situation with some German soldiers. They probably belonged to the 21. Panzerdivision whose command post was located near St. Pierre-sur-Dives. Their motorbikes, ready for the march, were camouflaged under the apple trees in our meadow. We thought that this chaos indicated a large-scale operation.
>
> At about 6 A.M. I witnessed a drama: a German He 111 was about to land at Carpiquet. Suddenly, a line of P-51 Mustangs showed up, we first thought they were German fighters, and dove on the hapless bomber. It was soon blown out of the sky.
>
> The martyrdom of Caen began at approximately 13.30 hours. Medium and heavy bombers dropped explosive and incendiary bombs on the city. I could clearly see the bombs falling from the bomb bays. The inhabitants were at their lunch tables. Because of that, the losses were grave. The center of the city, in particular, suffered greatly. Some 1,500 victims were buried under the ruins of the houses. After this air attack, refugees walked past our house.
>
> In the evening of this memorable day, our whole family went to the house of friends. They lived close to the church. My mother was afraid of air attacks on the main street of Verson.[11]

CHAPTER 1.02
Planning of the Counteroffensive by the I. SS-Panzerkorps

Even the general command of the I. SS-Panzerkorps was not aware of the developments in the situation in the Caen area when it was advised of the intentions of the 7. Armee. This information was received, upon the request of the I. SS-Panzerkorps, from the Ia of the 7. Armee on 6 June at 16.00 hours. It was only advised that the plan was to "unite" the three Panzerdivisions, the 21., "HJ", and Panzer-Lehr, plus the 716. Inf. Div., in the right sector of the LXXXIV A.K. under its command. At that time, the order of the 7. Armee to the Panzergruppen command West of 15.00 hours was still valid. It stated that the 21. Pz. Div. and the "HJ" Division, attacking under the command of the LXXXIV A.K., was to "drive the enemy who had broken through into the sea and destroy him". The Panzer-Lehr-Division was ordered only to initially capture the area Flers-Vire.

The chief of staff of the I. SS-Panzerkorps, Brigadeführer (1 star gen.) Fritz Kraemer, drove shortly after 16.00 hours via Mantes-Trun-Falaise to the area south of Caen. On the recommendation of the 7. Armee supreme command, the Korps battle command post was to be set up in the woods twenty kilometers northwest of Falaise (probably in the Forêt de Cinglais). The commanding general, Obergruppenführer (three-star gen.) Sepp Dietrich, drove to St. Pierre-sur-Dives where the command post of the 21. Pz. Div. was located. There he met its Ia, Oberstleutnant i.G. (lieutenant colonel, general staff) Freiherr (baron) von Berlichingen who informed him along general lines of the actions of his division. His commander was at the battle command post of the 716. Inf. Div. at the northwestern edge of Caen. Since he had not taken along any radio communications facilities, he could hardly maintain any connections with the three Kampfgruppen of his division, and he had only an incomplete picture of the situation. Brigadeführer Kraemer was trying in the meantime to establish a telephone connection to the AOK 7 (7. Armee supreme command) in Le Mans. He was successful only around 24.00 hours because the relay station in Falaise was hampered by fires and by the destruction of the city by the bombing raids.[1]

The Supreme Command West had informed the AOK 7 that the OKW (supreme command, Wehrmacht) had demanded the destruction of the enemy in the Calvados beachhead by the evening of 6 June through the concentration of all available forces. The chief of the general staff of the 7. Armee stated that this was impossible to achieve by the evening of 6 June in view of the immense superiority of the enemy. However, all measures had been taken to "commence a counterattack as soon as possible".[2] This was a fundamental change in the judgment of the situation. At 16.20 hours, the commander of the 7. Armee had still reported to the Heeresgruppe B his overall impression of the situation that strong enemy forces were located at the break-through spot, but that "at the present time, no special operational concerns" existed. He believed he could clear up the situation in the Cotentin with his own forces.[3] The only situation he considered to be critical at the time was in the Calvados sector, in the British/Canadian bridgehead.

Brigadeführer Kraemer was informed during his telephone call that it was the intention of the 7. Armee to attack the enemy who had broken through east of Bayeux with the "HJ" Division, the Panzer-Lehr Division and the 21. Pz.Div. "from the direction of Caen in the direction of Lion-sur-Mer" under the command of the I. SS-Panzerkorps.[4] The commander of the Panzer-Lehr Division, Generalleutnant Bayerlein, had received orders from the 7. Armee at approximately 17.30 hours "to further advance into the assembly area in a line Thury-Harcourt-Aunay-Caumont". He was initially assigned directly to the 7. Armee and was supposed to link up with the I. SS-Panzerkorps to which he would probably be attached later. After a long and unsuccessful search, this link-up was achieved only on 7 June at 16.00 hours. After the attachment of the Division, the I. SS-Panzerkorps sent a communications officer with the necessary documents to the Orne bridge in Thury-Harcourt during the night. The chief of staff found him dead on the road at approximately 7 A.M. on 7 June. He and his motorcycle had been run over by a truck.

It was the intention of the Panzerkorps to first await the assembly of the Panzerdivision and then, after all available air power had been brought in, the possible strength of which was unknown, to attack the bridgehead. The 21. Pz.Div. was ordered to hold the line it had reached, to carry out attacks with limited objectives on the enemy with the reinforced Panzerregiment and to give the impression of stronger Panzer forces. A continuous main battle line would not be necessary for this. The units in action to the right of the Orne river were to be pulled across to the left shore during the night 6-7 June. The 716. Inf.Div. was ordered to continue to hold the still defended strong points, to assemble the dispersed units and, with them, to prepare for defense north of Caen. All other troops still located there were assigned to it for this. The artillery Abteilung of the Korps (heavy SS-Artillerieabteilung 101) was given the order to take up positions south of Caen. The artillery commander would use it and the artillery of the 21. Pz.Div. and of the 716. Inf.Div. to support the attack and defense by the two divisions. The "HJ" division was ordered to assemble immediately southwest of Caen and to be prepared to attack. The Panzer-Lehr Division was given the adjoining area to the west around Evrecy. These orders, and the intentions of the Panzerkorps connected with them, could not be carried out. The 7. Armee informed Feldmarschall Rommel of the situation on 7 June at 04.00 hours. Generalleutnant Pemsel told him "that the three Panzer forces attached to the I. SS-Panzerkorps had been brought into the assembly areas and ordered to begin the counterattack without any other considerations and with all available forces."[7] The situation on the Cotentin was now also considered to be critical, caused by additional American landings. Three divisions, the 77. Inf.Div., the 17. SS-Panzergrenadierdivision "Götz von Berlichingen" and the 3. Fallschirmjäger-Division (paratroopers) were brought into this area for action. In view of the doubled serious threat—at the base of the Cotentin and at the coast of Calvados—the opinion of Feldmarschall Rommel won out. Namely, that the bridgeheads had to be smashed by an immediate attack of all available forces if the enemy had not already been destroyed at the beach during the landing.

A concerted attack by the three Panzerdivisions in the course of 7 June or even in the morning of this day was not possible. The 21. Pz.Div. was tied down in action on both sides of the Orne. The 716. Inf.Div. had no forces worth mentioning left who could have defended the northwestern part of Caen and the Carpiquet airfield. Only the 'coast defense sub-group Luc' still held its positions on both sides of Luc-sur-Mer in a width of approximately four kilometers, and the radar station near Douvres had withstood all attacks. The reinforced Panzer-grenadierregiment 25, units of the II. Panzerabteilung and the III. Artillerieabteilung of the "HJ" Division had reached the assembly area, originally ordered by the LXXXIV A.K., by early morning. Regiment 26, the I. Panzerabteilung, the I. and II. Artillerieabteilung, the Flakabteilung and the Pionierbataillon were still on the march. The advance units of the marching columns of the Panzer-Lehr Division had reached a line approximately Argentan-Domfront (fifty-five kilometers southeast and seventy kilometers southwest of Caen respectively) in the morning of 7 June. The division was strung out over a considerable length. Its first fighting units could reach the Caen area only in the morning of 8 June.[8] Thus, in the course of 7 June, the only units of the "HJ" Division able to attack were the Panzergrenadier-regiment 25 and a portion of the II. Panzerabteilung with fire support from the III. Artillerieabteilung. It was unclear if any part of the 21. Pz.Div. was in a position to join the attack.

CHAPTER 1.1
Attack by SS-Panzergrenadierregiment 25, the II. Panzerabteilung and the III. Artillerie-Abteilung North and Northwest of Caen on 7 June 1944, and Transition to Defense

Standartenführer (colonel) Kurt Meyer had rushed ahead of his regiment to the battle command post of the 716. Infanterie Division. It was located in a bunker in the la Folie area. He arrived around midnight of 6 June and met the commander of the 716. Inf. Div., Generalleutnant (two-star general) Richter and the commander of the 21. Panzerdivision, Generalmajor (one-star general) Feuchtinger. He was briefed on the situation. It was bleak. The 716. Inf.Div. had obviously been smashed. The way to Caen seemed open to the enemy. Feuchtinger did not have a completely clear picture of the situation of the various Kampfgruppen of the 21. Panzerdivision. He drew Meyer's attention to the possibility that the town and airfield of Carpiquet were already in enemy hands. Meyer ordered immediate reconnaissance. It reported an hour later that Carpiquet, Rots and Buron were free of enemy forces. Dispersed units of the 716. Inf.Div. had been found in Buron; les Buissons had been captured by the enemy.

Just as Meyer was about to leave the bunker to return to his command post, located in a small cafe in St. Germain-la-Blanche-Herbe at the west exit from Caen, he received a telephone call from Brigadeführer Witt. At that time, Witt was at the divisional command post of the 21 Panzerdivision in St. Pierre-sur-Dives. Witt was briefed on the situation. He informed Meyer of the order from the I. SS-Panzerkorps that the 21 Panzerdivision was to attack to the right of the railroad line Caen-Luc sur Mer, the 12. SS-Panzerdivision to the left, at 16.00 hours on 7 June and drive the enemy into the sea.[1]

The 21. Panzerdivision had attacked on the left of the Orne on 6 June with only two Kampfgruppen. Another one was in action against the airborne enemy to the right of the river. After breaking off the attack, the Division sought to reach the river. Its left flank was located near Epron. To the left of it there were only stragglers from the 716. Inf.Div. and small groups of the 21. Pz.Div., probably from Panzerjägerabteilung 200. A wide gap thus existed on the right border of the assembly area of the "HJ" Division, approximately along a line from the eastern edge of Verson-Rots. The division commander could not say anything at this time regarding the expected arrival of Panzergrenadierregiment 26, the I. Panzerabteilung and the other two Artillerieabteilungen. They had a significantly longer march route. Thus, he ordered the reinforced Panzer-grenadierregiment 25 to attack to the right of Regiment 26. To do this, it had to be pulled from its assembly area located on the left flank, to the right in order to link up with the left flank of the 21. Pz.Div. As a condition for the assembly, Brigadeführer Witt ordered that the area around the Carpiquet airfield had to be secured under all circumstances. It would likely be a priority objective of the enemy.

The attack by Regiment 25 was to be supported by the III. Artillerieabteilung, which was marching with the regiment, and those units of the II. Panzerabteilung which had arrived by then. The Mue creek was designated to be the dividing line between the two Panzergrenadier regiments.

Around 3 A.M. Standartenführer Meyer verbally issued the attack order to his reinforced regiment. Two Panzergrenadier battalions would attack in line, the I. on the right side, the II. on the left, and the III. staggered in the left rear. To do this, the I. Bataillon had to assemble on the left flank of the 21. Panzerdivision between Epron and la Folie. The II. Bataillon had to assemble near Bitot, the III. southeast of Franqueville on the back slope south of the road Caen-Bayeux. A platoon of heavy infantry guns (13./25) and a platoon of light Flak (14./25) was assigned to each battalion. The whole of the 16. (Pionier-) Kompanie was attached to the I./25. The III. Artillerie-abteilung was to take up positions so that it could have an impact on all of the attack sector of the regiment and on the open left flank. A battery of heavy field howitzers was to cooperate with each of the battalions. The Panzerregiment was ordered to support the attack on a wide front together with the units of the II. Abteilung which had arrived. The 15. (Aufklärungs-) Kompanie was ordered to secure the left flank. The forward regiment command post was set up in the Ardennes abbey.

The division moved its command post from the Forêt de Grimbosq, where it had been located during the night, to the southwest exit from Caen in the Venoix quarter, along the route Caen-Villers Bocage.

The Panzergrenadier battalions advanced during the night up to the road Caen-Bayeux. There they dismounted and marched on foot to their assembly areas. Their vehicles were camouflaged and left south of the city. Standartenführer Meyer observed these movements from his command post:

> The commander of the I. Bataillon of Regiment 25 reported to me. He is quickly briefed and informed of the situation. A short handshake expressed it all. We know that we must set out on a difficult course. The battalion jumps off the vehicles and the trucks disappear into the dark. No vehicles drive through the city, they all swing to the south . . . The grenadiers wave at me. Calmly, without overt emotions but with the firm determination to stand the test, they head for their baptism of fire.[2]

The III. (heavy) Artillerieabteilung set up its command post in the Ardennes abbey. From the two low towers of the abbey church one could observe all of the attack sector of the regiment. It was even possible to observe into the attack sector of the 21. Panzerdivision and to the left across the wooded valley of the Mue creek to the line of hills to the west. The attack sector covered a gently undulating plateau. As if on a theater stage, villages with their orchards, stands of trees and small wooded areas, were staggered into the distance, scattered among the corn and beet fields, and the livestock pastures. Tethered balloons were visible in the sky on the horizon. They were meant to secure the landing fleet from low level air attacks. The objective, the coast, seemed within reach. The 7. Batterie (heavy field howitzers) took up firing positions on the northwestern edge of Caen. Its observation post was located at the I. Bataillon. The 8. Batterie (heavy field howitzers) set up positions at the northern outskirts of St. Germain-la-Blanche-Herbe. Its observation post was located in one of the towers of the Ardennes abbey, a forward observer was with the II. Bataillon. The 9. Batterie (heavy field howitzers) had its firing positions at the southern edge of St. Germain-la Blanche-Herbe. Its observation post was also in a tower of the Ardennes abbey, one forward observer was with the III. Bataillon. The 10. Batterie (10 cm guns) established its firing positions in the Orne valley south of Venoix. Its observation post was located with one of the others in one of the towers of the Ardennes abbey.[3]

Standartenführer Kurt Meyer moved into his forward command post in the Ardennes abbey around 9 A.M. The drive there in his VW jeep resembled a rabbit hunt since numerous fighter-bombers kept the area under surveillance. In one of the abbey towers, Sturmbannführer (major) Bartling reported to him that the III. Artillerieabteilung was ready to open fire. The three battalions had already reported their completed assembly. The II. Panzerabteilung was still missing. Meyer saw the II. Bataillon in position in front of him. Its scouting parties were just disappearing into the undergrowth in the direction of the enemy. Around 10 A.M. the first Panzers finally appeared. Sturmbannführer Prinz reported that approximately fifty Panzer VIs were ready for action. The rest was expected during the course of the day and the following night. The Panzers rolled into their assembly areas: The 8. Kompanie with 5 Panzers into the sector of the I. Bataillon, the 7. and the 6. to the right and left of the Ardennes abbey, the 5. Kompanie southeast of Franqueville in a position on the back slope south of the road Caen-Bayeux with the III. Bataillon, the 9. as a reserve to the rear of the 5. Kompanie.[4]

In the meantime, the enemy had also assembled for the attack on Caen. The 3rd (British) Infantry Division was ready to attack in the sector assigned to the 21. Panzerdivision, its right flank reached into the sector of the 12. SS-Panzerdivision. The 2nd Battalion The Royal Ulster Rifles, reinforced by a company of East Riding Yeomanry (tanks) was to advance past the positions of the 1st Battalion The King's Own Scottish Borderers (K.O.S.B.) in Le Mesnil-1.5 kilometers northeast of Cambes-towards Cambes and on to Caen. This was right in the attack sector of the I./25.(5) During the night the Ulster Rifles had assembled at Hill 61 (1.8 kilometers northeast of Périers-sur-le

Dan). At 10.00 hours they reported the village free of the enemy, at 12.15 hours they reached the road Douvres-Caen. At 14.00 hours they were assembled in the woods northeast of Le Mesnil.[6]

The spearhead battalion of the 9th Canadian Infantry Brigade, the North Nova Scotia Highlanders, had reached the hill north of Villon-les Buissons at midnight of 6 June. A scouting party on Carriers, sent out toward Anisy, came under fire there and withdrew without its vehicles. The battalion The Queen's Own Rifles of Canada, part of the 8th Brigade but attached to the 9th, advanced via Anguerny and captured Anisy. The de la Chaudière Regiment, also part of the 8th Brigade, and the 27th Armoured Regiment settled down to rest for the night at Colomby-sur-Thaon.[7] The de la Chaudière Regiment was attacked on its left flank at approximately 02.00 hours by several armored personnel carriers of the 21. Panzerdivision. The Canadians lost one platoon, the Panzer grenadiers lost several prisoners.[8]

The spearhead of the 9th Brigade assembled on 7 June at 07.45 hours for a further advance, with the Carpiquet airfield as its objective. It consisted of the North Nova Scotia Highlanders and the 27th Armoured Regiment (The Sherbrooke Fusiliers Regiment). The Stuart tanks of the tank reconnaissance unit advanced at the point. They were followed by the "C" Company of the Highlanders, mounted on their Carriers. Next were a platoon of medium machine guns, a platoon of anti-tank gunners, two groups of engineers and four anti-tank guns (6 pounders). The main body, made up of the other three infantry companies, followed behind, mounted on their Sherman tanks.[9]

As it advanced, the spearhead came under rifle and machine gun fire from an orchard north of les Buissons, and from an 8.8 cm Flak or Pak immediately west of Villons-les Buissons. This resistance was broken by a pincer movement attack. Obviously, units of a Panzergrenadierbataillon of the 21. Panzerdivision were in action there since three armored personnel carriers were knocked out. Villons-les Buissons was cleared by 09.00 hours. When the Canadian spearhead left the town it came under fire from an 8.8 cm Flak or Pak at the entrance to the village of Buron. The gun was knocked out by a tank.[10]

Buron was captured after the weak resistance by stragglers from the 716. Inf.Div. had been overcome at approximately 11.50 hours. The spearhead pushed through the town and advanced further towards Authie. While the "D" Company combed the town, the "A" and "B" Companies on their Shermans drove around it and rolled forward in the direction of Authie. Buron was under heavy mortar fire. "D" Company suffered losses from rifle and machine gun fire. At approximately 14.00 hours, the point units of the North Novas and the "C" Squadron of the Sherbrooke Fusiliers found themselves in action against several machine guns. They were overcome by tanks. The North Novas requested artillery support but the observation officer reported that his artillery was still outside range. It needed more time to change positions. The only fire support available would be from a cruiser, but due to an error in the communications link it could not come into action. Several groups of tanks advanced further south and reached the entrance of the town of Franqueville, probably soon after 14.00 hours.[11]

Standartenführer Kurt Meyer tensely observed the battlefield through his binoculars. He had noticed a large tank unit assembling in the area south of Colomby-sur-Thaon. After some time he recognized that enemy tanks were rolling past the II./25 from Buron in the direction of Authie. He immediately directed that fire could only be opened on his order. In the meantime, Untersturmführer Porsch was reconnoitering with his four Panzer IVs along the road Franqueville-Authie. At around 14.00 hours he unexpectedly encountered Sherman tanks of the Sherbrooke Fusiliers which were approaching from Authie. In a brief fire fight three of his Panzers were knocked out, Hauptscharführer Müller, Oberscharführer Auinger and Unterscharführer Klempt. It would have been indefensible to wait until the planned start of the attack at 16.00 hours. The apparently surprised enemy had to be attacked right away. Meyer immediately ordered the commander of the Panzerregiment, Obersturmbannführer Max Wünsche, who was standing next to him, to assemble the Panzer companies which were located in the left sector. At the same time he ordered the commander of the III./25, Obersturm-bannführer Karl-Heinz Milius to join the attack by the Panzers with his battalion. Wünsche issued the order "Attention! Panzers, march!" by telephone to his command Panzer. It, in turn, issued the order by radio to the II. Abteilung and the assembled companies on the left. The 6. Panzerkompanie, located immediately to the left of the abbey, and the 5. started out without delay. Their fire caught the surprised enemy in the left flank. Within a short time several Shermans were in flames and exploded. The 6. Kompanie destroyed more than ten enemy tanks and lost five Panzer IVs. After this first halt to fire the Panzers advanced in the direction of Authie, accompanied by the Panzergrenadiers of the 9. Kompanie on foot. Authie was quickly taken. The Panzers of the 6. Kompanie bypassed the town and pushed forward in the direction of Buron. Sturmmann Hans Fenn, gunner in the I. Zug (platoon) of the 6. Panzerkompanie, wrote about this battle:

> Obersturmführer Gasch, who was not part of the originally planned exercise, had also arrived in the meantime. He took over the command of the point platoon, the I. Zug. We took a lot of prisoners whom we sent backwards to the grenadiers without getting out of our Panzers. We advanced further through the gently rolling terrain. I. Zug suddenly found itself on a wide open plain and under fire from the Canadian anti-tank guns. Four Panzer IVs of my platoon were immediately on fire. We, in the fifth Panzer IV, took a direct hit between the side and the turret as we were making the big mistake of trying to turn while under fire from the anti-tank guns.

We had been unable to knock out the Canadian anti-tank guns firing from 1,500 to 2,000 meters distance. The shell ripped off my Panzer commander's leg. He was Oberscharführer Esser. As I heard later, he still managed to get out of the turret. Because it was a phosphor shell, the whole Panzer was immediately in flames. I lost consciousness since the rubber cover of my gunner's hatch charred and jammed the hatch, preventing me from getting out immediately. Somehow, sub-consciously, I managed to crawl to the loader's hatch. I can only remember the moment clearly when I fell from the hatch to the ground, head first. With severe third degree burns I walked back in the direction of our grenadiers following behind. They stared at me as if I was a ghost, that is the way I must have looked. Our medic NCO drove me to the field hospital in the chief's car.[12]

Sturmmann (lance corporal) Karl Vasold of the 9./25 experienced the attack in this way:

The order came: Let's go! March! Attack on Authie with Panzer support. We came under a lot of fire and experienced our first losses. Canadian tanks at the edge of town were knocked out, the first house-to-house combat took place, the town was captured. The next attack was on the Château de St. Louet, west of Authie. There was concentrated defensive fire from Canadian anti-tank guns. Some of our Panzers were on fire. Critically wounded Panzer comrades were coming to the rear. They had lost hands, suffered severe burns. They were taken back to Authie. There was much coming and going. Only then we received fire from enemy artillery and the situation became risky. We also took fire from enemy tanks at Buron. They were poor gunners, the explosions were either ahead or behind us. We assembled at the edge of town and discussed the situation.[13]

The commander of the Canadian spearhead ordered his infantry companies to take up defensive positions north of Authie. "A" Company dug in southeast of Gruchy. "B" Company was held down in Buron by concentrated fire from German artillery and heavy infantry weapons.[14]

The 9., 10. and 11. companies of Regiment 25 and the two Panzer companies—6. and 5.—immediately continued the attack on Buron and Gruchy. They were supported by heavy concentrated fire from the III. Artillerieabteilung, directed by Sturmbannführer Bartling on the tower of the Ardennes abbey, and by heavy and light infantry guns, mortars, and heavy machine guns. The "A" Company of the North Nova Scotia Highlanders was overrun north of Authie. The Panzer-grenadiers thrust into Buron. As the Panzers approached the southern edge of town, a barrage from the Canadian artillery rained down on them. The Panzers and Panzergrenadiers suffered significant losses. The Canadian artillery occasionally fired on their own lines since the location of their troops was obviously unclear. Some Panzers took on wounded and withdrew in the direction of the Ardennes abbey. There they were ordered by Standartenführer Meyer to immediately attack again and to support the Panzergrenadiers in their hard struggle for Buron. A medic of the III. Bataillon, Rottenführer (corporal) Paul Hinsberger, reports on this action:

> The defense by the Canadians was so strong that the Panzers had to turn back. Accompanied by Canadian barrages, they drove back to their starting position along the country road in line with Cussy. My four stretcher bearers, among them temporary stretcher bearers I had appointed, loaded the seriously wounded onto the retreating Panzers. Among them were also Canadian wounded. As the Panzers arrived at their starting positions, Panzermeyer suddenly showed up and ordered the Panzers to counterattack. My stretcher bearers and I were worn out by the exhausting work and we did not manage to unload all of the wounded from the moving Panzers which barely stopped. A Panzer missed me by the width of a hair. Three of my stretcher bearers took part in the counterattack. The other one and I administered first aid to the wounded. Panzer-meyer ordered me to take the wounded immediately to the Ardennes abbey.[15]

Sturmmann Vasold continues in his report:

> We were on the attack on Buron with the remaining Panzers. Again, house-to-house fighting. Many prisoners were taken. We pushed past the edge of town. Heavy machine gun fire, we pressed our heads into the ground. There was no possibility of further advance. We had to withdraw again. A Panzer gave us cover fire.[16]

The dramatic battle is impressively described with few and matter-of-fact words in the War Diary of the 27th Armoured Regiment:

> C-Squadron was sent forward on the left to push into the enemy flank. Lieutenant Fitzpatrick's unit dropped off infantry immediately north of Authie and lost two of its three tanks within 60 seconds. He took up position with the remaining tank in an orchard just south of Authie. There he noticed that his 17-pound gun did not work because of damage to the locking mechanism. He observed the German attack and fought it with machine gun fire. The German attack consisted of two waves of infantry, then the Panzers advanced slowly and purposely. The infantry of the North Novas withdrew to positions directly south of les Buissons. As it turned out, only five men of

C-Company and few of A-Company made it there. German infantry pursued them, recaptured Buron and then attacked D-Company of the North Novas with bayonets. Our tanks rolled past D-Company and retreated with only minor losses.

The to and fro of the battle is also described in detail in the War Diary of the North Nova Scotia Highlanders:

We were unable to reach A-Company by radio, but Major Learment was in contact with it by his radio. We learned that A-Company was encircled by Panzers and infantry and unable to withdraw into the 'Fortress' just being formed by the battalion. Soon after, the positions south of Buron came under heavy artillery and mortar fire. When Panzers then attacked our flanks, the position became indefensible. Since the rest of the battalion did not have a field of fire towards the flanks, Major Learment had to expect encirclement if he stayed in his position. Major Learment who led the two point companies, with Captain Wilson who led the remains of B-Company, was ordered to retreat to the previously dug trenches behind D-Company. The battalion prepared to defend itself to the last. When the Panzers came around the flanks, the remaining tanks of the 27th Canadian Armoured Regiment, the self-propelled anti-tank guns in the woods of les Buissons, and all light infantry weapons opened fire over the heads of their own troops on the north edge of Buron. The enemy returned our fire with 7.5 and 8.8 mortars and with everything else he had. Under this fire, enemy infantry advanced and penetrated the trenches of D-Company. It was impossible to stop them since our men had to stay in their cover positions in order to avoid our fire which went over them and that of the enemy. Because of the high stands of grain they had no field of fire. Machine guns fired into the trenches and hand grenades were thrown into them. The 10th and 16th Platoon ran out of ammunition, were encircled and had to surrender. The guards had to take cover from the heavy fire by our artillery and two groups of 16th Platoon took advantage of this moment to flee and return to their company. At about this time a man from D-Company reported to the staff of the battalion that the forward positions had been overrun, were out of contact and needed help immediately. The commander ordered an immediate counter-attack without any further preparations. A savage battle followed as we attacked with the remaining twelve tanks under cover of strongly concentrated fire, directed by a forward observation officer, on the forward positions of D-Company. The artillery fire hit the enemy in the forward positions, and with the help of the tanks they were driven out of Buron towards Authie. Our tanks caused them heavy losses, and the large numbers of enemy soldiers were overrun in a few moments. Buron was recaptured, but since we could count only on a portion of D-Company and the remains of B- and C-Company which were not sufficient and since it turned dark, these positions could not be held through the night. For this reason, permission to withdraw was requested from the Brigadier.[18]

At 15.00 hours, Standartenführer Meyer had ordered the I. and II. Bataillon to also be ready for the attack as soon as the respective battalion on the left had reached the same line. The II. Bataillon did not have any enemy directly in front of it. The closest enemy units in its attack sector were at Anisy, namely the battalion The Queen's Own Rifles of Canada. However, the battalion on its left was exposed to the fire, on its left wing and during the advance on its left flank, from units of the North Nova Scotias and the 27th Armoured Regiment. These units had advanced via Buron on Authie or had remained in Buron. The right wing of the battalion bore the brunt of the 2nd Royal Ulster Regiment and the supporting tanks of the East Riding Yeomanry, attacking from Le Mesnil towards Cambes.

After the III./25 and the Panzers of 5. and 6. Kompanie had captured Authie and were advancing further on Buron, the II./25 of Sturmbannführer Scappini and the 7. Panzerkompanie joined the attack. The line-up was: to the right the 7. Kompanie under Obersturmführer (1st lieutenant) Heinz Schrott, to its left the 5. under Hauptsturmführer (captain) Kreilein, and staggered to the left rear the 6. Kompanie under Hauptsturmführer Dr. Thirey. The 8. (heavy) Kompanie, led by Hauptsturmführer Breinlich, had not yet arrived. The Panzers under the command of Hauptsturmführer Bräcker followed close behind in a wide wedge formation. St. Contest was captured without significant difficulties. Sturmbannführer Scappini was at the point platoon of the 7. Kompanie, together with its commander, his adjutant, Obersturmführer Franz Xaver Pfeffer, and the battalion physician, Dr. Sedlacek. Scappini ordered a short halt so that the companies to the left rear could catch up. While the staff was reconnoitering in the terrain, they were surprised by three advancing Canadian tanks. The staff took cover immediately, but they had obviously been already spotted. They came under heavy fire from the tank guns. Sturmbannführer Scappini received a fatal wound. The regimental commander, who had come forward by motorcycle to determine the situation, ordered Obersturmführer Heinz Schrott to take over command of the battalion. Obersturmführer Kurt Havemeister took over from him. The Panzers of 7. Kompanie forced the three tanks to retreat. The battalion advanced further and was able to take Malon and Galmanche without encountering serious resistance, bothered only by artillery fire.[19]

I. Bataillon, assembled to the right of II., had Anguerny, nine kilometers north of Caen, as its first attack objective. After II. and III./25 had eliminated the threat on the left flank, I. Bataillon began the attack at 16.15

hours. To the right was 1., to its left was 3., and to its left was the 2. Kompanie. The attack was supported by units of 8. Kompanie SS-Panzerregiment 12 under the command of Obersturmführer Hans Siegel. Five Panzer IVs had arrived prior to the start of the attack.

The advance went smoothly to the southern edge of the town of Cambes. After the Panzergrenadiers of 1. Kompanie had already pushed through the section of town extending south and reached a wooded area north of Cambes together with 3. Kompanie, Sherman tanks appeared to the left of the village ahead of 2. Kompanie and the wooded area and opened fire. Riflemen in the trees, light and heavy machine guns made a further advance very difficult. At the same time, strong artillery and mortar fire on the wooded area north of Cambes set in. Constant fighter-bomber attacks increased the impact of the enemy fire. Schütze (private) Emil Werner of 3. Kompanie reports on the progress of the attack, as his company experienced it:

> The time had come for the attack on Cambes. The order came 'Let's go! March!' Everything went well until Cambes. We could see the village very well from our location. At the edge of town we received infantry fire. All hell broke loose. We stormed a church in which sharpshooters were entrenched. Here I saw the first dead comrade from our company. He was SS grenadier (private) Rühl. I turned him over myself, he had taken a bullet in the head. We had not seen any Englishmen yet, but already we had dead comrades. Then the situation was becoming very critical. My group commander was wounded in the arm and had to go back. SS grenadier Grosse from Hamburg jumped past me towards some bushes, his machine pistol at the ready. He shouted 'hands up! hands up!', and was successful. Two English soldiers came out with their hands up. As far as I know, Grosse was awarded the Iron Cross II for this feat. Now, Untersturmführer (2nd lieutenant) Gscheider quickly came up next to me. Both of us took full cover next to a German Wehrmacht truck which had been abandoned under a tree. Untersturmführer Gscheider pointed at a house with his finger and said to me: 'Werner, fire into that'. This, I did. Untersturmführer Gscheider took an explosive bullet into the cheek. He could no longer talk and went back. A few seconds later, Unterscharführer (sergeant) Hatzke showed up and yelled: 'Let's go! March!' We spotted several enemy tanks sitting behind a high wall.[20]

The Panzers of 8. Kompanie now started the attack. One of them dropped out with a mechanical problem. The other four advanced to the west past Malon, spotted enemy targets west of the wooded area north of Cambes and opened fire on them. Obersturmführer Siegel reports:

Mine was the Panzer at the point. Since the stops to fire were becoming more and more risky, I raced towards the edge of the woods for cover. A shell exploding in the treetops turned out to be our undoing. The treetop fell down on us from great height and hit the center of the vehicle in such an unfortunate way that the leafy branches cut off our visibility completely, the turret got stuck, and we were thus out of action. We quickly turned back and forth but were unable to strip the monster from us. I bailed out and wanted to get into another Panzer. In the meantime, however, two of my vehicles had driven forward past me. They both were hit when they next stopped to fire. One lost a track, the other kept exchanging fire for a while yet. The fourth Panzer had slid sideways into a shell crater and was also stuck. The Panzers were out of action even before they were really involved in any.[21]

In the meantime, Panzergrenadiers had knocked out three Sherman tanks using Panzerfäuste (bazookas) in close combat. Sturmmann Köpke of 1. Kompanie knocked out two, Sturmmann Würfs of I. Zug (platoon) destroyed one enemy tank.

A report by Unterscharführer (sgt.) Helmut Stöcker, a member of I. Zug of the heavy Infanteriegeschützkompanie (infantry gun company) which supported the attack by the I./25, also shows the drive and the great dedication with which the attack was led.

"The attack was to be pushed forward as quickly as possible by the infantry. Because of the short range of our guns, we had to advance with the infantry lines into action without any armor, just with our prime movers. Everything went well until the infantry encountered heavy fire and the attack stalled. We now stood before Cambes on an open plain with our vehicles and guns. Under the assumption that the infantry would advance further, our platoon pulled ahead towards Cambes. We really had no choice since we would have probably been wiped out within the next ten minutes. We reached Cambes and dove into a ravine. Suddenly, there was the sound of tracks in the village. Some fifty meters in front of us, a Sherman came out of a side road. It stopped in the intersection and spotted us and our guns. The turret of the tank immediately swung towards us and before we knew what was happening, the first shell was fired. We saved ourselves by jumping to the left over a locked gate. We found ourselves on a farm. Some of the crews were only about one and a-half meter away from the guns when the first shell slammed through the tractors and guns. We were fortunate since it was probably an anti-tank shell which kept going. If it had been an explosive shell, we would have had it. Because of the great weight of our supplies we did not carry armor-piercing weapons. Fortunately, a single infantryman of the I./25 happened to be lost and joined us at the front. He had one Panzerfaust.

After some accurate planning, a Sherman was knocked out by this single Panzerfaust. This blocked the major intersection. We made our way back to the lines of the I./25. The guns remained with the enemy. Together with the commander of the Panzergrenadierkompanie we contemplated how to get to the one gun which was still ready for action. The decision was that it had to be brought back during the next night."

One of the anti-tank guns of the 14./25 was close to the heavy infantry gun platoon. The commander of the anti-tank platoon has been missing since.

The Ulster Rifles had come under heavy artillery and mortar fire as they crossed through Le Mesnil. In the diary of the 3rd British Infantry Division, "Assault Division", it is reported, among others:

> Nothing was known of the enemy's location since the woods and park at Cambes were surrounded by stone walls more than three meters high. The approach brought many losses caused by infantry and mortar fire from the small wooded area. Captain Aldworth led two platoons on the left side of the woods, Captain Montgomery led the other two on the right side. They immediately came under cross-fire from machine guns. When his company was forced to retreat, John (Aldworth) did not come back with it. When the battalion captured the small forest two days later, he was found dead at the point of his men. Right in front of him lay several dead 'SS-Stormtroopers'. He had pushed deeper into the woods than anyone else. Because of the high walls and the density of the woods, the tanks were unable to provide effective support. The battalion was ordered to retreat to Le Mesnil [where the battalion King's Own Scottish Borderers was in position] until the attack could be supported.[22a]

The I. Bataillon could not pursue this retreat. The enemy covered the small wooded area with strong barrages from artillery and mortars. The advanced observer of 7. Batterie, which depended on cooperation with I. Bataillon, was killed. His radio was destroyed, preventing further support by German artillery. German Panzers had been rendered inactive. The neighbor on the right, units of the Panzerregiment 22 of the 21. Panzerdivision, had not been assembled so that the right flank of the Bataillon remained open. Under these circumstances, Sturmbannführer (major) Waldmüller decided to halt the attack, disengage from the enemy and to take up defensive positions at the southern edge of Cambes. The commander of 1. Kompanie reported on this:

> The drive and determination of the attack were so great that disengagement from Cambes caused problems. Individual groups had doggedly worked their way forward. In some cases, and depending

on the terrain, they had advanced significantly, in the broken terrain-the village and the woods. They all had the will to reach the sea. It was difficult to enforce the order to withdraw. It encountered disbelief and was carried out only with hesitation. Still, the withdrawal movement did not have a negative impact on the superb fighting spirit.[23]

The withdrawal succeeded without enemy pursuit or significant interference. The companies dug in for defense along a line from the railroad embankment west of la Bujude—south of a crossroads 150 meters south of the southern exit from Cambes-crossroads east of the edge of the town of Galmanche. The sequence was 1. Kompanie, 3. Kompanie, 2. Kompanie. A link-up was established to Panzerregiment 22 on the right and to the II./25 on the left near Galmanche. The enemy covered the positions with barrages.

Since the point units of Regiment 26, the I. Panzerabteilung and the other two Artillerieabteilungen had only reached the assembly area at noon, or were even further to the rear, the Division had been anxious about the left, open flank of Regiment 25. At 16.00 hours it had ordered the Divisionsbegleit-kompanie (escort company), in positions to defend the Division command post in Venoix, to find out if the bridge across the Mue creek in the town of Rots was in enemy hands. If there was only a guard at the bridge, it was to be overcome, the bridge secured and reconnaissance conducted to the northern edge of Rots. A group of motorcycle riflemen and a 2 cm Flak gun were deployed to carry out this order. The Flak group and a machine gun group, led by the company commander, Obersturmführer Guntrum, pushed into the town from the east. In the center of town they received fire from all directions and were unable to advance to the bridge. The group of motorcycle riflemen, approaching the bridge from the south, also came under heavy fire. Two vehicles were destroyed by anti-tank shells. Since Rots was obviously occupied by at least two infantry companies and three anti-tank guns, the leader of the reconnaissance party decided to pull back. The motorcycle group was then used together with a newly brought up heavy machine gun unit, under the command of Untersturmführer Stier, for defense at the southern edge of the village. During this reconnaissance action, six NCOs and men were killed, one man was wounded, one missing.[24]

To the west of the Mue creek, the enemy had already reached or even crossed the road Caen-Bayeux. The neighbor to the right of Regiment 25, the 21. Pz.Div., had not commenced the attack. Since further forces were initially unavailable, the Division had ordered Standartenführer Kurt Meyer in the late afternoon to break off the attack for the time being, after reaching favorable position and to switch to defense. From one of the towers of the Ardennes abbey he had already spotted tanks rolling into Bretteville-l'Orgeilleuse from the north, and west of the Mue creek. They threatened his left, open flank. His I. Bataillon had to switch to defense already south of

Cambes and a counterattack by tanks on Buron was under way. Thus he had already ordered to break off the attack for the time being.

The 21. Pz.Div. had not reported to the I. SS-Panzerkorps that it would not commence an attack, nor had it informed the "HJ" Division of it. In a report by its commander there is only a short statement covering this:

> The Korps advised that the 12. SS-Division would link up with the Panzerdivision (21.) even during the night, and that both divisions would carry out an attack west of the Orne river before noon on 7.6.
>
> But there was no counteroffensive since during the course of 6.6. (this should read 7.6. Author) only one Panzergrenadierregiment and one Panzerabteilung from the 21. Pz.Div. arrived before 16.00 hours to link up on the left of the 21. Pz.Div. These forces were insufficient for a joint attack.[25]

The 9th Canadian Infantry Brigade had ordered the North Nova Scotia Highlanders in the evening to recapture the rest of les Buissons. The other battalions, the Stormont, Dundas and Glengarry Highlanders and the Highland Light Infantry of Canada, had linked up there and begun to dig in.[26]

According to reports from members of Panzerregiment 12 and the III./25, Panzers and infantry began a counterattack during the same evening and occupied Buron from which the Canadians had withdrawn. The 5. Panzerkompanie secured the northern edge of Gruchy.

When the order arrived at the II./25, which was on a speedy advance, to break off the attack and switch to defense, it was hard to understand. The Bataillon had the impression that it would not encounter any strong enemy forces during further advance. This was correct. The companies dug in along a curved line around Galmanche. The Bataillon command post was set up in Malon.

After nightfall, the battalions carried out reconnaissance to determine the whereabouts, behavior and intentions of the enemy. During this operation the heavy infantry gun, left behind in Cambes and expected to be still operational, was also to be retrieved. Unterscharführer Helmut Stöcker writes:

> The 1. Kompanie provided two assault parties which secured us to the left and right. The remainder of 1./25 opened some light gun fire to draw the enemy's attention to other targets. The crew of our I. Zug (platoon) of the 13./25 (heavy infantry guns) advanced as a body to the guns, led by Untersturmführer Markart. While the enemy was busy in the dark salvaging the Sherman, we stole our operational gun from just outside his positions. We also took all the equipment, aiming mechanisms, range finders, scissor telescope,

etc. The gun was brought back to the original position and joined the other two of our II. Zug.[27]

In the evening of 7 June, Regiment 25 held defensive positions along a curved line from the railroad Caen-Luc sur Mer to the Route Nationale No. 13 from Caen to Bayeux. The right wing of I. Bataillon was located at the railroad line south of Cambes. There was only a loose link-up with the 21. Panzerdivision. In the sector of II. Bataillon the line ran to the left along the northern edge of Galmanche, then along the northern edge of St. Contest in the sector of III. Bataillon and further along the northern and western edge of Buron. Its further course was along the western edges of Gruchy, Authie and Franqueville. Here, units of the 16. (Pionier-) Kompanie, the 14. (Flak-) Kompanie and the 15. (Aufklärungs) Kompanie of Regiment 25 were in position, together with parts of the II. Panzerabteilung and supported by the III. Artillerieabteilung.

The reinforced Panzergrenadierregiment 25 had been able to bring the attack by the English and the Canadians to a halt north and northwest of Caen. It had also succeeded in throwing back the tank spearheads which had advanced to close proximity of the Carpiquet airfield, inflicting heavy losses on the enemy. But the German losses, too, caused in particular by enemy artillery fire, were significant. The enemy suffered the most severe losses in the area of Buron-Authie-Franqueville. The North Nova Scotia Highlanders counted 11 dead, 30 wounded and 204 missing. The Sherbrooke Fusiliers lost a total of 63 officers, NCOs and men. According to their war diary, 15 of their tanks had been knocked out. The war diary of the North Nova Scotias shows 27 tanks destroyed. In the official Canadian War History the losses are registered as following: North Nova Scotias 242 casualties among which were 26 dead; 21 Cruiser tanks knocked out and a further 7 damaged.[28]

The companies of Panzerregiment 12 (5. and 6.) deployed in the left sector suffered 13 dead and 11 wounded. They lost a total of nine Panzer IVs, an unknown number was damaged. The III./25 counted twenty-eight dead, seventy wounded (among them five officers) and Twelve missing. 10. and 11. Kompanie had suffered the most severe losses in Buron. The II./25, in action to their right, had twenty-one dead, among them Sturmbannführer Hans Scappini, thirty-eight wounded and five missing. The 7. Panzerkompanie, which attacked there, counted two dead soldiers, two wounded officers, one wounded NCO and two wounded soldiers. Three Panzer IVs were probably total losses. The I./25, including the attached platoons (heavy infantry guns and Flak), suffered 112 casualties: fifteen soldiers were dead; three officers, eleven NCOs; and seventy-three soldiers were wounded. Of these, one officer, three NCOs and eleven men remained with the troop. One officer and nine soldiers were missing. After Untersturmführer (lieutenant) Gscheider was wounded, Unterscharführer (sergeant) Schott initially took over command of 3. Kompanie. The losses of weapons were not significant: three MG 42s, three assault rifles, two machine pistols, six rifles, one heavy infantry gun. Ammunition used was: 15,000 rounds for rifles and machine guns, seventy mortar shells, forty anti-tank shells (for the Pak), thirty shells for heavy infantry guns, 200 shells for 2 cm Flak, 300 shells for light infantry guns. The 8. Panzerkompanie, attached to I. Bataillon, lost four men dead, one NCO and one soldier wounded. Four Panzer IVs were temporarily out of action. 9. Kompanie, which had initially been held in reserve, also suffered losses: two NCOs and one soldier dead, three men wounded. One Panzer IV had been knocked out. It is not known whether it was a total loss.[29]

No figures are available on enemy losses in the attack sector of I. Bataillon. They were obviously significant. Three tanks were knocked out in close combat.

After the initial success of the attack it was important to bring up further forces as quickly as possible in order to re-commence the attack toward the coast and before the enemy could be significantly reinforced.

CHAPTER 1.2
Securing the Left Flank and Reconnaissance to the North and Northwest by the SS-Panzer-aufklärungsabteilung 12 on 7 June 1944

While the reinforced SS-Panzergrenadierregiment 25 fought its first large-scale battle against parts of the 3rd British Division and the 3rd Canadian Division to the north and northwest of Caen, Panzeraufklärungsabteilung 12 had its first engagement in action further to the west. Its enemy were units of the 69th Infantry Brigade which belonged to the 50th Northumbrian Division.

This division had landed on 6 June in the "Gold" sector between la Rivière and le Hamel. It consisted of Infantry Brigades 69, 151 and 231 and was reinforced by the 56th Infantry Brigade and the 8th Armoured Brigade. The units of the 231st Brigade, landed in the western portion of the sector near le Hamel, were facing significant problems. They were only able to break through the defensive positions on the dunes around noon, and then swing to the west. The hill south of Arromanches was taken in the afternoon in an attack by tanks and infantry against the determined defense by units of the 352. Infanterie Division. Units of the 69th Brigade had landed in the eastern part of the sector near la Rivière. The very effective preparatory fire had turned the town into a heap of rubble. Only one 8.8 cm gun was still in action on the western edge of town. It knocked out two "AVRE" bridge-laying tanks before it was overcome by a "Crab" mine-sweeping tank. Thereafter, the assault teams had to wrestle for the village in street combat for two more hours. A battery of four 15 cm guns, in position in partially finished concrete bunkers west of la Rivière—probably the Mont Fleury battery, had survived the bombardment during the night without damage. At the first light of day it opened fire on the approaching landing fleet. "Its first salvos hit to both sides of the ship which carried the sector command post and the commanding general. The 6-inch guns of the 'Ajax' answered immediately. After a 20 minute duel the battery fell silent."[1]

The 69th Infantry Brigade had not reached its objective, the railroad line Caen-Bayeux, on 6 June. It held the following line at midnight: the 7th Green Howards south of Creully, the 5th East Yorks south of Brécy, the 6th Green Howards to the west up to Vaux-sur-Seulles. The front line of the Division ran further from Sommervieu-St. Sulpice-Vaux-sur-Aure (three kilometers north of Bayeux)—la Rosière (3.5 kilometers southwest of Arromanches) to Arromanches-les-Bains. The greatest depth of penetration thus amounted to nine kilometers.[2]

The first English infantry unit engaged by the Aufklärungs-abteilung was the 6th Battalion the Durham Light Infantry (6th DLI). Entries in its War Diary on the embarkation at Southampton Water have been cited previously. The battalion was part of the second wave. The French coast came into view at 09.00 hours on 6 June. The battalion landed on the beach near la Rivière at 11.00 hours. The seas were rough. Most men felt unwell from the long journey. The waves made the landing difficult. Some groups were up to their hips in water as they went ashore. All of the bataillon was assembled west of Ver-sur-Mer by 13.00 hours. It began its advance at 15.00 hours, encountering only minor resistance. After a ten kilometers march via Crépon, Villiers-le-Sec, le Manoir it reached Esquay-sur-Seulles at 20.30 hours. The battalion was ordered to stop there and dig in since the first objective had been reached. It conducted reconnaissance ahead of its front line. The first prisoners were brought in. They were Russians from the 642 Ost-Bataillon (East Battalion).

At 05.00 hours on 7 June the battalion continued its advance and reached its objective of the day near Condé-sur-Seulles at 07.30 hours. It was attacked by one of its own aircraft and lost two Carriers. The bulk of the battalion arrived at Condé at 09.00 hours. A joint post was set up at the railroad bridge across the Seulles river one kilometer north of Choulain at 11.00 hours.[3]

After a quiet night which only saw fighting against cut-off German units and during which stragglers were taken prisoner, the other units of the 50th Division also began the advance again in the morning of 7 June. The 7th

Green Howards, reinforced by the 4/7 Dragoon Guards (tanks)—without its first company—pushed southwest via Coulombs. It encountered strong resistance near a farm 1.8 kilometers southeast of St. Léger (le Parc). That spot was secured by mine fields and it took some time before a path for the tanks could be opened under the cover of smoke. After attacks from the north and east the strongpoint was finally captured around 10.15 hours and forty-five prisoners were taken. The 6th Green Howards reached the area 1.8 kilometers northeast of Ducy-Ste. Marguérite at approximately 11.50 hours, the 5th E Yorks reached St. Léger. The 2nd Glosters and 2nd Essex had cleared Bayeux up to the railroad bridge at the southern exit of the town by 13.00 hours. At 16.45 hours, the Green Howards took a prisoner who said he had come from Caen and belonged to the 12. SS-Panzerdivision.[4]

When the point units of the 69th Brigade had advanced to within one kilometer of the road Caen—Bayeux in the evening of 6 June, it did not face an enemy ready for action. Units of the Aufklärungsabteilung of the "HJ" Division reached the southern edge of Caen and the Verson area, seven kilometers southwest of the city, during the night of 6 to 7 June. When daylight broke on 7 June, several scouting parties were sent out. An 8-wheel scouting party, sent in a northwestward direction, encountered and effectively fired on enemy defenses at the edge of town and the railroad station of Bretteville-l'Orgeilleuse around noon. A heavy anti-tank gun and a medium anti-aircraft gun were surprised in firing positions near Pûtot and knocked out from a distance of about 50 m.[5]

Another eight-wheel scouting party had last reported in the afternoon of 6 June from the area northwest of Caen. No message had been received since and there was no trace of it. An armored patrol of 2. Kompanie, using light armored reconnaissance halftracks, coming from le Mesnil-Patry and led by Oberscharführer Karl Jura, encountered Canadian jeeps at the southern edge of Pûtot and swung off to the southwest. At Cristot, where the Abteilung command post was located, it received orders around 15.00 hours to scout in a northwesterly direction to the Seulles sector up to Route Nationale No. 13 from Caen to Bayeux. It first reached the Seulles river near Tilly-sur-Seulles which was found free of the enemy. Jura advanced further via Buceels to Chouain and Ducy. There he had his first encounter with the enemy. The commander of the point halftrack which was equipped with a 2 cm gun, Unterscharführer Kurt Fischer, reports on this action:

> We drove in a westerly direction and reached Tilly-sur-Seulles which was abandoned. We had a look around in the town and then left it, having found nothing, on the road to Bayeux. The road climbed steeply even in town. When we reached the top , somewhere between Buceels and Jérusalem, we spotted white dots in the sky to the north which we took to be paratroopers. We added speed in

order to 'get them good'. After we had crossed through Chouain, we saw ahead of the railroad line Caen-Bayeux enemy tanks firing as they were moving. I checked out a dairy operation and brought back two barrels of butter, our only food supplies for the next few days. Then we drove cross-country through a three-pillar underpass under the railroad in a northerly direction. We always kept some 50 to 100 meters from the right shore of the Seulles river. The shore was covered with bushes and trees. (The Joint Post of the 6th DLI was supposed to be located at the railroad bridge, but no enemies were encountered there. Author) From these bushes we retrieved two Wehrmacht stragglers who climbed into the radio halftrack. On the hills of Ducy-Ste. Marguerite and Carcagny, which dropped towards the river, sat and stood enemy guards and smoked. We did not fire, and they did nothing to us. We were well camouflaged by the bushes and branches and they probably did not recognize us as Germans right away. But they did not quite trust the situation since they retreated slowly into their foxholes. We drove on for a while until we could see the 'paratroopers' again from a hill. They were at the same distance as before. I stopped and walked back to Jura who was driving 50 meters behind me. I told him that something had to be wrong here. He had also become concerned, and we turned around. We then drove to Ducy and slowly through the town. The road to St. Léger climbed gradually and had a slight bend to the right. To the right of the road were dense bushes. On a narrow lane, immediately next to the road, I spotted an enemy tank, its top hatch open. There was no sign of the crew. I stood on my seat, pulled the pin from a hand grenade and threw it into the tank. At the same time, my driver, Haacke, yelled: "Pak ahead!". An anti-tank gun had fired on us from road level at 200 meters distance. I had not noticed any of this since I was busy with the tank. I transmitted 'Tanks and Pak!' by radio, but no-one understood the message. Jura looked at us surprised as we backed around the corner. I reported to him, we turned around and drove back to Ducy. 100 meters south of the town, on the road to the railroad underpass, we turned right into a country lane leading to Pont de Conté. After driving some 200 m we stopped. We took up position, with our halftrack facing in the direction of our own lines, the turret at six o'clock, the engines running, and fired on anything that moved. We had tied boxes containing 300 rounds of gun shells with wires to the fenders on the outside. We wanted to get rid of them. It only took a few minutes before our fire was returned. Several mortars set their first salvo right between us. The drivers stepped on the gas and we raced off. The radio half-track drove into the ravine at such a high speed that its hull got caught on the ground and its tracks were turning in the air. My driver tried to get around it, ran up the embankment at an angle and the halftrack toppled. It came to a rest with its tracks up. I barely managed to get out of the turret, the crew was behind me. The second gun halftrack made it through all right. My driver lost his nerve and wanted to blow up the halftrack. No wonder, he had been at the steering wheel for more than thirty hours and it was his first time in action. A short dressing-down brought him back to his senses right away. During the few seconds between the salvos from the mortars we attached the rope from the front over the elevated front wheel. Frankowiak pulled the halftrack backwards at an angle and really managed to bring us back on the tracks. He had already pulled the radio halftrack clear previously. Jura had ordered anyone who was able to drive off immediately in the direction of the railroad line, without waiting for the others. We disconnected the rope and set off. As we did, we noticed the shear bolts had ripped off. With rattling track we drove to the closest cover and my crew tightened the track again while I stood guard with my machine pistol. After the repair was complete, we climbed in again and closed all the hatches, even the grating on top. I tied a few hand grenades to the grating by the pins so that I could use them with one hand. In the other hand I had the signal pistol so I could fire a flare as a signal and not be knocked out by our own anti-tank guns. We expected obstacles at the railroad line. The driver was ordered to make sure to cross under the railroad through a smaller underpass located a few hundred meters east of the arched bridge. We found nothing there and drove through the underpass without being bothered. After a few hundred meters we spotted armored personnel carriers and I fired a white signal flare. They were the other vehicles of the scouting party as well as some others, waiting for us. We drove to the Abteilung command post which had been brought forward to Audrieu in the meantime. After almost forty hours of driving in the halftrack, around 23.00 hours, we sank into the grass there, totally exhausted, and fell asleep immediately.[7]

The War Diary of the 6th Battalion The Durham Light Infantry notes that the Joint Post at the railroad bridge across the Seulles river had to be abandoned on 7 June because of enemy attacks. It was re-taken in the evening.[8] B-Company of the 6th Green Howards reported enemy tanks in the Ducy area at 20.00 hours. At 21.00 hours there was fire from a 20 mm Panzer gun across the company positions, with no losses.[9]

The main body of the Aufklärungsabteilung of the "HJ" Division also continued its march in the direction of Tilly-sur-Seulles after daybreak on 7 June along side roads. Constant fighter-bomber attacks delayed the advance and severed the parts of the column. Only small groups of vehicles advanced for short distances from one cover to the next. Heavy machine gun fire against the fighter-bombers showed no effect, they were obviously too well armored. The Italian 2 cm guns of the armored personnel carriers could only fire single rounds because of a lack of belts. They had no impact.

North of Cristot the spearhead knocked out a light English reconnaissance vehicle with a two-man crew. In Audrieu it encountered weak enemy infantry which was overcome in a surprise attack. Approximately twenty men were taken prisoner. An attack by the point company from Audrieu in a northerly direction got stuck even at the edge of town in strong defensive fire from the vicinity of the railroad line north of the small wooded area, two kilometers northwest of the town. The enemy opened artillery fire on Audrieu. The company took up positions at the northern edge. It was reinforced by a 7.5 cm anti-tank gun and a light infantry gun platoon.

At this time, the main body of the Abteilung was still advancing along the road le Mesnil Patry-Cristot and in Cristot. A heavy English armored reconnaissance vehicle with a 4 cm gun, coming from the southwest, encountered the column in a ravine at the southwest entrance to the town and destroyed two trucks. An Oberscharführer attacked it with a Panzerfaust. It missed its target, however, and exploded against the road embankment. The reconnaissance vehicle retreated to the southwest. In the afternoon, at almost the exact same spot, it was knocked out by a 7.5 cm anti-tank gun. The Abteilung prepared for the defense. The chain of strong points extended from la Rue (southeast of Audrieu) via the northern edge of Audrieu to the western edge of Pavie and into the area west of Hill 103 (southwest of Audrieu). The enemy artillery fire was aimed mainly on Audrieu and seemed to have the church steeple as its major target. Fighter-bombers, spotters and artillery aircraft were constantly in the air.[10]

During this first day of action the Aufklärungsabteilung lost two NCOs and four men dead, one NCO and twelve men wounded, six men missing.

A more pleasant experience should be reported at the end. Sturmmann M. of the communications company of the Abteilung recalls:

On 7 June I was ordered to intercept the NCO in charge (Fröhlich) with the field kitchen and the cook (Hilgers). Near the last house of Cristot in the direction of Audrieu fighter-bombers attacked my scout vehicle, driven by Tillenburg. We drove under cover. French civilians called us from there to an underground bunker in which the family had sought cover.[11]

CHAPTER 1.3
Assembly of SS-Panzergrenadierregiment 26 on 7 June, and Preparations for the Offensive on 8 June 1944

While the reinforced Panzergrenadierregiment 25 and Panzer-aufklärungs-abteilung 12 were already attacking and throwing back the enemy advancing from his bridgehead to the south, or were bringing him to a stop, Panzer-grenadier-regiment 26 was still on the march to the assembly area. The Regiment had the longest marching route to the area. Without taking into consideration the detour into the initially planned assembly in the area Bernay-Lisieux-Vimoutiers, the I./26, located in the Houdan area, had to travel 190 kilometers to Fontaine-Etoupefour. The Regiment had to move mainly during the day on this march. During the late afternoon of 6 June it was subjected to heavy air attacks. These grew even more severe during 7 June when the clouds broke up and the weather turned partly clear. Thus, the Regiment moved in small marching groups with large distances between vehicles, virtually jumping from cover to cover. This method was successful in keeping the numbers of losses and casualties low, but much time was lost. On 7 June, the Regiment lost one NCO and six men dead, two NCOs and nineteen men wounded. Of these, the III. Bataillon alone lost fifteen NCOs and men when driving through Falaise during an air attack on the city. The local administrations there, as elsewhere, had omitted establishing detours and marking them.

In the late afternoon of 7 June the I./26 reached Grainville-sur-Odon (12.5 kilometers southwest of Caen, immediately north of Route Nationale No. 175 from Caen to Villers-Bocage). A motorized scouting party of 1. Kompanie, led by Oberschar-führer Friedrich Hahn met an officer of the Panzer-Lehr Division in the evening. His mission had been to reconnoiter the road Caen-Bayeux. South of the road he had encountered enemy forces and suffered losses.[1]

The Bataillon had been ordered to assemble in Cheux early on 8 June for the attack. 3. Kompanie had been directed to secure the assembly area of the Bataillon. It advanced from Grainville towards Cheux, ready for action. They observed some German vehicles on the road Caen-Tilly-sur-Seulles being fired on by fighter-bombers with rockets. Weak enemy artillery fire was directed on St. Manvieu and to the east. The Kompanie established positions in the knee-high grain stalks along the slope immediately north of Cheux.[2]

During the evening and night, II. and III. Bataillon of Regiment 26 and the regimental units also arrived in the originally planned assembly area.

The enemy had been thrown back north and northwest of Caen with significant losses. He had been brought to a halt north of Audrieu. After he had recognized the presence of the "HJ" Division, the enemy had only advanced hesitantly. He had not taken advantage of the seven-kilometer wide gap between Rots and Audrieu. Obviously, the Panzer scouting parties of Aufklärungsabteilung 12 and the Panzer-Lehr Division had given the impression of a stronger adversary. Also, the missing link-up with the 9th Infantry Brigade to the east worried the enemy. The 7th Infantry Brigade only pushed forward to the rail line Caen-Bayeux, or just beyond it. In addition, it was the intention of the enemy to first secure the beachhead so that additional troops could be landed without danger, before advancing further.

CHAPTER 1.4
Intentions and Decisions on 7 June 1944

The factual progressions of events for the "HJ" Division have been described in the previous three chapters. Decisions of the supreme command were based on the picture it had of the developments. The following entries in the war diaries show an occasionally surprising divergence from the reality. This was probably caused by a lack of reports which can be explained, among other reasons, by insufficient communications connections. Air attacks on important centers had destroyed or damaged long distance communications systems.

The war diary of 7. Armee notes that the communications links with the LXXXIV. A.K. had been lost in the early morning hours of 7 June, preventing any reports on the developments of the night from being sent. At 4 A.M. the chief of staff of the Armee advised Feldmarschall Rommel that the three Panzerdivisions attached to the I. SS-Panzerkorps—21., 12. SS-, and Panzer-Lehr Division—had been brought into the assembly areas. Also, that they had been ordered to'begin a counter-attack with all available forces'. In fact, only the 21. Pz. Div. was in action against the enemy, west of the Orne river, where most of its forces were tied down in defensive actions. The other two were still on the march. Since radio silence had been ordered to conceal the assembly, units on the move could not report their positions. It cannot be said that the "HJ" Division and the Panzer-Lehr Division had reported their assembly during the night of 6 to 7 June. At 09.30 hours, General-leutnant Speidel reported to the chief of the operations section of the OKW about the situation, on request, that 'it can be expected that the attack by the 12. SS-Pz. Div. will begin even today.'[1]

The AOK 7 (supreme command, 7. Armee) was advised at 09.50 hours that it was the intention of the Heeresgruppe to assign Panzergruppe Command West to the Armee in order to take over command of the Orne-Vire sector. At 10.30 hours, General of the Panzer troops, Freiherr (baron) Geyr von Schweppenburg was briefed on his mission at the Heeresgruppe. It

should be remembered that the General, in opposition to the opinion of
Feldmarschall Rommel and Generalleutnant Speidel, had been and still was
of the point of view that the Panzerdivisions outside of the ships' artillery
range, should destroy the advancing enemy in a concentrated attack. It
could not be their objective to attack the landed enemy in the coastal sector,
much less to prevent further landings in cooperation with the divisions in
position. The intention of the 7. Armee—immediate counterattack with all
available forces—was in glaring contrast to this. These basic differences of
opinion had not been overcome.

The three Panzerdivisions intended for the Caen area were, by no means,
'all available forces'. A telephone conversation between the commander of
XXXXVII Panzerkorps with the Ia of Heeresgruppe B indicates that the 116.
Pz. Div. had advanced, as ordered, into the area northwest of Rouen, to the
right of the Seine river, at 03.00 hours on 7 June. The 2. Pz. Div. had deployed
'one Abteilung from the north bank of the Seine' (where to?). At 11.15 hours
the Heeresgruppe had requested from the OKW an additional mortar
brigade which was to be assembled at the 15. Armee (!). During this discussion, Feldmarschall Rommel imparted as his overall impression that 'it can be
expected that the enemy will launch a concentrated attack at another point'.[2]
He still had the mouth of the Somme river in mind. The static 346. Inf. Div.
was located in the area northwest of Rouen where the 116. Pz. Div. had been
deployed. The mobile Kampfgruppe of the 346. Inf. Div. was deployed, on the
suggestion of 15. Armee, to reinforce the 711. Inf. Div. for the counterattack
on the airborne enemy east of the Orne river. It was on the attack since 17.00
hours from Merville in the direction of Ranville. The remainder of the Division was to prepare for redeployment. However, the 116. Panzerdivision
appeared indispensable there, as was the 2. Pz. Div. which was still located to
the right of the Somme river.

At 12.00 hours, the 7. Armee reported to the Heeresgruppe that the "HJ
Division, beginning along the line Caen-Villers-Bocage, had its advance halted
by enemy aircraft. Pz. Lehr-Div. ready at 09.40 hours near Thury-Harcourt."[3]

The appendix to the war diary of the 7. Armee notes at 17.40 hours that
the I. SS-Panzerkorps intended:

Action by 21. Pz. Div. in direction Lion-sur-Mer along the road Caen-
Douvres as dividing line, 12. SS-Pz. Div. to the right and slightly to
the rear, Pz. Lehr-Div. on the left . . . I. SS-Panzerkorps wanted to
assemble at 16.00 hours, was however hindered somewhat by air
attacks. It is not known when the attack will take place.

The war diary of Heeresgruppe B notes for the same time:

In regard of the reported large Panzer assembly northeast of Caen,
the I. SS-Panzerkorps has directed 21. Pz. Div. to attack in the direc-

tion of Lion, SS-Pz. Div. "HJ" to the right of the road Caen-Douvres and Pz. Lehr-Div. to its left in direction of the coast. The attack, planned for 16.00 hours, has probably been delayed due to enemy aircraft activity. The lines at the beachhead north of Caen are largely unchanged from yesterday.

At 21.45 hours, according to the war diary of the Heeresgruppe, the 7. Armee reported:

According to messages received, I. SS-Panzerkorps with 21. Pz. Div. and 12. SS-Pz. Div. commenced an attack in a northerly direction at 16.00 hours.

Contrary to this, the war diary of 7. Armee notes:

The large-scale attack by I. SS-Pz. Korps, planned for 16.00 hours, from Caen to the north to eliminate the bridgehead could not be commenced at that time. Due to severe losses during the march and continuous air attacks, the assembly of the divisions of the I. SS-Pz. Korps in the planned assembly area was not possible on a timely basis. The counterattack was postponed to the morning of 8 June.[4]

Thus, the 7. Armee did not have a clear picture of the assembly and attack possibilities throughout the whole day and even during the evening. In the evening of 7 June the Heeresgruppe was under the impression that the attack by 21. Pz. Div. and the "HJ" Division was under way. The overall daily report states:

At 17.00 hours, I. SS-Pz. Korps with 21. Pz. Div. and 12. SS-Pz. Div. began an attack from the area north and northwest of Caen with the aim to break through to the coast. In the late evening hours it was in action against enemy tank forces near Douvres. Bringing up the Pz. Lehr-Div. has shown to be difficult and time consuming due to enemy air superiority. Because of this, it has not yet been in action.[5]

Based on this impression of its own situation and the assumption that the bridgehead had not been expanded significantly from the previous day, the Heeresgruppe had to expect that the initial success of this day could be enlarged the next day with the planned action by the Panzer-Lehr Division. This was a delusion.

In reality, the 21. Pz. Div. had not commenced an attack west of the Orne river on 7 June. Also, there could be no mention of an attack by the whole of the "HJ" Division. Only a reinforced Panzergrenadierregiment and an incomplete Panzerabteilung had attacked. The attack by the insufficient forces had only advanced to a line Cambes-Buron, approximately ten kilometers from the coast and eight kilometers from the Douvres radar station which was still being successfully defended. The enemy had significantly enlarged his beachhead and closed the gap between the 3rd British Division and the 3rd Canadian Division north of Caen.

The war diary of the I. SS-Panzerkorps did not survive. The Korps order for the attack on 8 June has not been found in other documents either. In the available divisional order of the Panzer-Lehr Division for the attack on 8.6.44 it is stated, inter alia:

3.) I. SS-Panzerkorps with attached 21. Pz. Div., SS-Pz. Div. HJ and Pz.Lehr-Div. will advance from the Caen-St. Croix area into the beachhead and capture the line St. Aubin-Vauvres-Creully. It will secure the left flank in line Carcagny-Ellon-Trungy by reconnaissance forces.

4.) Panzer-Lehr Division will assemble at 03.00 hours in the night of 7 to 8 June in such a manner that it can, on the order of the Division, attack in the direction of Courseulles.

5.) To be assembled: Pz. Grenadier Lehr-Rgt 901 on the right, Pz. Gren. Lehr-Rgt. 902 on the left; dividing line le Mesnil Patry-Putot (902)-Secqueville (901)-Lantheuil (902); forward line of the assembly: Road to Bayeux.

8.) Pz. ALA 130 (Panzer-Aufklärungs-Lehr-Abteilung = Panzer reconnaissance training Abteilung. Author) will advance via Villers-Bocage to the northwest and capture the line le Doucet-Ellon-Trungy and thus secure the left flank of the Division. Pz.Aufkl.Abt. HJ Division will link up to the east and secure up to the assembly area of the Division. Dividing line: Road Tilly-Bayeux.

13.) Division command post will locate in the Cheux area.[6]

Remarkable in this order is, that the Panzer-Lehr Division was to assemble in the same area as Panzergrenadierregiment 26 of the "HJ" Division. Further, that the forward edge of the assembly area was in enemy hands already on 7 June and that the Panzerregiment is not mentioned in the attack orders for the Panzer-Lehr Division. Based on this, one can conclude that the I. SS-Panzerkorps originally intended to move Panzer-grenadierregiment 26 from its initial assembly area, as ordered by the LXXXIV. A.K., to the right. The same move was planned for Panzergrenadierregiment 25, and for the same time, early on 7 June. They were to link up with 21. Pz. Div. Further, that the Pz.-Lehr Div. was to take over the assembly area of Regiment 26. However, the situation on both sides had changed significantly: the enemy had further advanced to the south, and the Pz.-Lehr Div. was still well back. This probably changed the intentions of the Korps. Its chief of staff, Brigade-führer Krae-mer wrote on this situation in his study that it was clear in the evening of 7 June that a gap of seven to ten kilometers existed in the attack sector of the Korps. Further, that the enemy could push through this gap at any time and smash the 12. SS-Pz. Div. and the Pz.-Lehr Div. in their assembly areas. Thus, the commanding general, Sepp Dietrich, had decided to attack before noon on 8 June without the Pz.-Lehr Div.[7] Obviously, all orders had not reached the troops in time. The first units of the Pz.-Lehr Div. arriving during the night of 7 to 8 June and in the morning of 8 June in their assembly areas were sur-prised to find units of the "HJ" Division there and turned back. On account of the considerable delays during the march and the overlapping orders which arrived at different times at the units, there was no possibility of a con-centrated attack on 8 June by the "HJ" Division and the Pz.-Lehr Division, not even to mention a joint attack by all three Panzerdivisions.

CHAPTER 1.5
Attack in the Left Battle Zone of the Division from 8 to 10 June 1944, and Transition to Defense

To the west of the Mue creek, the 3rd Canadian Infantry Division had reached its attack objective and changed over to defense in order to secure the beachhead and the further unloading of troops and materiel. Its 9th Infantry Brigade, reinforced by a tank unit, had however been thrown back by a counterattack of the III./25 and parts of the II. Panzer-abteilung on les Buissons. The 7th Infantry Brigade was in action west of the Mue creek. Its commander, Brigadier H.W. Foster, realized in the afternoon of 7 June that a dangerous gap existed in the Cairon area between his brigade and the 9th Infantry Brigade which was in bitter combat on the left. He directed a com-pany of the Canadian Scottish Regiment, his reserves, to secure the flank. It was reinforced by a tank company of the 6th Armoured Regiment and a number of anti-tank guns. The 1st Battalion The Regina Rifle Regiment had captured the towns of Norrey-en-Bessin and Bretteville-l'Orgeilleuse. To the west, the battalion The Royal Winnipeg Rifles had prepared for defense at the southern edge of Putot. The Brigade command post was located in le Haut de Bretteville. The 3rd Canadian Infantry Division intended to carry out a renewed attack on Buron with the support of all of the division artillery. For this reason, the 7th and 8th Infantry Brigades were to hold the positions reached on 8 June.[1] A loose link-up existed to the 50th (Northum-brian) Infantry Division west of Putot and north of Brouay.

ATTACK BY SS-PANZERGRENADIERREGIMENT 26 ON NORREY, BRETTEVILLE-L'ORGEILLEUSE, PUTOT AND BROUAY. SECURING NEAR AUDRIEU BY SS-PANZERAUFKLÄRUNGSABTEILUNG 12 ON 8 JUNE 1944

Panzergrenadierregiment 26 had been ordered to attack, while it was still dark, on 8 June. The attack was to be supported by the I. Panzerabteilung and the II. Artillerie-abteilung. However, the Panzerabteilung did not arrive before the start of the attack so the Regiment had to set out without Panzer support. The plan was that I. Bataillon was to capture Norrey, II. Bataillon Putot as their first attack objectives. The III. Bataillon (armored) had the mission to secure the left flank and to follow the advancing attack to the left rear of II. Bataillon. The I. SS-Panzerkorps had planned to have the Panzer-Lehr Division follow SS-Panzergrenadierregiment 26 staggered to the left rear. Depending on developments of the situation in this sector, it would push ahead of this regiment or pass it on the left and go into action on the enemy flank. This would also prevent an enemy attack into the open left flank of the "HJ" Division.[1a]

The terrain to the north and northwest of Caen, through which Regiment 25 and the II. Panzerabteilung had attacked on 7 June, was almost flat. The only obstructions to visibility were the villages with their adjoining orchards. West of the line Authie-Gruchy it was completely open and thus well suited for a Panzer attack. However, the terrain between the lines St. Manvieu-Rots and Fontenay-le Pesnel-Brouay was broken. Hill 99 was located at the northwest corner of Cheux. A flat ridge ran from there to the area southeast of Cristot, to Hill 102. The Mue creek runs from Cheux in a generally northeastward direction, west and north past St. Manvieu into the wooded valley near Rots. Near St. Manvieu, the creek is at an elevation of approximately sixty meters. A hollow extends to the west, it levels off between Cheux and le Mesnil-Patry at seventy meters. The terrain rises from the creek bed and the hollow to seventy-three meters near Norrey, le Mesnil is at the same elevation. From there, the terrain drops to the north to fifty-five meters near Bretteville while Putot is at seventy-four meters. Brouay is only located at an average elevation of sixty-five meters, however, Cristot is at eighty-five meters. The eastern and central sectors were covered with wheat and beet fields or clover pastures. Bushes and dense clumps of trees could only be found near the creek. Around le Mesnil, some hedges and rows of trees occasionally restricted the visibility. South of Brouay there were larger wooded areas and earth walls covered with hedges and trees short distances apart, enclosing pastures and fields. The railroad line Caen-Bayeux ran occasionally on elevated embankments or in hollows. It created an obstacle for the Panzers. The two to two-and-one-half meter high walls of limestone in the villages and around individual farms were considerable obstacles.

As ordered, the attack by the I./26 began on 8 June, probably at 03.00 hours. 3. Kompanie, led by Obersturm-führer Karl Düwel, was in action on

the right, 2. Kompanie under Leutnant Sauer on the left. 1. Kompanie followed on the right rear to secure the flank since there was no link-up with
Regiment 25. When 3. Kompanie reached the hill at St. Manvieu it came
under fire from the forward securing forces of the enemy. These withdrew to
Norrey as the attack progressed. The Kompanie received heavy artillery fire
during the further advance and had to stop half-way up the slope in front of
Norrey.

2. Kompanie on the left had initially advanced quickly. However, one platoon then got stopped in a clover pasture next to the rail line while the other
two succeeded in capturing a group of houses, Cardonville, along the railroad
line. Since 3. Kompanie had been stalled to the right rear, the Bataillon commander, Sturmbannführer Bernhard Krause, ordered the attack stopped.
The Kompanie dug in. It had stopped in a knee-high grain field.

At dawn, Obersturmführer Düwel, commander of 3. Kompanie, saw in
front the village of Norrey, surrounded by clumps of trees and towering above
it, the steeple of the old Norman church. On his way back from his platoon in
action on the right to the Kompanie command post, he was wounded by
infantry fire. When he arrived at his command post he requested fire on Norrey from the advanced artillery observer. The observer could not establish
radio contact with his battery since a Canadian radio transmitter started sending, breaking the connection. Düwel handed over command of the Kompanie to Hauptscharführer Kaiser and went back to the field first aid station
at Cheux.

1. Kompanie advanced to the right of the 3. to link up with the neighbor
on the right, but the advance stalled in concentrated artillery fire.[2]

The positions of the whole Bataillon were covered with brisk artillery
and mortar fire throughout the day. It slowed down any kind of movement.
The attack by the Bataillon on the positions of an equally strong enemy,
ready for defense, was thrown back. During this attack the battalion lost five
men killed, one officer, one NCO and eighteen men wounded.

The war diary of the Regina Rifles notes tersely: "The enemy carried out
a counterattack during the night on the positions of B-, C- and D-Company. It
was repulsed by our troops. The battalion was ordered to hold its positions."[3]

II./26, commanded by Sturmbannführer Bernhard Sieb-ken, assembled
during the night 7–8 June in and around le Mesnil-Patry. It had arrived, possibly because of the few available crossings of the Odon river and since the
Regiment had marched along several roads, by way of Fontenay-le-Pesnel
and Cristot. Since the situation was not clear, it marched in a staggered formation and ready for action. As the commander of 6. Kompanie, Obersturmführer Heinz Schmolke, reports, his company advanced in night battle
formation which had been practiced.[4]

The first attack objective of the Bataillon was the village of Putot-en-
Bessin, 1.5 kilometers north of le Mesnil (measured from church to church).
The battalion The Royal Winnipeg Rifles had prepared for defense at the

southern edge of Putot and along the railroad line with three companies. D-Company was located immediately east of the village, where the battalion command post had been set up, as reserves.

At approximately 06.30 hours, a battle-ready scouting party of the II./26 experienced the first contact with the enemy A-Company when it tried to push into the village across the railroad embankment. It was thrown back.[5] This indicated clearly that the enemy was ready to defend. The Bataillon assembled for the attack with 7. Kompanie, led by Leutnant August Henne, on the right and 6. Kompanie on the left. No information can be given on the initial action of 5. Kompanie which was commanded by Obersturm-führer Karl Gotthard. 8. Kompanie (heavy) took up positions so that it could support the initial attack across the open terrain, to follow later. Details on the artillery support are not known. The self-propelled heavy infantry gun Kompanie was probably not yet ready to fire since it marched with the tracked vehicles of III. Bataillon which moved at a slower speed.

The body of II. Bataillon arrived too late to attack before dawn together with I. Bataillon. When Schmolke was briefed at the Bataillon and received his attack orders he asked the commander when the start of the attack was to be. "Half an hour ago", Siebken replied. While Schmolke was away the company command post of the 6. took a direct hit. The commander of I. Zug, Obersturmführer Bayerlein, was critically wounded and died soon after in hospital. The company platoon commander, Unterscharführer Bernhaier, was killed, the battle field observer, Sturmmann Uschner, and the medic were wounded. Obersturmführer Schmolke reports on the development of the attack:

> Our first attack objective was the railroad line Caen-Bayeux, our second was the road Caen-Bayeux. The attack carried quite well to the railroad line. My point platoon took a lot of prisoners. Because of the time pressure, I could not interrogate them myself. They were sent directly to the rear. An infantry platoon of the Panzer-Lehr-Division attacked together with us and put itself under my command. I also met a Hauptmann (captain), a battery commander, who supported the attack with his fire.[6]

Oberscharführer Paul Dargel, commander of III. Zug of 6. Kompanie, remembers the further progress this way:

> The first target was the railroad embankment. Heavy artillery and rifle fire greeted us from the embankment. My Zug had the sector to the left of the road and of the underpass. Our II. Zug was the first to reach the railroad embankment. At 14.00 hours the message came back: 'Kompanie commander wounded!' Kompanie chief Schmolke

had received a flesh wound in the back caused by an artillery shell. I dressed it. The wound greatly bothered him. During the second stage behind the embankment we took some prisoners who were moved to the battalion command post. At 15.00 hours we observed thick clouds of dust in front of the sector of the Panzer-Lehr-Division. They were probably approaching columns of enemy tanks. Since we had now pushed our way into the positions, the artillery fire stopped. Also, there was hardly any rifle fire from the enemy lines.[7]

Through cooperation of all companies of the battalion, where the 7. Kompanie of Leutnant Henne had to do most of the fighting in town, the three Canadian companies, 'A', 'B', and 'C', were completely encircled in Putot in the early hours of the afternoon. They tried to withdraw under cover of artificial smoke when ammunition was running out. Only few men managed to make their way to 'D' Company which was still fairly intact and had set up defensive positions to the east of the village. At 14.20 hours, the commander of the Winnipegs still believed he could master the situation with his own forces. In the course of the afternoon the 3rd Canadian Infantry Division received reports that the troops in the right sector had been cut off by enemy Panzers.[8] This was a wrong impression. Very likely, the armored personnel carriers of the III./26 which had pushed into Brouay, had been mistaken for Panzers. An anti-tank gun of the III./26, in position near a railroad bridge east of Brouay, repeatedly fired on targets in Putot.

When parts of 6. Kompanie had almost reached the second objective, the Route Nationale, its left, open flank was attacked by numerous tanks. Oberscharführer Dargel, who commanded the III. Zug in action on the left, observed up to 18 enemy tanks at one time. These were a British tank unit, the 24th Lancers. They had assembled at 07.00 hours in the Martragny area (eight kilometers southeast of Bayeux). When advancing along Route National No. 13 from Bayeux to Caen, its point had taken heavy anti-tank fire immediately east of St. Leger. One Stuart tank had been knocked out. Despite concentrated artillery fire on the suspected positions of the anti-tank guns, the regiment could not advance any further at the time. One can assume that these German forces were a scouting party of SS-Panzeraufklärungsabteilung 12. Other German units had not pushed this far north across the Route Nationale. During the late afternoon the Lancers again rolled forward and encountered strong resistance at the western edge of Putot. They believed to have three battalions of a Panzergrenadierregiment of the "Hitlerjugend" Division in front of them. Parts of them, as is stated in the war diary of the British tank unit, had taken cover in the high grass of the orchards and in the tops of trees from where they fired on the tank commanders. After taking some forty prisoners, the regiment withdrew and was later ordered back into the Martragny area.[9]

Heinz Schmolke speaks about the tank attack by the 24th Lancers:

I took a fragment near my spine at the wrong moment. I tried to
keep going for a while and tried to find cover under a tree. But a
tank found me there almost immediately and I had to climb on it,
together with some other prisoners. At first, they drove with us some
distance towards our own lines, while our artillery fired on them
without regard for our own infantry. As far as I can remember, I saw
at least three tanks on fire. The previous sleepless days of the march
and the exhaustions of the attack had made us so fatalistic that we
did not care at all about the salvos exploding next to us. We were
even hoping for more of our own fire on the enemy tanks. In a
meadow near a group of bushes, the first dozen prisoners was assembled. Some were from my company and some were Heer soldiers,
while a Canadian with two pistols squatted in front of us and held us
in check. During a salvo from our own artillery exploding nearby I
managed to sneak away unnoticed into a ditch. While the other prisoners were loaded on tanks and carried off I was able to stay,
together with Unterscharführer Gauerke who had joined me, for a
few more minutes in our hiding place. However, the guard had sent
over another tank which brought us out of hiding again. We had
nothing at all, not a Panzerfaust, no magnetic mines, nothing which
could have helped us against the tanks in any way.[10]

At a prisoner assembly area at the beach, Heinz Schmolke was looked
after by a German medical officer. Oberscharführer Dargel continues the
report:

Half an hour later our armored reconnaissance vehicles showed up
from the direction of Putot. The enemy tanks probably mistook
them for Panzers and withdrew. Afterwards, I met four men of my
reserve units without their helmets and belts. They had run away
from captivity. I remember two of their names: Schäfle and Paul.[11]

More than anything else, it was probably the well aimed and effective
artillery fire which forced the enemy tanks to turn back.

At 17.00 hours the 7th Canadian Infantry Brigade ordered a counter
attack for 20.30 hours to recapture its old positions in Putot. The attack was to
be carried out by the 1st Battalion The Canadian Scottish Regiment, including the company in action at Cairon, reinforced by one company of the 6th
Armoured Regiment (tanks), a portion of the machine gun battalion The
Cameron Highlanders of Ottawa and the 12th and 13th Field Regiments
(artillery units). The Canadian infantry and tanks attacked behind a wall of
fire, effectively supported by the super-heavy machine guns and the artillery.

6. Kompanie had suffered heavy losses through a flank attack by the British tank unit. The company commander and one platoon commander were wounded, and on top of this, the company commander had been taken prisoner. 7. and 5. Panzergrenadierkompanie, supported by heavy machine guns, mortars and artillery, could not hold their positions against the superior attackers. Lacking any weapons for close-in anti-tank combat, they were helpless against the attacking Canadian tanks. Leutnant Henne writes on this:

> After we had captured the Canadian reserve company, we sat in their foxholes while five tanks stood in the ditch next to us for quite some time. We could do nothing about them.[12]

The Bataillon had to pull back to the railroad line. The Canadian war diary states that Putot was recaptured, despite determined resistance, by 21.30 hours.[13] During the night the Bataillon withdrew another 200 to 300 meters to the south of the railroad line to gain a field of fire, and dug in. The Canadian Scottish took over the Putot sector, the rest of the Winnipeg Rifles were pulled out as a reserve to the Brigade. They had suffered 265 casualties, among them 105 dead. The 1st Battalion Canadian Scottish Regiment had 45 dead among 125 casualties.[14] The II./26 of the "HJ" Division lost three NCOs and sixteen men dead, one officer, eight NCOs and forty-nine men wounded, one officer and twenty men missing. Except for one man, all missing were from 6. Kompanie, it also suffered the most dead, a total of forty-five losses. Total losses of the Bataillon were ninety-eight.[15]

The III. (armored) Bataillon SS-Panzergrenadierregiment 26 had reached Fontenay-le-Pesnel by midnight of 7 June and set up camp there. 10. Kompanie had marched at the point along the left advance route. Along side roads, it had arrived, likely by mistake, via Hottot at the bridge at the southern entrance of Verrières, 2.5 kilometers northwest of Tilly-sur-Seulles. The company commander, Oberleutnant Pallas, had driven his armored personnel carrier onto a mine there. Just before, he had taken two or three Canadians of the 3rd Canadian Infantry Division prisoner and sent them back to the Bataillon. South of Verrières, he then received the order to proceed to the assembly area of the Bataillon near Fontenay by way of Juvigny.[16]

The Bataillon had initially been ordered to assemble to the left rear of the II./26, to secure the left flank of the Regiment, and to follow the II./26 in the course of the attack. It was likely determined during the night that a wide gap existed between the II./26 and Panzeraufklärungsabteilung 12 near Audrieu. Obviously, the Regiment was not aware that portions of the Panzer-Lehr-Division were already advancing into this gap. Thus, III. Bataillon was ordered to attack to the left of II. Bataillon, capture Brouay as its first target and to close the gap between II./26 and A.A.12. After marching on foot, the Bataillon reached Cristot in the early morning hours of 8 June. The armored personnel carriers had been left in Fontenay since the Panzers had not yet arrived and the situation was completely unclear. It appears that timely reconnaissance had not been undertaken. The Bataillon commander, Sturmbannführer Erich Olboeter, had ordered the company commanders to the wooded area 500 m north of Cristot to receive their orders. Unfortunately, the assembled group of officers was caught by a violent fire attack by the enemy artillery. The chief of 10 Kompanie, Oberleutnant Wilhelm Pallas, and the chief of 11. Kompanie, Obersturmführer Hauser, were seriously wounded. Untersturmführer Helmut Mader, who was also wounded but remained with the troops, took over command of 10. Kompanie. Untersturmführer Karl Kugler assumed command of 11. Kompanie. Both companies received orders to advance in the direction of Brouay, supported by the armored personnel carriers with guns, to capture the town, and to prepare for defense there. The rest of the Bataillon was to remain in Cristot for the time being.[17]

The companies assembled for the attack at approximately 08.00 hours. The point platoon of 11. Kompanie advanced east of the road Cristot-Brouay through a high grain field. Some 500 meters north of the town it received fire from a single machine gun. It fell silent when the grenadiers singly worked their way forward. When the point had reached the crossroads 150 meters south of Brouay, soldiers were spotted at the northwest edge of town. It could not make out whether they were friend or foe. Engine noise could also be heard. Since there was no information about German troops it was assumed that the town was in enemy hands. The company commander ordered to storm Brouay. Without firing a single shot, the edge of town and then the railroad embankment was reached, running at the double. It was a great surprise to find two light machine guns at the embankment and a heavy machine gun at a bridge across the railroad immediately east of the village, all belonging to a battalion of the Panzer-Lehr-Division. The rest of the unit was encamped in a wooded area at the west entrance to Brouay. This unit of the Panzer-Lehr-Division had no contact with its own troops and believed it had been cut off.[18]

10. Kompanie, advancing to the left of the 11. through the harassing fire of enemy artillery, reached the wooded area southwest of Brouay around noon. Oberscharführer Hans-Georg Kesslau reports on this:

> Here we encountered the most terrible image of the war. The enemy had cut virtually cut to pieces units of the Panzer-Lehr-Division with heavy weapons. Armored personnel carriers and equipment had been ripped apart, next to them on the ground, and even hanging from trees, were body parts of dead comrades. A terrible silence covered all.[19]

The company advanced to the railroad embankment. Portions of a platoon with a cannon-equipped armored personnel carrier pushed forward along the rail line near a lineman's cottage. Another linked up at the railroad line and secured the western edge of the park of Château Brouay. 9. Kompanie secured to the left. There was no link-up to the Aufklärungs-abteilung, only contact. Enemy tanks approached the rail line from the Lou-celles area in the afternoon. Mortars of 10. Kompanie opened fire on them and they withdrew. Later, as Oberscharführer Hans-Georg Kesslau reports:

> A Sherman tank, followed by a carette, approached from le Bas d'Audrieu. We let them through our own lines. Unterscharführer Spary tried to knock out the tank with a Panzerfaust, but he was spotted by its commander, fired on with a machine pistol and wounded. Recognizing its desperate situation, the tank drove at full speed into the garden of the lineman's cottage and forced to a stop there, with nowhere to go. The carrette had followed it, like a foal would its mother, and was also forced to surrender. The tank was a command tank with a dummy gun. The crew, together with their maps, was sent to the Bataillon command post.[20]

The Pionierzug (engineer platoon) of the Bataillon was sent into action on the right flank of 11. Kompanie in the evening in order to better secure the railroad bridge. Since there was no link-up to II./26, scouting parties maintained connection during the night. The positions of the Bataillon were covered with harassing fire from artillery by day and night.

On 8 June the Bataillon lost one NCO and five men dead, two officers, one NCO and five men wounded.[21]

The authors of the war history of the Panzer-Lehr-Division, Franz Kurowski and Helmut Ritgen, could not find an explanation either for the confused situation on the left flank of the "HJ" Division. Helmut Ritgen writes:

> . . . the spearheads of II. Bataillon of the Panzer-grenadier-Lehr-Regiment 902—Major Welsch—[armored, as all four Panzer-grenadier battalions of the Panzer-Lehr-Division, while the "HJ" Division had six Panzergrenadier battalions of which only one was armored] had reached the Fontenay-Tilly area during the night 7 to 8 June. The regimental commander, Oberst Gutmann, marched with the battalion. I. Bataillon was far behind. After a briefing by the Division commander, SS-Panzeraufklärungsabteilung 12 secured a line from Brouay to the railroad line and to le Douet (seven kilometers west of Brouay, Author) in front of the sector. Portions of the defeated 352. Infanterie-Division also offered brave resistance during their retreat. When the Welsch Bataillon reached the railroad line near Brouay and le Bas d'Audrieu at 04.30 hours, it encountered a jumble of German and enemy troops. The enemy point units were advancing on both locations, the 8. British Armoured Brigade with

the tank battalion 24th Lancers in the east and the 61st Reconnaissance Regiment in the west. The report by the British states that they drew heavy fire as they approached the rail line and that they became involved in action against forces of the 12. SS-Panzerdivision which had also offered resistance at Loucelles (approximately two kilometers northwest of Brouay, Author) . . . The Welsch Bataillon was initially successful in preventing the enemy from crossing the rail line near Brouay. The regimental command post was being set up in the nearby park of the castle when British tanks rolled towards the park entrance and shot up all the vehicles parked under the trees. Then, a British artillery observation plane flew over the town and soon after the ground trembled from the explosions of heavy ships' artillery which concentrated its fire on the area of Brouay and south. It caused significant losses of men and materiel. Oberst Gutmann and several other officers were wounded.[22]

The Panzer-Lehr-Division suffered further heavy losses during this day through a terrible occurrence of a completely different nature. Two English scouting parties, numbers 2 and 6a, had crossed unnoticed through the thin security line of Panzeraufklärungsabteilung 12 on the left flank of the Division. They were part of the C-Squadron of the Inns of Court Regiment. As all other scouting parties of their company, they had been ordered by I Corps, to which they were attached, to destroy all bridges across the Orne river from the road bridge near Thury-Harcourt to the railroad bridge two kilometers south of Maltot inclusive. To achieve this, engineers had been attached to the scouting parties. This company had available forty-two Scout Cars and armored cars of various types.[23] Near a hill, probably Hill 102, one kilometer south of Cristot, the two scouting parties encountered a group of members of the staff of the Panzer-Artillerie-Regiment 130 of the Panzer-Lehr-Division. This group was made up of the regimental commander, Oberst Luxenburger, the Abteilung commander, Major Zeissler, the regiment adjutant, Hauptmann Graf (count) Clary-Aldringen and some six NCOs and men. They had driven ahead to this location which offered a view of the area to prepare the action of the Regiment for the attack which had been ordered for 9 June.

According to the report by Graf Clary, these German soldiers were completely surprised by the English scouting parties and taken prisoner. After the German officers refused to voluntarily ride on the English armored reconnaissance vehicles as shields against bullets, the badly disabled Oberst Luxenburger (he had lost an arm in the First World War) was bound by two English officers, beaten unconscious and tied to an English ARV, covered with blood. After respective orders had been received by radio, Major Zeissler, Graf Clary and the NCOs and men of the group were shot to pieces by the retreating British armored reconnaissance vehicles. Except for Graf

Clary who was saved from further bullets, after having received a number of wounds, by a dead comrade who had fallen on him, all German soldiers were killed. When the British reconnaissance vehicles crossed the German lines from the rear they were knocked out by a German anti-tank gun. Oberst Luxemburger, tied to one of the vehicles, was wounded. He was taken to a German hospital where he died soon after. Graf Clary regained consciousness after some time and crawled, badly wounded, in the direction of the village le Mesnil-Patry. Members of the II./26 found him and took him to the command post where he was given first aid by the battle reporter, Sturmmann Klöden.[24]

The war diary of the Inns of Court Regiment reports on this event on 8 June:

> 2 and 6a captured three German officers, among them a colonel and 3 [this probably means other ranks]. Upon withdrawing they were knocked out and lost all vehicles. Lieutenant Yodaiken and Lieutenant Wigram were killed, two other ranks missing. Four other ranks, led by Corporal Fowler, returned on foot using the compass for guidance.[25]

In retaliation, three Canadian prisoners of war were ordered shot near the command post of the II./26 on the following day. After the war, a so-called 'war criminals trial' took place because of this against Obersturmbannführer Siebken, Untersturmführer Schnabel and two men of the battalion. A report on this can be found elsewhere in this book.

✠

Panzer-Aufklärungs-Lehrabteilung 130 had received orders for 8 June to secure along the line Douet-Ellon-Trugny towards the north. It had been advised that SS-Panzeraufklärungsabteilung 12 would link up near Douet. Lehrabteilung 130 determined during the course of the day that a gap existed on its right flank to the Pz.A.A.12. It must be noted here that the Aufklärungsabteilung of the "HJ" Division had never received orders to establish a front to the north along the line Brouay-Chouain-Douet. Since the left flank of the Division would be open on arrival in the assembly area, it had been directed to bend its left wing backward and to reconnoitre to the north and northwest. Also, the left border of the Korps was, at the same time, the border between the 716. Inf.-Div. and the 352. Inf.-Div. This line ran from the crossroads near Fontenay-le-Pesnel to the west of Brouay to the coast east of Asnelles. Douet is located six kilometers west of Brouay. Thus, it was outside of the action sector of the Korps and also of the "HJ" Division.

During the morning of 8 June a scouting party of Aufklärungsabteilung 12 reconnoitered yet again in a northwesterly direction. The party was under the command of Oberscharführer Jura, commanders were Unterscharführers Löhr and Dörr. Jura rode in the point armored car, Löhr in the radio car behind. An entry in the war diary of the 6th Battalion The Durham Light Infantry states:

> An armored vehicle approached the Joint Post (near the railroad bridge across the Seulles river, Author) and knocked out two carriers. A weak infantry attack was beaten back, the armored vehicle was knocked out by mortar.[26]

After his return, Unterscharführer Löhr reported to Unterscharführer Kurt Fischer, who had remained behind because of repairs to his vehicle, that the point armored car had taken a mortar hit in front of the driver's hatch. The driver, Schütze (private) Bruno Lapzin, was severely injured and Jura was wounded in both legs. The gunner, Sturmmann Meyer, a cheerful Rhinelander, had pulled him from the turret and laid him on the ground behind the vehicle. He had applied tourniquets to both legs but had been unable to bring him back although he tried to do so under mortar fire. Jura was tall and heavy, Meyer was a not very strong eighteen-year old. The Abteilung commander, Sturmbannführer Bremer, immediately sent a scouting party from 3. Kompanie to the spot where the car had been knocked out. The party was unable to reach Jura and suffered losses itself. Obersturmführer Walter Hauck, commander of 2. Kompanie to which Jura belonged, led an assault party of sixteen men from Audrieu to the west to recover Jura. They were not able to reach the spot. The enemy had commenced an attack from the north in the sector between Brouay and the Seulles river in the meantime.

In the morning, at 10.30 hours, Lieutenant Kirk of the Durhams, had heard noises and interpreted them as an enemy assembly for an attack. Thus, he evacuated the Joint Post at the railroad bridge and withdrew to his company in Condé. One group was cut off and reached the company only later. Three men were missing.[27]

On orders of the 50th Infantry Division, the 8th Armoured Brigade Group (reinforced tank brigade) assembled in the St. Gabriel-Brecy-Martragny area on 8 June, beginning at 08.00 hours. Attached to the brigade were 147th Regiment Royal Field Artillery, the 1st Battalion The Dorsetshire Regiment, the 288th Anti-Tank Battery, the 'A' Company of the 2nd Battalion The Cheshire Regiment (machine gun battalion with heavy machine guns and heavy 10.7 cm mortars) and a portion of the 505th Field Company Royal Engineers. The mission was to attack from the assembly area to the south, to capture the Villers-Bocage area and to hold it in order to stop German reinforcements on their advance to the bridgehead. The first attack objective was the line from Hill 103 (southwest of le Haut d'Audrieu) to Hill 102 (0.5 kilometer south of Cristot, west to east). The spearhead consisted of the 61st Reconnaissance Regiment whose objective was to advance to the west via Loucelles, Audrieu, Hill 103 and St. Pierre and to reach Hill 111 (0.5 kilometer west of Tessel-Bretteville). Also, the 24th Lancers who would push ahead east of the 61st Reconnaissance Regiment together with one company of the Dorsets via the bridge on the eastern edge of Brouay, Cristot, Hill 102 to Fontenay-le-Pesnel.[28] The 61st Reconnaissance Regiment advanced towards the rail crossing north of le Bas d'Autrieu around 14.00 hours. It reached the crossing but was forced by the Aufklärungsabteilung to withdraw to the hilly area northwest of Loucelles. Aufklärungsabteilung 12 took approximately fifteen prisoners. The forces attacking Loucelles were stalled outside the town. It is not known which German troops fought there. It is probable that it was a small group of stragglers from the 352. Inf.-Div. The 24th Lancers were also pushed back near Brouay by the III./26 after they had become involved, probably by mistake, in the action near Putot and sustained losses. They limited themselves, together with the 1st Dorsets, to clear Loucelles. At 18.00 hours the Sherwood Rangers Yeomanry (tank unit) was ordered to bypass Loucelles and, moving to the west past Audrieu, to capture Hill 103. They crossed the railroad line west of the le Bas d'Autrieu station and advanced through the broken terrain west of Audrieu in front of the loose string of strong points of the Aufklärungsabteilung, sufficiently far removed, towards Hill 103. They encountered minimal resistance since they had found the gap between the Aufklärungsabteilung of the "HJ" and that of the Panzer-Lehr-Division. They pulled the anti-tank company and the mortar company into this position and prepared for the defense. Then they reconnoitered in the direction of St. Pierre where, according to reports by civilians, some 20 Germans were located.[29]

During these attacks, Audrieu and Cristot were under artillery fire. At 20.00 hours Audrieu came under the most concentrated artillery fire which included ships' artillery. Within one hour, the village was destroyed. Around 21.00 hours the fire was shifted to the castle gardens south of the village where the staff and the staff company of A.A.12 were located. They were shot to pieces. The fire attack lasted exactly one hour. Then there was a pause of five minutes, apparently to tempt the men to leave cover and retrieve the wounded. It was followed by another fire attack of twenty minutes. Most of the losses were incurred during that period. Based on the report by a British colonel who visited the then-chief of the staff company, Hauptsturmführer Gerd Frhr. von Reitzenstein in captivity, the fire attack was carried out by three artillery units and two battleships. The remains of the companies in action near Audrieu were pulled back, a number of armored personnel carriers and a 7.5 cm anti-tank gun were destroyed. The Abteilung was forced to abandon its previous lines in the face of high losses and the constant pressure of the superior enemy (tank unit with an attached tank reconnaissance unit and very strong artillery). It withdrew to the line southwest of Château Brouay-western edge of Cristot, western edge of les Hauts Vents to the area

500 meters northeast of St. Pierre. The Abteilung command post was moved to the area south of Cristot into terrain covered by meadows and hedges. Sturmbannführer Bremer, wounded in the shoulder, then handed over the Abteilung to Hauptsturmführer von Reitzenstein.

The assault party Hauck had observed the British advance to Hill 103 in its rear and was forced to break off the search for Oberscharführer Jura. It became known later that the critically wounded died on the same day. He was buried by the British near Condé-sue-Seulles and was later moved to the British war cemetery in Bayeux. The assault party took up a defensive position in an isolated farm. After risky attempts to break through, Hauck managed to rejoin the Abteilung with his men a few days later, probably on 12 June. Obersturmführer Hauck was awarded the Iron Cross I.[31] On 8 June 1944 the Aufklärungsabteilung lost four NCOs and fourteen men dead. Two officers, eight NCOs and thirty-eight men were wounded, one NCO and thirteen men missing. This was a total of eighty, a heavy toll.[32]

✠

While the fighting in Putot and at the Aufklärungsabteilung was still in full swing, Generalfeldmarschall Rommel arrived at the command post of the Panzer-Lehr-Division in Cheux. The time of his arrival is recorded as 19.05 hours in the diary of the Ib. Since Bayeux had been captured by the British during the night of 7–8 June and since they were facing almost no German troops in this sector, the Generalfeldmarschall ordered the Panzer-Lehr-Division not to continue the attack with the "HJ" Division. Instead, they were to re-assemble and attack from the area around Tilly in the direction of Bayeux on 9 June and to re-capture the city on the same day.

The commander of the Panzer-Lehr-Division, General-leutnant Fritz Bayerlein, testified during an interrogation by the Americans in 1948 that he had received the following order in the afternoon of 8 June from the I. SS-Panzerkorps:

> The attack together with the "HJ" Division northward to the coast will not be carried out. The Division will be removed from the Norrey-Brouay sector and shifted to the area around Tilly during the night 8–9 June. It will attack along the road Tilly-Bayeux in the morning of 9 June. Objective: capture Bayeux.

In the morning of 8 June the Panzer-Lehr-Division had the following forces ready south of the rail line Caen-Bayeux:
One Bataillon Panzergrenadierregiment 901 "near -Norrey" (no details are known),
One Bataillon Panzergrenadierregiment 902 near -Brouay,

Two artillery Abteilungen,

Panzeraufklärungs-Lehr-Abteilung 130 and

Panzer-Pionier-Bataillon 130 deployed in the Tilly-sur-Seulles area to secure the flanks.

Missing, mainly, were Panzer-Lehr-Regiment 130 and Panzerjäger-Lehr-Abteilung 130. The Panzer-Lehr-Division was not put into action as originally intended since the attack by Regiment 26 of the "HJ" Division near Norrey and Putot had not gained ground. Also, the enemy had begun an attack with strong tank forces, the 8th Armoured Brigade, on the left flank of the Division.[33]

NIGHT ATTACK BY THE 1. AND 4. KOMPANIE OF SS-PANZERREGIMENT 12, THE 15. (AUFKLÄRUNGS) KOMPANIE OF SS-PANZERGRENADIERREGIMENT 25 AND THE I./SS-PANZER-GRENADIERREGIMENT 26 ON NORREY AND BRETTEVILLE-L'ORGEILLEUSE ON 8–9 JUNE 1944

The 21. Panzerdivision was tied down in defense on both sides of the Orne river, as was Panzergrenadierregiment 25, linked up on the left. The II. Panzerabteilung of the "HJ" Division and the Panzer-Lehr-Division had been turned towards Bayeux. All this made an attack with limited objectives possible only for Panzergrenadierregiment 26 of the "HJ". This attack was considered necessary for two reasons: the Douvres radar station was still being doggedly defended but its relief required an early attack. In connection with this, there was the possibility of splitting the British/Canadian bridgehead. However, a successful attack required two to three new divisions. The terrain on both sides of the Mue creek and the lower Seulles river to its mouth near Courseulles-sur-Mer was favorable for such an attack. One condition for it was that la Villeneuve, le Bourg and Rots on the Rue Nationale from Caen to Bayeux and the two neighboring villages of Norrey and Bretteville–l'Orgeilleuse were in German hands. For the eventuality that the attack in this sector had to be halted for a time, it was necessary to establish a short connection between the inner flanks of Regiment 25 and Regiment 26. The left flank of the III./25 stood at the western corner of Buron, the right of the I./26 in St. Manvieu. Between them was a gap of 6.5 kilometers. It was secured, in a make-shift fashion, by the 16. (Pionier) Kompanie, the 14. (Flak) Kompanie and the 15. (Aufklärungs) Kompanie of Regiment 25 from Gruchy to Franqueville, and by the 2. and 3. Batterie (8.8) of Flakabteilung 12. The Divisionbegleitkompanie (escort company) provided a weak guard near Villeneuve. From there to St. Manvieu a two kilometers wide gap remained. Neither Panzergrenadierregiment had available any reserves since they had moved everything they had to their front lines because of the width of their sectors. If the right flank of Regiment 26 could have been successfully moved to the north of Rots the front line would have been shortened by 3.5 kilometers.

The Divisional commander had driven to the sector of Regiment 25 together with the Regimental commander. Thereafter, he ordered that, during the night 8–9 June, the Panther companies of I. Abteilung, expected to have arrived by then, together with a motorcycle company of Regiment 25 and supported by light motorized field howitzers (Wespen = wasps) were to attack and capture Bretteville. Because of the Allied air superiority and in order to surprise the enemy, the attack had to start at dusk in the evening of 8 June.

Only two companies of the I. Panzerabteilung had arrived and were ready for action. They were the 1. Kompanie under the command of Hauptsturmführer Berlin and the 4. under Hauptsturmführer Hans Pfeiffer. The 15. (Kradschützen Kompanie—motorcycle riflemen)/25 was led by Hauptsturmführer von Büttner. 2. Batterie of I. Artillerieabteilung under Obersturmführer Timmerbeil was attached. The Kampfgruppe was commanded by Standartenführer Kurt Meyer. The commander of the Panzerregiment, Obersturmbannführer Max Wünsche accompanied the attack by his Panzers since the staff of I. Abteilung had not yet arrived.[34]

The Regina Rifles had been observing the terrain ahead of them closely all day. At 08.85 hours they reported to the Brigade enemy Panzers approximately one kilometer west of Franqueville. D-Company in le Bourg and Villeneuve reported a significant number of enemy Panzers at 11.00 hours approximately 900 meters from its front lines. Based on this, the company was withdrawn at 17.00 hours to Cardonville on the rail line south of Bretteville, to reinforce the 'fortress' of the Battalion. C-Company was in positions at the southern edge of Norrey. It reported at the same time that it had repulsed an infantry attack but was under attack from Panzers. It requested artillery support. This was provided and the attack was beaten back. The "HJ" Division knew nothing of these two attacks, they must have been mistakes.

With the dusk (sunset was just before 22 hours) the Kampfgruppe began the attack from the area south of Franqueville. 4. Panzerkompanie moved on the right of the road, 1. Panzerkompanie to the left. Most of the motorcycle riflemem had mounted the Panzers. Standartenführer Kurt Meyer accompanied the troops in a sidecar motorcycle as he had promised to his 15. Kompanie during training for the first attack. The Regiment medical officer, Sturmbannführer Dr. Gatternig and Obersturmführer Dr. Stift also accompanied the Kampfgruppe. The Kampfgruppe rolled past the firing position of an 8.8 cm Flak battery of the Division. A group of motorcycle riflemen and the vehicle of the artillery observer drove behind Kurt Meyer, 100 meters further behind came the rest of the motorcycle riflemen. The Panthers drove at high speed through the open and flat terrain towards le Bourg. The Regimental commander Kurt Meyer raced into the small village on his motorcycle. The first group of motorcycle riflemen dismounted and advanced on foot to the bridge across the Mue creek. The town was free of the enemy, the bridge not destroyed. A few minutes later the Panzers arrived. They advanced across the bridge and assembled in the same formation as previously for the attack on Bretteville. In the meantime it was almost dark. The 4. Kompanie rolled along both sides of the road towards the village. Hauptsturmführer Hans Pfeiffer was on the road in the second Panzer, the platoons were staggered to left and right rear. 1. Panzerkompanie drove on the left of them. The Panzers stopped a few hundred meters from the town on the front side of an elevation sloping down toward the village. Fire from machine guns and anti-tank guns hit them. Both Panther companies concentrated fire on the entrance to the town, supported by the accompanying 2. Batterie. Then, 4. Kompanie raced toward the village at full speed. Sturmmann Hans Kesper, driver of a Panther in IV. Zug, remembers:

> My company advanced to the village along the road, the Panzers staggered one behind the other. We, of IV. Zug, were on the right side of the road which led to the village. I saw a church straight ahead of me. We were taking heavy anti-tank fire, some houses were in flames. I can still today hear commander Pfeiffer yell: 'Set the houses on fire so that we can see something!' The Panzer ahead of me took a direct hit.[35]

The point Panzers reached the edge of town where concentrated anti-tank fire hit them. Pfeiffer's Panzer took a hit and was quickly engulfed in bright flames.

One of the platoon (Zug) leaders, Untersturmführer Reinhold Fuss, reports on the fighting by the motorcycle riflemen:

> We were surprised by violent anti-tank fire. A great number of anti-tank guns seemed to be in positions along the edge of town. Canadian infantry was in position in the trenches to the left and right of the tree-lined road running from the northeast to Bretteville. They peppered the mounted grenadiers with wild rifle fire. I immediately ordered my Zug to dismount on their own and to advance in infantry style. Regrettably, we had already suffered some losses. In the meantime, Hauptsturmführer von Büttner was critically wounded at this same road. Among other comrades, SDG Waldvogel was killed there. All this happened still outside of Bretteville. It was impossible to push into the village. After only the first 50–100 meters we had to withdraw under the vast enemy fire superiority. Von Büttner had died by then. Panzermeyer then sent out two assault teams: I. Zug under my command was to swing right, II. Zug under Untersturmführer Fehling to the left, and both advance to the center of the village. There we would fire signal flares if we did not encounter enemy tanks. In that case, the Panzers, together with the rest of the infantry, would capture the town. Fehling was discovered and pulled back immediately,

as I learned later. I reached the church with only six men after a lot of violent shooting. The rest of my Zug, already decimated by the previous fighting, was lost along the way. I fired the arranged signal flares and withdrew with my six men into the interior of the church since we were getting fire from all sides. There I awaited the arrival of the Panzers. They did not show up.[36]

Max Wünsche ordered 1. Kompanie to detour the village by swinging left and to push into the center of town from the southwest. This was to revive the attack along the main road. The commander of I. Zug of 1. Kompanie experienced this as follows:

Hauptsturmführer Berlin ordered me by radio to drive around the village to the south and to penetrate into the town from the west. A few houses were burning on the southern edge of town, as was the railroad station outside the village to the south. The plan was that I should push through between the edge of town and the station. In order to offer a target for the shortest possible time against the burning buildings in the darkness, I ordered the Zug into line formation, and to break through as quickly as possible. Despite this, all three vehicles took anti-tank hits at almost the same moment, from the edge of town to the right, as they were driving through the dangerous line. The vehicle on the right burned as brightly as a torch, probably from a direct hit to the engine compartment. Its crew returned later, unscathed. My own vehicle took a hit which penetrated the turret. The loader was badly wounded, blinded, and had a number of broken bones. The electrical system failed. Unterscharführer Rust's vehicle on the left only took a hit to the gear cover and remained ready for action. I reported to Hauptscharführer Berlin from this vehicle by radio and received orders to turn around. We pulled my loader from the interior and rested him on the rear. Then, we drove back to the road with the two remaining vehicles. There I made sure that my loader received medical attention.

Somewhat north of the road I spotted a slit trench in the dim light of the explosions. In this trench lay Canadians, strangely with their faces down. When I asked whether they intended to sleep through the war, they got up and surrendered. They were six or eight, and I had them transported back to the Division.

I then took the submachine gun from the vehicle and ordered the crew to repair the electrical system. I walked forward to Hauptsturmführer Berlin to give him a verbal report. Then I left on foot to take a closer look at the situation in the village. Just after I set out I met Untersturm-führer Nehrlich, orderly officer with the regimental staff, who joined me. His weapons were a Canadian rifle and a rifle grenade in his pant pocket.

At the entrance to the town we found stacks of ammunition crates. We entered the village along the walls which bordered the gardens and houses on the street side. As we advanced along the southern edge of town, two troop transport trucks of 15. Kompanie passed us. This Kompanie had arrived in the meantime and they planned to push into town in this manner. At an intersection in the center of town sat a Panzer V, probably from 4. Kompanie. It was still glowing weakly. When the first truck reached this Panzer, it was hit by two explosive charges, probably coming from the houses. Some Panzergrenadiers ran back, yelling. The second truck pulled back. At the same time, lively infantry fire set in. We rushed through a gate and took cover behind a two-meter high garden wall. When the noise of fighting died down, and the calls for help from Canadian and German wounded grew weaker, Nehrlich and I found ourselves in the center of town among Canadians. We could not pull back along the street, and wherever we looked across the garden wall, we encountered Canadians.

Daylight came around 04.00 hours. We jumped across a garden wall to the east into another garden which was free of Canadians. We took cover at a wall to the east, in a willow tree. This tree extended to the other side of the wall and across the path behind it which was being used by the Canadians. After some time, one or both of the Kompanies carried out another attack on the town from the south. It was not successful, but it distracted the Canadians so that we managed to cross the path. We reached the street through an adjoining market-garden and reported back to Obersturmbann-führer Wünsche.[37]

Sturmmann Leopold Lengheim, gunner in the second Panzer of III. Zug of 1. Kompanie, recalls his experience of the attack:

We were firing from all barrels. Untersturmführer Teichert's II. Zug attacked south of the village. We were located more to the west of town. Zugführer Dietrich in Panther 135 ordered us by radio to follow him. Teichert was immobile in the village, surrounded by enemy infantry. His Panzer had taken a hit to the tracks. We drove behind Panther 135 in the direction of the village to get Teichert out. Panther 135 was hit from a row of bushes, approximately 100 meters away. The crew had to bail out. All, except the radio operator, made it. Obstructed by the heavy smoke from the knocked out vehicle, we nevertheless fired a few anti-tank shells in the direction of the row of bushes. Untersturmführer Dietrich and his crew came running towards our Panzer and waved us back. We did a 180 degree turn and got out of firing range of the Canadians. After some 500 meters we found cover at a row of trees and set up a firing position.

Through my gunner's sight I watched a virtual wall of fire coming at us from about 900 meters away. We no longer had time to think, load-fire, load-fire, as fast as we could. Then it was over for us, too. Hits to the hull and the gun had destroyed the accuracy of the aiming mechanism. We were firing much too short. The next hit came just below the cupola. The cupola and the head of our commander Hohnecker were gone. Our driver, Binder, understood the situation. He turned around at full throttle and drove into cover. We were ordered by radio, no longer ready for action, to drive in the direction of the repair shop. With our nerves on edge and our dead comrade in the Panzer, we drove in the direction of Martinville. There we buried our comrade Hohnecker.[38]

The attack by I./26 left no discernible impact in Bretteville. In particular, infantry was lacking. If it had arrived then, the initial success could have been enlarged and the objective could probably have been accomplished. Wünsche drove with his command Panzer to Norrey. He came under heavy fire, but found no German troops and had to turn back. With heavy hearts, Kurt Meyer and Max Wünsche had to make the decision to break off the attack. They withdrew behind the Mue creek. Obersturmführer Chemnitz reports further:

The Panzers were now coming back from the attack. Since the road was running on an embankment, the drivers had to rely on signals to drive onto the road. Obersturmbannführer Wünsche was doing this first, then I took over. One of the Panzers had turned around on the road. I was standing in front of it and giving signals to the driver. Behind me, on the right, stood Wünsche. On the left, Nehrlich. Just then the Panzer was hit by a shell from a Canadian tank on the front armor. Wünsche was slightly wounded by the fragments, I took fragments from my head down to my knees. Nehrlich, however, was so badly wounded by fragments that he bled to death during his immediate transport to the dressing station by side-car motorcycle.

I drove in the car of the medical officer via Ancienne Abbaye to the dressing station at the entrance of Caen. There, Untersturmführer Dr. Jordan looked after the wounded.[39]

For unknown reasons, 3. and 2. Kompanie of I./26 could not take advantage of the attack by the Panzers and motorcycle riflemen on Bretteville. However, 1. Kompanie, led by Hauptsturmführer Helmut Eggert, was able to capture Rots against only minimal resistance after advancing via la Villeneuve and le Bourg. It dug in for defense at the north and northwest edges of Rots. I. Zug and the heavy Zug were in positions west of the Mue creek near le

Hamel. II. Zug was located at the northern edge of the town, its front line facing north. Some Panthers of 4. Kompanie took up ambush positions. Two each sat south of the church, at the crossroads in the northeast corner of the castle park, and near the road intersection in le Bourg. An attached anti-tank gun of 4./26 was spotted by the enemy as it went into position. This gun and the village immediately came under heavy fire from artillery and from tanks in position on a line of hills west of the village. There were considerable losses. A wide gap still existed between 1./26 and the two Kompanies of I./26 which were stuck south of Norrey. In order to close this gap and to secure the important road bridge across the Mue creek in le Bourg, the Divisionbegleit-kompanie was ordered on 9 June at 22.00 hours to link up with 1./26 in the southwest sector of Rots and in le Bourg and to prepare for defense. Available for this mission were the Schützenzug (riflemen), the Kradschützenzug (motorcycle riflemen platoon), and a heavy machine gun squad. This small Kampfgruppe was attached to I./26. The commander of the Schützenzug, Unterscharführer Leo Freund, reports on his experiences:

> I was checking on our machine gun positions at the edge of town when one of our men suddenly shouted: ' There's someone walking towards us from the front!' A glimpse through the binoculars showed that it was an unarmed Canadian moving towards us along the road ditch. We all took full cover and jumped out when he was right in front of us. I addressed him in German: 'Well, buddy, what are you looking for on this side?' Laughingly, he promptly replied in German: 'I've had it up to here.' Of course, we were initially at a loss for words, then everyone joined the laughter. I later took the prisoner to the divisional command post and handed him over to the Ic. During the afternoon of the same day, a jeep carrying two Canadians drove along the same road towards our position. We let it through and challenged it between the houses. When the surprised Canadians went for their weapons, we had to open fire. The jeep became an item of great interest to us, and many took it for a drive. Thereafter, it served the Kompanie chief, Obersturmführer Guntrum, as his official vehicle.[40]

The war diary of the Regina Rifles records the following for the night 8–9 June:

> The battalion command post was under attack by Panthers and infantry from 22.30 hours onward. At 00.30 the battalion command post came under grenade and machine gun fire when the enemy pushed into the town with Panzers and infantry. One Panther pulled up next to the command post. It was knocked out by a PIAT (anti-tank rocket). In the meantime, everyone had a hot time. The Panz-

ers took out the men in the slit trenches throughout the village. They also knocked out our anti-tank gun. The whole sky was lit by burning roofs and Panzers on fire, as well as by our parachute flares. At 03.15 hours a Sonderkfz. 140 (armored car) came racing up from Bretteville. It was knocked out in front of the command post by a PIAT. During the battle we lost seven carriers, one of which was loaded with ammunition. Five enemy Panzers were knocked out in the vicinity of the command post.

At 04.23 hours the Panzers pulled back from the area of the command post and stopped some distance away. We requested artillery fire on the Panzers. This was approved. We were informed that tank support would arrive at dawn. At 04.45 the enemy directed determined attacks against all companies. They were thrown back.[41]

Lt. Col. Matheson, a member of the Regina Rifles who experienced the battle, reported to the editor of the history of the 3rd Canadian Infantry Division:

A total of twenty-two Panthers circled the battalion command post and the positions of A-Company during the night. It is difficult to describe the existing confusion. The connection with all the others, except D Company, was lost. Fires and flares lit up the terrain and several times the enemy seemed to believe that the resistance had faltered. A daredevil German dispatch rider raced through Bretteville on a captured Canadian motorcycle. He was only stopped by the commander's submachine gun. Some time later a German officer drove directly up to the battalion command post. He got out and looked around for a few seconds until an excited anti-tank soldier fired his rocket at him and scored a direct hit.[42]

Kampfgruppe Meyer/Wünsche and I./26 had suffered heavy losses.

	Dead			Wounded			Missing		
	Officers	NCOs	Men	Officers	NCOs	Men	Officers	NCOs	Men
Pz.Rgt.	2	3	7	4	3	23	-	-	-
Rgt. 25	1	5	13	1	1	14	1	1	7
2./A.R.	-	-	-	-	1	4	-	-	-
I./26	-	2	10	-	6	42	-	1	-
Total	3	10	30	5	11	83	1	2	7

Total losses were: 43 dead, 99 wounded, 10 missing, for a total of 152 lost.

The severity of the battles in the Norrey sector are also reflected in this further report by Untersturmführer Reinhold Fuss. He had lost contact with the Kompanie in Bretteville during the withdrawal and remained in the church with six men. He writes:

> I found myself on the balcony together with six men of my Zug. After three sleepless nights, they were now exhausted and asleep on the floor. I could barely keep my eyes open to watch the immediate vicinity of the church and the through-road close-by in the falling dawn. I completely missed the priest entering the church at approximately 05.30 hours. I noticed him when he uttered a shout. He threw up his arms and ran, yelling constantly, out of the church. I immediately woke my comrades. As we ran down the stairs from the balcony to the interior of the church, some Canadian soldiers already came storming into the church, firing wildly. We fired a few salvos from our submachine guns and the machine gun and were able to leave the church through a side door. We were running, in a group, across the street into the cemetery, accompanied by wild firing from the masses of Canadians standing in the street. Two comrades, Zimmermann and Ziermann, did not make it.
>
> In the cemetery we found a bush-covered hollow and prepared for the defense to the last. But, while we did come under fire, even from anti-tank guns, they finally and miraculously left us alone. The Canadians probably figured that we would eventually come out on our own, driven by hunger and thirst.
>
> So we were lying there, exhausted and emaciated. One of our boys wanted to fire a bullet from his 08 pistol through his head. We barely managed to stop him. Unterscharführer Flixeder seriously requested me to transfer him to II. Zug. He wanted to express that it had been an idiocy to push through to the center of the village under these circumstances. One can imagine how I felt inside, we had certainly arrived at the lowest point our nerves could endure. Thus, we spent six days in this hollow. We took turns sleeping to prevent each other from snoring. On the second day we already felt somewhat better. All the time, of course, we were hoping that the town would finally be captured by our unit. It was impossible to break out. During the nights we could hear a large number of guards wandering about in the immediate vicinity, waiting for us. During the days we were grimly listening to the artillery observer shouting from the church: 'one-hundred more, two-hundred more' etc. From the houses came the sound of radio music, among others a constant repetition of the Blue Danube waltz, and loud yelling by the soldiers. On the sixth day, after constantly taking turns working, we had completed digging a hole into the adjoining wall with a bay-

onet to the point where we could break out during the night. Two
comrades begged to be left behind. They were too exhausted. We
were unable to change their minds. After crawling through a cellar
we reached a pasture, covered with vehicles. Despite the many
shouts of 'stop!' we made it to the edge of town and after some difficult jumps, we reached the woods near Norrey. There we spent, the
three of us left, the next day in thick bushes. During the following
night we made it to the Krause Bataillon, overjoyed. There we
received food and liquids for the first time.

I was certain to have seen Zimmermann lying dead in the street.
After my return to the Regiment I then wrote the usual letter to his
parents. Twenty years after the war I learned that he had been taken
prisoner, badly wounded. He had been looking for me for years.
After locating me through the Red Cross we have been meeting reg-
ularly and are keeping in close contact. Through hear-say I found
out later that Ziermann was also captured. If and where he returned
to after his release, I do not know. He was from Eastern Germany
and would have certainly contacted me if it had been at all possible.

The names of the two men who made it back with me were Hans
Derkogner and Wittich, whose first name I have forgotten. While
Wittich was killed in action later, Derkogner, who was from Wolfs-
berg in Carinthia, returned home after a short imprisonment. He
was an outstanding skier, downhill and jumping. He captured the
title of academic world champion in ski-jumping in St. Moritz in
1947. He died in 1956 from injuries sustained in a motorcycle accident.[43]

The daring surprise attack by the small Meyer/Wünsche Kampfgruppe
had scored a significant initial success. The enemy had been maneuvered
into a very difficult situation. However, because of the lack of German
infantry, full advantage could not be taken of the situation. The tactic of surprise, using mobile, fast infantry and Panzers even in small, numerically inferior Kampfgruppen, had often been practiced and proven in Russia. This
tactic, however, had not resulted in the expected success here against a
courageous and determined enemy, who was ready for defense and well
equipped. Through good battle field observation, the enemy had recognized
the outlines of the preparations for the attack and drawn his own conclusions. The deployment of D Company to Cardonville had prevented a breakthrough by 2./26 from the farm south of the rail line to Bretteville, only
1,000 meters away. The anti-tank defenses all around the village were strong
enough to thwart all attempts by the Panzers to by-pass the town to the south
and north. The surprising use of parachute flares with glaring magnesium
light blinded the Panthers and clearly outlined them to the enemy Pak. This
enemy was especially strong in the defense and could not be taken by sur-

prise. He fought with determination and courage. The question remained, how the success of the capture of Rots could be enlarged.

On 8 June the Division came into possession of valuable enemy documents. When searching the battlefield of Authie and Franqueville, the complete radio documentation had been found undamaged in a knocked-out tank.

In the evening of this day, two Canadian Carrettes, coming from Putot, drove across the mined bridge at the eastern edge of Brouay right in front of the barrel of an anti-tank gun of the 12./26. They were knocked out. One of them burned out with the crew inside. The other was almost undamaged. Its crew, a first lieutenant and his driver, was killed. A coded map was found inside the Carrette. It showed the terrain on both sides of the mouth of the Orne river to the area south of Caen. Code names which started with the same letters as the names of the real villages, rivers, etc. were printed on the map. For instance, the Orne river was called Orinoco on the map. Terrain impassable to tanks was particularly marked. The positions and fortifications of the Atlantik-Wall were also shown. Their armament, down to the machine guns and mortars, was indicated.

This obviously perfect enemy reconnaissance frightened the troops. These details could not be the result of airborne reconnaissance but only of spying. Later, there was an explanation for this. Counter-intelligence reported that they had arrested a Frenchman and convicted him of espionage. He testified that, as a vegetable dealer, he had daily driven up and down the coast near the mouth of the Orne river for years until the start of the invasion. During these drives he had scouted the German positions and subsequently reported on them. This had been possible, despite the order by Feldmarschall Rommel when he took over Heeresgruppe B that all French civilians be evacuated from the vicinity of the coastal positions.

A notebook with entries was found on a captain killed in action. It contained notes on the treatment of civilians and prisoners. According to these notes, no prisoners were to be taken if they might impede the attacking Allied forces.

The code names on the map and codes for tactical operations were used in the enemy radio transmissions for some time. This made it easier for the communications intelligence section of the Division to interpret enemy radio exchanges.

All other documentation, not needed by the Division, was passed on through regular channels.

ATTACK BY 3./SS-PANZERREGIMENT 12 ON NORREY ON 9 JUNE 1944

In the evening of 8 June, the supreme commander of Panzergruppe West, General der Panzertruppen Freiherr Leo Geyr von Schweppenburg, took over command in the right sector of 7. Armee. In the morning of 9 June, he judged the situation as follows: The enemy would only commence an attack on a broad front when he was thoroughly prepared. One could not wait for this attack, but had to forestall it through one's own attack from the Caen area to the north. He expected that the Americans would not push into the open left flank of the Panzergruppe. However, this possibility had still to be considered. General von Geyr drove to the Caen area and surveyed the terrain from a tower of the Ardennes abbey. He ordered the Panzerdivisions to be prepared, as of the evening of 10 June, for a night attack to the north along both sides of the narrow gauge rail line from Caen to Luc-sur-Mer. From the Ardennes abbey, General von Geyr observed the start of an attack by Panzers of the "HJ" Division. As soon as they had left the western suburbs of Caen, they were attacked by bombers. This reinforced his opinion that, without Luftwaffe support, only a night attack was possible.[44]

The Panzer attack was an action by 3. Panzerkompanie which had arrived only during the previous evening, not in time to take part in the attack on Bretteville. It can no longer be clarified how the plan for this attack came about. The commander of the Panzerregiment had been at the main field dressing station before noon of 9 June to have his wounds looked after. As he expected, the order for the attack was issued by Standarten-führer Kurt Meyer. It seems likely he believed that an attack south of the rail line, somewhat shielded from Bretteville, could be successful in capturing Norrey. More so, since the enemy was weakened by the fighting of the previous night. The capture of Norrey was a basic condition for the renewed attack to the north. Kurt Meyer's judgment was probably reinforced by the plan for 10–11 June on which General von Geyr had briefed him at the Ardennes monastery.

3. Panzerkompanie had moved in on 8 June via Thury-Harcourt. It advanced to Authie by way of Carpiquet and Franqueville. Unterscharführer and leader of a half-Zug, Alois Morawetz, remembers this day as follows:

> We drove past an airfield, located to the left of the road, and turned northward. We were traversing an area where a tank battle seemed to have taken place the previous day. A number of knocked-out light tanks, probably English, were scattered through the terrain. I think that I also saw knocked-out Panzer IVs. We turned towards the northwest and traveled through completely open terrain. We had not seen any German units for a long time when a Kübelwagen (jeep) approached us from ahead. It was Panzermeyer. On his orders we continued in a northwesterly or westerly direction. After approximately one kilometer we reached a village. It was Château de St. Louet, on the outskirts of Authie. The Kompanie took up defensive positions on its northwest edge. For approximately half-an hour we came under heavy fire, probably from ships' artillery. Although we were located on the front slope, we were unbelievably lucky and

suffered no losses. We then pulled back to positions on the back slope, immediately at the edge of the village. The night passed quietly in our positions. From some distance to the southwest we could hear loud battle noises, also Panzer guns. As we learned later, it was an attack by our 1. [and 4.] Kompanie on Bretteville.

On 9 June, at approximately 09.00 hours, we were relieved by a Panzer IV Kompanie of II. Abteilung. We drove in a southwesterly direction towards Rots. I was driving as the last vehicle of our Kompanie. We had gone less than 200 meters when I turned to look back and saw that the first Panzer IV began to burn. The artillery fire had started again in the meantime.

In the vicinity of Villeneuve, the commanders were briefed on the situation and ordered to attack Norrey which was held by strong enemy forces. I./26 was to carry out an attack simultaneously with theirs. The attack was to start at 13.00 hours. The Kompanie was to be commanded by Hauptmann Lüddemann since Obersturmführer von Ribbentrop, the Kompanie chief, was wounded. He had left the hospital without being discharged and had just arrived at the Kompanie. But, with his arm in splints, he was unable to lead it. At least, he wanted to be close to his men. Alois Morawetz continues his report:

We crossed the rail line Caen-Bayeux through an underpass, turned right and took up positions on a back slope.

The twelve Panthers were lined up next to each other at a right angle to the rail line. My vehicle sat at the right flank, close to the rail embankment. I. Zug under Untersturm-führer Bogensberger was on the left. II. Zug under Untersturmführer Alban was in the center. III. Zug, led by Untersturmführer Stagge, was deployed on the right. Hauptmann Lüddemann sat somewhere in the middle. The time was approximately 12.30 hours. In front of us it was relatively quiet. There were almost no fighter-bombers in the air, as was usual for noon-time. A short time later we set out through the slowly rising terrain. After approximately 500 meters we reached completely open and level terrain, meadows and fields. Half left ahead of us lay Norrey. I was driving approximately twenty to fifty meters to the left of the rail line. It ran through a gully, beginning at a lineman's cottage. On the left edge of the gully was probably a hedge which provided us with some cover against being spotted. The whole Kompanie drove as a body, at high speed and without any stops, in a broad front. When the left flank was just outside the village, the order came in: 'Wartesaal (waiting room), swing to the left!' (Wartesaal was the code name for our Kompanie). I ordered my driver to go at full speed and pull slightly to the left. Until then we had not experienced any resistance. Approximately 1,000 meters ahead was a railroad station where some movement could be spotted. I was driving already approximately thirty meters ahead of the Kompanie in a slow left turn, in order not to fall behind. At that moment, after a muffled bang and a swaying as if the track had been ripped off, the vehicle came to a stop.

It was quiet inside the vehicle. I thought we had driven onto a mine. When I looked to the left to check the situation, I happened to see the turret being torn off the Panzer driving on the left flank. At the same moment, after another minor explosion, my vehicle began to burn. The machine gun ammunition caught on fire and there was a crackling noise like dry wood burning. Since we were to push into the town, I had closed the turret hatch moments before. I tried, without success, to open the turret hatch. I could only lift it with the spindle but could not swing it out. Paul Veith, the gunner sitting in front of me, had apparently been seriously injured by fragments from the hit. Veith did not move. I tried for a long time with all my energy to swing out the hatch. I was only successful when I tried different height settings on the lift crank. It had probably been damaged by the hit. I jumped out, fell on the rear and was unconscious for a short time. Then I saw flames coming out of the open hatch as if from a blowtorch. I got up and tried to jump off. However, I could not keep my balance and landed, head-first, on the ground. I do not know how long I lay there. Then I got on my feet and saw to my left, along the same line as my vehicle, other burning Panzers. Among them was Stagge's. Approximately 200 to 400 meters behind the Panzer, I spotted the sidecar motorcycle of our medic, Unterscharführer Gose. I walked towards it. Members of the crews from the other knocked-out Panzers also arrived there. They were burned, without exception, in their faces and hands. In the meantime we had noticed that the whole area was under infantry fire. The medic's driver (Unterscharführer Harting, Author) was trying to start the motor again. It had stalled after taking a hit to the left cylinder head. After a few tries, the motor started again. Gose glanced at the men standing around and, since I was apparently the worst burnt, he put me in the sidecar. We turned around and drove back. After a few meters, Gose, who sat in the rear seat, dropped backwards off the moving motorcycle. I drew the driver's attention to this since he had not noticed it. We drove on another 200 meters or so back to the lineman's cottage. There we stopped. I kept the motor running, using both my hands on the twist-grip, while the driver made his way forward to the medic. After approximately ten minutes the driver came back again and told me that Gose did not have a chance. He had been critically wounded in the stomach. The remaining five

Panzers were now withdrawing, firing rapidly. When I left with the motorcycle driver from the lineman's cottage in the direction of la Villeneuve, the Panzers were approximately at the same line as the cottage. Seven of the 12 attacking Panzers were left at the front. From what I can remember, all seven were on fire. We made it back to la Villeneuve. I think we met some men of the Kompanie baggage train near a restaurant. The motorcycle driver left me there and returned to the front to pick up more wounded. As I learned in the late afternoon at the main dressing station, 15 of the 35 crew members from the knocked-out Panzers had been killed. The rest, with few exceptions, were wounded, almost all with burn wounds.[45]

The history of 3. Kompanie supplements this report in specific points:

After bailing out, the wounded, mostly more or less seriously burned, tried first to reach the cover of the railroad embankment. Initially, they were prevented from getting there by an enemy machine gun which had taken up position in the lineman's cottage on the road Norrey-Bretteville. Only after Unterscharführer Hermani had removed this obstacle with a few hand grenades did the situation become more bearable. While the whole sector was under concentrated enemy fire, some of it from ships' guns, the wounded dragged themselves along the rail line back to the starting point of the attack at the railroad underpass.[46]

Obersturmführer von Ribbentrop observed the attack and writes on the subject:

After the attack had advanced a few hundred meters, five or six Panzers went up in flames within a short period of time. The attack was broken off. As far as I remember, Hauptmann Lüddemann returned and was sent to the hospital afterwards. I did not see him again.[47]

He was killed in action on 14 June near Fontenay.

Max Wünsche had just returned from the main dressing station. He had suffered wounds from fragments and a slight concussion. He saw the first Panzers in flames. In a letter, he wrote: 'I could have cried for rage and sorrow.'[48]

Without doubt, this attack was an unfortunate operation right from the start. Once again it was proven that surprise raids had no expectation of success here. As has been quoted from the war diary of the Regina Rifles, the battalion had been promised tanks for the morning of 9 June. They had arrived at 05.15 hours.

On this day, 3. Kompanie lost one NCO and one soldier dead, two officers, four NCOs and eleven men wounded. One officer, two NCOs and eleven men were missing. Most of these were probably killed. Seven Panthers were totally lost.[49]

The losses of Panzers in the first battles required fastest possible repairs in order to always have the largest possible number of action-ready vehicles. It now showed, how valuable it had been that so much emphasis had been placed on the fitting of the repair companies and the training of their members at the time of setting up the Division. However, these men were not only superb and skilled mechanics and technicians. They had also received thorough training as soldiers since they had to do their work close to the front lines, under enemy air activity and, occasionally, artillery fire. When recovering knocked-out or damaged Panzers from the battlefield, these men could also find themselves within the field of fire of light and heavy infantry weapons or tanks. So they had to be able to behave in an appropriate manner under fire. This, then, also required the fighting morale and stability of a fighter. How much emphasis was put upon this soldierly attitude was indicated by the fact that the Stabsscharführer of the maintenance company of I. Panzerabteilung, Haupt-scharführer (1st sergeant) Georg Fahrbach, was awarded the Iron Cross I and the Wound Badge in Gold. The fighting troops owed these men a debt of gratitude. A report by Sturm-mann Helmut Pock of the maintenance company of I. Panzer-abteilung, which was commanded by Untersturmführer Dipl. Ing. (graduate engineer) Robert Maier, offers an insight. He wrote:

> We were at the southern edge of the town of Venoix, not far from the city of Caen. Our small squad had made camp in a meadow covered with trees and shrubs. The terrain gradually sloped from the road to the Odon river. We parked our prime movers, well dispersed, under the numerous groups of trees and bushes. Some of the men had gone to look for quarters while the rest of us made sure that the equipment was well camouflaged. When this job was finished, I went with my comrade to see what quarters they had set aside for us. We were pleasantly surprised. Ours was a small villa named 'Sanssouci'. Its inhabitants had fled, but almost all furniture and fixtures were still there. We were not lacking anything. A soldier profits from the ability to quickly feel at home anywhere. So we were particularly well off there. My secret hope, to get some rest, regrettably did not come true. Immediately, the order came: 'You, you and you, outside. There's a Panzer out there! It must be repaired.' We objected that we could do nothing in the darkness. But there were several Panzers by then, waiting for us. This meant lots and lots of work. I was given one of them. It had a damaged steering gear which had to be repaired. To get into the interior of a vehicle we often

climbed in through the turret. As I climbed up and was feeling for a hold, my hands gripped a wet, slippery substance. I asked the gunner about it. 'Our commander was killed in action. His head was ripped off. I know that the whole interior is a mess,' the poor guy answered. It had been his first time in action. 'It's all right, there's nothing you can do,' I tried to console him. I slowly wiped my hands and was suddenly out of words to say.

Working in the interior of the Panzer with the hatch closed made me sweat a lot. The steering gear could only be reached from the driver and radio operator side of the Panzer. There was hardly enough room to sit. So I worked like a contortionist and had to twist my body and hands into impossible positions to reach everywhere.

'Bastl' was wandering around, checking to see if we needed advice or help. I showed him the damaged parts I had removed. Bastl gave me valuable pointers which had to be remembered when putting the complicated mechanism together. I was surprised to see Bastl wandering about like this, the explosions of shells were close-by.

I only saw Oberscharführer Hermann when I reported to him that I had carried out my orders. 'You can lie down now. I want everyone to be washed and shaved in the morning. Tell the others also.' With this, I was dismissed for the moment. We did not use the beds in 'our' villa. We preferred the hard floor, we had got used to it. As a special luxury we used one of the carpets, which could be found in almost every room, to sleep on.[50]

The members of 2. Panzerkompanie, which had arrived as the last of I. Abteilung at the invasion front, also had a memorable event on 9 June. During its advance the Kompanie passed by the command post of Panzergruppe West in la Caine, six kilometers northwest of Thury-Harcourt, as reported by Standarten-oberjunker (officer cadet) Paul Dienemann. Located there was the previous chief of 2. Kompanie, holder of the Knight's Cross, Hauptsturmführer Wilhelm Beck. He had lately directed the officer cadet course of the Division. The course was disbanded at the start of the invasion. He then was assigned as the liaison officer of I. SS-Panzerkorps to the Panzergruppe:

Full of joy, he waved his arms in greeting and shouted: 'Let's get at it, boys! Show them what the Second can do!' This would be the last time I met him. I had been with him since early 1940. During the Russian campaign in 1941 and 1942 I was his gunner with an assault gun in the LAH (Leibstandarte Adolf Hitler Division).[51]

Helmut Pock, who had probably met his former chief before noon, remembers it this way:

In the vicinity of the Divisional command post we met Hauptsturmführer Beck. We knew him from Russia where he had earned his
Knight's Cross near Charkow. Beck was one of those officers who
combined the personality of officer and human in a rare, magical
manner, exemplary in all his actions. Oberscharführer Hermann
personally knew Beck very well and exchanged a few words with
him. Unter-scharführer Sebastian and I stood a respectful distance
away. Hauptsturmführer Beck asked if we had anything to drink for
him. 'Pock, have a look in the vehicle. There has to be a bottle of
mineral water. Bring it here!', Hermann ordered. He almost always
had everything handy a soldier needed. I remembered when, coming back from Russia in 1943 by rail transport to Berlin, the train
stopped somewhere in Posen province. It was a medium-size station
and we soldiers sat, well behaved, at the open doors of the freight
cars. The civilians gaped at us, among them, of course, quite a few
girls. At least, that is what we imagined. Beck walked up and down
the transport train in his usual erect bearing. Then he stopped at
our car and asked: 'Well, boys, will you show your appreciation when
the young girls wave at you?' As a chorus, we replied with a loudly
shouted: 'Jawoll (yes, sir!), Hauptsturmführer!' This characteristic
behavior, unimportant as it may seem, impressed us from this officer. If Beck had asked for it, we would have let ourselves be cut to
pieces immediately for him.[52]

ATTACK BY SS-PANZERPIONIERBATAILLON 12 ON NORREY ON 10 JUNE 1944

As stated previously, the jutting Canadian position in Norrey was a major
obstacle to a renewed attack northward, which would best have been initi-
ated along both sides of the Mue creek. The supreme commander of Panzergruppe West, General Geyr von Schweppenburg, also came to this
conclusion when he surveyed the terrain from the Ardennes abbey. He had
an excellent knowledge of the terrain, gained during the preparations for
'Operation Seelöwe' ("Sea Lion," the planned invasion of England), in 1940.
In preparation for this attack he ordered that the Panzer-Lehr-Division had
to take over the battle sector St. Manvieu-Putot-Brouay. "HJ" Division would
keep the attack sector from le Bourg on the east bank of the Mue creek to
the narrow gauge rail line Caen-Luc-sur-Mer. The 21. Pz.Div. would link up
on the right. The plan for Regiment 26, still in defensive action in the Rots-
St. Manvieu-Putot-Brouay sector, was to move it between the left flank of
Regiment 25 near Franqueville and the Mue creek, after it had been relieved
by the Panzer-Lehr-Division.[53]

In preparation for this attack, scheduled for the night 10–11 June, "HJ"
Division was given the task to attack the jutting front near Norrey even

before the general deployment. This jutting front line also flanked the positions of II./26 in a very disturbing manner. The only available unit for this attack was the Pionierbataillon which had not yet been in action. The Pionierbataillon was attached to Regiment 26, which had been ordered to attack Norrey before dawn on 10 June, for this task. The Bataillon, commanded by Sturmbannführer Siegfried Müller, deployed at the front line south of Norrey behind 3. and 2. Kompanie of I./26. On the right was 2. Kompanie under Obersturmführer Kuret, in the center was 1. Kompanie of the Holder of the Knight's Cross, Oberleutnant Otto Toll, on the left, 3. Kompanie led by Hauptsturmführer Tiedke. Obersturmführer Herbert Bischoff's 4. Kompanie deployed its Granatwerferzug (mortar Zug) with 3. Kompanie. Based on entries in the diary of the Divisionsbegleitkompanie, the attack started at 05.00 hours, according to other reports, at 03.00 hours. It is possible that the Companies, because of the varying distance from the attack objective, may have staggered the start of their attacks. A member of 1. Kompanie, Sturmmann Helmut Schuck, provided the following report:

> The attack started when it was still dark. When the enemy figured out what was happening, they were probably listening to our radio transmissions, the heaviest possible barrages from artillery and mortars set in immediately. Since 1. Kompanie sat right in the center of the barrages, the only way out was to dodge the fire. In this, the Kompanie was successful, thanks to the leadership of Oberleutnant Toll. 1. Kompanie continued the attack and approached to within 100 meters of the Canadian positions. The enemy seemed surprised, machine gun and rifle fire set in only then. The Kompanie set up positions in a gully and opened fire on the spotted enemy positions. After approximately ten minutes, the defensive enemy fire slowed down. At that moment, Toll issued the order to capture the Canadian positions at the edge of Norrey through a frontal assault. After synchronizing their watches, 1. Kompanie attacked five minutes later. The enemy seemed to have expected this, since heavy machine gun fire set in, some of it from the right flank. The Zugführer of I. Zug, Untersturmführer Kurz, was seriously wounded. He handed I. Zug over to Unterscharführer Schima who was also wounded almost immediately. Unterscharführer Lenhard of 2. Gruppe (squad) had previously been lost due to a leg wound. Sturmmann Pflug was killed by a bullet to the head. At the same time, Oberleutnant Toll was seriously wounded by a machine gun salvo. II. and III. Zug did not fare any better. They lost, as did I. Zug, almost all NCOs. Machine gunner Weigt of 1. Gruppe, I. Zug, was killed. Sochau, Schmidt and Janzenberger were wounded. Without leadership, 1. Kompanie was facing the Canadian position when the order came to retreat to the gully. There, a terrible scene awaited. Approximately

fifteen to twenty wounded, most of them seriously, lay there. Among them was Oberleutnant Toll who died thirty minutes later. Untersturmführer Kurz also died from his critical wound, a bullet to the stomach. 1. Kompanie changed over to defense in the gully facing the Canadian positions. During the attack and the defense, there was no contact at all with 3. and 2. Kompanie. The connection was probably lost during darkness and mainly because of the heavy enemy barrages. 2. Kompanie, to the right of 1., also suffered heavy losses. It, too, got stuck in the defensive fire.

At that point, the medical officer Dr. Zistler arrived in the position of 1. Kompanie and began looking after the wounded. Some of them, he carried to the dressing station on his back, without being fired on by the Canadians.

At approximately 16.00 hours, 1. Kompanie withdrew to its starting positions, taking all wounded with them. It took up defensive positions southwest of Norrey. 3. -Kompanie took up positions to the left of 1. Kompanie. Untersturmführer Bruno Asmus was made commander of 1. Kompanie.[54]

Sturmmann Alois Banz of 3. Kompanie wrote on the progress of the battle:

Despite heavy mortar fire, we managed to advance to the edge of town. II. Zug of our Kompanie was located in a gully leading to the town. 1. Gruppe, led by Unterschar-führer Klein, formed the right wing. It soon encountered a tank advancing from the village toward the gully and opened fire. Although this was the first time in action for all of us, the courage displayed in trying to spot and neutralize enemy firing positions, was exemplary. Even today, I can vividly recall the image of the machine gunners Pail and Langbauer. Both, in order to have a more favorable field of fire, stood erect in front of a hedge and fired salvo after salvo into a suspected enemy position. 3. Kompanie had to record the first dead and wounded already during this morning. The attack stalled at the edge of town.[55]

It could not be determined how the attack by 2. Kompanie progressed.

The attack by the Pionierbataillon had initially advanced without use of firearms or support from heavy infantry weapons or artillery. In the last phase of the attack, when it had been spotted by the enemy, it was supported by artillery and mortars and probably by infantry guns of Regiment 26. The attack finally broke down under the barrages of Canadian artillery, mortars, machine guns and tanks. During the course of the day and after the onset of darkness, the Kompanies were pulled back to their starting positions.

Sturmmann Schuck has already reported on the brave actions of the medical officer of the Pionierbataillon, Ober-sturmführer Dr. Friedrich Zistler. Zistler wrote later on this:

> I received the report on the fighting by our 1. Kompanie, led by my best friend Otto Toll. Those days still seem very recent to me. I can still see Otto lying before me, unfortunately already dead. He had tried to make a tourniquet using the ribbon of his Knight's Cross and a flashlight, obviously to stop the bleeding from an artery. Otto died from a bullet which penetrated both his chest and abdominal cavity.[56]

The losses of the Pionierbataillon were significant. Three officers, three NCOs and twenty-two men had been killed in action. One officer, six NCOs and thirty-five men were wounded; one officer, one NCO and eight men were missing. The total losses were eighty.[57]

Four attempts to capture Norrey, one of the cornerstones of the Canadian defensive position, had failed. This village, together with Bretteville, formed a strong barrier, blocking the attack plans of the Panzerkorps. For this reason, repeated attempts were made to take these positions through a number of attacks. They failed because of insufficient forces, partly because of rushed planning caused by real or imagined time pressures. Last but not least, they failed because of the courage of the defenders which was not any less than that of the attackers. It was effectively supported by well-constructed positions, strong artillery, anti-tank weapons and by tanks.

DEFENSIVE FIGHTING BY SS-PANZER-AUFKLÄRUNGSABTEILUNG 12 AND III./SS-PANZER-GRENADIERREGIMENT 26 ON 9 AND 10 JUNE 1944

The Aufklärungsabteilung had taken up a new security line during the night 8–9 June. At approximately 01.00 hours, the Abteilungsadjutant Obersturmführer Buchheim, an assault squad and several drivers attempted to retrieve several still mobile Panzers from the castle park of Audrieu. The castle and the park were still free of the enemy. However, the vehicles which had not been burnt out were wedged in by fallen trees. They could not be moved by either human strength or by towing them. Thus, only important documents were saved and the radio equipment was destroyed.

An armored car scouting party had been attempting to establish contact with Panzeraufklärungs-Lehrabteilung 130 near Tilly-sur-Seulles in the morning of 8 June. It spotted enemy tanks on the road Bayeux-Tilly in the area of the creek crossing one kilometer northeast of Folliot. Because of a damaged tire, it dodged into Folliot and let the tanks roll past. After the damage was repaired, the party returned to the Abteilung during the night by way of

Tilly, Juvigny, Vendes, and Cheux. At the Abteilung the party found its second armored car which it had to leave in Cheux during the morning with a damaged clutch.[58]

To continue the attack to the south, the 8th Battalion The Dorsetshire Regiment had been attached to the Armoured Brigade Group. The 4/7 Dragoon Guards (tanks) and 1st Dorsetshires had cleared the western attack strip by noon. They joined up with the forces located on Hill 103. The Hill had been captured on 8 June. In the morning, another tank unit, the 24th Lancers, had been pulled forward to the Hill. In the afternoon they attacked, together with the 8th Battalion of the Durhams, to the south. At 17.30 hours they captured Saint Pierre, located two kilometers southwest. However, I. Bataillon of Panzergrenadier-Lehr-Regiment 901, in position there, was able to hold the bridge across the Seulles river on the road to Tilly. The Durhams set up defensive positions in Saint Pierre. One tank company remained with them as support. The rest of the forces were pulled back to the area around Hill 103.[59]

During the course of the day, scouting parties, probably from III./26, penetrated into le Bas d'Audrieu, Pavie and le Haut d'Audrieu. This caused the 8th Armoured Brigade Group to abandon the eastward advance route. In its place, it established a new route from the crossroads one kilometer southeast of St. Leger via the railroad crossing 800 m west of le Bas d'Audrieu station, the road fork 500 m west of Pavie to Hill 103. Action by tanks was prepared to secure the supply vehicles using this route.[60] The Aufklärungsabteilung was linked-up to its neighbor to the left, the Panzer-Lehr-Division, only through scouting parties. In order to reinforce the Aufklärungsabteilung, the 2. Panzerkompanie, which had arrived last in the Caen area, was moved up to Fontenay-le-Pesnel, probably during the night 8–9 June. It was attached to the Aufklärungsabteilung. During the attack by the 24th Lancers on Saint Pierre, which also threatened the security of the Aufklärungsabteilung's left flank in les Hauts Vents, the Panther-Kompanie was alerted. It was moved into the gap between the Aufklärungsabteilung and the Panzer-Lehr-Division near Parc de Boislonde. The only existing report on this action comes from Sturmmann Hans-Ulrich Dietrich, gunner in the Panther of Oberscharführer Günter Stumber. He remembers it this way:

> It was so hazy that no details could be made out, even through the telescope. Stumber, using his binoculars, had the same problem. We all knew that the enemy was in the woods ahead of us. But where exactly? Nothing moved, either here or there. The waiting was a drag on our nerves. After some time, Stumber ordered the driver to advance slowly straight ahead. He said something like: 'Let's find out now where they're hiding.' We had advanced twenty to thirty meters. I had pointed the gun into approximately eleven o'clock

position, when we were hit from approximately one o'clock direction. Initially, I only noticed that the hit had landed on the front right turret. I had not yet contemplated its consequence. As the driver stopped, I swung the turret to 1 o'clock. While rotating, we were hit a second time, again from the front right. It felt to me as if someone had hit the right half of my face with full force. The jolt, which went through the Panzer, made my left upper leg hit the grip of the hand wheel for the gun's precision adjustment. At least, that is what I thought. Only later, when the according weakness set in, did I notice that a fragment had got me. It continued to cause me a lot of problems in later days.

After the second hit I wondered why there was no reaction from Stumber. I turned back toward him. He was dead. His chest was completely ripped apart. Obviously, both shells had gone right through him.

I ordered the driver: 'Backward, march!' and reported the event by radio. As we were driving backward I noticed that the loader had been wounded in the hip. He indicated, however, after I had crawled over to him, that he could manage for a while. I also spotted two holes, immediately beside each other, next to the turret machine gun where the armor was thickest. The two shells must have gone through it like through butter. The poor visibility forced me to climb out the rear hatch and to sit next to the driver, on the outside. He had his hatch open, for better visibility. Tragically, the driver, Hase, also climbed out and stood next to the turret on the right, the enemy side. I yelled at him repeatedly to get back in. But there was no way he would sit in his seat again. And so, what had to happen, happened. Shortly after, on the move, another shell hit us at turret level, exactly from the right. It ripped one of Hase's legs off, close to the hip, and threw him high into the air. I can still see it today, how he tumbled and then slammed into the ground. I jumped off immediately, the way I had learned it with the paratroopers in Mailly-le-Camp, ran over to him and pulled him into the ditch. I applied a tourniquet to his leg stump, using a belt. There was no way of telling whether Hase had internal injuries. He was only fully conscious for a few more moments. During one of them, he suddenly had his pistol in his hand. He wanted to shoot himself. This, he said very clearly. Of course, I took the pistol away from him. It took some time, it seemed very long to me, before we were found by our comrade Dienemann and another member of the Kompanie. Dienemann stayed with Hase. The other caught hold of me, lifted me up, and carried me like a small child, I am 183 centimeters tall, into the woods a few meters away. Some Panzers from our Kompanie were sitting there.[61]

On 10 June, after a fire attack by mortars and artillery, I./901 of the Panzer-Lehr-Division attacked the 8th DLJ in Saint Pierre at first light and captured the town. By 11.30 hours, after a counterattack supported by the 24th Lancers and land and ships' artillery, the Durhams had retaken the village with the exception of its southeast section. This is reported in the war diary of the 8th Armoured Brigade Group.

According to statements by Ritgen, the British were able to hold only the northeastern part of Saint Pierre.[62]

In the morning, at approximately 10.00 hours, the commander of the Panzer-Lehr-Division, Generalleutnant Bayerlein, visited the command post of the Aufklärungsabteilung. He wanted to determine why the link-up between his right wing and the Aufklärungsabteilung had not been achieved. He was briefed on the location of the positions. Soon after, officers of the neighbor regiment to the right reported to the command post of the Aufklärungsabteilung to establish contact. Enemy tank reconnaissance was repulsed by German anti-tank forces during the course of the day. The heavy enemy artillery fire also caused losses during 10 June.[63]

DEFENSIVE FIGHTING BY SS-PANZER-GRENADIERREGIMENT 25 FROM 8 TO 10 JUNE 1944

Panzergrenadierregiment 25 had to change over to defense already in the evening of 7 June along the lines it had reached during the attack. Its right neighbor, 21. Panzerdivision, had also not yet started its attack. Panzergrenadierregiment 26 and I. Panzerabteilung were still on the march. The Canadians had already crossed the road Caen-Bayeux west of the Mue creek. While Regiment 26, parts of the Panzerregiment, 15./25, and the Pionierbataillon were attacking to the north to capture the area for the planned deployment of the Panzer-Lehr-Division, some of them had to temporarily change over to defense, the enemy renewed his attack in the sector of Regiment 25. It was obviously the enemy's intention to still capture Caen. Regiment 25, supported by III. Artillerie-abteilung and, initially, II. Panzerabteilung, prepared for this. The Panzerabteilung had to act as a mobile anti-tank force since the Panzerjägerabteilung (tank hunters) of the Division was still awaiting delivery of Jagdpanzers (tank destroyers) in its assembly area.

During the night 7–8 June, I./25 reinforced its positions since a renewal of the enemy attack had to be expected the next day. Scouting parties reconnoitered towards Cambes and determined that only the woods north of the village were in enemy hands.

Also on 8 June, the English artillery was firing barrages. During the course of the day the enemy attacked with a force of approximately two companies, supported by tanks, at the dividing line between I. and II. Bataillon. Two tanks were knocked out. Obersturmführer Hans Siegel reports on this:

Tank alarm through Bataillon messenger, Waldmüller, with the request for support through an immediate attack in a northerly direction. I ordered Hauptscharführer Drebert, commander of III. Zug, and his four vehicles immediately to proceed to the front. I would brief them there. The Kom-paniechef and the messenger were to walk ahead on foot to determine the battle situation. Arriving at a glade in the forest, Siegel spotted approximately twelve enemy tanks approaching, their point still 800 meters away. They would reach our lines before our own Panzers could. We had two 7.5 cm Paks in position, and they were not reacting. Why the hell not? One reported: 'Out of ammunition', the other: 'No field of fire'. A few choice words resulted in those standing around quickly carrying ammunition over from the gun without field of fire. Already, the first enemy tank was in flames. The gunner was directed to knock out some of the tanks at the point and then the ones at the rear. The attack stalled. Every shell into the stationary tanks in front of us was a hit and caused renewed panic. Hastily, the enemy retreated. We were not fired upon and had no losses. Our own approaching Panzers were ordered back to the starting position. There, an artillery fire attack surprised them. Hauptscharführer Drebert was killed outside his Panzer.[65]

The following day, 9 June, the Royal Ulsters started an attack from Anisy at 15.15 hours in order to capture Cambes. They were supported by preparatory fire from the artillery of the 3rd Division and from a cruiser. That fire landed in no-man's land.

When the battalion had approached to within one kilometer of its objective, it received concentrated fire from artillery, mortars and machine guns (probably from II./25). The enemy suffered significant losses, among them company commanders. The commander of the attached artillery unit, 33rd Field Regiment, was killed as was the forward observer. "The intensity of enemy fire in the woods (north of Cambes, Author) was as devastating as anything experienced anywhere throughout the campaign." With the arrival of darkness, the K.O.S.B.s moved forward to reinforce the Ulsters. The enemy apparently expected a counterattack.[66]

The war diary of I./25 does not mention this attack. Instead, two attacks on the neighbor to the right, Panzerregiment 22, are reported. The first attack started at 16.00 hours, resulting in two enemy tanks lost. The second attack began at 20.30 hours. The neighbor on the right knocked out 15 tanks during the attack. The Zug of 16. (Pionier) Kompanie, in action on the right flank of I./25, destroyed a tank in close combat using a T (Teller) mine. Both attacks were thrown back.[67] No mention of these battles was found in the war history of the 3rd Infantry Division.

During the fighting of 8 and 9 June, I. Bataillon lost one NCO and four men killed. Four NCOs and sixteen men were wounded. Of them, four NCOs and five men remained with the unit.

The following days were remarkable mainly because of the industrious building of positions. The numerous fire attacks by enemy artillery forced the Panzer shelters to be constructed like bunkers. They were propped up on the inside with railroad ties from the close-by line Cane-Luc-sur-Mer. Trees had to be cut down to open up fields of fire. Sturmbannführer Waldmüller himself was on his feet day and night, to the point of dropping dead, to supervise and direct the building of the positions. His Bataillon command post, too, was an earth bunker in the open field, just behind the front line. His example, his inexorable insistence saved the lives of many of his men at the time.

Scouting parties were active every night to determine the enemy positions and movements. A terse entry for 10 June can be found in the war diary of the Bataillon:

Scouting parties sent towards Cambes. Fire fight with enemy scouting party. The northern section of the town is held by enemy forces.

The visit by the regimental commander on 10 June was a worthy conclusion to the first period of fighting by the Bataillon. He carried decorations, and Sturmbannführer Waldmüller was able to issue thirty Iron Crosses II. Class to the bravest of his young soldiers.[68]

Obersturmführer Kurt Havemeister, commander of 7. Kom-panie, reports on the building of positions and the actions in the sector II./25, adjoining on the left:

Making use of the unbroken ground between the fields, the positions of I. Zug were located approximately eighty meters in front of the buildings, facing Buissons in the northwest. Those of II. and III. Zug were approximately forty meters from the manor and the park wall, facing towards Cambes. To the left, close contact existed with 5. Kompanie under Hauptsturmführer Kreilein. The contact to I. Bataillon remained loose since it abutted a tank trench further to the rear, and the gap to us was never completely closed.

The enemy artillery fired on St. Contest, which we had captured but whose center was not firmly in our hands, for three more days. This caused us some wounded from mortar fire. However, we were able to dig day and night, taking turns. We also managed to open a field of fire by cutting down the grain fields during the night. As well, we placed Teller mines at the edges of the grain fields, with thin wires running from the mines to the bunkers. The Kompanie squad dug a narrow trench on the manor side away from the enemy. They blasted a hole into the foundation wall and set up the Kompanie command post in the coal cellar. Although the young crew believed that the project was finally complete, connecting trenches to the units were dug later. In the other cellars, facing the enemy lines, doors were installed and the rooms were readied for the wounded, for the issuing of supplies and ammunition, and temporary lodgings for forward observers and prisoners. In the hope to get some peace from me, the young soldiers had furnished my command post very comfortably. They had covered the coals with carpets from the manor and brought in a settee in the style of some Louis or other, covered with silk damask material, and set up a portable bar. After repulsing two scouting parties and an unsuccessful enemy assault, we daily expected heavy fire and larger scale operations. Instead, we enjoyed a surprise visit from the rear by Standartenführer Kurt Meyer with a small entourage. The Regimental commander was obviously satisfied that we had not set up our positions in close proximity to the buildings. In his well known, terse manner he commended the Zug leaders and NCOs on what they had achieved in such a short time. On his departure, however, he restricted himself to shaking my hand. All the greater was my joy a few weeks later when I was awarded, together with Hein Schrott, Xaver Pfeffer, Dr. Alex Sedlacek and other comrades from all ranks, the Iron Cross I . . .

The advanced artillery observers, whom we did not really like close to us because of their radio traffic which gave them away, did what they could, directing barrages. When we reported to the Bataillon enemy tank reinforcements in Buissons, and our apprehension, we immediately received a Pakzug. It took up positions, safe from fragments and camouflaged, behind the southern park wall. When the commander of the Pakzug reported to me only two days later, at the command post of I. Zug, a tank assembly at Buissons, I was initially skeptical but then believed his assertions. We quickly brought the three Paks, under cover of the southwest park wall in the orchard, behind I. Zug into the prepared open firing positions. We had barely taken cover when 10 tanks started to move out of Buissons. I was so startled that I did not immediately recognize the angled direction of their movement.

The attack was obviously not meant for us, but for I. Bataillon on our right. The Canadians had apparently no knowledge of the protrusion of our front line, almost abreast of the northwestern edge of Cambes. In any case, their commanders led the attack from open hatches with visual contact, in the direction of Cambes. I held back the Pak commander until the ideal distance existed and ordered I. Zug to join in with machine guns and sharpshooters as soon as the first Pak shell was fired. The Pak commander opened the fireworks

at his discretion almost immediately from all three guns simultaneously on the enemy flank. Within a few minutes, six tanks were
knocked out and the others were driving in wild curves, their commanders dead. Crews who bailed out suffered heavy losses from the
fire of I. Zug. Only then did artillery fire on I. Bataillon set in. We
were able to bring the guns under cover during the enemy confusion. When the fire swung over to us and the 'innocent' 5. Kompanie, all of us were in complete cover. The medic had to look only
after three minor casualties. In the early morning we noticed, to our
surprise, that all the tank wrecks had been towed away during the
night. A single knocked-out tank still sat only 100 meters in front of
the white walls of Buissons. This did not give us cause for contemplation. During the next day, however, we received conspicuously
well aimed fire from a rapid-fire gun. I remembered 'Trick 17' from
Russia. As a courier there, driving alone, I had come under fire
from knocked-out tanks. The same situation here was confirmed by
I. Zug. Of course, it was a question of honor for our tank hunters to
set out the very next night. Three of them were able to creep close
enough to observe ammunition being supplied to the two men who
climbed into the tank. Its tracks were damaged, but its turret was
intact. After the ammunition carriers had left, and after some
period of further observation, Sturmmann Enders, covered by his
comrades, managed to attach a hollow charge to the turret. This
knocked out the tank and its unfortunate crew for good. The squad
returned unscathed after approximately two hours, to the justified
celebration by their comrades.[69]

III./25 also started to reinforce its positions immediately. Forward positions were set up in the tank trenches which were located north of Buron
along both sides of the road to les Buissons. The main line of resistance was
set up outside the edge of town since the town itself was a frequent target of
enemy artillery. Sturmmann Karl Vasold reports on the events during these
days:

We moved into positions in the tank trench to the left and right of
the road. There was heavy machine gun fire. We dug in under
extremely difficult circumstances. We cut down the 'Rommelspargel'
(Rommel asparagus) to cover our foxholes. The first enemy scouting
parties showed up during the night. They slid into the tank trench.
Hand grenades flew this way and that. Then it turned quiet again.
9.6.: enemy artillery was finding its range, not even a mouse could
have moved throughout the day. Gruchy, to our left, was most often
under fire although there was no-one inside. In this manner, one day

followed the other. Forceful enemy scouting assaults were fought back by us with machine guns. A machine gunner of the neighbor Zug set a Canadian tank on fire with tracer bullets. The distance between us and the enemy was approximately 600–700 meters. One evening, two Canadian tanks approached on the road from Cairon. Machine gun fire whistled above our heads. Riflemen fired anti-tank grenades at them. They hit accurately, but their impact was more moral than anything else. The rifle grenades made a terrible noise. The tanks turned back in the direction of Cairon.[70]

On 9 June, II. Panzerabteilung suffered a severe loss which had a special significance beyond the Division and the circle of its members. The Kompanie commander of 7. Kompanie, Obersturmführer Heinz-Hugo John, was killed in action on this day. He was an Obergebietsführer (superior regional commissioner) in the Reichsjugendführung (Reich youth directorate). Born in Erfurt in 1904, he was a member of the German Reichstag (parliament) since 1932. Since the outbreak of the war he had served in the front lines of the Heer and had been awarded the Iron Cross I. and II. When the "Hitlerjugend" Division was set up, he was transferred there at his own request. He had participated in the attack of 7 June as commander of I. Zug 7. Kompanie. After Hauptsturmführer Bräcker had been wounded, he had taken over command of the Kompanie. The Kompanie reported on his death:

> SS-Obersturmführer Heinz John was killed in action on 9.6.1944 at approximately 20.00 hours near la Folie, as Kompanie commander of 7./SS-Panzer-Regiment 12.
>
> The mission of the Kompanie was to secure against enemy tanks and infantry. The front slope, where the Kompanie was in securing positions, was under heavy mortar fire. Obersturmführer John was ordered by radio to report to the Abteilung command post to receive orders. At the very moment the Obersturmführer was about to climb out of the Panzer, it took a direct hit to the radio operator's hatch. A large fragment from the explosion cut through Obersturmführer John's spine and killed him on the spot.
>
> Others killed by this direct hit were the radio operator, SS-Sturmmann Mende and the loader, SS-Schütze (private) Noa. The driver and gunner bailed out immediately and reported back to the Abteilung command post.
>
> Since the sector which the Kompanie secured was under heavy artillery fire, the mortal remains could be retrieved from the knocked-out Panzer only after darkness had set in.
>
> SS-Obersturmführer John and the other comrades were buried in St. Germain near Caen.[71]

During these days the heavy SS-Artillerie-Abteilung 101/501 also reached the operations area. It had come from the Beauvais region via Paris and took up positions in the area of Bretteville-sur-Odon (4.5 kilometers southwest of Caen). The 1. Batterie—21 cm mortar with a range of up to sixteen kilometers—established its observation post in one of the towers of the Ardennes abbey. Obersturmführer Hinrich Garbade, as the forward observer, was located northeast of Malon close to the tank trench. A member of the communications squad, Sturmmann Erich Hüttner, reports on the first action by this battery:

> Two of our comrades remained at the observation post of Ardennes abbey. The rest of us continued to push the phone line forward. A small village appeared in front of us. It was Cussy. Explosion after explosion from enemy artillery shook the village. Without hesitation, we thread the wire through the ruins of Cussy. Then, open terrain lay ahead of us, visible to the enemy. We had to crawl the 300 to 400 meters to the main front line. Machine gun fire was raking overhead. Mortars were plowing the terrain.
>
> Then we reached the brave grenadiers of the 12. SS-Pz.-Div. "HJ" in a tank trench. We dropped down, completely exhausted. A few meters further ahead, our forward observer, Obersturmführer Garbade, sat in a foxhole. We crawled across to him and installed our telephone. My comrade Walter Rades and I remained at the front. The other boys of our installation group crawled back to Cussy where they set up a relay station.
>
> And then the fun began! We rapidly gave the precise fire orders from our forward observer down the line, and in quick succession the 21 cm shells howled across to the Canadians. The other batteries, too, had taken accurate aim and over there, at the other 'field post number, explosion followed explosion, throwing dust high in the air. An enemy battery was spotted and knocked out by the 21 cm shells. Tank assemblies were bombarded and blown apart. The infantry men of 12. SS-Pz.-Div. heaved an audible sigh of relief: Finally, those on the other side had to face the music for a change. Ever new fire orders—barrages as fast as the barrels allow. Heaven only knew how many of our batteries had joined the action.[72]

The 2. and 3. Batteries, 17 cm guns with a range of thirty-two kilometers, probably fought a cruiser, securing the mouth of the Orne river, from their positions near Bretteville-sur-Orne on 12 June. The fire was directed from an old tower of a manor located on the right bank of the Orne river. Hits were observed, as was exploding ammunition on board of the cruiser. The cruiser laid a smoke screen, preventing any further observation. The enemy immediately sent artillery observer aircraft to locate the batteries. The batteries of our guns were not spotted, however, a firing mortar battery was severely hit. Members of 3. Kanonenbatterie (gun battery) found a 38 cm dud shell.[73]

With the attack by the Pionierbataillon on Norrey on 10 June 1944, the first battle for Caen was ended for the 12. SS-Panzerdivision. We must, however, take a final look at the overall situation at the I. SS-Panzerkorps.

As already mentioned, the Panzer-Lehr-Division was initially scheduled to attack to the north in the battle sector between Norrey and Brouay, adjoining the "HJ" Division to the left. The enemy had captured Bayeux in the meantime and was advancing in the developed gap to the west, southwest, and southeast. The I. SS-Panzerkorps, probably prompted by the Heeresgruppe, ordered the Panzer-Lehr-Division to attack approximately along the road Tilly-Bayeux in the morning of 9 June and to take the city. According to the report by Helmut Ritgen, the following were assembled for the attack in the morning of 9 June:

on the right: Panzergrenadier-Lehr-Regiment 901,

Panzerjäger-Lehr-Abteilung 130,

along both banks of the Seulles river;

on the left: armored Gruppe (group) Schönburg, consisting of

II. Abteilung Panzer-Lehr-Regiment 130,

I. Bataillon Panzergrenadier-Lehr-Regiment 902, (the remainder of Panzergrenadier-Lehr-Regiment, after the confused fighting and severe losses of 8 June, was apparently not yet ready for action).

Panzeraufklärungs-Lehr-Abteilung 130 secured the left flank of the Division, linking up with Gruppe Schönburg in the west.

In the late afternoon of 9 June, armored Gruppe Schönburg started the attack. Since enemy pressure on Tilly had increased in the meantime, Panzergrenadier-Lehr-Regiment 901 did not take part in the attack. Gruppe Schöburg captured Ellon, six kilometers southeast of Bayeux, without encountering any resistance. As they were leaving the town to the north, enemy tanks were spotted to the northeast. It could not be determined, subsequently, to which unit these tanks belonged. The divisional commander, Generalleutnant Bayerlein, ordered the attack stopped at this moment. The armored group was pulled back to its starting positions. It is not clear, as Ritgen states, whether the order to withdraw was an individual decision or whether it had been ordered from above.[74]

This question deserves further investigation. In the war diary of AOK 7, the plans for 8 June were recorded as follows: ". . . to attack to the north and west of Caen with Panzer units of 12. SS-Pz.Div. and of the Pz.-Lehr-Div. in the direction of Bayeux." This can only be interpreted to mean that, in the context of the attack by both Panzerdivisions, the target of the Panzer-Lehr-Division was Bayeux. Generaloberst (four-star general) Dollmann, the supreme commander of the 7. Armee, informed Generalleutnant Speidel at 01.25 hours on 9 June of his intentions and requested the concurrence of the Feldmarschall to ". . . penetrate from the Caen area with the units of

Panzergruppe West, in action there, northward and to initially clean up the situation on the east wing of the all-over invasion area." At 06.30 hours, Feldmarschall Rommel advised the Generaloberst ". . . of his concurrence regarding the proposal by the Armee for action in the Caen area." He emphasized: "Point of main effort on the left, the point of main effort on the right wing remains unchanged."[75] At that time, the attack by the Panzer-Lehr-Division had not yet started. It is inexplicable why it nevertheless took place. However, it can be established that the attack was broken off in the afternoon on orders of the Armee.

✠

The attack from the Caen area to the north, proposed by the 7. Armee did not take place. The war diary of Panzergruppe West, which starts on 10 June, notes for this day: "After discussion with Gen. Feldmarschall Rommel, the planned attack by I. SS-Panzerkorps during the night 10–11 June will not take place. Reasons are lack of forces and enemy reinforcements."[76] It is surprising that the war diary of Heeresgruppe B contains vastly different sounding and partly contradictory entries. There it is stated, regarding a conversation of the Feldmarschall with Generaloberst Jodl, chief of the Wehrmacht operation staff, at 21.45 hours of the same day: "The situation there is thus that the Panzergruppe West has now been pushed into defense." Even at 22.15 hours, he advised the chief of staff of the Supreme Command West in a telephone conversation that: ". . . the Panzergruppe West will attempt the attack in the course of the night. The supreme commander [Feldmarschall Rommel] has approved and sanctioned the planned attack. He is, however, convinced that a decisive success cannot be forced because of the enemy air activity and the superior enemy artillery."[77] A reasonable explanation of these contradictory pieces of information given to the OKW and the Supreme Commander West is not possible. Based on this, however, the conclusion can be drawn that Heeresgruppe B had wide-ranging decision-making powers at the time.

The enemy, or fate, relieved those in responsibility from having to clarify the contradictions, in an unfortunate manner. At 20.30 hours, the command post of Panzergruppe West was attacked by fighter-bombers and smashed. The supreme commander, General Geyr von Schweppenburg, was wounded. His chief of staff, Generalmajor Edler von Dawans, and the Ia, Major i.G. (general staff) Burgsthaler, were killed. Among the total of seventeen killed was also the liaison officer of the I. SS-Panzerkorps, Hauptsturmführer Wilhelm Beck. The rest of the staff was pulled out. The command in the sector of the Panzergruppe was transferred to I. SS-Panzerkorps.[78] Today it is known that the air attack was the result of the efforts of the British radio intelligence group "ULTRA". At 04.39 hours on 10 June, this group conveyed the following message to the British army group: "Command post of Panzergruppe West in the evening of 9 June in la Caine."[79]

The attack, hoped for by the 7. Armee, planned by Panzergruppe West, and approved by Feldmarschall Rommel had been canceled even before the bomb attack on the command post of the Panzergruppe. It would really have been hopeless since the units available for action in the Caen area were not sufficient for it. The 21. Panzerdivision was tied down in defense and could hardly free up significant forces for the attack. Major parts of the Panzer-Lehr-Division were fighting off continuous attacks in the area north of Tilly. This would surely have prevented it from making available strong forces for the attack next to the "HJ" Division, which, in addition would have had to relieve Regiment 26. Two half Panzer-divisions were not sufficient to achieve the task. In contrast, the Heeresgruppe had available two Panzerdivisions which had not yet been put into action, 2. and 116. Panzer-divisions. They were still located along both sides of the Somme river.

After his inspection visit to 7. Armee, Feldmarschall Rommel had briefed the OKW—Generaloberst Jodl—on his impressions. This took place on 8 June at 23.10 hours. At that occasion, Jodl stated that the OKW was convinced that no further landings would occur in the Supreme Command West sector. Rommel pointed out that the enemy had only one army group in action so far. This meant that no forces should be moved from the Pas de Calais, as had apparently been recommended by the OKW. Jodl persisted in his point of view. Previously, at 20.45 hours, the Supreme Command West had already affirmed to the Heeresgruppe its judgment: ". . . that the necessity exists to bring further forces forward [to the invasion front] even though this meant recklessly exposing other fronts." Generalleutnant Speidel had agreed. Even during the night 8–9 June, Heeresgruppe B ordered the deployment of 2. and 116. Panzerdivisions. The 2. Panzer-division was set in march for action at the invasion front under the XXXXVII. Panzerkorps. The 116. Panzerdivision remained in the sector of 15. Armee. On its request, and with the approval of the Heeresgruppe, 116. Panzerdivision was advanced to the line Yvetot-Neuf Chatel (thirty kilometers northwest and forty kilometers northeast of Rouen respectively, i.e. northeast of the Seine river). Once again, the disastrous results of the falsified enemy picture provided by Fremde Heere West (foreign armies west) were shown.[80]

The order to deploy 2. Panzerdivision to the invasion front was issued too late. The Division could not arrive in time for the planned attack at Caen. The initiative there was completely in the hands of the enemy. This initiative could only be recaptured if the reinforcing of German forces was quickly possible. The Panzerdivisions in action had to be relieved by infantry divisions and further Panzer forces had to be brought in.

2. The Second Battle for Caen from 11 to 18 June 1944

After the attack by SS-Panzer-Pionierbataillon 12 on 10 June had been repelled, the offensive operations by Panzergruppe West to smash the

British-Canadian bridgehead came to an end for the moment. The enemy had been forced onto the defensive in the right and central sectors of the Division, without having reached his initial attack objective, Caen. However, along both sides of the dividing line between the "HJ" Division and the Panzer-Lehr-Division, the enemy had been on the attack since 8 June. Dempsey wanted to enlarge the initially minor successes through the deployment of stronger forces and through expanding the attack front, beginning on 11 June.

With this he followed the plans already decided on before the invasion. The objective of this attack was to capture the hilly terrain around Villers-Bocage, Hill 198 (4.5 kilometers southwest) and Hill 192 (2.5 kilometers south). Put into action to achieve this were: 7th Armoured Division with the attached 56th Infantry Brigade to the west of the Seulles river, 69th Infantry Brigade of the 50th Infantry Division with the 8th Armoured Brigade to the east of the Seulles river. In the sector of 3rd Canadian Infantry Division adjoining to the east, the 2nd Canadian Armoured Brigade was to secure and support this operation through a limited attack on the flank.

SECTION 2

The Second Battle for Caen from 11 to 18 June 1944

CHAPTER 2.1

Attack on the Positions of SS-Panzeraufklärungsabteilung 12 near Cristot and of III./SS-Panzergrenadierregiment 26 near Brouay on 11 June 1944

Since the major thrust of the British/Canadian attack was on the left sector of the Division, the developments of 11 June are being reported, exceptionally, in a sequence from left to right.

In the morning of 11 June, Brigadeführer Witt visited the Aufklärungsabteilung. He was accompanied by Sturmbannführer Bremer who had somewhat recovered. The Divisional commander handed the first decorations to members of the Abteilung.

Hauptsturmführer Freiherr (baron) von Reitzenstein briefed the two commanders on the situation. Losses caused by mortars and fighter-bombers were tremendously high, almost all company chiefs and platoon leaders were already out of action. The companies were only at half of their fighting strength. Enemy field- and ships' artillery were firing shells with highly sensitive impact detonators. Thus, the shells exploded in the tree-tops and the fragments would frequently wound the men in their foxholes. The fire was flexibly and effectively directed by artillery spotter aircraft. Firing at these was practically impossible since ammunition belts for the Italian 2-cm guns were not available. Since the troops had camouflaged themselves very successfully against being spotted by fighter-bombers, the aircraft looked for other targets. French civilians, among them women with baby carriages, fleeing from the combat area were chased on the roads and shot. Even cows which were still in the pastures were being 'hunted'. The enemy had repeat-

211

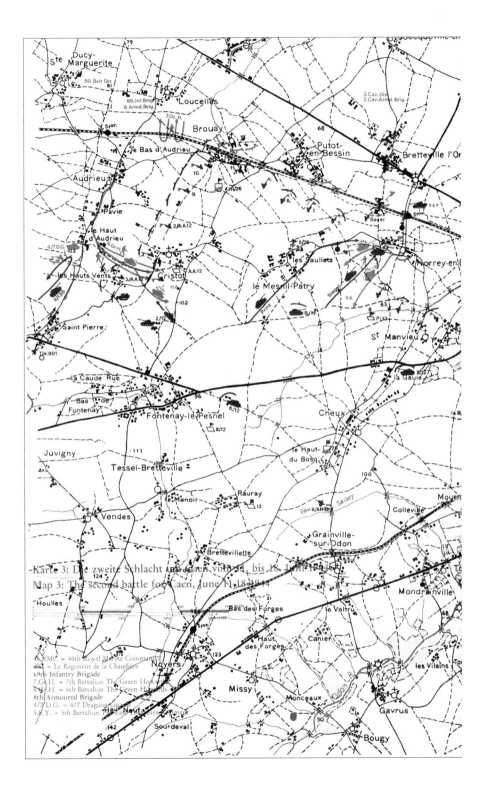

Karte 3: Die zweite Schlacht um Caen, vom 11. bis 18. Juni 1944
Map 3: The second battle for Caen, June 11–18 1944

46 RMC = 46th Royal Marine Commando
RC = Le Régiment de la Chaudière
69th Infantry Brigade
7.G.H. = 7th Battalion The Green Howards
6.G.H. = 6th Battalion The Green Howards
8th Armoured Brigade
4/7 D.G. = 4/7 Dragoon Guards
5.L.Y. = 5th Battalion The East Yorkshire Regiment

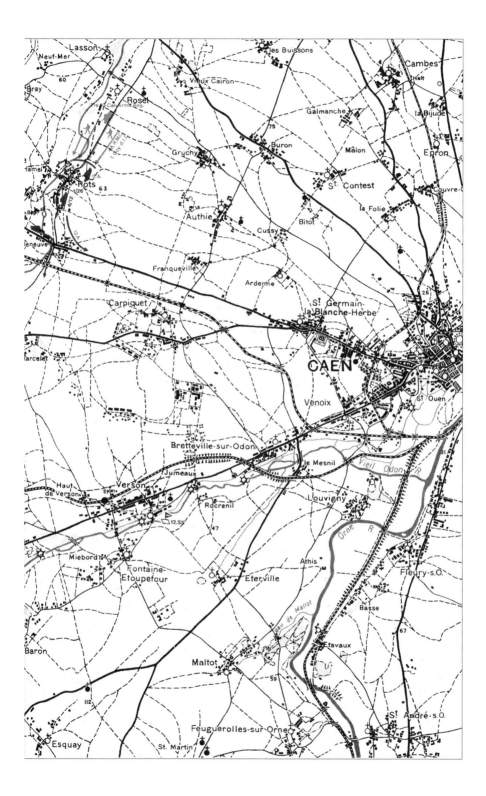

edly reconnoitered with tanks but had been repelled by fire from the anti-tank guns. Support from German artillery was sorely missed.[1] The Divisional commander drove on to III./26. Sturmbannführer Bremer took over the command of the Abteilung again.

In the course of the morning, a radio message from the communications intelligence platoon of the Division arrived at the staff of the Panzer-regiment in Rauray. Monitoring of enemy radio traffic had indicated that enemy artillery would direct concentrated fire on a command post detected in Rauray at 12.00 hours. All non-essential personnel in Rauray and all vehicles which could be spared were sent to a hastily established alternative command post in Bretteville, one kilometer south of Rauray. The command Panzers and the radio armored car were dug in at Rauray. The staff remained in the citadel-like buildings of the manor. The predicted fire set in punctually. It lasted fifteen minutes. "The tall trees and the thick walls stopped the blessing. The Panzers also survived all this without damage", reported the Regimental adjutant, Hauptsturmführer Georg Isecke.[2]

The 69th Infantry Brigade, too, had a visit by its divisional commander in the morning. He issued an order to the Brigade at 07.15 hours to advance further, and to clear St. Pierre, Cristot and the woods east of the town, as well as the terrain in between. The Brigade, in turn, ordered the 6th and 7th Green Howards (infantry battalions) at 10.00 hours to attack simultaneously at 14.30 hours. The 6th Green Howards were to attack via Audrieu towards Cristot, the 7th Green Howards towards the small wooded area east of this village. The 5th East Yorkshires (infantry battalion) were ordered to cross the railroad line behind the 6th Green Howards and to take over St. Pierre from the 8th DLI. The enemy was expected southwest of Tilly-sur-Seulles and southeast of Audrieu. The attack by the 6th Green Howards would be supported by the 4/7 Dragoon Guards (tank unit).[3]

The commander of the 4/7 Dragoon Guards, Lieutenant Colonel R.G. Byron, had scouted the area around Hill 103 together with "B" Squadron and determined possibilities of approaching Cristot. The tanks encountered considerable resistance from well camouflaged riflemen and machine gunners ". . . who seemed to be hidden in every hedge." At the same time, a scouting party of the Aufklärungsabteilung with a Panther of 2. Panzerkompanie was on its way. Standarten-oberjunker (officer cadet) Paul Dienemann reported on this mission:

My Zug of 5 Panthers was assigned to Sturmbannführer Bremer of the Aufklärungsabteilung. Ahead of us we had open terrain of approximately 100 meters. Behind that were thick rows of bushes and trees which obstructed our vision, with a village behind them. A 10-men scouting party of the Aufklärungsabteilung under the command of an Ober-scharführer was sent out at approximately 18.00 hours to determine the enemy location and intentions. One of my

Panthers, commanded by Unterscharführer Helmle, drove on the left flank to provide cover and protection. After approximately 150 meters, the scouting party came under rifle fire. The commander dropped to the ground, hit in the stomach. The Panther continued to advance in order to get out of a hollow. At a bend in the path, the Panther's gun became entangled with that of a Sherman tank. Neither tank could knock out the other. The English tank commander had left his tank and was bending over the badly wounded scouting party commander, dressing the wound. He said, in German: 'You're all right now, you'll be going home to hospital. For you, this bloody war is over.'

The Englishman climbed back into his tank and waved at Unterscharführer Helmle to indicate there would be no shooting. Both tanks pulled back. The wounded Ober-scharführer was laid on the Panzer. On its return, the scouting party reported: ' contact with the enemy after 150 meters'.[4]

Another scouting party, led by Unterscharführer Kretschmer of 4. Kompanie of the Aufklärungsabteilung, was ordered in the afternoon of 11 June to establish contact with the battle outposts of Untersturmführer Karl-Walter Becker of 2. Kompanie. Even before they were reached, Kretschmer spotted a large tank assembly west of les Hauts Vents. It was reported to the Kompanie. The two anti-tank guns still fit for action were alerted.[5]

The Green Howards had marched through Ducy-Ste. Marguerite at 14.30 hours. At 16.00 hours they marched through Audrieu on their advance towards Cristot. There they were to change over to defense in order to ". . . prevent the enemy from using Hill 102 [one kilometer south of the town]".[6] They were advancing along both sides of a path leading from le Haut d'Audrieu to the south exit of Cristot. They reached the road fork immediately northeast of les Hauts Vents at approximately 18.30 hours. There they came under extremely violent machine gun fire from the hedges and orchards west of Cristot. They fought their way forward, with difficulty, from hedge to hedge. Finally, the company advancing on the left succeeded in knocking out a machine gun in position at the foot of an old oak tree at a bend in the path at the southern edge of town. They continued their advance on Hill 102. To the south of it, the other companies fought their way from one hedge to the next. They suffered considerable losses.[7]

The tank attack, which started at 17.20 hours, was accompanied by two companies of the 6th Green Howards. The outposts of the Aufklärungsabteilung and the crews of the widely scattered strong points in the hedges opened fire on the accompanying infantry with rifles and machine guns. The tanks and their guns were quite ineffective since the terrain was quite broken and made it impossible to spot the enemy. "C" Squadron, attacking on the left, reached the edge of town where it stalled since the infantry could only penetrate the outer parts of the town. A Sherman was knocked out by an anti-tank gun in position close to the Abteilung command post. "B" Squadron, on the attack to the right of "C" Squadron, lost seven tanks during its advance across open terrain towards Hill 102 through a counterattack by a few Panthers of 2. Panzer-kompanie and anti-tank gun fire. The Green Howards, having suffered severe losses, in particular among the company commanders, stopped the attack and retreated in the direction of le Haut d'Audrieu. On the request of the commander of the 6th Green Howards, several tanks drove back to the battlefield. They were able to retrieve numerous wounded and the dead commander of the 5th E Yorks, as well as pick up other infantrymen who had been pinned down by the fire.[8]

The Aufklärungsabteilung established contact with the individual strong points through scouting parties and recovered its dead and wounded. Unter-scharführer M. found Unter-scharführer Hans Binder of 4. Kompanie who had been -wounded in the afternoon. A hand grenade had wounded him in the right upper arm and left knee. English soldiers had administered first aid. M. and his driver, Matthias Tillenburg, laid the wounded on the hood of their one-ton armored car and brought him back. It was necessary to amputate the arm.

The 7th Green Howards, advancing on the left of the 6th Green Howards, had come under heavy fire from the Brouay area and south of it from III./26 as they approached the rail line. The company on the right was forced to take cover approximately 100 m south of the rail line. The left company, further behind, was kept down by the fire from III./26. After the fall of darkness, the 7th Green Howards withdrew to the area northwest of Brouay.

The advance of the 5th E Yorks on St. Pierre had triggered a counterattack by II./Panzer-Lehr-Regiment 130. Despite the unfavorable, broken terrain it was possible to penetrate into the British positions on Hill 103 in the late evening. Two Panzers were knocked out. One of them was that of the commander, Major Prinz (prince) Schönburg-Waldenburg. A 'confused situation' developed on Hill 103. The attack had to be broken off and the Panzerabteilung pulled back into its starting positions. To the left, Tilly-sur-Seulles had been held against an attack by a mixed battle group of the 56th Infantry Brigade after eventful fighting. However, the 22nd Armoured Brigade of the 7th Armoured Division had captured Verrières, approximately one kilometer northeast of Lingèvre. It could not be re-taken through a counterattack during the night.[9]

The III./26 and the Aufklärungsabteilung had held its widely dispersed and sparsely manned chain of strong points. The attacker had been thrown back and suffered severe losses. The commanders of "A" Company of the 6th Green Howards and of "C" Company as well as the deputy commander of "B" Company had been killed. The commander of "B"Company was wounded. The number of noncoms and men killed is not available to the author. The

7th Green Howards, too, had suffered significant losses. The 4/7 Dragoon Guards had lost 7 tanks and a number of crews.[10]

Losses on 11 June 1944:

	Killed			Wounded			Missing		
	Officers	NCOs	Men	Officers	NCOs	Men	Officers	NCOs	Men
III./26	-	-	1	-	-	4	-	-	-
Aufkl.-									
Abt. 12	-	4	22	-	6	10	1	-	4
2.Pz.Kp.	-	-	-	1	-	4	-	-	-
Staff I.Pz.									
Abt. & 5.									
& 9.Pz. Kp.	-	-	-	1	-	4	1	1	3

The total losses of this day: 27 killed, 30 wounded, and 10 missing, for a total of 67.

It had been reported that a Sherman tank had been knocked out by an anti-tank gun in position near the Abteilung command post. Hauptsturm-führer von Reitzenstein and the commander of the Stabskompanie (staff company), Untersturmführer Wieneke worked their way forward to the knocked-out tank during the night 11–12 June, starting out at approximately 02.00 hours. While Wieneke covered, von Reitzenstein started the tank. They drove it back to the command post and set it over the earth bunker as protection from shrapnels. A dead soldier was found in the Sherman. He was buried in Cristot. The tank could not be used for anti-tank operations since hits to the turret had destroyed the traverse and gun elevation mechanisms. For safety reasons, the ammunition was unloaded. The boxes holding provisions, found tied to the rear of the tank, were joyfully secured. The men marveled at the equipment and provisions of the British.[11]

CHAPTER 2.2
Repelling the Attack on le Mesnil-Patry on 11 June 1944

The 3rd Canadian Infantry Division had prepared an attack by the 2nd Canadian Armoured Brigade for 12 June. Its objective was to capture the high terrain south of Cheux (Hill 107). As a requirement for this attack, the Mue valley near Rots had to be cleared on 11 June. In order to support the attack by the 69th Infantry Brigade of the 50th Infantry Division against the Brouay-Cristot sector, both attacks were scheduled for 11 June.[1] In the early morning hours of 11 June, the 2nd Canadian Armoured Brigade received the order to commence the attack on the high terrain south of Cheux as early as possible. At 08.00 hours, the participating troops were ordered to start the attack at 13.00 hours. The time for preparing this attack was very short, apparently too short to plan artillery support.[2] Only on 10 June, the 6th Armoured Regiment had received twenty replacement tanks with crews. They had to be made ready for battle. The men had to be introduced to their first battle experiences.[3]

The attack was to be carried out by the 6th Armoured Regiment (The First Hussars Regiment), a tank unit, and The Queen's Own Rifles of Canada, an infantry battalion. After marching through Norrey and passing through their own minefield along a predetermined path, the mission of the attacking troops was first to capture le Mesnil-Patry. Then, swinging to the left, proceed via le Haut du Bosq to take and hold the high terrain south of Cheux.[4] The attack point was formed by "B" Squadron of the Hussars and the mounted "D" Company of the Rifles. After passing along the path through the minefield, "C" Squadron was to follow to the right rear in order to secure the right flank against the troops located south of Putot. "A" Squadron and the unit staff followed behind.

The assembly was detected by the radio surveillance of "HJ" Division and reported. The artillery had spotted the marching units. The Hussars, coming from Bretteville, crossed the rail line near the station north of Norrey. They had to detour around a Panther of 3. Panzerkompanie which had been knocked out here during the attack of 9 June. Just as the point tanks rolled through the narrow village streets, they had to maneuver back and forth at the church to get around a sharp corner, heavy fire from German artillery and mortars set in. It was impossible to find another way, the village had to be traversed under fire.[5]

The attack began at 14.30 hours. The Pioniers, located closest to the enemy in the attack strip, had been ordered to let the tanks roll by and only fight the infantry following behind with rifles and machine guns. They were in position in a field of wheat. Their well-camouflaged foxholes could not be spotted. Since the enemy infantry did not follow the tanks but was mounted on them instead, the men opened fire immediately. The Canadian infantrymen jumped off. The tanks rolled, their machine guns firing wildly in all directions, at high speed towards le Mesnil. Bloody hand-to-hand combat between the Pioniers and the Canadian infantry broke out. At the same time, the Pioniers detailed to fight the tanks attacked them with anti-tank rifles, Panzerfaust and magnetic mines. Pionier Gassner attached a magnetic mine to a Sherman. As he jumped off into cover he came under the direct fire of the tank gun and was killed. Immediately after that, the Canadian tank blew up.[6] Pionier Horst Lütgens was fortunate enough to survive. He describes the battle with a Sherman in this way:

> Our Pionier scouting party had dug in at an orchard. The main battle line was 200 m in front of us. I sat outside my foxhole and was writing a letter to my relatives. Suddenly, the Canadians opened fire on our front lines from all barrels. Since I had not yet seen very much action, I felt pretty uneasy. Almost immediately, Unterscharführer -Vogel who commanded the Zug, yelled: 'Tanks from ahead!' Then I could also hear the engine noise and the barking of the machine guns.
>
> 'Lütgens, Panzerfaust ready, let's go!' came Unter-scharführer Vogel's voice. I was the only one in the Zug who had gone through extensive training with this weapon and knew it well. I had been taught that detonators and explosives had always to be kept separately. Now, we had the mess! Theory and practice are indeed quite different. I planned to overcome this later, if I was still alive. The detonator was with Walter Stinner, in his foxhole 20 m away. In the meantime, the tanks were coming closer and closer.
>
> 'Lütgens, get out, attack the first tank!', Unterschar-führer Vogel shouted urgently. Gathering all my courage, I jumped out of my hole and crawled, while machine gun salvos whistled above, close to the ground, to Walter Stinner. 'Walter, quickly, hand me the detonators!' He threw them over to me and shouted: ' Horst, good luck!' I really needed it, these giants had arrived in the meantime. Now I was suddenly very calm, but a rage quelled inside me. I asked myself what had happened to my comrades up front. Were they dead or had they let the tanks roll past? I crawled back to my hole and grabbed my first Panzerfaust and made it ready. I had three of them in my foxhole. Then I looked for a victim. There it sat, the Sherman, huge and mighty. Its turret was pointed in the direction of our battalion command post. Its gun fired round after round. I had to get closer to it. I started to crawl. To my right, Unterscharführer Mathoni appeared. He had obviously figured out what I planned since he shouted at me: 'Horst, look after yourself. I'll give you cover!' These words helped me a lot, they showed that I was not all by myself in this inferno. Now, there were even more tanks! One, two, three, four, five of these Shermans could be seen in the blue haze of the air saturated by gunpowder smoke. When I was within twenty meters, I aimed and fired. But nothing happened. Jam! Just what I needed! Once more, I cocked and fired. Jammed again! Now I was getting nervous. I cocked the weapon again and this time it roared off. I could not watch the hit. The tank providing cover had spotted me

and was firing on me. I did hear the explosion, and then ran in zigzagging jumps back to my foxhole. All of a sudden, the Canadians turned away. I could immediately make out the reason for this. Three German Panzers had joined the battle. It was a feast for the eyes. Within a short time, six Shermans were in flames or had blown up. The order to counterattack was a relief. Now we could come to the help of our comrades up front. The Canadian infantry had penetrated together with the tanks, so we held little hope for our boys. We took several prisoners, among them a wounded Captain. The prisoners were taken to the rear by an escort.

After the powder smoke had lifted, I inspected 'my' Sherman. It had been hit from the front, directly under the driver's seat. The shell had drilled through a set of spare tracks and the armor. Suddenly, the battalion commander stood in front of me. His arm was in a sling. 'Thanks a lot, Lütgens. This guy was giving us hell. He was just about to zero in on my bunker. Who knows what would have happened if you hadn't knocked it out.' He handed me an Iron Cross II. and assured me that the tank-killer stripes would follow later.[7]

A squad leader of the Granatwerferzug (mortars) of 4. (heavy) Pionierkompanie also disabled a Sherman. It was later taken over, fit for action.[8]

The chief of 8. Panzerkompanie, Obersturmführer Hans Siegel, was on his way to the command post of II. Abteilung of Panzerregiment 12 south of Fontenay around 14.00 hours. War decorations were to be awarded there. He had with him one Panzer and several noncoms and men. Just outside the town he encountered his commander, Sturmbannführer Prinz. Prinz told him that the commander of SS-Panzergrenadierregiment 26, Obersturmbannführer Mohnke, had just been to see him. Mohnke had requested Panzer support against an attack by enemy tanks and infantry near le Mesnil. Siegel was ordered to turn around immediately, to determine the situation and clear it up if necessary. After he returned to the Kompanie, his squad leaders reported that heavy infantry and artillery fire had been heard for some time from the right of le Mesnil.

The 8. Kompanie sat in ambush position behind the sector of II./26, approximately one kilometer south of le Mesnil. The squad leaders were celebrating Untersturmführer Jeran's birthday. The battle noise grew ever louder and was getting closer. Mushrooms of smoke, generated by knocked-out tanks, could be spotted. Obersturmführer Siegel decided to 'check things out'. He took the three Panzers sitting furthest to the right. Among them was Untersturmführer Jeran. He reports:

As we rolled forward, and during an observation stop, I recognized from the agitated gestures of some grenadiers who were pointing in the direction of the enemy with their spades, that acute danger was facing us. 'Ready for action!' On this order, the hatches of the three Panzers closed as by themselves. The gun barrels were wound down to firing elevation. Anti-tank shells were loaded on the move. A hedge was still obstructing our vision of the enemy on the left. When the hedge suddenly disappeared and the point Panzer was already in the midst of our own infantry, several Shermans were spotted rolling at a dangerous distance toward us through the orchard of a farm. We had driven right in front of their barrels and were showing them our vulnerable flanks. 'Enemy tanks from the left—nine o'clock—200—open fire!' This was all the chief of the 8., who was also the commander of the point Panzer, could do. But nothing else was required. The months-long drills and battle experience of the crews now proved themselves. The driver jerked the Panzer to the left, bringing it into firing position. Even before the fighting compartment ventilation fan, crucial for the survival of the crew, got to full speed, the closest enemy tank had been hit. Within a minute or so, four or five Shermans were burning. Only the last one, which had worked its way to within 100 meters on the far left, brought the sweat to the commander's brow. It had only just been spotted as it was already swinging its turret toward us. 'Enemy tank hard left—ten o'clock—100!' Barrel was now turning toward barrel, muzzle against muzzle. Through the gun sights they were close enough to touch. For another blink of an eye, the gunners may have aimed the cross hairs of their gun sights at each other. Then came a blow, a flash of fire from the breech of the gun, the cartridge dropped into the sack, the enemy tank exploded!

Only now, the other two Panzers could close in. They had stood behind the hedge, unable to observe what happened right before our eyes. Even before our infantry was ready to storm ahead, the three Panzers drove past the burning wrecks and between the fruit trees to our own main line of resistance. As we were advancing, the command Panzer knocked out two more Shermans from a distance of 1,200 meters. They had tried to get away.

The enemy was retreating and in considerable confusion. It was important to take advantage of this situation. The other two Panzers were ordered to follow, staggered to the left rear, and to push through a field of wheat at full speed without stopping. Once they reached a bordering row of trees and a hedge, 1,600 meters away, they were to halt. During the advance, the command Panzer came under anti-tank fire from a line of trees on the right. The commander informed the crew through his throat microphone: 'Pak fire from the right!' Once again, the driver reacted immediately. He pulled the Panzer around into firing position. And now a duel of fire started. After five exchanges, our Panzer took a direct hit from a second or even third anti-tank gun. The crew bailed out, regrettably without the radio operator who had fallen victim to the hit to the right front. The Panzer was in flames, and fire from all kinds of weapons covered the spot where it had been knocked out. The other two tanks had also stopped to fire and had been hit. They were stuck approximately 800 meters to the rear.[9]

At the same time as the Panzer IV of Obersturmführer Siegel, those units of 1. Pionierkompanie which were ready for action, began a counterattack. They pushed back the Canadian infantrymen who had broken through or took them prisoner.

The Hussar's "C" Squadron had recognized the predicament of "B" Squadron which had pulled ahead, and closed up on the right. They came under fire from the right flank from anti-tank guns or Panzers. The commander thought he had, by mistake, come under fire from members of the 69th Brigade which was simultaneously attacking toward Brouay and -Cristot. He ordered messages be sent using signal flags. He climbed out of his tank to verbally inform all the other tanks. The fire grew more intense and one tank after the other was hit. In reality, he was caught in the counter-attack by further units of II. Panzerabteilung. Immediately after Sturmbannführer Prinz had ordered Obersturmführer Siegel to check things out in his sector, he obtained additional situation reports. Then he gathered the units of his Abteilung not yet in action for a counterattack and attacked with them past le Mesnil to the west, or through the town. He was just in time to destroy "C" Squadron before it could come to the aid of "B" Squadron. Its point tanks had already advanced to the command post of 7./26 under Leutnant Henne. The coordinated efforts of Obersturmführer Siegel, an anti-tank gun of II./26 in position at the edge of le Mesnil, and of tank hunting parties, the remaining tanks of 'B" Squadron were knocked out. The order from the commander of the Hussars, Lieutenant Colonel Colwell, to withdraw to the starting -positions arrived either too late or did not reach the troops.[10] The two point companies of his unit were destroyed, as was "D" Company of the Queen's Own Rifles. Only few could save themselves by retreating behind their own lines. The Hussars lost thirty-seven Sherman tanks. All officers and noncoms of "B" Squadron, with the exception of three, were missing. The unit had eighty losses, of these fifty-nine were killed or wounded. "D" Company of the Queen's Own Rifles lost ninety-six men, of these fifty-five were killed or wounded.[11]

The defenders, too, had suffered heavy losses. Regiment 26 recorded two officers, one NCO and fifteen men killed, six NCOs and twenty-six men wounded, one man missing. Among the dead were the commander of 2. Kompanie, Leutnant Sauer, one NCO and two men. They had held their position at the Cardonville estate near the rail line since the attack on 8

June. Now, they had been overrun. The Pionierbataillon reported one officer, one NCO and twenty-seven men killed, one officer, Dr. Zistler, the medical officer, three NCOs and forty-five men were wounded, five men were missing. The list of II. Panzerabteilung showed one man killed, seven men wounded, one officer and four men missing. This amounts to a total of 189 losses. Three Panzers had been knocked out. One of them was later retrieved and repaired.[12]

Obersturmführer Siegel reports on the final phase of the battle:

After I had reached our own lines again, together with a Canadian corporal who had surrendered, an uncommonly impressive scene could be observed. The Canadians were driving ambulances onto the battle field. Each of them had a man standing on the running board, waving a large Red Cross flag. Medics with stretchers jumped off while the flag carriers continued to wave their flags. For approximately half an hour, the wounded were found and removed, as if it were a peace-time exercise. Not a shot was fired to disturb this activity.[13]

In contrast to this, the next day again brought an example of inhuman battle conduct. Pionier Herbert Wendel was at the main dressing station. A machine gun salvo had penetrated both his upper legs on the previous day. His right eye was irreparably injured. He had bruises from tank tracks on both legs. Next to him, Pionier Klumpler, also wounded, had been bedded down. Suddenly, the dressing station, well and visibly marked as such, came under attack from fighter-bombers. There were a number of casualties. Pionier Klumpler was killed.[14]

CHAPTER 2.3
Defense and Withdrawal from Rots on 11–12 June 1944

Rots had been captured on 9 June by 1. Kompanie of SS-Panzergrenadier-regiment 26. Together with two attached 7.5 cm anti-tank guns of 4./26, one Zug of Pioniers of 16./26, and the 4. Panzerkompanie, 1. Kompanie prepared for the defense. The Divisionsbegleitkompanie (escort company) had taken up defensive positions at the western edges of the Château park and of la Villeneuve. A forward observer of III. Artillerieabteilung had set up his observation post in the loft. A rifle Zug had taken up position at the northern edge of Rots. From there, the valley of the Mue creek, running northeast and covered with trees and bushes, as well as the open terrain in the direction of Rosel and Vieux Cairon, could be watched. A gap of almost 2.5 kilometers existed from there to Gruchy where parts of III./25 were in position. The other two rifle Züge had set up defenses west of the Mue creek, facing northwest. They were located on the other side of the road from le Hamel to Lasson and in the northeastern sector of le Hamel. On the order of Hauptsturmführer Helmut Eggert, commander of 1. Kompanie, two anti-tank guns of 4./26 had taken up positions well forward in order to have a firm link-up with the Pioniers. Hauptsturmführer Hans Pfeiffer, commander of 4. Panzerkompanie, had placed a number of Panthers in Rots in such a manner that they could be effective, from their cover, to the north and northwest. Some of them were sitting at the road junction at the southeast corner of the park. Others were at the intersection near the school and several were close to the church in the northern sector of Rots.[1]

This forward German position in Rots threatened the deep flank of the Canadians in Norrey, Bretteville l'Orgeilleuse and Putot. Thus, the 3rd Canadian Division ordered its elimination. For the attack on Rots, the 8th Canadian Infantry Brigade put the 46th Royal Marine Commando, reinforced by a company of the 10th Canadian Armoured Regiment, into action. They were to advance along the valley of the Mue creek from north to south, drive back the forces there, and clear the creek valley. The two infantry battalions, de la Chaudière and North Shore, were ordered to advance into the villages in the creek valley as soon as the attack by the Marines moved forward. For this reason, the de la Chaudière battalion was assembled near Bray, two kilometers northwest of Rots.[2]

Since the commando units were special troops, here is some background information for ease of understanding. The commandos consisted of twenty-four officers and 440 NCOs and men. They were divided into platoons of three officers and sixty NCOs and men each, with light weapons, light equipment and only the most essential vehicles.[3]

The troops in action in and around Rots were under heavy fire throughout the night of 9 to 10 June. During 10 June, too, the positions were subjected to massive artillery shelling. Brisk air activity prevented all movement during the day. Toward the evening, enemy tanks were spotted. They fired, from a depression in the ground, at suspected positions approximately 800 meters north of Rots. There were no losses.[4]

In the morning of 11 June, the commander of a heavy Zug spotted a Sherman, with two artillery observers mounted on the turret, on the road from Lasson to le Hamel, driving in the direction of le Hamel. The anti-tank gun could not find a field of fire. Instead, the mounted artillery men came under effective fire from a machine gun. Soon after, barrages of medium and heavy caliber concentrated on the position of the heavy Zug. When the fire died down, the men noticed the assembly of a dozen Sherman tanks and strong accompanying infantry forces on their right flank in the Mue valley.

This was also observed by a Panther sitting near the church. The driver, Sturmmann Hans Kesper, remembers it this way:

> We were sitting in ambush position, well camouflaged, near a farm. The church was to our right. After a violent artillery attack, ten to fifteen Sherman tanks attacked us from dead ahead. My vehicle, our gunner was Unterscharführer Ecki Stuhldreher, knocked out four or five of this group. The others turned away. In retaliation, the enemy concentrated horrific fire on us. Our infantry suffered severe losses. During the afternoon, the village was attacked once more. Our Panzers of III. Zug were battling in the town with Shermans and infantry which had penetrated. The vehicles of I. Zug, among them the command Panzer, held on to a small hill. My Panzer had damage to the tracks. We were sitting, somewhat covered, on the rear slope. I asked two grenadiers to help me mount the track. Despite the artillery explosions all around us, they did. On the radio I heard, even outside, the urgent orders from Hauptsturmführer Pfeiffer: 'Speed it up! The pressure is getting too strong!' Our own infantry was already coming down the hill. I drove off, uphill, to assist the command Panzer. A group of our own infantry was lying in a ditch, helpless, in the fire of explosive shells from British tanks. We opened fire on the Shermans and the attacking infantry. When I glanced to the left for a moment, the command Panzer was driving down the hill. One minute later, word of its demise arrived. The British or Canadians were already in the village, but our forward repair squad brought the dead commander in on a Carette.[5]

The Marines, together with Sherman tanks, penetrated into the northern part of Rots. After suffering severe losses, 1. Kompanie in action there, could no longer hold on. The chief of the Divisionsbegleitkompanie, Obersturmführer Guntrum, with two squads of his infantry and several Panthers, began a counterattack. They managed to clear the edge of town from west to east. The Panthers knocked out six Shermans, forty prisoners were taken. In a renewed attack, supported by eight Shermans, the Marines again pushed into the village. The forces of the defenders were no longer sufficient for another counterattack.[6]

Attacked in the flank and threatened from the rear, the two rifle Züge, the heavy Zug and the two anti-tank guns could no longer hold their positions. Under the fire of five Shermans, IV. Zug of 1./26 fought its way back to the position of the anti-tank gun. It was impossible to move the gun into a new firing position as required by the changed situation. Also, the attempt to recapture the positions of I. Zug through a counterattack faltered in the presence of a superior enemy who was already in the rear of the heavy Zug. Oberscharführer Hahn and his men fought their way back to the bridge in the center of town. There he encountered the Kompanie commander, Hauptsturmführer Eggert, who ordered him to hold the bridge for as long as possible and then to fight defensively from the houses to the right of the Mue creek. Oberscharführer Karl Friedrich Hahn describes the ensuing battle in the town as follows:

It was not very long before the Canadian tanks started rolling towards the bridge, spreading wild fireworks ahead of them. I ordered individual withdrawal to the houses in our rear, each would give the other covering fire. I remained, together with the machine gunner Sturmmann Isterling, who had only just shown his mettle, until the tanks reached us, or had even passed us. Ahead and in between the steel giants we managed the almost impossible, we made it to the houses behind us. There I encountered Untersturmführer Groß who was just firing a Panzerfaust at a Sherman. I suddenly found myself inside a house together with another comrade. Only a low wall separated me from the tanks rolling by and from the infantrymen with them. I had made my decision, during the next gap between them, I would fight my way to the other side of the street using a hand grenade and my submachine gun. Just then I heard tank noises and wild shooting. Crouching below the window ledge, I watched the street, spellbound. Then, when a tank rolled in front of my window and I spotted the Balken cross, it was almost beyond my imagination that I had been saved by a Panther. I jumped onto the street, and suddenly all my comrades were around me again. Then began a battle of Panzer against tanks, while we fired on the British infantry which was scattering into all directions. Death reaped a rich harvest among these young Marine infantrymen. Many seemed to have forgotten their training and ran into our fire. After the Panther had knocked out two Shermans and a Carette, it drove on in the direction of le Bourg. Suddenly, two Shermans appeared which pursued it at high speed. It was knocked out by a hit to the engine compartment. I took cover, together with Forth, behind a house until the Canadian tanks had passed. Then we spotted Unterscharführer Tauschwitz lying wounded on the ground, all by himself. French civilians had dressed his wounds. We bedded him on a wheelbarrow and I rolled it down the village street. But again came the shouts: 'Tanks!' I raced down the street at a hell of a speed, behind me the tank noises coming closer. Now, three of the beasts showed up and I wheeled to the left into a farm. The tanks drove around it to the right. I bedded Tauschwitz down in the road ditch next to the house wall and covered him with the wheelbarrow. The tanks were firing wildly, then drove back into the village center after a while. There I met up again with Untersturmführer Groß and the other comrades.[7]

The commander of the Pak-Zug (anti-tank gun), Ober-scharführer Erwin Wohlgemut, reports on the violent fighting in the village:

We reached 1. Kompanie in the center of the village after crossing through some gardens. There was heavy fighting in the streets. The street surface was virtually covered with dead and wounded. They were mostly English. Suddenly, a Panther showed up, to support us. It was a terrible scene as the Panzer, crushing the dead and wounded, made its way to the intersection. There was no escape on the narrow street, framed by houses and walls. With the Panzer's support we started a counterattack. Soon after, a shout came: 'Tanks from behind!' Our Panzer was in a difficult situation. It could not turn around in the narrow street. So it backed up to a spot where it could at least swing the turret around by 180 degrees. With this, it rolled slowly toward the village exit. Suddenly, a Sherman showed up ahead. Our Panzer crew must have spotted it, since the engine was gunned to a howl in an attempt to gain the edge of town where the turret could be traversed. They did not make it, our Panther was knocked out. Whether from ahead or behind, I do not recall. As I heard later, Hauptsturmführer Pfeiffer was reported to have been killed in this Panzer.[8]

The fighting inside the village raged all night. At dawn of 12 June, the last of those who had held on in the town reached the outposts of 15./25 west of Franqueville. The Begleitkompanie, too, which had been attacked in its positions in the park of the Château by tanks and infantry, and had held these positions, was ordered by I./26 to withdraw from the southwest sector of Rots. Panthers had knocked out 2 Shermans during the fighting. It took up new positions approximately 1.000 meters to the south.[9]

The severity of the fighting was also confirmed by a report from the other side:

Infantry of the de la Chaudière Regiment and tanks of the Fort Gary Horse were quickly assembled behind the battered 6th Armoured Regiment. They were dug in between Bray and Rots for the eventuality that the 12. SS would take advantage of the confusion and break through to the coast. For the Chaudières it was their first encounter with the Waffen-SS, and not a happy one. Only a few wounded returned from its first scouting party to Rots. The Grenadiers had let them come up very close before opening fire. Later in the evening, the outstanding 46th Royal Marine Commando attacked the hand-picked boys of the Hitlerjugend. 'They fought like lions on both sides. The dead were lying body to body', wrote the historians of the Chaudières who reached the village the next morning. 'We searched every house, every yard, to prevent ambushes. That is the confirmation of how brutal the fighting of last night must have been. The commandos were lying dead in rows next to the dead SS-men. Hand grenades were scattered everywhere in the streets and front doors of the houses. At one spot we saw a commando and an SS-man who died virtually arm-in-arm, one killing the other. At another spot we found a German and a Canadian tank, having crushed each other. They were still smoking and from each of the smoke-blackened turrets hung the dead bodies of the machine gunners. Over there was a squad which had run toward a small wall to seek cover. They had been shot down before they reached it. And then, at the church, as the vanguard of "C" Company and the Carettes swung around the corner, they encountered three Germans. Only three. But one of them immediately drew his pistol and hit one of our men. A machine gunner killed two of the three SS-men, but the survivor did not surrender. He tricked us and disappeared. Now you will understand what fanatics we were facing.[10]

French villagers reported on the fighting:

The whole battle for Rots took place between the church and the schoolhouses (northeast corner of the Château park). They fought with cold steel, with Panzerfaust, shot each other in the cellars. A German Panzer went up in flames in the church square, as did a Canadian tank. The number of dead on both sides surpassed one-hundred.[11]

During a discussion between the 3rd Canadian Division and the 8th Brigade the desirability of holding Rots was pondered. As a result, the Régiment de la Chaudière was ordered to take over the sector. Claims are that it buried 122 killed Germans. Its own losses were reported as seventeen killed, nine wounded and thirty-five missing. The Glengarrians captured Vieux Carrion, three kilometers east of Rots, in the course of 11. June.[12]

The German losses were also severe:

	Killed			Wounded			Missing		
	Officers	NCOs	Men	Officers	NCOs	Men	Officers	NCOs	Men
1./26, Pak-Zug, Pionierzug	-	3	14	-	7	18	-	-	15
Div.Bgl.Kp.	-	-	3	-	-	2	-	-	-
4.Pz.-Kp.	1	-	1	-	1	2	-	-	-
Totals	1	3	18	-	8	22	-	-	15

The total losses were: 22 dead, 30 wounded, and 15 missing. All together, these amounted to 67 losses.

The Panzerjägerzug (tank hunters) had lost two anti-tank guns. The number of lost Panthers is not known, at least one was a total loss.[13]

CHAPTER 2.4
Repelling the Attempted Breakthrough by the 7th Armoured Division via Villers-Bocage to Evrecy on 13 and 14 June 1944

The counterattacks by parts of 21. Pz.-Div. on 6 June and by the 12. SS-Pz.-Div. from 7 to 10 June had prevented the planned capture of Caen and the Carpiquet airfield. The enemy had been unable to achieve any advances in the sectors northeast, north, and northwest of Caen. The three Panzer-divisions of the I. SS-Panzerkorps had been sent too late to mount a counterattack which would have had any expectation of breaking through on a wide front to the coast, and to prevent the link-up of the two British/Canadian bridgeheads, and to subsequently smash them. After Bayeux had been captured on 7 June, and the Panzer-Lehr-Division had been unable to re-take it, the initiative in the Caen area was in the hands of the enemy. The enemy had moved the point of major thrust to the left sector of the "HJ" Division and the sector of the Panzer-Lehr-Division. In occasionally heavy fighting, inflicting losses on both sides, the main line of defense of the "HJ" Division, except for the forward bulge position in Rots, had been held. The Panzer-Lehr-Division had successfully defended the line from south of St. Pierre-Tilly-sur-Seulles-Lingèvres-la Sanaudière to the Aure creek against concentrated attacks. The contact to 352. Infanterie Division to the left had been lost. This division, which had successfully resisted for a long time on the day of the invasion, had been weakened by constant attacks by superior enemy forces. It had reached a point where it could no longer hold its sector, despite reinforcements which had trickled in. The approaching infantry and Fallschirmjäger (paratroopers) divisions marched partly on foot, partly on bicycles or on vehicles, even civilian busses. This required much too much time. A successful counterattack here could have only been conducted by Panzerdivisions. They were not there. The 2. Pz.Div., part of the Heeresgruppenreserve (army group reserve) was only put on immediate marching readiness on 9 June. The majority of the wheeled units marched through Paris in the evening. The tracked units (Panzerregiment, Schützenpanzerbataillon [armored cars], parts of the Aufklärungsabteilung) had to be transported by rail. Significant delays occurred, caused by a shortage of locomotives. At the same time, 116.

Pz.Div. which also belonged to the Heeresgruppen reserve, advanced to the line Neufchatel (forty kilometers northeast of Rouen)-Yvetot (thirty kilometers northwest of Rouen). Thus, it remained east of the Seine river. The 17. SS-Panzergrenadierdivision "Götz von Berlichingen" and the 2. SS-Panzerdivision "Das Reich" advanced from the areas south of the Loire river. Both had significant problems transporting the tracked vehicles by rail. In addition, "Das Reich" Division had been ordered to take part in putting down the uprising by the Maquis (French underground) in the Limoges area. Because of this, the wheeled vehicles could only begin their march from the Limoges area to the invasion front on 12 June. The tracked vehicle units, completely inadequate for fighting the Maquis, had to drive 300 kilometers through hilly terrain to the loading area Périgieux-Angoulême. Before loading there, they had to await the arrival of the initial issue of spares to repair the damaged Panzers and get them ready for action. Thus, the transport trains could only leave on 15 June. Approximately one third of the Division had to remain behind in the Montauban area since only a portion of the vehicles to refit the Division had arrived. The war diary of the 7. Armee contains the following entries regarding the progress of the march in the evening of 11. June:

> Bulk of 3. Fallschirmjägerdivision located in the area northeast of St. Lô, parts of 17. SS-Panzergrenadierdivision are in the assembly area southwest of Carentan, Kampfgruppen 265. and 275. Inf.Div. have reached the St. Lô area, first units of Werferbrigade 8 (mortar brigade) have arrived after land march from the Chartres area.

An additional entry on 12. June states that wheeled units of 2. Pz.Div. would probably arrive early on 14. June and that:

> Wheeled units of 2. SS-Pz.Div. would be available for action at the earliest in the morning of 15 June.

In the evening of 11 June, the 7. Armee had learned that the enemy had penetrated into Carentan. Only at 06.20 on 12 June, the report arrived there that the city had fallen into enemy hands the previous day at 18.00 hours after bitter hand-to-hand combat. Lack of ammunition at Fallschirmjägerregiment 6, in particular, was the cause. With this, the wedge which separated the two American landing areas had been penetrated. Based on the situation, as it was known in the evening of 11 June, the 7. Armee reported to Heeresgruppe B the following intentions for 12 June:

> I.SS-Panzerkorps will hold its present line, releasing Panzer forces for the counterattack. The left wing (Pz.-Lehr-Div.) will close the gap to 352. Inf.Div. with Aufklärungs units.

The right flank of 3. Fallschirmjäger-Div. will advance to the Vire-Elle sector.

The 17. SS-Panzergrenadierdivision will assemble south of Carentan for the attack to the east or north.[2]

While the attention of 7. Armee was centered mainly on the development of the situation at the base of the Cotentin and a major attack was expected on Caen, based on reports of tank concentrations by I. SS-Panzerkorps at its northern front, the Americans and British took advantage of the gap between the Pz.-Lehr-Div. and 352. Inf.Div. on 12 June. Reconnaissance by Pz.-Lehr-Div. determined 'weak enemy reconnaissance forces' in the area near Caumont. The commanding general of LXXXIV A.K., General der Artillerie (general of the artillery) Marcks, was killed during a fighter-bomber attack on the march to Caumont with hastily assembled units. While the Armee still believed that only weak enemy reconnaissance forces existed, the Supreme Commander West ordered the gap between Pz.-Lehr-Div. and 352. Inf.Div. to be closed as quickly as possible using all available forces. The immediate goal had to be the creation of a clear coherent front. The Armee reported that, to achieve this, it had sent into action the Aufklärungsabteilung of 2. Pz.Div., parts of Panzer-Aufklärungs-Lehrabteilung and the reconnaissance of 3. Fallschirmjäger Division. The wheeled units of 2. Pz.Div. and 2. SS-Pz.Div. would be put into action immediately after arriving.

The attacks by the 50th Infantry Division and the 7th Armoured Division, supported by units of the 3rd Canadian Infantry Division from the north on the left flank of the "HJ" Division and the sector of the Pz.-Lehr-Div., with the objective of Villers-Bocage, on 11 June had brought no successes. Since they also failed in the morning of 12 June, the Second British Army ordered at noon of 12 June to take advantage of the gap which had developed further to the west. Regarding this, a report of the 22nd Armoured Brigade of the 7th Armoured Division states:

> Because of the difficult terrain and the resulting slow advance, it was decided that the 7th Armoured Division would by-pass the left flank of the Pz.-Lehr-Div. to the left of the American sector. The Americans were just to the north of Caumont and there were positive expectations that this success could be used in the direction of Villers-Bocage and, if possible, to capture Point 213 [2.5 kilometers northeast of Villers-Bocage].[3]

If this was successful, the Division was to advance further on Evrécy (twelve kilometers east-northeast of Villers-Bocage). Units of the 50th Infantry Division would follow, a reinforcement by the 1st British Airborne Division was planned.[4] Evrécy is located in a depression of the range of hills between the Odon and Orne rivers, three kilometers southwest of Hill 112 which would take on great importance. The success of this daring plan would have severely threatened the rear of the front near Caen.

The first marching group consisted of a battle group of the 22nd Armoured Brigade. Formation, and also marching order, of the battle group:

8th King's Royal Irish Hussars (reconnaissance unit),

4th County of London Yeomanry "Sharpshooters" (tank unit), battle staff of the 22nd Armoured Brigade,

5th RHA (artillery unit) without one battery,

1/7 Battalion The Queen's Royal Regiment (infantry),

5th Battalion Royal Tank Regiment,

1st Battalion The Rifle Brigade (armored infantry) without two companies,

260th Anti-Tank Battery.

This battle group assembled at 16.00 hours on 12 June. Its vanguard encountered an anti-tank gun and infantry near Livry (3.5 kilometers northeast of Caumont). When the situation had been cleared up at 20.00 hours, it seemed too late for further advance. The column took until midnight to catch up. The battle group rested in Livry and established contact with the 1st US Infantry Division in the Caumont area. Apart from the late hour, it appeared advisable to the brigade commander to stop the advance since this would keep the enemy in the dark on his further intentions: advance to the south or to the southeast.[5]

At 05.30 hours on 13 June the battle group started its further advance. The "Sharpshooters" were at the point, the 8th Hussars (without two companies) secured the right flank. The 11th Hussars, the reconnaissance unit of XXX Corps, scouted along both sides of the route of advance. The Brigade had expectantly ordered, in case it was possible to capture it, how the area around Villers-Bocage would be secured:

4th "Sharpshooters" capture and secure Hill 213 northeast of Villers-Bocage,

1/7 Queens capture and secure the exits from Villers-Bocage, except those west of the church,

1st Rifle Battalion (without two companies) capture and secure the remaining three exits from town,

5th Royal Tanks capture and hold the high terrain around Maisoncelles-Pelvy (three kilometers southwest of Villers-Bocage, meant is probably Hill 174, approximately 1.2 kilometers southeast of the town),

260th Anti-Tank Battery will close the gap between the "Sharpshooters" and 5th Royal Tanks.

There was no contact with the enemy during the march and in Villers-Bocage except for the units securing the flanks.[6]

Despite the lack of aerial reconnaissance, the I. SS-Panzerkorps was aware of the threats to its deep flank. None of the three Panzerdivisions in action at the front had available reserves which could have been used to secure the flanks. Thus, the general command saw itself forced to move the parts of the Korps-Tiger-Abteilung (Schwere SS-Panzerabteilung 101) which had just arrived, behind the left flank of the Panzer-Lehr-Division during the night of 12–13 June. The Abteilung had left the area near Beauvais (approximately seventy kilometers north-northwest of Paris) by road during the night 6–7 June. During a night attack in the woods near Versailles, 3. Kompanie and the repair company had suffered significant losses. The long march on land also brought about considerable technical losses. The companies arrived at the front only with a portion of their Panzers. Before an action, several days of technical servicing would have been necessary, but there was no time for it.[7]

Under the leadership of Hauptsturmführer Rolf Möbius, 1. Kompanie was resting on the morning of 13 June approximately ten kilometers northeast of Villers-Bocage after a night march. Seven to nine Tigers had arrived by then.[8] The 2. Kompanie of Obersturmführer Michel Wittmann had made camp at the same time in a small wooded area directly south of the tiny village of Montbrocq, located immediately south of the Route Nationale and two kilometers northeast of Villers-Bocage. Extremely heavy artillery fire had forced them to move positions three times during the night. One Tiger secured northwest of the town along a country-lane running parallel to the Route Nationale. Obersturmführer Jürgen Wessel, leading I. Zug, had been attached to I. Panzerkorps as liaison officer. On its orders, he immediately established contact from there with the Panzer-Aufklärungs-Lehrabteilung which was in position to secure the left flank of the Panzer-Lehr-Division.[9] It had been forced to extend its left flank on 12 June from Torteval (6.5 kilometers northeast of Caumont) to Anctoville (7.5 kilometers northeast of Caumont) since the enemy had attacked near Torteval with tanks and infantry. In the morning of 13 June, the Abteilung observed and successfully battled tanks, armored cars and trucks northwest of Torteval. The reconnaissance reported constant contact with the enemy in a southwesterly direction.[10] This was likely the securing of the flanks by the 11th Hussars. Obersturmführer Wessel drove to the Korps command post via the most direct route possible. The Korps had obviously been informed previously by telephone. It alerted the two Tiger companies and ordered the "HJ" Division to have two Panzer companies ready for departure. One Panther and one Panzer IV company were assigned to this.[11]

In the meantime, the vanguard of the 22nd Armoured Brigade had reached Villers-Bocage and passed it unhindered. The main column, traveling on the road Livry-Amaye sur Seulles-Villers-Bocage, did not encounter any enemy forces. One company of the "Sharpshooters" and a motorized company of the 1/7 Queen's marched along Route Nationale on to Hill 213 (217) where it was to establish securing positions.[12] The further developments are described in detail in the submission of 13 June by the general command I. SS-Panzerkorps to award the Knight's Cross with Oak Leaves and Swords to Obersturmführer Michel Wittmann. There it is stated:

At 08.00 hours, a security post reported to SS-Ober-sturm-führer Wittmann that a strong column of enemy tanks was marching on the road Caen-Villers-Bocage.

Wittmann, who was in cover with his Tiger 200 m south of the road, identified an English tank unit followed by an English armored car battalion.

The situation demanded immediate action. Wittmann was unable to issue any orders to his dismounted men. Instead, he immediately pushed into the English column with his own Panzer, firing on the move. Through this quick action the enemy column was initially separated. At a distance of eighty meters, Wittmann knocked out four Sherman tanks. Then he maneuvered his Tiger into and parallel to the column at 10-30 m, and drove alongside, in its marching direction, firing on the move. He was successful in knocking out fifteen heavy enemy tanks within a short period of time. A further six tanks were knocked out and their crews forced to bail out. The accompanying battalion of armored cars was almost completely destroyed. The four Panzers of the Wittmann Kompanie, following behind, took approximately 230 prisoners. Wittmann advanced further, far ahead of his Kompanie, into the town of Villers-Bocage. In the center of town his Panzer was rendered immobile by a heavy enemy anti-tank gun. Despite this, he still destroyed all enemy vehicles within range and dispersed the enemy unit. Then, he and his crew bailed out. They made their way on foot approximately fifteen kilometers to the north to the Panzer-Lehr-Division. There he reported to the Ia, turned around with fifteen Panzers of the Panzer-Lehr-Division and advanced again on Villers-Bocage. His Schwimm-Volkswagen (amphibian VW) had caught up in the meantime. In it, he made his way to 1. Kompanie in action along the main road to Villers-Bocage. Using his recent fighting and situation experiences, he directed 1. Kompanie into action against the enemy tank and anti-tank gun forces still in the town.[13]

After being alerted in the morning, 1. Kompanie of the Tigerabteilung was marching along the Route Nationale in the direction of Villers-Bocage. As it approached Hill 213 (217), the men spotted burning tanks and half-tracks. The four point Tigers drove into Villers-Bocage. Oberscharführer Werner Wendt, Panzer commander and half-platoon leader in 1. Kompanie, reported:

At the edge of the city a street led to the left. Another Tiger and I remained there. The British had withdrawn into the town. There was fire from all corners. We were battling anti-tank guns and infantry. Even today, I can still picture Untersturmführer Lucasius as he was knocked out by close-range weapons. He bailed out. His burns looked frightening. The whole racket was over in the late afternoon.[14]

As the Kompanie commander reported, 1. Kompanie lost three Tigers to close-range weapons.[15] The Panzer losses of 2. Kompanie are not known. The use of Panzers for combat within towns, in particular of Tigers meant to battle tanks at long distances, was obviously inexpedient. Since German infantry was not available, it was correct for Wittmann and Möbius to penetrate into the town with their Tigers. In particular, while the enemy was still under the devastating impression of seeing his vanguard totally destroyed in such short time. The cooperation of the two Tiger companies—a total of only thirteen vehicles at the start of the attack—and hastily assembled units of the Panzer-Lehr-Division was successful in driving the enemy out of the city by noon, with the exception of the western part of town.

The first units of 2. Pz.Div. joined the fighting from the south in the afternoon. Subsequently, the 22nd Armoured Brigade evacuated the city and assembled its remaining forces near Tracy-Bocage (approximately 2.5 kilometers southwest of Villers-Bocage) where the tank unit of the 5th Royal Tanks and artillery had set up defenses in the meantime. The 131st Infantry Brigade prepared for defense in the area around Torteval-la Paumerie (six and three kilometers northeast of Caumont respectively). The divisional commander, General Erskins, assigned the 1/5 Queen's, an infantry battalion, to the 22nd Armoured Brigade. The 1/5 and 1/7 Queen's, the remaining tanks of the "Sharpshooters" and anti-tank guns set up defen-ses at Amaye-sur-Seulles and at Hill 173 (174). A briefing on the situation took place in la Paumerie on 14 June at 16.00 hours. Divisional commander Erskins ordered the 22nd -Armoured Brigade to withdraw to the area of les Orailles (nine kilometers northeast of Caumont) during the night 14–15 June. There it would link up with the right wing of 50th Division and close the gap to the 1st US Infantry Division together with the 13th Infantry Brigade. Erskins cited as the reason for this withdrawal that the frontal attack by the 50th Division against the positions of the Panzer-Lehr-Division was progressing too slowly and that the contact of his Division with the rear was thus too greatly endangered. In order to cover and camouflage the withdrawal, fighter-bombers would attack Villers-Bocage before dusk and heavy bombers at around midnight. The retreat took place as planned and without any significant interruptions from the German side.[17]

The attacks by the 50th Infantry Division and the 8th Armoured Brigade on 12 and 13 June against the positions of the Panzer-Lehr-Division from the north had also had an impact on the left wing of the "HJ" Division, mainly through concentrated artillery fire. The Pionierzug of the Aufklärungs-abteilung positioned mines in front of the most endangered sectors.[18] The war diary of 7. Armee notes for 12 June:

> Enemy attacks against the left wing of 12. SS-Pz.Div. and on both sides of Tilly-sur-Seulles (Pz.-Lehr-Div.) were repulsed, thirty-two tanks knocked out.[19]

The battle of Villers-Bocage was a significant defensive success. It has to be measured against the long-term objective. The letter by General Mont-gomery of 12 June makes it clear that this was not a localized operation, but that it had wide ranging significance. The overall operations plan envisaged that the British Second Army, in this phase, had as the primary objective to tie down German forces. This would offer the First US Army the opportunity to cut off the Cotentin peninsula, capture Cherbourg and finally to break out of the landing area. The Third US Army was standing by in England for this operation. However, Montgomery had doubtlessly not given up the intention and hope to break out of the beach-head first with the British Sec-ond Army. "Operation Perch", as the action at Villers-Bocage/Evrécy had been named, was too daring to just tie down German forces. A great decision was sought, dared, and hoped for. The operation failed primarily through the brave decision by Obersturmführer Michel Wittmann, the most success-ful Panzer commander of the Second World War. It failed because of his courage, his tactical and technical abilities and because of the valor, the expertise and the camaraderie of his Panzer crew. Justifiably, the Oak Leaves with Swords were awarded to Wittmann on 22 June, as the seventy-first sol-dier. As stated in the submission by I. SS-Panzerkorps, he had "knocked out 138 enemy tanks and 132 enemy anti-tank guns" by 14 June.

His success was the condition for the effective actions by parts of the Panzer-Lehr-Division and the first units of 2. Panzerdivision. They would hardly have been successful in resisting the bulk of the concentrated 7th Armoured Division, if it had been able to continue its march unimpeded, and the simultaneous pressure of the 50th Division. There were certainly a number of factors which led to the abandonment of "Operation Perch":

1. The destruction of the vanguard of the 22nd Armoured Brigade by Obersturmführer Wittmann together with other Tigers of 1. and 2. Kompanie/Schwere (heavy) SS-Panzerabteilung 101 and parts of the Panzer-Lehr-Regiment 130.
2. The counterattack by the first units of the just arrived 2. Panzerdivi-sion, not expected by the enemy.

3. The unbreakable resistance by Panzer-Lehr-Division against all attacks by the 50th Infantry Division and the 8th Armoured Brigade on 13 and 14 June.

4. The lack of protection on the left flank of the 7th Armoured Division during the planned advance on Evrécy, caused by the failure of the attacks on the positions of Aufklärungsabteilung 12 near Cristot and on the link-up between II./26 and Pionierbataillon 12 near le Mesnil and Norrey.

5. The collapse of the attack by the 51st (Highland) Division eastward of the Orne river.

As shown in the loss reports, the two Tiger companies remained in the area near Villers-Bocage until 16 June. During this time they lost:

| Date | Killed | | | Wounded | | | Missing | | |
	Officers	NCOs	Men	Officers	NCOs	Men	Officers	NCOs	Men
13.6.	-	3	7	1	2	9	-	-	-
14.6.	-	-	-	-	1	4	-	-	-
15.6.	-	1	2	1	-	3	-	-	-
16.6.	1	1	2	1	-	3	-	-	-
Total	1	5	11	3	3	19	-	-	-

Total losses amounted to: 17 killed and 25 wounded, for a total of 42 casualties.

CHAPTER 2.5
The Death of Brigadeführer Fritz Witt on 14 June 1944

All surviving members of the Division recall 14 June as an unforgettably tragic day. The Divisional commander, SS—Brigadeführer and Generalmajor of the Waffen-SS Fritz Witt, holder of the Oak Leaves to the Knight's Cross, the German Cross in Gold, the Iron Cross I. and II. and of other decorations, was killed during a fire attack by British ships' artillery on the divisional command post in Venoix near Caen.

The commander had visited different units every morning since the start of the invasion in order to get to know their positions, to learn exact details on enemy observations and to listen to situational briefings. He inquired after the concerns and wishes so as to help where possible, or he discussed plans for upcoming actions and how they would be carried out. While Witt was away, the first general staff officer remained at the command post. In the evening of 13 June he asked the divisional commander for the opportunity to survey the terrain in the sector of Regiment 26 in order to study the planned course of a new main line of resistance which had been suggested to the Korps. The commander agreed.

The next morning, after the first reports had been received and evaluated, the Ia, Sturmbannführer Hubert Meyer, set out with his driver, Rottenführer (corporal) Helmut Schmieding, in his VW-Kübelwagen. The commander remained at the command post. The Ia visited the command posts of the Panzerregiment in Rauray, of the Aufklärungsabteilung in Cristot and of III./26 south of Brouay. Then he drove to the command post of Regiment 26 which was situated, well camouflaged but uncomfortably, in earth bunkers in an orchard near le Haut du Bosq. From there he drove back to the main road which ran in a straight line from Frontenay-le-Pesnel to St. Manvieu and then, with a number of bends, on to Caen. The Ia surveyed the terrain, but also observed the skies. The road was lined by rows of tall poplars which restricted aerial observation. Just before the road dropped off slightly toward the Mue creek southwest of St. Manvieu he spotted, looking back, a fighter-bomber flying toward the car at high speed out of a turn. At his order, Helmut Schmieding braked sharply and pulled over to the left shoulder and down the gently sloped embankment. Both sought cover in the road ditch, even as the on-board guns of the fighter-bomber were already clattering and their bursts were throwing up dirt on the road. At this instance the two heard raging fire from light anti-aircraft guns and watched the fighter-bomber, trailing smoke, pull off to the left toward its own line and go down. At that moment they spotted to the right of the road, at the edge of a pasture bordered by hedges, a Zug of four-barrel Flak (anti-aircraft guns) on Panzer IV chassis. They had made out the fighter-bomber in time and shot it down. These Flak-panzers were individual constructions of the Panzerregiment. They were the prototypes for "Wirbelwind" (whirlwind) after the regimental commander, Obersturmbannführer Max -Wünsche had introduced a model and photos at the Führer-hauptquartier (Führer headquarters). The Zug, part of II. Panzerabteilung, was led by Hauptscharführer Karl-Wilhelm Krause who had been Adolf Hitler's personal orderly for years since 1935 and had been transferred to the fighting forces during the war. One of the gunners of this Zug which consisted of three Panzers, i.e. twelve 2-cm Flak, was Sturmmann Richard Schwarzwälder. He wrote in a report to the author:

> On 14 June 1944, when you were being chased by a fighter-bomber,
> I already had downed seven aircraft and been awarded the Iron

Cross II. I had a total of fourteen kills . . . At the start of the invasion it was still easy to shoot them down, the guys were flying low and were inexperienced. However, this was to change soon.

Schwarzwälder was wounded during the Ardennes offensive on 15 January 1945 in the Eifel mountain range. His right upper arm had to be amputated.[1]

The Ia thanked his rescuers and drove on to the command post of I./26. Together with Sturmbannführer Bernhard Krause he walked to his observation post at the northwest edge of St. Manvieu. On the other side of the Mue creek, half-way up the slope toward Norrey, sat the downed fighter-bomber. During the briefing on the terrain and the location of the German troops, a Canadian ambulance approached the aircraft from the direction of Norrey. A medic, waving a large Red Cross flag, stood on its left running board. The vehicle stopped next to the fighter-bomber in no-man's land. The medic continued to wave his flag. Others got out of the vehicle with a stretcher and, sometime later, carried the pilot to the ambulance, pushed the stretcher inside. The ambulance drove off slowly cross-country, just as it had arrived. Not a shot was fired, everything was as quiet as during the deepest peace on a summer day in the country.

Then came a call from the command post. The Ia was to telephone the Division immediately concerning an urgent matter. He walked back quickly with Sturmbannführer Krause. The first orderly officer, Obersturmführer Bernhard Meitzel, answered the telephone: "Please come back immediately. Something has happened here." Because of the danger of enemy monitoring of telephone calls, no details were offered or questions asked. All those present felt a great, uncertain anxiety. Something extraordinary had to have happened, but no-one suspected the terrible truth. The Ia drove back the few kilometers as fast as possible. Neither he nor his driver paid much attention to the skies above. What had happened? This was the only question on their minds.

As they approached the command post they noticed branches ripped off by shell fire on the road. The house appeared to be intact, but in the yard behind it, again ripped-off branches and dismayed men. Bernhard Meitzel reported: "The commander has been killed. We had an attack by ships' artillery." The commander's orderly officer, Obersturmführer Georg Wilhelm Hausrath, one NCO and one man of the staff company had also been killed. Three NCOs and six men of the staff company and the Nachrichtenabteilung (communications) had been wounded. The wounded had already been transported to the main dressing station at Louvigny. The dead lay, covered, in the yard.

Meitzel described the events. While the Brigadeführer and most members of the staff were inside the house, they suddenly heard artillery shells of apparently heavy caliber fly over the command post. The commander and

Meitzel walked behind the house to observe. The 10. Batterie (10 cm guns) was in position in the Odon valley, a few hundred meters to the southeast. The commander assumed that the enemy would concentrate on this target. One of the next salvos hit north of the road on which the command post was located. Now it looked as if the command post was the target after all. The Brigadeführer ordered everyone to take cover in the prepared anti-shrapnel trench, dug immediately behind the house under tall trees. He was the last one to jump into the trench. At that very moment a shell exploded in the treetops and a hail of large and small shrapnel whistled about, mostly downward. A large piece of shrapnel hit the Brigadeführer in the head. This shell and others exploding in the garden also hit the other men, one NCO and one man of the Funkstaffel (radio communications), on the other side of the road. The fire attack lasted only a few minutes. Meitzel had returned to the house since he expected safer cover there than in the trench. When the command post was set up, the Ia and Meitzel had found a spot in the center of the house behind several chimneys where a number of walls offered cover in the direction of the enemy. He had remained unhurt.

Immediate action was now necessary. The Ia reported to the chief of staff, Standartenführer Fritz Kraemer, by telephone and barely encoded, what had happened. There was a telephone connection to the Korps command post by cable which was fairly secure. The chief ordered that the ranking officer would take over the command initially. The Ia suggested that the command post be moved further west since the present location was known to the enemy either through the betrayal by civilians or by radio direction finding. The chief agreed. Standartenführer Kurt Meyer, commander of Panzergrenadierregiment 25, was requested to come to the divisional command post because of a 'special occasion'. The report of the Brigadeführer's death moved him deeply. The new responsibility meant a heavy burden to him. This became even more obvious when the Ia described the personnel and materiel situation of the Division. Not one man had arrived to replace the high losses, no replacements whatever for the lost Panzers and guns. Ammunition and fuel had to be brought in from far away, they were not available in sufficient amounts.

Standartenführer Meyer drove back to his Regiment. He handed over its command to the commander of III. Bataillon, Obersturmbannführer Karl-Heinz Milius. Hauptmann Fritz Steger took over III. Bataillon. The Ia ordered Obersturm-führer Meitzel to set up a new command post in Verson, also on Route Nationale No. 175 and four kilometers southwest of the present command post. The Funkstaffel was to be located some distance away, connected by a telephone wire.

In the afternoon, all members of the Divisional staff present in Venoix bade farewell to their dead. The commander of staff headquarters, Hauptsturmführer Albert Schuch, a front-line soldier of the First World War, had brought back his dead friend, Fritz Witt, and his killed comrades. For some time, the commander found a dignified resting place in the park of the small castle in Tillières-sur-Avre. He had lived there since his arrival in Normandy, had celebrated his thirty-sixth birthday there on 27 May, and had been able to spend a few days together with his wife. After the town was captured by the Allies in August, his remains were buried in a corner of the village cemetery. Later, they found a resting place at the German War Cemetery Champigny-St. André de l'Eure (twenty kilometers southeast of Evreux).

The Division had lost the man at the top. During many months of effort, together with his commanders, officers, platoon and squad leaders, he had built the Division. He had determined the principles of training and education and had supervised them being put into practice. He had been molded, to a large extent, by the school of Standartenführer Felix Steiner, then commander of the "Deutschland" Regiment. Having advanced to regimental commander in the Leib-standarte which he had joined in 1933 and amassed valuable battle experience, he had mastered his objectives in a progressive and exemplary manner. As a cool, thoroughly deliberating and planning tactician, Witt led in battle with unshakable calm. He was a rock in the sea, the totally accepted leader, trusted by all and admired by his young soldiers. After a battle had started, he led from the front, as the commander of a mobile unit should, but he never lost the total picture. At the hot spots of the fighting he spread security and confidence, and he ensured the courage for total engagement through his calmness and seeming unconcerned attitude. Even during difficult times he remained upright and undaunted, instilled new hope and confidence. The well-being of all members of his Division, in particular of the young soldiers to whom he was a shining example and a considerate father, was his concern. He gave his attention to the supply troops as he did to the fighting troops; he was always there for them all.

Brigadeführer Witt may have had a premonition that he would be killed in the battle of Normandy. In the morning of 6 June he was sitting on the terrace behind his house where he had received his birthday guests only ten days before, and had joyfully celebrated with them, at a small table, his head resting on both his hands. He only got up when one of his commanders arrived, battle-ready, to take his leave. Witt certainly knew that his Division was facing a difficult time and he was aware of the full extent of his responsibilities. Maybe he felt what fate held in store for him. A few days later, all this had disappeared like a bad dream. Then the steel hit him, after having lived through many dangerous battles. This outstanding soldierly leadership personality remained a living model to his Division.

CHAPTER 2.6

Withdrawal of the Left Flank of the Division to the Line St. Manvieu-Parc de Boislonde. Repelling British Attacks between 15 and 18 June 1944

It had become obvious that the situation for the neighbor to the left, the Panzer-Lehr-Division, was getting more and more critical. The simultaneous attacks, frontally from the north and enveloping from the west, indicated the objective to be the area behind the left wing of the "HJ" Division. The hot spot of the fighting with the neighbor was Tilly-sur-Seulles. The dividing line between the two divisions ran along the le Bordel creek west of Brettevillette through Tessel and Fontenay-le-Pesnel. The easterly part of this town belonged to the "HJ", the westerly, Bas de Fontenay, to the "Panzerlehr". The line continued east of les Hauts Vents and le Haut d'Audrieu. The enemy was firmly holding the northern section of Saint Pierre. The point units of the "Panzerlehr" stood at the road Fontenay—Tilly. The left wing of the "HJ" with 2. Panzer-kompanie was located near Parc de Boislande. The front line ran from there in a generally northern direction, west of Cristot, to the western edge of Brouay. In the neighboring sector, forward outposts had been set up near les Hauts Vents since the terrain to the east of there was broken and difficult to survey. The Aufklärungsabteilung was holding the sector from south of les Hauts Vents to the fork in the road east of Pavie, a width of more than three kilometers. The contact on the right was III./26 of Sturmbannführer Olboeter with two companies to the western exit from Brouay and one company in Brouay to the railroad crossing at the town's eastern exit, and a guard to the right. This Bataillon's sector was four kilometers wide. To the neighbor on the right, II./26 of Sturmbannführer Siebken, there was only visual contact during the day, scouting parties went back and forth at night. The positions of II./26 ran approximately 400 to 500 meters south of the rail line. It was obvious that these advance positions could not be held in the face of an attack by strong forces. The Aufklärungsabteilung was neither meant nor equipped for defensive duties. For this reason, the Division had requested from the Korps that the front be moved back to a line St. Manvieu-south of le Mesnil Patry-northern edge of Parc de Boislande. This would additionally lead to the Aufklärungsabteilung being pulled out since the Division had no reserves of any kind available. This request was initially not approved. Brisk enemy reconnaissance activity and intensive radio communications pointed to a forthcoming attack in this sector. Finally, the Korps approved the shortening of the front line for the night of 15–16 June. At the same time, the Panzer-Lehr-Division received permission to move back the left flank of its northern front line. Under pressure from the enemy, the front line near Tilly was moved back by 1.5 kilometers already on 14 June. The town, however, remained in German hands.[1] The Division moved back its left wing during the night 14–15 June.[2] In order to allow III./26 as much time as possible to set up in its new positions, the Divisionsbegleitkompanie (escort company) was attached to Regiment 26 on 14 June and ordered to relieve III. Bataillon for a while. During the course of the day the Begleitkompanie took over the Brouay sector. It was only possible to set up a system of strong points. For instance, only fifteen men of the Begleit-kompanie were available for the sector of 10. Kompanie instead of 130 men. At 23.00 hours, III. Bataillon withdrew and prepared for defense at the northern edge of the Parc de Boislande during 15 June.[3]

In the morning of 15 June the enemy, approximately in battalion strength, attacked the dividing line between the Divisionsbegleitkompanie and the Aufklärungsabteilung and then swung north in order to roll up the position of the Begleitkompanie. The enemy was thrown back in a counterattack. After the previous main line of defense had been re-established, the Kompanie pulled back from the enemy. During this action it lost five killed and fourteen wounded who were moved to the main dressing station, and six wounded who remained with the Kompanie. Six men were missing. An interesting note can be found in the diary of the Divisionsbegleitkompanie:

English infantrymen shy away from fire. They only feel strong when protected by their tanks. During one's own attack one must attempt to get close to the enemy infantry so as to evade enemy artillery fire.[4]

After the withdrawal, units of the Begleitkompanie were attached to 4. Panzerkompanie, others to I./26.

The British 49th (West Riding) Infantry Division, part of XXX Corps, had arrived in the bridgehead. It had not been spotted by intelligence on 14 June. In the 'enemy location' map of 7. Armee it was wrongly assumed to be in the area southwest of Bayeux, even, surprisingly, still on 21 June. Only on 22 June was it shown in its real operational area. This division had been ordered to link up to the left, i.e. east, of the 50th Division, with the previous objective of Noyers.

It is interesting to read what the situation report of the 49th Division had to say about the enemy and in particular about the missing scouting party of the Divisionsbegleitkompanie in strength of one NCO and five men. In the morning of 15 June, two members of the Sicherungskompanie (guard company) of the staff of 12. SS-Panzerdivision "Hitlerjugend" had been captured in the Brouay area. "It cannot be explained', it was stated, "how troops of the divisional headquarters could penetrate so far to the northwest. A more intensive interrogation may determine where the headquarters is located. These two Hitlerjungen were only too eager, after some waving of the pistol, to start telling all. But they assured us that they were regrettably poorly informed about the situation and even where they were. The Divisionssicherungskompanie is equipped with VW-Schwimmwagen and motorcycles."[5] These brave young soldiers who had the misfortune to be captured in the broken terrain, had been at the new Divisional command post in Verson only on 14 June. Their determination and quick thinking could be thanked that the new command post did not immediately become known to the enemy.

In this report it is also of interest what a young Frenchman from Audrieu stated. He and five other Frenchmen had been arrested by German troops and interrogated by a major in Cristot. They had spent the night in a command post in the Parc de Boislande. There, he said, he had overheard a German plan of action. It stated that armored cars would be assembled on 15 June in Brouay to attack the Château Loucelles. One can see just how unreliable such sources are. However, the report of the 49th Division contains a number of accurate findings which confirm the quality of aerial surveillance and the thorough work of the enemy counterintelligence and monitoring services. They had determined that their enemy opposite was the left wing of 12. SS-Pz.-Div. "HJ". The troops, so the report stated, were not located in villages but were well dug in and under cover in wooded areas, camouflaged shrapnel trenches and along the assumed advance routes of the enemy. The Canadians had observed and reported that the German Panzers (probably south of le Mesnil-Patry) were dug in up to the turret and would be difficult to fight. In North Africa, the use of phosphor smoke had proven effective since it would seep through the hatches.

One of the prisoners was reported to have had a stripe on his sleeve with the name "Adolf Hitler". This had started the rumor that the 1. SS-Division had moved in. Interrogations and his pay-book had indicated, however, that he had transferred from 1. to 12. Division.

The 50th Division, in position to the west of 49th Division, had reported that the enemy had withdrawn from its front line and contact had been lost. The 49th Division assumed that the same was the case along its front and it sent out battle-ready scouting party. A company of the 4th Lincolns encountered resistance in Saint Pierre and lost two carriers to mortar fire. The scouting party advancing along the road Saint Pierre-Fontenay came under Panzer fire from the southwest corner of the Parc de Boislande and lost four carriers. It was assumed, with certainty, that Brouay, Cristot and Fontenay would be held by the enemy and that weak enemy forces were located in Saint Pierre.[6]

In the morning of 15 June the new Divisional commander, Standartenführer Kurt Meyer, visited the SS-Panzeraufklärungsabteilung 12 in Cristot. He ordered the withdrawal for the night 15–16 June. It started at approximately 21.00 hours, unnoticed by the enemy. The Pionierzug mined the roads leading towards the enemy, in particular the through-roads in Cristot. Around midnight, it left the town as the last unit. Its members observed an enemy scouting party run into the mine obstacle. The mines exploded.[7] During the following day, units moved further south to the area around Missy.[8]

During the night of 15–16 June, the three other battalions of Regiment 26 also took up positions along the shortened main line of defense. The I. Bataillon connected with Regiment 25 on the right wing south of Franqueville. The main line of defense ran south of the Mue creek to the northwest corner of the small woods northwest of St. Manvieu. There it connected with the Pionierbataillon. The Pionierbataillon's main line of defense also ran south of the Mue creek. Its sector extended to to the left to a country lane which forked toward le Mesnil-Patry and to Cristot. There, it connected with the II./26. The forward edge of the positions of II./26 ran parallel, to the north, to the road from St. Manvieu to Fontenay at a distance of approximately 1,000 meters. In order to extend its left wing to III. Bataillon, the 15. (Aufklärungskompanie)/26 was inserted. The connection with III. Bataillon was approximately south of Hill 102. Behind the front line of Regiment 26, II. Panzerabteilung was installed in ambush positions as an anti-tank force. The Panther companies of I. Abteilung were completely withdrawn and assembled near Noyers to be deployed at the hot spots. The 2. Kompanie which had been located in the Parc de Boislande was relieved by 8. Kompanie which assembled south of Fontenay. To the right, 6., 5., 7., and 9. Kompanien linked up, extending up to Marcelet. The Pioniers of the Pionierbataillon mined the terrain to the east and west of the southern exits from le Mesnil-Patry.

The 49th Division ordered the attack to capture Cristot for 16 June. The attack was to be carried out by the 146th Brigade. Available for the attack were: 1/4 The King's Own Yorkshire Light Infantry (KOYLI), an infantry battalion, reinforced by the heavy weapons of the Brigade; one platoon 6-pounder anti-tank guns of the 220/55 Anti-Tank Regiment; "D" Company (mortars) 2nd Kensingtons; fourteen Centaurs (Cruiser Tank Mk VIII-A 27 L with 95 mm howitzer gun of the Royal Marines Armoured Support Group),[9] supported by: 24th Lancers without one squadron, unless the complete unit was required (tank unit); Division artillery of the 49th Division (seventy-two guns, 25-pounders); 121st Medium Regiment (sixteen guns, 5.5 inch); 5th AGRA (Army artillery) as far as available; division artillery of the 50th Division as far as available; 76th Anti Aircraft Brigade; one to three cruisers; fighter-bombers and rocket-equipped aircraft.

The fire support was planned as follows: From 23.00 to 04.00 hours, short and very violent fire attacks on selected targets, including the Cristot area, to prevent the enemy from sleeping. The 5th AGRA and "D" Company would concentrate preparatory fire during the last quarter hour before the start of the attack on selected targets in and around Cristot, in particular on the open fields on the northern and western edge. The attack by infantry and tanks would be supported by a moving wall of fire from 164 light guns of the 49th and 50th Divisions and from sixty-four medium guns of the 5th AGRA. During this time period, the 76th Anti-Aircraft Brigade would hold the enemy down in the Parc de Boislande and on Hill 102 with twenty-four heavy guns. For fifteen minutes, until twenty minutes before the start of the attack, the cruisers would fire on the Parc de Boislande. During the last quarter hour before the attack started, fighter-bombers would attack known targets. Attacks by medium bombers on the artillery positions in the areas around Grainville and Fontenay had been requested. The attack was to start at 12.00 hours. A fake attack by the 147th Brigade from the direction of Brouay and an attack by the left neighbor of the 3rd Canadian Division had been planned as support.[10]

The attack by the 49th Division and the 3rd Canadian Brigade found a void. The shortening of the front line had been accomplished just in time. The enemy reported that the 1/4 KOYLI had taken Cristot. The 147th Brigade with the Royal Fusiliers (infantry) had captured Brouay and were in the process, during the afternoon, of clearing the woods south of the town. The enemy had left a number of traps and mines behind in Brouay.[11]

The left neighbor, the Canadians, had taken le Mesnil-Patry from which the enemy had withdrawn the same day. Enemy losses had been reported as seventeen dead, two armored cars and one other vehicle. A mortar position near le Haut du Bosq had been destroyed. In an armored car, found knocked out near Hill 103, 500 meters southwest le Haut du Bosq, the British discovered the pay-book of one of the dead. He was identified as a member of the SS-Panzeraufklärungsabteilung 12. In the vehicle log book an identification mark was found: an emblem showing the victory rune and a skeleton key (Dietrich) with two oak leaves below. It was assumed, correctly, that this was the insignia of 12. SS-Panzerdivision "HJ". Someone had ventured, trying to explain the two victory runes on the collar patches, that the unit in question was the 44. Panzergrenadierregiment. This wrong identification was unfavorably mentioned in the reports by the enemy as a "not exactly shining attempt' at an explanation.[11] The 49th Division now planned to reach the line of the road Juvigny-Fontenay by the afternoon of 18 June in three stages.

During the night 16–17 June, one company of the 4th Lincolns would capture les Hauts Vents while the 1/4 KOYLI would reconnoitre the woods southwest of Cristot.

The capture of these woods by the 1/4 KOYLI had been ordered for 17 June. The 6th Duke of Wellington's Regiment—6DWR—(infantry) with the attached 24th Lancers (tanks) had been ordered to capture the Parc de Boislande from the direction of le Haut d'Audrieu. In the meantime, the 11th Scots Fusiliers, with fourteen Centaurs assigned to them, would clear out the woods south of Brouay.

On 18 June, the 146th and 147th Brigades would advance one battalion each to the road Bas de Fontenay-Fontenay.[12]

For the attack by the 6th Duke of Wellington's, the 147th Brigade had at its disposal: the heavy weapons of the Brigade; "D" Company 2nd Kensingtons (mortars); two platoons self-propelled anti-tank guns of the 235/73 Anti-Tank Regiment; fourteen Centaurs; one company 24th Lancers (tanks). As support, the following had been ordered to cooperate: the division artillery of the 49th Division (seventy-two guns, 25-pounders); 121st Medium Regiment (sixteen guns, 5.5 inch); and, expected, one Medium Regiment 5th AGRA.

Initially, the attack had been ordered to start at 15.00 hours. This was later advanced to 14.00 hours.[13]

A British artillery spotter aircraft had not detected any enemies during a low pass over the Parc de Boislande. It was thus assumed that the German troops had withdrawn from the woods and from Saint Pierre to the Fontenay area. This was the reason for the 146th Brigade to scout the Parc de Boislande in the morning of 17 June. In case the enemy had pulled out of the woods, the preparatory artillery fire would not be required.

In this case, it would be the mission of the 146th Brigade to advance to the right of 147th Brigade to the road Juvigny-Fontenay and to be ready for a further advance on Noyers. The 10th Battalion Durham Light Infantry would then become responsible for clearing Saint Pierre. In case of the least favorable situation, the two battalions would not carry out their attack to the road mentioned above before 18 June.

The 8th Armoured Brigade (tanks) without one company was attached to the 49th Division. It had to be ready, from 14.00 hours onward, to march into the area near Hervieu (two kilometers west of Audrieu). One company of the 49th Reconnaissance Regiment was ordered to close the gap to the left neighbor between Parc de Boislande and le Mesnil-Patry.[14]

The main line of defense of III./26 ran north of the Parc de Boislande. On the right was the 11., to the left the 10. Kompanie. The 9. Kompanie remained in the northern section of Fontenay as a reserve. The 15./26, assigned to the Bataillon, was located to the right of 11. Kompanie. The 16. (Pionier-kompanie) was also in action near Fontenay as its list of losses shows. It can be assumed that the Kompanie was used to reinforce the positions, in particular to place mines. To the left, there existed only a loose connection to the Panzer-Lehr-Division near Saint Pierre.

The men of III./26 in their slit holes at the northern edge of the Parc de Boislande and the forward orchards watched a wall of fire rolling towards them from Cristot at approximately 15.00 hours. As it reached the park, it concentrated there for a lengthy period. Most of the Panzergrenadier positions and almost all heavy weapons positions were smashed. When the steamroller of fire continued rolling into the woods, several waves of tanks followed it through the destroyed orchards. Behind them strolled the infantrymen openly across the terrain, hands in their pockets, cigarettes between their lips. Fire from some of the outposts which were still battle ready forced them into cover. The enemy fought the survivors in the positions with tanks and artillery, then pushed his attack forward and broke through. Violent hand-to-hand combat erupted. When the resistance had been broken, the enemy advanced to the southern edge of the woods. There, he stalled under the fire of the Reservekompanie, the 9./16, and the artillery.[15]

At dusk, III./26 and 9. Kompanie carried out a counter-attack, supported by a few Panzers of 8. Kompanie. While the enemy, according to estimates from artillery men, had fired 1,500 to 2,000 shells in support of his attack, the German artillery—probably II. Abteilung—could only use 300 shells. Effective support by Panzers was impossible in the broken terrain of the park. Apparently, however, some Panzers of 6. Kompanie together with units of 15./26 accompanied the counterattack past the park to the right. The attack initially advanced well but was then smashed by the concentrated fire from the superior enemy artillery. A forward securing position was held on Hill 102, 500 m southeast of Cristot. It harassed the enemy with rifle fire.[16]

After the failed attack, the Division asked III./26 whether it could recapture the Parc de Boislande with its own available forces and under which conditions. Sturmbannführer Olboeter believed that this would be possible with sufficient artillery support. The Division agreed and arranged for I. Abteilung to hand over ammunition to the II. since it had already become scarce there. Also, 8. Panzerkompanie was assigned for the latter phase of the attack, when the previous positions had been reached, as an anti-tank force.

After a short fire attack by artillery and mortars, 9. and 10. Kompanie started a counterattack on 18 June from the -northern section of Fontenay west of the road to Cristot. The Panzergrenadiers penetrated into the woods where violent hand-to-hand combat developed. Some units pushed through to the northern edge of the park. Barrages set in and prevented the arrival of reinforcements. The units of both Panzer-grenadier companies which had broken through were wiped out. The retreating English infantry was picked up by tanks of the SRY north of the park. The 7th Battalion The Duke of Wellington's and a company of the SRY attacked the weak positions on Hill 102 and captured them. Counterattacks by a few Panzers of 6. Kompanie and 15./26 were repelled.[17] The III./26 was ordered by the Division to withdraw to its starting positions. There, it prepared for defense.

The Kompanietruppführer (company chief) of 10./26 at the time, Oberscharführer Hans-Georg Keßlau, reports on the counterattack:

The Kompanie reached the assembly area at approximately 12.00 hours. To the right of the Kompanie was 9. Kompanie. At 14.15 hours we began a sparse fire attack with our heavy weapons. Our attack started out well through a knee-high grain field. Alarmed by the battle noise, an enemy artillery observation aircraft flew in from the north. It spotted our attack and directed concentrated, heavy artillery fire on us. The spearheads of the Kompanie had already reached the wood and were in hand-to-hand combat with the British who were dug in there, spades against machetes. The commander of 9. Kompanie, Obersturmführer Zantop, was also killed during this carnage. A comrade of 9. or 10. Kompanie told me later that he had seen Zantop being attacked by an Englishman with a machete and received a slash to the neck. The messenger, right behind his Kompanie chief, felled the attacker at almost the same instant with a burst from his machine pistol. Too late! The enemy artillery fire intensified, our attack stalled. We were ordered to return to our assembly areas. After some time, the enemy appeared to believe that we had taken the wood. He moved his fire and concentrated it on the wood for one and one-half hours. The 10. Kompanie had suffered significant losses during this attack. The Kompanie commander, Untersturmführer Mader, was wounded for the third time. A search party was sent into the wood during the following night to look for the missing men. It had no contact with the enemy and returned with four dead. They were buried in the creek valley. A comrade who was missing at the time told me about his experiences later in hospital, in 1945: 'During the night after our attack on 18 June I came to on the battlefield in the rain and with severe leg and head pains. One of my legs was smashed, I had been hit in the head by a shell fragment. I was terribly thirsty. In my steel helmet I gathered some rainwater and drank it. This refreshed me somewhat. I oriented myself and crawled toward the wood in the direction of the attack. At the wood's edge I found the abandoned enemy positions and dead soldiers from both sides. A graveyard-like silence covered the wood. I crawled back and was found, somewhere, by comrades from a unit of the Heer.[18]

After the war, in 1945, the defense for the Waffen-SS at the Nürnberg Trials collected evidence of Allied violations against the laws of war at the American prisoner of war camp at Auerbach. At the time, a former member of III./26 provided the following statement:

Our Kompanie chief, Obersturmführer Zantop, was badly wounded by a bullet in the stomach on 18 June during our attack on the town of Fontenay. We were initially repelled and returned to our starting positions. Later, when we captured the Canadian (should be: British, Author) positions, we found our Kompanie chief dead, his throat had been slit.[19]

As can be seen in the report on the counterattack by 9. and 10. Kompanie of 18. June, the assumption on the death of Obersturmführer Zantop is based on an error. This is herewith being rectified.

The war diary of the 49th Division on the fighting of 17 and 18 June contain several remarkable notations.

Today (17 June) a prisoner was taken in the Parc de Boislande. He was brought in yelling and was marked for special treatment. The results of his interrogation are as follows:

15. Kompanie 16. SS-Panzergrenadierregiment, known as Vorausabteilung (advance Abteilung), similar to the already identified Sicherungs-(guard) Kompanie of the Divisional staff. His first battle. Joined 12. SS-Div. from 1. SS LAH in October of last year. Arrived at the location where he was taken prisoner two nights ago. Does not know the extent of the positions to other battalions. Kompanie leader is Oberleutnant Beyer. The Kompanie has thirty Schwimmwagen (amphibious vehicles) equipped with heavy and light machine guns MG 42, anti-tank rifles. He does not know their make. He seems to know nothing about the new rocket firing positions. He did not fight in Russia, but one or two NCOs and officers were there. The 5. and 8. Kompanie are also in position, but he does not know where. The 14. Kompanie is a gun Kompanie.

The prisoner, who was in deep shock for various reasons, asked after the interrogation whether he would now be shot. Since this had been indicated as a possibility, no conclusions (on his question, Author) could be drawn.

Along our front line, the enemy today violently attacked the Parc de Boislande with infantry and Panzers, supported by mortar and artillery fire. Throughout the day it was difficult to determine the real positions. Even now, not all details on the enemy situation are available.[20]

During the fighting in the Parc de Boislande, the German troops suffered heavy losses. The lists of losses show:

	Killed			Wounded			Missing		
	Officers	NCOs	Men	Officers	NCOs	Men	Officers	NCOs	Men
9.&10./26	1	1	15	2	5	41	-	-	14
15.&16./26	-	1	22	-	2	42	1	-	3
6.Pz.-Komp.	-	-	-	1	-	-	-	-	-
Total	1	2	37	3	7	83	1	-	17

Total losses were: 40 killed, 93 wounded, and 18 missing, for a total of 151.

According to enemy reports, only seven prisoners were taken. Thus, it has to be assumed that eleven missing were killed.[21]

No figures are available here on the personnel losses of the enemy. Documentation indicates that the 24th Lancers had lost 7 Sherman tanks of which 4 had exploded.[22]

In an overview on the battles in the Parc de Boislande, the war diary of the 147th Infantry Brigade states the following:

The 6DWR undertook a daring attack on a troublesome wooded area called Parc de Boislande. It was successfully captured, not without significant losses which included all officers of one company. On 17 June [must be 18 June], the 6DWR were violently attacked in the Parc with devastating effect. After lengthy fighting they were driven out. This battalion continued to be luckless. Wherever it went, it was pursued by enemy mortars and launchers. As a result of losing most of its officers and cadre personnel, its morale suffered significantly. The 7DWR rectified the situation through a skillful counterattack on Hill 102, the hill dominating the park. Hill 102 was captured and held against all resistance. During the following week there was brisk reconnaissance in the park and most of the equipment lost by the 6DWR was recovered.[23]

As an example of the degenerated thinking spawned by the Second World War, the report on the enemy situation by the 49th Division of 19 June contains the following:

An award is being offered for SS-Obergruppenführer Sepp Dietrich, the notorious commander of I. SS Pz.Korps, dead or alive.[24]

On 18 June the 50th Division again attacked the neighbor to the left at Saint Pierre and Tilly. Both towns were captured by the enemy. After an unsuccessful counterattack by the Panzer-Lehr-Division to recapture Tilly, it abandoned the rubble of the town during the night of 18 to 19 June. Violent fighting had raged for days. The Pz.-Lehr-Div. set up new positions to the south and southwest near Montilly and Sagy.[25] There was now the danger that the enemy would attack the left flank of III./26 from the direction of Saint Pierre. This danger would have been even greater if the Bataillon had again advanced to the northern edge of the Parc de Boislande after the park had not been occupied by the enemy again. This terrain, hard fought-for during two days, remained no-man's land until 25 June. The III./26 only left advanced guards in the northern section of Fontenay and prepared for defense in the southern section. The park was kept under surveillance by scouting parties.

The 8. Panzerkompanie was located in the northern section of Fontenay as an anti-tank force. Its commander, Obersturmführer Hans Siegel, reports on this action:

We did not move for more that twenty-four hours but sat, 'ready for action', in our Panzers. This was a never-before experienced, extremely difficult physical burden: always on the look-out, not speaking to anyone. The crews isolated, not knowing what was happening elsewhere, and time and again, concentrated fire attacks. The limbs turned stiff in the narrow, uncomfortable seated position, the eyes grew tired and the senses turned dull. Despite all this, I only allowed leaving the Panzer for the physical necessities. I wanted to prevent losses from shrapnel and infantry bullets and, above all, not to give the enemy any indication of our presence. It paid off, there were no losses.

Around midnight I received the order to withdraw with the Kompanie before dawn. The difficulty was to disengage unnoticed. Thus, all drivers were ordered to back their vehicles at a predetermined time for a set distance without steering movements. This process took over an hour and was completed without setting off an alarm on the enemy side.[26]

Just how confused the situation in and around Fontenay was, is shown in a report by Oberscharführer Rudolf Polzin, Zugführer in 8. Kompanie:

Across a small bridge we entered Fontenay. The town seemed completely dead. Later, I learned that a German with a 'Ofenrohr' (anti-tank weapon) had been in ambush at the bridge. He wanted to knock me out, thinking the British had sent in a captured Panzer. Luckily, the firing mechanism failed. The houses of the town had been largely destroyed by shelling. Suddenly, we spotted an enemy Pak (anti-tank gun), not even thirty meters ahead. [Polzin had probably reached the eastward defenses of Saint Pierre.] I gave the order: 'Forward! quick! Ram the Pak!' just as we felt the hit and my Panzer slowly came to a standstill. We had been hit but were not on fire. I ordered: 'Bail out to the right!' From the ruins of close-by houses came several infantrymen, gaping at us. Later, an officer from the Panzer-Lehr-Division arrived, Oberleutnant Philipp. From him I learned that we had been hit by our own Pak, approximately 300 meters away. The shell had grazed the driver's hatch, the driver was mortally wounded. The shell then hit the turret, destroying the traversing mechanism. It then bounced off and damaged an oil line, immobilizing the Panzer. Oberleutnant Philipp told me, as if apologizing, that the town had already changed hands a number of times. Several enemy artillery attacks followed, I was badly wounded in the left lower leg and taken to the field dressing station.[27]

The civilian population, too, suffered greatly from the fighting. Whenever possible, civilians were evacuated from the battle areas, but occasionally, events overtook them.

The lord of Château de Boislonde and his family lived in the cellars of the castle throughout almost all of the battles in this area. A German officer had once told him to leave. He had answered: "What good would that do? If you demand that I leave, I will. But tomorrow I will be back!" Thus, the family stayed and lived through the fighting. The lady of the castle recorded her experiences and observations for her daughters in her diary. Despite the subjective approach it is still an historic document. Some sections are of general interest.

Wednesday, 7 June. Cloudy skies. A motorized German squad is under cover along a hedge at the exit from the Parc de Boislande. English aircraft are circling over Tilly and then drop their bombs. The Germans are in headlong flight in groups of three or four in the direction of Caen. Tilly is destroyed, on fire. The residents are fleeing in panic. I can see that the English are in Audrieu and le Pont Roc, the Canadians in Haut Vents. The sky is full of aircraft. At dusk, a German motorized column of cars, motorcycles and tracked vehicles takes cover in the lower part of the park along the garden and the small woods near the horse stable. They stay overnight and move on to Cristot the next morning.

Thursday, 8 June. Raymond wants to go to St. Martin to get news. A German guard stops him: 'Retour! No promenade!' The castle is cut off from the rest of the world. Some SS men arrive. They demand water, cider, milk and they kill the chickens. Just after noon, four German soldiers ask for something to drink. They are part of the crew of a Panzer in position. They are almost dead from exhaustion and fatigue. They say that reinforcements will arrive and the attack will take place in the afternoon. They sit down and fall asleep immediately. An hour later, a soldier arrives to wake them up. Aircraft are circling overhead and a terrible barrage can be heard from the direction of Mesnil-Patry. Later in the afternoon the village was completely leveled.

Friday, 9 June. The noise of the battle very close by is increasing as the sun is rising. The previous evening was quieter. The nightly bombardment set in around 10 P.M. and lasted until dawn. It has been this way throughout the battle. Around 2 P.M. there is a long droning noise. It is a German column of Panzers, trucks, cars, etc. coming down from Cristot. They drive around the park and set up position in Bas-Clos. At the same time a terrible artillery barrage set in, raining down on Fontenay. Roofs are whirling through the air, houses are in flames. Everyone prepares to bed down in the cellar for the night.

Saturday, 10 June. One Panzer is hidden at the entrance to the park, others in the field. Germans are coming and going. Around 7

A.M. one Kompanie marches into battle. They cross the grassy square and walk up to the wood, in groups of eleven men and in single file. Every eleventh man of each group carries a long barrel (anti-tank weapon, my husband says). At 11 A.M. terrible artillery fire sets in. Our window panes are blown out. We all assemble in the cellar and pray our rosaries. A huge piece of the house facade has been shot off . . .

Sunday, 11 June. We are saying mass. Refugees arrive, we are now twenty-seven . . . The barrages last for hours. We pray and whisper our rosaries. The children are playing at dominoes.

Monday, 12 June. I walk up to the garden to cut some cabbage. A shell explodes a few meters away at the corner of the horse stable. Two, three, four shells, I have just enough time to jump back into the cellar. The ground is shaking. The cellar is full of dust, bricks are dropping off the windows. After all is quiet again, Georges finds a huge piece of a shell, measuring 38 cm in diameter. The northeastern wing of the castle no longer exists. The 380 mm shells of the Rodney have brought that about. In the evening, at 9 P.M., aerial bombardment.

Tuesday, 13 June. Passing Germans descend into the cellar and ask Aimé Leborgeois to serve as their guide, he would be away for two days. Two-hundred people have sought cover in the lime-kilns. During the day, the men reinforce our shelter. In the late afternoon, heavy shelling started. Suddenly, during the night, ten Germans arrive, led by an Unteroffizier (sergeant). He points his flashlight at us and says: 'We will sleep here!' The cellar is filled to the bursting point. They look for straw bails and go to sleep at the entrance.

Wednesday, 14 June. The Germans sleep through the morning at the cellar entrance. To get out, we have to step over their bodies. Their faces are black, their faces are tense, their despair is deep. At 11 A.M. their comrades arrive and shake them awake. They pick up their helmets and rifles and leave. We, too, speak of leaving, but where to?

Thursday, 15 June. Around 11 A.M. four Germans arrive and ask if they could have some chickens cooked. The German, who speaks such correct French, is Alsatian and belongs to a Panzer unit. While he is talking, the other three Germans fall asleep. Other Germans, among them an officer, take over the upper floors. In the evening, they all take their helmets and rifles and march into battle. Other Germans soon after take their place.

Friday, 16 June. Roger is taken out by the Germans at 5 A.M. to dig a shelter in the woods. An officer shows up: 'I want two monsieurs, to work'. Four men go off and work the whole day, digging the hole, cutting down trees, sawing off branches and build a solid shelter. At noon, a shell explodes near to the cellar window, a fragment injures M. Carville. Falling bricks smash the cooking pot in the chimney. All the refugees swear to dedicate themselves to Holy Jesus. During the evening I discuss with the Oberleutnant the subject of cows.

Saturday, 17 June. The Unteroffizier comes over from the shelter at 9 A.M., looking for a jar of cider. Raymond brings him to the shelter built yesterday. At 9.30 A.M. terrible artillery barrages set in, everyone is shaking, jumping about. We could see nothing in the smoke. At 2 P.M. the scene changes again. Rifle fire, salvos, engine noise, and a shout: 'There, an Englishman!' The Englishman topples over and falls down on the stairs, killed by a salvo. Above our head we hear the noise of running feet, confusion, salvos. A hand grenade explodes very close-by. 'Don't shoot! Civilians! Civilians!' Georges walks outside. The English are suspicious. Fifteen soldiers are there, faces blackened, the helmets covered with twigs, bayonets at the ready. 'We are thirty-one civilians and seven German soldiers!' 'All right! Children come up first!' Each one grabs a blanket and mounts the fifteen steps from the cellar. An English soldier stands on each second step, with a bayonet or sub-machine gun. We have to sit down behind a coach-house. These soldiers have an embroidered bear and the words 'Duke of Wellington's' sewn to their upper sleeves. One of them is from Sheffield, the others from Manchester. At 7 P.M. the English allow us to return to the castle. There is nothing left of the trees in the park. A parachute is dangling from a linden tree, a dead soldier attached to it. On the grassy square we count some twenty English tanks.

Sunday, 18 June. Refugees arrive. They are surprised to find Englishmen. Prayers are at 9 A.M. A child has been killed by a shell. The English bring in one wounded. Four English soldiers wander about, looking for their unit. The English tanks are still immobile, without life. There is thunder from guns. The English ambulance does not arrive. Why have the English abandoned the tanks in the meadow? The shelling is terrible, again, throughout the night. The refugees leave again at dawn. Parts of the castle walls have collapsed under the shell fire. The four Tommies who were looking for their units yesterday, slept in the horse stable while the wounded Englishman has bedded down in our shelter, waiting for an ambulance which does not arrive.

Monday, 19 June. The English tanks have not moved. However, the four Englishmen showed up from the horse stable to talk to the wounded. 'The tanks are filled with supplies and rations!' They return with two civilians, arms loaded with canned food. When the people at the lime-kilns learn that Boislonde has been liberated, they send a messenger to ask the English not to shell the lime-kilns since 350 civilians were hiding there. The four Englishmen say that they are stragglers, do not know where there units are, and cannot carry the message. At 3 P.M. Buratti arrives to tell us that the Germans are withdrawing from the lime-kilns: 'The whole population must leave for Vendes, Evrécy, Villers, Thury-Harcourt, etc. There are no Germans between Boislonde and Fontenay, except for one outpost at Calvaire. The English tanks are abandoned. The shelling will again be terrible'. If the Germans ever came back to Boislonde they would find the wounded Englishman in our cellar and we would all be shot. We explain to the Englishmen that it would be very dangerous for us if they stay here. Only the wounded man can stay since he cannot walk. In the evening there is a renewed terrible shelling.

Tuesday, 20 June. Four English soldiers arrive at 9 A.M., their helmets covered with grass, the faces smeared with dirt. They speak to the wounded man and take along the four 'stragglers' in the horse stables. A quiet day. A tracked armored car arrives in the evening to pick up the wounded.

Wednesday, 21 June. A civilian who had passed through the lines, arrives. He tells us that people on the other side of the front are making hay and are working in their fields. This news baffles us since we have been buried in our cellar for fifteen days without being able to go outside. Suddenly, an English officer arrives. He salutes and takes off his headgear. 'You're in great danger here', he says. 'We'll be starting a major attack. We'll lead you far away from the danger.' This takes our breath away. 'I'll take the first twelve along with me.' At first, we all resisted, but then there is nothing here that has to be done, forcing us to stay. Within moments, everybody has a small parcel in their hands. We leave the cellar, forty-one people. Except for the beautiful trees, nothing remains other than enormous craters. The abandoned tanks are still sitting on the castle lawn, the carcasses of the sheep, the body of the pilot, arms crossed, are still there. At the exit from the park, English helmets and rifles appear from the shelters. Stop! Suddenly, a column of English soldiers surrounds us and we climb up through the fields. Here we spot the skeleton of 'Admiral', our beautiful horse. All our apple trees have been ripped out, hundreds of shell fragments lie about, burnt-out tanks and cars, dead soldiers everywhere. Every fifty meters the soldiers signal a stop and we lie down in the grass. After a wide detour through the fields the civilians reach the road to Cristot. Our personal documents are checked in a field at the entrance to Cristot. Then, trucks arrive to transport the refugees to Léger-Caragny and Rucqueville.

Sunday, 25 June. All attempts to return to the castle fail. The battle makes it impossible to approach. The English capture Fontenay.

Thursday, 29 June. A renewed attempt is successful. We look after the animals and take some clothing. Nothing has changed around the castle.

Monday, 3 July. Our second journey to Boislonde. This time the castle is nothing but a huge pile of smoking bricks. We learn that the English had mined the castle and blown it up on Saturday, 1 July, in the afternoon. That is all we know. Nothing remains for me except a medallion, a crucifix and a photo of our Château de Boislonde. May you, my daughters, have the fortune to build your own families and to preserve your Christian homes with inner peace.[28]

In the diary of the lady of the castle of Boislonde, mementos are found. They are a Waffen-SS sleeve stripe with the name "Adolf Hitler", a black and white woven sleeve badge showing a bear, another sleeve badge, oval, white with three trees, and two red and white bands with the inscription "Duke of Wellington's" which the English had on their epaulets.

The diary entries do not offer any information on what happened to the German soldiers who were in the cellar with the civilians when the English arrived at Boislonde on 17 June. One of the civilians who was there at the time, reported later on this:

With us in the cellar were four German soldiers, two of whom were wounded. They had been unable to reach their own lines south of the Parc de Boislande and were hiding with us. One day, and English patrol showed up. They surrounded the castle ruins and threw smoke grenades through the cellar windows. We shouted with all our force: 'Civilians! French! Civilians!' A frightful, blackened face of an English commando bent down, the barrel of a sub-machine gun pointed. Shaking, we climbed out, one after the other. When the two young German soldiers stepped out: 'Rara . . . Rrrrr'. They were felled by a burst of fire. The two wounded, however, were led away. I had the impression that the English were not taking many prisoners in the Boislonde sector. The English buried their dead in the southern section of the park, near a barn. There were sixty graves.[29]

The killed British were transferred after the war to a British war cemetery south of Fontenay. Next to them, some of the dead of III./26, killed on 18 June, also found their last resting place. The Commonwealth War Graves Commission had laid out and decorated their graves with the same dignity as those of the killed British soldiers. Former members of the "HJ" Division, during a visit to the battle fields in July 1975, laid a wreath at the cenotaph of the war cemetery in honor and memory of the dead of both nations.

6 June 1944. The dug-in and camou-flaged panzers of the "Hitlerjugend" Division wait for the orders to march to the front.

The Panzerregiment marches to the front by day as well, with big intervals between the vehi-cles. A Panzer IV halts under cover during a rest break. Front left, the iden-tification sign of the division.

June 1944. Artillery observer on a twoer of the church of Ardenne Abbey.

Marauder bombers approaching, 6 June 1944.

The young soldiers of the 12th SS soon learned to fear and respect the Allies' air power.

Panzer IV moving up to the front. A swastika flag is used as an identification sign for aircraft.

6 June. Panzer-meyer's first command post in St. Germain la Blanche Herbe, on the road leading out of Caen (today on its northwest outskirts).

The attack for midday on 7 June northwest of Caen is prepared. From the left: Sturmbannführer Eric Urbanitz (CO, 1st Artillery Battalion), Sturmbannführer Karl-Heinz Prinz (CO, 2nd Panzer Battalion), and Sturmbannführer Karl Bartling (Co, 3rd Artillery Battalion).

Panzer No. 536 of 5th Company (Panzer IV) SS Panzerregiment 12 directly before the attack on Authie, northwest of Caen on 7 June 1944: Unterscharführer W. Kretzschmar (tank commander), Sturmmann Schweinfest (gunner), Sturmmann Gaude (loader), Sturmmann Schreiner (driver), and Sturmmann Stefan (radio operator).

A knocked-out Sherman tank near Authie, northwest of Caen, 7 June 1944.

Normandy, Summer 1944. Amphibious vehicle of Kraderkundungs-Zug of Panzerregiment 12.

Caen, early June 1944. A knocked-out Sherman Firefly tank.

Waffen-SS Combat Cameraman.

Long-range observation.

Panzer No. 536 receives a direct hit from artillery fire on 7 June 1944 at Buron, northwest of Caen. A return roller and a suspension arm are shattered. The crew remove the damaged parts and the maintenance unit repairs the Panzer in one and a half days. This was the Caen-Bayeux, Caen-Villers Bocage crossroads.

Panzer IV No. 536 of 5th Panzer Company in a wheatfield in the Caen area, June 1944. Good camouflage was vital because of Allied mastery of the air.

"INVASION! German countermeasures in action!" The panzergrenadiers of SS Panzer Division "Hitler-jugend" have already fought superbly right from the first battles. The harshness of what is happening has swiftly impressed itself upon their young faces.

June 1944. A briefing from Hans Waldmüller, CO of 1st Bn.Regt. 25, in the field south of Cambes.

June 1944. Grenadiers drag an ammunition trailer to the gun position, past a knocked-out Sherman tank.

Early June 1944. The corps artillery battalion, Heavy SS Artillery Battalion 101, supports Regiment 25. Third from left: the battalion commander, Sturmbannführer Steineck; Sturmbannführer H. Meyer; Panzermeyer; Obersturmführer Bernhard Meitzel; and Hauptsturmführer Günter Reichenbach.

Early June 1944. Panzermeyer drives the divisional commander to the battalions of Regiment 25 on a motorcycle-sidecar combination. Sturm-bannführer Dr. Erich Gatternigg, the regimental medical officer, mounts the rear seat.

June–July 1944. Entrance to the courtyard of the former Ardenne Abbey, northwest of Caen. A camouflaged Volkswagen passes the sentries. On the right mudguard the divisional insignia, and next to it a blackout headlight.

A 15-cm heavy infantry gun enters the courtyard of Ardenne Abbey.

A one-ton tractor with a mounted crew tows and infantry gun.

The gun is brought into position.

Lunch in the field.

June 1944.
Wounded soldier
waits for an ambu-
lance at the north-
ern exit of Abbaye
d'Ardenne.

June 1944. The leader of a reconnaissance group briefs motorcyclists on enemy positions.

Grenadiers prepare for an attack, weapons are checked once again. They are carrying light assault packs. The grenadier on the left already has the base plate of a 8-cm mortar strapped on his back.

Caen area, June–July 1944. Tent of Kraderkundungs-Zug of SS Panzerregiment 12. Next to the tent is an amphibious vehicle.

Caen area, June 1944. Tasting German army bread.

June 1944. Grenadiers in house-to-house fighting near Caen.

After the unsuccessful attack by 3rd Panzer Company: the Panzerregiment CO, Obersturmbannführer Max Wünsche, who was wounded on 9 June, and Obersturmbannführer Rudolf v. Ribbentrop, who commanded 3rd Company. He was wounded on 4 June and could not take part in the attack.

Command post of SS Panzer Reconnaissance Battalion 12 in Cristot. Under a knocked-out Sherman tank, which Hauptsturmführer Gerd v. Reitzenstein and Untersturmführer Albert Wienecke have salvaged, are Sturmbannführer Gerd Bremer (CO) and Obersturmführer Kurt Buchheim (adjutant).

"British soldiers watch a burning farmhouse in Cristot, after entering the village. The Germans resisted strongly before they gave up the village, 17 June 1944." (English description on photograph)

Conferring on the field situation at the divisional command post in Caen-Venoix on 13 or 14 June 1944: Obersturmbannführer Max Wünsche, Brigadeführer Fritz Witt, and Standartenführer Kurt Meyer.

June 1944. Motor-cycle messenger in a burning village near Caen.

A shot-down Spitfire near Caen.

June 1944. The grave of Brigade-führer Fritz Witt in the park of Château de la Guillerie in Tillières sur Avre.

Standartenführer Kurt Meyer takes over command of the Division after the death of Brigadeführer Fritz Witt on 14 June 1944. He received the Oak Leaves to the Knight's Cross on 27 August 1944.

A wounded Allied airman is brought to the dressing station. On the right is Wilfried Woscidlo, a war correspondent.

Motorcycle soldier.

Obersturmbannführer Heinz Milius, who has taken over command of Regiment 25 from Standartenführer Kurt Meyer, discusses the situation with Sturmbannführer Hubert Meyer, war correspondent Herbert Reinecker, and orderly officer No. 1 Obersturmführer Bernhard Meitzel (Demyansk Shield on upper arm).

From the diary of Madame Demesnil of Château de Bois-londe: Badges of the British battalion which fought here against 3rd Battalion Regt. 26 on 18 June 1944.

The Château de Boislonde at the conclusion of the fighting at the end of June 1944.

The Iron Cross, Second Class, for bravery in combat.

Unterscharführer Otto Knof, panzer commander in the 5th and 9th Companies.

Unterscharführer Horst Lütgens, of the engineers reconnaissance platoon in the Engineers Battalion, knocked out a Sherman tank with a Panzerfaust on 11 June near le Mesnil.

Oberscharführer
Georg Fahrbach,
staff sergeant of the
Panzer Maintenance
Company.

Sturmmann Jochen
Leykauff, NCO can-
didate of 15/25.

Maltot, Normandy, July 1944. Young soldiers of SS Panzerregiment 12 receiving the award of the Iron Cross from the regimental commander, Obersturmbannführer Max Wünsche. On the left is the regimental adjutant, Hauptsturmführer Georg Isecke.

By means of the Field Post, a newspaper even gets to a foxhole.

The section leader.

The leader of an MG Squad just before an attack: ammunition belt around his neck, spade attached to the chest. On the MG 42 is an ammunition drum for firing from a standing position.

Shouting orders and staying low to the ground.

Observation platform of SS Panzerregiment 12 in Rauray after the capture of the village on 27 June 1944.

Wounded POWs from the "Hitlerjugend" Division on 27 June 1944.

Mid-June 1944. Camouflaged amphibious vehicle of Kraderkundungs-Zug of SS Panzerregiment 12 in Rauray.

SS Sturmbannführer Gerd Bremer, commander of SS Panzeraufklärungsabteilung 12.

Standartenoberjunker Paul Dienemann, here as Oberscharführer and Zugführer in 2. Panzerkompanie.

Sturmbannführer Erich Olboeter, commander of 3rd Battalion Regt. 26. He received the Knight's Cross on 27 July 1944 and was killed in action on 2 September 1944.

Hauptsturmführer Hans Siegel, commander of 8th Company, SS Panzerregiment 12. He received the Knight's Cross on 23 August 1944.

Untersturmführer Jeran's knocked-out Panzer IV being towed by a British Cromwell tank.

Schutzenpanzer-wagen 251/7, a vehicle of the engineer troops, with crossing rails fasted to the side. Note the blackout headlight on left fender and the divisional insignia next to co-driver's hatch.

Rauray, regimental command post of SS Panzerregiment 12 from 24 to 27 June 1944.

CHAPTER 2.7
Actions of SS-Panzergrenadierregiment 25 and 21. Panzerdivision

During the heavy fighting on the left wing of "HJ" Division, the enemy did not attack in the sector of Regiment 25, apart from some local actions. Both sides carried out brisk reconnaissance. The Divisional situation report for 16 June states the following: "The enemy reconnaissance during the night was unsuccessful in penetrating our positions anywhere. The scouting parties were either destroyed or forced to turn back."[1]

Sturmmann (lance corporal) Emil Werner of 3. Kompanie reports on a scouting mission to Cambes, located in no-man's land in front of the sector of I./25:

> We were one NCO, Unterscharführer Galter, and ten men. We were led to the Kompanie command post and Hauptsturmführer Peine-mann took our pay-books so that the enemy could not determine our unit in case one of them fell into their hands. The chief was still limping, he had been wounded during a fighter-bomber attack. We had much respect for this man. He was always there for his young soldiers which gave us courage. As we left his earth bunker, his last words were: 'Good luck, boys!' We started out at 23.30 hours. We followed behind our squad leader, first along the sector of 3. Kompanie, past the tank trench to the graveyard and then through a mine barrier. There we met another squad laying mines. The Unter-scharführer said: 'You'll have to come back to this spot. Everything else is mined already'. There was a wood approximately 300 m further. We wanted to move in but at the same moment an English scouting party was coming out. I saw a few figures run across the path, not ten meters from us in a grain field. Already, the first shots were fired. Unterscharführer Galter was hit, he was probably dead. I was next, with my MG 42 (machine gun), and took a bullet in the stomach. I had seen the muzzle flash. I was lying on the path through the fields and noticed that I was bleeding. I felt no pain, only fear. I never got to fire a shot, only heard the shouting from both sides. After twenty minutes, everything was quiet. Suddenly, I heard Germans talking. One of them said: 'Werner is also missing.' Now I was sure, they were my comrades, and I called out. Two men came over and I put my arms around their necks. They pushed a rifle under my behind and carried me back immediately. They still had me sitting on the rifle when another one shouted: 'Werner, is that you?' That was my Spieß (top kick), Benno Gerl from Munich.

He had come to the front line with hot food, which was impossible to do during the day because of the fighter-bombers. Benno gave me a bottle of Schnaps and several packages of cigarettes. His last words were: 'Werner, give my love to the homeland.' I was then loaded into an ambulance and taken to the field dressing station in a forest. I was operated on during the same night. The doctor asked me how old I was. I answered eighteen years and ten days. That was my farewell to the 12. SS-Panzerdivision. I was moved to a hospital in St. Wendel. After two months I met a comrade from my Kompanie, SS-Grenadier Beierl. He told me much more about the scouting mission. The Canadians had played a trick on us. We had been sent to find out what the noises were we heard every night. As my comrade Beierl told me, the Canadians had set up a concrete mixer on the road, filled it with large rocks and let it run. It had made the noise and was spotted by another scouting party from 3. Kompanie.[2]

The war diary of I./25 states tersely:

Increasing enemy reconnaissance activity during the night. Fire exchanges with enemy scouting parties in front of the sectors of 3. and 1. Kompanie. A strong enemy scouting party in front of the neighbor Kompanie on the right (of 21. Pz.-Div., Author) was forced to turn back. Only weak enemy air activity, caused by the weather situation. During the night increasing artillery and mortar barrages on all of the sector. Our entrenchment building had probably been spotted. Excavation noises on the enemy side also indicate building of entrenchments. Barbed wire obstructions are being installed ahead of the positions of the Bataillon, T- and S-mines are being laid. Hand grenades were fixed to the barbed wire. A connected system of trenches is being built. In case of an enemy attack, the position must be held under all circumstances.[3]

Obersturmführer Kurt Havemeister, commander of 7. -Kompanie, reports on an attack against the positions of II./25. Concentrated enemy artillery fire had announced an attack. When the noise of breaking trees and crumbling walls suddenly stopped, the time had come:

Together with the Kompanietrupp (squad) I was able to get out of the command post. Outside, in the first light of day, we were lost for words. All the buildings had been turned into heaps of rubble, the connecting trench was buried, the park a chaos of fallen trees. The messengers had been instructed during the long waiting periods. They had just disappeared, crawling and leaping, into the ruined terrain when MG and infantry fire could clearly be heard from I. Zug. I must have shouted with relief, a shout which Oberjunker (officer cadet) Meyer interpreted as the order for immediate departure into this direction. I only saw him again hours later in the cellar dressing station. After a noticeable decrease of the battle noise I realized that the artillery fire had stopped and I spotted, to my joy, the messengers from II. and III. Zug. No fighting noise had so far been heard from their direction. While they reported destruction and losses, they were ready for defense. This report was answered with the admonition of extreme vigilance, without regard of the developments at I. Zug, and with best wishes. Obviously, the mortars had only suffered minor damage. They were firing, as ordered, from among the fallen trees of the park, into the terrain ahead of our lines.

Finally, when a happily grinning messenger from I. Zug reported to me, I was able to picture the situation and my apprehensions disappeared. The Canadians had still no idea of our forward bunkers and our positions behind the edges of the fields. It also appeared that Tommy was not taking part in the game this time, leaving the Canadians to enjoy their revenge by themselves. These believed that, after the barrages, all they had to do was to move into the building and they suffered terrible losses. We were helped not only by the field of fire we had opened up by mowing the grain, but also by the anti-personnel mines and the remotely activated Teller mines which proved to be devastating weapons, to the joy of our men. The squads following behind did obviously not want to leave the cover of the tall grain for the open terrain but as soon as they assembled, mines exploded immediately. We could not only hear the urgent orders of the enemy NCOs but also, sadly and clearly, the shouting of the wounded.

Suddenly, when I heard MG- and rifle fire from II. and III. Zug, I had to expect a relief attack from Cambes. I was able to reach the command post of III. Zug through the park. On my way I found a messenger who had obviously wanted to get to me. When I arrived there was still firing at II. Zug, but an attack from Cambes could be ruled out. The enemy artillery now concentrated heavy fire on the area of our Bataillon command post in la Folie. A platoon of Canadians, with three squads, obviously wanted to squeeze by I. Zug, after their terrible experience, and make their way to Cambes. This brought them almost abreast of our positions and they were almost completely wiped out by our fire on their flank.

I returned to my own command post. The dressing station in the cellar looked bad, the bewildered medics had their hands full. Several dead were already bedded down in the entrance to the cellar. Their sight drove me out to I. Zug. Even during this tiring journey, an unusual silence set in, broken only by some individual shots.

While making my way through the orchard I spotted, from the direction of les Buissons, low vehicles with large, waving Red Cross flags. I immediately sounded my well-known signal whistle to stop fire. To open fire was allowed only after a different version of the whistle had been sounded. The Canadians approached the edges of the grain fields at high speed to recover their wounded and dead, putting their justified trust in our fairness. We used the unusual silence for the same bitter purpose. After approximately one-half hour, a Canadian officer standing upright in a vehicle saluted toward us as they drove off. I returned this with the German salute, from the edge of the field. The expected artillery fire did not set in during the night. It was aimed, with long intervals, far behind our positions. Our joy was great when our Bataillon doctor suddenly showed up at the southern wall of the park, together with vehicles and medics. He administered first aid and ensured proper loading and transport of the wounded in vehicles to the hospital. This brave Dr. Sedlacek from Vienna did not only inspire new courage in our desperate medics, but also in all of us, for further actions. Several comrades owe their lives to his untiring efforts.

Sadly, I had subsequently to write letters to a number of relatives of our dead and this really impressed on me who these victims were. Dead were Oberscharführer Durnhammer, two other married NCOs, and five young soldiers. Severely wounded, and thus lost to us, were Untersturmführer Harter, one NCO, and six soldiers. Several lightly wounded could remain with us, but they were only conditionally ready for action. During the two weeks since our action began we lost more than a third of our total strength.[4]

Occasionally, scouting activity also resulted in amusing experiences. For this reason, the 'Story of the flour-Canadian' in Buron at III./25 is retold here. It was written by Untersturm-führer Franz-Joseph Kneipp of the staff of Regiment 25:

This happened in the early morning hours of a day at the invasion front in Normandy in June 1944. The village in which this smile-causing story took place is called Buron.

Heavy defensive fighting was raging at the invasion front. Our Division found no rest. As a member of Regiment 25 I was leading a scouting party of one NCO and three Grenadiers through the town at approximately 04.00 hours. Since it was already light and I wanted to make my way back without being spotted, we set out for the command post of III./25. Although we had to hurry, the fighter-bombers fired even on individuals if they spotted them, I went into a house along the way to see if I could possibly find some special edible treat. My soldiers remained in the street, under cover. I looked around in the kitchen of the abandoned house, but could not find anything useful to us. Leaving the kitchen, I turned around once more. Some movement had caused this instinctive reaction. My glance fell on a large barrel, covered in white dust. On top of it was a big round cover which was moving very slightly. I called one of my men in and, weapons cocked, I lifted the cover of the barrel. Now I had found something special after all, even if it was not edible, a Canadian soldier totally covered in flour dust. At first I saw two hands rising slowly higher and higher. In one hand, the young soldier—he was no older than our young Grenadiers—held a fountain pen which he offered me as if to appease me. In the other hand he had a children's picture book with thick cardboard pages on which a horse, a cock, chickens and various farm animals were depicted. In his terror, the young warrior was unable to utter a sound. He only stared with fearful eyes at the death's-head on my field cap. He was trembling like an aspen leaf. We helped him out of the barrel. He dusted off his uniform, disappearing for a moment in a thick cloud of flour. He had crawled into a flour barrel to hide from us.

He had written on every blank spot in the picture book: to the residents of the house asking forgiveness for having eaten a glass of marmalade he had found, to his parents, to say good-bye on the assumption he would not get out of the village of Buron alive. When he was finally convinced we would not harm him, he thawed a little but could still not say a coherent sentence. Then, in the evening hours we took him to the command post at the Ardennes abbey. My hope for him is that he may have lived through the war.[5]

Just how costly the artillery and mortar fire and the scouting activity on both sides were, is shown by the losses of I./25 during the period 11 to 18 June: Killed were one NCO and six men, wounded two officers, four NCOs and twenty-three men of whom one officer, two NCOs and five men remained with the unit.[6]

The war diary of I./25 offers some indication of the general situation in the sector northeast and north of Caen:

A rocket launcher Abteilung has been attached to the Regiment, VB to the I./25. The commander of the rocket launcher Abteilung visits the Bataillon commander at 19.00 hours for a briefing on the situation. Enemy troop concentrations have been spotted to the north and northwest and successfully engaged by our own artillery and heavy infantry weapons. Strong enemy air activity during the day,

continuous artillery fire on the Bataillon sector during the day, quiet
during the night. Our Flak (anti-aircraft gun) shoots down one four-
engined and one two-engined enemy bomber. Parachutes with supplies are dropped at 23.00 hours from transport aircraft, probably
east of the Orne river. Scouting parties of 13. Kompanie in Cambes
are fired upon during the night. The positions are being reinforced
in the course of the night. The 1. Kompanie advances to the rail
embankment on the right to fill the gap created by the withdrawal
of 16. Kompanie . . . The 16. Kompanie has been pulled out to take
up position between Regiment 25 and 26.[7]

The rocket launcher Abteilung was part of Werfer-regiment 83, commanded by Oberstleutnant (lieutenant colonel) Böhme. It was attached to
the "HJ" Division. Together with Werferregiment 84 it formed the Werferbrigade 7. Of the Division's own Werferabteilung, the SS-Werferabteilung 12,
only 1. Batterie of Obersturmführer Reinhold Macke, had been brought
along at the start of the invasion. This was caused by the shortage of the
majority of the vehicles. It was attached to Werferregiment 83 and saw action
within that Regiment's activities.

An entry in the Bataillon's war diary for 13 June is remarkable:

Artillery barrages throughout the whole day, minor air activity over
the areas to the rear. Concentrated bombardment on Caen, flares
over the sector of I./25.[8]

An enemy attack north and northeast of Caen was predictable.

The war diary of 7. Armee notes on the further fighting in the right sector of I. SS-Panzerkorps on 12 June:

As ordered by the Führer, the enemy bridgehead between the Orne
and Vire rivers must be attacked piece by piece and smashed. As a
first step, the enemy east of the Orne river must be destroyed in
order to free up 346. Infanterie Division.

The Armee ordered, among others, the I. SS-Panzerkorps, which was
responsible for the Troarn-Orne sector (Kampfgruppe Luck, Pz.Gren. Rgt.
125 of 21. Pz.Div.), to reinforce this sector ". . . so that an enemy breakthrough to the south becomes impossible." After the attachment of Werferbrigade 7, the LXXXI. A.K. was scheduled to attack the Bois de Bavent. The
I. SS-Panzerkorps was ordered to join this attack with strong forces.[9]

In the morning of 13 June, the 51st (Highland) Division had started an
attack east of the Orne river against the sector of the units of 21. Pz.-Div. in
position there. It had thus obviated the attack by 346. Inf.-Div. This division
was ordered to begin the attack to relieve 21. Pz.-Div., planned for the

evening, immediately. The attack by the Highlanders was repelled. In the sector of 21. Pz.-Div., east of the Orne river, and of the "HJ" Division, it was a quiet day with the exception of strong artillery and reconnaissance activity.[10]

Just outside of the mouth of the Orne river, active unloading was spotted on 15 June. This indicated renewed attack plans in the sector to both sides of the Orne river. The heavy SS-Artillerieabteilung 101 of I. Korps severely harassed the unloading, until it was finally stopped.[11]

The 21. Pz.-Div. attacked in the early morning of 16 June east of the Orne in order to reduce the British bridgehead. Herouvillette was re-captured. Enemy resistance increased near Esocville and the attack stalled. Localized successes were achieved through assault-party actions on 18 June. The link-up to 346. Inf.-Div. was re-established near Bavent.

In order to guarantee a uniform conduct of the fighting in the total landing area, Heeresgruppe B moved the right border of 7. Armee on 17. June from the Orne to the Seine river. The command in this sector was given to the general command of LXXXVI. A.K. With this, all units of LXXXI. A.K. and I. SS-Panzerkorps, fighting in this area, came under its command. The new general command was ordered to destroy the enemy beachhead between the Dives and Orne rivers and ". . . as soon as possible, to free up the initially attached attack forces of I. SS-Panzerkorps."[12]

CHAPTER 2.8
Actions by the Divisionsbegleitkompanie with the Panzer-Lehr-Division from 16 to 20 June 1944

Before noon on 16 June, the enemy had broken through the thin line of the neighbor to the left, the Pz.-Lehr-Div., and had advanced to the road Fontenay-Caumont near Hottot.[1] The Begleitkompanie of the "HJ" Division had just been withdrawn and returned to Divisional reserve status. It was alerted at 13.00 hours and set in march to the Aufklärungsabteilung of the "Panzerlehr". The Kompanie took over a 1,500 meters wide sector. It was a quiet day except for artillery and mortar fire.

On 18 June, the Kompanie was ordered to counterattack and clean up a breakthrough between 3. and 4. Kompanie of the Aufklärungs-Lehr-Abteilung. This counterattack was conducted by the Schützenzug (rifle platoon) with a strength of one officer (Untersturmführer Erwin Stier, four NCOs and twenty-four men, together with the light Infanterie-Geschütz-Zug (infantry gun). The main line of defense was restored and 120 prisoners taken, among them were a colonel, two majors, and four more officers. Captured were: thirty-two rifles, eight machine guns, eight mortars, one anti-tank rifle, ten sub-machine guns, one radio, and a folder with maps and secret orders.[2] Unterscharführer Leo Freund took part in the counterattack and reports:

> The enemy had broken through southwest of Tilly on 18 June. In the afternoon, the Divisionsbegleitkompanie received orders to counterattack. The Kompanie chief, Obersturmführer Fritz Guntrum, issued this order to the Schützenzug and the light Infanterie-Geschütz-Zug and determined 20.00 hours as the start of the attack. Considering the strength of the enemy, an immediate attack would have been pointless, in particular as a counterattack was expected. Our only chance was an unexpected surprise attack, and this seemed only possible during the evening. So we moved into our assembly area and observed the terrain ahead of us throughout the afternoon. The front line ahead of us at the breakthrough point was completely dissolved. Time and again, individual soldiers and even whole squads of the Panzer-Lehr-Division appeared, retreating. We questioned them on the enemy's locations. When they heard of our intention to counterattack, they looked at our small group of twenty-nine men unbelievingly, and hurried on.
>
> The terrain in front of us was covered with many hedges. A path cut through it in our exact direction of attack. The Kampfgruppe was divided so that the first squad was to the left, the second squad to the right of the path. The third squad and the Zug squad under Untersturmführer Stier assembled along the path. With us was also Unterschar-führer Kurt Breitmoser as the forward observer of the light Infanterie-Geschütz-Zug. It had taken up positions with its three guns (7.5 cm) behind us.
>
> The attack started on time and advanced quickly. The first enemy positions were virtually overrun. Now it became apparent how right we had been with the element of surprise. The enemy was leisurely setting up positions, i.e. the individual men were busy making themselves comfortable in their foxholes, since a counterattack was no longer expected at this time. The attack went extremely well. We advanced irresistibly and were often involved in hand-to-hand combat. The forward observer Breitmoser provided us with excellent service. He managed to have his light guns fire on each individual hedge where stronger resistance was shown, even if these enemy position were only thirty meters in front of us. His directions to the firing position were so accurate that we had to admire him. Our men had been gripped by an irresistible drive to attack. Suddenly, the attack stalled on the left side, at the first squad. An enemy machine gun position with an excellent field of fire forced the squad to take cover. A Sturmmann of this squad moved off without

special order, gave the machine gun position a wide berth and suddenly appeared behind it. With his hand grenade armed, he was hit by pistol bullet from the machine gun nest and dropped, mortally wounded, on the enemies. The exploding hand grenade wiped out the position and the attack rolled on. Inside the machine gun nest, our comrade and three enemies lay dead. Then the attack stalled on the right side, at the second squad. Together with Unterscharführer Breitmoser and two men of the Zug squad I raced over to help. After a few well-placed salvos from our guns the attack continued there also and we stormed in intervals across the meadows from hedge to hedge. Together with a machine gunner of the second squad who had the machine gun on his shoulder harness and was firing from the hip, I was racing towards a large hedge under covering fire from our comrades. We already knew that we had to fight for each hedge, but we were not prepared for what we found behind this one. We suddenly found ourselves at the edge of a wide trench with approximately forty Englishmen in it. They stared at us as frightened as we stared at them. However, we regained control more quickly and after a short burst of fire from our machine gun and my machine pistol (MP44) and after our loud yells of 'Hands up!', they all surrendered. The Englishmen immediately in front of us had been hit and had collapsed on the ground. Some shots had also been fired at us and my comrade, a Rottenführer (corporal) whose name I have sadly forgotten, had been hit. He was bleeding from a wound in the left cheek, but with all the excitement and tension, had not even noticed it yet. When I saw the blood on his face, I covered the English soldiers with the machine gun and sent him back to find the medic. Soon after, the second squad caught up with me and we noticed that some of the Englishmen had embroidered stars on their epaulets. We did not give this much thought, the attack had to continue since we needed to take advantage of our successful surprise and recapture our previous main line of defense. The objective was achieved and then we determined that we had lost one killed and two wounded. The enemy, however, was totally annihilated. Those who were not lying dead or wounded behind us had been taken prisoner. After we had some rest from the events, I inquired from the medic as to the whereabouts of the wounded Rottenführer. He answered that he had sent him on to the main dressing station. I was somewhat disappointed since I had considered the wound only as a scratch. My disappointment grew the next day when I checked with the main dressing station and was advised that the Rottenführer had been transported to the field hospital. I just could not understand why they made such fuss about a mere scratch. Some weeks later I received a field post letter from this same Rottenführer,

mailed from the home town hospital of Leipzig, in which he virtually apologized for not having returned that evening. His wound was
a clean shot through the head. The bullet had entered in the left
cheek and exited behind the right ear. As I read this letter a cold
trembling feeling ran through me.

At dawn we were relieved at the recaptured main line of defense.
At an isolated farm, we fell into a deep sleep until we were found by
a small column of vehicles in the afternoon. We had to assemble in
the farm yard, the commander of the Panzer-Lehr-Division had
arrived. Incredulous, he surveyed our small group and demanded to
know whether we had really not been more. He then told us with a
few short words that we had wiped out an enemy battalion and captured one colonel, two majors, two captains and two lieutenants. He
expressed his appreciation, and we, ourselves, were surprised about
the extent of our success.

Untersturmführer Stier received the E.K.I. (Iron Cross I.) from
the hands of the Generalleutnant. He also awarded two E.K. II. of
which I received one. The successful counterattack was also mentioned in the Wehrmacht report where it was stated: 'An enemy elite
battalion was annihilated southwest of Tilly and the battalion staff
captured'.[3]

The Kompanie remained in action in the Hottot area until 20 June. At
times, its neighbor to the left was the Korpsbegleit-kompanie of I. SS-Panzerkorps.[4] Between 18 to 20 June it lost three men killed, one NCO and five
men wounded, and one man missing.[5]

CHAPTER 2.9
Final Observations on the Second Battle for Caen

During this time period, a completely new event occurred. During one
night, possibly 15–16 June, an unknown flying object was observed from the
Divisional command post. It flew at an altitude of a few hundred meters and
at a distance of approximately 1,000 meters from a southwesterly into a
northeasterly direction. The trail of fire was clearly visible and a loud droning noise could be heard. Only a few days later we learned that it had been a
V1. The age of the rocket had begun, but the troops knew nothing of this.
After a failed first launch on 13 June, the attacks were started again during
the night 15–16 June. Within the first twenty-four hours, 244 flying bombs
were launched on London of which, however, only a portion reached their
target.[1]

The defensive fighting during the second battle for Caen had made clear, above all, two difficulties: the superiority of the enemy artillery and the anti-tank capability.

On the first point, the Division reported through channels to the Heeresgruppe in its situation report for 17 June 1944, among others:

It has been shown again that the enemy can achieve successes exclusively by use of his incredible superiority in material, and that the fighting value of his infantry is minor. One of the major conditions for a successful defense and later attack is effective supression of the enemy artillery. Required for this are:
    1.) Observation batteries, if possible aerial reconnaissance;
    2.) Sufficient amounts of artillery ammunition.

In the situation report for 18 June it is stated:

The cause for the failure of our own counterattack, despite strong artillery support, can be found in the fact that reconnaissance and supression of enemy artillery was impossible and that its barrages could not be -prevented.[2]

The vast material artillery superiority of the enemy was effectively increased even more through artillery observation aircraft, as it was shown during the fighting for the Parc de Boislande.

The enemy artillery superiority also had a negative effect on the German anti-tank capability. Whenever the enemy attacked with tanks and infantry behind the moving wall of artillery fire, the anti-tank guns of the defenders had, for the most part, already been knocked out before they could fire their first shell. The infantry was kept down by the fire and could, often enough, not fire their Panzerfausts quickly enough or it was wiped out by covering tanks and the infantry following behind. Effective anti-tank activity was possible only by Jagdpanzers (tank destroyers) and Panzers. To do this properly, they would have had to sit so close behind our own forward lines that they could effectively fight enemy tanks when these opened fire on the German infantry. In the flat, open terrain, the Jagdpanzers and Panzers would have been spotted immediately by enemy artillery observers, would have come under concentrated fire and been knocked out. Thus, they had to be held back at a distance which allowed adequate camouflage. This was more easily possible with the Jagdpanzers, because of their low silhouette. For this and other reasons, anti-tank activity was the fundamental objective of the Jagdpanzers, and not of the Panzers. Under cover, and in rolling terrain, both could be kept closer behind even if they did not always have a good field of fire. Even in rolling terrain, when no covering hedges, bushes, clumps of trees or buildings were available, the Jagdpanzers and, especially, the Panzers had to seek ambush positions on the back slopes so as not to be spotted by the enemy artillery and taken under concentrated fire. They then required sufficient distance from the ridge so they could open fire on enemy tanks immediately after these came across the hill, without having to move the Panzers, thus avoiding having to show the enemy the more weakly armored sides. For the Jagdpanzers this was necessary, in addition, because of the restricted traversability of their guns.

Above all, the mission of the Panzers during defensive fighting was to knock out enemy tanks which had broken through from ambush positions to the rear or in a counterattack. To do this, they had to be concentrated in the vicinity of expected hot spots, they had to be out of range of ground-based artillery observers, set up facing in a favorable direction, and brought forward under cover. Since the German Panzerjägerabteilung was still waiting for its Jagdpanzers and was not ready for action, the Panzerregiment had to take over these responsibilities as well. It was unable to fully carry out both missions.

During the second battle for Caen, the enemy had attacked with tanks and infantry in the broken terrain of the Bocage on 11 and 17 June. The tanks which had broken through on 11 June had been successfully knocked out when they entered open terrain during the attack on Hill 102. Several Panthers caught them from the flank. On 17 June, the wooded terrain of the Parc de Boislande prevented a counterattack by tanks or support of the counterattack by assault guns. In both cases, the enemy had deployed his tanks to accompany the infantry, as if they were assault guns. During this period, the enemy undertook real tank attacks twice: near Norrey and le Mesnil-Patry on 11 June and near Villers-Bocage on 13 June. In the first case, the Canadian tanks attacked across mostly open terrain, with infantry mounted. They had only dared to do this since they had been told that "Jerry" was on the run. Since the infantry was mounted, it could not be separated from the tanks and arrived simultaneously with them right in the middle of the positions of the Pioniers and Panzergrenadiers. This breakthrough would have succeeded, despite the destruction of a few tanks by brave tank hunters and a Pak, had not some Panzers shown up just in time and counterattacked without coming under artillery fire. This deployment in the classical manner was almost an ideal case, if the inevitable need for improvisation at the time is disregarded.

The second battle for Caen was a clear German defensive success. The initial frontal attacks on the positions of the Panzer-Lehr-Division, coupled with a flank attack on the left wing of the "HJ" Division, had not achieved the desired breakthrough. Instead, they resulted only in minor territorial gains and caused heavy losses to both sides. Thereafter, the attempt was made to break up the German defensive front line near Caen through a wide pincer movement using insufficient forces, in order to encircle the three Panzerdivisions in action there, or to smash them. Contributing to the eventual retreat of the 7th Armoured Division after the defeat at Villers-Bocage were a mistaken judgment of the situation and a lack of valor of XXX Corps. Only the first wheeled units of the newly and surprisingly arrived 2. Panzerdivision had shown up, the Panzers were still far behind. The Corps had the opportunity to use the just landed 49th Infantry Division to reinforce the 7th Armoured instead of ordering it into the attack near Cristot and the Parc de Boislande, without any appreciable territorial gains. On the German side there were not sufficient Panzer and almost no infantry available to launch a successful counterattack. Panzergrenadierregiment 25 had not been seriously attacked since 8 June, apart from localized actions. Together with parts of 21. Panzerdivision, it should have been relieved by an infantry division, but none had arrived so far. The operative reserves of the OKW (supreme command Wehrmacht) were tied down in defense since 11 June.

The losses of "HJ" Division until 16 June were 403 killed, among them 17 officers; 847 wounded, among them 29 officers; 63 missing, among them 5 officers; and 6 ill—a total of 1,149 losses.

Armored vehicles ready for action on this day were 52 Panzer IVs, 38 Panthers, 10 Wespen (Wasps, 10.5 cm howitzers on PzII chassis), 5 Hummeln (Bumble bees, 15 cm howitzers on PzIV chassis), 304 armored cars, armored reconnaissance vehicles and artillery observation Panzers, and 23 heavy Pak.[3]

Until then, neither personnel nor material replacements had arrived while the enemy constantly replaced his losses.

It was necessary, once again, to bring in reinforcements more quickly than the enemy. On 18 June, the three Panzer-divisions and the 346. Infanteriedivision (the 716. Infanteriedivision had been almost completely destroyed) in the area of Caen were facing five infantry divisions, one airborne division and three tank brigades of the enemy.

CHAPTER 2.10
Between Two Battles

Since there was virtually no German aerial reconnaissance, any information on the situation and intentions on the enemy side could be gained only through scouting parties and from prisoners taken by them, from captured documents and monitoring of communications. The Division had—as was not usual for Panzerdivisions of the Heer—a Nachrichtennah-aufklärungszug (close-distance communications monitoring platoon), led by Untersturmführer Siegfried Schneider. The platoon consisted of a listening squad with four receivers to monitor radio communications, three translators, and one listening device for wire communications interception. The vehicles of the platoon were Fiat cars, modified in a makeshift manner.

The squad monitored the enemy radio communications. The coded morse traffic was not monitored, even after code documents had been captured during the first days as well as later. This work was probably done at the Supreme Command West. For this, Nachrichten-Aufklärungs-Abteilung 13 (communications monitoring Abteilung) was available. Schneider had, at times, received training and briefings at its offices in Tourcoing, Vitre and Le Mans.

For the monitoring of the radio traffic, in particular that of the tank units and the artillery, the captured code names for towns, individual farms and castles, rivers, wooded areas and hills, were a valuable asset. Some of these names were changed after some time, in particular the code names of the units. Even if no concrete tactical information was exchanged, after some experience was gained, valuable conclusions regarding the general intentions could be drawn from the often careless and undisciplined radio traffic. For instance, the preparations for the attack on 16 and 17 June were clearly recognized. Untersturmführer Schneider reports on the difficulties imposed on this activity by the German troops:

> Only a few days after the start of the invasion, the commanders and chiefs had already become aware that the enemy had available considerable means of radio direction finding. This resulted in an aversion to anything using an antenna. My Zug moved from St. Germain-la Blanche-Herbe, to where Panzermeyer had 'banned' me since he did not want me in the Ardennes abbey, to the I./26. When I reported to Sturmbannführer Krause at his command post at St. Manvieu, I was unable to convince him either that only radio transmitters, but not radio receivers, could be located by taking bearings. In his fatherly manner, but unequivocally and direct, he told me that sufficient distance had to exist between his command and my antennas. He 'banned' me and my Zug to Marcelet.
>
> Regrettably, we did not have the capability of direction finding, a technique which deeply impressed our officers.[1]

When the front line in the sector of Regiment 26 was shortened during the night 15/16 June, in some spots moved a few hundred meters to the rear, there was an opportunity to deploy the telephone monitoring squad. There were three means of intercepting wire messages: tapping of the enemy wire using a specially developed clamp to attach to the wire, through under-the-ground listening devices or monitoring wire loops which were located close to the enemy wire connections and worked through induction. Since there could not yet be any enemy wire network in the area to be given up, and since the special clamps were not available to the Zug, only the other two possibilities could be considered. A large monitoring wire loop was to be installed, using the rail line Caen-Bayeux. Untersturmführer Schneider reported on this:

> The listening device sat in Marcelet (a park with a manor house), not far from the Carpiquet airfield. Along the rail line east of Rots and Brouay, all remaining telegraph wires and the rail itself were switched to a parallel mode. Our own communications squad set up the wire connection from east of Rots. In Brouay, the line was connected under my supervision, and a connecting wire was laid to a spot north of le Mesnil-Patry. Another connecting wire was put in place by the communications Kompanie since the Zug did not have enough of the required heavy field cable. The total time required to set up the listening loop was approximately five hours. The loop worked, as we confirmed through the field telephones hooked up at both ends. The call went through. After connecting it to the listening device, nothing further was heard. Another check, after approximately two hours, indicated that the loop had been broken. I do not know the reason for this, so I can only speculate. Even when we worked on the connection in Brouay, strong enemy pressure was directed onto that bulge in the front line. After handing over the line north of le Mesnil-Patry to the communications Kompanie for its continuation to Marcelet, heavy artillery fire was concentrated on le Mesnil-Patry as we passed through it. It is possible that Brouay was abandoned a few hours later, that the Canadians detected our plan and cut the wire at the rail line. It is more probable, however, that the relatively long connecting wire to Marcelet (approximately seven kilometers) was cut several times by the heavy artillery fire on the le Mesnil-Patry area.[2]

Several days later, on 18 June, an attempt was made to use the underground listening devices. Untersturmführer Schneider wrote on this:

> Three underground listening devices were installed approximately 150 meters in front of the forward lines of 15./25, the right neighbor of I./26, in the Rots area during the night. The receiver was set up in a trench close to a machine gun position. Here I spent the quietest day at the invasion front. We had finally found some peace from the ships' artillery and fighter-bombers. Our attempt was without success.[3]

The efficiency and effectiveness of any fighting force depends largely on its supply units. Both are dependent upon each other. In recognition of this, the supply troops, in the same manner as the fighting forces of the Waffen-

SS, were led by officers and not by civilian officials. As well, NCOs and men were subjected to thorough combat training and could be expected to act in a battle-ready manner. This proved to be valuable because of the Allied air superiority and later during the withdrawal fighting.

The supply troops, the repair installations and the provisions battalion of the Division were located, since the invasion started, in the Forêt de Grimbosq and the Forêt de Cinglais, fifteen to eighteen kilometers south of Caen. They were installed outside the range of the artillery—in particular the ships' artillery—and well camouflaged against aerial observation. They worked as directed by the Ib, Sturmbannführer Fritz Buchsein. The supplies, especially fuel, ammunition and spare parts, had to be brought in from a long distance away. Since the invasion had been expected by the supreme commanders of the Heeresgruppen West to take place at the Pas de Calais, the Oberquartiermeister (supreme quartermaster) West (O.Qu.West) had established the large supply depots primarily behind this sector of the coast. Only when the insistence of the OKW forced more attention to be given to Normandy, a portions of these supplies were moved behind this sector. But even after a short time, neither the depots of the 7. Armee nor those of the O.Qu. West were sufficient to meet the demand. In addition, the ammunition supplies for the OKW reserves, i.e. the "HJ" Division, were stored by O.Qu. West in the Paris area. The troops had only one supply unit of ammunition. Based on prior experience, the daily requirement of the troops was approximately 1/8 of one supply unit, which then lasted for eight days of fighting. According to accounts from O.Qu. West, fuel available at the troop level were 3.5 consumption units for the wheeled vehicles and five consumption units for the tracked vehicles. This equaled a driving distance on the road of 350 kilometers and 250 kilometers respectively.[4] The frequent stops, having to leave the roads to take cover from fighter-bombers, and the detours required by destruction of roads, had caused a higher consumption.

The enemy air superiority forced, except when rain occasionally prevented fighter-bomber activity, supply runs to be made during the few hours of darkness. The result was that, together with the reduced speed possible at night and the long distances, the available transport capacity was insufficient. The destruction of rail lines by air attacks forced a replacement of the lost rail capacity through vehicle columns which were already overloaded and used up fuel themselves. The war diary of 7. Armee repeatedly notes these supply problems. For instance, an entry on 12 June, 15.40 hours states:

> Chief of I. SS-Pz. Korps submits a request to the Chief of the General Staff, under all circumstances, possibly by Ju (air transport, Author) to bring forward Panzer ammunition and charges for Panzerfaust."
> At 16.05 hours: "Chief of the General Staff orders O.Qu., using any means available, to supply the ammunition requested by I. SS-Pz. Korps from the Reich." On 13 June, 17.15 hours: "Chief of the Gen-

eral Staff advises O.Qu.: the Ia of 2. SS-Pz.-Div. will arrive at O. Qu. to pick up urgently needed fuel. Anything possible is to be handed over. O.Qu. reports that the closest fuel depot which can supply is located near Nantes." At 17.15 hours: "For 2. Pz.-Div. (advancing near Villers-Bocage, not 2. SS-Pz.-Div., Author), twenty cubic meters of fuel will be flown in tonight." On 15 June, 21.50 hours: "Units of 3. Fallschirm-Jäger Division on foot have not yet arrived. All column vehicles, without exception, are needed for supply." 22.45 hours: "O.Qu. reports to Ia that, after discussion with Chef LXXXIV. A.K., all available vehicle capacity of the Korps is in tactical use. O.Qu. requests a decision whether available Armee transport capacity is to be used to bring up ammunition or fuel. Both, simultaneously, is impossible. If -ammunition is brought up, supply of fuel will stop for a few days."[5]

In a report by Division-Nachschub-Truppen 12 (Division supply troops), the activity of this Abteilung is tersely stated:

In view of enemy air superiority, supply runs are carried out almost only during night hours and in small columns. They often required days since loading took place, among others, at depots near Le Mans, Compiègne, and Sens. The delivery, in particular of the heavy ammunition, occasionally took place at, or just behind, the firing positions.[6]

Obersturmführer Emil Maître, commander of 4. Kraftfahrkompanie (motor transport), reported on the actions of the men:

The supply of the fighting troops was carried out, as a rule, during the night. However, activity during the day could not always be avoided. Battalions and batteries which had almost or totally run out of ammunition, were waiting longingly for the vital ammunition so as to continue to be ready for the defense. After returning from the nightly action, sleeping in exhaustion, the drivers were pulled from their resting places. They sat down behind their steering wheels without grumbling and drove off. These were often 'trips without return'.

The squadrons of fighter-bombers and the twin-fuselage Lightnings ruled the skies and dove down whenever they spotted any movement on the ground. They chased single vehicles and even individual men on the roads and in the fields. They were hunting from an altitude of 200 meters with bombs, rockets and on-board weapons, hardly ever missing a target. Despite this, the men behind the wheels, driving calmly in leaps from cover to cover, reached their destination in most cases. They never thought of their highly explosive loads. Sometimes a bit of luck was missing and the load took a hit. Our moves took place at night as soon as the patrolling fighter-bombers had returned to their bases. Often, the vehicles returning from their night mission at first light, had to find our new location. If a vehicle had not returned after a twelve hour tour, a search party was sent after it. We were all full of joy if the vehicle showed up, but full of sadness and pain when another comrade had to be -buried.[7]

The Wirtschaftsbataillon 12 (provisions battalion) was located in a forest south of Putanges near le Menil-Jean (fifteen kilometers west of Argentan) since the start of the invasion. The provisions were picked up at the Armee provisions depot, flour and slaughter cattle were occasionally drawn from the countryside as per regulations.[8]

Of particular importance was the repair of the vehicles, especially of the Panzers. Hauptsturmführer Georg Isecke, adjutant of the Panzerregiment, noted on this:

The Regiment repair company and the Abteilung maintenance pla-toons deserve particular appreciation. Because of the air superiority, it is important to ensure good camouflage of the locations in the woods. Hauptsturmführer Sammann and his men have here achieved an accomplishment without parallel. All movements, espe-cially the reco-vering of knocked-out or immobile Panzers, could only be carried out at night. The excellent cooperation between the repair and the fighting troops proved itself time and again. It was frequently possible to recover under enemy fire. After the start of the fighting, the recovery tractors were reinforced by captured Cromwell tanks which served as tractors after the turrets had been removed. Twenty-ton cranes allowed the lifting of the turrets when guns needed to be repaired. The frequent direct fire, the hits from fighter-bombers or bombs exploding close-by led to gun damage which was then repaired by re-adjusting.[9]

The medical facilities, too, had to perform well beyond ordinary require-ments. This was true all the way from the medic level in the companies through the Bataillon/Abteilung medical doctors with their helpers at the field dressing stations, the regimental doctors and their assistants, the main dressing stations of Sanitätsabteilung 12 (medical Abteilung), its ambulance units, the ambulances of the battalions, Abteilungen and regiments, the SS-Feld-Lazarett 101 (field hospital) of the Korps right up to the base hospitals in Alençon and Bagnolles. The two main dressing stations of 1. Sanitäts-kom-panie in the Préaux-Bocage area, eighteen kilometers southwest of Caen, and at Notre-Dame-de Coursson were ready for action already in the afternoon of

7 June. The I. H.V.P.-Zug (main dressing station Zug) of 2. Kompanie, despite the prescribed and clearly visible markings of the Red Cross on circular white background, had been subjected to a violent air attack from low-level aircraft on 6 June. It was out of action for quite some time. The II. Zug set up a main dressing station initially in Missy (15.5 kilometers southwest of Caen on the Route Nationale No. 175 from Caen to Villers-Bocage). Then, because of the danger from the near-by front it moved the main dressing station to the Château de la Motte near Acqueville (twenty-four kilometers south of Caen). The fighting troops brought their wounded to the main dressing stations either with their own ambulances or with those of the three ambulance platoons of the Sanitäts-abteilung, after first aid had been administered. There, they were cared for to the point where they could either return to their units or be transported to the Korps hospital in Sées (twenty kilometers north of Alençon, eighty road kilometers southeast of Caen). Those wounded who could not be transported, in particular stomach wounds because of the danger of infection, were operated on at the main dressing stations and nursed there until they were in a condition to be moved.

The main dressing station of Dr. App, II. Zug of 1. Sanitätskompanie, moved, after the Division had shifted to defense, to the Château Louvigny, three kilometers southwest of Caen, to remain close to the fighting forces. During the first day, already, the dressing station was so flooded with wounded from both sides that a tent had to be set up in the castle park. During these days, the I. H.V.P. (main dressing station) of 1. Kompanie in Préaux was attacked by low flying aircraft. This resulted in a number of dead and wounded, also from the medical personnel. Among others, the Kompanie motorcycle messenger, Sturmmann Gebken, was killed by a shot in the head. When a command post, located in the vicinity of Louvigny (it is not known of which unit) was shelled by enemy artillery and ships' artillery, some shells also landed in the castle park. There were some minor casualties among the medical personnel and some damage to vehicles from fallen trees.

One day, when wounded Canadians were to be transported to the Korps hospital, they refused to travel by day. Through an interpreter they were asked for their reasons and they stated that ground and air forces had orders to also fire on vehicles marked with the Red Cross since these were transporting weapons, ammunition and supplies to the fighting forces. There is no question, ambulances of the Division were never used to transport ammunition or other supplies, except medical supplies and, of course, wounded. The same is true, without doubt, for all other units. The result of the interrogation and reports on the attacks on medical installations by fighter-bombers, contrary to international law, were submitted to the International Red Cross through regular channels. The situation did not change. For instance, during the first weeks of the fighting—the date cannot be determined with certainty—a column of fifteen ambulances was attacked by Allied aircraft. The vehicles were transporting critically wounded, among them

Canadian pilots, from the area Louvigny-Mondrainville-Missy to the evacuation hospital at Argentan. The fighter-bombers initially flew a fake attack. The medics and drivers unloaded the wounded quickly to bring them to safety. This was only partially achieved when the aircraft started a low-level attack. There were several dead, and some of the wounded were hit again, among them Canadians. Killed, among others, were three ambulance drivers. Two vehicles burned out, the other received hits but were still mobile.[10] In contrast, the ground forces, as the reported examples have shown, behaved in a proper and militarily fair manner.

A report by Unterscharführer Kurt Fischer of 2. Kompanie of the Aufklärungsabteilung describes the path and fate of some of the wounded. It was 13 June 1944, the Abteilung was in position in the Cristot area. He writes:

> I had sent out my crew to find something edible. The two returned soon after with two chickens. We started to prepare them. We had a pan in the Panzer, and poured gasoline into two empty 200-gram meat cans, to be used as a stove. During a refill with the gasoline bottle, my driver Döring burned his right hand so badly that the skin could be pulled off like a glove. I was mad! I was supposed to receive my gas line, which had been damaged, back from the repair squad so that I would be mobile again. Now, I no longer had a driver. But being mad did not help. Also, I did not have much time for being angry. For the first time ever, our Kompanie kitchen showed up, and there was to be food. Sadly, we did not get that far. At the same moment, as so often, the routine call echoed through the hedges:
>
> 'Everyone to the front with small-arms!'
>
> I collected a few men from my Kompanie and was about to set out with them when one of our cooks, the eighteen-year old Silesian Hanke, came over to me and practically begged to be taken along. He also wanted to get to the front for once. I told him to grab a carbine quickly and so he set out with us.
>
> After only a few steps we heard a fighter-bomber which we had not spotted before because of some tall trees. I glimpsed it diving at us and shouted:
>
> 'Get out of the way! He's coming at us!'.
>
> I dove into the hedge and already heard the explosions. Even before I hit the ground again I felt a hard hit to my right leg but managed to slide the other two or three steps into the hedge. There I crawled into a shallow depression, my feet sticking out. I noticed that I was bleeding but, since I could move both legs a little, I figured that it could not be too bad. A few meters away, Hanke was yelling as if he had been stuck. He had been hit in the arm and leg. The medic, Rottenführer (corporal) Zacharias, came immediately,

dressed Hanke and calmed him. As he was about to leave I shouted at him:

'Hey, Zacho! Don't you want to dress my wounds?'

'Did you get it, too?'

'Sure!'

'Oh, sh . . .!

So he put my dressings on. This was at 10:50 A.M.

Now I was mad yet again since I had to leave the Kompanie. And we had not even won the war yet!

Like a good head of the household, I looked after my house, i.e. my Panzer. The gunner, Haake from Clausthal-Zellerfeld, received my pistol and machine pistol. I got my black uniform out of the Panzer (we wore fatigues under the camouflage) and went over to Untersturmführer Becker to have the E.K. II, awarded on 11 June, entered in my pay-book. Then we were carried a few meters further to the Abteilung doctor who gave us the obligatory shots. My driver Döring, his hand dressed, trotted sheepishly alongside. He must have been in fairly bad pain. Soon, an ambulance arrived which took all three of us off. There was a short stop at our repair squad, approximately twenty kilometers from Cristot where I had been on 9 June. Our supply squads were probably stationed there. They always wanted to know who had gotten it. They opened the rear of the ambulances and looked in on us. One of them had a piece of copper line in his hand and showed it to me with the remark that my fuel line was fixed again. Of course, I no longer needed it.

At 17.00 hours I arrived at the main dressing station of 1. Sanitätskompanie. As I recall it, the dressing station was located in a massive two-story house, next to it were one or more shacks with large Red Crosses on them. It may have been in Préaux-Bocage, west of Grimbosq.

I spent quite a long time on my stretcher in the hallway and asked occasionally when it would by my turn and how serious a case I was. But, they had better things to do than to make conversation. Later I woke up in one of the shacks. I was lying at the end of a row of fifteen to twenty wounded, nicely laid out like sardines, under a window, on a straw sack or mattress on the floor.

In the long, narrow room there was just enough space for the medics to walk through. They had implanted a draining device in my right calf and cut out a shrapnel, the size of a five Mark coin, which had gone through the calf into the left foot. Actually, I was not feeling too bad at all.

Suddenly, we heard a fighter-bomber circling above us and then our shack was already being hammered. Everything was filled with smoke and wood splinters. The machine gun salvo had penetrated less than a meter above my head. I could reach the holes with my hand. This was not a nice feeling. After all, the fighter-bomber must have had at least six machine guns which he had raked us with. I knew this feeling already. The Kanonenpanzers (gun Panzers) of the 2./ Aufklärungsabteilung (half-tracks) had always to take over covering the flanks during fighter-bomber attacks since we could elevate the 2-cm-KWK to almost 90 degrees. Thus, during the decisive moments when it thundered, the driver and the commander were pretty helpless while the gunner, at least, could do something. But the armor gave us some confidence, even if our feeling of security was more of a moral kind, since the hits from Fighter-bombers penetrated even our fronts where the armor was somewhat stronger. On 7 June, when we suffered two killed in this manner just outside Fontaine-Etoupefour, Kompanie chief Walter Hauck prohibited us firing at low-level aircraft.

But, to be lying around wounded, unable to do anything, immobile, that was something different altogether. The medics of the dressing station soon came rushing over. They each grabbed a straw sack by the foot end, shouted: 'Hold tight!' and dragged the straw sack and the man on it outside, down a few stairs and into the park or under a bush. There we stayed, scattered, for hours. It had turned dark. From time to time we could hear the shouts for a medic. Some, of course, were afraid of being forgotten or not found again. Finally, a truck arrived. We were loaded onto it, packed, sitting or stretched out, and driven off. There was no medic with the truck, only the driver. When dawn came, the driver said: 'We'll stay here until dusk', and positioned his truck under a tree.

So we were waiting again, without being cared for, without food. The driver had found us something to drink, probably cider. But other than that he did nothing. From time to time we heard fighter-bombers and hoped they would not spot us. Bodily functions continued, there was a terrible stench on the truck.

What does one think of in such a condition, during such times? I don't remember any more. Our senses were probably dulled, on top of that we were under the influence of medication. We probably also slept. The night before we never closed our eyes, and the days and nights in Cristot had not exactly been restful. The sense of total helplessness must be one of the worst feelings. And we were helpless. This probably lasted for more than twelve hours.

Well, the day went by. It turned dark and the truck started to move again. We drove throughout the night and reached Sées in the early morning of 15 June. The doctor at the central station examined me after cutting away the dressings. He waved his hand in a dismissive gesture and said: 'Into the hospital, immediately!'

So I was given a special ambulance and felt quite honored, although I probably did not look too honorable in my condition.

At 06.00 hours I arrived at the Korps hospital 501 at Sées. The first person I saw, still outside, was Hauptsturmführer Dr. Hugendubel whom I knew very well from Charkow. He was a ward physician at Sées. He also recognized me immediately and said: 'Fischer, you will be in my ward!'

He had me carried inside and kept looking after me very well while I was there. Later I woke up in a huge hall with large windows, just as in a church. A Red Cross nurse was sitting at my cot.

Gradually, I noticed that I had a splint and a dressing on my right hip. I could not understand this. It came to me that I had been wounded in the right calf, after all. Finally I managed to raise myself a little and saw that my right leg was gone. I asked the nurse:

'Nurse, where is my leg?' (Stupid question!)

'It is gone.'

She said, tears in her eyes. I felt the urge to comfort her. Dr. Hugendubel explained to me later that he had been there during the amputation. The whole knee joint had been full of pus. Too long without medical attention. Any more delay would definitely have led to gangrene.

So the Allied fighter-bomber attack on the main dressing station had been crowned by success after all.

We were doing quite well in Korps hospital 501 (field post number 56 886), after we had gotten through the first few bad days. We were cared for by German Red Cross nurses who were often on duty around the clock. Transports of wounded arrived almost exclusively at night. A nurse was on duty in our hall every night also. Some wounded died each night, sometimes noisily, sometimes quietly. I remember one in particular. He was an 18-year old member of a Panzer crew, critically burned. The headboards of our beds were next to each other. He did not have a chance and died after a few days. Dr. Hugendubel told me later that, if it had been in his power, they would have awarded the E.K. to this boy who had died so courageously, fully conscious.

Some of the personnel were Russian women and girls. They had joined the hospital in Charkow in 1943. More of them than we needed wanted to come along when the Division was moved to Germany later. We took as many as possible, young lads also. The women were helpful, clean and highly respectable. I also remember a somewhat older Danish lady who devotedly worked there. Finally, there was also French staff. One French nurse greeted me very happily one morning and said that my cheeks were pink again for the first time. The day before I had been in poor shape (letter to my parents of 28.6.44) That was true, the previous day I suffered severe after-bleeding. A French barber organized some perfume for me. The stench from my dressing bothered me. Mostly, cráp paper dressing was used which did not absorb anything. But the mixture of pus and perfume was even worse.

The only problem at Sées was that there were no potatoes to be had. We had not been fed any for weeks, only noodles, rice, spaghetti and such stuff. I was quite tired of it. With the Kompanie, we had already been fed a lot of milk rice, seminola and similar food. But potatoes were not to be had!

Dr. Hugendubel had once said to me that I would only be transferred when transport to Paris became available. Otherwise I would only end up in a different hospital. One day, the time had come. In the evening a truck would leave for Paris with wounded, and I was to be among them. I was happy, of course, but then the nurse came and said: 'Mr. Fischer, tomorrow we will have the first potatoes.' That was a real dilemma! What to do? Although it was not my decision, I still thought about it. But then I figured, if there were potatoes in Sées, there would be potatoes in Paris and I was transferred.

We arrived at the central depot in Paris at 06.00 hours and were excellently provided with food and drink. And there were potatoes at lunch! On 13 July 1944 I was transferred to the Kriegslazarett 1/680 (base hospital) which was located in the Hopital de la Piété. On 18 July I was already moved to Merzig by hospital train. So I was back in the Reich.[11]

One more example may show the attitude of the young soldiers of the "Hitlerjugend" Division as they staked their lives and died. The medical officer of the Pionierbataillon, Hauptsturmführer Dr. Friedrich Zistler, himself wounded as he was looking after wounded men on 11 June near le Mesnil-Patry, reports on a moving experience:

I was lying, badly wounded, in a collection room of a field hospital and momentarily came out of my morphine-induced slumber. Next to me I heard a comrade, moaning from pain, speaking very clearly: 'Mother, mother, but I mean Germany.' While thinking about these words I fell asleep again. After some time I woke up again and found that these had been the last words from the mouth of this boy.[12]

The comradely bonds lasted beyond death. Frequently, scouting parties would retrieve killed comrades during the night when they had been unable to so during the day because of the fighting. They risked their lives without hesitation during these operations. All the killed who were found received a dignified burial from the troops. The Stabsscharführer (staff sergeant) of 10. Kompanie of SS-Panzergrenadierregiment 26, Oberscharführer Walter Schwabe, wrote on this:

> In Normandy, we were able to bring supplies to the Kompanie in action at the front line only during the night. There were three of us, the armorer, the driver, and myself in the armored car. We were taking provisions, ammunition, and mail to the front. On the way back we took the killed comrades who had been retrieved with us to the supply troops. We safeguarded the personal property which the dead had with them and sent it later, with the rest of their belongings, to their families. One half of the identification tag was broken off and saved.
>
> At an open and easily found spot, for instance at a crossroads, members of the supply unit dug a grave for each killed man, if possible. If the losses had been very high we were forced to use collective graves. We buried the dead wrapped in a tarpaulin. We decorated the grave-mounds with flowers and quietly said our good-byes. On each grave we set a wooden cross in the shape of an Iron Cross into which rank, name, birth date and day of death were burned.
>
> The Kompanie chief wrote a letter to the families advising them of the death. He reported when and under what circumstances the comrade had been killed and tried to comfort. At home, the letter was delivered, whenever possible, personally by a comrade from an office of the Waffen-SS or by a member of another organization.
>
> From time to time we submitted, through channels, loss reports to the Wehrmacht information office. These contained lists of all killed, wounded and missing members of the Kompanie. They also contained the location and date of the loss, unit, number of the identification tag, rank, first- and family name, date and place of birth, address of the closest relatives, cause of death or nature of the wound. For the wounded, we reported whether they had remained with the unit or to which medical facility they had been transferred. For the killed, we noted the location of the grave. We included the broken-off half of the identification tag. We sketched the location of the graves for the officer responsible for war graves in the Division, so that the graves could later be found again.[13]

The enemy, too, had difficulties with supplies and bringing up reinforcements. Cherbourg, with its big deep-sea port, was still in German hands. It had to be assumed that, in case it was captured by the Americans, the harbor could not be used for weeks or even months. For this reason, the Allies had planned and prepared the construction of man-made ports as far back as the summer of 1943. One of them was to be built for the British troops near Arromanches (nine kilometers northeast of Bayeux) and one for the Americans near St. Laurent-sur-Mer (fifteen kilometers northwest of Bayeux). They were to be ready for use a few days after the successful landing. Indeed, outside the shallow beaches of the Normandy coast, piers and breakwaters were constructed from huge pre-built caissons and sunken ships. To do this, the sixty meters long and up to 5,000 tons heavy caissons had to towed across the Channel and assembled at the site with other construction material. This was an amazing technical achievement which was neither prevented or even hampered by either the German Marine (navy) or the Luftwaffe. The only really effective obstacle was the sea.

The first of these parts had already been towed across the Channel of 7 June and unloading started on 18 June in both harbors. Only the piers to unload the tanks from the ships were not yet ready so that the landing craft had to be beached, causing long delays. On 19 June, when a large amount of construction material for the piers was brought across the Channel, based on a favorable weather forecast, an unexpected heavy storm set in and destroyed them close to the Normandy coast. The storm lasted for three days. Trains of barges sank, ships were thrown on the beach, the American "Mulberry" harbor was destroyed and could not be re-built. Parts which could still be used served to repair the British harbor. After that, only minor amounts of supplies could be unloaded, they dropped to 20 percent of the amount prior to the storm. The Allied actions on the southern front came to a standstill. A dangerous shortage of ammunition set in.[14]

The Third Battle for Caen from 25 to 30 June 1944

CHAPTER 3.0
Planning

The German units in Normandy had been forced into defense since 10 June. The enemy had been able to strengthen his forces more quickly than the German side. In addition, the attack divisions in action there, 21. Pz.-Div., 12. SS-Pz.-Div. "HJ", and the Pz.-Lehr-Div., were tied down in the Caen area in difficult defensive fighting. In the long run, the front line could not be held with the forces deployed, not even along river sections further to the rear. It had proved impossible to repel the landing on the first day, or to smash the bridgeheads piecemeal during the next days before the enemy could significantly increase his forces. Thus, the objective of the German side had to be the destruction of the man-made enemy harbors with newly brought-in forces. Thereafter, to destroy the enemy, cut off from his bases, unit by unit. Although Cherbourg with its large deep-sea port was highly endangered, it would be weeks after it was captured before it could be used for enemy supplies. The defense of Cherbourg could thus be considered to be of secondary importance, although the engagement of American troops there had to have a favorable impact on the actions against the sector between the Orne and Vire rivers.

On 11 June, Feldmarschall Rommel, in a teletype message to the chief OKW, Feldmarschall Keitel, had provided his judgment of the situation and said, among others:

> The conduct of the fighting until now clearly shows the enemy intentions:
>   1) to secure a deep beachhead between Orne and Vire, to be used later as the starting point for an attack with strong forces into the interior of France, probably in the direction of Paris,

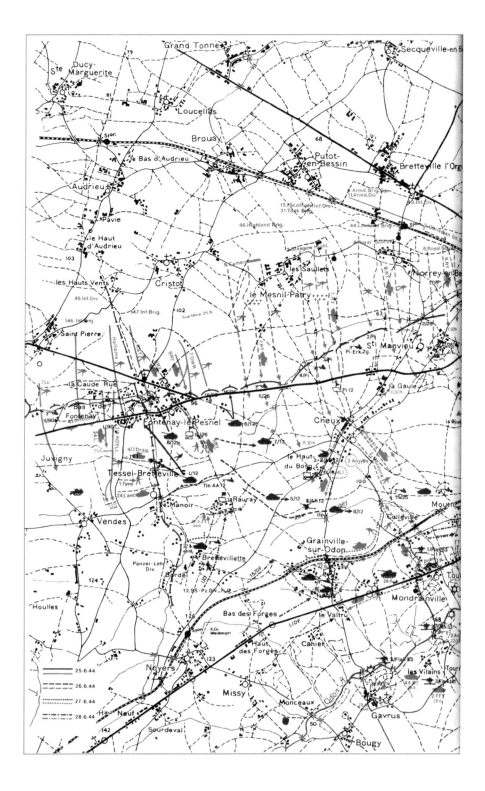

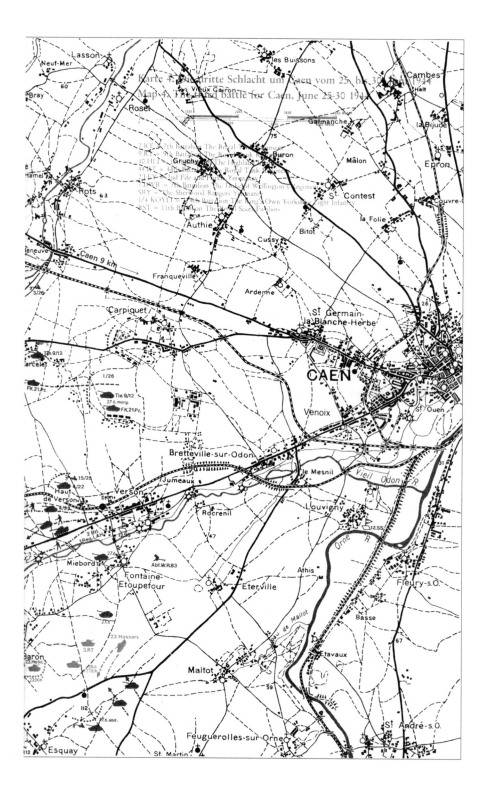

Karte 4: Die dritte Schlacht um Caen vom 25. bis 30. Juni 1944
Map 4: The third battle for Caen, June 25-30 1944

7.KT = 7th Battalion The Royal Tank Regiment
9.RT = 9th Battalion The Royal Tank Regiment
10.HLI = 10th Battalion The Highland Light Infantry
44.RT = 44th Battalion The Royal Tank Regiment
2.FY = 2nd Fife and Forfar Yeomanry
7.DWR = 7th Battalion The Duke of Wellington's Regiment
SRY = The Sherwood Rangers Yeomanry
1/4 KOYLI = 1/4th Battalion The King's Own Yorkshire Light Infantry
RST = 11th Battalion The Royal Scots Fusiliers

2) to cut off the Cotentin peninsula and capture Cherbourg as quickly as possible in order to have a large and effective harbor. Depending on developments it appears possible, however, that the enemy will forego capturing the Cotentin peninsula if the fighting there becomes too difficult, and will push into the French interior early, using all available forces.

Because of the determined fighting by the troops in action in the coastal defense sectors and the immediate counterattacks by the available major reserves, the development of the enemy operation has progressed considerably more slowly than originally hoped by the enemy, despite the use of the heaviest war material. It also appears that the enemy is throwing more forces into action than originally planned.

Under the cover of very strong air units, enemy forces on land are noticeably gaining strength. The German Luftwaffe and Kriegsmarine (navy) are unable, especially during the day, to impede this to any extent. Thus, the enemy land forces are growing more quickly than we can bring up reserves to our front lines. The immense enemy air superiority has prevented the quick deployment of I. SS-Pz.-Korps, Werferbrigade 7, III.Flak-Korps (anti-aircraft), as well as II. Fallsch.-Jg.-Korps Meindl (paratroopers) into the area between Orne and Vire in order to start a counterattack on the landed enemy. Werfer-Brigade, Flak-Korps and Korps Meindl are still approaching. The I. SS-Pz.-Korps has been forced into defense under bitter fighting. Its open western wing is being attacked by superior tank forces.

The Heeresgruppe has to be content initially to form a cohesive front line between Orne and Vire with the forces becoming slowly available, and to wait for the enemy. Under these circumstances it is, regrettably, impossible to reinforce the units still holding many of the positions along the coast. The Heeresgruppe plans to relieve the Panzer units in action by infantry units as soon as possible, and to form mobile reserves with the Panzer units again.

The Heeresgruppe plans to move the concentration of German actions into the Carentan-Montebourg area in order to destroy the enemy there and avert the threat to Cherbourg. Only when this has been achieved, can the enemy between Orne and Vire be attacked.[1]

A Führer briefing took place on 17 June in a Führer headquarters, built in 1940 for the Operation "Seelöwe" (sea lion)—the planned landing in England—in Margival near Soissons. In addition to Adolf Hitler, the chief of the Wehrmacht operations staff, Generaloberst Jodl, the field marshals von Rundstedt and Rommel with their chiefs of staff, generals Blumentritt and

Speidel, as well as several officers of the Wehrmacht operations staff, and the escorts of the supreme commanders took part. The report by Major i.G. (general staff) von Ekesparre, the Ib of Heeresgruppe B, indicates:

First, Feldmarschall Rommel reported on the enemy and German situation, condition of the German troops, battle readiness and progress of deployments. During this he reported on the high infantry losses, the delays in bringing up reserves due to the over-whelming enemy air superiority, and the strong enemy material deployment. He stressed the lack of Luftwaffe support and the absence of any kind of aerial reconnaissance.

Verbatim, the report continues:

Supreme Commander West provides further back-ground information. Based on the situation, he requests the Führer's approval to withdraw our own front line from the northern part of the Cotentin peninsula in the direction of Cherbourg.

The Führer determines that the stranglehold on the Cotentin, as the situation now stands and because of the German inferiority in the air which cannot be quickly overcome, cannot be prevented.

The Führer approves the plans submitted by Supreme Commander West.

A change in the situation is only possible by cutting off enemy supplies or pushing back the enemy naval forces.

In this respect, the Führer orders a reckless deployment of new mines by Marine and Luftwaffe between Le Havre and the east coast of the Cotentin in order to prevent the enemy from sailing the area unimpeded. This area is no longer of interest to the German Marine in any case. The Führer also states that the Marine had hesitated too long regarding this action. It is also planned, as soon as possible (in approximately six weeks), to deploy a new bomber weapon against the enemy unloading and naval units.

The holding of Cherbourg gains its full rationale only with respect to these two measures. Every day gained by holding the fortress is of great value to our own operations.

Regarding the rest of the front, the Führer stresses that cleaning up the situation east of the Orne river, in particular, appears important to him.

10.30 hours. When questioned by the Führer, the Supreme Commander West judges further enemy landing possibilities as follows:

At the Wehrmacht command Netherlands, our own defensive front line is weak. Enemy landings are possible.

At AOK 15, our own defense is stronger than in Normandy. However, no sufficient fast mobile units are available any more. The enemy will encounter significant difficulties there.

In Bretagne and at AOK 1 and AOK 19, enemy landings are easily possible since our own forces there are too weak. A landing at AOK 1 is, however, not probable.

The Führer is of the opinion that the enemy will not throw his last forces into action, since this is not how he normally conducts his operations. The fact that all his battle-proven units are already in action in Normandy indicates that he has already committed himself there to a large extent. It is possible that the enemy will be forced to also land at AOK 15, because of the just started long range bombing.

On the Führer's request for further intentions regarding present actions, the Supreme Commander West requests the following directions (not verbatim):

The expansion of the enemy beachhead is to be prevented under all circumstances. Tactical changes to our own front line are to be made as circumstances require. The reserves for the attack on the enemy beachhead are to be assembled (chief of the general staff Supreme Command West states on this that the Führer has given his approval).

It is intended to conduct the attack in such manner as to split the enemy beachhead east of St. Lô and then, depending on the situation, roll it up either to the east or west.

The Supreme Commander Heeresgruppe B warns not to conduct a re-alignment of our own front lines through attack action since this would use up the forces of the Panzer divisions. Proposal: put the Inf.-Divs. into action in the Orne sector, leave the Pz.-Divs., in action west of Caen, in their present position, assemble the reserve units on the wings. After completion of assembly, limited withdrawal to the south in order to push into the enemy flanks with the Panzer units and to fight the battle outside the range of the enemy ships' artillery.

In closing, the Führer stressed that it was important to hold the southern front on the Cotentin peninsula as far north as possible in line with the swamp area Prairies Narecageuse de Gorges. It is out of the question to conduct the fighting at the bridgehead Caen-Carentan only in a defensive manner since the enemy would smash everything with his superior deployment of materiel. For this reason, all means have to be used to block the sea at the bridgehead to the enemy through use of mines and new airborne weapons in order to cut off the enemy supplies and enable our own counterattack.

Following this, there was a briefing by the commanding general LXV. Korps on long range bombing.

Then followed a communal meal.

Around 15.00 hours the Führer bade us farewell.[2]

In the assessment of the enemy situation by Adolf Hitler it is remarkable that he drew, from the deployment 'of all battle-proven units in Normandy', the correct conclusion that 'the enemy had already committed himself there to a large extent'. He added, however, that the long range bombing by V1 might force the enemy to land in the 15. Armee sector, for instance at the Pas de Calais. The field marshals von Rundstedt and Rommel also still considered this as a possibility. This is not surprising when one evaluates the enemy situation map West. Copies of sections of the map of 19 June are attached on page D-8.

Above all, it is remarkable that forty-four infantry divisions, five airborne divisions, eleven tank divisions and twelve tank brigades were still assumed to be in England. This meant a factor of 3.6 for the infantry divisions, and more than twice the tank units, which had already arrived in Normandy. Only for the airborne divisions the relationship was almost one to one.

Considering that thirty-seven divisions were available to Eisenhower on 6 June in reality, the result is that forty-four divisions were invented. Nevertheless, the supreme and high commands had to seriously consider the possibility of a second landing at the Channel coast and commit unnecessary forces there.

The impact of the wrong figures was increased even more by the 'Short assessment of the enemy in the west by the supreme command of the Heer general staff/department Fremde (foreign) Heere West of 19.6.44'. In it there is a statement on 'assembled armed forces group in southeast England':

There is further information from southeast England regarding the movement by the American Army Group I (Fusag) in the direction of the southeast coast. The suggested move, yet unconfirmed, of the units of the English II. Army Command in Kent county is within the frame of this concentration in the southeast. The report from an especially reliable source warrants consideration. It states that the actions of the Fusag will be supported by strong sections of heavy air force units. This points at action against strong fortifications and thus remains within the present assessment (central Channel coast). Information on the date of action is still missing. As well, it cannot yet be determined that the German rocket attack will bring about an advancement of the date of the Fusag action.[3]

The creation of these figures has already been discussed.

Plans for a counterattack were drawn up after the Führer briefing of 17 June. Their objective was a splitting of the beachhead at the border between the Second British Army and the First U.S. Army and the subsequent destruction of both armies.

Based on the 'Plans for the deployment and further conduct of fighting in the eastern half of the beachhead', submitted by Heeresgruppe B, the AOK 7 briefed the respective subordinate general commands of I. SS-Panzerkorps, LXXXVI. A.K., and XXXXVII. Panzerkorps on 19 June. A copy of the transcript of the teletype message from the chief of staff, Generalmajor Pemsel, initialed by the supreme commander, Generaloberst Dollmann, is reprinted below.

Details on the expected progress of the operation were not given.[4]

Feldmarschall Rommel submitted two studies with proposals on the conduct of the fighting to the Supreme Commander West on 19.6.44. A copy of the covering letter follows below, copies of sketches of the accompanying maps are attached on pages D-9 and D-10.(5)

The OKW disclosed its intentions on 20 June. The two most important sections read:

1.) It is the Führer's intention to conduct a concentrated counterattack with 1., 2., 9., 10. SS, 2.Pz. and Pz.-Lehr-Div. in such a way as to destroy initially the American forces (II. U.S. Army Korps) in the Balleroy area. For this, it is necessary to relieve 2. Pz. and Pz.-Lehr-Div. by the Inf.-Divs. arriving first. Deployment, starting point and time, as well as attachment of Heer forces are to be reported.

2.) Previously to this, the enemy east of the Orne is to be destroyed, using heaviest possible attack means, on a timely basis and in such a manner that participating Heer forces will again be available for the main attack.[6]

On 21 June, Feldmarschall Rommel reported on this:

The aim of Study I, submitted on 19.6., was a split of the Montgomery Army Group at the border between 2. English/1. U.S. Army, followed by a concentrated swing to the west to destroy the American forces in the Balleroy area. In this study it was planned to have 12. SS and 21. Pz.-Div. participate, relieved by the Inf.-Divs. In accordance with the OKW order, the Inf.-Divs. will now relieve 2.Pz. and Pz.-Lehr-Div. For this, action by 276. and 277. Div. will be required. It must be reported that the total width of the sector of the two divisions will be approximately thirty kilometers. Considering the weapons and equipment of the Inf.-Divs. and the tactical importance of the sector, this width appears to be too great without the availability of a Panzer unit as a 'fire-brigade'. Deployment and starting point for the counterattack ordered by OKW would have to take place as shown on the attached map. The starting positions immediately before the attack are located close and to the south of the front line.

Deployment order:

Command: Panzergruppe West

Right: I. SS-Pz. Korps with 12.SS, 1.SS-Pz.-Div. and Pz.-Lehr-Div.

Center: XXXXVII. Pz. Korps with 2. Pz.-Div., 276. and 277. Inf.-Div., the two Inf.-Divs. are to be brought forward immediately the Pz.-Div. crosses the front line.

Left: II. SS-Pz. Korps with 9.SS, 10.SS and 2.SS-Pz.-Div. The II. Fallsch.Jg. Korps will take part on the western wing against the Forêt des Biards ou de Cérisy

Artillery: For deployment see Appendix 2 and pages D-4 to D-6. Werfer-Brig. 7,8,9, at the point of major thrust—Caumont sector.

Time: Not yet possible to determine since units and ammunition have to be brought up. At the earliest, 10–14 days.

It continues: "The attack east of the Orne depends, as the Führer was briefed verbally, on the previous elimination of the enemy ships' artillery. Without this measure, as I determined personally yesterday, any attack is bound to fail." The Feldmarschall thought it necessary to put the 16. Luftwaffenfelddivision and 21. Panzerdivision into action east of the Orne, since 346. Inf.-Div. had lost most of its fighting capacity. He stated that, because 16. Lw. Feld-Div. had to be brought forward, and for other reasons, this attack could not be carried out in time. This meant that both attacks—east and west of the Orne—would have to be carried out simultaneously.[7]

It is remarkable that, in both studies and the accompanying notes, reports and orders, the man-made harbors of Arromanches and St. Laurent are never mentioned as an attack objective. Without them, a sufficient supply of the troops in the bridgehead would have been impossible. If they had been captured and destroyed, the landing troops in the bridgehead could have been destroyed sooner or later. This destruction could not have been prevented by ships' artillery or air support.

Without examining in detail the developments to this point, the proposition by the supreme commander Panzergruppe West from 26 June to the Heeresgruppe B must be noted. He did not, as Heeresgruppe B had done, commit himself prematurely to the conduct of fighting in a second or third phase. In addition, the proposal by the Panzergruppe notifies an important intention: Attack at night![8]

After the situation on the Cotentin had developed in a critical manner, the OKW inquired from Supreme Command West on the possibilities of a counterattack to relieve Cherbourg. Feldmarschall von Rundstedt replied the same day that sufficient forces, including the required supplies, could not be made available. Also, any forces used now would not be available for the planned July offensive. He recommended that 'it should be examined if, after a successful attack on Balleroy and to the northwest of it, the attack could be continued in the direction of Carentan. Until the start of the major offensive, the area around and east of Caen remains the most important for Supreme Command West.' The Feld-marschall expected that the enemy would concentrate his attacks there. In his opinion, the direction of an attack from the Caen area to the south and southeast would be operationally most favorable. 'For this reason, we must be strong in this area.'[9]

Here too, any reference to the man-made harbors and their decisive importance for the enemy—more important than Cherbourg or the whole of the Cotentin—is missing. It can only be assumed that, because of the lack of aerial reconnaissance, these harbors, or at least their importance, had not yet been recognized. However, prisoner statements could have offered sufficient insights if the required attention had been paid to this question. An in-depth examination of the problem could provide important conclusions.

All attempts by the British and Canadians to enlarge the beachhead in its eastern part, or even to take Caen and the high plain south of the city through repeated pincer attacks, had failed in the face of the determined resistance by three Panzerdivisions, 21., 12.SS, and Pz.-Lehr-Div. The defender suffered heavy losses during this fighting, in particular from the devastating fire from land- and ships' artillery. The losses had not been replaced. The enemy, too, had high losses, but they, as well as material losses, had continuously been replaced. In the eastern beachhead, however, the enemy could only achieve advances after new forces had been brought in.

General Montgomery issued Directive No. M502 on 18 June on how the operations in the beachhead were to be continued. In it, he expressed the opinion that, after the small beachheads had been joined up into one large one, after repelling the first counterattacks and assemblies of reinforcements behind the attack divisions, "we are now in a position to proceed to other objectives and reap the harvest." After a briefing on the difficulties on the German side he described his possibilities and intentions as follows:

> At the present, our two armies are facing in different directions. Once we have taken Caen and Cherbourg, and are all looking in the same direction, the enemy's problem will be overwhelming. At that time, the present threat to Normandy will become his major preoccupation and will likely rank ahead of other threats, such as to the Pas de Calais. Then we will have a great opportunity to threaten the German Armee and destroy it between Seine and Loire . . . It is clear that we will now have to capture Caen and Cherbourg as the first step in the execution of our overall plan. Caen is really the key to Cherbourg. Its capture will set free the forces which are now tied down in securing our left flank. On Wednesday, 21 June, the Sec-

ond British Army and the First U.S. Army will have new reserves available.

The objectives of the Second British Army were determined to be:

The immediate mission of this Army will be to take Caen and create a strong eastern flank for the army group. The operations against Caen will be carried out by a pincer movement from both flanks. The aim will be to have the VIII Corps, well equipped with tanks, establish itself southeast of Caen in the area Bourgebus-Vimont-Bretteville sur Laize (nine kilometers southeast, fourteen kilometers southeast, and sixteen kilometers south of Caen, respectively). The flank of the Army will run from Vimont to the north in the general direction of Troarn, then along the Dives river to the sea near Cabourg. The right wing of the Army will form the western arm of the pincer movement against Caen. It will then advance southeastward via Aunay-sur-Odon and Evrécy on the two Orne bridges between Thury-Harcourt and Amayé-sur-Orne, and encircle both bridges. These operations will start on 18 June and reach their maximum on 22 June when the VIII Corps will commence realization of its objective, through the beachhead, east of the Orne river.

During this time, it would be the mission of the First U.S. Army to cut off the Cotentin peninsula from all supplies, to capture Cherbourg, to maintain close contact with the Second British Army on its left flank, and to cover the right flank of the 7th Armoured Division during its advance on Aunay. Of secondary importance, the Americans were to attempt to advance in the direction of St. Lô in order to create a favorable starting situation for the XV U.S. Corps for a push across the line St. Lô-Caumont to the south and southwest. The landing of this corps was planned for Omaha Beach from 24 June onward. At the end of Montgomery's order it was stated:

The enemy divisions are weak and there are no reserves. We are reinforced, have a large number of tanks, and can call on a strong air force for support. I hope to see Caen and Cherbourg in our hands on 24 June.[10]

This directive was followed by another, M 504, as early as 19 June. It contained a major revision. In its introduction it was explained that a detailed examination of the problem had shown that it would be difficult to assemble the VIII in the beachhead east of the Orne, and to function as the left arm of the pincer against Caen. The enemy there was strong and preparatory operations would take time. Based on this it had been decided that the VIII Corps would form a part of the western arm of the pincer. The attack objec-

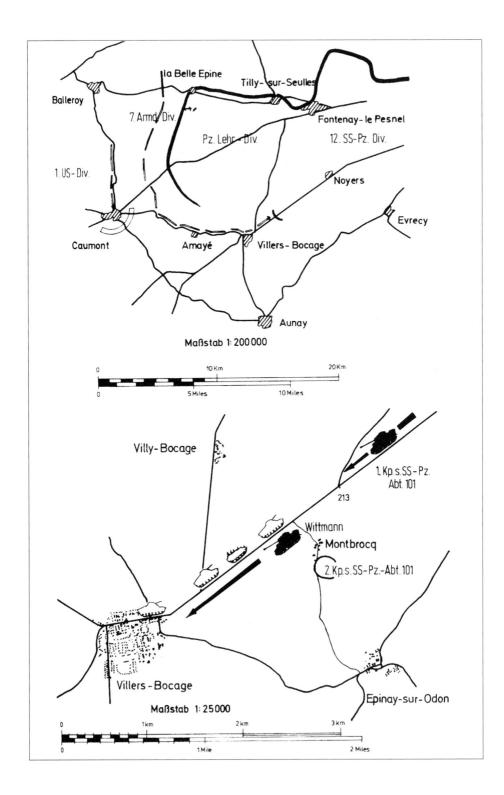

Maßstab 1 : 200 000

Balleroy — la Belle Epine — Tilly-sur-Seulles — Fontenay-le Pesnel — 12. SS-Pz. Div. — 7. Armd. Div. — Pz. Lehr - Div. — 1. US- Div. — Noyers — Evrecy — Caumont — Amayé — Villers - Bocage — Aunay

0 — 10 Km — 20 Km
0 — 5 Miles — 10 Miles

Maßstab 1 : 25 000

Villy - Bocage — 1. Kp. s. SS - Pz. Abt. 101 — 213 — Wittmann — Montbrocq — 2. Kp. s. SS - Pz. - Abt. 101 — Villers - Bocage — Epinay-sur-Odon

0 — 1 km — 2 km — 3 km
0 — 1 Mile — 2 Miles

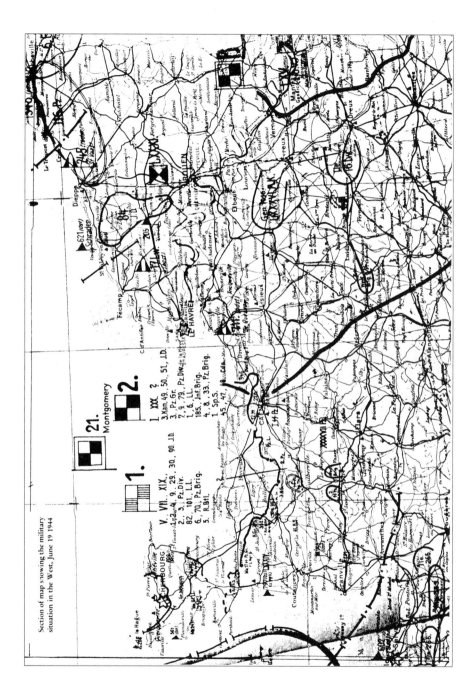

Section of map showing the military
situation in the West, June 19 1944

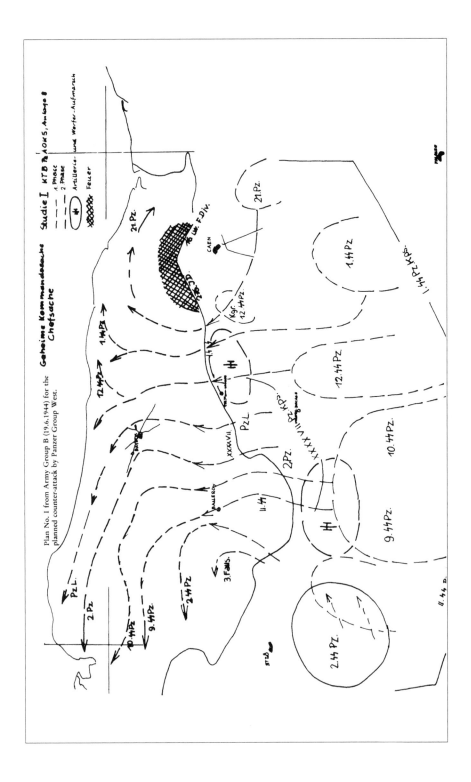

Plan No. I from Army Group B (19.6.1944) for the
planned counter-attack by Panzer Group West.

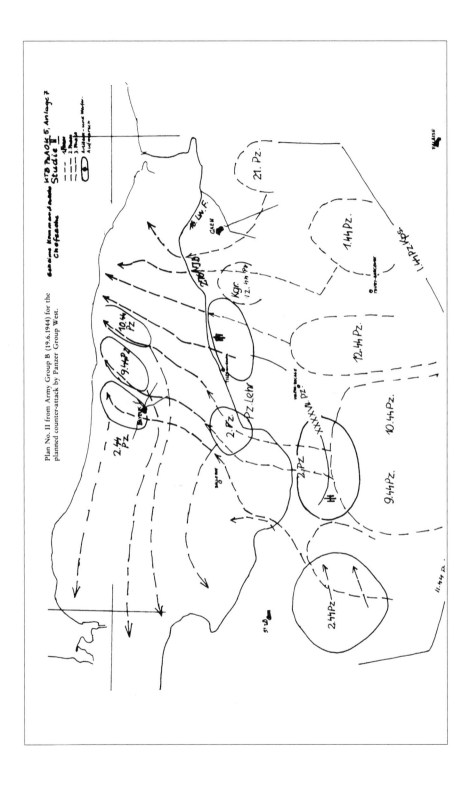

Plan No. 11 from Army Group B (19.6.1944) for the planned counter-attack by Panzer Group West.

Plan from Panzer Group West (26.6.44) for the
planned counter-attack by Panzer Group West.

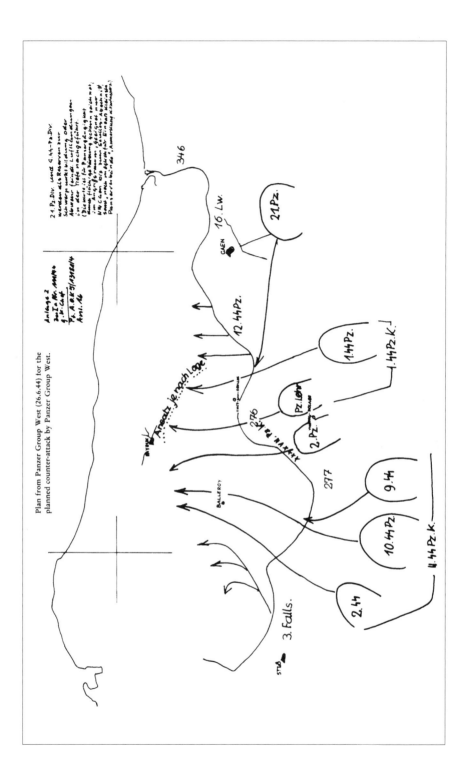

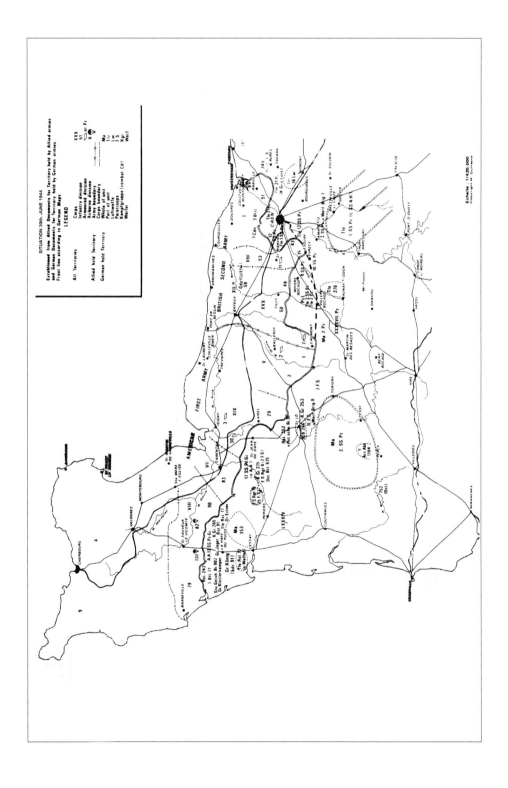

tive remained unchanged. The Corps was now to advance via St. Manvieu-Esquay-Amayé sur Orne. The forces of the I Corps, already assembled east of the Orne, would attack there as it became possible. The start of the total operation was ordered for first light on 22 June, for the attack by VIII Corps it was the morning of 23 June.[11]

Thus, a major operation, which could have brought the end of the campaign, had been prepared by both the German and Allied sides. The German supreme command assumed that it would be ready for the attack during the first days of July. Montgomery expected to be ready on 22 June. The race to assemble began. Of the German Panzerdivisions scheduled for the offensive, the following were in action on 21 June when Feldmarschall Rommel submitted his revised proposal to the Supreme Command West: 12. SS-Pz.-Div. and Pz.-Lehr-Div. defending northwest and west of Caen, and 2. Pz.-Div. whose bulk was defending east of Caumont. Those units having been brought up by rail had been unloaded in the Le Mans area on 19 June and were marching into the assembly area. The 2. SS-Pz.-Div. "Das Reich", except for the units delayed in the Montauban area, was still on the advance. It assembled in the area west of Torigni (twelve kilometers southeast of St. Lô) as a Heeresgruppenreserve (army group reserve). The 1. SS-Panzer-division was advancing from the former assembly area of the "HJ" Division in Belgium to the area east and southeast of Evrécy. The II. SS-Panzerkorps with its corps troops, with the 9. SS-Panzerdivision "Hohenstaufen" and 10. SS-Panzer-division -"Frundsberg" had been withdrawn from action with the Heeresgruppe Nordukraine (army group Northern Ukraine). Beginning on 12 June, it had been moved to France by rail. The wheeled units were unloaded approximately on 16 June at Epinal and Nancy. From there, they had to march by road via Orléans, Alençon and Troyes as well as Fontainebleau, Chartres, Sées into Normandy. The tracked units were transported by rail into the Dreux area. On 20 June, the Korps was still hundreds of kilometers away. The infantry divisions assembled, detailed by 1. Armee in Southern France, were 276. Inf.-Div. in the Domfront-Flers area and 277. Inf.-Div. in the Carrouges-La Ferté-Macé area. The 16. Luftwaffenfelddivision (Luftwaffe field division) was moved from the sector of the Wehrmacht commander of the Netherlands into the area around Mezidon-Livarot (twenty-three and forty-two kilometers, respectively, southeast of Caen). The advances were considerably delayed by the destruction of rail installations, air attacks during the day, and shortage of fuel. All the advancing Panzerdivisions were either coming out of action in the east (9. and 10.SS) or from incomplete refitting after bloody -fighting (1. and 2.SS). The Pz.-Lehr-Div., still tied down in defense, was supposed to receive parts of the Feldersatz-bataillon (field reserve battalion) to replace its losses of 2,300 Panzergrenadiers.[12]

The storm which started on 19 June and lasted for three days, had, as described in the previous chapter, delayed the assembly on the British side.

Only a portion of the troops scheduled for the start of the attack on 22 June had been landed. There was also a shortage of the required ammunition, so that the main attack had to be postponed to 26 June.

The commanding general of II. SS-Pz.-Korps, Obergruppenführer (three-star general) and General der Waffen-SS Paul Hausser, arrived at the command post of 7. Armee on 23 June. He reported that his Korps was expected to be assembled on 25 June in the area around Alençon (ninety kilometers southeast of Caen). Units of 276. Inf.-Div. had reached their assembly area.

On this day the Heeresgruppe B issued orders to Panzergruppe West on how the relief operations were to take place:

> In accordance with verbal directives, A.O.K. 7 will relieve 21. Pz.-Div. at the present front line by 16. LW. Feld-Div. and Pz.-Lehr-Div., 2. Pz.-Div. by 276. and 277. Inf.-Div. Required land march by 16. LW. Feld-Div., 276. and 277. I.D. of 150-200 kilometers will delay arrival of the infantry divisions.

All available column transport space was to be used.[13]

A meeting took place on 24 June at the Panzergruppe West. Taking part were the supreme commander, General der Panzertruppen Freiherr von Geyer, the commanders of XXXXVII. Pz.-Korps, the I. and II. SS-Pz.-Korps.[14] They were briefed on the plan of operations. No-one knew that the preparatory attack for the British operation "EPSOM" would start the next day, that the race to assemble had already been lost. The decisions, taken too late from the very first day of the invasion onward, had caused the German assembly to lag behind by fourteen days. A German offensive on 20 or 21 June would have caught the enemy at a moment of extraordinary weakness. This favorable situation could not be exploited.

CHAPTER 3.1
Preparations

"HJ" Division faced the "EPSOM" operation along an unchanged broad front line sector. The severe losses, especially of Panzergrenadiers, and of materiel had not been replaced. The losses until 24 June had amounted to 2,550 men.(1) At an authorized strength of a Panzergrenadierregiment of 86 officers, 605 NCOs and 2,502 men, one can assume that the Panzergrenadier regiments were lacking two battalions, the losses of the Aufklärungsabteilung and the Pionierbataillon were along the same lines. Regarding the strength in Panzers, the Division reported on 24 June as ready for action:

58 Panzer IVs,

44 Panzer Vs (Panthers),

233 armored personnel carriers, armored scout cars and artillery observation vehicles, and

17 heavy anti-tank guns.

Compared to the resources available on 6 June, this amounted to
losses of:

36 Panzer IVs,

19 Panzer Vs,

44 armored personnel carriers, etc., and

11 heavy anti-tank guns.

Approximately half of the Panzer losses were total, the rest were being
repaired.[2]

The map on the third battle for Caen in the map section shows the front
line in the sector of 12. SS-Panzerdivision. The positions in the sector of SS-
Panzergrenadierregiment 25 from Epron to Franqueville had been well reinforced over two weeks of hard work using available means. In addition to the
foxholes, positions for riflemen and machine guns had been set up in
houses. The positions for the heavy infantry weapons had been carefully
selected, camouflaged and prepared for close defense. Mine barriers and
barbed wire obstacles had only been set up to a minor extent. The battalions
and companies attached to Regiment 26, I./26, Pionierbataillon and II./26,
had only been able to prepare for defense since 16 June, the 15. and 16./26
as well as III./26 since 19 June along the shortened front line. The Pionierbataillon had reinforced its positions in a particularly expert manner.
Despite and because of the shortage of time, strong points for light and
heavy infantry weapons had been established through extraordinary efforts
in the often badly damaged or destroyed houses in Fontenay, especially
south of the creek valley.

To the rear of the sector of Regiment 26, the Panzer IVs of II. Abteilung
of Panzerregiment 12 were aligned, well dug-in and camouflaged, in
sequence 9., 7., 5., 6., 8. Kompanie for anti-tank action. Alternate positions
with covered approaches had been prepared. The I. and II. Abteilung of the
Artillerieregiment, which was in position behind Regiment 26 and depended
on good cooperation with it, had also prepared for close defense and were
well camouflaged. Because of the width of the sectors of the Panzergrenadier companies, their positions did not have much depth. So the heavy
infantry weapons, the Panzers and the artillery were to form the strong
points of the main battlefield. The only, and weak, infantry reserve available
was Aufklärungsabteilung 12 near Bretteville and Missy. The Divisionbegleitkompanie was in action with the Panzer-Lehr-Division.

The I. Abteilung of Panzerregiment 12 was ready as an operational
reserve in the Noyers area in order to be available in the left sector of the
Division, where an enemy attack was expected.

To the rear of the sector of 12. SS-Pz.-Div. and Pz.-Lehr-Div. between St. André-sur-Orne and Aunay-sur-Odon, the III. Flak-korps with Regiments 2, 4, and 3 had taken up positions. The Flak-Sturm-Regiment 4 with three Abteilungen had prepared for anti-aircraft action and, if necessary, ground target action in the area Mouen-Noyers-Evrécy. The Werferbrigade 7 (rocket launchers) was still in action east of the Orne river.

The enemy attack plan had to take into consideration the varying characteristics of the terrain, as the defenders had done with the deployment of their units and the determination of the course of the forward front line and the establishing of positions in the depth. The terrain south of the rail line Caen-Bayeux in the Norrey-le Mesnil-Patry sector drops off slowly in a southeastern direction toward the valley of the Mue creek. The only, minimal, cover available south of Norrey was offered by grain fields which had already been devastated during the previous fighting. South of le Mesnil-Patry, individual clumps of bushes were scattered through the fields. The terrain rises again slowly from the Mue creek in a southeasterly direction toward St. Manvieu, more quickly in the southwesterly direction. It forms a ridge which slopes down gradually from Rauray, at an elevation of 120 meters, to the area south of Cheux. Rauray commands the terrain which drops off to approximately sixty meters elevation along the creek bed in the northeast. The road Caen-Bayeux, lined with tall trees, cuts through the terrain. The town of Cheux is bedded into a valley. Two roads run through the town along the slopes, the farms are stretched out along the roads. The ridge south of Cheux and le Haut-du-Bosq was more extensively covered with bushes, clumps of trees, hedges and earth walls. It drops off slowly toward the Salbey creek and then rises again in its western part toward Grainville while the slopes fall away further east toward the Odon valley. There, the adjoining towns of Mouen, Tourville and Mondrainville with their houses, trees, hedges and gardens make the terrain very difficult to survey. South of the Odon valley, whose edges are covered with thick bushes, groups of trees and small wooded areas, slowly rising slopes lead up to Hill 112 from where visibility is excellent. One can look across large fields, across the deep-cut valley of the Orne river to the high open plain which extends from Caen to Falaise. The villages to the west of the Orne disappear in the valleys of the creeks, depressions, and the slopes falling off toward the river. This view would make the Panzer men, who have found their way painfully through the broken terrain up to here, heave a sigh of relief.

The plan of the VIII British Corps provided that the 15th (Scottish) Infantry Division with attached 31st Tank Brigade, the 11th Armoured Division with attached 4th Armoured Brigade Group (4 tank units), and 43rd (Wessex) Infantry Division would attack along a narrow strip from St. Manvieu to le Mesnil-Patry across the positions of the 3rd Canadian Infantry Division. The center line was St. Manvieu-Esquay-Amayé-sur-Orne. Because of the great threat to the flank, the 49th (West Riding) Infantry Division with attached 8th Armoured Brigade (three tank units) was scheduled to capture the high terrain around Rauray on the day before the start of the main attack. Further objectives of this division were Noyers and Aunay-sur-Odon. The I. Corps had been ordered, together with the 3rd Canadian Infantry Division and the 2nd Cana-dian Armoured Brigade, to capture the Carpi-quet airfield as soon as the main attack was advancing well. In order to estab-lish a more favorable situation for an attack by the 51st (Highland) Division from the beachhead east of the Orne to the south—the eastern arm of the pincer—this division had been charged with capturing St. Honorine (6.5 kilometers northeast of Caen) on 23 June, during darkness and without artillery preparation.[3]

A total of 900 artillery pieces, including those of three cruisers and one gunboat, were available to support the attack by the VIII Corps.

The following relative strengths resulted:

"Rauray" sector (Fontenay-St. Pierre):
    British: 9 infantry battalions,
    4 tank units.
    Germans: 2 infantry battalions (III./26 and I. Bataillon Panzer-Lehr-Regiment 901, units of 15./ and 16./26),
    1 Kompanie Panzer IVs (8. Kp.).
Sector St. Manvieu-Fontenay (exclusive):
    British: 22 infantry battalions,
    11 tank units.
    Germans: 3 infantry battalions (I./26, Pionierbataillon, II./26),
    4 Kompanies Panzer IVs (9., 5., 7., 6.).
Divisional reserve:
    1 Aufklärungsabteilung,
    1 Panzerabteilung (Panzer Vs).
Facing each other, in total:
    British: 31 infantry battalions,
    15 tank units
    900 artillery pieces.
    Germans: 5 1/2 infantry battalions,
    2 Panzerabteilungen, and possibly 1-2 -Panzer companies of the Panzer-Lehr-Division,
    36 artillery pieces and possibly 6 of the -Panzer-Lehr-Division.
Thus, the relation of forces was
    Infantry 6:1,
    Tanks 7.5:1, and
    Artillery 21:1,
in favor of the attacker. Nothing needs to be said about the—albeit weather-dependent—enemy air superiority. The III. Flak-Korps, in action in the operations area, could also be used against ground targets. Whether the

Werferbrigade 7, still in action east of the Orne, would be able to join the defensive fighting west of the river later, in whole or in part, depended on the development of the situation.

In short, the numerical superiority of the enemy was so overwhelming that the success of the offensive operation could be seen as a certainty. The period between 19 and 25 June was relatively quiet. The German side used it to further reinforce its positions. The situation reports of the Division show:

19 June: The enemy is refraining from any offensive operation in the sector of the Division . . . Our own reconnaissance indicates that the enemy has pulled back 1,000 to 1,200 meters in front of the left wing of the Division and has left only weak forward positions in the Parc de Boislande under cover of tanks. An enemy tank was destroyed by our scouting parties in close combat and a heavy machine gun was captured. Enemy air activity was very minimal, caused by the adverse weather. Enemy attack intentions were not determined. The Division continues to reinforce its positions and is holding them.

20 June: The enemy did not attack in the sector of the Division during 20.6. Enemy reconnaissance activity was minor. There was a continuation of hostile harassing artillery fire at the previous levels. Caused by the adverse weather, enemy air activity was very weak.

Our increased reconnaissance determined that the enemy, leaving in place weak forward positions which are also used, it appears, by enemy forward artillery observers, has withdrawn 1,500 to 3,000 meterse from his own main line of resistance. In front of the right portion of the Division's sector, the enemy has partly mined his old positions.

This reinforces the impression gained until now that the enemy, at this time, does not have any offensive intentions in the sector of the Division, after having apparently suffered very heavy losses during his previous offensive attempts.

The Division is reinforcing and holding its positions. Brisk preparatory reconnaissance is being carried out in all of the sector.

21 June: "Apart from our own brisk, and minor enemy reconnaissance activity during the night from 20 to 21 June as well as the usual harassing fire from the enemy artillery and our own fire attack on suspected artillery positions in the Audrieu area (4.5 kilometers northeast of Tilly), 21 June passed quietly.

Our reconnaissance confirmed the deductions of the previous day that weak enemy security guard positions—probably forward outposts—are positioned approximately 1,000 meters in front of our own main line of defense. Our reconnaissance, planned for the night 21 to 22 June, will attempt to determine the course of the enemy main line of defense. Statements by a French civilian who crossed the front line indicate that tanks are being unloaded continuously at Bernières-sur-Mer (fifteen kilometers west of the mouth of the Orne). They are assembled in the Douvres-Bény sur Mer-Thaon-Colomby. These reports could so far not be confirmed by statements from prisoners or our own air reconnaissance. The Division does not consider it practical to capture the narrow strip of terrain between our own and the enemy's main line of defense, although it is only weakly defended. No major advantage would be gained, but on the other hand, the Division would be exposed for a considerable time to superior enemy artillery fire in a terrain unfavorable to defense, after leaving its fortified positions. The severe losses which would have to be expected cannot be made up by the insignificant gain in terrain. Considering the short distance of the right wing of the Division to the coast (twelve kilometers), an attack would appear advisable only when there is an expectation that a push would carry through to the enemy artillery positions or even to the coast. The Division continues reinforcing its positions through use of barbed wire and mines, and is holding them.

22 June: The sector of the Division was quiet during 22 June, apart from the usual harassing fire by enemy artillery and minor enemy scouting activity.

Our own reconnaissance activity during the night 21 to 22 June 1944 was successful in locating forward enemy positions ahead of the sector of the Division along a line: town center of Cambes-les Buissons-Vieux Cairon-Rosel-Rots-Norrey-le Mesnil-Patry-Parc de Boislande. It could not be determined if stronger enemy forces are assembled behind the forward positions for defense, or if they are meant for an attack. The reconnaissance planned for the night 22 to 23 June should clarify the assembly of the main enemy forces and give an early indication of enemy attack preparation. The Division continues to hold and reinforce its positions using barbed wire and mines.

23 June: It was a quiet day in the sector of the Division. The reconnaissance of the night 22 to 23 June indicated that the enemy has reinforced his own positions, weak until now, in front of the sector of the Division. This appears to be the result of our own brisk reconnaissance activity.

Thus, it was impossible to penetrate the reinforced positions and reach the main enemy forces.

The Division considers an enemy attack on both sides of the Orne to capture Caen as a possibility. It has, however, no proof that the enemy intends an attack with this objective.

The Division is reinforcing its positions, using all available means, and is holding them.

24 June: It was a quiet day in the sector of the Division.

The results of our own air reconnaissance confirm the picture of the enemy gained until now.

There was brisk activity by our Luftwaffe in the morning hours. In comparison, the activity by the enemy air force was minor despite favorable weather.

The enemy harassing fire continued at the previous level.

Indications of a pending enemy attack, reinforcement or regrouping could not be determined. There are no new reports regarding the tank assembly in the area west of the mouth of the Orne, reported by the French civilian.

The Division is reinforcing its positions using all available means, and holding them.

An entry in the war diary of I./25 of 22 June is worth a mention. It reads:

The Division relayed an intercepted enemy radio message indicating that the enemy wants to be in Caen within 24 hours.[5]

There is no indication on the origin of this radio message. Presumably, it came from the listening surveillance of the communications close-intercept Zug of the Division and was related to the attack by the 8th Infantry Brigade of the 3rd British Infantry Division on Château de la Londe (five kilometers north of Caen) on 23 June.

The Allied expectations regarding operation "EPSOM" are indicated in two documents. On 23 June, General Montgomery wrote to 'Freddie', his chief of staff, General Francis de Guingand:

The whole of the south-facing front of the Army Group, from east of Caen to the west and all the way to the sea south of Barneville (on the west coast of the Cotentin, Author) will burst into flames the day when the VIII British Corps starts its attack.[6]

The supreme Allied commander, General Eisenhower, radioed General Montgomery on 25 June 1944:

I have been informed that your attack on the eastern wing has started this morning. All the luck in the world to you and Dempsey. Please do not hesitate to make major demands for air support of any kind which could possibly be helpful to you. Whenever a justifiable opportunity offers itself, we must destroy the enemy with everything we have.

I hope that Bradley will be able to quickly clean up the Cherbourg mess and turn around in order to attack to the south, while you have grabbed the enemy by the throat in the east.[7]

ENEMY FORCES IN GREAT BRITAIN, NORTHERN IRELAND AND AT THE INVASION FRONT

		Inf. Div.	Inf. Brig.	Airld. Div.	Para. Btl.	Armd. Div.	Armd. Brig.	Cmndo & Rngr Btl.
In Great	British	34	4	4	5	7	11	10
Britain and	Americans	10	-	1	-	4	1	3
Northern Ireland	French	-	-	-	2	-	-	1
	TOTAL	44	4	5	7	11	12	14
Invasion Front	British	5	1	2	-	3	3	5
Mouth of	Americans	7	-	2	-	2	2	1
the Seine	French							
	TOTAL	12	1	4	-	5	5	6
TOTAL FORCES Great Britain, Northern Ireland, Invasion Front		56	5	9	7	16	17	20

Transcript
Teletype Message
From: AOK 7 Ia
To: I.SS-Pz.Korps
        LXXXVI. A.K.
        XXXXVII. Pz.Korps

For the deployment and conduct of further fighting in the eastern half of the bridgehead it is planned:
1) Action by 16.Lw.Feld.Div. on both sides of the Orne. Width of sector 10–12 km, to relieve 21.Pz.Div. This Div. will initially remain behind the front line as operational reserve.
2) 276.Div. to link up with 16.Lw.Feld.Div. to the west to relieve the bulk of 12.SS-Pz.Div.
   Border on the left: rail line Caen-Bayeux.
   Deployment of the I.D. has to take place in such a manner that it can set up positions under the cover of the Pz.Div.

I.SS-Pz.Korps will report the most favorable locations, in terrain and fighting aspects, for the I.D. positions using map 1 : 80,000.

Both divisions will later be attached to LXXXVI. A.K.

3) Deployment of 277.Div. will be decided depending on the situation and will be ordered later.

4) After completed relief, I.SS-Pz.Korps will be withdrawn and will assemble with 1.SS-Pz.Div. and 12.SS-Pz.Div. as well as 21.Pz.Div. on both sides of the Orne.

1.SS-Pz.Div. is attached with immediate effect.

The Div. has been ordered to reach the Evreux-Laigle-Dreux area as the first assembly area. Arrival of the first units (Pz.Rgt. 1) at the earliest on 20.6.

5) XXXXVII.Pz.Korps with Pz.Lehr-Div. and 2. Pz.Div. will take over command in the sector between the rail line Caen-Bayeux and Drome river. They will later join the attack by I. and II. SS-Pz.Korps.

Preliminary dividing line to I.SS-Pz.Korps:

Villers-Bocage (47.)-Longraye (I.)-along the Aure river.

6) Planned deployment order:

To the right, Pz.-Gruppe West, between Seine and Drome rivers with LXXXVI. A.K., I.SS-Pz.Korps, II.SS-Pz.Korps, XXXXVII.Pz.Korps.

West of the Drome, AOK 7.

AOK 7 Ia Nr. 3196/44 g.K. (geheime Kommandosache = top secret)

signed: Pemsel

Appendix 6 to the War Diary
Panzergruppe West

Heeresgruppe B

Chief of General Staff

Ia Nr. 3558/44 g.Kdos.Chefs. (top secret, commanders only)

Ref: FS Obkdo.H.Gr.B (supreme command Heeresgruppe B) Ia Nr.3672/44 g.Kdos. of 15.6.

Subj: Plans for conducting the attack by Pz.Gr.West

Att: 2 maps

To the

Chief of General Staff of Supreme Command West

With this, two map studies by the supreme commander on possible conduct of an attack are being provided.

Study I will be used if the present front line in Calvados remains generally stable.

As the first phase, the breakthrough by XXXXVII.Pz.Korps and II. SS-Pz.Korps across the road Caen-Balleroy, simultaneously tying down the enemy north of Caen, is projected.

Second phase: Assembly of all Pz.Divs. with concentration on Bayeux to split the Montgomery Army Group at the border of 2.English/1. U.S. Armies, followed by a concentrated swing to the west, I. SS-Pz.Korps to the east.

Study II takes into account an enemy push into the direction Falaise-Paris. The difficulties of a later re-deployment (in green) must be accepted.

signed

CHAPTER 3.2

Attack by the 49th (West Riding) Division on Both Sides of Fontenay-le Pesnel on 25 June 1944 and Defensive Fighting by III./SS-Panzer-grenadier-regiment 26, Panzerregiment 12, Panzer-aufklärungsabteilung 12 and Panzer-grenadier-Lehr-Regiment 901

The 49th Division planned to conduct the attack to capture the high ground around Rauray and to break through to Noyers and Aunay-sur-Odon as follows:

Two infantry brigades with an attached tank unit each will be in action in the attack strip from the western edge of Bas de Fontenay to the group of houses at St. Nicolas Ferme (600 meters south of the road fork at the eastern exit from Fontenay). The 146th Infantry Brigade with the 24th Lan-cers will attack in the western sector, the 147 Infantry Brigade with The Sherwood Rangers Yeomanry in the eastern sector.

The attack on Rauray will take place in four phases.

In Phase A, the 146th Brigade will take la Caude Rue and Bas de Fontenay. The 147th Brigade will take Fontenay-le Pesnel.

If the skies are clear, the attack will start at 04.15 hours, in case of cloudy skies, at 04.30 hours.

In Phase B, the 146th Brigade will take the northern part of the woods west of Tessel-Bretteville ('Tessel Woods'). The start time for the attack will be set after the capture of Fontenay.

In Phase C, the 147th Brigade will take the crossroads northwest of Rauray and conduct reconnaissance toward Rauray. The 146th Brigade will advance to the west along the same line to the eastern and southern edge of the Tessel Woods. The start time of the attack will be set after completion of Phase B.

In Phase D, the 147th Brigade will capture Rauray.

Divisional reserves are 70th Infantry Brigade and 4/7 Dragoon Guards (tanks) less one company. They will assemble in the area west of Audrieu in order to repel a German counterattack into the eastern flank.

In each phase, the battalions will attack behind a moving wall of fire which will be provided by nine light and five medium artillery units, among them also American and Canadian units. The wall of fire will move forward every twelve minutes.

Attached for support are: engineers to place anti-tank mines, a company of anti-mine tanks, and an anti-tank battery.

The Allied air force will support the attack with fighter-bomber action on Juvigny, Tessel Woods and Cheux from first light until 06.30 hours, on Juvigny, Rauray and Cheux from 06.30 hours to 08.00 hours, on the road Villers-Bocage-Noyers from 08.00 hours to 12.00 hours.

Simultaneously with the 49th Division, the 50th Infantry Division will attack, adjoining to the west, with its left wing from the Tilly area and take Montilly (one kilometer south of Tilly).

Rauray will be captured before midnight on 25 June. On 26 June, the 70th Infantry Brigade will attack past the 146th Brigade and capture Monts (five kilometers south of Juvigny), the 147th Brigade will take Noyers. For this, a tank unit will be attached to each brigade. The second part of the operation will take place in cooperation with the neighbor to the east, the 15th (Scottish) Infantry Division.[1]

The 49th Division prepared the attack very carefully. The 146th Brigade conducted reconnaissance every night. It had several encounters with the enemy without suffering any losses. The plan of action was explained to each man by use of a model which had been set up in a barn. The forward edge of the assembly area was marked with white tape and dimmed lights. Guides led the troops to their areas. Another white tape was laid as a guide line for the attack. The assembly proceeded as planned.

After an immense artillery preparatory fire, the enemy started the attack on 25 June at 05.00 hours.[2] With increasing daylight, it became more and more foggy. Visibility was soon only four to five meters. At the Hallamshire Battalion, which was to capture the western part of Fontenay, the companies lost direction during the course of the advance. Link-up was lost and the battalion commander and his staff eventually reached the road Fontenay-Tilly first. He had barely crossed it when he came under fire from machine guns and Panzers from "all directions". The infantry fire came primarily from units of I. Bataillon Panzergrenadier-Lehr-Regiment 901 of Major Uthe, who was killed during the fighting, and from units of III./SS-Panzergrenadier-regiment 26 from the flank, supported by several Panzer IVs of 8. Kompanie, commanded by Obersturmführer Hans Siegel. One after the other, the individual companies of the Hallams arrived. They crossed the Bordel creek and reached their first attack objective, the road Fontenay-Juvigny, at approximately 09.15 hours. To the west, the Lincolns had reached their attack objective even earlier.

When the Hallams sought to link up with their neighbor to the east, the 147th Brigade, at the bridge crossing the creek along the road Fontenay-Juvigny, they found none of their own troops. Instead, they came under fire from Panzers of 8. Kompanie. Some men were injured. Firing rockets at the Panzers proved unsuccessful. The Hallams had set up their command post in the church in the western section of Fontenay. The Panzers opened fire on it, but a British Pak in position there, using the new anti-tank shells "sabot", managed to knock out the point Panzer IV. The following Panzer destroyed the anti-tank gun. The Pak crew thought they had knocked out the first Panther which was apparently thought of as something special. They were given five Pounds Sterling as a reward by the division commander, at the exchange rate of the time, approximately fifty Reichsmark.[3] In the meantime the 1/4 Battalion The King's Own Yorkshire Light Infantry of the 146th Brigade had arrived and was advancing on the Tessel Woods. The woods were free of German troops and occupied before noon.

The 11th Battalion The Royal Scots Fusiliers of the 147th Brigade had started its attack at the same time as its neighbor to the west, the Hallams. The Battalion lost its way in the fog. Some units showed up at the Hallams. It finally dug in at the northwestern exit of Fontenay. When the visibility improved and the companies had been reassembled, the Battalion attacked the eastern section of Fontenay. It was caught by concentrated fire from I. Artillerieabteilung, from heavy infantry guns of Regiment 26, and from mortar and machine guns of III./26. Despite their own moving wall of fire, the Scots were able to advance only slowly. In the war history of the Royal Fusiliers it is stated: "it was bloody man-to-man fighting. . . . The losses were severe. . . . The fighting was particularly violent along the road Caen-Tilly."[4] Reserves were brought up. Despite this, the grenadiers were able to hold the southern part of Fontenay, through which the main line of defense ran. They were entrenched in the houses which offered them some cover. They defended each house and each machine gun and rifle position with all their force and skill. British engineers blew up several houses and other strong points using special vehicles (AVRES). Despite this, the Scottish attack stalled.

The breakthrough by the 146th Brigade at the Panzer-Lehr-Division also had a negative impact on the left wing of III./26. The enemy stood deep in the left flank of the Bataillon after he had taken the northern edge of the Tessel Woods. Sturmbann-führer Olboeter led his small reserve into a counterattack. He was supported by 8. Panzerkompanie and parts of the 9. and 6., as well as by artillery and heavy infantry weapons. The situation was cleared, five enemy tanks and two guns were destroyed. In order to protect the left flank, Olboeter bent his left wing slightly to the rear along the Bordel creek since his forces were limited.[5]

The bitterness of the fighting is illustrated in a report by SS-Panzerobergrenadier (corporal) Hans Kempel which appeared on 9 November 1944 in the first issue of the Divisional newspaper "Panzerpimpfe" (Panzer-HJ-youths):

25 June 1944—at the observation post near Fontenay. The two of us form a radio squad. We had dug into the ground so deep that we felt safe from any artillery fire. It had been quiet for days. Such weird calm could not last very long. And so it was, at 3 A.M. the barrages set in. They lasted for hours. Our radio equipment was not yet functioning. It could drive you to despair.

Around 6 A.M. the hellish fire moved to the rear positions. The attack had to start any time now. Already, the first machine gun salvos were rattling across our foxholes. Let's get out . . .With all possible haste we set up our equipment under favorable cover. Tommy had fired smoke, you could not see your own hand in front of your eyes. Now came the order to establish contact with the firing position. But there was no reply from the other end! Damned hard luck.

There was only one solution: repair the telephone line to the command post. The British were still covering the area with artillery and mortar fire. But that could not dissuade us. We jumped out, into the noisy chaos.

It was not easy to cross a distance of 300 to 400 meters which the enemy can observe. After several failed attempts we managed, crawling a couple hundred meters on our stomachs, to make our way to a road. Fortunately, the overhead telephone line which crossed over the road, was still undamaged. It would have been a tough job to repair it. Was the worst now behind us?

After a short breather we wanted to cover the rest of the distance. Suddenly, there was fire from tanks less than 300 meters away. In addition, the artillery fire was coming closer again. There was no time to think. We raced forward, jumping, letting the wire slide from our hands. Finally, finally, we reached—miraculously uninjured—the command post. The line was working again.[6]

Since the frontal attack on Fontenay in the sector of III./26 was not advancing, the 147th Brigade pulled the 7th Battalion The Duke of Wellington's Regiment (7DWR) to the front and directed it to attack the right flank of Sturmbannführer Olboeter's battalion. This put Olboeter into a very difficult position. Just then, contact with the Division command post in Verson was lost. The Ia ordered the Aufklärungsabteilung to re-establish contact. Sturmbannführer Bremer directed Untersturmführer Karl-Heinz Gauch, who was commanding 1. Panzerspähkompanie (armored car company) temporarily at the time, to establish contact with Sturmbannführer Olboeter.

Karl-Heinz Gauch describes his experience this way:

I reported to the commander. 'Good, Gauch, that you are here! Have a look at this!' He pointed to the map. 'The enemy has broken through here, at our neighbor to the left, with infantry and tanks. The III./26 of Sturmbannführer Olboeter is located here, near Fontenay. There must be a dangerous gap between him and the Panzer-Lehr-Division. We have no details. There is no contact with the battalion.' Instinctively, I thought of 'Pütti', the youngest in our officer cadet course. Untersturmführer Gädertz was now the orderly officer of III. Bataillon. Sturmbannführer Bremer continued:

'One of your Zug leaders has to try to make contact with Olboeter. He must take a squad of motorcycle riflemen along. If necessary, force must be used. You understand? Who will do this?'

'Sturmbannführer, may I be allowed to do this myself? I think that much depends on this!'

'No, you lead the Kompanie!'

'May I point out that Bartsch can do that for the time being. I will be back soon! Sturmbannführer, my friend Gädertz is also over there. May I ask again for this mission. I can't help it. I feel this gnawing restlessness, I have to do something.'

'Well, all right, get going, but hurry back!'

I snatched the map from the table and saluted. Back to the company, quickly into the camouflage suit. Where the hell is the steel helmet? Never mind, it will have to be done without!

'Quenzel squad, mount. Let's go!'

I jumped on the motorcycle behind Unterscharführer Paul Quenzel and quickly briefed him on the mission. I shouted my orders at Bartsch as we drove off. We set out through Missy across the rail line Caen to the west. The ripped telephone wires hung from the posts, tangled. We had to drive slowly. Our route took us through a ravine. In the meadow to the left were many craters from shells. Dead animals were lying about, their corpses bloated. The sun shone directly on them, the stench was terrible. Ghastly, how the dead cows and bulls pointed their stiff legs toward the sky. It was absolutely quiet. My three machines left a long trail of dust behind. It was fortunate that we were among trees and it was still too early for the fighter-bombers. We drove through Tessel-Bretteville. The village was almost completely deserted, in the middle of the flat Normandy plain. Only the occasional inhabitant darted by, like ghosts in a dead fable city. In its quiet and abandoned state, the village was simply eery. Then, we were back in the open fields. Pastures and hedges, always in squares. To the left was a farm. I did not know then that it would almost seal my fate. Suddenly, there were soldiers running toward me. They directed me to the command post of III. Bataillon. Ahead of me was the town of Fontenay.

Careful! The enemy can spot us now. It did not help very much that I took along only one machine. Shells were suddenly hitting the ground next to me, ahead and behind. Dirt was thrown into the air. Let's go on, no hesitation. Smoke, explosions, and more dirt! Into the chaos and through it! That was our only chance. I did not have to tell the driver anything, he knew himself how to handle such situations. The motorcycle was put into cover, the driver flat on his stomach next to it. I hurried onward. With a few leaps I crossed the meadow. A whining in the air, then the explosion—down! A stack of straw next to me caught on fire. I had to go on. My tongue was sticking, hanging from my mouth. During this effort I remembered that I had not yet eaten anything that day. Quickly, I pushed through a hedge. A twig cut my face, there was some bleeding. Then I reached the Olboeter command post! An earth bunker with a pile of straw over it to protect against exploding shells. I virtually dropped down at Olboeter's feet. My sudden entrance extinguished the candle which had barely illuminated the interior. Someone was looking for matches, cursing. I reported after the candle had been lit again:

'Untersturmführer Gauch, Panzeraufklärungsabteilung. Ordered to establish contact. I request your present situation. Why is there no contact with the Division? Do you have contact to the left?'

I was trembling. My breathing came in jerks. It seemed as if all the cigarettes of the last eight days were trying to get out of my lungs at the same time. Dirty, unshaven, their eyes deep in their sockets, tanned by the sun, several officers were sitting in front of me. The one with the black hair and the almost delicate body, that was Olboeter, nicknamed 'Püttmann'. Of the others, I only knew the tall Lehmann. The commander took both my hands:

'The situation? Tell Gerd he must help us under all circumstances. Tell him we are in very bad shape! I can barely hold on. I had to withdraw the left wing to here an hour ago'.

He indicated it on the map. I took notes.

'But here is a gap right up to the chestnut woods. I can't do any more, the losses are too high! It's a bloody mess! Gerd must help! And now, can you maybe spare one more cigarette?'

Sturmbannführer Olboeter was speaking as if out of breath. His eyes flickered restlessly. I did not need to ask what happened in the previous hours. He, who loved each one of his men like a father, had to use them now in reckless action. 'Pütti' (Untersturmführer Gädertz) was at the front with 10. Kompanie, I could not see him. An hour ago he was still alive. And now! An hour has sixty minutes, each minute in action has a thousand dangers! Hastily, we smoked our cigarettes. Above us, the enemy artillery is howling. With each explosion, the miserable candle threatened to go out. Messengers were coming and going without pause. Every time one of them scurried through the narrow entrance it was getting still darker there, one meter below ground. That took away more of the meager daylight coming in. Reports were coming from the front line:

'Artillery fire on all Bataillon positions!'

'11. Kompanie: chief wounded, continues to command. Four enemy tanks at the edge of town.'

'12. Kompanie: shortage of ammunition!'

'10. Kompanie: one Panzer knocked out.'

'9. Kompanie: infantry attack repelled, suffered losses.'

'12. Kompanie: with this kind of attack, ammunition left will last only a few hours.'

'10. Kompanie: chief is out of action, Untersturmführer Gädertz in command of Kompanie.'

Now 'Pütti' led the Kompanie. Obersturmführer Hopf had only recently arrived at III. Bataillon. What a great guy! In the meantime, 12. Kompanie reported that the tanks had turned away. All Kompanie commanders demand simultaneously what should be done next. They requested further orders. These orders could only read:

'Hold positions, hold them under all circumstances!'

Sturmbannführer Olboeter shouted it, he roared it into the telephone. His voice was breaking, he was more than excited. I registered everything. Now I knew what was going on. I took my leave. I gave my last cigarettes to the officers and men in the bunker, one meter below ground, two meters below the straw. What ridiculous protection against a shell from a heavy British gun.

'Don't forget anything, Gauch! Don't forget us and tell my friend Gerd everything!'

I arrived back at the motorcycle. A shrapnel had cut through the side-car. We raced back at full speed, past shell craters and burning heaps of straw. On the way we picked up a wounded man who was going back. I was carrying inside everything I had seen and heard and lived through during the past minutes. Yes, they did need help out there, help without delay. A Pak or a tank sent its shells after us.

The wounded, made overly nervous by his injuries, jerked with each explosion.

I found the commander again at the command post of Panzerregiment Wünsche. I reported in terse words, not leaving any doubts. I was sure not to have forgotten anything Olboeter had instructed me to do. Next to Gerd Bremer stood Obersturmbannführer Wünsche. He, too, was listening, outwardly quiet.

'By tonight we'll have looked after this matter! Gerd, please give me one of your infantry companies to cover the Panzers. I'll attack left of Tessel-Bretteville! We'll throw the enemy back to the road!'

My commander had already turned to a messenger:

'Obersturmführer Beiersdorf to report to me immediately! 4. Kompanie, get ready!'

'Well then, Gauch, let's do it one more time!'

He, too, appeared absolutely quiet. And then we were back at our command post and orders were virtually raining down.[7]

The enemy had broken through the positions of Panzer-grenadier-Lehr-Regiment 901 to a depth of three kilometers. There was not only the danger that the enemy would push into the back of III./26, but also that he would advance—almost unhindered—in a southerly direction toward Noyers and Villers-Bocage. In order to close this dangerous gap between the "HJ" Division and the Pz.-Lehr-Div., the I.SS-Panzerkorps ordered a counterattack by "HJ" Division with I. Panzerabteilung and the sole infantry reserve of the Division, the Aufklärungs-abteilung 12. Simultaneously, a counterattack by the Panzer-Lehr-Division was started. The two components were to meet at Juvigny. Because of its own difficult situation and because an expansion of the enemy attack further east was expected, the Division requested the Korps to send other forces into action. It had no reserves left and could not receive any support from the Armee in time. Thus, there was no choice but to stick with the attack by the Wünsche Kampfgruppe as ordered.

Under the command of Obersturmbannführer Max Wünsche, the Division started the counterattack from the area of Tessel-Bretteville toward Bas de Fontenay with I. Panzer-abteilung with three companies, the Aufklärungsabteilung with the 3. and 4., units of 5. (heavy) Kompanie and units of III./26. The attack started in the course of the afternoon. The 2. Panzer-kompanie under Obersturm-führer Gaede drove at the point. The spearhead Zug was led, at his express request, by Untersturmführer Schröder. Immediately west of Tessel-Bretteville, resistance stiffened. The point Panzer was knocked out at short distance. Untersturmführer Schröder was killed as he bailed out.[8]

By 22.30 hours, the advance had reached a distance of 500 m from the road Fontenay-Juvigny and contact to the left wing of III./26 had been established. Contact with the Panzer-Lehr-Division near Juvigny had not been possible.[9]

In the meantime, the Duke of Wellington's attacked the right sector of III./26, and of 15./26 and 16./26—the Aufklärungs and Pionier companies—adjoining to the right. By 21.00 hours they had taken a section of eastern Fontenay. But some strongpoints were holding in the village and St. Nicolas Ferme, 300 meters southeast of the exit from the village. The Wellingtons stopped their attack and were ordered to clear the village the next morning and to capture the Ferme (farm).[10]

Obersturmführer Hans Siegel, chief of 8. Panzerkompanie, reported on his experiences with the Grenadiers of III./26:

> During these battles, I learned to value the young Grenadiers. During the enemy fire attacks they cowered in their foxholes, often for half an hour. They lasted through the hail of shells which was joined by branches from explosions in treetops, and pieces of bricks from destroyed houses. At the decisive moment, however, when the banging from the enemy infantry announced the impending attack, they came out of their foxholes as if lifted by ghostly hands and, like moles, machine guns and steel helmets, with almost indiscernible faces below, pushed toward the enemy. There was no shooting, since ammunition was short. But then, when the figures with the flat helmets were moving about in the chaos of the houses and streets, many almost at touching distance, well-aimed machine gun salvos whipped out of the German foxholes, believed to have been destroyed. A few of these were generally sufficient to end the racket. From the turret hatch of my Panzer I observed that, occasionally, one of our Grenadiers would jump into the next foxhole to help a wounded comrade or take his position, quite matter-of-course and without orders.[11]

The courageous battle for Fontenay is aptly relayed in the war history of the Royal Scots with few words:

> Because of the violence of the fighting, the toughness of the enemy and the vehemence of the artillery fire from both sides, this battle will forever remain in the memory of those who took part in it.

The Bataillon had lost seven officers, and 194 NCOs and men. It was withdrawn and only put into action again on 28 June to protect the right flank of the Division.[12]

The fighting of these days is described in the English enemy situation report as follows:

> The enemy had reinforced houses and turned them into fortified strongpoints. These were still being defended [at midnight]. Approximately thirty Panzers had been in action in Fontenay during the course of the day. Some were still fighting there during darkness. Since the fighting is still going on, it is difficult to judge the enemy strength. We assume that he does not have more than fifty men. But these few men under the cover of the fortified houses and supported by mortars, machine guns and Panzers, will be overcome only with extreme effort.[13]

Of the seventy prisoners taken by the enemy this day, one was a member of the Aufklärungskompanie of Panzergrenadierregiment 26 and one of the Aufklärungsabteilung 12. The rest were from the Panzer-Lehr-Division. In one of the enemy situation reports is a remark, worth noting, that 276. and 277. Infanterie Divisions had apparently departed from their -operational areas in the Pyrenees. The 16. Luftwaffen-Feld-Division had left its area in Holland. Enemy intelligence obviously had it easy in the occupied territory and was, in addition, effectively supported by the ULTRA radio surveillance.[14]

The units of the "HJ" Division, in action on the German side in the Fontenay sector, had also suffered heavy losses.

They are compiled in the following table.

Unit	Killed Officers	NCOs	Men	Wounded Officers	NCOs	Men	Missing Officers	NCOs	Men
II./26	-	2	8	2	18	-	-	1	-
III./26	1	-	9	1	6	28	-	-	3
15.&16./26	-	-	14	1	6	24	-	-	7
A.A.12	-	1	3	1	2	17	1	-	9
Pz.Rgt.	-	1	6	1	1	12	1	-	1
Totals	1	4	40	6	33	81	2	1	20

The total losses amounted to 45 killed, 120 wounded and 23 missing, altogether 188.[15]

The 49th Division had not reached its attack objectives as far as they were located in the sector of "HJ" Division. Fontenay had not been completely captured, strongpoints were holding out. There could be no thought of capturing Rauray. The III./26 and the units of the heavy infantry gun company, the Aufklärungskompanie and the Pionierkompanie of Regiment 26 in action with it, had defended their positions with incomparable valor. According to enemy testimony, the artillery had effectively supported them, despite the fact that it could not be compared with the enemy's either in the number of guns nor the amount of ammunition. The Panzers of II. Abteilung, in particular those of 8. and 6. Kompanie, had always been at the hot spots, had strengthened the resolve of the Grenadiers and had knocked out several enemy tanks—at least five. It had proven correct to keep the only reserves, I. Panzerabteilung and Aufklärungsabteilung, assembled on the left wing in expectation of an enemy offensive there. They were sufficient to stabilize the situation in the sector, but not enough to restore it in the sector of the neighbor to the left.

The Panzer-Lehr-Division had no reserves available at all. For this reason, the Divisionsbegleitkompanie of the "HJ" and the Korpsbegleitkompanie had been sent into action there, and the Korps expanded the sector of the "HJ" Division to the left by 1.5 kilometers to the bridge across the creek one kilometer east of Montilly. At the same time, orders were issued to move the main line of defense into the area south of the road Fontenay-Juvigny. Since the positions in Fontenay could not be held with available forces, the Division reinforced the protective positions along the line south of St. Martin (eastern section of Fontenay)-Tessel-Bretteville-Vendes. The III./26, temporarily attached to Panzerregiment 12, took over the sector on the right. Along the eastern bank of the Bordel creek were securing positions of I. Panzerabteilung and Aufklärungsabteilung from Grande Ferme to le Manoir (1.5 kilometers west of Rauray). From there, a link-up to the Panzer-Lehr-Division in Vendes was to be attempted and held. The 2. Kompanie of the Aufklärungs-abteilung pushed a securing position forward into the area southeast of Juvigny.[16]

The Tessel woods were in enemy hands. Enemy strength was estimated to be at least one infantry battalion and twenty tanks. The Division expected the enemy to continue his attack toward the south on 26 June and to attempt to widen the established gap. An enemy attack from le Mesnil-Patry on the position of 12. SS-Panzerpionierbataillon, started simultaneously with the attack on Fontenay, had been repelled. A repeat on 26 June had to be expected.[17]

The general command of I.SS-Panzerkorps ordered a counterattack by the "HJ" Division and the Panzer-Lehr-Division for 26 June in order to achieve the planned new main line of defense. The Divisional command of the "HJ" reported that its own forces were insufficient for this. The Panzerkorps promised its Tigerabteilung as reinforcements.[18] The Division planned to attack early on 26 June. As it turned out, the Tigers could not be assembled in time. Thus, the general command ordered that II. Abteilung of the Panzerregiment, in addition to I., would take part in the attack. The 5., 6., 7. and 9. Kompanie were assembled behind the right and central sectors of Regiment 26 and the attached Pionierbataillon as the only mobile anti-tank forces. The Divisional command thus requested urgently to do without II. Abteilung and to make other forces available instead. Obergruppenführer Sepp Dietrich and Brigadeführer Kraemer showed full understanding for these concerns. However, since other forces had still not arrived, "HJ" and Panzer-Lehr-Division had to carry out the attack to clear the situation with their own forces before the enemy continued his offensive.

The supreme command of 7. Armee also fully understood the serious-ness of the situation. It informed the Heeresgruppe in its daily report that the counterattack in the afternoon had taken place by ' concentrating all still available forces and seriously weakening the other front sectors'.[19]

A speedy clearing of the breakthrough at the dividing line between the "HJ" and Panzer-Lehr divisions was also necessary for another reason. The Supreme Command West relayed the following order from the OKW to the Heeresgruppe B on 25 June:

> It must be expected that the enemy will start an attack either from the area north and northwest of Caen to the south or southwest, or from the Carentan area to the southwest and south, even before our own assembly is accomplished.
>
> The advance and assembly for the planned offensive operations must thus be conducted in such a manner that a counterattack into the deep flanks of enemy breakthroughs can be carried out at any time with those units which have already arrived.[20]

The phrase "counterattack into the deep flanks" should be kept in mind. It will carry major importance in the pages ahead.

The "HJ" Division ordered the Panzerregiment for 26 June, to bring for-ward 5. and 7. Kompanie and to attack in the morning, together with the attached forces—III./26 and A.A. 12—and the I./A.R. 12 which was depend-ent on joint action. The objective was to gain the line south of St. Martin-Juvigny and to hold it. Subsequently, the Tessel woods would be cleared of the enemy. The units of 9. Panzerkompanie in position at the western edge of the Carpiquet airfield were left in their ambush positions, in order to have an effective anti-tank force at least in that location. As ordered by the Divi-sion, Regiment 26 reinforced its III. Bataillon by I. Zug of 1. (armored) Kom-panie of Pionierbataillon 12. The Zug took up position near St. Nicolas Ferme during the night.[21] The forces for the counterattack marched into their assembly areas during the late hours of the night.

CHAPTER 3.3

Attack by the VIII (British) Corps—Operation 'EPSOM'—and the 49th Infantry Division in the St. Manvieu-Fontenay Sector, and Defensive Fighting by SS-Panzergrenadier-regiment 26, SS-Panzerpionierbataillon 12 and SS-Panzer-regiment 12 on 26 June 1944

The planning and preparation for Operation "EPSOM' have been discussed previously.

The VIII Corps had orders to attack, one day after the 49th Infantry Division, in the le Mesnil Patry-St. Manvieu sector beyond the positions of the 3rd Canadian Infantry Division. The 15th (Scottish) Infantry Division would attack first and initially capture the high ground south of Cheux. Then it would take the Orne crossings near Gavrus and Tourville and hold them. The 11th Armoured Division (tanks) had been ordered, together with the attached 4th Armoured Brigade (tank brigade), to capture, from the two bridgeheads, the Maizet-Esquay area and to hold it. This was the high terrain between Odon and Orne. They were then to establish bridgeheads across the Orne between the bend in the river southeast of Maizet and Feuguerolles-sur-Orne. The 43rd (Wessex) Infantry Division was the reserve of the VIII Corps. Provided the attack was making good progress, the I Corps would secure the left flank by capturing Carpiquet.

The attack plan of the 15th Division provided:

Attack with two infantry brigades at the point:

> to the right (west) the 46th Highland Brigade with
> 9th Battalion The Cameronians,
> 2nd Battalion The Glasgow Highlanders,
> 7th Battalion The Royal Tank Regiment,
> 2 companies (medium machine guns) of the 1st Battalion The Middlesex

Regiment;

> in reserve: 7th Battalion The Seaforth Highlanders;
> to the left (east) the 44th Lowland Brigade with
> 8th Battalion The Royal Scots,
> 6th Battalion The Royal Scots Fusiliers (RSF),
> 9th Battalion The Royal Tank Regiment,
> 2 companies medium machine guns, as above;
> in reserve: 7th Battalion The King's Own Scottish Borderers (KOSB);

Engineers: 2 companies 'Thresher' tanks to remove mines,
1 company AVRES to hurl explosives against obstructions and to lay
bridges across -ditches;
Artillery: each infantry brigade has one Field Regiment (light artillery)
attached. It will fire moving walls of fire from 344 light and medium
guns;
total fire support from approximately 900 guns including the artillery
of 3 cruisers and 1 gun boat;
Air support: By medium bombers stationed in England, and by 12 Spitfire and 3 Mustang squadrons departing the beachhead.[1]
The attack by the division would proceed in three phases:

Phase 1: both brigades at the front will cross the 'starting line', rail
line Caen-Bayeux, between the western edge of Putot and Norrey
station, in a width of approximately 2.5 kilometers. They will initially
capture the line le Haut du Bosq-St. Manvieu;

Phase 2: the 15th Reconnaissance Regiment Royal Armoured Corps
advances to Mouen (three kilometers southeast of Cheux). It is followed by the 227th Infantry Brigade, advancing beyond the 46th
Brigade. The 227th will capture the Odon crossings near Gavrus and
Tourville.

Phase 3: the 44th and 46th Brigades will be relieved by two infantry
brigades of the 43rd Infantry Division. The 46th Brigade takes over
the sector of the 15th Reconnaissance Regiment and later advances
to Evrécy. The 44th Brigade takes over the Colleville-Tourville-
Mouen area.

Action by the 11th Armoured Division was planned as follows:
The Division follows the 15th Division along two routes of advance. The
29th Armoured Brigade crosses the Odon, after the bridgeheads have been
established by the 15th Division, and captures Hill 112. It is followed by the
4th Armoured Brigade which will capture Hill 120 north of Maizet. The
159th Infantry Brigade of the 11th Armoured Division, marching behind the
4th Armoured Brigade, must be ready to support the two point brigades in
establishing the bridgeheads across the Orne.[2]
During the last days before the start of the offensive, the reconnaissance
units of the 15th Division surveyed the terrain from the position of the forward units of the 3rd Canadian Division. They found it difficult to find their
attack targets with use of the map in the broken attack strip. The 'starting
line' was under constant German surveillance and under fire, which made
scouting it difficult. Le Mesnil-Patry turned out to be a perfect obstruction to

tanks. The rifle companies of the Cameronians and their supporting tanks would have to find different approaches. The left open flank and the very broken terrain there would come under fire from the direction of the airfield.

During the night from 24 to 25 June 1944, the infantry of the 15th Division advanced from the area around Cully and Secqueville (nine and 7.5 kilometers north of Cheux respectively) into the assembly areas behind the 'starting line'. The artillery advanced into its assembly areas but remained under cover of barns and trees and hedges during the day. Because of the reinforcement of the troops in the front line of the 3rd Canadian Division, the reconnaissance of the "HJ" Division had been unable, since 23 June, to penetrate into the depth of the main enemy battlefield. Thus, the preparations for the attacks had not been recognized. During the night of 25 June, the Scottish infantry advanced into its assembly areas. Firing positions for the guns were dug and occupied, ammunition was brought forward.[3]

Although the 49th Infantry Division had not reached its attack objectives, in particular the hill near Rauray, and thus the threat to the flanks from the west had not been eliminated, the start of the offensive was not postponed. Montgomery was aware, in large measure, of the advance of new German units through aerial observation and his intelligence service. He had to forestall their assembly.

During the night, Obersturmbannführer Max Wünsche had assembled his Kampfgruppe for the attack in the morning of 26 June. It was still dark when Standartenführer Kurt Meyer left the Divisional command post to drive to Rauray. Prior to this, he had been briefed by the Ia on the latest reports. At the time, the front was still quiet. The radio surveillance by the Nachrichtennahaufklärungszug (communications monitoring) had not offered any new insights either. It could not provide a definitive confirmation of the reported tank assembly northwest of Caen. Despite this, the Divisional command was convinced that a large-scale operation was being prepared. The barrages which had prepared the attack of the 49th Division near Fontenay the previous day, and had lasted for three hours, could not have served to support a purely local attack. The fire had vastly surpassed anything experienced until then. The Division commander again urged the Ia to maintain close contact with the Panzer-Lehr-Division so that both attacks would be coordinated. He could be reached through the command post of the Panzerregiment in Rauray. He would attempt to make sure that the counterattack would advance well so that II. Panzerabteilung could soon return to its ambush positions behind Regiment 26.

Since the 49th Division had not been able to completely capture Fontenay by the evening of 25 June, while the Hallams to the west had reached the southern edge of the Tessel Woods already in the afternoon, it changed the plan for the continuation of the attack. It ordered the 1st Battalion The Tyneside Scottish, supported by both tank units 4/7 Dragoon Guards (without one company) and the 24th Lancers, to attack the left flank of III./26 in order to weaken the positions in and south of Fontenay. The right flank of the attacker would be protected by the 12th KRRC at the southern edge of the Tessel Woods. The attack of Kampfgruppe Wünsche from the Rauray area to clear the woods, and that of the British from the woods toward Tessel-Bretteville and le Manoir unfortunately met head on at dawn.

The chief of 6. (Panzer IV) Kompanie, Obersturmführer Ludwig Ruckdeschel, experienced the attack in this way:

> We were pulled from our favorable assembly area where we awaited enemy tank attacks and directed to a spot where more than one hundred enemy tanks were supposed to have broken through between our Division and the Panzer-Lehr-Division. We arrived there still at dawn without losses. The enemy tanks were reported to have taken cover in a wooded area." Ruckdeschel scouted the terrain near le Manoir on foot. He reported further: "I surveyed the woods through my binoculars and spotted tank tracks outside the woods, running to the right in the direction of a large orchard. Fortunately, there was a cemetery wall near-by where I could let my Panzer take cover. I got out of the Panzer and walked alone, with my binoculars, along the tank tracks, from tree to tree. Suddenly, automatic weapons fire from enemy sharpshooters hidden in the trees burst around me. Instinctively, I dropped to the ground and crawled back. Suddenly, there were bangs and enemy explosive shells were hailing down. We could locate the enemy tank position by the muzzle flash. My Panzers were well protected from it. I was still 50-60 meters away from my Kompanie when there was another bang. An explosive shell had hit a tree I was just walking under. My right arm was minced meat. I was taken to the main dressing station. The Divisional medical officer, Sturmbannführer Dr. Rolf Schulz, said to me: 'Medical experience would not allow you to still be alive. You have lost far more than half of your blood, and that is normally the end.' My being wounded had as its only positive result the revision of our attack plan.[4]

The attack by I. Panzerabteilung and units of II. Abteilung together with 3. and 4. Kompanie initially advanced well. It stalled, however, when the enemy had also started the attack. The intelligence officer of I. Abteilung, Untersturmführer Rolf Jauch, was wounded during this attack. He reported:

> The attack stalled and we came under fire from three sides. Because of damage to the gun of my Panther (the pinion was defective), I had to get out with my gunner to remove a pinion from a knocked-out Panzer sitting at the eastern side of the valley. On the way back,

we came under fire from the right. My gunner Gumpert was killed immediately. I took it to the right elbow and the chest (minor). I took the pinion to my Panzer. Jürgensen (the Abteilung commander) advised me to make my way to the east and from there to the south since it was impossible to have me transported from there by ambulance. I managed to work my way through the hedges and to the road along which we had advanced on Tessel-Bretteville. In the afternoon, an ambulance picked me up there and took me to the field dressing station and then to the main dressing station.[5]

The Divisional commander had observed the attack and experienced here the start of operation "Epsom". In his book "Grenadiere" ("Grenadiers") he wrote:

The morning was already dawning. Everything is still quiet. I am standing near Rauray with Max Wünsche and watch the last Panzer roll into the assembly area. It is growing lighter and lighter. The first tethered balloon already hangs in the sky. It can't be long now before the deadly dance continues.

The German batteries are firing barrages. English low-level attack aircraft roar above and send their rockets howling into Rauray. The hell of the battle of materiel has begun.

The first Panzers are rattling to the front. The attack initially advances well, but it is stalled by an English counterattack. It turns into a battle of tank against Panzer which fought with great determination. The broken terrain, covered with hedges, does not allow our Panzers to take advantage of the longer range of their guns. In particular, the lack of infantry forces becomes noticeable. The concentrated artillery fire greatly inhibits any cooperation and later makes direct command almost impossible.

Nothing can be heard from east of Rauray. All of the fighting has moved to the west. Again, give-away columns of smoke hang in the sky. Each column means the grave of a Panzer. I am concerned about the situation in the sector of Regiment 26. There is not even one exploding shell to the right of Rauray. It is starting to rain. Thank God, this protects us from the fighter-bombers.—But, what is this? The ground seems to open up, to devour all of us. Within a few seconds, all hell breaks loose. Rauray consists only of fragments of ripped trees and buildings. I am lying in a road ditch, listening to the din of the battle. Barrage follows after barrage, without let-up. The fog mixes with the gasses of exploding shells. I can still not determine the situation, all wires are cut. There is no longer any contact with the Divisional staff and the point units. A messenger from II. Bataillon comes running at me and yells: Tank after tank on the right wing of the Bataillon! His report is made inaudible by the noise of the exploding shells. My ears are trying to analyze the battle noise, without success. All I can hear is an ongoing hissing, banging, and booming of shells exploding, mixed with the creaking tracks of rolling tanks.

This is the expected major offensive! We are now fighting for the cornerstone of the German front in Normandy. Caen is the objective of the attack. Caen is to be throttled by a pincer attack. Caen is to be Montgomery's prize and will bring down the German front. All around me, men are staring in fascination at the murderous spectacle. Red-hot steel is whistling above us, digs into the wet ground with a hissing noise.

I call for Wünsche. Messengers jump across the road and disappear into the thicket of green hedges. It does not take long and Wünsche is at my side.

I do not have to go into detailed explanations for this old front soldier. We have spent too much time together—he knows me and what I want.

With a few words I brief him on my assessment of the situation. It reads: The enemy is trying to break through with strong tank forces in the sector of Regiment 26 and to bring down Caen. I order: 1. The attack on Juvigny is to be stopped immediately; 2. Rauray, the cornerstone of the Division, must be held under all circumstances; 3. You are responsible for Rauray.[6]

The Divisional commander ordered Obersturmbannführer Wünsche to stop the attack immediately, to hold Rauray under all circumstances and to return the Panzer companies, which had been withdrawn from their ambush positions behind Regiment 26 during the night, to their old positions at all possible speed. He then drove back to the Divisional command post at Verson, fortunately unmolested by the fighter-bombers whose activity was curtailed by drizzle and a low cloud cover. Enemy fighters were only in the air to protect the airspace above the assembly area.

At 07.30 hours, enemy artillery had opened preparatory fire with several hundred guns on the German positions in the attack strip of VIII Corps. One of the British soldiers described his feelings, and those of comrades, as they were waiting for the order to attack:

The artillery fire had been hammering from the direction of the front line without interruption since dawn. We were listening with a mixture of excitement and apprehension. . . . Between the rain showers we watched the reflection of the gun fire from the low clouds: the horizon was trembling and a thousand eerie lightnings crisscrossed the night sky. For a long time we watched in silence.

Then, someone said what we were all thinking: 'We have to go into that!' Our breathing became a little faster, our hearts were beating a little harder. Those eighteen-year olds of the "Hitlerjugend" Division, strong in their youthful trustfulness and youthful fire, were selling their lives at a high price.[7]

It is unimaginable for anyone who has not lived through such barrages just what impact they have on the man in his foxhole. The British wall of fire concentrated at its first target line for ten minutes. Then it moved forward every three minutes by 100 yards (ninety meters). The two tank companies of the 7th Royal Tanks which attacked, together with the Cameronians, near le Mesnil and were then scheduled to advance further, encountered mine fields 350 m southwest and southeast of the village at 07.00 hours. These had been set by Pionierbataillon 12. The British lost nine tanks.[8] The British infantry had to attack without tank support. Finally, the outer edges of the mine fields were determined and they could detour them. But the tanks could only get to the point of the infantry when the left battalion had reached the road Caen-Fontenay, even later at the battalion to the right. In the meantime, the contact with the moving wall of fire had been lost. Surviving Panzergrenadiers of Regiment 26 and individual anti-tank guns opened frontal fire from the area south of Fontenay. The II. Artillerieabteilung and the heavy infantry guns as well as the Flaksturmregiment 4 (anti-aircraft assault regiment) laid barrages in front of their own positions and concentrated fire on the advancing tanks and their accompanying infantry in order to separate them. The III. Artillerie-abteilung, in position in the sector of Regiment 25, and I. Abteilung which supported the Kampfgruppe Wünsche in its attack and defense in the Rauray area, were not able to take part. At approximately 11 A.M. the Glasgow Highlanders reported that they had reached the northern edge of Cheux. The Cameronians were at the same line to the right. Their right wing was further back. Their tanks were even further back since they had come under defensive fire from well camouflaged anti-tank guns and, as they thought, Panzers. The Cameronians then reported that they had reached the northern edge of le Haut du Bosq at approximately 11.30 hours. The Glasgow Highlanders reported that they had pushed through Cheux and had begun to clear the village.

Based on these favorable reports, the VIII Corps ordered at 11.50 hours that one company of the 1st Northamptonshire Yeomanry were to conduct reconnaissance along the planned advance route of the Corps. The 11th Armoured Division was ordered to move ahead the 29th Armoured Brigade into the area north of Cheux and to prepare its further advance. The company first encountered a minefield which prevented an approach to the village from the north. Then, the ruins of the destroyed town impeded crossing through it. It came under close attack with hand grenades, Panzerfausts, and fire from rifles and reached the southern exit of Cheux only at approximately 13.00 hours. When it then advanced against the hill to the south, the scouting party in the center was destroyed by Panzer fire from the southwest and southeast. Two others were held down, while the fourth managed to reach the edge of the town of Grainville at 15.00 hours. It, together with the rest of the company, was withdrawn at approximately 15.50 hours.[9]

According to the entries in the enemy war diaries, Phase 1 seemed to run in accordance with the plan. The German enemy was neutralized, even destroyed. There was surprise not to have found stronger resistance. In particular, there was initially no explanation where the Panzers of the "Hitlerjugend" Division were. Their counterattack was still expected. The assembly of all of the Panzerregiment in the Rauray area was in fact the reason that the attackers, using the impact of devastating barrages and with the support from numerous tanks, were able to overcome the positions of the infantry and of the Pioniers, acting as infantry, in a relatively short time period. Most of the anti-tank guns had been destroyed by the enemy artillery fire before they could enter the battle. The Pioniers and Panzergrenadiers suffered heavy losses from the barrages although they were well dug-in. As the barrage moved closer they had crawled into their foxholes. After it had moved by, they appeared from their foxholes to fight the attacking British infantry. Often, they already found themselves surrounded by the enemy. Apparently, the last salvos had been shells which did not disintegrate into shrapnel on exploding. This had enabled the tanks and the accompanying infantry to follow close behind without danger. Some of the men were captured before they could use their weapons, others took up the fight from close distance.

The commander of Granatwerferzug (mortar Zug) of 4. Kompanie, Oberscharführer Ernst Behrens, had also been captured in this manner. He witnessed the fighting for his observation post which the enemy had obviously not spotted at first. He reported:

> SS-Pionier Pelzmann was the forward observer in the shelter on that day. His observation post was located on a low rise under a tree. It was covered with an armor plate from a Panzer IV which he had found himself. This position could almost not be spotted since the armor plate itself was covered with grass. There was only an observation slit in the direction of the enemy, no larger than that of the driver of a Panzer.
>
> Although my Zug command post was located approximately 40-50 meters behind Pelzmann's observation post, and I had already been captured, I could see that Pelzmann was still fighting. Many dead English soldiers were lying in a semicircle in front of his position. Suddenly, the cover was lifted and Pelzmann came out of his shelter. He grabbed his rifle with its telescopic sight by the barrel and slammed it with full force against the tree so that the butt broke off. He was left with only the barrel in his hands and threw it away.

Then I heard him shout loudly: 'Well, I'm out of ammunition! I've gotten enough of you—now you can shoot me!' I was completely convinced that Pelzmann would join our group as a prisoner. That did not happen, but what followed was horrible. A tall, red-haired Englishman walked toward Pelzmann, grabbed him by the jacket collar with his left hand and shot him in the temple with a pistol. As he let go of Pelzmann, the body dropped backward to the ground, his right arm in the air.

Several men of my Zug and I were ordered by an English officer to place the just killed comrade as well as the other dead, friend and foe, into prepared sacks and carry them to a spot he indicated. When we came to the spot where our comrade Pelzmann lay, I saw almost thirty dead English soldiers in front of his observation post.[10]

A descriptive report on the fighting for the command post of the Pionierbataillon was provided by Untersturmführer Hans Richter of the Bataillon staff several days after his escape. It was recorded by a war reporter. The command post was located approximately 200 meters south of the road Caen-Fontenay between two country lanes, running north-south approximately one kilometer west of la Gaule. The post was inside an earth bunker which had been dug into the northern slope of a hill some time before the invasion and which fit perfectly into the surrounding landscape. In front of the bunker was an observation post with a scissor telescope. The position was well camouflaged by a natural growth of bushes. The bunker and observation post were connected by a covered walk, at right angles. A communication trench ran to a grain field to the south. It had not been cultivated for quite some time and was overgrown with weeds and small bushes. The terrain to the north, falling off slowly at first and then relatively flat, to the road Fontenay-Carpiquet, as well as the southern edge of the Parc de Boislande and the villages of le Mesnil-Patry and Norrey-en-Bessin, could be well observed from the post. Because of this favorable observation situation, the command post was repeatedly visited by the Divisional commander, the commander of the Artillerieregiment, and other officers. The battery commanders, Obersturmführer Timmerbeil and Oberleutnant Haller, set up observation posts in the bunker and repeatedly directed the fire of their batteries from there with substantial success.

To both sides of the command post, II. and III. Zug of 1. Pionierkompanie, as battalion reserve, were well dug in and ready for action. The I. Zug had been attached to III./26 during the night 25/26 June in the area north of Rauray. The position of 2. Batterie of I./SS-Panzerartillerieregiment 12 under Obersturmführer Timmerbeil was located in an orchard at the southwestern edge of Cheux, approximately 800 m behind the command post. This battery of 6 light field howitzers (10.5 cm, self-propelled) depended on cooperation with the Pionier-bataillon.

Here follows the first part of the battle report:

Enemy harassing fire was concentrated on the positions of SS-Pz.-Pionier-Bataillon 12 and on the command post from 02.45 hours. The night was clear. The commander, Sturmbann-führer Siegfried Müller, immediately requested a report from the companies on what they observed. The companies reported no observations or actions. The wires to the units were broken by the harassing fire. Contact with the units was maintained by field radios.

Telephone connection to the units was re-established at 04.30 hours.

Enemy barrages started at 06.00 hours. Impact explosions were close together. Slowly, the fire came closer and closer. The wires to the units were not yet cut.

At 06.15 hours, the commander spotted through the scissor binoculars an assembly of enemy tanks at the southern edge of le Mesnil-Patry and the southern edge of the Parc de Boislande. The commander reported this to the Ia and requested release of the artillery. At the same time, the commander requested Panzers or armor-piercing weapons. The artillery was given the go-ahead and fired a few salvos. The salvos were well aimed into their targets.

From 06.15 hours on, constant requests to the companies for observations or if enemy attacks can be spotted. The companies report: 'Negative!'

At approximately 07.00 hours, Obersturmführer Bischof (commander 4. (heavy)/SS-Pz.-Pionier-Bataillon 12) reported that his neighbor on the left had pulled back approximately 200–300 m during the night and that his left flank was open. The commander reported this immediately to the Ia. Contact with 2./SS-Pz.-Pi.-Btl. 12 was lost at 07.00 hours. Enemy tanks were advancing slowly on the positions of the neighbor on the left and of the Bataillon. The commander requested Panzers from the Ia. The Ia referred him to the commander of SS-Pz.-Gren.Rgt. 26. The wires to the Regiment were destroyed, radios are not available. Thereupon, the commander ordered the adjutant to bring up the Panzers assembled behind our sector for a counterattack.

Contact by radio with 3./SS-Pz.-Pi.-Btl. 12 was good. The squad leader, SS-Sturmmann Pötsch, did a particularly good job. A request to 3./SS-Pz.-Pi.-Btl. if an enemy attack had been spotted was still without result.

At 08.15 hours, no Panzers had yet arrived. The commander sent two messengers in quick succession with the order to bring up the Panzers. The command post was now coming under extremely heavy barrages. Enemy machine guns were firing close-by. Huge clouds of dust and fog covered the command post. They prevented the battlefield observer from seeing anything.

At approximately 08.30 hours, the leader of the Pi.Erk.-Zug (Pionier reconnaissance Zug), Oberscharführer Vogel, reported to the commander with some of the men of his Zug. He was wounded and he reported that individual enemy tanks were sitting on the road Fontenay le Pesnel—Carpiquet. Oberscharführer Vogel was ordered to take up positions with his men to the left and right of the command post.

At 09.00 hours, SS-Unterscharführer Hemken reported 'Enemy tanks!' The commander jumped from the bunker and saw, to the left and right of the bunker, tanks, armored cars and infantry on foot advancing on Cheux. The commander immediately ordered the trenches and the observation post to be manned and fire to be opened on the enemy infantry. The enemy was attacking the bunker and trenches with tanks and opened heavy fire from tank guns and machine guns. The men withdrew, fighting, to the bunker. The last man was barely inside the bunker when an enemy tank fired its gun into it three times. Oberleutnant Haller and one man were killed, a majority of the crew was wounded.

Hand grenades were thrown into the bunker, filling it with smoke and fumes. Some men received minor injuries from the hand grenades (since a woolen blanket was hanging in front of the entrance, the hand grenades exploded outside the entrance, Author). It was just like a miracle. Tense and determined, the crew awaited another attack. Nothing happened. The tension increased, the wounded were moaning. Enemy infantry took up positions left and right of the bunker. Artillery and self-propelled guns were firing very near-by. Orders could be clearly heard, occasionally a man was laughing. Tommy felt quite safe. Tanks were rolling without pause in the direction of Cheux.

Suddenly, there were noises from the rear entrance to the bunker. The senses tensed, pistols were leveled at the entrance. A man pushed through the entrance with difficulty. He was a comrade (Sturmmann Eberle, Author). He reported that two enemy armored cars, hit by hand grenades, were on fire outside. He picked up our last hand grenade and disappeared again. He wanted to watch what the enemy was doing. The commander ordered the entrances guarded by two men who had not yet been wounded. They had knives in their fists. Any enemy who dared come into the bunker was to be eliminated without noise. The men had calmed down somewhat, any noise was avoided. Some of the wounded had fallen asleep, exhausted. The others were smoking.

After one hour, our man returned. He reported that all of the hill was covered with enemy tanks, armored cars and infantry.

Slowly, very slowly, the hours passed. The guards were stood, without movement, quietly at the entrances and watched. Time and again, there were voices quite close to the bunker. Some curious enemy soldiers inspected our scissor binoculars and played with them. In between, there were the harsh discharges from guns very close by. But nothing else happened. Ammunition was exploding in the enemy armored cars. This was holding the Tommy off. Sporadic explosions from our own artillery made us heave sighs of relief. Never before had we yearned for our artillery in this manner.[11]

The already mentioned harassing fire was fired by the Haller and Timmerbeil batteries which were in position southwest of Cheux. Portions of the two squads of 1. Pionier-Kompanie had withdrawn, fighting, to Cheux and were defending from the houses. They were fighting the company of the 2nd Northamptonshire Yeomanry which was advancing through the town. This Kampfgruppe was led by Untersturmführer Asmus. The technical officer for engineering matters, Untersturmführer Lorenz, had put together another Kampfgruppe from parts of the supply unit. He had tried, without success, to relieve the Bataillon staff. The rest of the Pionierbataillon supply unit was located in Mouen, forming a Kampfgruppe there.

At the same time as the 46th Brigade, the 44th Brigade together with tanks of the 9th Royal tanks, had started the attack. Their first objectives were the villages of la Gaule and St. Manvieu. The 6th Royal Scots Fusiliers reached the northern fringe of St. Manvieu at approximately 07.30 hours. Throughout the morning there was heavy fighting for the village. Each house and each farm was struggled for. The war diary of the VIII Corps states:

Two houses, in particular, were defended with great determination and finally cleared by flame throwers. The 8th Royal Scots reached la Gaule at approximately 08.30 hours. Here again, the push through the town was possible only after bitter fighting. At 11.30 hours, both battalions had reached the southern edges of their villages. It appeared that the towns were firmly in their hands, but numerous points of resistance were still being doggedly defended and had to be fought. This fact, and a number of counterattacks made the situation less favorable than had initially been expected.

The 9th Royal Tanks reported three damaged tanks in St. Manvieu.[12] Oberscharführer Erich Wohlgemuth, commander of the Panzerabwehrzug of the 4/26 (anti-tank Zug), reported on the fighting of I./26:

Heavy artillery fire woke us at a very early hour. Based on its intensity, we recognized that an attack was coming. We drew back into our slit trench which we had covered with farming implements, beams, girders and dirt. This would prove to be advantageous since we took at least four direct hits on our approximately 1.5 square meter trench. Since the shells were outfitted with highly sensitive impact detonators, nothing much happened. There was only an immense amount of dust every time. The whole terrain was covered by explosions, one could say, two per square meter. As the fire moved further to the rear, we jumped out of our trench and ran to the Kompanie command post. Behind the moving wall of fire came tanks and infantry. A farm, adjoining the school, was already occupied by the British. They tried to get across a wall into the school. When we were unable to hold them off with our hand weapons, I fired a Panzerfaust at the wall, but it did not explode. The attack at this spot slowed down, but we suddenly had a number of enemy tanks in our back. The Kompanie chief, Obersturmführer Alois Hartung, ordered us to withdraw to the Bataillon command post. Alois Hartung ended up behind enemy lines. Our medic, Unterscharführer Geßwein, two dead soldiers and five or six wounded remained at the Kompanie command post which we had built ourselves. We never learned what had become of them.

We had to abandon an attempt to recapture our last anti-tank gun. It was sitting outside the park where the Bataillon command post was located. An enemy tank had stopped approximately thirty meters from it. As reported to me later by the gun's commander, Unterscharführer Laube, it did not return to action, having been damaged by artillery fire.[13]

Unterscharführer Heinrich Bassenauer of Granatwerferzug 4./26 (mortar Zug) experienced the enemy attack in this way:

Three of our mortars had already been lost to direct hits. Many of the comrades of our Zug had been killed or wounded. The enemy had already advanced to the trees and hedges of our position. We were encircled by tanks which were pointing their guns at us from a respectful distance. With the remaining two mortars we withdrew to the Bataillon command post and set up position between the barns, well out of sight. We crawled back to our previous positions repeatedly to retrieve mortar ammunition, again suffering losses from enemy rifle and machine gun fire. Our surface fire prevented the enemy infantry from advancing further. When the English flame-thrower tank pushed into the entrance to the Bataillon command post, it was as if the world was about to disintegrate, amid the roar and whistling, the horizon turned red and black.[14]

A messenger of 1. Kompanie of Regiment 26 who was at the Bataillon command post, also reported on the battles in St. Manvieu. The command post was located in a big house along the road Rots-Cheux, adjoining a park-like garden. Sturmmann Aribert Kalke wrote:

The artillery fire was constantly increasing, finally concentrating on the center of the village. Explosions hit the front yard, directly ahead of the entrances to the command post. The house was shaken by hits. Between the explosions we could hear the short, harsh barking of tank guns. The Bataillon staff had sought cover in the cellar. Only a few men had remained in the upper levels. Radio contact with the companies had been lost, the situation was not clear. The Bataillon commander, Sturmbannführer Krause, was just about to send a messenger to 2. Kompanie when a messenger from that Kompanie dropped into the command post through the smoke and fumes. He was wounded himself and reported that the Kompanie chief, Obersturmführer Gröschel, and his deputy had been killed. The Kom-panie, engaged in bitter hand-to-hand combat, had been overrun. The enemy had broken through at 2. Kompanie and at the connection to 1. Kompanie with strong tank and infantry forces. Enemy tanks were immediately outside the command post.

The commander (Sturmbannführer Krause, Author) ordered his adjutant to establish contact with a Panzer-kompanie located in the la Bijude area (two kilometers southeast of St. Manvieu, Author). It was requested to counterattack immediately. Untersturmführer Hölzel took me along as his messenger. An Untersturmführer who was at the Bataillon staff as the liaison officer of the Regiment, accompanied us.

When the artillery fire weakened a little, the three of us left the command post by a rear exit at short intervals. A small, dense wooded area immediately behind the house offered us cover. After scaling a high fence, we found ourselves in a grain field which also gave us cover from being spotted. There, I lost sight of the two officers. As I crossed the road Fontenay-Caen, I came under machine gun and rifle fire from the right. I passed by a field dressing station which was being disbanded because of the proximity to the enemy. Shortly thereafter, I met again Untersturm-führer Hölzel and we reached the Panzerkompanie together. The Kompanie chief categorically declined a counterattack into the village without infantry cover. Without accompanying infantry, Panzers were not suited to fight in the streets. While Untersturmführer Hölzel set up a new strong point with a few stragglers, I was ordered to establish contact with 1. Kompanie. I encountered I. Zug of Untersturmführer Groß. When I arrived, the Zug no longer had contact with its neighbor squads on the left and the Kom-panie command post. Repeatedly, messengers were sent. They merely brought back a critically wounded comrade, Sturmmann Hans-Joachim Forth.[15]

While the two officers and Sturmmann Kalke attempted to bring in rein-forcements, the battle for the Bataillon command post blazed. The hero of the day was Unterscharführer Emil Dürr, gun commander in Panzerab-wehrzug of the 4./26. A war correspondent, whose name is not known, describes Emil Dürr's fighting in a report.

The tank has to go!
They had carried him from the burning house, which the enemy tank guns had picked as their target in the St. Manvieu park, to a hollow under the old shady trees. There he lay, both thighs wrapped in make-shift dressings, quiet and withdrawn. His blue eyes clear and calm, his lips pale, pressed together in pain. His comrades stood around him. They would have liked to do something to help him through those last moments he had to live. But there was nothing to do or to say. Yes—he only had moments left to live. Sighing, the medic had turned away from him, the dressings dripping with unstoppable blood. . . . Did he know that he had to die?!
The Kompanie commander asked him if he had a wish. Yes— please lift his head a little. If only they had a pillow to offer him a soft headrest—but there was only a gas mask which they carefully pushed under his head.
The guns of the enemy tanks surrounding the park sent shell after shell, without pause, into the tree-covered terrain. The gable of the house in which the Bataillon command post was located, blew apart with a bang. The beams were smoldering. Here and there the dry ground, set afire by the searing tongues of the flame thrower tanks, was burning. Smoke and dust were creeping through the trees to the hollow. A fine rain drizzled with hopeless monotony on the leaves.
The wounded man turned his head a little. He sought to see something. But he only spotted the smoke, the fumes, and the clouds of dust.
'You must not let them into the park'—he said. He spoke calmly, as if there was nothing to worry about for him. Then he asked for a cigarette. Many hands were extended toward him. He smiled. Yes—

the comrades—they knew he was about to begin a long journey, but they did not sense that he, too, knew it.

He smoked, composed, as was his manner. He held the cigarette in his right hand, black with Norman soil, a few blood stains on the crust of dirt. His hand, too, was steady, eerily so. His left caressingly stroked the grass on which he was bedded. Under this grass, he would soon be sleeping, sleeping forever. . .

'There is nothing behind us', he said. 'You must hold on until they have set up a new line behind us'. . .

He seemed to want to say more as his lips continued to move, but no words were formed. His left hand gripped the grass more firmly as if it was looking for a hold . . .

'Give my love to my wife'—he said—'and the little one . . . take care of them . . .

And do not be sad—there is nothing sad' . . .

Then the cigarette dropped from his hand. He closed his eyes. Once more he breathed, deep and heavy. Then the blood stopped, as did his heart.

His comrades took off their helmets and instinctively folded their hands. And tears were running down quite a few cheeks. They were not ashamed in front of each other.

Heavier and heavier, the shells from the tanks hammered the park. The beams of the house were splintering, bricks were flying from the park wall. The earth was trembling.—In the early morning hours of 26 June 1944, while the sun was still resting behind the Norman hills, the English barrages had set in. For almost three hours they laid salvo after salvo on the line of main defense outside of St. Manvieu and on the village itself. And on the Grenadiers of I. Bataillon of a regiment of the SS-Panzer-Division "Hitler Jugend", which had been awaiting the major enemy offensive on the Carpiquet airfield and the Orne river for days now, in front of the gates of Caen. Foxholes were filled in, machine guns smashed, men were mercilessly ripped apart. Ammunition depots blew apart, telegraph posts tumbled with hollow screams, and wires ripped singing across the roads . . . Houses caught on fire, gables came crashing down. The earth moaned with its wounds, dug into the ground in countless numbers. When, three hours later, the enemy guns fell quiet and only shrapnels were whirling and howling through the air, enemy tanks advanced through the smoke, the stench, and the fog. They broke through the positions and overran St. Manvieu. Like a pack of hungry wolves they surrounded the park. The hand-full of men in the Bataillon command post could count fifteen Shermans, with their naked eyes. They were sitting in front of the wall which enclosed one side of the park, and in the grain field on the other side.

Whoever had arms left to fight was sent into action in the park, messengers, clerks, orderlies.

If they roll over the hedge, thought the Grenadiers, if they break through the walls, if they push into the park—well, then it will be over. Then, the battered Bataillon would lose its leadership, the cornerstone of the uneven battle would be overthrown. Then, the desired English breakthrough would succeed, because that is what they wanted—to break through here, to the Orne river, to the last undamaged bridge near St. André, to reach the road Caen-Falaise, to encircle Caen from the south. The Bataillon command post had suddenly become an important bastion—and it had no heavy weapons. They had sub-machine guns and rifles. They had Panzerfausts and magnetic explosives. And only a hand-full of men. This could only have a minor effect against a few dozen tanks. Minor effect? Who could predict it?

And they had Unterscharführer Dürr. But no-one could foresee the outcome during this critical hour. The young, blond-haired Unterscharführer himself did not know of it . . .

But two mortars were still sitting in the park, massive and mighty. And their crews had twenty-five shells left. These they fired among the tanks, into this corner and that. The shells exploded with bangs and caused confusion. Sharp-shooters crept to the hedges and wall ledges and fired at the commanders who came out of their hatches too soon.

Some of the tanks turned away. They assumed the forces in the park to be much stronger and did not dare to break through. But the calm did not last long, the tanks returned and fired from all barrels. They picked the house as their target and damaged it so badly that the wounded had to be carried out.

Then, suddenly, there was a shout of alarm within the doggedly defending troop. A flame thrower tank had set up at the entrance to the park, dominating the path to the command post, and able to harass any movement. 'That tank has to go', the commander ordered. He said it as he was walking by, he had no time to stop. He was needed out there with the men, here and there and everywhere.

Unterscharführer Dürr had heard the order. He did not hesitate. 'I'll go', he said, and he was gone. He took a Panzerfaust and went to scout the situation. It was difficult to get close to the tank. It was sitting in a position which dominated the terrain on all three sides.

Unterscharführer Dürr did not calculate for long. He jumped across the inner wall of the yard and ran straight at the tank. But the

Panzerfaust did not pierce the tank. Maybe he had not aimed accurately enough in his excitement.

Then Dürr felt a blow to the chest, and immediately a warm substance was running down his thighs.

Hit! Shot in the chest!

Angry, Dürr pulled himself up and ran back the path he had come. He picked up another Panzerfaust and ran up to the tank a second time. This time, since the distance was unfavorable, he aimed at the tracks. The tank rattled, the track ripped. But again, Dürr was covered by violent machine gun fire. Crawling, he worked his way back. With one jump he scaled the wall, out of the range of fire. He spotted a magnetic charge and quickly grabbed it. A comrade wanted to hold him back: 'You are bleeding—'

Dürr did not let himself be stopped. The tank had to go . . .

For a third time he set out on his dangerous journey. For the third time, already quite weakened, he jumped across the wall. He ran, stumbling, toward the tank, paying no attention to the bullets. Now he was very close, one more jump—attached the charge—he was about to get away when he heard a rumbling sound behind him—the charge had dropped to the ground . . .

Not even seconds were left for him to consider, no time to contemplate his duty, desires, wishes . . . the tank had to go—And once again, he was at the flame thrower tank like a flash. He grabbed the charge with a strong fist, pressed it against the tank, staggered once, pushed, gasping, against the diabolic dynamite . . .

Then came the roaring bang—flickering fire, flames, darkness in front of his eyes . . .

As he hit the ground, he saw that the tank was burning. He wanted to jump up—but he could not, as if paralyzed he lay on the ground. He tried it once more, felt a stabbing pain in his thighs . . . he looked down on his bleeding legs and his heart turned cold with shock . . .

Was it desperation which gave him superhuman strength now? He crawled back down the path, now open, to the command post. The comrades spotted him, pulled him in, took him to the medic.

Four hours later his life came to an end. Not a word of complaint had come across his lips.

'You must not let them into the park!' he said.

And he calmly smoked a cigarette as if he was saying good-bye to his comrades before going on an extended leave. They were silently standing around him, watching this brave man slide into immortality . . .

Over his grave, the commander awarded him the Knight's Cross to the Iron Cross—as the first non-commissioned officer of the SS-Panzerdivision "Hitlerjugend". . .

And beyond his grave shines the quiet readiness of this absolute soldier.[16]

On the course of the fighting at II./26, which was in action to the left of the Pionierbataillon, only a short report by a combatant is available. Oberscharführer Paul Dargel of 6. Kompanie wrote:

The enemy tank attack had been repelled. The enemy tanks did not have a field of fire in the ravine. Two of them were knocked out by a Sturmmann with Panzerfausts. Sadly, Untersturmführer Lütschwager and Zugführer Claußen were killed on that day. I took a bullet in the lung. During the transport back to Paris, even the ambulances were attacked by fighter-bombers.[17]

The 5. and the 7. Panzerkompanie had been in ambush positions behind the sector of the Pionierbataillon until nightfall on 25 June. After the counterattack was broken off near Tessel-Bretteville, they tried to regain these positions. The Panzer IVs had been dug in there, well camouflaged, a field of fire had been cleared. The 7. Kompanie had been in position immediately west to the northern section of Cheux, able to control the road Fontenay-Caen. Now, enemy tanks were sitting there. The ambush positions of 5. Kompanie were located to the southwest, near le Haut du Bosq. Untersturmführer Willi Kändler reported:

Even as we approached, numerous enemy tanks of various sizes could be seen on the hill to our left. They had come from le Mesnil, pointing in the direction of Cheux. Before we could turn into our old position by the hedge, we became involved in a violent duel of the tank guns, with successes and losses. Cruising a few meters ahead of my Panzer, Untersturmführer Buchholz was standing in his turret. His Panzer took a direct hit, Buchholz's head was ripped off. Since a column of English tanks had already broken through toward Cheux, the Kompanie withdrew, fighting, for two or three hedge-bordered pasture squares to the south. We took up new positions on both sides of Route Départemental No. 83 (from Noyers to Cheux, Author). The platoons of Untersturmführer Porsch and of Untersturmführer Kunze took up positions north of Point 112 (400 meters southwest of the Ferme le Bosq, Author). I went into position with the remaining four or five Panzers of my Zug south of them, slightly staggered to the rear. As I recall, Oberscharführer Junge encountered, on the way to the new positions, Sherman tanks advancing in a southwesterly direction on a parallel path. At very close distance he knocked out five of them.[18]

As already mentioned, two Artillerieabteilungen were in position behind the sector of Regiment 26. The firing positions of I. Abteilung with 2. Batterie, self-propelled 10.5 cm field howitzers with six guns each, and of 3. Batterie, self-propelled 15 cm field howitzers, also of six guns each, were located, at the start of the attack, at the fringes of Cheux, approximately 500 meters southwest of the church. Since 25 June, 1. Batterie was attached to Kampfgruppe Wünsche to support its counterattack. During 26 June, the Abteilung had to withdraw to new firing positions northwest and west of Grainville. This was reported by the then orderly officer of the Regiment, Oberscharführer Max Anger.[19] The II. Abteilung with three batteries of six each light field howitzers 10.5 cm, pulled by tractors, was in position immediately southwest of le Haut du Bosq. The positions of the batteries had been wired and prepared for close combat. Oberscharführer Hans Hartmann of 5. Batterie reported on his experiences on 26 June:

> Our battery commander, Obersturmführer Kurzbein, had set up the observation post in a house in Cheux. Our firing position was located immediately to the right of the road Bretteville-Cheux. The pasture was bordered by high hedges on the left and by a row of trees on the right. We had dug an earth bunker to the right of the row of trees and covered it with heavy oak boards. A few hundred meters behind us, two anti-aircraft batteries were in position. They had shot down several Allied aircraft during the previous days.
>
> The battery officer was Oberscharführer Werner Nitsche. He was the only NCO in the firing position, there were no Zug leaders, the gunners were rank and file. It was for this reason that the commander had ordered me to the firing position although I had initially been scheduled as the forward observer.
>
> In the morning, our commander advised us that the observation post would be abandoned. Thus, we were on our own. I went to the soccer field in front of us and climbed onto a goal. Approximately four kilometers away, south of le Mesnil, I spotted an assembly of some twenty armored enemy vehicles. We started a fire attack with all four guns. It was so well aimed that the tanks dispersed in no time. Judging by the explosions, one tank must have taken a direct hit. As the vehicles pulled away, they stirred up so much dust that we could no longer observe anything.[20]

After the German counterattack had been broken off in the morning, the fighting also continued in the left sector of the Division. The English attack from the Tessel Woods, started at the same time as that of Kampfgruppe Wünsche, came to a halt after bitter fighting. The 4/7 Dragoon Guards (tanks) only advanced to the Bordel creek west of Tessel-Bretteville. This creek proved to be an obstacle to the tanks, except for a few spots. The 24th Lancers (tank unit), attacking to the right, managed to bring a few tanks across the creek near le Manoir, but it proved impossible for them to evade the fire from German Panzers (only I. Panzerabteilung was left) from the hedge-covered terrain on the eastern bank. The infantry battalion 1st Tyne Scots, accompanying the two tank units, was pinned down behind the creek by the Panthers and the securing positions of the Aufklärungs-abteilung.[21]

Since this attack out of the Tessel Woods from the west toward Rauray was stalled, the 49th Division ordered an immediate attack by the Sherwood Rangers Yeomanry, a third tank unit, from Fontenay along both sides of the road to Rauray, and to capture the town.[22] Its attack was accompanied by an infantry battalion, the 7th Duke of Wellington's. This attack took place in conjunction with that of parts of the 7th Royal Tanks which attacked past le Mesnil-Patry to the west and had been stopped by the mine field there for a long time. When the attack by the Sherwood Rangers started, the 6th Panzerkompanie had not yet returned to its ambush positions southeast of Fontenay. Unterscharführer Heinz Berner, who was the chief of the repair squad of 6. Kompanie, was waiting for his Kompanie. He wrote obout his experience:

> During the absence of the fighting unit, one Panzer and the repair squad remained behind under my command to secure the position. The Panzers had not been gone very long when the enemy tried to break into our position with infantry and tank support. Our Panzer took up the fight but had to withdraw under the enemy pressure. The repair squad, which also had to guard our Panzer against tank hunting parties, was pinned down by machine gun and rifle fire. Two men were wounded. When the pressure continued to increase, we had to abandon the Kompanie command post. During the attempt to drive off in the VW-Kübel, a rifle shot ripped the peaked cap from my head. I continued to wear the cap, as a good luck charm, until being critically wounded in Hungary.
>
> We had already reached the rear border of our assembly area when, virtually at the last minute, our fighting unit returned. It immediately went on the counterattack and cleared our assembly area again.[23]

Since morning, alarming reports had arrived at the Divisional command post from all corners, with the exception of Regiment 25. There, no attack had started and there were no preparations which would indicate any serious enemy plans. By noon, approximately the following picture had emerged: The positions in the sector St. Manvieu to east of Fontenay had been overrun. St. Manvieu, where the command post of I./26 was located, had been captured by an attack from the north and southwest. Some strongpoints were apparently still holding out. The 1. and 3. Kompanie, in position east and northeast of the village behind the Mue creek and adjacent to Regiment 25 on the right, were outside the attack sector of the Scots. The 9. Panzerkompanie (without one Zug), in position behind the Bataillon sector, could have probably repelled a tank attack on the Carpiquet airfield for the time. A counterattack on St. Manvieu, understandably demanded by Sturmbannführer Krause, would have led to destruction during the fighting in the town without infantry accompaniment. Contact to the Pionierbataillon had been lost when enemy tanks had tried to knock out the Bataillon command post. It was located on a small hill immediately south of the road Fontenay-Caen, one kilometer west of la Gaule. The enemy had pushed into Cheux with tanks and infantry. The supply units of the Pionierbataillon and Regiment 26 were still resisting there. There were no reports on II./26. Parts of II. Panzerabteilung had obviously stopped the attack by enemy tanks at and west of le Haut du Bosq. Their left flank, however, was threatened by enemy tanks attacking west of le Mesnil toward the south. Kampfgruppe Wünsche was successfully defending, so far, north and west of Rauray. As a consequence of the failures of his attacks on Rauray from the west and from the north out of the Tessel Woods, the enemy had not advanced further south. The danger of a breakthrough by enemy tanks thus existed mainly southeast of Cheux in the direction of the Odon crossing near Verson, or south of Tourville. The Division had no reserves of its own to prevent this. It moved the 15. (Aufklärungs-) Kompanie of Regiment 25 into action southeast of Cheux, but there were no Panzers available to support it. The general command was constantly informed on the situation and was requested to send reinforcements. Initially, one company of the Korps Tiger Abteilung was promised and moved to the area near Grainville, 2.5 kilometers south of Cheux. Later, Brigadeführer Kraemer, chief of staff of I. Panzerkorps advised that one company each of Panzers and assault guns from 21. Panzerdivision would be attached to the "HJ" Division. Their move into the Verson area was requested and promised.[24]

Even on the previous day, the general command had requested infantry reinforcements for action with the Panzer-Lehr-Division from the Armee. The Armee could only advise at noon on 26 June that the Heeresgruppe had approved infantry reinforcement for the Pz.-Lehr-Div. and ordered the attachment of Werferbrigade 7. Two battalions of the "LAH" had been released for the "HJ" Division, but they were still a long distance away.[25]

The enemy had moved the 29th Armoured Brigade of the 11th Armoured Division forward into the area north of Cheux around noon. It received orders from the Division to advance on Gavrus with the 2nd Battalion Fife and Forfar Yeomanry—FFY—(tank unit), and on Tourmauville with the 23rd Hussars (tank unit). The third tank unit, 3rd Battalion Royal Tank

Regiment, was to follow. The 2nd FFY kept to the west of Cheux and was involved in fighting with parts of II. Panzerabteilung before it crossed through the village. The situation was confused. The 23rd Hussars rolled through the center of the town, but were stopped by fire from anti-tank guns, and probably from artillery, as they were about to exit the village to the south. Both units were greatly impeded in their advance by the ruins of the village and the resistance which restarted time and again. The VIII Corps was convinced that the time was still unfavorable for an advance by the tank brigade. It ordered the 15th Division to bring the reserve brigade, 227th Highland Brigade, forward.[26] The anti-tank guns mentioned in the war diary of VIII Corps were likely Panzers of 5. and possibly 7. Panzerkompanie. The guns which had been in action in the front lines had long since been knocked out.

It was the mission of the 227th Infantry Brigade to capture the Odon river crossings. The 2nd Argyll and Sutherland Highlanders were scheduled, in accordance with the operational orders, to take the bridges near Gavrus and Tourmauville. It was hoped that this would succeed before dark on 26 June. Le Haut du Bosq had not yet been taken. Panzers and Panzer-grenadiers of the "HJ" Division were scattered northwest, west and southwest of this village in small fighting groups. They attacked time and again. For this reason, the Brigade sought to find a way through Cheux. The infantry advanced only very slowly under the fire of hidden Pioniers and Panzer-grenadiers. It was almost impossible for the tanks and carriers to make their way through the ruins. Before the 10th Highland Light Infantry, advancing on the right, could reach its assembly area south of le Haut du Bosq, it was stopped by fire from Panzers. The 2nd Gordon Highlanders, reinforced by a company of the 9th Royal Tanks, was advancing on the left. They came under violent fire from Panzers and machine guns as they reached Hill 100 south of Cheux. The road to Mondrainville runs across this hill. A number of tanks were knocked out, the infantry suffered losses. The battalion had lost contact with the left forward company which had broken through to Colleville at approximately 22.00 hours and had been temporarily encircled. The tanks retreated. The commander of the Gordons assembled whatever he could find of his battalion and formed a hedgehog defensive position on the hill south of Cheux. The battalion had suffered significant losses. Four officers had been killed, one was wounded.[27]

The "C"-Squadron 9th Royal Tanks had lost nine tanks.[28]

This attack by the 227th Brigade was repelled by the Aufklärungskom-panie of Regiment 25 of "HJ" Division and the two companies of Panzers and assault guns of 21. Panzerdivision which had arrived just in time.[29]

In the afternoon, the Divisional commander, Standartenführer Meyer, drove to the Aufklärungskompanie of Regiment 25. There, north of Mouen, was the First Orderly Officer of the Divisional staff, Obersturmführer Bern-hard Meitzel with an assault squad formed from members of the Divisional staff. They had got caught in the middle of an attack by the Gordons, the tanks of the 9th Royal Tanks and the 23rd Hussars. Meitzel recorded his fighting experiences in his diary in this way:

> I was on the ground next to my Divisional commander when, a few hundred meters away, the remains of the Aufklärungskompanie of his former Panzergrenadierregiment were squashed by British tanks and the accompanying infantry. We could not even help with artillery fire since we were out of ammunition. The Divisional commander knew everyone of these seventeen- to eighteen-year old soldiers who were fighting their last battle in front of us now. When I looked at the Standartenführer, I saw tears in his eyes. When we returned to the Divisional command post in Verson, we came across two British tanks. Messengers of the Divisional staff had knocked them out with Panzerfausts. The wrecks were sitting not even 200 meters from the command post. The Divisional staff had set up a hedgehog position.[30]

The attack by the tanks accompanying the Gordons was finally stopped by a single, unexpectedly appearing, 'Tiger'.

One of the young soldiers of the Aufklärungskompanie, Sturmmann and officer candidate Jochen Leykauff, experienced this battle and had the misfortune to be taken prisoner in a hopeless situation. He described his experiences:

> 26 June, in the afternoon. The 15. Kompanie is disengaging from the enemy along a shallow trench bordered by a bulky hedge. Over there is a tank assembly, on the other side, the flanking English position. After many jumps and a fall, I am alone. The rest of my squad, led by Boigh, has disappeared. First, I have to catch my breath. From behind, there is track noise, then burst of fire along the hedge. I jump into cover, press myself under some branches. Two, three small armored personnel carriers rattle past, a white, five-pointed star on the side wall. Suddenly, it is quiet, then, the howling of engines, automatic weapons fire. Then, quiet again. Rain is beginning to drop on the leaves. I crawl further in the direction of the withdrawal. To the right, a soldier in a camouflage jacket is on the ground, moaning quietly. Carefully, I pull him into cover, feeling blood. I look for his first aid pack, push tunic and shirt up on his back, put on a dressing. The bullet has exited at the level of his kidneys. I rip open my first aid pack as well. 'Thirsty', he says. I take off my helmet and set it in the rain, putting on my small camouflage cap. Tanks are coming closer, single and in groups. They are assembling to the left, not far away. Suddenly, it becomes very noisy in the

field bordered by the hedge. A light tank approaches at high speed and breaks through the bushes in front of us. We cannot stay here. Behind us, the hedge bends into a low meadow. Can we get there at dusk? Or even now, through the veils of haze? I tell him that I am going to scout for a better spot, and crawl from the cover.

A machine gun salvo rattles just above my head. I press into the furrow, crawl on. Again, the rattle and the ground is hit all around me. A flash through my brain: It's over! The fire comes as from above, tank machine gun. From the right, close, a shout comes through the rain: 'Hands up!' I press even further into the dirt. More fire, and again: 'Hands up!' An engine is being started, it howls. Noise from tracks, I spot the tank to the right. A soldier is watching me from the turret. I get up slowly, knowing that the end is near. The guy in the turret waves me off. I sense that they will shoot me in the back. I walk toward the tank, looking straight at the man in the turret. Standing below him, I say:

'A wounded comrade lies in the bushes over there!' The radio is cackling through the noise of the engine. A hatch opens in front of me. A man jumps out, pulls out his pistol. He rips open my ammunition pack, grips a magazine, looks at the points of the shells, throws it away. I ask: 'Do you make prisoners?' He points with the barrel of his pistol, I take off my belt. He will probably not shoot. He pushes me in the direction of the tank assembly. I stop" 'My comrade!' He pushes me with the pistol and I walk on, ashamed.

A man in a leather helmet, whom they address respectfully, is standing, half crouching, between two tanks and points his pistol, secured by a string, at me. English soldiers are standing in a circle around me, pistols, sub-machine guns, and carbines in their hands. A Major addresses me in German, I automatically reply in English. He jumps back when artillery shells explode. His index finger is on the trigger, I keep looking at it. He is not satisfied. 'Let's speak German to each other', he says. He asks: 'Where are your tanks?' This is a question I will hear time and again. I do not know. I proudly name the killed Kompanie commander.

I climb on an armoured car, sit down in front of the turret, holding on to the machine gun barrel. We roll through the rain. The commander addresses me. He had been working in Hamburg as a business man. We drive past infantry digging trenches. They look up in surprise, their equipment orderly piled next to them. They are wearing bulky oil skins.

Two short and sturdy men, bayonets fixed, take me further to the rear. The bayonets look like huge nails. We stumble cross-country. When shells howl toward us, they sometimes drop into the dirt and I keep standing. Or I drop down and they wave their weapons impatiently. We come to a dirt road on which a long column of tanks line up. 'Shermans', I say and they nod. This is the entrance to town, in the middle of the supply troops. A tall, fat soldier is walking over, the sleeve covered with chevrons, drunk. He pulls out his pistol: 'Fucking SS!' Immediately, the carbine barrel of one of my escorts hits him in the back. 'Snell', says one of them, and they push me on. I am handed over.

From the rear of a tank, a Colonel wearing a black beret, looks grimly down on me. I notice the small stick he carries. More questions. I am standing at ease. 'Attention!', the Colonel orders, and he is right. Dusk has come, we are waiting for a car. Around us, well-trained men in leather vests, rain coats and sweaters instead of the uniform pieces we are used to. I climb on the front seat next to a sergeant. The Englishman drives off at high speed, a cigarette in the corner of his mouth, calls me 'boy'.

We arrive in the darkness. I am standing between parked vehicles. A tall, slender soldier comes strolling over to me. He is a young officers, addresses me in German. Asks for my age and rank, and after our Panzers. He speaks in a reserved and friendly manner. many new things were ahead of me, he said. Besides, as a soldier, I would know that I did not have to divulge anything during interrogation. Then he leaves again.

I am led to a tent. Two NCOs are sitting at a table on which some kind of coal oil lamp is standing. My personal data is recorded, my pockets emptied. I cannot translate 'anti-poison pills' for them, and they push the plastic container carefully to the side. I am still wearing my ripped camouflage suit. My pay book and the watch, broken since the start of the invasion, remain on the table as I am led out and to a wire fence.

The gate is opened and I walk inside. They lock up behind me. I spot comrades standing in a group. Some are lying on the ground. I walk to the side in the rainy night. I bed down on the wet grass, putting my swollen hands in my pockets. I am cold. I roll on one side, pull up my knees and try to sleep.[31]

There was no prospect of re-gaining the old main line of defense with the remains of the over-run battalions and the few Panzers and assault guns of II. Panzerabteilung and 21. Panzerdivision, assembled near Mouen, and 1. Panzer-kompanie of the Tigerabteilung. Thus, the Division ordered, with approval from the Korps, the establishment of a new position along the line Marcelet-Hill southeast of Cheux-Rauray-Vendes.

The remains of the staffs of I./26, the 2. and 4. Kompanie, encircled at the command post in St. Manvieu, had been able to hold out there until the evening. An attempt in the afternoon by 1. Kompanie and the assault gun battery of 21. Panzerdivision, to break through to St. Manvieu from Marcelet, had broken down in the concentrated enemy artillery fire. The 181st Field Regiment, a light artillery unit of the 15th Division, had fired forty salvos ". . . as fast as the gunners could load."

The 44th Infantry Brigade had sent its reserve battalion, the 7th Battalion The King's Own Scottish Borderers, to St. Manvieu. It had arrived there near 17.00 hours. Subsequently, the Royal Scots Fusiliers, were pulled back. This battalion had lost four officers killed, among them two company commanders. The total losses of the battalion were twenty-one killed, 113 wounded and nine missing. During the night, the 7th Scottish Borderers were relieved by the 129th Infantry Brigade of the 43rd (Wessex) Division. During the brief period of action, the battalion had lost among others, one company commander.[32]

Since the I./26 had no prospects of being relieved, and since there was no contact with the Regiment or the Division, Sturmbannführer Krause ordered the remains, assembled around him, to break out during the night. Unterscharführer Heinrich Bassenauer took part. He wrote about it:

> After darkness fell we assembled for the break-out: at the point, Papa Krause, a huge figure and a shining fatherly example, followed by the rest of his Bataillon, including our wounded comrades and the prisoners. Unnoticed, we slipped through the English lines in a tall grain field, crossed the road Caen-Fontenay, and reached the Marcelet-Verson road, where we were welcomed by our own units. During the following day, we moved into new positions at the southern slope of the Carpiquet airfield.[33]

On the left wing of the "HJ" Division, at the Wünsche Kampfgruppe, the heavy fighting continued throughout the day. The men of III./26 and the attached Pionierzug repelled all attacks, often in conjunction with a counterattack together with Panzers of the 6. and 8. Kompanie and I. Panzerabteilung. In the afternoon, Wünsche had to let go 8. Kompanie of his Panzerregiment to support the companies of II. Abteilung in battle near Cheux. The northern front of the previous line could not be held against the constant pressure by the superior enemy. On the order of the Division, the Grenadiers, Pioniers, reconnaissance squads with their heavy weapons and the Panzers of 6. Kompanie and of the Zug of 9. Kompanie, in action there, were withdrawn to the area north of Rauray. The situation report of the Division noted:

> While I./SS-Panzerregiment 12, encircled southwest of Fontenay, fought its way south, III./SS-Panzergrenadier-regiment 26 and SS-Panzeraufklärungsabteilung 12 under SS-Sturmbannführer Olboeter

and SS-Sturmbannführer Bremer repelled all attacks by the superior enemy near Rauray.[34]

During the night, the Panzerregiment moved its command post, which had eventually been located in the front lines, to Grainville.

The British tank unit, The Sherwood Rangers, reported having reached its attack objective, Rauray, at 21.00 hours. This was an error. It was pulled back to Fontenay for the night. One company of tanks and the infantry battalion 7th Duke of Wellington's took over securing the road fork at the eastern exit from Tessel-Bretteville in its place. The 24th Lancers, not having advanced near le Manoir, had been pulled back to Fontenay to support the attack by the Sherwood Rangers, but had not been called in. They remained in the area north of Saint Pierre for the night, together with the 4/7 Dragoon Guards, the 12th KRRC and the forward command post of the 8th Armoured Brigade. They reported, as successes: three Tigers, two Panzer IVs, three Panthers, one Panzer of unknown type, and one self-propelled gun knocked out.[35] The real losses of German Panzers are not known. However, Tigers were not in action there at all.

The Kompanie commander, Hauptsturmführer Hans Siegel, reported on the actions of 8. Panzerkompanie, beginning in the afternoon of 26 June, in the area west and southwest of Cheux:

It is late afternoon. Four Panzer IVs, the only battle-ready ones of the Kompanie at the time, are being refuelled hastily northeast of Rauray, and filled with ammunition to the brim. The crews hardly find time for a sip from the canteen. The enemy has been pushing since the early morning hours, always with fresh forces. The faces are marked by the fighting. The Kompanie has been in continuous action for more than 24 hours.

Just as the ready-for-action reports from the individual units arrive, and they are to be sent forward again, Regimental commander Max Wünsche arrives. He orders the chief of 8. Kompanie, Siegel, to clear up a very recent enemy breakthrough southeast of Cheux through a counterattack with these four Panzers. The situation there is confused. Infantry to accompany the Panzers is not available. There is no time to be wasted. Anything further will be a reaction to the situation as it occurs, and is the responsibility of the chief of 8. Panzerkompanie, as the commander of these four Panzers.

A quick briefing of the crews, the chief's Panzer will be at the point. Then they mount. The engines howl, the hatches are pulled shut, barrels and turrets are swung into combat position. The last shouted good wishes from the Regimental commander are swallowed up by the clanking of Panzer tracks pulling ahead.

The first firing stop took place after only a few hundred meters. We fire upon targets we have spotted, armored vehicles already give off the well-known dark clouds of smoke. Staggered, and at full throttle, we cross a plain without any cover. Firing, we break into a large stand of trees at the bottom of the valley. Three carriers, innocently coming opposite, loaded with supplies and ammunition, are quickly knocked out. Across a small meadow in the woods, on the left of the path leading to Cheux, we cautiously advance to the forward line of trees on the enemy side. There, an embankment as high as a man, offers such cover that only the gun barrels and the machine guns top it. Everything below them is under complete cover. Ahead of us, a wide and slowly rising meadow lies wide open, leading to the enemy. Behind it—distance approximately 1,200 to 1,500 meters—the gabled roofs of Cheux. We stop here, the Panzers ready to fire.

The chief of 8. dismounts, together with his gunner. They cross through the small wooded area on the right while two other crew members, led by a commander, scout to the left. Initially, neither friend nor foe is found. Chief and gunner creep past the knocked-out carriers to an abandoned VW-Kübelwagen, belonging to the artillery of our Division. Further ahead, to the right, sit our own abandoned guns. Empty cartridges, dug-up dirt, no shells and no tractors—an eerie silence at the falling dusk. There—a bunker and voices—friend or enemy? The gunner gives cover, the chief jumps at the bunker and rips the door open, pistol at the ready, yelling: 'Password!' Instead, happy shouting from our own infantry men, out of ammunition, who have dug in there against the advancing enemy.

After returning to our own Panzer, the other scouting party, which had gone to the left, reports that parts of Regiment 26 were encountered on a hill approximately 500 meters further. They can, however, not link up with us since they do not have enough soldiers available. We find ourselves in the forward front line, without contact on the left or right. The enemy has withdrawn, probably to the southern fringe of Cheux. The breakthrough spot is closed, mission accomplished. It is getting dark.

The report on this to the Panzerregiment results in the order to hold this position and to haul back the remaining guns of our artillery behind the rail line by midnight, using a Panzer. This is done as heavy rain sets in and under a pitch-black sky. The gun crews are sitting exhausted inside the Panzer, weapons at the ready. The driver and radio operator are guarding outside, tarpaulin pulled over their heads, machine pistol stuck through the slit, to keep it out of the increasingly violent rain. There is radio silence.

The chief of 8. Panzerkompanie drives back to the Regimental staff and reports in person to Regimental commander Wünsche in Grainville. The room is darkened, flickering light from burnt-down candles illuminates the map on the table, over which the commander is leaning, pensively. Cupboards have been pulled in front of the windows as protection from shrapnel. Orderlies and officers are hanging, exhausted, across the chair backs or are bedded down on make-shift resting places. A cup of coffee is being offered, without a sound. It tastes good. The time is just before midnight.

Then the door creaks, and into the unusual quiet after the din of battle we are used to, an Obersturmführer stumbles, saluting hastily. He is the Zug leader of an anti-tank gun unit in position along a rail line. Out of breath, he reports engine and track noise from approaching tanks!

A questioning look from the commander to his Panzer commander—'Calm down, these are our own Panzers from 8. Kompanie, bringing back the guns!—Siegel, you drive forward again, keep your eyes open—good luck!'

As I arrive at the position, ammunition and provisions are being brought in. The commander of the Artillerie-abteilung, Sturmbannführer Schöps, is there also. He thanks the chief of 8. Kompanie after the last of the guns is in safety. He has personally directed this transport from the front lines and is about to leave. His VW is sitting in a narrow pass, bordered along both sides by bushes. The car is pointing in the direction of the enemy, about thirty-five meters behind the chief Panzer, which is also in the way. A few of those standing around lift the Kübelwagen and turn it by 180 degrees on the narrow path. At that very moment, suddenly, a shout: 'Hands up!' Several figures jump from the bushes at the surprised group which jumps apart and seeks cover behind the chief's Panzer. Only the chief of the Pz.-Kp. jumps, in a reflex movement, at the attackers who are already firing their automatic weapons from their hips. On the run, he grabs the one closest to him by the throat with his left hand. With his right, he pushes the gun barrel down and away, and throws the man to the ground, falling at the same time. During the fall, the fixed, three-cornered bayonet penetrates the Panzer chief's leather pants. While the attacked man, lying on the ground, fires the whole magazine through the pant leg, without being able to hit anything since the barrel is being pushed away, the left hand of the attacker throttles his neck. The clip is soon fired and the Englishman gasps 'Help me—help me'. Thereupon, a figure approaches the two men wrestling on the ground, pulls the trigger and fires from above. 'Oh—I'm wounded', and with this his resistance ebbs, he lets go. Only then, the German remembers his own pistol, rips it from his pant pocket. He cocks it with his right hand, the left is still grasping the neck of the man lying beneath him, and fires the whole clip of the 08 in the direction of the dark figure which is disappearing as quietly as it showed up. Only now can the Panzer commander free himself from the enemy bayonet sticking in his pant leg. He gets up, leaving the other one lying on the ground, not moving—shot by his own comrade who hit the wrong man in his panic.

Suddenly, there is a ghostly silence. Only the rain rustles in the tops of the deciduous trees above us. We can feel our hearts beating in our temples. 'Back to my own Panzer!', it flashes through the chief. Ten meters from it, a figure crouches on its knees on the ground, supported by its arms—the artillery commander. He lets his head hang down and gasps quietly. Kneeling next to him, the Panzer chief tries to lift him with his right hand. But the man kneeling on the left slides away in a slippery puddle—blood! He drags the wounded into cover under his Panzer and leaves him there for the time being.

But where are the others? There is no sound, no movement, only the rain! A sprint across the wet meadow to the other Panzer, approximately seventy meters further on the left. The gunner is sent to the right, the loader must look after the wounded. The Panzer crews must be alerted. On the way to the Panzer on the left, another clip is pushed into the pistol. What a bright idea! Two figures wearing flat helmets are standing on the Panzer, clearly visible against the night sky. As if paralyzed, the chief stands next to the Panzer to the side and watches as the figures are pulling on the turret hatch which is obviously being held down from the inside. There is an almost rhythmical metallic banging—up-down, up-down! 'Hand grenade!' one of them hisses to the other in English. Then the tension eases: Just a moment, friends! And quietly, as so often practiced on the firing range, the hand is lifted with the pistol, one bullet each, that is enough, the turret is clear! Then, suddenly, a salvo from a German sub-machine gun rattles across the turret, sparks flying. The Panzer provides sufficient cover from it to the chief. The salvo came from ahead! It was our own guard on the outside, only awakened from his lethargy by the two pistol shots. The crew inside the Panzer had been surprised by the scouting party creeping up. No wonder: rain—exhaustion—midnight!

Suddenly, the engine of the chief's Panzer, sitting by the path, howls. Screeching, someone tries to put it in gear. That cannot be the driver. The chief is about to jump there. He assumes his Panzer was captured. But then, the Panzer pulls ahead. Not into the direction of the enemy, not to the rear, it turns and drives to the center of the meadow. It stops after a few meters, the engine is turned off, it's over. There is no movement, only the rustle of the rain in the deep dark night. Pistol at the ready, jumping to the Panzer, from the rear and under it. First of all, cover! And then crawling forward to the exit hatch in the hull, the stomach sliding across the dripping wet grass. If he starts out again and turns on the spot! Cautious knocking signals with the pistol grip against this hatch are initially not answered. Then—Password! 'It's us!—There was trouble over there and since the chief was not with us, we got away from the road!'

'Where's the gunner?'—'Not here either!'

He reports in after about half an hour: 'Back from captivity!' What had happened? On the way to the right he had been grabbed, without a sound, by the straggling enemy scouting party. Not a sound—a smack into the back with the rifle butt was enough, his hands ripped upward on the back, led away! As they were approaching the enemy position, giving light signals with a flashlight, a machine gun covered the returnees with salvos. This caused the two Englishmen to jump into cover, and with them, our gunner. But he jumped into the small streamlet, rolled up like a ball and remained lying motionless in the water. 'God damn it! Where's our prisoner?' 'Where are you?' Again, they waved their flashlight in the bushes, causing more covering fire, hit the ground again, and finally took off. This allowed our gunner to return unharmed, even if his arm was worn out and he had a pain in the back. But he was so exhausted that the chief exchanged him for a messenger who had just arrived, and sent him back. The messenger was taken into the Panzer.

The enemy, probably alerted by the guns being pulled out and suspecting a Panzer assembly, had obviously withdrawn. Order is quickly restored. The artillery commander is dead. He bled to death from an artery wound, as it was established later. He is taken back by his men, who are also wounded. The Panzer crews are uninjured and fully combat-ready. The situation remains as tense as before. After this enemy reconnaissance, an attack can be expected in the morning hours. This, the chief reports back, and personally informs his neighbor on the left, probably II./Rgt. 26. The gap still exists, it cannot be closed.[36]

The order by the Division to move to the new line further south had not reached the Pionierbataillon by way of Regiment 26. The Bataillon commander, Sturmbannführer Siegfried Müller, decided to break out with his staff during the night in pouring rain. This breakout is described in the report by Untersturmführer Richter, which has already been quoted.

Everything is all right until 21.00 hours. Then, suddenly, voices, very close. The tension is there again. The voices abate, lucky once again. All of a sudden, a Tommy stands in front of the entrance. 'Hey, boys!' he shouts. The wounded men give a start, there are noises in the bunker. The Tommy fires. Then he rips the blanket from the entrance and throws hand grenades. With the explosion, he jumps into the bunker, a knife flashing in his fist. The commander fires, once, twice. The Tommy sinks to the ground, dead. Track noise, a tank sits in front of the other entrance. A machine gun fires into the entrance, hand grenades explode. Miraculously, the men suffer only minor injuries. Tommy demands that we surrender, a discussion for and against begins among the men. The commander orders resistance to the last man. A man loses his nerve and surrenders. With the help of this soldier, the Englishman repeatedly demands our surrender. There is no question of giving up. The man shouts at us: 'Boys, surrender. There is no way out, forty tanks are sitting out here. If you don't come out, they'll smash the bunker.' Several men want to give up, but the commander admonishes them with a few short words. Everything is all right, the attitude of the men is restored. Hand grenades are dropped into the bunker. Tommy sends our man forward, behind him an Englishman with a sub-machine gun. The Englishman fires, some of our men are wounded again. One of our men fires from the bunker. Frightened, Tommy drops his sub-machine gun and runs off. Then, the tank pulls back and fires a few shells from its gun on the bunker. Suddenly, the man who had wanted to surrender reports back and apologizes to the commander, stating that he wants to fight on. All is back in order. Hours of tension follow. A bottle of champagne is being handed around. The minutes only crawl by, there is no new attack. The commander asks for his steel helmet and puts it on. All are determined, ready for battle and the last fight. Rain sets in again, darkness falls.

The breakout is ordered for 24.00 hours. The men are ready, the commander covers. At exactly 24.00 hours the crew of nine men leaves the bunker. Minutes of extreme tension follow. Will the enemy notice us or not ? The commander is at the point, pistol in one hand, compass in the other. We want to reach our own lines again, direction south. Time and again, the point has to stop, the wounded cannot keep up. Every foxhole is searched, the enemy could be inside. And it rains and rains, we are wet through and through after only a few minutes. Now and then, an English signal flare lights up the sky and we press into the ground. We have been going for four hours already and still have not reached our own lines. Then, a figure in front of us. The commander crawls around it and then shouts: 'Hallo, Password!' The figure disappears, does not answer. Again, extreme tension, followed by muted shouts. We hear: 'Untersturmführer Richter, over here!' The figure comes up, not a Tommy, but one of our NCOs [Unterscharführer, later Oberscharführer, Peter Mathoni of the Pionier reconnaissance squad, he was awarded the Iron Cross I]. We all catch our breath.

Ahead of us, a hedge and tall trees. Next to us, tank tracks in the ground everywhere. The commander sends two men ahead. They soon return and report: 'English voices everywhere by the hedge'. But we move on, the men creeping from hedge to hedge. Then, sharp silhouettes ahead of us. Tanks? We look more closely. Yes, tanks! We detour again.

Daylight has come. We are located between two British tank assemblies. It is useless to push on. Again, a guard ahead of us, no question, an Englishman. Exhausted, wet through and through, we lie down in a ditch, camouflage ourselves and fall asleep. We want to start out again in the evening. Then, twenty minutes later, tank noises, very close. We are startled, a tank gun fires. The commander looks up, 'Panzers, German Panzers', he shouts. Yes, they are really German Panzers. Delivered and laughing, we run toward them. Half an hour later we arrive at the command post of Regiment 26.[37]

Untersturmführer Richter supplemented this report later:

Only nine men took part in the breakout. The two seriously injured were totally exhausted and could not be transported. They had been looked after as well as we could and remained behind, with their agreement. As far as I know, one of them was an artillery man. I do not know his name. He was a brave young man. The other was Sturmmann Thile from Hamburg. He, too, was brave and patient, one of my best men in the bridge-laying squad.

When the Pionierbataillon was located in the Nienburg-Liebenau area in autumn of 1944, I received information from the hospital that he had been exchanged as a seriously wounded, and that one of his legs had been amputated. He was awarded the wound medal in silver and the Iron Cross II in hospital.[38]

After nightfall, the enemy stopped his attacks. As already described, night and rain made it possible for the encircled smaller or larger groups of the "HJ" Division to make their way to the German lines, more or less unmolested by the enemy. They were incorporated, as far as they were still combat-ready, into the newly set up line Marcelet-Hill southeast of Cheux-Rauray-Vendes. This line consisted, especially in the central sector, of a chain of dispersed strongpoints without any depth. It could not withstand a renewed strong attack, in particular of strong tank forces. The Division stated in its situation report:

> While strong enemy tank forces advanced in the area northeast of Norrey until 20.00 hours (fifty-three enemy tanks were counted), the remains of SS-Pi.-Btl. 12, of SS-Pz.-Gren.-Rgt. 26 and the SS-Pz.-Aufkl.-Abt. 12, and in particular SS-Pz.-Rgt. 12 under the command of SS-Obersturmbannführer Wünsche, repelled all enemy attacks. After all these crises had been overcome, the new main line of defense was in our hands in the evening of 26.6.1944, despite the weak available forces.
>
> During the fighting of the day, at least 50 enemy tanks were knocked out by Panzers and Pak. It cannot be determined how many tanks were destroyed in close combat and by mines.
>
> Our own losses of Panzers, and in particular of Panzergrenadiers, are high. SS-Pz.-Pi.-Btl. 12 must be regarded as being wiped out. The extent of the extremely heavy losses of SS-Pz.-Gren.-Rgt. 26 cannot yet be determined. The II./SS-Pz.-Art.-Rgt. 12, encircled south of Cheux, which had been fighting on with determination in both an artillery and infantry mode, could be relieved in the course of the night and take up new positions. During this operation, the Abteilung commander, SS-Sturmbannführer Schöps, was killed.
>
> The Panzergrenadiers, Pioniers and parts of the artillery fought in the breakthrough area until their own total destruction.
>
> Especially distinguished were:
>   SS-Obersturmbannführer Wünsche,
>   SS-Sturmbannführer Olboeter,
>   SS-Sturmbannführer Bremer,
>   SS-Sturmbannführer Krause,
>   SS-Hauptsturmführer Ruckteschel,
>   SS-Hauptsturmführer Siegel,
>   SS-Unterscharführer Dürr, 4./SS-Pz.-Gren.-Rgt.26.
>
> The Division expects that the enemy will renew his attack on 27.6.1944 from the Cheux—St. Manvieu—Norrey area, despite his high losses, in order to capture Caen.
>
> The Division will defend its positions using all available forces.
>
> Combat-ready are:
>   30 Panzer IVs,
>   17 Panzer Vs,
>   233 armored personnel carriers, armored cars, -armored artillery observation vehicles,
>   14 heavy Pak.
>
> Signed: Meyer SS-Standartenführer

Using the casualty lists, the losses of those taking part in the defensive fighting of 26 June can be determined. The following table shows them:

Unit	Killed			Wounded			Missing		
	Officers	NCOs	Men	Officers	NCOs	Men	Officers	NCOs	Men
R.E.26	-	-	17	3	6	40	-	1	22
I./26	-	-	6	-	5	18	-	5	35
II./26	1	-	14	-	5	21	2	1	57
III./26	-	2	6	-	4	19	-	-	-
Pi.Btl.	-	6	12	1	1	21	1	14	266
A.A.12	-	1	4	2	-	16	-	-	6
Pz.Rgt.	-	4	7	5	9	28	-	-	-
A.R.12	2	-	6	-	2	24	1	-	1
Total	3	13	72	11	32	187	4	21	387

The total losses were 88 killed, 230 wounded and 412 missing. This amounted to a total of 730 losses.

The general command was not in any doubt about the threatening situation in the sector of the "HJ" Division. For the Panzer-Lehr-Division, the day had been relatively quiet. The enemy had undertaken "numerous reconnaissance drives, supported by artillery. . .", but they had all been beaten back. A breakthrough near Château de Cordillon (1.5 kilometers north-west of Hottot) had been cleared up, partly through hand-to-hand combat. The report for 26.6.1944 of the Pz.-Lehr-Div. continued:

> The line of Divisional positions offers the enemy the opportunity of a push into the deep flanks of the Division. Based on this it is requested:
> a) to allow the 12. SS-Pz.-Div., after clearing up the breakthroughs, to link up at the northern edge of the Tessel Woods and
> b) to arrange for 2. Pz.-Div. to strengthen the right wing.
> The Division does not have reserves available to counter these possible encircling attacks.[39]

This conclusion is surprising. In the Divisional order of the Pz.-Lehr-Div., issued on 25.6.1944 for 26 June, it is stated under Item 2.):

> Pz.Gren.Lehr-Rgt. 901 with attached Pz.Pi.Btl.130 and one company Pz.Gren.Rgt. 192, as well as units of the Pz.Lehr-Rgt. 130, to be

brought in, will attack from the area southeast of Juvigny and will capture . . .

. . .

c) I./Pz.Gren.Lehr-Rgt. 901 is to be moved to the supply base for refitting.

In the "Additional order to the Divisional order of 25.6.44" it was stated:

1.) On the order of the Korps, the counterattack to clear the gap is to be discontinued.

. . .

4.) Pz.Pi.Btl. 130 is to be removed from the sector of Pz.Gren.Rgt. 901 during the night from 26 to 27 June, and to be made available to the Division.

5.) Panzer-Lehr-Rgt. 130 will secure the sector of the Division against tanks, concentrating on the right sector.

To achieve this, one Abteilung is to be shifted into the area of Pz.Gren.Lehr-Rgt. 901. A second Abteilung is to be held in readiness so that it can be shifted quickly to the right wing.

6.) Pz.Jg.Lehr-Abt. 130 will take on tank hunting duties in the sector of the Gerhard Gruppe (group).

The situation report of 21. Panzerdivision for 26.6.1944 reports that it ". . . had again handed over two weak companies [Panzergrenadiers] to the Panzer-Lehr-Division".[40]

The Divisional orders of the Pz.-Lehr-Div. indicate that its Pionierbataillon was not in action on 25 June and that it was available again in the evening of 26 June. At that time, the Divisionsbegleitkompanie (escort company) of the "HJ" Division was attached to the Pz.-Lehr-Div. It was in action on the front line north of Sermentot where it had relieved two companies of the Pz.Gren.-Lehr-Rgt. on 23 June. The "HJ" Division had no infantry available to close the gap southeast of Cheux in even a make-shift fashion.[41]

At 20.10 hours, the chief of staff of I. SS-Panzerkorps, Brigadeführer Kraemer, reported to the Ia of 7. Armee on the situation:

Enemy breakthrough between St. Manvieu-Tessel-Bretteville to the south. Two hours ago, the spearheads were in Grainville. Our own units are still located to both sides of Cheux.

If new forces are not brought up tonight, a breakthrough on both sides of Cheux cannot be prevented.

The forward units of 1. SS-Panzerdivision are located in the St. Germain area, however, without fuel. Werferbrigade 7, with one Abteilung, can be put into action on 27.6.

Ia stated that new forces are not available. Infantry, on the advance at this time, will only arrive in the Villers-Bocage area two nights later. It cannot be expected before that. The I. SS-Panzerkorps is to attempt to get help through 2. Pz.-Div.[42]

One hour later, the supreme commander of 7. Armee, Generaloberst Dollmann, spoke with Feldmarschall Rommel and described the threatening situation to him. He suggested using II. SS-Panzerkorps in a counterattack. The Feldmarschall demanded that an encirclement of 12. SS-Panzerdivision and of 21. Panzerdivision of the Heer had to be prevented at all costs. He approved action by the II. SS-Panzerkorps with the objective of attacking the enemy advancing to the south and east. Since the Korps had not yet arrived, he approved a suggestion by the Armee to put into action immediately a Panzerabteilung of 2. Panzerdivision of the Heer and a Kampfgruppe of the 2. SS-Panzerdivision.[43]

Brigadeführer Kraemer advised the Ia of the "HJ" Division that a Panzer Kampfgruppe of the 2. Panzerdivision and a Regimental Kampfgruppe would be brought in. They would attack the enemy flank near Cheux across the line Noyers-Rauray. The Ia requested that these Kampfgruppen should, at all cost, establish contact early with the Wünsche Kampfgruppe, or with him if they were attached to the Division, in order to be briefed on the latest situation and receive their orders. This was promised. Until the arrival of these reinforcements then, the "HJ" Division would have to beat off the expected enemy attack, with the objective of breaking through, using its own, totally insufficient forces. The arrival of units of the "LAH" could only be expected on 28 June, that of II. SS-Panzerkorps only on 29 June.

Brigadeführer Kraemer had moved his command post from Baron-sur-Odon (four kilometers southwest of Verson) 2.5 kilometers to the south. It had come under artillery fire. He requested that the Division move its command post further to the rear as well. Standartenführer Meyer and the Ia stated that this was completely impossible under the present circumstances. The overtaxed troops had to have the impression that the Divisional command had confidence in the further development and was not giving up. Kraemer finally agreed but ordered that all measures were to be taken to ensure that contact with the Korps command post would be maintained.

The following enemy situation existed at nightfall on 26 June: The 46th Brigade of the 15th Division had captured Cheux. However, some individual German squads were still fighting there, preventing an unmolested march through the town. The 227th Brigade had, for the time being, set up defensive positions between Cheux and le Haut du Bosq and on Hill 107 south of Cheux. The 44th Brigade was located in the area around la Gaule and St. Manvieu and was to be relieved by the 129th Brigade of the 43rd Armoured Division in the course of the night.

The 11th Armoured Division was assembled with the 29th Armoured Brigade immediately north of Cheux and with the 4th Armoured Brigade in the area Norrey-le Mesnil. The 159th Infantry Brigade was located further to the rear, near Secqueville (four kilometers north of Norrey).

The 214th Infantry Brigade of the 43rd Division had been ordered to advance into the Cheux area from the Rucqueville area (9.5 kilometers north of Fontenay) at 01.00 hours on 27 June. The 130th Infantry Brigade, located behind it, was to advance to Bretteville and relieve the 8th Canadian Infantry Brigade by noon on 27 June. It, in turn, was scheduled for an attack on Carpiquet.

Assembled for the attack on 27 June, apart from the 15th (Scottish) Division with attached 31st Tank Brigade, and having not yet been in action, were two tank brigades and four infantry brigades. Facing them in the Marcelet-Grainville sector were, from the "HJ" Division, the worn-out remains of I./26, II./26 and the left-over squads of Pionierbataillon 12, II. Panzerabteilung (without 6. Kompanie), a weak Tiger company, a weak Panzer company, and an assault gun company of 21. Pz.-Div. On the western wing, with the Wünsche Kampfgruppe, the I. Panzerabteilung, the III./26, the Aufklärungsabteilung and parts of the Regimentskompanie 26 were tied down by the 49th Division.

The war diary of VIII Corps summons up the result of the first day of its offensive in this manner:

All units (except the 3rd Royal Tanks) were in action for the first time. The majority of the officers and NCOs gathered their first battle experiences. All reports indicate that the units were well led and that the troops fought bravely, skillfully and daringly. They were facing an enemy who fought, with fanatic determination, in a terrain which he knew well and had prepared for the defense. The broken terrain and inaccurate maps made orientation difficult . . . causing first reports to indicate greater progress than had in reality been the case.

The broken terrain was to the advantage of the defenders and the enemy made full use of this advantage. The fighting was mostly carried out at short distances. . . . The enemy was holding his positions and let us pass when he was not directly attacked, overwhelmed or overrun. He only showed up when he detected promising targets or had himself been spotted. There were numerous nests of resistance which had to be fought long after the attack objectives had been reached, in the forward as well as the rear areas. . . . It was remarkable that, in all cases, these nests of resistance fought until the crews had been killed or the positions captured.

When there were indications of a breakthrough in a narrow sector, both flanks were open and the broken terrain again helped the enemy. He missed no opportunity to harass our flanks. There were many examples of enemy Panzers being dug-in, and for each of these positions there was an alternate position. These positions had been carefully chosen and prevented any close approach.

The bad weather prevented the air support to the Corps, which it would otherwise have had for its operation.[44]

Sturmmann Jochen Leykauff captured the desperate fighting of the Aufklärungskompanie of the SS-Panzergrenadierregiment 25 in the Mouen area of 26 June 1944 in a poem. It is located here at the end of this report on the hard day of battle.

26 June 1944, afternoon—
The Kompanie assembles to the left—
The position can no longer be held—
Grenadiers cling to the rocky trench.
Mortar shells explode in the tree tops.
Heavy machine guns saw through the position.
Tanks break through,
roll right across the trench,
here, now,
smash through the hedges.
Explosions all around.
The last Panzerfaust whistles off.
A few Shermans sit
and give off smoke.
We Grenadiers have no heavy weapons.
We cling to our carbines.
The position can no longer be held—
Kompanie—
assemble to the left.
'Destroy the remaining weapons', he says to me.
Boys under steel helmets,
jumping past,
from the right wing.
Explosions.
Our squad's machine gunner,
bleeding from ripped camouflage gear.
A noisy racket.
In the back of the trench, steel slabs,
semicircle,
explosions just ahead of our muzzles.
Shouts—
Two carbine locks,
ripped open,
away, across the hedge.
One is crawling down the ditch,
quiet.
Emptiness on the right.

No-one left. Are they coming? No-one left.
Are they already advancing?
Empty ditch.—
The position can no longer be held—
Nothing is behind me.
Must not lose contact!
Explosions.
A terrible racket!
What a choice:
remain in the empty ditch,
but fire, along it—
or to the right,
to be seen by the machine guns—
or on the left,
in front of the spitting monsters—
I can see the tanks, not the machine guns,
so, out of the ditch to the right,
up through the hedge—
and I am among thick branches,
blackberry branches.
Jumping deeper into it,
falling,
thicket of branches,
as wide as two men are tall,
and along the ditch,
but offering me cover.
Entangled.
Explosion.
Jump—fall—
becomes the routine.
Up, and jump across branches,
carbine crosswise
in front of the chest,
falling.
Working forward, piece by piece.
Camouflage gear rips,
bleeding hands on the carbine,
in front of the face.
Kompanie
assembles to the left.
I can't see anyone.
The position cannot be held any longer—
Over there,
on the left,

someone is lying;
two men are on their knees.
The Kompanie commander!
I have to get there.
Blood from the heel on the boot.
We grab him.
He curses and yells
through the explosions.
We drag him along the ditch,
in front of the muzzles.
He shouts at me:
'Get rid of your bloody rifle—
get a real hold on me!'
I grab him with both hands.
Further,
along the ditch,
the terrain drops off,
hedges are jutting.
There—tall and calm,
stands Boigh,
others are lying on the ground,
catching their breath.
The Kompanie commander
at our feet.
Boigh takes over the rest,
the chin-strap under his nose,
machine pistol under his long arm,
muzzle pointing down.
The position could not be held any longer—
Vehicles,
over there in the grain field,
smashed.
Among them, Panzers.
Flixeder's bright, sharp voice,
to me:
'Thrown the rifle away already?!'
Boigh standing next to me,
hands me his machine pistol.
Pick up the wounded—Lets go!
Explosions roar.
We have no contact at all.
Back.—
Position abandoned—

CHAPTER 3.4

'EPSOM'—the Second Day of the Offensive by the VIII (British) Corps, Breakthrough by the Enemy to the Odon River and Establishing a Bridgehead near Tourmauville. Abandoning Rauray and Moving to a New Position north of Brettevillette on 27 June 1944

The enemy did not continue his attack during the night from 26 to 27 June 1944. This enabled the stragglers of the "HJ" Division to make their way back to their own lines and to reinforce the positions along the new line to the rear, as much as their exhaustion and the rainy weather allowed. One must really speak of a line here, since there was no depth to the main battle field, apart from the positions of the heavy infantry weapons and of the artillery. The backbone of the position was formed by the thirty battle-ready Panzer IVs and seventeen Panzer Vs of the Division, together with the Panzer IVs and the assault guns of the two companies of 21. Panzerdivision, whose strength is unknown. The Korps-Tiger-Abteilung, at this time, had 18 Tigers which were concentrated and in action throughout the Korps sector. Approximately 6 of them probably fought in the Verson—Grainville sector.[1] Most of the combat-ready heavy anti-tank guns were located in the sector of Regiment 25 north and northwest of Caen.

Further support was provided by the Flaksturmregiments 2 and 4 (anti-aircraft assault troops) of the III. Flak-Korps of the general of the anti-aircraft artillery Pickert, in as far as they were in position in the central sector, mostly south of the Odon river. These Flak positions cannot be defined as anti-tank barriers, as often depicted in the war historical literature of the other side. The Flak was effective in self-defense against enemy tanks at short and medium distances for only a short time. At long distance, across open terrain, the 8,8 cm guns could be spotted, by their high barrel elevation, immediately after opening fire and could be fought effectively by tanks, artillery and fighter-bombers. The Flak's major significance lay in firing at airborne targets and ground shelling from covered, camouflaged, positions.

One Abteilung of Werferregiment 83 of Oberstleutnant Böhme took up fire positions in the course of 27 June in the area south of Verson. However, it cannot be determined when it was ready to open fire.

The British VIII Corps had not reached its objective on 26 June. Thus, it ordered the 15th Division, supported by the 29th Armoured Brigade (tanks) of the 11th Armoured Division, and two units of the 31st Tank Brigade to go on the attack again at 03.00 hours on 27 June. The objective was to capture the Odon river crossings. From out of the bridgeheads, the 11th Armoured Division, as originally planned, was to capture the Evrécy—Esquay area in order to subsequently form a bridgehead across the Orne river.

The plan, in detail, was:

The 10th Battalion The Highland Light Infantry of the 227th (Highland) Infantry Brigade will attack on the west together with tanks of the 31st Tank Brigade. They will capture the Odon crossings near Gavrus. Start of the attack at 04.45 hours;

the 2nd Battalion The Argyll and Sutherland Highlanders will attack to the east, with tanks and as previously scheduled, and will cross the Odon south of Tourville. Start of the attack at 05.30 hours;

the 29th Armoured Brigade of the 11th Armoured Division will support the attack by the 227th Infantry Brigade,

the 159th Infantry Brigade will advance via the Odon crossings and establish bridgeheads, as soon as the first tank units have crossed the Odon river.[2]

The 49th Infantry Brigade, adjacent to, and west of, the VIII Corps, ordered the continuation of the attack for 27 June, with a concentration in the eastern section of the 70th Infantry Brigade. The attack objective of the day was Noyers. It was to be reached in four stages:

Stage 1: Rauray, unless it had already been captured in the evening of 26 June;

Stage 2: Capture of Brettevillette;

Stage 3: Capture of Hill 124, 2 km northwest of Noyers, and

Stage 4: Noyers.

To support the attack by the 70th Brigade: 8th Armoured Brigade (tanks) with a tank unit. Fire support by concentrated fire from 4 field regiments, 4 medium regiments, 1 heavy regiment, for a total of nine artillery units.

The neighbors: The 49th Reconnaissance Regiment will maintain contact with the neighbor to the east, the 15th Division. The 146th Infantry Brigade will attack to the west of the 70th Brigade and capture Monts. The 147th Brigade, having fought in Fontenay, will assemble in the area around Fontenay as a reserve and be held in readiness.[3]

In the morning of 27 June, when the 10th Highland Infantry (10HLI) had reached its starting positions for the attack on Gavrus by way of Grainville, the terrain was under fire from German machine guns and mortars. It suffered losses and did not advance further. It reported being under attack by four Tigers from an orchard southwest of Cheux. At 07.00 hours, reports arrived that the company on the right had been encircled by Panzers and that one of the Panzers had advanced to within 150 yards (130 meters) of the Battalion command post. Later, the 10HLI again attempted to cross its 'starting line'. Again, it came under heavy fire and suffered losses. It withdrew to its starting positions and was pinned down there throughout the day.[4] The battalion suffered 112 losses.[5]

The four "Tigers" mentioned were four Panzer IVs of Hauptsturmführer Siegel and his 8. Kompanie. They had taken up positions immediately to the north of the narrow creek bed of the Ruisseau de Salbey behind a hedge, interspersed with trees, along both sides of the road from Cheux to Grainville. Siegel reported on the events of the late night hours and the repulsion of an attack by the 10HLI:

> At approximately 04.00 hours, the Panzer commander once again proceeds, alone, to the neighbor on the left. There is no contact to the right, after the artillery, too, has been withdrawn. After some 300 meters he encounters the first of the guards, covered by a tarpaulin, asleep along the ditch. It does not look any different in the Bataillon command post, set up in a bunker. They are all asleep, exhausted. On his way back the Panzer commander tries to wake up the men, to cheer them up. Regarding a possible attack, he replies that our Panzers are sitting over there, and they will look after it! Just before arriving at the Panzer position, the enemy artillery 'blessing' sets in. Shell after shell comes howling in, whistling frighteningly across our heads, exploding behind us. All of them wide—fortunately. Those exploding in the tree tops are more dangerous, but the wet soil swallows most of it. Fountains of dirt and rock combine to form a macabre curtain.
>
> Even from a distance, working his way through the barrage of howling shells, seeking cover time and again, the commander, approaching his Panzers, notices that these were suddenly pulling to the rear one at a time. He races after them—what are they doing? They are already pushing up on the back slope, they will be spotted by the enemy at any moment now. Finally, he is spotted and his gestures, demanding a stop, are understood. The commander was gone. The men in his Panzer believed that he would not return. The crew decided to get away from the artillery fire. The other Panzers joined the withdrawal movement since they received no orders to do otherwise. This, conversely, reinforced the action of the leaderless crew of the command Panzer. The Panzers are ordered back into their starting positions. They arrive there just in time as an infantry attack begins from the heights south of Cheux, accompanied by tanks which are, however, still holding back.
>
> They let the attack approach them frontally. Fire only from machine guns, not from the Panzer guns, so as not to betray the presence of Panzers prematurely. Open fire only at the commander's orders. We let them come close and then hammer, at short distance, concentrated fire from four machine guns at the massed attackers who are anxiously firing bullets into the terrain, without aiming. Experience has shown that our tactic works, and the conse-

quence here is, too, that they run back in panic, right under the salvos from our machine guns. We open fire from our Panzer guns only on the tanks attacking with the second wave. Again, we achieve full success, without losses of our own. The crews bail out in panic from burning and exploding tanks. The rest of them turn away and, with them, the infantry disappears behind the hills.

In the meantime, the sun is climbing higher. The chief sends back a short report, requests ammunition and asks for reinforcements to secure the open right flank. Danger is threatening there! Assemblies of new enemy forces are spotted on the right. This requires the chief to pull at least his own Panzer out of the secure cover where it had been sitting until now, to the right, in order to gain better visibility and a field of fire against a possible outflanking move. A less perfect cover has to be accepted for this. Observation through the field glasses indicates a strange assembly of infantrymen. They are dropping their heavy backpacks and sit down on the ground. Distance 1,200. At that very moment, the Panzer sitting further to the left sends a shell from its gun which turns into a direct hit. A flash and explosion, bodies are hurled high into the air, turning like windmill sails, arms and legs stretched out, then dropping to the ground. All this indicates that they were engineers who had been handling anti-tank explosive charges.

Soon after, the expected attack, again with tanks, starts and, indeed, further to the right. The third wave does not fare any better than the previous ones. It is allowed to get close and is then sent back in panic flight. A dozen burning tanks are sitting in the field. The chief spots one, however, straight to our right. Its optics and a part of the turret can barely be made out, using the binoculars, through the twigs and branches. It is sitting still, has obviously not spotted us. Initially, it is not considered dangerous, and why fire shells through the branches which would deflect them in any case, reducing the accuracy of the aim.

At approximately 10.30 hours, the fourth wave prepares for the attack. This time, it appears, there are more tanks. The same drama as before is repeated, but, during the frontal tank duels, an anti-tank shell suddenly rips open, coming from the right, the floor of the chief's Panzer. The lone tank, mentioned before, had sneaked close and, while our turret is still being swung to the three o'clock position, a shell hits the front right and, like a flash, the chief's Panzer is engulfed in flames. Hatch covers fly open, the gunner bails out to the left, in flames, the loader dives out to the right. The chief wants to get out through the top turret hatch but is caught by the throat microphone wire. He then tries to make it through the loader's hatch to the right but bumps heads violently with the radio operator who could not open his own hatch. The barrel, having been turned half-right, is blocking it. The chief has to move backward. He pushes the radio operator through the hatch, is engulfed in flames for some seconds, in danger of fainting. Still, he manages the jump to freedom. But he still has the steel boom of the throat microphone at his neck, he cannot pull it over his steel helmet. So he is hanging at the Panzer skirt, almost strangling himself, while machine gun salvos are slapping against the Panzer. With a desperate jerk, he rips loose. The wire, almost finger-thick, dangles in front of his chest. In the hollow, scene of the attack at night, the crew assembles, except for the driver, Sturmmann Schleweis, who remained in the burning Panzer. He was probably wounded, or killed by the impact. His hatch was free, he would have made it out otherwise. The gunner lies on the ground, still in flames. The crew covers him with their own, partly burned, bodies, trying to smother the flames. He was not wearing leather gear, but only fatigues, since he was taking the place of the regular gunner only for the night. The Regiment had to thank its commander, Max Wünsche, for the leather clothing. He understood the value of such gear. It was booty from Italian navy supplies, and saved the lives of quite a few men. The gunner died of his burns later in hospital.

Initially, the chief as well as the others, do not notice their own burns on their faces and their hands. The tank attack is still rolling ahead, it has not been stopped. However, this is soon looked after by the other three Panzers. They seem not to have noticed the drama which just ended. The excitement of combat holds everyone in its grip. Almost helplessly, the chief stands in the middle of the action and observes, to his reassurance and joy, how courageously the commanders—all NCOs—are doing battle, and how well the shells are aimed by the crews. Almost each shot is a hit. They have been spotted behind this excellent cover, but only by their muzzle fire. The embankment covers them, it would have to be a direct hit to the turret.

This attack, too, is repelled. The hatch of one of the Panzers opens. A face looks out, barely recognizable, blackened by powder smoke, marked by the exertions, and shocked by the view of the chief who resembles more a baked potato than a human.

After handing over command to the senior Panzer commander, an Unterscharführer, the chief drives the wounded men back to the Regimental command post in the VW-Kübel of the artillery commander. It was still sitting there from the night before. There is no need to report off duty. The Regimental commander, Obersturmbannführer Max Wünsche, is there. He slaps the chief on the shoulder and the medics administer the pain-killing morphine injections to all.[6]

As previously mentioned, the Korps had informed the Division the previous evening that a Panzerabteilung of 2. Panzerdivision of the Heer would be brought in early on 27 June. Its mission was to push into the enemy flank from the west near Cheux. This Abteilung never established any contact with the Division although the Divisional command post was still located, as during the previous day, in Verson. It must be assumed that this unit established contact with the Panzer-Lehr-Division and received its orders from there although there is no documentation available for this assumption.

In the morning, at approximately 09.00 hours, a Hauptmann (captain) of Panzerregiment 3 of 2. Panzerdivision had received a briefing on the situation by Hauptsturmführer Siegel in his field position. He had advanced with his Kom-panie during the night from the St. Lô area. His Kompanie with 17 Panthers was resting, at this time, somewhat further west in the vicinity of the positions of 5. Panzerkompanie, as indicated in a report by Untersturmführer Kändler. The Hauptmann had orders to clear the situation in the southern section of Cheux through an attack. Siegel had previously observed that the enemy had established a new point of concentrated force further to the right, probably the 2nd Argylls advancing on Tourville. Siegel would have thought it sensible if the Panthers had taken up positions to the right of him in such a manner that they could have put pressure on the flanks of the enemy advancing to the south. This would have contradicted the orders of the Panther chief, but these had surely been issued by an authority ignorant of the local situation, especially at this time. The Hauptmann thus decided to attack along the path through the fields, leading from le Haut du Bosq to Cheux, probably also expecting support from the infantry in action there.

At approximately 09.30 hours, according to reports from the enemy side, German Panzers attacked from the west (?) on Cheux, penetrated into Cheux, ". . . caused temporary confusion and knocked out several guns which were on the move. The attack was repelled, six enemy Panzers were knocked out. A German report indicated that the I. SS-Panzerkorps had attacked with 60 Panzers that morning."[7] In the war diary of the 7th Royal Tanks it can be read that its 'C' Squadron, which supported the 10HLI, had knocked out two Panthers.[8] The Intelligence Summary of the 49th Division of 27 June notes that a Panzerkompanie of 2. Panzerdivision had attacked. A captured radio operator of 4. Kompanie of Panzerregiment 3 had provided information on strength and losses of the Kompanie (four of seventeen Panthers) and on the departure point of the unit (advance from the St. Lô area during the previous night). From the captured documents, code numbers for the units of the Division ". . . for coded exchanges during difficult situations . . ." had been gained.[9]

This attack was a failure and it was broken off after several Panthers had been lost. While the reports of 7. Armee and the discussion notes in the appendices to its war diary repeatedly mention the addition of one Abteilung of the Panzerregiment of 2. Pz.-Div., in reality, action by only one Kompanie could be documented. In the Divisional Orders of the Panzer-Lehr-Division from 27.6. for 28.6., only the attachment of ". . . one Pantherkomp. of I./Pz.-Rgt. 3 . . ." to the Weidinger Kampfgruppe is mentioned.[10] Whatever the case was, the order for this attack was an obvious mistake. In this situation, not even an Abteilung accompanied by infantry at battalion strength could have achieved lasting success. The enemy superiority was much too great. Instead, the Pantherkompanie could have extraordinarily contributed, from favorable positions, in the defense against the attack from Cheux via Colleville on Tourville. This was a case where, with best intentions, wrong actions had been ordered in ignorance of the real situation and the local conditions. One of the reasons why the Divisional command staff had remained in Verson was to be able to direct operations close to the quickly changing circumstances.

The attack by the 10HLI and the supporting tanks from Cheux in the direction of Grainville with the objective of taking the Odon crossings had stalled in Gavrus under the fire of the four Panzer IVs of Hauptsturmführer Siegel. Members of Regiment 26 and the Pionierbataillon 12, as well as I. and II. Artillerieabteilung had also taken part in the action. The 2nd Argylls, to the east, were faring better. Although they had to cross through the 10HLI, already attacking, on their way to the assembly area, which caused a terrible confusion in Cheux, they had finally gotten free and advanced quickly past the positions of the 2nd Gordons.

They encountered a particularly weak spot in the German defense. Only weak guards of the Aufklärungsabteilung, which had been moved from the operations area Rauray during the night in order to close a dangerous gap here as best they could, were located north of Colleville. The command post of the Abteilung was situated in Mondrainville. The 1. Batterie of Flakregiment 53, part of Flaksturmregiment 4, was also in position there. Other than that, only members of supply units and stragglers had prepared for defense in the town. In order to keep the area under surveillance, Sturmbannführer Bremer had ordered a Panzer reconnaissance squad, under the command of Oberscharführer August Zinßmeister, to the railroad crossing north of Tourville.

After the 2nd Argylls, supported by the 23rd Hussars, a tank unit of the 11th Armoured Division, had captured Colleville in house-to-house combat, they advanced further toward Mondrainville.[11]

The diary of August Zinßmeister contains the following entry on the fighting in this area:

Dead and wounded Tommies are lying at the railroad crossing (north of Tourville, Author). They are members of an assault squad which was caught by the British artillery fire on the dam. A heavy artillery barrage is raining on Mondrainville and our sector again. The whole area is full of smoke. We want to repair a flat tire on the

eight-wheeler at the southern fringe of Tourville, but the artillery
fire drives us to the other hill at Baron. The tire is completely
ripped, useless. Back to Tourville. We encounter a squad of riflemen
withdrawing along our path from the railroad crossing. A counterattack with Panzers and motorcycle riflemen on the railroad crossing.
But Tommy is able to get into the village on our flank. We fire everything we have, with devastating effect, from close distance at the
infantry. The Tommies send up smoke signals and hammer us with
heavy caliber shells. I drive to the command post south of
Mondrainville to report. We are reinforced by the Flanderka scouting party and return for another counterattack along the path to the
northern edge of town. The bushes and hedges are full of English
infantry and the fire fight continues without pause. One of the
wheels on my 8-wheeler '121' is blown away by a hit and I bail out
and move over to '122' which has pulled up in the meantime. The
English infantry manages to advance further through the hedges
and now we are coming under fire from anti-tank weapons from
ahead. We return to the main road, constantly firing on Tommies
trying to jump across the road in the fog. We inflict heavy losses on
them until a period of quiet sets in.

I receive orders from Untersturmführer Flanderka to drive to
Mouen and establish contact there with our own Panzers and assault
guns. I drive up and down among the Tommies for a short while, firing. Then, I order 'Let's go—Step on it!' and we run into a Sherman,
face to face. I look into its muzzle, as Dey shouts: 'Oberscharführer, is
that a German?' The gunner sends a salvo of anti-tank shells across
its bow and we are surprised when we see the crate disappear behind
the corner of the house. Then we take off. While I am reporting to
Flanderka, six Shermans push out from behind the house and rattle
down the street. It is twelve noon. A group of armored cars is trying
to make its way to us in Tourville. As they turn, one of them is hit on
the road and catches on fire. We race past them along the embankment to south of Grainville, to report there. On my own, I send 3
Panthers out against those beasts in Tourville. The Abteilung issues
new orders for 1. and 2. Kompanie: Go to the Divisional staff and
secure there! The Panzers are refueled, then we set out via Bougy
and Gavrus. There we again find the Tommies advancing and fire on
them until calm sets in, then we drive on.[12]

The 2nd Argylls continue their attack at approximately 15.00 hours. At
around 17.00 hours, the two point platoon reached the undamaged bridge
across the Odon northwest of Tourmauville, covered by a company of the
23rd Hussars. The anti-aircraft battery in position in the vicinity at the northern shore of the Odon—2. Batterie Flak Regiment 53—had changed posi-

tions together with the whole Abteilung. An anti-tank gun was supposed to be in position at the bridge. If this was so, it had been unable to prevent the crossing of the bridge. By 20.00 hours, two companies had crossed the creek and a company of the 23rd Hussars prepared to cross. By 22.00 hours, all of the 2nd Argylls Battalion, 23rd Hussars and six anti-tank guns had crossed the creek. The anti-tank guns remained there to secure the crossing. The 23rd Hussars and a company of the 8th Rifle Brigade advanced, against some resistance, on Hill 112. As darkness fell, they had prepared for defense at the northern slope between Baron and the ridge.[13]

A radio message from the 23rd Hussars regarding the crossing of the Odon had been intercepted by the radio communications monitoring unit at the Divisional command post in Verson. Somewhat later they heard the inquiry: "Do you still require a fast operation at Verson?" Apparently, the enemy was aware that the command post was located there and intended to clean it out. A reply was not heard. All still available men of the staff were in securing action near Fontaine-Etoupefour. The Panzerregiment received orders to release units and, by occupying Fontaine and Hill 112, to prevent an enemy breakthrough to the Orne bridges. After the first Panzers had arrived in Fontaine, the Division removed its command post to Louvigny since it was no longer possible to direct operations from Verson.[14]

It has already been reported that Hauptsturmführer Siegel and his four Panzers had repelled the attacks by the 10HLI, together with tanks, from Cheux to the south in the morning and before noon. The subsequent attacks, too, during which an attempt was made to detour the anti-tank obstacles, faltered before the few Panzers of the 8. and the 5. Panzerkompanie. Untersturmführer Willi Kändler, commander of III. Zug of 5. Kompanie, reported on the development of these battles. He sat, with his Zug, to the right of the road leading from Cheux via le Haut du Bosq to Noyers, approximately in line with Siegel's Panzers. He wrote:

> The meadow I sat on was bordered by a ravine running in an east-northeasterly direction. A well-reinforced command post was located there [probably the abandoned command post of II. Artillerieabteilung, now used by the staff of an infantry battalion, possibly II./26 of Sturmbann-führer Siebken]. My Kompanie chief, Obersturmführer Bando, was there also. Since our Panzers were sitting in the front lines we were under constant intense fire from anti-tank guns and tank guns. My head was injured by shrapnel from a hit. I could remain there, but my seriously injured gunner, Koloska, had to be transported away. At approximately 11.00 hours, my Kompanie chief Bando came to my Panzer. He indicated an enemy machine gun to the right of a farm ahead of us as a target and ordered me to attack it. As he was walking away, only a few meters from my Panzer, a salvo from this machine gun caught him in the

back of the head and killed him. I personally reported Bando's death to the other two Zug commanders, Porsch and Kunze. When I returned, I saw that my Panzer had been hit again and knocked out. It had already been pulled out of the position. The Panzer of commander Wichmann was approaching and I took it over. My new gunner was now Willi Schnittfinke from Cologne, the loader was Jansen from Essen. In the morning there had been five Panzers of my Zug sitting at the hedge. This number had now melted down to three, the commanders were Kändler, Jürgens, and Biback.

The anti-tank fire on our hedge increased more and more. We figured the intention was to force our hidden Panzers out through systematically moving fire. In order not to lose the three remaining Panzers, I pulled them back into a hollow in the far corner of the meadow where they were safe from direct fire. I posted a few soldiers in the front line, men from knocked-out 'Wespen' (wasps) of I. Artillerieabteilung. I ordered them to report anything important immediately to me.

In the early afternoon one of these men knocked on my Panzer and reported that three Sherman tanks had approached to a distance of 600 meters to the right of the farm in front of us. They were sitting there, the crews standing on the tanks. Together with the other two commanders and the three gunners, I crept on foot to the observation spot. We found the observation confirmed and, indeed, the British tank crews could be seen moving about on their tanks without a care. I indicated the targets: 'Biback, you take the tank on the right; Jürgens, you take the left, I will take the one in the center. Approach the hedge, with as little noise as possible in second gear, along one line, fire simultaneously. Each will knock out his tank and immediately return to the cover of the hollow!' Biback got stuck with the hull on a tree stump in the ravine. Jürgens, too, was hanging back initially to my right rear. I had to also knock out 'Biback's tank' myself. Jürgens had caught up in the meantime, his round on 'his tank' was a direct hit. All three Shermans were in flames. We had not made it back to our hollow when raging fire from numerous unseen tank guns from both sides of the farm concentrated in our direction.

As a reward, I released some chocolate from our Iron Reserves with the direction: 'But don't touch the last piece, otherwise we'll get knocked out ourselves.' No-one, myself included, touched that chocolate. Even superstition has its place in dangerous situations.

In the late afternoon, three Panzers appeared on the right of the ravine. I believed, for a while, they were reinforcements for us, but they were looking for 8. Kompanie. I pointed them in the general direction, since I did not know the exact position.[15]

These were probably Panzers of 8. Kompanie. They had been readied for action again in haste by the repair units. They contributed significantly to the successes.

The British brought up reinforcements to guard their flanks and, as planned, to gain a second bridgehead across the Odon. In the early afternoon the Gordons advanced to Colleville. ". . . Rifle fire was raging, as everywhere . . .", it is stated in the history of the 15th Division, ". . . for instance, the Royal Fusiliers surrounded twenty-five riflemen in a wood in their assembly area which had supposedly been cleared out twenty-four hours previously . . ."[16] After having been relieved by the Seaforths, the Gordons then advanced on Tourville. By 15.00 hours, the Glasgow Highlanders had taken up positions in Colleville. They were followed by the Cameronians, mounted on their tanks, to clear out Grainville. They advanced along the rail line and encountered grenadiers and a few Panzers in the western sector of the town which was firmly held by these. As darkness fell, the British withdrew in order to keep the town under surveillance.[17]

The 49th Division had ordered, for 27 June, the 70th Brigade, together with tanks, to attack. The objective was to take Noyers. The first stage was to capture Rauray. On both sides of Rauray and immediately north of it, only III./26 of Sturmbannführer Olboeter with the Zug of 1. Panzerpionier-kompanie, parts of 13., 15., and 16./26 together with Panzers of 6. Panzerkompanie, one Zug of the 9., and with 2. Panzer-kompanie were in position. The Aufklärungsabteilung had been pulled out during the night into the area north of Mondrainville. Parts of I. Panzerabteilung had also been moved to Grainville. The remaining weak forces had the difficult mission of preventing a breakthrough to Noyers. Such a breakthrough would have grave consequences for the defense of the sector south of Cheux and for the right wing of the Panzer-Lehr-Division.

Today, a British war cemetery is located between Fontenay and Rauray. Many of the dead of the 49th Division, as well as dead of the "HJ" Division, have found their last resting place on it, next to each other. In July 1974, former members of the "HJ" Division, during a battlefield inspection in preparation for this Divisional history, visited the cemetery. They laid a wreath at the memorial for the dead of both sides during a ceremony. They found the following entry from a member of the 11th Battalion The Durham Light Infantry of the 70th Brigade, which attacked on 27 June, in the visitors' log:

> The attack on Rauray started at 8 A.M. on 27 June. The 'A' Company of the 11th Durham Light Infantry advanced from the southeastern corner of the present cemetery toward the row of trees. After twenty minutes, only six of the seventy men of the two point platoons were still alive. Then, the whole Battalion attacked and was caught in the crossfire of the riflemen. Very heavy losses.

As several former members of the Bataillon of Sturmbannführer Olboeter, the III./26, remember, a short cease-fire was agreed between the Germans and British—probably on 27 June—in the Rauray sector, to allow recovery of wounded and killed. It lasted from approximately 12.00 to 14.00 hours. Oberscharführer Hans-Georg Keßlau recalls:

> We watched British medics, Red Crosses on the chest and back, carry their wounded and dead to ambulances in the forefield half right of us. Immediately after the cease-fire expired, the attacks set in again with renewed force. Sturmmann Walter Frobel, who had brought me the order for the cease-fire, was also wounded.[18]

After the heavy losses of the previous days and the withdrawal of Panzers and the Aufklärungsabteilung, Rauray could not be held against the attack by the 70th Brigade and the supporting tanks. In the course of the afternoon, the Kampfgruppe, in action around Rauray, pulled back to a line immediately north of Brettevillette. After capturing Rauray, the 70th Brigade did not continue its attack. In the enemy situation report of the 49th Division, it is stated, in regard to the attack on 27 June:

> Today, we have captured Rauray which has been defended by the enemy with determination for almost two days. His infantry and Panzers defended each inch of soil in the north and east of the town against all attacks.[19]

Oberscharführer Keßlau continues his report:

> The combat strength of 10 Kompanie on 27 June was approximately two NCOs and twenty men. In the evening hours, I was ordered to the command post of Sturmbannführer Olboeter. He instructed me to guard the command post with a few men since it was no longer known if there was still contact between the individual companies. I took off with two comrades. About 200 meters in front of the command post we captured three Englishmen, but they did not know where their own troops were located. As they stated during the interrogation, they thought that this area had long been taken by their own forces. During the withdrawal to the new position, I was wounded and picked up by a Panzer [armored car] of our battalion. Sturmbannführer Olboeter shook hands with the wounded before they were driven to the dressing station at Missy. The main dressing station was guarded, at a radius of approximately 300 meters, by military police. They did not allow any fighting vehicle to enter. Fighter-bombers flew surveillance in the airspace above.

During these combat action, our supply troops were in a valley near Gavrus (five kilometers southeast of Rauray, Author) on the Odon. There, our dead were laid to rest.[20]

No reports are available on the Panzer combat in this sector for 27 June. The diary of 2. Panzerkompanie indicates that Unterscharführer Süße and his crew knocked out three Shermans during this day. He was then knocked out himself, and wounded. He had already been knocked out once during the previous day, when his whole crew was able to bail out.

The 146th Brigade had attacked the Panzer-Lehr-Division in order to capture Monts. In its Divisional order for 28 June it is stated that the enemy had attacked east of Juvigny in battalion strength. This attack had faltered under the concentrated fire of the Scholze Kampfgruppe, causing high and bloody enemy losses.[21]

The enemy situation report of the 49th Division, already cited, also contains interesting entries. They refer to the activities of the communications monitoring platoon of Untersturmführer Schneider. It is stated there:

During the night of 24 June, the radio contact between the fire position of the mortars and the observation post was interrupted by a stranger on the same frequency we were using. I am sure he was a German. I was in contact with him for ten minutes without noticing anything wrong since he had the same manner of speaking as the radio operator at my opposite unit. I only became suspicious when he asked for the password of the night which, of course, I did not give him. Then, my opposite unit reported in and stated that they had not transmitted at all for the last fifteen minutes. When the strange voice called in again I requested that they leave the frequency, and it replied: 'OK Tommy out'.

After that, contact was normal for a while until the same voice called in again and I was requested to cancel a fire order. I did not do that. He then jammed our frequency by constantly sending morse code. This lasted for about thirty minutes during which no contact was possible. After that, contact was normal.

The stranger seemed to be using a strong transmitter since he came in very clear. It was not the first time that we were jammed or interrupted, but it was the first time that English was spoken.[22]

Marcelet was abandoned during the night of 26 to 27 June. The remnants of I./26 of Sturmbannführer Krause, which had withdrawn from St. Manvieu, established defensive positions at the western fringe of the Carpiquet airfield. To the right, 3. Kompanie linked up with Regiment 25. The Panzers of 9. Panzerkompanie of Obersturmführer Büttner and the radio company of 21. Panzerdivision also abandoned Marcelet. Reconnaissance from the 43rd Division had reported Marcelet and la Bijude to be clear of the Germans. The enemy did not attack in this sector on 27 June. The 130th Infantry Brigade of the 43rd Division had relieved the units of the 3rd Canadian Infantry Division in action in the Norrey-Putot sector, so that they would be available for the planned attack on the airfield.

As the night of 27 June fell, the parts of the Division in action in the sector of the British "EPSOM" offensive, stood along the following line:

I./26 with 9. Kompanie/Panzerregiment 12 and radio company of 21. Pz.-Div.: Western edge of Carpiquet-western edge of the airfield;

15./26 and one Panzer IV-Kompanie of Panzerregiment 22 of 21. Panzerdivision: on the left of I./26 to the area west of le Haut de Verson, the 4. Kompanie of Panzerregiment 22 arrived with five combat-ready Panzer IVs at le Haut de Verson in the evening;

parts of Panzerregiment 12: western edge of Fontaine Etoupefour-south slope Hill 112-Esquay;

Aufklärungsabteilung 12, II./26, stragglers of Pionierbataillon 12, staff company 26, parts of Panzerregiment 12, in particular 5. and 8. Kompanie: north of Gavrus-Grainville-south and west of Cheux (listing not in sequence of operational locations);

III./26 with attached elements and parts of Panzerregiment 12 (6. Kompanie, 1 Zug of 9. Kompanie, 2. Kompanie): southwest of le Haut du Bosq-north of Brettevillette to the Bordel creek;

Artillery, mortars and Luftwaffe Flak were in position: III./Artillerieregiment 12 unchanged at the western edge of Caen, II./A.R. 12 probably in the Esquay area, 5. Batterie had lost its guns at the Route Nationale and was fighting as infantry;

I./A.R. 12 in the Grainville area;

mortar Abteilung of Werferregiment 83 southeast of Verson;

the Flak-Sturm regiments, as far as they were in the operational area, had moved positions southward; near Hill 112, a 8.8 battery had been blown up and abandoned, further details are not available.

Enemy forces were, at the time, distributed as follows:

44th Infantry Brigade in the le Mesnil-Patry area;

227th Infantry Brigade with the 10HLI, as in the morning, in the southern section of Cheux;

2nd Gordons in Colleville, 2nd Argylls in the Tourmauville bridgehead;

46th Infantry Brigade with 9th Cameronians in the western sector of Colleville;

Glasgow Highlanders east of Grainville, 7th Seaforths northwest of Mouen;

4th Armoured Brigade with 44th Royal Tanks west of Colleville;

3rd City of London Yeomanry northwest of Mouen, The Greys in le Haut du Bosq;

31st Tank Brigade with 7th Royal Tanks in the vicinity of le Mesnil-Patry;

29th Armoured Brigade of the 11th Armoured Division with 3rd Royal Tanks in Colleville, two companies of the 23rd Hussars between Hill 112 and Baron, location of 2nd Fife and Forfar unknown, one company of the 8th Rifle Brigade at the bridge near Tourmauville;

159th Infantry Brigade of the 11th Armoured Division with 4th Shropshires and units of the 1st Herefords in the Tourmauville bridgehead, 3rd Monmouthshires on the march to Mouen.

Also in the bridgehead were two companies of tanks, one company armored infantry, one whole battalion infantry and parts of two others.

Two tank units were located in the gap between Grainville and Mouen, another one immediately to the north of them, as well as four infantry battalions with another one on the advance.

Facing this superior force were a few Panzers of Panzer-regiment 12 and two companies of the Aufklärungsabteilung in a semicircle around the southern slope of Hill 112. To prevent an enlargement of the breakthrough in the direction of Verson and Grainville, one Panther company and 7. Panzer IV Kompanie of Panzerregiment 12 near Grainville, and one Panzer IV Kompanie of 21. Panzerdivision west of Verson were lined up. In Grainville, stragglers and parts of the regimental units of Panzergrenadier-regiment 26, and near Verson, the remains of 15./25 were facing the enemy. The remains of two Panzer companies, the 8. and 5., stood with approximately fifteen Panzer IVs south and southwest of Cheux. At least two Panzer companies were tied down on both sides of Brettevillette.

The worn-out battalions, II./26 and III./26, were located from south of Cheux to the Bordel creek, at the left border of the Division. A dangerous gap existed between Verson and the southern edge of the Carpiquet airfield, secured only by scouting parties.

On 27 June it had been possible to contain the breakthrough on both sides of Colleville, which had led to the establishment of a bridgehead near Tourmauville, initially near Hill 112. However, the forces available there could not withstand a continuation of the attack from out of the bridgehead. It was obviously the intention of the enemy to widen the breakthrough in order to be able to bring more forces quickly across the Odon. The bridge across the Odon south of Tourville was very narrow, the approach and exit from it were very winding, and fell steeply toward the Odon river. It seemed most important to the Division to prevent an enlargement of the breakthrough area, if possible, to reduce it and then to cut it off. No forces of its own were available for this.

The course of the fighting and further intentions were described in the daily report of Heeresgruppe B for 27 June 1944 as follows:

On 26 June, I. SS-Panzerkorps, throwing into action its last reserves and with the extreme exertion of all forces of the outstandingly fighting 12. SS-Pz.Div. "HJ" and Panzer-Lehr-Division, achieved a complete defensive success and knocked out more than fifty tanks. The enemy breakthrough area was contained by night-fall.

At 08.15 hours on 27 June, the enemy started another attack after preparatory artillery barrages and low-level aircraft attacks south of Fontenay-le Pesnel. During fierce fighting, enemy point units crossed the road Caen-Villers-Bocage near Mondrainville in the evening hours. An armored squad of 12. SS-Pz.Div. is in combat in the Cheux area. All available units of 1. SS-Pz.Div. "LAH" are advancing toward the breakthrough.

The continuation of the enemy attack in an east-southeasterly direction is expected for 28. June, coupled with an attack from the area north of Caen.

. . .

I. SS-Panzerkorps: armored battles in the Mouen-Cheux area are continuing.

In the breakthrough area, the enemy has crossed the road Caen-Villers-Bocage east of Rauray, between Mondrainville and Tourville, and has reached Baron late in the evening. Countermeasures: advancing units of 1. SS-Pz.Div. "LAH", one Pz. Abt. of 2. Pz.Div.— under way.

Toward evening, enemy attack west of Hottot. Countermeasures against localized breakthrough are under way.

Since 19.30 hours, enemy attacks, supported by tanks, south of Juvigny. Fighting on-going.[22]

On 27 June, too, the Division had suffered high losses:

Unit	Killed			Wounded			Missing		
	Officers	NCOs	Men	Officers	NCOs	Men	Officers	NCOs	Men
R.E.26	-	-	3	-	3	9	-	1	20
I./26	2	1	8	-	2	5	-	1	1
II./26	-	-	2	-	-	3	-	-	4
III./26	-	-	8	-	-	23	1	-	-
Pi.Btl.	-	-	1	-	-	2	-	-	-
A.A.12	-	-	2	-	3	10	-	-	-
Pz.Rgt.	2	2	10	2	6	17	-	-	-
A.R.12	2	-	1	1	2	21	-	1	9
Total	6	3	35	3	16	90	1	3	34

The total losses amounted to 44 killed, 109 wounded and 38 missing. This was a grand total of 191 losses.[23]

The appendix to the daily report of 7. Armee for 27 June noted, regarding the intentions of I. SS-Panzerkorps:

> Defense of existing main line of resistance, containment of the breakthrough near Cheux through offensive action.[24]

The SS-Panzergrenadierregiment 1 of 1. SS-Panzerdivision Leibstandarte SS "Adolf Hitler" (LAH), without one battalion, was attached to the "HJ" Division for the counterattack against the breakthrough.

The Regimental commander, Sturmbannführer Albert Frey, reported to the command post of the Division at Louvigny in the evening of 27 June. He was briefed on the situation and personally went to survey the terrain. His mission was: counterattack with the support of one Panzerkompanie of 21. Panzerdivision, the available units of the Artillerieregiment and the mortar Abteilung of Werferregiment 83 from the area west of Verson. Recapture Mouen and Colleville and establish contact with the units of the Weidinger Kampfgruppe in action near Grainville after assembly in the morning of 28 June.

The following developments led to the Weidinger Kampfgruppe being sent: In the evening of 26 June a deep breakthrough near Cheux had become obvious. Feldmarschall Rommel approved, at approximately 21.00 hours, that the 7. Armee dispatch one Panzerabteilung of 2. Panzerdivision and two battalions of 2. SS-Panzerdivision "Das Reich" for a counterattack. Before noon on 27 June, the 7. Armee had judged the situation more positively. At 10.10 hours it informed the Heeresgruppe B on the situation and that ". . . yesterday can be considered an outstanding defensive success . . ." Thus, the Armee asked the Heeresgruppe to stop the already advancing units of 2. SS-Panzerdivision. Also, 1. SS-Panzerdivision was no longer to advance across the Orne to the west. At 12.50 hours, Generaloberst Dollmann, the supreme commander of 7. Armee, informed the commanding general of II. SS-Panzerkorps, -Obergruppenführer Hausser, that ". . . the situation at I. SS—Panzerkorps has developed differently from what was expected. Primarily, a fine defensive success has been achieved there. At the present time, a Panzer counterattack is under way. Thus, it is initially no longer necessary that II. SS-Panzerkorps goes into action as ordered yesterday. The Korps is to stop, staggered to the left as much as possible, so that it can be turned back into the direction of its original objective." At 13.30 hours, the Armee advised the Panzer-Lehr-Division that the Kampfgruppe of 2. SS-Panzerdivision ". . . has not been released for action . . ." The I. SS-Panzerkorps reported at 16.05 hours that ". . . it is planned to push back the enemy, who has advanced to the line Mondrainville-Tourville, during the night. In addition to 1. SS-Pz.Div., two battalions of 2. SS-Pz. Div. are requested for this." At 17.00 hours, the Armee, with the agreement of the Heeresgruppe, approved the intentions of I. Panzerkorps. When the 1. SS-Pz.Div. was named, only the two approved battalions were, of course, considered. In the daily review of the Armee it is thus stated: "For the containment and counterattack during the night 27–28 June, two battalions each of 1. and 2. SS-Pz.Div. and one Panzerabteilung of 2. Pz.Div. are attached to I. SS-Pz.Korps, as requested." At 23.00 hours, I. Korps reported that the counterattack would start early on 28 June. Finally, the chief of staff of the Armee briefed the chief of the Heeresgruppe on the situation at I. SS-Pz.Korps at 23.50 hours. He stated that he believed ". . . contrary to the judgment in the morning, more extensive measures against the enemy pressure are required."[25]

In the afternoon of 26 June, the 2. SS-Panzerdivision received orders for the seconding of the Kampfgruppe. It was set in march to the 2. Panzerdivision at Jurques (9.3 kilometers southwest of Villers-Bocage) at 21.00 hours of the same day. The Kampfgruppe consisted of the staff of SS-Panzergrenadierregiment 4 "Der Führer" with 13., 14., 15., and 16. Kompanie with all their half-tracked vehicles, I. Bataillon of Regiment 4 and the attached I. Bataillon of SS-Panzergrenadierregiment 3 "Deutschland". The Kampfgruppe arrived at Jurques around midnight. From there it was directed onward to the Panzer- Lehr-Division and arrived at dawn of 27 June in the area south of Monts (5.5 kilometers northeast of Villers-Bocage).

The commander of the Kampfgruppe, Sturmbannführer Otto Weidinger, was briefed at the Divisional command post near Monts by Generalleutnant Bayerlein. Little was known about the situation at the "HJ" Division. In the General's opinion, there could be no thought of a counterattack during the day. It was more important to stabilize the front line and re-establish its cohesiveness, before the enemy continued his attempts at breaking through.

The mission of the Kampfgruppe was formulated in the Divisional order of the Pz.-Lehr-Div. for 28.6. as follows:

Kampfgruppe Weidinger, including the two battalions of SS-Pz.Div. 'Das Reich', attached to the Panzer-Lehr-Division, will relieve the securing line of the neighbor on the right (Kampfgruppe Mohnke) and parts of Pz.Pi.Btl. 130 during the night 27/28 June. It will then defend the line Mondrainville-Grainville (south)-Rauray (south)-Tessel-Bretteville (south)-road intersection 350 meters south of the Tessel Woods (inclusive). For this, one Panther company of I./Pz.-Rgt. 3 will be attached to the Kampfgruppe. The attached Pz.-Komp./Pz.-Lehr-Rgt. 130 is to be released.[27]

Apparently, the advance by the Weidinger Kampfgruppe was spotted by enemy aerial reconnaissance.

The war diary of the 8th Armoured Brigade noted that a German Panzer unit was spotted on the march from Villers-Bocage to the north on 27 June at approximately 13.00 hours. The 49th Division expected an enemy Panzer attack into its left flank to develop. It thus ordered the 8th Armoured Brigade to assemble in the northern part of Fontenay in such a manner that it could face a Panzer attack from the south or east.[28]

Regarding the deployment of German units, the enemy had learned that the II. SS-Panzerkorps with 9. SS-Panzerdivision "Hohenstaufen" and 10. SS-Panzerdivision "Frundsberg" were on the march in the Paris area on 20 June.

"They will not be in action yet against our offensive within the next few days. No details are known regarding 1. SS-Panzerdivision 'Adolf Hitler'. It keeps its pseudo-virginal coyness regarding its intentions. . . . All three SS-Divisions are probably held ready for a joint counterattack."[29]

CHAPTER 3.5

'EPSOM'—the Third Day of the Offensive of the VIII (British) Corps, Expansion of the British Bridgehead Westward to Gavrus. Our own Counterattacks near Hill 112, West of Verson, near Grainville and South of Rauray on 28 June 1944

The opposing intentions of the two sides clashed on 28 June: The British VIII Corps endeavored to expand its bridgehead to the south and west while, at the same time, enlarging the breakthrough which, at its narrowest spot, was only three kilometers wide. In contrast, the 12. SS-Panzerdivision wanted to prevent capture of Hill 112 and a further breakthrough to the Orne river. In addition, in cooperation with the Weidinger Kampfgruppe, it wanted to carry out a counterattack from Verson to the west in order to cut off the enemy forces located in the bridgehead.

In the early morning, the 159th Infantry Brigade of the 11th Armoured Division took over the bridgehead near Tourmauville from the 2nd Argylls. This infantry battalion had orders to advance along the broken and impassable bed of the Odon creek to the west and take the crossings near Gavrus. The bulk of the 1st Battalion The Herfordshire Regiment and the 4th Battalion The King's Shropshire Light Infantry (KSLI) had advanced across the Odon and relieved the Argylls. They enlarged the bridgehead at the crossing point, but were constantly harassed by fire from riflemen. The 23rd Hussars (tanks) advanced onto the knoll of Hill 112. They came under fire from

Panzers of Panzerregiment 12 from the area south of Fontaine-Etoupefour and from the wooded areas northeast of Baron. By approximately 12.00 hours, they occupied the northern section of the Hill with two companies. However, they were unable to advance further on the knoll of the wide and, in its upper part, flatly curved hill. Finally, their ammunition was getting scarce. They were relieved by the 3rd Royal Tanks, another tank unit of the 29th Armoured Brigade, at approximately 15.30 hours. The Hussars moved to a resting position in an orchard in the southern part of Tourmauville. They had lost four killed, five wounded and six missing.[1]

The 3rd Royal Tanks had been located south of les Vilains (600 m northwest of Tourmauville) and had been relieved by a third tank unit of the Brigade, the 2nd Fife and Forfar Yeomanry. They arrived at the northern slope of Hill 112 at approximately 17.00 hours.[2]

In the meantime, Panzerregiment 12 had pulled the 5. and 8. Panzerkompanie from their positions south of Cheux and south of le Haut du Bosq, as well as the companies in action in the Rauray sector, after the Weidinger Kampfgruppe had taken over the Mondrainville-Tessel-Bretteville sector. One Panther company was guarding the eastern slope of Hill 113, two kilometers west of Esquay, to the north. This was confirmed by enemy observations, according to which five Panthers had been spotted there at 07.50 and 16.30 hours. As reported by Oberscharführer Willy Kretzschmar, 5. Kompanie had arrived in Esquay at about 8 A.M. At approximately 10 A.M. the Panzerregiment with II. Abteilung of Sturmbannführer Prinz, without 9. Kompanie, and with 2. Kompanie of I. Abteilung attacked Hill 112 from the southeast and south. One Panther company, as already mentioned, was located west of Esquay. The other battle-ready one was in action west of Verson along both sides of the road Caen-Villers-Bocage.

Untersturmführer Willi Kändler reported on the advance of 5. Panzerkompanie from its positions south of le Haut du Bosq to Esquay:

The whole 5. Kompanie, now led by Untersturmführer Porsch in the point Panzer, had only about ten armored fighting vehicles left. I had orders, the gun pointing at six o'clock, to secure to the rear as the last Panzer and to pay special attention to the paths and roads from the east. The drive was intense. We observed intensely, sometimes believing to have spotted tank targets. We fired a few shells in that direction but could not make out any details. I did not notice crossing the Odon, in any case I cannot remember it. We probably crossed the Odon in the early morning between le Valtru and Gavrus. We certainly reached the center of Esquay without any problem. There, we stayed for about half an-hour. Completely exhausted from the intensive days and nights of fighting I fell asleep on a grassy square amidst a group of houses opposite the church. A member of my Panzer crew woke me up: 'They've gone already!' By this time it was probably around 09.00 hours. We immediately set out with our Panzer and spotted the others about 200 m ahead of us already, swinging to the right from Esquay, advancing on the hill. We caught up, and even passed them on the right.[3]

Oberscharführer Willy Kretzschmar described the advance and the attack as he experienced them:

Under the tall, thick trees and well camouflaged against being spotted from the air, we spent only a short period of time in the town. We then marched in a southeasterly direction to the assembly area approximately 1,200 to 1,500 meters south of the square wooded area on Hill 112.

After a very short assembly, we started the attack in a broad wedge formation on that wooded area at 09.30 or 10.00 hours. We worked our way forward, each Panzer giving the other covering fire. Without firm targets, we fired anti-tank and explosive shells into the wood. The attack moved forward briskly. When we had approached to within 300 to 400 meters, we spotted retreating English soldiers between the trees. We fired the turret and forward machine guns into the wooded terrain. At approximately 100 meters from the woods, we changed from the wedge into a staggered line since the opening in the forest was only 80 to 100 meters wide. The incline on our left was covered with bushes and trees. I was now driving as the point Panzer. Our direction was approximately northwest. The gun was pointing at twelve o'clock, an anti-tank shell was ready in the barrel. We cautiously made our way forward along the small forest which was 150 to 200 meters wide. Behind me drove the vehicle of Unterscharführer Jürgens. His gun was pointing at three o'clock in the direction of the forest so as not to be surprised by a grenade from an enemy 'stove pipe' (bazooka). At the end of the forest I ordered an observation stop. I searched the terrain to the right in front of us with my binoculars for tanks and Pak. Since I did not spot anything suspicious, I ordered 'Panzer, march!' After a drive of only ten to fifteen meters there was a sudden bang, sparks were flying and we noticed a hit from the right, three o'clock direction. I shouted at the driver, Sturmmann Schneider: 'Backward, march!' He reacted at lightning speed, threw the Panzer into reverse, and backed into the cover of the forest at full throttle. Not one second too soon, otherwise the British would have nailed us directly. Immediately in front of our bow, anti-tank shells ripped ugly black furrows into the green grass.

Now, the forest came back to life. Fire from rifles and machine guns was pinging against the armor, we were covered by mortar and artillery fire. We did not hold back either and briskly returned the fire as we were backing away. We returned to our assembly area without any losses. There, we inspected our damages—a clean hit, gone through between the engine and fighting compartments approximately twenty-five centimeters below the turret. Except for a small shrapnel stuck in my right thigh, we all escaped with just a scare. The driver took the vehicle to the repair shop. I remained in Esquay with the rest of the crew, the gunner Sturmmann Schweinfest, loader Sturmmann Gaude and radio operator Sturmmann Stefan. In the afternoon, more Panzers of 5. Kompanie arrived. My crew and I took over a Panzer which had come back from the repair shop.[4]

Untersturmführer Willi Kändler also took part in this attack. The commander of his half-Zug was Oberscharführer Willy Kretzschmar. Kändler experienced it in this way:

We detoured around a small wood approximately three quarters up the hill and approached the square wooded area in a wide loop without being bothered much. I had come within 100 meters of it when I suddenly spotted the brown uniforms of Tommies rushing to and fro. We came under violent fire, had losses, and were pushed back under constant fire from armor piercing weapons to the base of Hill 112, behind a hedge. To the east, approximately 1,000 meters away, was a depression in the terrain which offered cover against the hill. A mortar unit was also in position there, they were getting ready to move out. I stretched out again, exhausted, and fell asleep.

Our numbers had shrunk to four Panzers. The commanders were: Untersturmführer Porsch, Untersturmführer -Kunze, Hauptscharführer Müller, and Untersturmführer Kändler. The other Panzers had been lost to enemy fire or technical problems.

Kompanie commander Porsch wanted to start a second attempt to capture the square wooded area and the hill. We then attacked from our position in a direct line on the square wooded area. It was around noon. Just after we set out, my gunner, Sturmmann Willi Schnittfinke, reported to me that there was a mechanical defect in our electric gun firing mechanism. We had to stop and, even after a quick repair, we were lagging behind the other three Panzers of the Kompanie maneuvering in front of us. This was a bad situation to be in. Hauptscharführer Müller, too, fell behind Kunze and Porsch. From Kunze, in the point Panzer, we could hear on the radio, probably regarding the lagging behind of the others: 'I don't give a damn—Panzer march!' Kunze's Panzer was knocked out 200 m away from the square woods. The attack was broken off, the three Panzers returned to their starting positions. Both Kunze's driver, Sturmmann Gröter (?), and the radio operator were able to bail out of the Panzer. Gröter was visibly moved, he said: 'The shell went right between my legs.' (Amazing, what details remain as fragments of memory. In this case, the fact that I was worried about my friend Kunze, would have contributed.) I decided immediately to get to his Panzer as soon as possible.[5]

A renewed attack with Panzers of II. Abteilung which had arrived in the meantime, was planned for the afternoon. Around noon, four Panzers of 6. Kompanie, under the command of Standartenoberjunker (officer cadet) Kurt Mühlhaus, scouted Hill 112 from a southeasterly direction. Sturmmann Heinz Nußbaumer took part and reported:

> The Panzers stopped in a line along one of the willow hedges which were common there. The commander sent me into the hedge to reconnoiter. In the next hedge I spotted enemy tanks, some of whose crews were sunbathing. Enemy artillery was constantly dropping scattered fire. I reported my observations to the commander of 648. He passed them on. At approximately 17.45 hours, 648 took an artillery hit on the left front corner. The flash of the explosion wounded the driver, radio operator and the gunner. The vehicle did not catch on fire. The Kompanie even brought it back all the way to Germany.[6]

The report by Untersturmführer Willi Kändler continues on the progress of the third attack of this day, in which 5. Kompanie took part:

> At around 17.00 hours, our total number, through newly arrived Panzers, was back to nine. The 6. Kompanie under Untersturm-führer Helmut Buchwald with Zugführer (platoon leader) Kurt Mühlhaus was also there. This time we tried to attack the hill by swinging wide to the left around the small wood in front of the square wooded area. Despite being covered from view to the right toward the square wood, we again came under heavy fire from tanks, had a few Panzer losses and had to withdraw again to our starting positions.
>
> As one of the details of this attack, the exemplary behavior of the gunner, Sturmmann Schmid, who lost a leg in this attack, has stuck in my memory. Despite his serious wound, he turned the gun to twelve o'clock so that the driver and radio operator were able to bail out of their otherwise blocked hatches above.
>
> In the late evening hours, our Regimental commander Wünsche drove up to our hedge and praised our action. He told us that 36 enemy tanks had been counted on the hill.

After we had pulled our Panzers into the hedges, I agreed with Untersturmführer Porsch that I would establish contact on foot with our neighbor to the right, 6. Kompanie, located close by, also in hedges. On the way there, I encountered a Schwimmvolkswagen (amphibian VW) of the reconnaissance Zug of the Abteilung. The two men in it reported having come down from the hill. They had seen a Panzer IV with its engine running and a dead soldier sitting in front of it. This could only be the Panzer of Helmut Kunze. After reporting to Porsch, I drove immediately with the two in the Volkswagen in the dark up the hill to the Panzer. It was really Kunze's. In front of the Panzer, the loader, Howe, was lying dead on his back, his blue eyes open. He had spots from blood in his face. Helmut Kunze sat dead in the commander's seat. The shell seemed to have hit him directly in the back. To his left sat his dead gunner. The Panzer engine had been running since noon. The driver and radio operator's hatches were lit. I had the two scouts cover toward the enemy and drove the Panzer under its own power almost to our position. Just before I got there, it ran out of fuel and stopped. Unterscharführer Heinz Berner, the leader of the repair squad of 6. Kompanie, pulled me the rest of the way to the hedge with his tractor. Our comrades Kunze, Howe and the gunner, whose name I do not remember, were buried in the castle garden of Coultru next to the killed Kompanie commander Helmuth Bando. The Panzer, with a new turret, was back in action a few days later.[7]

It could not be established how many enemy tanks and German Panzers were knocked out during this day. The diary of 2. Panzerkompanie only noted: "Streiber knocks out a 'Churchill'. A total of twenty-one enemy tanks have been knocked out by 2. Kompanie."

A great number of observations of German Panzers in the area of Hill 112 were noted in the war diaries of the other side. Some of them are quoted here:

Five Panthers in the vicinity of the curve in the road 1.5 kilometers west of Esquay and several Tigers and 8.8 guns in Esquay; they made a further advance in the western attack sector of the enemy impossible.[8]

At 16.40 hours, four Tigers, two self-propelled tank destroyers and armored personnel carriers spotted one kilometer west of Maltot advancing to the west: they prevented detouring Hill 112 from the east. In the evening hours, threeTigers were spotted on Hill 112. Machine guns and rifles were fired from the same area. At midnight, six Tigers, supported by machine gun and mortar fire, again attacked the positions of the 3rd Royal Tanks from the hill. The 8th Battalion The Rifle Brigade (equivalent to the German Schützenpanzerwagenbataillon = armored personnel carrier battalion) arrived, mounted, at this very moment. The attack was repelled, the Tigers withdrew.[9]

It must be noted, regarding these observations, that Tigers were most probably not in action on Hill 112. Those attached to "HJ" Division fought in the Verson area. In the context of the battles on Hill 112 it is worth noting that the tank unit 23rd Hussars was facing the attacks by parts of Panzerregiment 12 before noon and in the afternoon. From approximately 17.00 hours on, when the third German attack on the hill was under way, the just arrived 3rd Royal Tanks were also in action there. The third tank unit of the 29th Armoured Brigade and the Fife and Forfars moved over into the area around Baron in the course of the day. There, they could be observed from Carpiquet where an artillery observation post of Artillerieregiment 12 was located, and they came under artillery and mortar fire. They then withdrew to the less steep slope.[10]

The 29th Armoured Brigade of the 11th Armoured Division lost seventeen killed, forty-eight wounded and two missing during these battles. In the evening, it had 165 battle-ready Sherman and Stuart tanks.[11]

An estimated total of thirty Panthers and, in the vast majority, Panzer IVs (which were often mistaken for Tigers by the enemy) of Panzerregiment 12 were in action here.

Earlier, it was mentioned that the 2nd Argylls had been relieved in the bridgehead in the morning. They had the order to advance along the Odon creek bed to the west and capture the Odon crossings near Gavrus. The battalion initially sent two scouting parties, led by officers, to the bridges near Gavrus. They reached the bridges at approximately 14.00 hours and found them undamaged and unguarded. The battalion followed along both sides of the creek along the broken and difficult terrain. It reached the bridges before nightfall and prepared for defense with three companies on the southern creek bank and with one company and the staff on the northern bank. It may be surprising that these bridges were not guarded by German forces and prepared for demolition. Very likely, sufficient forces were not available to properly guard them. Demolishing them would have delayed the enemy advance only by a few hours, but would have proved positive to the German defense effort. However, the few existing bridges were also needed for German supplies and movement of troops. This prevented a pre-emptive demolition. Its preparation also required securing forces, and these had to be stronger, the more broken the terrain was. A German guard of a Pak and weak close-combat forces had proved to be insufficient at the bridge at Tourmauville on the previous day. The catastrophic shortage of forces had made any strong securing effort impossible. Every man had been in action at Tourmauville, Colleville and Mondrainville. As the example shows, forces have to be held in reserve, without regard, for such a mission, in particular when the available forces are barely sufficient to hold the main line of defense.

An attack from the north and northeast was planned to combine with the attack by the Argylls along the creek bed. At the first light of day, the 9th Cameronians started another attack from the western section of Colleville, together with a tank company, on Grainville. During their second attempt, with strong artillery support, they were able to take the town. Two of three Panzers spotted there were reportedly knocked out when the town was abandoned. It can be assumed that at this time, the enemy attack started at 03.30 hours, the parts of Regiment 26 and the Panzerregiment in action there had not yet been relieved, since Sturmbannführer Weidinger, according to his report to the author, had no Panzers there. The Cameronians prepared for defense at Grainville.

The 46th Infantry Brigade had to carry out this attack. It now put into action its reserve battalion, the 7th Battalion The Seaforth Highlanders. It would advance via Colleville in order to capture le Valtru (south of Grainville) and the connecting road to Gavrus. The battalion started its attack, supported by Churchill tanks, immediately after first light. It made its way with difficulty through the bottleneck at the railroad crossing near Colleville which had also to be used by the 11th Armoured Division. Attacking, it reached le Valtru along both sides of the road from Mondrainville after violent fighting and heavy losses to the point company. The main body of the battalion, following behind, was just able to prevent losing the town again to the counterattack of I. Bataillon of the SS-Panzergrenadierregiment 4 "Der Führer". One company of the Seaforths secured in front of the hill west of the creek bed. Toward the evening, an armored scouting party established contact with the Argylls in Gavrus.[12]

The resistance which the attacking units of the VIII Corps encountered everywhere, and the numerous German counterattacks, caused anxiety to the Corps. It appeared dangerous to let the 11th Armoured Division advance in the direction of the Orne as long as the situation north of the Orne had not been clarified. During a discussion at the command post of the 15th Division at 10.00 hours, the Corps thus ordered the 11th Armoured Division to hold its established positions in the bridgehead and to reinforce them, and not to advance on the Orne without express order. The 15th and 43rd Divisions were ordered to clear the area between Cheux and the Odon.[13]

The 15th Division handed over the mission to clear out the terrain between Cheux and Grainville to the 44th Infantry Brigade. Through this, it wanted to open up the western route of advance, which had, so far, been blocked successfully and with high enemy losses, by 8. and 5. Panzerkompanie, together with Grenadiers of Regiment 26, Pionier stragglers and support from artillery, in particular I. Abteilung. Until then, all of the traffic into the bridgehead had to use the railroad crossing at Colleville. The 6th Battalion The King's Own Scottish Borderers (KOSB) was ordered to relieve the 10HLI in the southern section of Cheux. The 6th Battalion The Royal Scottish Fusiliers received orders to move to the right of the KOSB. Both were then to penetrate to the south to Grainville. Cheux, in particular its northern sections, was destroyed to such an extent that the two battalions were able to advance only with great difficulties and delays.[14]

Around 14.00 hours, the KOSB relieved the 10HLI in the southern section of Cheux. The 10HLI were ordered to occupy Mouen. At approximately 19.00 hours, the Royal Scots moved up to the line of the KOSB, and both battalions advanced to the south.[15] They encountered considerable resistance and had to fight their way from hedge to hedge. They stalled at approximately 22.30 hours because of stiffening resistance at the line of the Salbey creek. They were to resume the advance at first light on 29 June.[16]

The 2nd Battalion The Glasgow Highlanders had relieved the 2nd Gordons of the 227th Brigade the previous day in Colleville and was supposed to attack Mondrainville on 28 June. Just as they assembled for the attack, they were in turn attacked by I./"DF" with Panzer support. The Glasgows repelled the attack with the support of a few tanks. A captured German Panzergrenadier had stated that he belonged to II./"DF". This was an apparently intentional deception since this battalion was not part of the Weidinger Kampfgruppe.[17]

The 3rd Battalion The Monmouthshire Regiment, part of the 159th Infantry Brigade of the 11th Armoured Division, had been ordered in the evening of 27 June to follow the main body of the Brigade into the area south of Tourville. It was to move into a defensive position behind the other two battalions of the Brigade, north of the Odon river.[18] During the night, with poor road conditions and because of outdated maps, the battalion had lost its way and found itself in Mouen. Mr. J. J. How, then company commander and a captain in this battalion, wrote in its history:

> At approximately 03.00 hours we arrived at an abandoned village. The battalion commander called a stop and ordered setting up of an all around defense. In that way, we could wait for daylight and better determine where we were. The men were tired and hungry. They had been on the march since the previous morning, had dug in three times and not been given anything to eat since the field kitchens had not been able to make their way through. When the morning came, we encountered a farmer and his family. They were surprised to see 'Tommies' in this area and stated excitedly that, only the evening before, German troops had been there. We learned from them that the village was called Mouen. Until then, no British troops had been in this village. It was located too far to the left. Obviously, the enemy had withdrawn only a short time before we arrived there.
>
> In consideration of the uncertainty of the location of enemy positions, 'C' Company was left behind in the village to secure the flank of the route of advance of the Brigade. The remainder of the battalion withdrew to Mondrainville in order to move into the positions

on the hill immediately north of the Odon river. It arrived there at 07.30 hours.[19]

No reliable and detailed information on the counterattack by the SS-Panzergrenadierregiment 1 of the 'LAH" on 28 June from the Verson area to the west can be provided. The Regimental commander, then-Obersturm-führer Albert Frey, was very seriously wounded on 20 July. He believes that his capacity to remember this time period had been impaired. The commander of I. Bataillon, Sturmbannführer Wilhelm Weidenhaupt, died before the examination of these developments. The commander of II. Bataillon, Sturmbannführer Max Hansen, was once more seriously wounded during this attack and cannot reliably remember details. Thus, only an overview of the situation can be put together, based on reliable reports, for portions of the sector.[20]

The Regiment had been ordered to attack along both sides of the road Caen-Villers-Bocage. Then, in cooperation with the Weidinger Kampfgruppe which was to advance to Mondrainville, it was to cut off the enemy forces which had crossed the Odon. Available for this were: SS-Panzergrenadier-regiment 1 (without one battalion), two weak companies of Panzerregiment 22 with Panzer IVs (one of the companies only had five Panzers available), one Pantherkompanie of Panzerregiment 12, and a few Tigers (probably no more than three) of the heavy SS-Panzerabteilung 101. Since the two other Artillerieabteilungen were tied down in other sectors, only III. Abteilung, with what little ammunition was available, could provide fire support. The Werferabteilung, as far as it was not engaged in the fighting on Hill 112, also provided support. Based on the limited artillery support which the "HJ" Division could offer him, Sturmbannführer Frey wanted to await the arrival of his "LAH" Artillerieabteilung. It would, under no circumstances, be ready to fire in the morning of 28 June. The Korps, as did the Armee and the Heeres-gruppe, pushed for the earliest possible start of the attack, before the enemy could bring further reinforcements forward. The objective was to prevent an enemy breakthrough to and across the Orne, and to gain time as well as favorable starting positions for the counterattack by II. SS-Panzerkorps. The Supreme Command of 7. Armee, with justification, had not wanted an attack during the night. This would not have been possible, since Regiment 1 could not arrive in a timely manner. The Allied bomber squadrons in England had been prevented from taking off by the bad weather. However, the fighter-bombers departing the airfields in the beachhead had been able to effectively fight and delay the advance of the reinforcements. The results of this were now being felt.

The attack started at approximately 06.00 hours after assembly west of Verson. Lance corporal Werner Kortenhaus experienced this attack as the radio operator in one of the five Panzer IVs of 4./Pz.-Rgt.22. He reported that they were driving in file as they approached the railroad crossing north of Mouen. There, the point Panzer IV knocked out three enemy tanks. The accompanying Panzergrenadiers of the Waffen-SS, supported by the Panzers, captured the northern section of Mouen which had been occupied by the Monmouthshires. The enemy tried to withdraw along the railroad line and suffered heavy losses during this fighting.[21]

The war history of the Monmouthshires states on this:

> Soon after the withdrawal of the battalion from Mouen, 'C' Company encountered strong enemy infantry and -Panzer forces. . . . An extremely violent battle followed during which the company was encircled. The men fought bravely against a much superior force, but finally the situation became so hopeless that the company commander, Major Richards, decided to fight his way out with the few who were not yet wounded. Only he and 14 men eventually arrived at the battalion. It is known that twenty-one were killed, and it appears certain that the other were wounded during this fighting.[22]

Werner Kortenhaus reported as follows:

> We crossed the rail line north of Mouen and took up positions in the meadow between the rail line and the path to Cheux. We were uncomfortably exposed in the open terrain. All around us we saw English equipment, dance music was coming from their radios. I spotted several bodies on the ground near the three knocked-out English tanks.[23]

Parts of 1. Regiment of Sturmbannführer Frey had obviously advanced to Colleville. At 16.30 hours, the 10th HLI started out from Cheux to occupy Mouen. One hour later, they had to stop before reaching the bridge across the Salbey creek when they came under rifle fire from Colleville. After clearing the situation and issuing of orders again, the battalion started its attack on Mouen at 19.45 hours behind a moving wall of fire from British artillery. Two companies advanced to the right, the other two on the left of the railroad embankment without encountering any resistance. The attack was supported by tanks of the 3rd Battalion The City of London Yeomanry. One of the Shermans advancing on the left was knocked out, ". . . probably by an anti-tank gun."

The companies and the battalion staff advancing on the left then came under heavy machine gun fire from the houses and the railroad embankment, whistling through the ears of the grain. These companies could not advance any further. Three Shermans were knocked out, five Panthers were reported knocked-out. There were heavy losses. Before the units advancing on the right could reach the clumps of trees west of Mouen, they came under machine gun fire which they assumed came from a Panther dug in at an orchard. The commander of the point company was wounded, two men were killed. A further advance appeared impossible, the companies withdrew to a hollow. The attack was broken off at 21.00 hours.

Werner Kortenhaus reported on this:

> Our gun was facing northwest. Suddenly, we took a hit. The fire came from the left. Our turret was stuck, we could no longer turn it. We received permission from the Kom-panie commander to withdraw to a hollow to repair the damage. As we drove back, we came under more fire. I could see the explosion of shells ahead of us through my telescope. We later found that we had also been hit in the rear. Fortunately, the shells ricocheted off. When we advanced again to the rail line approximately an hour later, the other four Panzers of my Kompanie had withdrawn behind the rail embankment. The Panthers of the SS were no longer with us, I assumed they had pulled off to the left. One of our Panzers took two hits in this position and burned out. Unteroffizier (sergeant) Eichler, the Panzer commander, had his head ripped off by a shell as he was observing from the hatch of the commander's cupola. The Panzer rolled backward. Finally, the Kompanie commander was also wounded by a hit. A front drive sprocket of one of the Panzers was shot off. Under cover from the Panzergrenadiers, two men of the crew shortened the tracks in the middle of enemy fire and put it back on. That was heavy work! This last of the Panzers then had to pull back also. As we withdrew, further SS-Panzergrenadier rein-force-ments arrived. We had one total loss and two damaged Panzers which were later fully repaired. We also had one killed and two wounded. This included myself, with a fractured ankle.[25]

The war diary of the 4th Armoured Brigade, of which the 3rd City of London Yeomanry (CLY) was a part, noted the loss of three Stuart tanks before noon. There was no mention of the three knocked-out Shermans, they were noted in the war diary of the 10HLI.[26] The 3rd CLY remained in the area northwest of Mouen. The second tank unit of the Brigade, the Greys, were located one kilometer northwest of Mouen. The third unit, the KRRC, was at la Bijude (2.5 kilometers east-northeast of the church of Cheux). The armored reconnaissance unit of the 11th Armoured Division, the 2nd Northamptonshire Yeomanry, was positioned at the road fork 800 m southeast of the Cheux church. Thus, there were three tank units and armored reconnaissance unit in the attack sector of 1. Panzergrenadierregiment or on its right flank, in addition to the infantry battalion before its front line. When the threat by this attack was determined, probably after the capture of Mouen, the Grenadiers came under annihilating British artillery fire of a severity not encountered before. They suffered high losses and had to withdraw. It cannot reliably be determined along which line they then prepared for defense.[27]

The 70th Infantry Brigade had gone on the attack in the Brettevillette sector in the morning, starting from Rauray. The attack had been repelled. It can be assumed that this took place before the scheduled relief of the Olboeter Kampfgruppe by the Weidinger Kampfgruppe. The report on the enemy situation of the 49th Division indicates that a German counterattack had thrown back the Brigade shortly afterwards. That can only have been the Weidinger Kampfgruppe. The British enemy situation report described this as follows:

> After a difficult battle for Brettevillette, our troops came under a swift and violent attack. They had to withdraw to the Tessel-Bretteville area to re-assemble. They are now firmly established there. Prisoners taken during this phase have stated that the counterattack was led by newly arrived troops of the 2. SS-Panzerdivision, This Division had been located near St. Lô for some time and had not yet been in action. They were moved to our front sector yesterday to stop the threat posed by our Division and the divisions to our left in the last few days. Initially, it seemed that it was a well prepared attack by SS-PGR (Panzer-Grenadier-Regiment, Author) 'Der Führer' on the right, and the SS-PGR 'Deutschland' on the left. However, our neighbor division on the left took 25 prisoners of SS-PGR 'Deutschland' in the grid square northeast of Gavrus and today located units of the other regiment in the western section of Mondrainville. This seems to indicate that the enemy is not acting in accordance with a prepared plan, but is sending parts of the unit into action when they arrive, 'a little bit here, a little bit there'. This does not show the vigor we had expected from these troops.[28]

This third day of the "EPSOM" offensive, the fourth day in the left sector, was also its end. The attempt to capture all of Hill 112 from the bridgehead near Tourmauville, gained the previous day, had faltered under the counterattack of Panzerregiment 12, led by Obersturmbannführer Max Wünsche. Certainly, no more than thirty Panzer IVs and Vs took part in the defense in this sector and the counterattack at any time. The Luftwaffe Flak had moved positions, Panzergrenadiers were initially not involved in this fighting. The III./26 with Sturm-bannführer Olboeter would have arrived only during the course of the day. Parts of the Aufklärungsabteilung were taking part in defense in the Verson-Fontaine sector, in particular along the broken creek bed. Although it had been impossible, against the superior enemy tank forces, to capture the hill, the enemy could only hold the northern slope. In the evening of 28 June, four tank units with 165 battle-ready tanks were located inside the bridgehead. After replacing the losses, which had occurred, by repaired Panzers, Max Wünsche had available, at most, thirty Panzer IVs and Vs. A significant defensive success had been achieved there.

The enemy had managed to secure his flanks at the three-kilomter wide breakthrough section and to hold them in the face of the counterattacks by Panzergrenadierregiment 1 and parts of the Weidinger Kampfgruppe, somewhat further west, but had been unable to enlarge it. The bridges near Gavrus were in enemy hands but no contact to the north existed there as yet. The pockets of resistance of the Pioniers and parts of Regiment 26 in Cheux and le Haut du Bosq, which had held out for three days, had finally been cleared out. These fighters, who remained unknown, and who were killed or finally overwhelmed and taken prisoner, deserve particular admiration.

After capturing Rauray in the afternoon of 27 June, the 49th Division had been unable to break through or to push the front line further back. The division, itself, had been thrown back there by parts of the Weidinger Kampfgruppe.

The failure of the attempts to enlarge the breakthrough section, the numerous German counterattacks, the great efforts required in clearing out the terrain in between, the arrival of new units whose size were not determined (individual battalions were believed to be parts of advancing divisions) and the approach of II. SS-Panzerkorps caused the enemy to suspend his offensive for the time being. Further, the intention to enlarge it to the Carpiquet and Caen areas was temporarily abandoned. There is really no doubt that it would have been possible, by putting the remaining 500 tanks into action, to smash the left wing of the "HJ" Division from Esquay to Carpiquet and thus gain a more advantageous starting base for the subsequent battles. This false estimation by the enemy of his possibilities must, without doubt and to a large extent, be credited to the outstanding valor of the soldiers from all branches of the "Hitlerjugend" Division which smashed Montgomery's high hopes.

This day of battle, too, had demanded its victims. The following table shows the losses of the "HJ" Division units fighting in this sector:

| Unit | Dead | | | Wounded | | | Missing | | |
	Officers	NCOs	Men	Officers	NCOs	Men	Officers	NCOs	Men
R.E.26	-	-	-	-	-	-	-	-	-
I./26	-	1	3	-	3	4	-	-	-
II./26	-	-	1	-	-	2	-	-	2
III./26	-	-	1	-	1	3	-	-	-
Pi.12	-	-	2	-	-	-	-	-	-
A.A.12	-	-	4	-	5	3	-	-	-
Pz.Rgt.	1	-	6	-	2	15	-	-	-
A.R.12	-	1	2	-	1	15	-	-	-
Total	1	2	19	-	12	42	-	-	2

The losses amounted to 22 killed, 54 wounded and 2 missing, for a total of 78.[29]

Since the daily summary of AOK 7 offered only little detail regarding the battles of 28 June, the respective paragraph of the morning report of 29 June is quoted below:

> In the afternoon hours of 28. June, the massive tank attacks to the northeast, southeast and south from the breakthrough area, were brought to a stop through daringly executed counterattacks by 12. SS-Pz.Div. 'HJ', reinforced by parts of 2. Pz.Div., Pz.Lehr-Div. and 2. SS-Pz.Div. 'Das Reich'. Severe losses were inflicted on the enemy and temporarily lost terrain was recaptured. Our own attack along both sides of the road Caen-Villers-Bocage was stopped by enemy tank attacks along a line Mouen-creek bed two kilometers east of Tourville.[30]

An important change in the superior command occurred on 28 June. The Supreme Command of Panzergruppe West, with General der Panzertruppen Leo Freiherr Geyr von Schweppenburg as Supreme Commander, took on a new command responsibility. The previous area of 7. Armee was divided. The Panzergruppe Command West took over the sector from the Seine river to the Drôme river which runs west of Caumont, of Balleroy and of Bayeux, and thus came under the direct command of Heeresgruppe B of Feldmarschall Rommel. It commanded:

The LXXXVI.A.K. with the divisions
- 711. Inf.-Div.,
- 346. Inf.-Div.,
- 16. Luftwaffe Feld Div.,
- 21. Pz.-Div.

The I. SS-Panzerkorps with the divisions
- 1. SS-Pz.-Div. "LAH",
- 12. SS-Pz.-Div. "HJ",
- Pz.-Lehr-Div.

The XXXXVII. Panzerkorps with the divisions
- 2. Pz.-Div.,
- 276. Inf.-Div.,
- 277. Inf.-Div.

The II. SS-Panzerkorps with the divisions
- 9. SS-Pz.-Div. "Hohenstaufen" and
- 10. SS-Pz.-Div. "Frundsberg".

The divisions in action to the west of the mentioned border line remained under the Supreme Command of 7. Armee. The 2. SS-Pz.-Div., with the exception of the Weidinger Kampfgruppe, remained as a reserve of the Heeresgruppe.

The first objective of the Panzergruppe command was:

    A) Defense of existing positions,

    B) Preparations for a concentrated counterattack to destroy American forces in the Balleroy area, as well as the enemy forces east of the Orne river,

    C) Preparation for a counterattack into the deep flanks of possible enemy breakthroughs

        1) from the Caen area and west, to the southeast . . .[31]

Regarding Point A), the Panzergruppe Command West, after taking over command at 17.00 hours on 28 June, ordered the attached general commands:

    1) Panzergruppe West intends to attack across the line Gavrus-Noyers early on 29 June with II.SS-Pz.-Korps (9.SS-Pz.-Div. and 10.SS-Pz.-Div.) in order to take the Baron, Mouen, Cheux areas and to destroy the enemy who has advanced across the road Caen-Villers-Bocage.

In order to carry out this attack, the II. SS-Panzerkorps was attached to the I. SS-Panzerkorps. The border line between I. SS-Panzerkorps and the XXXXVII. Panzerkorps to the left was determined on 29 June at 08.00 hours: Aunay (to XXXXVII. Pz.-Korps)-Tournay (to I. SS-Pz.-Korps)-Cristot (to I. SS)-Rucqueville (to XXXXVII.). With II. SS-Panzerkorps being in action, the parts of 2. and 21. Pz.-Div. attached to I. SS-Panzerkorps, were to be returned to their divisions.[32]

The plan for the counterattack by II. SS-Pz.-Korps had been worked out by the Supreme Command of 7. Armee. It had ordered the Korps at 08.10 hours on 28 June ". . . to attack immediately in order to clear out the breach south of Cheux . . ." after such an order had been temporarily withdrawn at noon on 27 June. The general command reported that the Korps was not yet fully assembled. After this back and forth, the commanding general, Obergruppenführer Hausser, took a wait-and-see attitude. The chief of staff of the general command, Standartenführer Pipkorn, reported to the Armee supreme command at 13.00 hours that the attack could start early on 29 June. At 17.35 hours, the chief of staff of Panzergruppe West, Generalleutnant Gause, informed the 7. Armee during a briefing on the situation that the I. SS-Pz.-Korps could no longer hold the front line with its own forces, the involvement of all of II. SS-Pz.-Korps was required. The Ia of the Armee supreme command advised that the Armee had already issued orders to this effect.[33]

On 28 June at 10.00 hours, the Supreme Commander of the 7. Armee, Generaloberst Dollmann, died at his command post ". . . of a heart attack . . ." In reality, he had committed suicide, as the chief of the general staff, Generalleutnant Pemsel reported after the war (v. Deutsches Soldatenjahrbuch 1974, page 19). At 15.00 hours, the Heeresgruppe informed the 7. Armee that ". . . the Führer has appointed Obergruppenführer Hausser to Supreme

Commander of the 7. Armee Supreme Command . . ." Generalleutnant Speidel, chief of staff of the Heeresgruppe, informed the chief of staff of 7. Armee
that ". . . until the return of the two Feldmarschalls from the Führer, Obergruppenführer Hausser will take over supreme command for the existing
Armee sector." The chief of staff of the Armee, Generalleutnant Pemsel,
thought it ". . . practical that Obergruppenführer Hausser remain at the front
for -today, so that parts of II. SS-Pz.-Korps will be properly deployed during
the existing situation." (16.35 hours). The Heeresgruppe approved the suggestion, but also agreed with the request from Generalleutnant Pemsel that
Ober-gruppenführer Hausser arrive at the Armee even during the night. At
18.00 hours, the commander of Panzergruppe West asked for confirmation
from the commander of the Armee ". . . that the plan still was to have the II.
SS-Pz.-Korps attack to half-right (northeast). The chief of the general staff
confirmed this".[34]

As already mentioned, II. SS-Panzerkorps was assigned to the general
command of I. SS-Panzerkorps for the attack on 29 June. ". . . directions will
be issued by Panzergruppe West . . .", Generalleutnant Pemsel ordered the
chief of staff of II. SS-Panzerkorps.

All this meant, in few words: Feldmarschalls von Rundstedt and Rommel
were at the Führer headquarters for a Führer briefing. The Supreme Commander of 7. Armee, Generaloberst Dollmann was lost to sudden death. The
chiefs of staff of Supreme Command West, Heeresgruppe B and AOK 7 had
to lead their supreme commands by themselves. The newly appointed
Supreme Commander of 7. Armee was recalled, during the night, from the
assembly area of his Korps while it was preparing its first, and an important,
attack in the west, in order to take over command of the whole front in the
invasion sector. In this situation, a campaign-decisive operation had to be
decided on by the afternoon, at the latest. The previously issued orders
remained in force. It cannot be determined that the Generalleutnants Speidel and Pemsel considered other solutions and requested decisions on them
from their supreme commanders. Generalleutnant (ret.) Dr. Speidel does
not mention anything of the kind in his book "Invasion 1944", (Tübingen
and Stuttgart 1949).

There is no doubt that a wrong decision had been made. In view of the
ratio of forces, as already described, the attack by II. SS-Panzerkorps was
doomed to failure. The two Panzer-divisions, coming out of action in Russia
and after difficult advance and short assembly, were supposed to attack an
enemy by day, who had spotted the assembly and prepared for the attack.
They were facing eleven tank units with some 500 battle-ready tanks. The II.
SS-Panzerkorps had a maximum of half that number available for combat. In
addition, there was the great enemy artillery and air superiority. The German Luftwaffe flew an unusually high number of missions during these days
under extremely adverse circumstances, but was unable to penetrate. It was

reported that 26 German planes were shot down by the 83rd Group on 28.6. in the operations area.[35]

The enemy situation map of 7. Armee, as of 22.00 hours on 28 June 1944, indicated in the breakthrough sector and up to the left border of the Panzer-Lehr-Division:

2 tank divisions (7th and 9th Armoured Divisions),
1 tank brigade (141st Armoured Brigade),
3 infantry divisions (15th, 49th and 50th Infantry Divisions).

In reality, the following were located in this area:
2 tank divisions (7th and 11th Armoured Divisions),
3 tank brigades (4th and 8th Armoured Brigades, 31st Tank Brig.),
4 infantry divisions (15th, 43rd, 49th, and 50th Inf.Div.).

The decisive enemy tank forces had been underestimated by half. At the same time, the strength of the enemy forces facing the Panzer-Lehr-Division was incorrectly estimated. Instead of the 9th Armoured Division, the 50th Infantry Division was in action in the front lines, and the 7th Armoured Division was in reserve.

Even the incorrect image of the enemy indicated a ratio of 7:4 with regard to the tank and Panzer forces in favor of the enemy. This had to indicate the futility of a counter-attack against the breakthrough sector. What other counter-measures offered themselves in its place? The soft spot of the enemy was near Caumont, as the 7. Armee map on the enemy situation of 22.00 hours on 28.6. indicates. An attack in this sector, as originally planned and with the Mulberry harbors as the objective, would have pushed into the deep flank of the enemy and not just hit him in the shoulder. In view of such a threat to his supply depots, to the airfields in the bridgehead, and even to the artillery positions of the VIII and XXX Corps, the enemy would have had to break off Operation "EPSOM" immediately and re-deploy his troops in action there. The German forces in action in the breakthrough sector could have retaken their old front lines.

Available for such a counterattack in the Caumont area were: the II. SS-Panzerkorps with the SS-Panzerdivisions "Hohenstaufen" and "Frundsberg", the 2. Panzerdivision, the 2. SS-Panzerdivision "Das Reich", without the Weidinger Kampfgruppe, and parts of the Panzer-Lehr-Division.

The SS-Panzergrenadierregiment 1 of the "LAH" Division and the Weidinger Kampfgruppe were available for containment attacks and to penetrate into the breakthrough sector. In addition, parts of 21. Pz.-Div., which was just being relieved, were free.

While, in total, the units available for an attack in the west were weaker than the original plan had foreseen, one enemy tank division, two infantry divisions and three tank brigades were tied down in the breakthrough sector.

They had been considered available at the planned start of the German counterattack at the beginning of July. The whole situation could be changed in favor of the Germans only through an attack, and the sooner, the better, since enemy forces were reinforced at a faster rate than the German forces. The favorable situation, brought about by the early enemy attack and the outstanding defensive fighting by the "Hitlerjugend" Division, was obviously not recognized by either the supreme command of the 7. Armee, which was responsible, nor that of Heeresgruppe B.

CHAPTER 3.6
Counteroffensive by the I. and II. SS-Panzerkorps to Cut Off the British Odon-Bridgehead on 29 June 1944

The counterattack by the two SS-Panzerkorps on 29 June can be described only in broad terms. As far as II. SS-Panzer-korps was involved—and it was in the center of the fighting—the battles of this and the subsequent days were portrayed in detail in the book by Wilhelm Tieke : "Im Feuersturm letzter Kriegsjahre" (Inside the fire storm of the last war years), Osnabrück, 1975. The I. SS-Panzerkorps was involved in this counterattack only with parts of the "HJ" Division and units attached to it. They were Panzerregiment 12, one Kompanie of the Korps-Tiger-Abteilung 101, the Aufklärungsabteilung 12, the III./26, the SS-Panzergrenadierregiment 1 "LAH" (without one battalion), two Panzer companies Panzerregiment 22 (21. Pz.-Div.), the SS-Artillerieregiment 12 and the Werfer-regiment 83. The other battalions and Abteilungen were tied up in defensive action in other sectors.

The VIII Corps had the following intentions for 29 June:
1) Enlargement of the bridgehead across the Odon river;
2) Clearing the area Colleville—Tourville—Tourmauville—Gavrus—Bougy—woods 500 m southwest of Cahier (all towns were included) by the 15th Division;
3) Clearing the area Bas de Mouen—Gournay—Baron—excluding Tourville—excluding Colleville by the 43rd Division;
4) As soon as the 15th Division had accomplished its mission, the 11th Armoured Division—as foreseen in the original plan—would further advance toward the Orne.[1]

On the German side, the deployment and assembly of II. SS-Panzerkorps for the counterattack continued through the night and forenoon of 29 June. The planned start of the attack at 06.00 hours had to be postponed to 14.00 hours because of a delay in the deployment.[2] The units of I. SS-Panzerkorps, which were to attack together with the II. SS-Panzerkorps from the east and south, had to await the completion of the assembly and the start of the attack from the west. They were attacked by the enemy prior to this happening.

In the meantime, the British attacks to clear the towns in their attack sector began. The 8th RS and the 6th RSF reached the railroad embankment west of Grainville at approximately 10.40 hours. In the course of the day, the 2nd Gordons in Tourville and the 10th HLI in Colleville were relieved by parts of the 214th Brigade. They assembled south of Mondrainville in order to be available and ready for the advance on Gavrus.[3]

The Worcesters of the 43rd Division attacked Mouen and had the town cleared by 11.00 hours. The 129th Infantry Brigade attacked from the area south of Mouen in the direction of Baron. It captured the town in a slow advance, facing moderate resistance, by 18.30 hours. The 159th Infantry Brigade reinforced the bridgehead near Tourmauville, disturbed only by mortar fire.[4]

The 29th Armoured Brigade of the 11th Armoured Division wanted to capture Hill 112 and Esquay before noon. At 04.40 hours, the 44th Royal Tanks (assigned from the 4th Armoured Brigade)—without one company— tried to outflank Esquay, without success. The 8th Battalion Rifle Brigade, without 'F' Squadron but supported by the 3rd Royal Tanks, attacked the small wooded area 300 meters east of Hill 112 at 10.15 hours. This was the small square wood which would later be so violently fought for. A few Panzers of SS Panzerregiment 12 had held up the advance there until then. At the same time, the 2nd Fife and Forfar Yeomanry, swinging to the left, planned to support the attack, but was stopped by fire from the Château de Fontaine area. At approximately 11.00 hours, the Panzers of Panzerregiment 12 had to withdraw in the face of the superior enemy who then occupied the square wood. Fierce and accurate fire from artillery and mortars was concentrated on the wood throughout the day.[5]

As indicated in the reports by Kändler and Kretzschmar, the square wood was in enemy hands the previous day. Apparently, it had been captured during the night by parts of Panzerregiment 12 and of III./26. The 8th Battalion The Rifle Brigade tried to re-capture it, but was repelled at 03.30 hours. In the morning, the British then attempted again to take the wood, supported by tanks, and were successful. Oberscharführer Kretzschmar of 5. Panzerkompanie observed some of the fighting and reported on it:

On 29.6. we were in covering position at the base of Hill 112. Artillery fire was raining down on us. Around noon, some eight to ten fighter-bombers showed up and circled overhead the square wood. They then attacked in a dive with bombs, rockets and onboard weapons. We sat in our hatches, marveling at the spectacle. '. . . it's better they blast their own troops than us!', my gunner commented.[6]

At approximately the same time, tanks of the 3rd Battalion The Royal Tank Regiment were attacking from the area 750 m northwest of Hill 112 to the south and southwest. They encountered six Tigers situated west of Hill 112 which fought them off.[7]

The evening report of Panzergruppe West stated, regarding the battle at Hill 112, that ". . . an enemy column of approximately 50 tanks and infantry from Baron in the direction of Château de Fontaine was destroyed by artillery and mortar fire."

According to the evening report of Panzergruppe West, the attack by II. SS-Panzerkorps started at 14.30 hours. The daily report of 7. Armee fixed the time to be 15.30 hours.[8]

The 9. SS-Panzerdivision attacked along both sides of the road Noyers-Cheux. SS-Panzergrenadierregiment 20 was on the right, SS-Panzergrenadierregiment 19 was in the middle and the Weidinger Kampfgruppe was on the left. SS-Panzerregiment 9 supported the attack.

A breakthrough succeeded between le Valtru, defended by the 7th Seaforths, and Grainville where the 9th Cameronians were in position. The breakthrough was sealed off with the support of the 9th Royal Tanks (without one squadron), from artillery and the air force. By approximately 18.00 hours, the enemy had re-established himself in his previous position.

Further to the north, at the railroad embankment near Grainville, the attack by the "Hohenstaufen" ran into the relief of the 8th Royal Scots by the 6th Royal Scotch Fusiliers. Two companies of the 8th RS were overrun. But the breakthrough was sealed off there, too. Since 14.00 hours, two units of the 4th Armoured Brigade—the 4th CLY and the 44th Royal Tanks—and self-propelled anti-tank guns of the Anti Tank Regiment were ready, in the sector of the 44th Infantry Brigade, to repel the expected counterattack.

To the left of it, a few Panzers were able to break through to Cheux, but they were stopped there and knocked out.[9]

In the course of the afternoon, the attack by the "Hohenstaufen" Division broke down at the tank and anti-tank gun barriers, in the barrages of the superior artillery and the hail of bombs from the air force. The troops had to be withdrawn to their starting positions.

To the south of the Odon river—probably somewhat later, since the advance of SS-Panzergrenadierregiment 21, which had been relieved at the eastern front as the last, had been delayed—the "Frundsberg" Division attacked. Regiment 21, reinforced by Panzers and Pioniers, succeeded toward the evening in capturing Evrécy and Hill 113. A further advance toward Esquay was not possible. To the left, Panzergrenadierregiment 22, also supported by Panzers and Pioniers, took Gavrus. However, it was driven out by a counterattack and set up defensive positions immediately south and southwest of the town.[10]

At 16.00 hours, an officer of III./SS-Panzer-Gren.Rgt.19 ("Hohenstaufen) had been captured in the area west of le Haut du Bosq. The map found on him, and notes in his notebook, indicated that this was an attack by three battalions of SS-Pz.Gren.Rgt.19 along an axis Feuguerolles-Brettevil-lette with the starting line le Valtru-Vendes. The objective was to capture and hold Cheux. Another captured document showed that one battalion of SS-Pz.Gren.Rgt.20 was also taking part. A prisoner stated that Panzers of SS-Panzerregiment 9 were also fighting alongside the infantry.[11]

Based on the impression of the fighting of the afternoon and the results of aerial reconnaissance, statements from prisoners and captured documents, the enemy decided on new plans. At approximately 21.00 hours, the VIII Corps received orders from the Second Army, in view of the overall situation, to halt the attack toward the Orne for the time being and to consolidate in the captured area. The 29th Armoured Brigade was to withdraw to the northern bank of the Odon and the Odon bridgehead be held by infantry. The four tank units were carefully pulled back across the only bridge near Tourmauville, in driving rain, between 23.00 and 04.00 hours. They assembled south of Norrey.[12]

Effective 00.00 hours on 30 June, the following changes in assignment occurred on the enemy side:

53rd Division—until then with XII Corps—to VIII Corps;

159th Infantry Brigade from 11th Armoured Division to the 15th (Scottish) Division;

86th Anti Tank Regiment from XII Corps to the 53rd Division;

one battery from the 91st Anti Tank Regiment to the 43rd Division;

one battery from the 91st Anti Tank Regiment back to the 21st Anti Tank Regiment;

72nd Medium Regiment (artillery) from I Corps to VIII Corps;

68th Medium Regiment from VII Corps to I Corps;

32nd Guards Brigade Group remained attached to the 43rd Division.

As the first unit of the 53rd Division, the 158th Infantry Brigade was to arrive and assemble in the Norrey-Putot-le Mesnil area.

The plan of the VIII Corps for 30 June was to hold the positions captured on 29 June and to reinforce them. Two infantry brigades were to hold the bridgeheads across the Odon and two tank brigades were to assemble in such a manner that they could secure the le Haut du Bosq-Cheux area.[13]

The Supreme Command of the 7. Armee judged the situation in its daily summary for 29 June 1944 in this way:

The armor battle for Caen, for which the enemy had brought in several new divisions from the Tilly-sur-Seulles area on 25 June, has passed, for the time being, its greatest intensity. This was brought about by the counterattack of II. SS-Panzerkorps whose combat-ready point forces entered the fighting at 14.00 hours.

The arrival of the divisions of II. SS-Pz.-Korps, barely in time, made possible the prevention of the enlargement of the break-through area on all sides. Further, the breakthrough was compressed against an enemy who was superior on the ground and in the air.

New, and large, loads from ships west and east of the Orne indi-cate the arrival of further forces. It can be assumed that the enemy will continue his attack from the breakthrough area and, in connec-tion with it, possibly east of the Orne in order to capture the impor-tant road junction center of Caen.[14]

The plans of I. SS-Panzerkorps for 30 June 1944 is recorded in a noted telephone call:

> 22.20 hours: I. SS-Panzerkorps intends to continue the attack after regrouping. Because of the difficult terrain, the concentration will be on the left. The breakthrough area is eight kilometers deep, six kilometers wide. Newly arrived English divisions: 11th Armour Divi-sion, 15th and 43rd Infantry Divisions and 4th Tank Brigade.

Another note indicates the intentions of II. SS-Panzerkorps:

> 23.00 hours: Plan of II. SS-Panzerkorps: Attack tonight in the Ver-son-Mouen-Baron area, with concentration at 12. SS-Pz.-Div.[15]

This last entry is incomprehensible since 12. SS-Pz.-Div. was not attached to the II. but to I. Korps. The "HJ" Division did not have forces available for a concentrated attack. It is likely true that the attack by II. Korps was sched-uled to continue during the night and be supported by the "HJ" Division in the vicinity of Hill 112.

CHAPTER 3.7
Continuation of the Counteroffensive by the I. and II. SS-Panzerkorps on 30 June 1944. Breaking Off the Attack, End of the Third Battle for Caen.

As planned, the II. SS-Panzerkorps and parts of I. SS-Panzerkorps resumed the attack during the night 29–30 June 1944. The objective was to cut off the breakthrough.

On the right wing of the "Frundsberg" Division, Panzer-regiment 21 started its attack at 01.30 hours and succeeded in occupying Avenay and

Vieux. In Vieux, contact with III./SS Panzergrenadierregiment 26 of the "HJ" Division was established. After assembly and preparatory fire from Artillerie-regiment 12 and Werferregiment 83, as well as parts of Werferbrigade 8 which had been directed to support the "Frundsberg" Division, II. Abteilung SS-Panzerregiment 12 with parts of III./26 attacked Hill 112 from the east and southeast. At the same time, parts of SS-Panzergrenadier-regiment 21 and II. Abteilung of SS-Panzerregiment 10 attacked from the south and southwest. Except for a few tanks, the enemy had already withdrawn his tanks units from Hill 112. It was still occupied by the 8th Rifle Battalion The Rifle Brigade. The artillery and rocket barrages had a devastating impact. When the Panzers started out, they were able to quickly capture the hill, which had been fought over for days. The hilltop was taken by 07.30 hours, the north slope by noon.

Untersturmführer Willi Kändler of 5. Panzerkompanie of Panzerregiment 12 reported on this attack:

Early in the morning, rockets from our launchers, trailing veils of smoke, howled into the English positions in the small square wood. These launchers decided the success of the attack during that morning. This was our fourth attack on Hill 112, and it was crowned by the capture of the square wood and the hill. As we drove up, we saw numerous destroyed vehicles, among them knocked-out Sherman tanks.[1]

Oberscharführer Willi Kretzschmar of 5. Kompanie experienced it in this way:

The attack advanced at a swift pace. Without any resistance worth mentioning—no comparison with the previous attacks-we reached the square wood and Hill 112. We saw destroyed tractors, armored personnel carriers, Pak, as well as Sherman and Churchill Mark III tanks. When the situation on the hill quietened down, our radio operator, Erich Stefan, went exploring. He brought back several large tins of chocolate cookies from the knocked-out tractors. For the next few days of fighting, we were well supplied.[2]

Sturmmann Erich Fugunt of 6. Kompanie of Panzerregiment 12 wrote on this:

Our own artillery first fired right among us until we sent up a white flare. There was a terrible din in the early morning light. The rocket launchers were firing right above us toward the hill. The Grenadiers reported that the 'Tommies' were on the run. Without waiting for an order, Oberjunker (officer cadet) Mühlhaus said: 'Let's go!'

When we reached the top, it was all over. Some tank engines were still running, but no-one could be seen inside. Grenadiers of the 'Frundsberg' were already coming up the other side. Some hours later they came under a heavy artillery barrage and suffered heavy losses.[3]

To the left of Regiment 21, SS-Panzergrenadierregiment 22 again attacked Gavrus. Artillery and mortar fire, as well as hand-to-hand combat, caused the 2nd Argylls to suffer high losses. They were forced to abandon Gavrus and withdrew, as ordered by the Brigade, under cover of their tanks, which had been brought up for this reason, to Colleville by way of le Valtru.[4]

The "Hohenstaufen" Division had also started its attack to the left of the "Frundsberg" at 01.30 hours. SS-Panzer-grenadierregiment 19 was stalled near Grainville, in particular when fire from the flank from the Baron area set in with first light. The attack by SS-Panzergrenadierregiment 20, to the left, was also unable to advance further after some initial successes, facing an enemy prepared for defense, who had considerably fortified his positions.

In the afternoon, II. SS-Panzerkorps, whose command had been assumed by the previous commander of the "Hohenstaufen" Division, SS-Gruppenführer and Generalleutnant der Waffen-SS Bittrich, ordered the attack, which had become hopeless, to be stopped. The forward line in the sector of I. and II. Panzerkorps ran as follows in the evening of 30 June, starting at the right wing of "HJ" Division: Southern edge of Cambes-northwestern edge of Buron-northwestern edge of Gruchy-1.5 kilometers northwest of Carpiquet-center of Verson-western edge of Eterville-Hill 112-crossroads 200 meters southeast of Tourmauville-southern edge of les Vilains-northern edge of Gavrus-crossroads le Valtru-group of houses southwest of Grainville-southern edge of Tessel-Bretteville-crossroads one kilometer southwest of that town-immediately west of the Tessel Woods-Juvigny (incl.)-road fork one kilometer northwest of Longraye-northwestern corner Bois de St. Germain.

In the addendum to the daily report of Panzergruppe West, from which the account of the location of the forward line was taken, it was stated as the intention of the Panzergruppe: ". . . continuation of the attack with II. SS-Panzerkorps during the night 30 June to 1 July . . ."[5]

The enemy expected the continuation of the attacks by II. SS-Panzerkorps. At 11.00 hours, the VIII Corps issued orders at the command post of the 15th (Scottish) Division to representatives there of the 11th Armoured Division, the 15th (Scottish) Division, the 43rd (Wessex) Division, the 53rd (Welsh) Division, and the 31st and 33rd Tank Brigades. The Second Army had advised that, according to information ". . . from very reliable sources . . .' a more forceful counterattack than that of the previous day, with the same direction of thrust, was possible. The information indicated that the attack of the previous day had only been a probe. Thus, it was ordered that further advances were to be stopped for the time being and the present positions be held.

Overall, the plan envisaged:

the artillery remained in its present positions;

the anti-tank activities in the sector of the Corps were to be coordinated under the direction of the commander of the 91st Anti Tank Regiment;

the 4th Armoured Brigade was to be held in readiness in the area northwest of Cheux in order to confront any tank attacks from the southeast and southwest;

the 29th Armoured Brigade was assembled in the area northeast of Cheux in order to meet any tank attacks from the east. Both of the brigades were prepared to assist the other;

on the right flank, a tight connection with the left wing of the XXX Corps was to be maintained;

during the nights 30 June to 1 July, and 1 to 2 July each, one infantry brigade of the 15th (Scottish) Division was to be relieved by a brigade of the 53rd Division.[6]

This attack by II. SS-Panzerkorps did not come about. The third battle for Caen had come to an end. The enemy had been unsuccessful in forcing the breakthrough to the Orne river or even beyond to the high plains south of Caen, despite the fact that he had assembled vastly superior forces for this. This was primarily the achievement of all elements of 12. SS-Panzer-division "Hitlerjugend" in action there. They had prevented for two and one-half days, through the battles near and south of Fontenay, the capture of Rauray which was a significant requirement for Operation "EPSOM". The breach of the line of the neighbor to the left had brought about the order putting the whole of the Panzerregiment into action, thus robbing the front line in the attack sector of the VIII Corps, on 26 June, of any mobile anti-tank capability. Despite this, I./26, Pionier-bataillon 12, II./26 and units of Regiment 26 had held off a deep penetration until 5., 7., and 8. Panzerkompanie had returned. These few Panzers had prevented any enemy attempt to break through to Grainville until the morning of 28 June, inflicting heavy losses on the vastly superior enemy forces. However, they and the few Tigers of Hauptsturmführer Möbius were too weak to close the gap which had developed on the right. There, the enemy had been able to break through and form a bridgehead across the Odon river on 27 June. That this succeeded only so late was the achievement of the stragglers who made the town of Cheux difficult to pass through for the enemy until 28 June and defended themselves in their resistance positions to the bitter end. Many members of the supply troops, although normally charged with other duties, stood the test. The Artillerieregiment, although short of ammunition, effectively supported the Grenadiers, Pioniers and Panzers, often at very close range. Werferregiment

83 provided invaluable assistance during defense and counterattack during the last phase of the battle. Time and again, the communications crews of the battalions, regiments and the Division had maintained contact, and re-established it. Without this, any kind of leadership would have been almost impossible. The medical services performed their difficult duties for days in a devoted manner, for days without a break. The supply troops brought forward whatever the fighting troops needed and whatever they had available, day and night. The repair services of the Panzerregiment, from the repair squads of the companies in the front lines to the repair companies, brought disabled Panzers back to battle-readiness, without taking a rest and often under enemy fire. The Panzers and assault guns of 21. Panzerdivision supported 15./25 in a comradely manner when the objective was to prevent the enlargement of the breakthrough area near Mouen. They also supported the two battalions of SS-Panzergrenadierregiment 1 when the attempt was made to cut off the enemy who had broken through. Although this attack did not achieve its objective, it did contribute to making the enemy delay his advance. During the battles for Hill 112 and near Esquay, Obersturmbann-führer Wünsche with the decimated Panzerregiment 12, the Aufk-lärungsabteilung and III./26, fought off all enemy attacks, as previously at Fontenay and rauray. His 30 Panzers, at most, were facing the 165 tanks of VIII Corps in the evening of 28 June. Finally, it must be emphasized that the determined fighting by I./26 of Sturmbannführer Krause significantly contributed to the enemy dropping his plan to capture the Carpiquet airfield with the 3rd Canadian Division. Finally, II. Panzerabteilung and III./26 had the privilege, together with Panzers and Grenadiers of the "Frundsberg", to recapture the dominating Hill 112. It would then be the focal point of heavy fighting for weeks to come.

The "Hitlerjugend" Division had suffered heavy losses during these battles. Those of 29 and 30 June are shown in the table below:

Units	Killed			Wounded			Missing		
	Officers	NCOs	Men	Officers	NCOs	Men	Officers	NCOs	Men
R.E.26	-	-	-	-	-	2	-	-	-
I./26	-	-	-	-	2	-	-	-	-
II./26	-	1	2	-	-	1	-	-	-
III./26	-	-	1	-	2	3	-	-	-
A.A.12	-	1	-	-	-	-	-	-	-
Pz.Rgt.	2	-	1	2	5	19	1	1	1
A.R.12	-	-	2	-	2	6	-	-	-
Total	2	2	6	2	11	31	1	1	1

The total losses of the Division during the defense and counterattack in the sector of the British offensive are compiled in the following overview:

Date	Killed			Wounded			Missing		
	Officers	NCOs	Men	Officers	NCOs	Men	Officers	NCOs	Men
25.6.	1	4	40	4	17	99	2	-	21
26.6.	3	13	72	11	32	187	4	21	383
27.6.	6	3	35	3	16	90	1	3	34
28.6.	1	2	19	-	12	42	-	-	2
29. & 30.	2	2	6	2	11	31	1	1	1
Total	13	24	172	20	88	449	8	25	441

The total losses amounted to 209 killed, 557 wounded and 474 missing, for an overall total of 1,240 losses.[7]

No figures are available for the British losses, except in those cases where they were indicated in the war diaries used.

The French civilian population was also affected by the fighting, in particular the inhabitants of the villages in the battlefield area who did not want to abandon their houses or farms.

As has already been mentioned, a young Frenchman living in Verson and attending secondary school in Caen, watched the heavy air bombardment of the city on the day of the Allied landing. His family experienced particularly painful circumstances during Operation "EPSOM". He wrote on this:

On 26 June 1944 at approximately 7 A.M., the Allied artillery started to shell with increasing vehemence. Then, there was a pause in the fire. My father, responsible for civil air defense in the village, left the house of our friends to determine what damage had occurred. He returned after completing this mission. At 7.30 A.M., renewed heavy harassing fire started. I watched a team of horses gallop down the street without a driver. My father picked up his helmet and disappeared. That was his last mission.

A few minutes prior to this barrage I spoke to an SS-Obersturm-führer who had brought us a bottle of gasoline, since we used a gasoline lamp. Suddenly, all hell broke loose! My mother, her friends, my friend, the SS-Obersturm-führer and I disappeared into a shelter trench. This artillery fire lasted for 1/2 or 3/4 of an hour. At the Odon river, behind the church, a truck was burning with bright flames. Some houses were damaged or destroyed. When quiet set in again, I came across the priest: 'I have heard that your father was mortally wounded. He is already dead. A man found him in the Rue des Ruettes and brought him into the cellar of your house'. I found my father dead, he had been shot through the chest. The fall had broken his teeth and the force of the explosion had burst his lungs. On 26 June 1944, Verson suffered ten killed and thirty wounded.

Our house was destroyed on 28 June.

During the night from 1 to 2 July, brisk artillery fire from both sides set in. Rockets howled overhead. At about 5 a.m. I no longer wanted to remain under cover. I decided to catch a breath of fresh air and went for a walk in Verson. I had friends who were in the trenches. Now and then, I heard machine gun salvos and in the Rue de Dîme some bullets whistled by. The former recreation center opposite the church stood in flames. Together with some other residents we decided to cross the German front lines since life there had become unbearable.

At 6 A.M. we formed a procession of approximately 150 persons. Smoldering beams and collapsed houses blocked the streets. When we reached the western edge of the village, Allied artillery fire forced us to the ground. I crept into a hollow tree trunk and waited for the end. Then we fled on. In the ravine at Colleville (near Mouen), two British Sherman tanks were on fire. Suddenly, at the entrance to Mouen, several British soldiers aimed their weapons at us. They were equipped with submachine guns.

The following day, we were distributed among the villages around Bayeux. A month later we returned to Verson.[8]

The general command of I. SS-Panzerkorps requested from the Armee supreme command on 27 June, that the "Hitlerjugend" Division be mentioned in the Wehrmachtsbericht (armed forces report) with the following wording:

In the bitter fighting west of Caen on 26.6.1944, the SS-Panzerdivision 'Hitlerjugend' under the command of Standartenführer Meyer has particularly proved itself and inflicted maximum losses on the enemy. Sixty enemy tanks were destroyed, some of them in close combat. During this action, the Kampfgruppen of SS-Obersturmbannführer Wünsche and of Sturmbannführer Olboeter especially distinguished themselves as the cornerstones of the armor battle.[9]

A part of the Wehrmachtsbericht of 29 June 1944 read:

. . . In Normandy, the enemy expanded his strong attacks to a width of almost twenty-five kilometers. The fighting in the area southwest of Caen, where the enemy had achieved a narrow penetration, was particularly bitter. The counterattack by German armored Kampfgruppen, which started in the evening hours, compressed the enemy spearheads into a very narrow area. The enemy suffered grave losses of men and materiel. One Panzerabteilung alone destroyed fifty-three enemy tanks. During the fighting of the last few days, 12. SS-Panzerdivision 'Hitlerjugend' under the command of SS-Standartenführer Meyer and, in particular, the Kampfgruppe of SS-Sturmbannführer Olboeter fought outstandingly . . .[10]

In its situation report of 26 June, the Division had listed the names of those who especially distinguished themselves. These were:

the commander of Panzerregiment 12, Obersturmbannführer Wünsche;

the commander of III./SS-Panzergrenadierregiment 26, Sturmbannführer Olboeter;

the commander of Aufklärungsabteilung 12, Sturmbann-führer Bremer;

the commander of I./SS-Panzergrenadierregiment 26, Sturmbannführer Krause;

the chief of 6. Panzerkompanie, Hauptsturmführer Ruckdeschel;

the chief of 8. Panzerkompanie, Hauptsturmführer -Siegel;

the leader of a Pak of 4./SS-Panzergrenadierregiment 26, Unterscharführer Dürr.

To this list should have been added the names of the commander of Pionierbataillon 12, Sturmbannführer Müller who only reached his own lines again during the following day, and of the chief of 4. Kompanie of SS-Panzergrenadierregiment 26, Obersturmführer Alois Hartung who only returned to his own lines days later.

These names are also representative of the troop branches they belonged to. For all those whose quiet valor was not rewarded with a medal—and those were certainly many, above all those killed and wounded—Unterscharführer Emil Dürr must be representative. He was awarded the Knight's Cross posthumously.

At the end of this battle, the following were submitted to be awarded the Knight's Cross: Sturmbannführer Erich Olboeter, Sturmbannführer Bernhard Krause, and Hauptsturmführer Hans Siegel.

The Oak Leaves were proposed for Obersturmbannführer Max Wünsche. All four submissions were approved. The text of the submission for Obersturmbannführer Wünsche's Oak Leaves follows:

During the difficult attacks and defensive fighting of 12.SS-Pz.-Div. 'Hitlerjugend' west of Caen, SS-Panzer-Rgt.12 under the leadership of its commander, Obersturmbannführer Max Wünsche, has destroyed 219 enemy tanks until now. This success must be credited solely to the flexible leadership and determination of its com-

mander. With resolute personal involvement he mastered the most
difficult situations. The action of SS-Panzer-Rgt.12 on 28–29 June
1944 southwest of Caen foiled the enemy intention of forming a
bridgehead near Amayé and St. André across the Orne river. Kampfgruppe Wünsche, through constant counterattacks and skillfully
executed thrusts to the flank, was successful in smashing the enemy
tank spearhead. Without the action of SS-Panzer-Rgt.12 under the
command of SS-Obersturmbannführer Wünsche, the Division
would not have been able to destroy the enemy forces southwest of
Caen. The achievements of SS-Panzer-Rgt.12 must be valued especially highly since it is a young regiment with a very young corps of
non-commissioned officers and even younger men. The losses suffered by SS-Panzer-Rgt.12 bear no relationship to the enemy tank
losses. SS-Obersturmbannführer Wünsche was already wounded on
the second day during close hand-to-hand combat. Despite this, he
remained with his regiment and continued to lead it with brave personal engagement.

I submit that the personal valor of the commander of SS-Panzer-
Rgt.12, Obersturmbannführer Max Wünsche, and his skillful leadership be recognized with the awarding of the

Oak Leaves to the Knight's Cross of the Iron Cross
signed: Meyer
SS-Standartenführer
and Division Commander[11]

Despite all the valor of the involved elements of the "HJ" Division, the
Tigerkompanie, Werferregiment 83, the three Panzer- and assault gun companies of 21. Panzerdivision and parts of III. Flakkorps, the British breakthrough across the Orne could not have been prevented without the
engagement of the Weidinger Kampfgruppe, the SS-Panzergrenadier-regiment 1 (without III. Bataillon) and, in particular, of II. SS-Panzerkorps. But
this also had the consequence that these units were weakened by the counterattacks to the point where they could no longer be considered for the initially planned offensive operation. Thus, despite the failure of his offensive,
the enemy had achieved a great success: he had prevented the counteroffen-
sive. Another solution which could have been considered on the German
side has already been indicated previously. Even if the desired success had
not been achieved, the effect of an attack at a weak spot of the enemy, threatening his supply basis, had to be more positive than a counterattack, almost
as a continuation of the advance, against a vastly superior enemy who was
prepared for defense.

While the Second Army, overestimating the strength of the forces available in the breakthrough area, was still expecting a major attack, the leader-

ship of Panzergruppe West had come to the conclusion that the earlier planned attack to separate the British and American beachheads was no longer possible. Given the existing ratio of forces, even cutting-off the penetration area of the VIII Corps could no longer be achieved. New decisions became necessary.

At the end of this section, a sentence by the British military author Chester Wilmot on the actions by the soldiers of the "Hitlerjugend" Division from his book "The Struggle for Europe" should be cited:

> The 12. SS-Panzerdivision, which defended this sector, fought with a determination and ferocity which would not be encountered again throughout the whole campaign.[12]

The Chief of the General Staff   HQ, 15 August 1944
of the Heer

Dear Wünsche!

On the occasion of the renewed noble honor which was awarded you by the Führer on 11.8.44, I express to you and your brave Regiment my sincerest congratulations.

All the best for the difficult battles and continued good soldier's luck!

In comradely solidarity and with

Heil Hitler!
Yours
Guderian

SECTION 4

The Fourth Battle for Caen from 4 to 10 July 1944

CHAPTER 4.0
Preparations

The objective of the British "EPSOM" Operation, the breakthrough to the Orne bridges and the capture of the high plain south of Caen, had not been achieved. The British had forestalled the German intention to separate the British-Canadian bridgehead from the American through an attack by the concentrated Panzerdivisions. Among those forces scheduled to take part in this action; all of the SS-Panzerdivisions "Frundsberg" and "Hohenstaufen", as well as parts of the "LAH" and "Das Reich" had been put into action to prevent the enemy breakthrough. Both sides had to reach new decisions.

The picture of the enemy held by the OKW and the supreme command authorities in the west were based on the Lagebericht West Nr. 1308 (situation report west) by the general staff of the Heer/Abteilung Fremde Heere West (department foreign armies west) of 26.6.1944. In it, the situation in England was described as follows:

> Determination of location of forces have lately made more and more apparent the strong concentration of forces in the southeastern part of England. The army in the sector London-Brighton-Dover, attached to the Canadian army supreme command, is constituted mainly of English and Canadian units. The 3rd US Army, assembled northeast of London, is made up mainly of American units. Also, the composition of these two armies indicates a plan for action in the central Channel sector, in-as-much as the army located closer to the continent is composed of the more highly valued British units.
>
> The fall of Cherbourg will soon have greater implications on the Normandy peninsula. The 4–5 American units, tied down in the battle for Cherbourg, can now be brought into action for the further

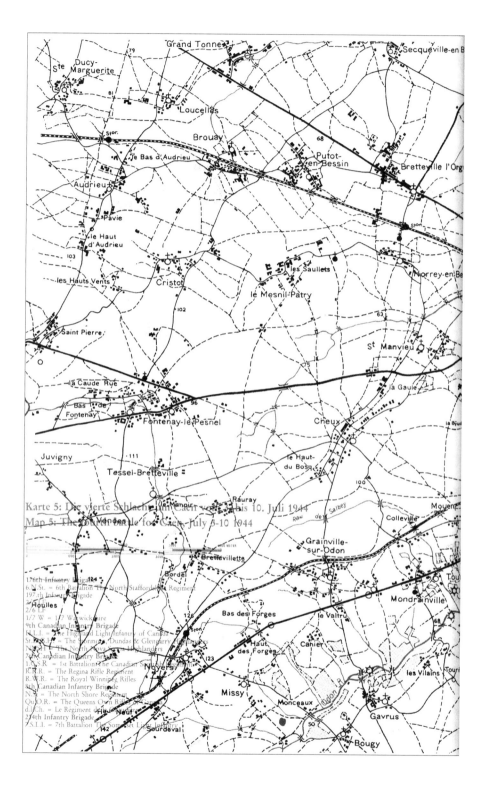

Karte 5: Die vierte Schlacht um Caen vom 5. bis 10. Juli 1944
Map 5: The Ditt Battle for Caen July 5-10 1944

176th Infantry Brigade
6. N.St. = 6th Battalion The North Staffordshire Regiment
197.th Infantry Brigade
2/6 LF
1/7 W = 1/7 Warwickshire
9th Canadian Infantry Brigade
H.L.I. = The Highland Light Infantry of Canada
St. D. & G. H. = The Stormont, Dundas & Glengarry Highlanders
N.N.S.H. = The North Nova Scotia Highlanders
7th Canadian Infantry Brigade
1.C.S.R. = 1st Battalion The Canadian Scottish Regiment
R.R.R. = The Regina Rifle Regiment
R.W.R. = The Royal Winnipeg Rifles
8th Canadian Infantry Brigade
N.Sh. = The North Shore Regiment
Qu.O.R. = The Queens Own Rifles of Canada
d.l.Ch. = Le Régiment de la Chaudière
214th Infantry Brigade
7.S.L.I. = 7th Battalion The Somerset Light Infantry

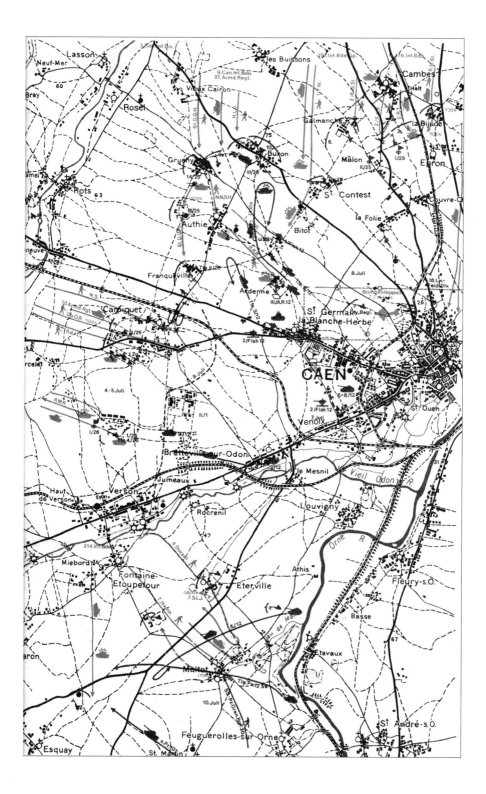

fighting to capture the peninsula, in a generally southern direction.
. . . An imminent use of Cherbourg harbor, based on the present
level of destruction, should, however, not be expected. Thus, transport of supplies and additional forces for all of the Normandy area
will have to primarily take place through landing craft cargo space
for probably several weeks to come.[1]

Supreme Command West informed the attached commando authorities
on 27 June of an OKW order of 26 June which was obviously based on the
judgment of the enemy situation by Fremde Heere West. In it, it was stated:

The grouping of enemy forces in England as well as in Normandy
indicates with increasing certainty that the enemy will concentrate
his second major landing between the Somme and Seine rivers.
    The fighting in Normandy has shown that a major landing can
only be repelled if a sufficient number of large units are assembled
as a reserve immediately behind the coastal front line. For this, the
reserves assembled between Somme and Seine (116.Pz.Div. and
84.I.D.) do not appear sufficient.
    Supreme Command West will propose which other units can be
brought into this area. The resulting weakening of other front lines
is accepted, but not that of the Kampfgruppe which is being assembled facing the beachhead.[2]

The fact that Heeresgruppe B also shared this judgment of the enemy is
shown in a teletype message which it sent to the Supreme Command West
on 25 June. Apparently, Supreme Command West had ordered the move of
89.Inf.Div. into the area east of Le Havre. The Heeresgruppe objected
against this and wrote:

The withdrawal of these forces prevents the planned, urgently
required reinforcement of the defensive strength of 15. Armee at its
present weak spots, namely:
    a) in the Ostend area (possible enemy starting point, according
       to reports from informers, etc.),
    b) in the Somme-Seine sector. This sector appears of particular
       importance in the context of the enemy operation in Nor-
       mandy whose planned enlargement from the Caen area in an
       easterly and southeasterly direction can be expected as indi-
       cated in monitored orders for aerial photo missions. The
       increased aerial reconnaissance in the coastal sector between
       Somme and Seine of the last days indicates the intention of
       the enemy to start an operation north of the Seine, using the
       army group which has not yet been deployed. In cooperation

with the Montgomery army group operating south of the Seine, it aims at a breakthrough to capture Paris.[3]

The agreement with the OKW assessment of the enemy situation and his plans is not surprising when one remembers that the Ic of the Heeresgruppe was the former department chief for England in the office for Fremde Heere West, Oberstleutnant i.G. Staubwasser. This must not be interpreted as saying that he had been made aware of the falsifications by Oberst von Roenne and Major Michael.

The situation map of Supreme Command West of 26.6.1944 indicates only minor changes compared to that of 26.6. whose tabular listing is shown in Chapter 3.0. The listing of 26.6. merely indicates one extra infantry brigade in its total. The units still available in England are reduced by one infantry division and one tank brigade, and increased by one airborne division. It is revealing to look at a comparison of the units of the Second British Army, assumed to be in the beachhead, and those available in reality. In this context, attention is immediately drawn to the fact that the name of the supreme commander is given as Anderson instead of Dempsey.

Division in the beachhead

Indicated by Supreme Command West	In reality
4 infantry divisions	8 infantry divisions
1 tank escort infantry division	— — —
3 tank divisions	2 tank divisions and parts of another
1 airborne division	— — —

Of the available divisions, these were not recognized: 15th, 43rd, 53rd Infantry Divisions, 11th and parts of Guards Armoured Divisions.

Of those assumed to be available, these were not there: 9th Armoured and 6th Airborne Divisions.

The unit called "3.Pz.-Gren.-Div." was very likely the 3rd (British) Infantry Division. The Allies did not have any "Panzergrenadier" Divisions. All infantry divisions were motorized and were normally strengthened by tank brigades. The "79.Pz.-Div.", named by Supreme Command West, was probably an assembly of armored special units which were assigned as required but could not be put into action together. These were, for instance, tanks for the removal of mines, laying of bridges, or flame-thrower tanks.

While the total figure of the Allied divisions, based on the falsified information from Fremde Heere West, was vastly exaggerated, too few divisions were assumed to be in the beachhead. Invariably, this had to lead to wrong conclusions and decisions.

Finally, it is also remarkable that Lagebericht West No. 1308 (situation report west) of 26.6., from the department Fremde Heere West, assumed that reinforcements and supplies would be brought in by landing craft; there was no longer any word concerning the existing man-made harbors.

As already mentioned, the two supreme commanders in the west, Field Marshals von Rundstedt and Rommel, were at the Führer headquarters for a briefing at the height of the crisis during the British "EPSOM" offensive. In a report put together by Major i.G. Wolfram, who had accompanied Feldmarschall Rommel but not taken part in the discussions, on 1 July, the following Führer directives were noted. They had been issued in the evening of 29 June:

> a) Above all, the Führer indicated that it was necessary to initially bring the enemy attack to a halt, as a precondition for a later elimination of the beachhead.
>
> b) The Luftwaffe will constantly harass the enemy beachhead using the most modern aircraft (jet-and rocket bombers). They will intercept enemy aircraft over the beachhead and destroy them.
>
> c) Sea lanes are to be mined.
>
> d) Special bombers are to be sent into action to combat battle ships.
>
> e) Flak positions are to be set up along the supply routes.
>
> f) Immediate deployment of 1,000 fighters from the new production in order to establish air superiority for at least a few days each week. Flying three missions per day, the then-available fighters could fly up to 1,500 missions per day.
>
> g) The Kriegsmarine will deploy all available naval units into action, further units are to be brought in.
>
> h) Supplies. Transport columns from all units are to be concentrated from the Reich and to be brought into action in the area of Supreme Command West. The supply of ammunition for four Werfer brigades is assured, but has, however, to be brought in from the Reich. The four Werfer brigades will be put into action together in a mobile manner.[5]

On his return to la Roche-Guyon, where his headquarters were located, Feldmarschall Rommel found the proposals of the Supreme Commander Panzergruppe West which had been worked out on 30.6., even while the counterattack by I. and II. SS-Panzerkorps was still under way. Because of its importance, this teletype message is quoted here in full:

> 1.) The situation at Caen and to the west demands new basic decisions. They must be decisive and realistic. Undoubtedly, the enemy intention is to initially wear down the Panzer divisions which are the first to block the way to Paris. Based on this, it is

necessary to maintain their combat strength. Our own objectives are offensive thrusts, such as the one by II. SS-Pz.Korps, in order to gain operational time.

2.) It appears possible and promising to:

   a) land severe blows on the enemy while maintaining the combat strength of the Pz.-Divs.

   b) After a purposeful straightening of the front line, the worn-out Pz.-Divs. can be quickly refitted, brought back to combat readiness and burn-out to their personnel and material prevented.

3.) Proposal:

   Withdrawal from Caen-North and the bridgehead.

   It must be pointed out that the enemy has left only one bridge across the Orne intact behind the Caen bridgehead. He dominates this bridge with artillery and air force and it is likely meant for his own use later.

   Defense of Caen-South and the Orne river.

   Further general front line, initially, approximately: Avenay—Villers-Bocage—area around Caumont. The II. SS-Pz.Korps is to be left at this front. Parts of 21.Pz.-Div., 12.SS-Pz.-Div. and Pz.-Lehr-Div. are to be deployed as soon as possible as reserves and for refitting.

   Then, renewed shift to offensive thrusts outside of the effective range of ships' artillery.

4.) It is no longer possible

   a) with the existing ratio of strength to achieve a breakthrough to the coast and, after the fall of Cherbourg, to subsequently take operational advantage of it.

   b) in view of the effective range of the enemy ships' artillery (up to thirty kilometers inland) the enemy air effectiveness and the effectiveness of the enemy artillery based on aerial observation, to hold front lines in the manner of the 1918 trench warfare with Panzer divisions. Their decimated or shrinking units, in particular the Grenadiers, would burn out in a very short period of time.

   c) to expect a change in the situation through the use of poorly equipped and less than outstanding Inf.-Divs. which, while promised, would only arrive at a time which cannot be predicted.

5.) A clear choice must be made between tactical patchwork which invariably brings about an immobile defense and leaves all of the initiative with the enemy, and flexible combat which seizes, at least temporarily, the initiative.

   It is the opinion of the Panzergruppe that flexible combat is not only the more proper but also the more promising decision rather than that of inflexibly defending the present line. The relevant experiences in the East contribute their own understanding.

It is particularly important that a decision is not carried out too late and in such a manner, that it can only take place, and achieve success, with the offensive action by II.SS-Pz.Korps.

An early approval is requested.

The Supreme Commander of Panzergruppe West
signed: Freiherr von Geyr
Ia No. 116/44, Secret Command Matter, Chiefs.

The supreme command of 7. Armee, to which the Panzergruppe was attached, essentially agreed with this proposal in its appraisal of the situation of 30 June. Feldmarschall Rommel relayed both reports to the Supreme Command West and wrote:

I fully agree with the judgment of the supreme commanders and request earliest approval for a purposeful straightening of the front line:
    Withdrawal from the Caen bridgehead,
    Setting up the line Caen-South-Orne-Bully-Avenay-Villers-Bocage-area around Caumont.
    Assembly of mobile reserves behind the eastern wing in order to counter the expected enemy thrust from the eastern bank of the Orne river in the direction of Paris.[6]

A discussion on this matter between Feldmarschall Rommel and General von Geyr took place on 1 July. General von Geyr once more explained his own judgment of the situation. He saw the possibility to remove and refit the "HJ" and Panzer-Lehr divisions through the shortening of the front line. The Feldmarschall considered it necessary to leave the Panzer divisions at the front for the time being, but also thought that parts could soon be pulled out and be left close to the front as battle reserves. The infantry divisions, on the advance, would also have to be put into action at the front. Later, the Panzer divisions would have to be placed immediately behind the front line so that ". . . they could directly (constantly with artillery and Pak) support the fighting . . ." Further, the file note of Panzergruppe West on this discussion continues:

The Feldmarschall reported on his discussions with the Führer: Conduct of fighting in an offensive manner is, for the time being, no longer possible in the west. Because of our use of retaliatory

weapons, the enemy has been forced to act. It is important to anni-
hilate him through fire and quick counteroffensives, when possible.
Caen will be the pivotal point for the enemy thrust toward Paris. It is
important to move more and more forces there.[7]

On 30 June at 24.00 hours, General Speidel had already informed the
chief of staff of 7. Armee that the planned withdrawal from Caen would be
approved by the Heeresgruppe.[8]

It is surprising that the Feldmarschall, despite the shortening of the
front line, initially did not want to pull out and refit any of the Panzer divisions. The Caen bridgehead had prevented the enemy from starting his
"EPSOM" operation, as first planned, with the point of major concentration
east of the Orne. An abandonment of the bridgehead would make it possible
for the enemy to carry out such an operation unobserved, or at least unhindered. There would then be no available free Panzer forces to face such an
attack east of the Orne.

The Panzergruppe West received orders, based on a Führer order, from
Heeresgruppe B in the afternoon of 1 July to halt all preparations to withdraw from the Caen bridgehead. Consequently, General von Geyr sent a
message to the Heeresgruppe, relayed by Generalleutnant Speidel without
comment to Supreme Command West. It read:

If the requested straightening of the front does not occur within a
few days, the 9., 10., 12. SS-Pz.Divs. and the Pz.-Lehr-Div. will burn
out to the extent that they will no longer be usable.

We are here not talking about 'running away', but rather about a
sensible and methodical removal from the fire of ships' artillery for
which the men are helpless targets at the present.

This same message has been sent to Generaloberst Guderian.[9]

A decisive change occurred on 3 July through replacing of the two
supreme commanders: based on a hint out of the Führer headquarters, Generalfeldmarschall von Rundstedt had asked for a suspension from office for
health reasons and was replaced by Generalfeldmarschall Hans von Kluge.
General der Panzertruppen Freiherr Geyr von Schweppenburg was relieved
as the Supreme Commander of Panzergruppe West. As his successor, General der Panzertruppen Heinrich Eberbach took over their command.

The "Hitlerjugend" Division owed a debt of gratitude to General von
Geyr. He had supported all the plans of the Division to fashion the training of
the young soldiers as close to the realities of war as possible. Further, he had
contributed many suggestions which had been favorably and eagerly accepted
and turned into actions. His strategic ideas for the defense against the invasion had been accepted with conviction and became ingrained in the commanders of the units. The General had been granted only a few days to lead

the Panzer troops in battle, carried by the confidence of the troops. It was his tragic fate that he was unable to gain acceptance of his convictions at the very beginning of the invasion. Instead, he was forced to lead his Panzergruppe in accordance with the defensive concept of Heeresgruppe B, which was contrary to his own. The troops greatly regretted the replacing of the General and continued to feel gratitude to him, as he also maintained his affectionate bonds with them. He wrote to the Author on 20 February 1971:

> Through its devoted fighting spirit, the 'Hitlerjugend' Division has merited that its actions be recorded in a book.

In the person of General Eberbach, a combat-proven and responsible Panzer leader took over supreme command of the Panzergruppe. The troops did not know him then, but immediately felt confidence and were never disappointed.

On 1 July, the Panzergruppe had judged the enemy intentions as follows:

> After the enemy attempt, to by-pass Caen and attack from the south in order to cut it off, has faltered, he will now try to attack from the west and out of the bridgehead on the eastern bank of the Orne and capture Caen.[10]

General Montgomery's plans and the measures to be taken were recorded in Directive M 505 of 30 June 1944. It stated that is had been possible, as planned, to pull the main German forces to the eastern flank of the beachhead, allowing the 1. US Army to take Cherbourg without being hampered by advancing German reserves. Montgomery established three requirements:

1.) We must maintain the initiative and, in addition, conduct offensive operations.
2.) We must not suffer any setbacks. That is especially true for the eastern wing where the enemy has assembled strong forces. Any setback there will have a direct impact on the quick execution of our plans on the western wing.
3.) We must continue to carry out our plans without any delays and must not be maneuvered into a position where we merely react to the actions of the enemy.

It would be the objective of subsequent operations to tie down the German divisions between Caen and Villers-Bocage. Further, it would also be to advance with the western wing of the Army group to the south and in a wide sweep to the east in order to threaten the route of withdrawal for the German divisions in the area south of Paris. The Seine crossings below Paris had been destroyed and would be kept unusable.

In the framework of this general plan, the Second British Army received the directive to "develop operations for the capture of Caen as opportunity arises, the sooner the better."

A German counterattack with strong forces was expected between Caen and Villers-Bocage. In order to have a mobile reserve at hand, the 7th Armoured Division was pulled out of the right wing of the Army and its sector taken over by the First US Army. That Army received orders to start an offensive on 3 July. Its first objective was to reach a line Caumont-Vire-Mortain-Fougères. An attack from Vire to take the important railroad junction of Flers (thirty-two kilometers southwest of Falaise) was to be planned. Two points in the operational orders are remarkable. Firstly, despite the radio monitoring by "ULTRA", Montgomery was not aware of the real intentions of the German leadership. The operational directives had been delivered verbally or in writing ("Chiefs' matter! Through officers only") Secondly, Montgomery was forced to remove the 7th Armoured Division in order to have any kind of mobile battle reserve at all. It had suffered a severe defeat near Villers-Bocage from the actions of the heavy SS-Panzerabteilung 101 under Hauptsturmführer Michel Wittmann. Thus, in case of an attack by II. SS-Panzerkorps and 2. Panzerdivision near St. Lô on 29 June in the sector of the 7th Armoured Division, Montgomery would not have had any forces available for countermeasures.

CHAPTER 4.1
Fighting for the Carpiquet Airfield on 4 and 5 July 1944

With the end of the third battle for Caen, the front line of the defensive positions of the "HJ" Division in the right sector ran unchanged; from the railroad line Caen-Luc sur Mer opposite la Bijude at the southern edge of Cambes-north of Galmanche-northwestern edge of Buron-northwestern edge of Gruchy-western edge of Authie-western edge of Franqueville to the Route Nationale No. 13 from Caen to Bayeux.

South of it, the positions of I. Bataillon SS-Panzergrenadierregiment 26 started at the rail line Caen-Bayeux. The 3./26 and I. Zug of 1./26 were in position at the western edge of the village of Carpiquet. They were supported by two light infantry guns of 4./26 in firing positions at the eastern edge of the village. No infantry had been placed on the level and cover-less airfield. The Bataillon staff of I./26, the remnants of 2. Kompanie, 1. Kompanie (without I. Zug) and of 4. Kompanie (without one Zug) had set up defensive positions at the southern edge of the airfield after giving up Marcelet. The defenders were able to use some of the fortifications which had been built before the invasion by the Luftwaffe in the defense of the airfield against enemy air actions. These positions could, however, only be used as shelters or trenches, but not as firing positions.

Panzer action as an anti-tank defense within the town of Carpiquet was out of the question and Pak was not available. Thus, 2. Batterie (8.8 cm) of Flakabteilung 12 was brought into position at the road fork at the west exit from St. Germain-la Blanche-Herbe in such a manner that it dominated the eastern edge of Carpiquet. At the southeastern corner of the airfield, but outside of the barracks, approximately five Panzer IVs of 9. Kompanie of Panzerregiment 12 were in ambush positions from where they could observe the whole width of the airfield. The Panzers were led by Obersturmführer Buettner, the commanders of the other Panzers were Untersturmführer Modes, Oberscharführer Richard Rudolf, Unterscharführer Ernst Haase and Unterscharführer Urban.[1] If required, parts of 4. Panzerkompanie (Panthers) could be moved in from Bretteville-sur-Odon, located immediately southeast of the airfield.

The III. Abteilung of SS-Panzerartillerieregiment 12 and parts of Werferregiment 83 of Werferbrigade 7 under the command of Oberstleutnant Böhme were available to provide artillery support to defenders of the airfield area. Böhme detected "heavy projectiles" in the vicinity of the airfield. They had been installed before the invasion to blow up bridges and other important installations. These projectiles were fifty-kilogram rockets, filled with explosives or flammable oil, and fired from a wooden frame rather than a barrel. Such projectiles were occasionally placed on the sides of armored personnel carriers and were adjustable in height. Oberstleutnant Böhme had these projectiles removed and installed them, in a makeshift fashion, in position so that they could be fired at the village of Carpiquet.

The terrain drops approximately fifty meters from the airfield elevation to the Odon valley in the south. At the northern edge of the valley runs Route Nationale No. 175 from Caen to Villers-Bocage. Along this Route, the towns of Vernoix, Bretteville-sur-Odon, les Jumeaux and Verson are located. A battalion of SS-Panzergrenadierregiment 1 of the "LAH", assigned to the "HJ" Division since 28 June, stood near les Jumeaux. The left wing of the Regiment extended to the southwestern exit from Eterville. At that point there was loose contact with the "Frundsberg" Division. The positions of I./26 at the southern edge of the airfield were flanked by the enemy to the south, located in Verson and Fontaine-Etoupefour. The positions north and northwest of Caen could only be held if the airfield terrain remained in German hands. As one requirement for this, the flanking positions to the south had to be eliminated. SS-Panzergrenadierregiment 1 received orders, with the support of parts of the Panzerregiment, III. Artillerieabteilung and Werferregiment 83, to attack along both banks of the Odon to the west on 1 July

1944, and to capture Verson and Fontaine-Etoupefour. The daily report of Heeresgruppe B of 1 July 1944 states:

> Parts of 12.SS-Pz.Div. HJ advanced along both sides of the road Caen-Villers-Bocage to Verson. Their left wing captured Fontaine-Etoupefour and established contact with 10.SS-Pz.Div. immediately south of the town.[2]

During the planning of operation "EPSOM", the enemy had envisaged that, if the attack by VIII Corps progressed well, two further operations would be started: "ABERLOUR", attack by the 3rd British Infantry Division with attached 9th Canadian Infantry Brigade against the German bulge in the front line north of Caen, and "OTTAWA", an attack by the 3rd Canadian Infantry Division (without the 9th Brigade) and the 2nd Canadian Armoured Brigade from the north on the village of Carpiquet. Because of the unsatisfactory progress of the attack by VIII Corps, both operations were canceled. A new plan to clean out Caen was developed by the I Corps. Part of this plan was an attack by the 3rd Canadian Infantry Division on Carpiquet from the west under the code name "WINDSOR". It was postponed on 30 June, and ordered, along the lines of the new directive by General Montgomery but using stronger forces, for 4 July. "The mission was difficult since the attack objective was held by units of 12. SS-Panzerdivision . . . and the defenders were well dug-in. Thus, the plan envisaged strong support", Stacy wrote in the Canadian war history.[3]

The attack was to be carried out by the 8th Infantry Brigade under the command of Brigadier K.G. Blackader. Attached, in addition, were: The Royal Winnipeg Rifles Regiment of the 7th Brigade, the 10th Armoured Regiment of the 2nd Armoured Brigade, reinforced by special tanks of the 79th Armoured Division, consisting of one company of "Flails" (mine removal tanks), one company of "Crocodiles" (flame thrower tanks), and one company of "AVREs" (bridge-laying tanks). Proposed fire support would be by: Royal Navy battleships, twelve light, eight medium and one heavy artillery units, three companies of The Cameron Highlanders of Ottawa regiment with heavy machine guns and mortars and 1/2 platoon of the 16th Field Company Royal Canadian Engineers. Air attacks on selected targets were planned and an additional two squadrons of Typhoon fighter-bombers were available to the Brigade. A report by L.R. Gariepy of the 6th Armoured Regiment of the 2nd Canadian Armoured Brigade indicates that parts of this regiment were probably also involved in the attack although this was not mentioned by Stacy.[4]

During the first phase of the attack, the village of Carpiquet and the hangars at the northern and southern edges of the airfield were to be captured. During the second phase, The Queen's Own Rifles of Canada regiment, held in reserve, were to advance through Carpiquet and take possession of the buildings and the barracks at the eastern edge of the field. The infantry was to cross the starting line at 05.00 hours behind a moving wall of fire which was to be provided by six light and two medium artillery units.[5]

Significant enemy movements were detected on 2 July 1944 to the west of the airfield by close-range radio monitoring and ground-based observation. Reconnaissance thrusts by armored reconnaissance forces were repelled. The daily report of Panzergruppe West states:

> The enemy is reinforcing again on the left wing of 12. SS-Pz.Div. The enemy is attempting to determine the line and strength of our positions through (armored) reconnaissance thrusts from the Marcelet area and south of there. He was repelled by artillery and mortar fire. Significant enemy movements (sixty tanks and vehicles) were observed at approximately 14.50 hours from the direction of Bretteville (l'Orgeilleuse) in a southerly direction toward St. Manvieu. Tank assemblies in the woods southwest of Marcelet . . . Throughout the day, brisk enemy artillery activity (surprise attacks) on positions and rear areas of 12. SS-Pz.Div. Brisk enemy air activity. Reports on spying activities by the civilian population have been provided to the Ic.[6]

There was also a pleasant surprise on this day, as Unter-scharführer Heinz Förster reported. He had led II. light Infanteriegeschütz (infantry gun) Zug until the guns had been destroyed, and was then attached to the staff of the battalion Sturmbannführer Krause. He wrote:

> One day after our withdrawal from St. Manvieu we reached the Carpiquet airfield where the remnants of the companies had set up rear positions. The Bataillon command post was installed in a concrete bunker on the airfield.
>
> I spent much time at the observation post which was located in the top of the bunker and could be reached through a duct. From there, any change in the enemy situation had to be reported to those below.
>
> During the first days it was still very quiet. Individual shells exploded in close vicinity and low-level aircraft fired their on-board machine guns and cannons at us.
>
> In the early morning of the fourth or fifth day, when I was in the observation post, I spotted Obersturmführer Hartung who had been missing since the attack on St. Manvieu. He was approaching us from the enemy lines. We all, Sturm-bannführer Krause included, were full of joy. Obersturmführer Hartung reported to the commander that the enemy was preparing for an attack.[7]

Obersturmführer Alois Hartung told how he lived through the attack of 26 June in St. Manvieu:

> Through a hole in the wall of the house, in which the Kompanie command post was located and where the entrance to the bunker was located, I watched a platoon of Englishmen climb across the garden fence. I aimed fire from my machine pistol at the enemy and they withdrew immediately, laying a smoke-screen. Soon after, I heard armor noises and believed that von Ribbentrop was arriving with his Panzers. I jumped out into the corn field in order to direct them. However, they were English tanks. They spotted me and converged on me in the corn field, constantly turning in order to crush me. I crawled and leaped back and forth next to the tank tracks, following the movements of the tanks in the dead ground. Amidst the fog and powder smoke I managed to jump into a road ditch overgrown with nettles. I then crawled into a culvert where I remained until darkness fell. I was not spotted by the enemy infantry and tanks which constantly passed by. During the night I retreated into a corn field and found cover again in a pasture covered with tall grass. All around me, cows were grazing peacefully.
>
> During the following night I found another hiding place in a castle park in which a British command post was located. It had to be a castle in or near Marcelet, located along the road Caen-Tilly. I remained in this hiding place for two days and nights and watched the activity at this command post. The close-by noise of fighting confirmed that I was in the immediate vicinity of the front line. During the fourth night I recognized that the enemy was preparing for an attack. In the morning fog I mingled with the advancing British and reached the positions of my own 4. Kompanie.[8]

Obersturmführer Hartung reported where he had spotted the artillery firing positions and the tank and infantry assemblies. These observations went to the Division and from there to the Artillerie- and the Werfer regiments.

The description of an episode from the life of Hauptsturmführer Heydrich, chief of 10. Batterie (10 cm guns) of the Artillerieregiment, by Untersturmführer Gerhard Amler is indicative of the aerial preparation for the Canadian attack. The battery chief's observation post was located in the control tower of the Carpiquet airfield.

> One day, as fighter-bombers were attacking Carpiquet airfield, Heydrich had been hit in the head by a piece of brick. He arrived at Bartling's Abteilung command post with a bandaged head. Bartling's

physician determined: concussion, and ordered Heydrich to drive back to the closest field hospital. Heydrich then cried on my shoulder: this was a terrible shame to happen to an officer! Not even a proper wound! How would it look, him standing there and having to admit that a chunk of brick had fallen on his head. But, what could he do? Bartling had ordered, Heydrich had to obey. This, he did, but soon after he returned to the command post behind the abbey wall. This time, however, his arm was in a plaster cast. He was properly wounded and would not have to be ashamed any longer. The ambulance column had been set on fire by fighter-bombers. Heydrich, one of the few who could walk, got away, although he was wounded. Heydrich wanted to stay with us. He said his arm did not bother him and he did not want to even hear any more about the concussion. But Bartling remained unmoved, and Heydrich was sent to the rear once more. This time, too, he did not get very far.

On one of the following days I rode with my driver, Keßler, on the side-car motorcycle without the sidecar to my supply troops in the rear. On this cycle we had both learned to survive fighter-bomber attacks by getting off it in a flying leap. We had just weathered an attack in an orchard by three fighter-bombers using rockets and on-board cannon. They used up an immense amount of material with only the two of us in their gun-sights, so we seemed to be quite important to them. We withdrew to a farm to celebrate this 'birthday', and who should we find already lying in the straw but Hauptsturmführer Heydrich. He had been knocked out and wounded for the second time while on a transport for the wounded, and he was playing the role of the superior being, quite aware now, he said, how to get to a hospital: only by motorcycle. Said and done, the next messenger on a motorcycle took him along. It was almost unbelievable, but the motorcycle, too, was shot out "from under his ass'. That was the last we heard of Heydrich, but somehow he made it after all. I don't know how Bartling found out later that Heydrich was in hospital in Brussels. But, when the large withdrawal in the direction of the Westwall was under way and the Americans were rolling towards Brussels, Bartling said to me: 'Heydrich has always been your friend. The Amis must not catch him! Go and get him out of Brussels! I'll look after your battery.' So I set out to bring Heydrich out of Brussels.[9]

On 3 July, the enemy attack units moved into their assembly areas behind the front line which was manned by units of the 43rd (British) Infantry Division. In the evening, the battleship "Rodney" fired fifteen salvos of its 16-inch guns from a distance of 26,200 yards (approximately twenty-four kilometers) on the installations around Carpiquet.[10]

In the early morning hours of 4 July, enemy radio traffic increased. The content of the messages indicated an impending attack. Based on previous experience, the Division calculated the start of the attack for 06.00 hours. The wooded areas east and southwest of Marcelet were considered to be the assembly areas. In order to smash the assembly, or at least to inflict painful losses on the enemy, squeezed into a narrow space, two fire attacks by artillery and mortars carpeted these areas at approximately 05.00 hours. The III. (heavy) Abteilung SS-Panzerartillerieregiment twelve fired some ten salvos (approximately 220 shells) and the mortars fired two half-salvos. Ground observation of the target areas was not possible but the enemy radio traffic indicated that the fire had been effective. A repetition of the fire attacks was not possible because of a lack of ammunition.[11]

Canadian sources indicate that the attack started at 05.00 hours. The war diary of the Panzergruppe indicates the start at 07.15 hours with annihilating fire on known or suspected positions, and an immense moving wall of fire. Our artillery and mortars sent barrages into the area immediately behind the moving wall of fire. These caught the forward attack wave and caused it serious losses. According to Canadian sources, the enemy reached the edge of Carpiquet at 06.32 hours.[12]

The barrages, fired by 428 guns of the ground troops, the 40.6 cm guns of the battleship "Rodney", the 38 cm guns of the monitor "Roberts" and other warships,[13] inflicted heavy losses on the defenders. Many of the survivors had to first dig themselves and their weapons out of the rubble. A bitter battle for the town, which was completely destroyed, started. The flame-thrower tanks played a decisive role in it.

Sturmmann Karl-Heinz Wambach of 3. Kompanie describes his experiences of this day as follows:

By 4 July 1944, all NCOs except for two, were either wounded, missing or killed. At this time, Obersturmführer Baumgardt was company chief of 3. Kompanie. He had replaced the wounded Obersturmführer Düvel. Untersturm-führer Kaiser led I. Zug.

Except for a few reconnaissance attacks on our positions, 3. Kompanie was generally spared. Before the attack of 4 July, I led two scouting parties in the area east of Marcelet and was able to report important details on the enemy assembly. During the night of 3 to 4 July, the tanks which had been moved to the very front indicated clearly that an attack was about to start immediately. Even during the night, our positions were moved back approximately 100 meters. Still, the immense fire at the start hit our positions with devastating effect. Based on my own judgment, I was to fire a green flare for fire support, and a red one to call fire on our own lines. Immediately after the barrages, the point tanks rolled towards us, accompanied by infantry. The 3. Kompanie, already badly weakened, could withstand the enemy material superiority for only a short time. Firing a green flare caused an enemy tank to roll toward my foxhole, do a full turn and cover me with dirt up to the chest. The fire support never came. I managed to free my arms. Only scattered fire still came from the positions of 3. Kompanie. Enemy tanks were sitting everywhere in the terrain. Three of them were on fire and, above the dug-up edge of my foxhole, I could see tanks advancing in the direction of the airfield. From a clump of trees a 8.8 fired on the hesitant enemy. This had to be about 11 A.M. and I was still not able to free my legs and hips. Suddenly, a voice yelled behind me: 'SS bastard, hands up!' Two Canadians pulled me from my prison, tied my hands and then hit me in the face with full force. I could hardly move my legs since I was wounded in the back, but they drove me to the rear without any regard, hitting me with their rifle butts. Then, I was tied to a fence post in the immediate area of exploding 8.8 cm shells. I must have stood there for a good three hours before they brought me further to the rear.

The number of dead Canadian still strewn throughout the terrain indicated that the enemy, too, had suffered extremely high losses during his attack.

Without a pause, the bitter battle continued in the distance. For me, the sad and uncertain journey into captivity began. It would last four and a half years.[14]

In a letter of 18 August, the Kompanie commander informed the parents of Sturmmann Wambach that their son was missing.

At the front, 18 August 1944

Dear Wambach family,

After the heavy fighting which the Kompanie and I survived on 4.7.44 west of Caen, I must now inform you, after an anxious wait, that your son Karl-Heinz has been missing since these battles. As the Kompanie commander, I continued to hold out the hope that your son would return to the unit. Regrettably, mine and the Kompanie's wait has so far been in vain, but I hope that your son is still alive and will return to our beautiful homeland after this great struggle.

With the Kompanie, your son Karl-Heinz served as squad leader and carried out his responsibilities to my unreserved satisfaction. In action, his courage and valor were outstanding and I watched his impeccable behavior with pleasure. I regret that I cannot have your son with me during future battles.

I know, dear Wambach family, that this message will be difficult for you. However, together let us hope that your son and our comrade Karl-Heinz is alive and will return to us. With this strong hope I remain,

Heil Hitler!
Yours
Baumgardt
SS-Obersturmführer
and Kompanie commander.

According to Canadian statements, Carpiquet was in their hands at 14.00 hours. The Queen's Own Rifles of Canada regiment had started out at 11.00 hours with the aim of taking the installations on the eastern edge of the airfield. Fire from an 8.8 cm Flak battery at the road fork near St. Germain-la Blanche-Herbe prevented the advance of tanks beyond the eastern edge of Carpiquet. Fire from artillery and mortars made any advance across the open field impossible. The radio monitoring branch heard the commander of the de-la-Chaudière regiment report the capture of the village from its center to his brigade. He was ordered to report in person to the brigade. However, fire attacks by artillery and mortars, caused by this message, tied him down. As soon as he reported that he would try to drive off, another fire attack prevented this.

The mortars, rocket launchers and artillery never ceased firing. For the next five hours, Carpiquet was an inferno. There was not a square of ground the size of a thumb which had not been hit. The bombardment was so intensive that hardly anyone dared to leave the trenches and shelters.

In the evening, we tried to place a ring of mines along the front line but the fire inflicted so many losses that we had to postpone this to the next day. And, the next day was just as bad.[15]

The attack by The Royal Winnipeg Rifles of Canada regiment on the hangars at the southern edge of the airfield was, right from the start, badly hampered by artillery, mortar, and machine gun fire. The attached tank company was initially held in reserve and only supported the action by firing from the rear. Only at the demand of the commander of the Winnipeg Rifles, one platoon was released and advanced. At approximately 09.00 hours, two companies reached the closest hangar. But even with the support of Crocodiles and tanks, they were unable to dislodge the Panzergrenadiers from their positions. Thus, they withdrew to the sparse cover of a small wooded area approximately 800 meters west of the hangars. At approximately 16.00 hours, the Winnipegs and the tanks renewed the attack and again encountered bitter resistance.[16]

Both times, the tank attacks were repulsed by the few Panzers of 9. Kompanie and, probably during the second attack, also by several Panthers of 4. Kompanie which had been brought in from Bretteville-sur-Odon. The Panzer IVs of 9. Kompanie fired partly from their ambush positions at the southern edge of the airfield but, twice, they advanced on the attack and reached the hangars at the southern edge of the airfield, once even the command post of Sturmbannführer Krause. During this battle, Oberscharführer Rudolf knocked out 6 Shermans. At one of these, sitting at the northern edge of the airfield, he fired from a hangar in the south. Rudolf was awarded the Knight's Cross since his action, in particular, was instrumental in throwing the attackers back to their starting positions. Untersturmführer Modes of 9. Panzerkompanie was wounded during this fighting.[17]

Some of the combatants reported on the defensive battles of the Panzergrenadiers, the forward observers and the communications crews.

A messenger of 1. Kompanie of SS-Panzergrenadier-regiment 26, Sturmmann Aribert Kalke, describes his experiences during the fighting as follows:

> The enemy was hammering us from all barrels. He concentrated his fire on our positions around the bunkers of Krause and Eggert (chief 1. Kompanie). I was in position as battlefield observer, located in an old anti-aircraft machine gun position from where I had a good view of the terrain dropping off to the south. There, a wide gap existed towards our neighbor on the left.
>
> The fire reached such intensity that there was no way back for me into the cover of the bunker. Besides, I was not allowed to leave my observation post. I had no other choice but to crouch, as small as possible, in the old ammunition bunker of the Flak position. It was open to one side.
>
> Suddenly, a terrible explosion! I was pushed against the ceiling of the bunker, my mouth full of the taste of gun powder. The bunker was filled with smoke and fumes. I was happy when I determined that I was not wounded. Only a short time later did I notice blood trickling from my ears, nose and mouth, brought about by the pressure of the detonation. My hearing, too, had greatly suffered.
>
> Then, a pause in the fire set in and I heard a babble of voices, as if far away. In my immediate vicinity, enemy infantry was running about. Widely dispersed, they had passed my observation post without spotting me. Several tanks accompanied them. It looked as if they were going to a hunt as they casually marched right through our position, obviously believing that the immense moving wall of fire had extinguished all life. They walked in a westerly direction toward the command posts of the Kompanie and the Bataillon. While the

infantry disappeared in the direction of the small wood, some of the tanks remained sitting directly in front of the bunkers, two tanks at the Bataillon's and one at the Kompanie's.

Then, new track noises. A single German Panzer, coming from the Odon valley, advanced on the hill to a point where it could knock out at least two of the tanks. While I was still contemplating what should be done, I spotted Sturmmann Köthe of my Kompanie who carried a wounded comrade. He shouted that, up there at the hangars and bunkers there was no longer any movement and that they were likely the last two survivors.

I helped him carry the wounded comrade to the rear. On the road Carpiquet-Bretteville sur Odon we encountered a Hauptsturm-führer of the 'LAH' with his unit.[18]

Oberscharführer Erwin Wohlgemuth, leader of the Pak Zug of 4. Kompanie, reported on this battle:

In the morning of 4 July, barrages of never before encountered intensity set in. I was located in a former ammunition bunker. The explosions were of such violence that bits of concrete inside the bunker burst from its walls. Once the artillery fire had moved on to the rear, I leaped ahead some ten meters to the front squad of the mortar Zug to repel the expected attack. Scharführer Daniel and Unter-scharführer Kordahs of the mortar Zug had been killed. Also, our artillery observer was dead from a twenty-five-centimeter-long fragment of a ships' artillery shell sticking in his back. There was no problem repelling the infantry attack. We concentrated our fire at the massed groups of attacking infantrymen until they retreated. In return, more artillery fire came down on us. I established contact with Oberscharführer Karl Hoffmann who led 2. Kompanie. Tanks had broken through on the right wing of his Kompanie. We realized that it was impossible to hold the position and ordered a withdrawal. After I had made sure that the wounded were being transported back, I had approximately ten men from our Kompanie available. During the withdrawal we encountered the 7.5 cm Pak of 13. Kompanie. It was unmanned, two dead crewmen were lying behind the gun. I wanted to fire the Pak at the approaching tanks. It did not work, the lock had been damaged by a hit and was stuck.

Since the order stated that the airport had to be held at all cost, we picked new positions for ourselves. At this very moment, a salvo from our artillery hit near-by. We had two wounded. I had them taken to the rear, and this left me with only five men from our Kompanie assembled around me. Based on the fact that our own artillery was already firing on our positions, I determined that the airfield had been given up by us. I withdrew to the positions of the 'LAH' to our rear. There, I met an old 'LAH' comrade with whom I had been in Russia in 1941. He could not believe that anyone could have lived through the hellfire rained down on Carpiquet airfield.

Five men were with me. All the others were wounded or killed. Two men had been cut off, they made their way back to us two days later.[19]

It is possible that the following report by Unterscharführer Herbert Kraft speaks of the rescue of the two wounded from 2. Kompanie, mentioned previously. Herbert Kraft had lost contact with the SS-Panzerregiment 2 of the "Das Reich" Division and fought for a while in the lines of the Panzerregiment of the "HJ" Division. He wrote:

After we had not been able to leave our Panzers for days, I had crawled under the Panzer during a break in the fighting in order to finally stretch my tired limbs properly. After not even ten minutes, violent enemy artillery fire started. My comrades, who knew that I was lying under the Panzer, did not move it in order not to endanger me. It was impossible to climb into the Panzer. Suddenly, I spotted four young Grenadiers carrying a seriously wounded comrade through the fire. I yelled at them to take cover under the Panzer, which they did. One of them explained to me that the wounded man had to be taken as quickly as possible to the dressing station. He had a shrapnel wound in the abdomen and was bleeding to death. They asked me for the blanket I had with me so that they could better transport him. Bedding the wounded on it, they set out jumping through the fire. I watched them disappear into the smoke and had no hope that they could possibly make it through. Three days later I met a young Sturmmann. He addressed me and I recognized him to be one of the four Grenadiers who wanted to transport the seriously wounded man to the dressing station. Radiant with joy he told me: 'We got him through!'[20]

The communication crews also significantly contributed to the success of the defense. The Division received important information through radio monitoring on the enemy intentions and situation. The telephone squads established, time and again, contact with our front line, despite the terrible artillery fire, thus allowing transmission of important reports and orders. A report by Sturmmann Oswald Beck, member of a telephone installation squad of the Regiment Nachrichten (communications) Zug of SS-Panzergrenadierregiment 26, indicated the immense stress these men suffered as they carried out their work, relying only on their own resources:

Two installation squads were assembled. Obersturmführer Griebel, the communications officer, was looking for volunteers for a special mission. Beck, Riedel and Thide stepped forward. The problem was the telephone line on the airfield. The command post of I. Bataillon 26 was encircled in a bunker. The line had to be cleared from interference one more time. All of the installation squad accompanied us to a house from where the road led in a straight line up to the airfield. There we went through our preparations. Pieces of cable of approximately twenty meters in length were cut off a roll and the insulation removed from both ends. This was done to overcome having to patch up many short pieces. Each of us had four or five of the lengths hanging from his belt. As well, electrical tape was cut into strips and simply stuck to the belt. Initially, it was still quite easy. The road rose in elevation and could not be observed from the airfield. Only the last piece of road up ahead would be dangerous. From there on, the road was level with the airfield. The 'Tommies' were all around, only our immediate vicinity was still clear. Three or four patches were quickly completed and we pressed on. Just before we reached the top bend, we left Riedel behind. In case both of us were wounded, he would inform the installation squad. We got down on our stomachs and crawled along the cable. We advanced slowly, without any sudden movements. There was no cover anywhere, everything was covered in concrete. 'If anything explodes here, we'll see a lot of fragments!', Günther Thide said.

The last thirty meters were strewn with mortar shells whose wings were sticking out of the concrete road surface. We went on crawling, the cable always in our hand. There, a patch is needed, if we're lucky, the only one. We patched and hooked up out handset, but our call only reached our installation squad. We had found one cable end, the other end was nowhere to be seen. Now, our pre-cut cable pieces came in handy. We patched and went on, two or three times more, then we found the other cable end. The sparse grass cover on our left was almost black from the explosions, shrapnel had ripped deep furrows into the ground, everything stank of explosions and powder. Again and again, more pieces to be patched and then, suddenly, the connection to the bunker was there. I did not even let the comrade in the bunker begin to talk but shouted: 'Quickly, quickly, report!' Any second, the firing could set in again and everything would have been in vain. Now that the connection had been re-established, no time was to be wasted in getting away from the airfield, but caution was required. If they spotted us they would fire their guns at us as if at sparrows. It only took a few minutes before the artillery started to direct harassing fire on the airfield. When we reached our comrades again, we were first given a swig of Calvados. This, we had richly deserved. Although the line had not lasted as long as it took us to return to our squad, the time had been sufficient to inform the men in the bunker at the time our Panzers would try to get them out.[21]

Obersturmführer Herbert Engemann had been attached to III. Artillerieabteilung of Sturmbannführer Krause as forward observer. He had been ordered to set up his observation post at the Bataillon command post although the visibility from there was inadequate. But Krause wanted to have the artillery man and his communications hook-up with him. Engemann remembered it as follows:

> In the morning of 4.7.1944, after intensive barrages, the Canadian infantry attack started, supported by tanks. Sturmbannführer Krause ordered all of the remnants of his Bataillon which he could reach to pull back to the Bataillon command post bunker.
>
> Radio contact, for me, was possible only outside of this bunker. I issued orders, during the enemy attack, to fire on our own positions, upon which all the infantry, and ourselves, returned to the bunker. After the artillery fire on our positions, we stormed outside to the earth mound we had built three to four meters around the bunker, to fight off enemy infantry. After several repetitions of this, both the radio and a radio operator were lost, so that no contact of any kind could be established. Amazingly, the enemy had reached our bunker and enemy tanks had even driven by; however no enemy forces attacked our bunker. So we were able to secure the bunker and only retreat into it when there was a significant enemy superiority. Because of the losses, Sturmbannführer Krause tried to bring all the men of his Bataillon who might still be outside, into the bunker. As I recall, we were still twenty to twenty-five men, in addition to some thirty wounded whom we looked after and cared for to the extent possible.[22]

Unterscharführer Förster describes the fighting for the Bataillon command post in this manner:

> Our infantry in the southwest corner of the airfield pulled back to the Bataillon command post. Most of our comrades were caught in a straight trench outside the command post and killed or wounded by flame throwers or tank machine guns. Two of our Panzers also entered the fighting. Those of us from the Bataillon command post, Papa Krause at the point with his pistol in his hand, started a coun-

terattack to help our hard-pressed comrades. After bitter fighting, the enemy pulled back.

Now we could, under constant fire, rescue the wounded and dead. We brought them back to the Bataillon command post which began to look like a dressing station. During the battle, we knocked out two Canadian Paks and one tank.

Even then, enemy aircraft flew low-level attacks against us and fired on anything that moved. There was great excitement at the Bataillon command post, the telephone connection to the Regimental command post had been re-established. Papa Krause requested reinforcements, adding: 'In case we receive no reinforcements, we will disengage from the enemy!' The Regimental commander was unable to send us reinforcements but ordered us to hold the position until nightfall.[23]

At 18.30 hours, I. SS-Panzerkorps reported to the Panzergruppe that the enemy had taken up positions in Carpiquet with forty to sixty tanks. Desperately needed ammunition to combat the enemy was not available after the extensive artillery and mortar actions of the previous day. The chief quartermaster of 7. Armee was unable to provide the requested amounts of ammunition. The Panzergruppe advised that the chief quartermaster west would attempt to bring forward light and heavy mortar ammunition to fight the enemy, who had penetrated into Carpiquet during the night.[24]

Since a continuation of the attack appeared hopeless, the 8th Canadian Infantry Brigade ordered it to be halted at 21.00 hours. It directed The Royal Winnipeg Rifles, who had attacked at the southern edge of the airfield, to withdraw to their starting positions. Forty-four fighter-bombers were sent into action to knock out 17 Panzers or self-propelled guns, reported to be dug in at the edge of the airfield, with rockets.[25] This attack, if it took place (no information is available on this), had no effect.

It was obvious that the enemy planned to break through to the Orne bridges in Caen from the west with strong forces and on a wide front. The question was, whether he would be satisfied with the partial success, achieved with probably significant losses, start anew at a different spot, or restart the attack from Carpiquet with fresh forces. In any case, the forward position in Carpiquet was a serious threat to the German bridgehead position. Thus, the general command ordered that the village of Carpiquet was to be recaptured and contact be established along a favorable line to the forces in action in the Odon valley. "HJ" Division directed SS-Panzergrenadierregiment 1 to capture Carpiquet in a night attack from the north, and to defend it. Further, to establish contact on the right with Regiment 25 and to the positions near Verson on the left. The remnants of I./26, in action on the southern edge of the airfield, would then be pulled out.

The mission to take Carpiquet in a night attack from the north was handed to III. Bataillon of Panzergrenadierregiment 1, led by Obersturmbannführer Wilhelm Weidenhaupt. The II. Bataillon, commanded since 28 June by Obersturmführer Herford after Obersturmbannführer Max Hansen had been wounded, moved into positions at the eastern edge of the airfield after nightfall.

The pull-out of the remnants of the Bataillon, in action at the southern edge of the airfield, took place without any problems. All wounded and weapons were brought back. Obersturmführer Engemann reported on the details:

At approximately 2 A.M. on 5 July 1944, Sturmbannführer Krause ordered that all those wounded in the legs or stomach be prepared to be transported, using sticks, poles, and whatever else was available. All other wounded were to walk by themselves, or supported while walking. Sturm-bannführer Krause ordered to freely step outside the bunker. We had our weapons hanging from our shoulders as we walked, with the wounded, in the direction of our own front line.

Nothing happened when we stepped outside. There was total quiet. I could clearly make out three Canadians standing about ten meters away. Neither we, nor the Canadians, fired. Since we had no idea of the overall situation, we could not determine whether the Canadians let us pass with our wounded, since we certainly did not give the image of a battle-ready force, between their lines, or if they were just a Canadian scouting party we encountered there by chance. We reached our own lines, bringing back all our wounded.[26]

After assembly immediately south of Route Nationale No. 13, the night attack by III. Bataillon of 1. Regiment started shortly after midnight. Right after the attack started, 1. Kom-panie, advancing in the center, was hit by German artillery fire and suffered considerable losses. In its place, 3. Kompanie with Hauptsturmführer Maurer took over the point of the attack. Despite heavy defensive fire, it reached its first attack objective, the railroad embankment along both sides of the country lane from Franqueville, at first light.

The attack was continued across the rail line but came to a halt at the edge of the village. Violent enemy barrages smashed 1. Kompanie. On orders of the Division, the Bataillon stopped the attack and took up a defensive position at the Route Nationale. The unsuccessful attack allowed the remnants of 3. Kompanie of SS-Panzergrenadierregiment 26 and several survivors of I. Zug of 1. Kompanie and 4. Kompanie to disengage from the enemy.

Two reports, from both sides, illustrate the course of this bitter night battle. A messenger of I. Zug of 3. Kompanie of SS-Panzergrenadierregiment 1, Sturmmann Gerhard Franz, described his experiences:

The 'Tommies' had woken up, our element of surprise had gone to hell. Violent defensive fire from the right and dead ahead hammered us. We could not make out our attack objective in the dark. Our only reference points were the enemy muzzle flashes; we had to move forward precisely into that! Untersturmführer Harrer, leader of I. Zug and 2.09 meters tall, was the tower in the battle. On his long legs, he was always a few meters ahead of us and we had problems keeping up with him. 'Keep up, pick up the speed, we're almost there! We'll only take cover when we've reached the enemy!' Thus he encouraged us when the temptation was high to just pull down one's head and stay put. And time was running out, the shadows of our comrades following us grew fewer and fewer. Then we had done it, a narrow hollow took us in. Enemy fire from close distance was silenced by the machine gunner, firing from the hip. We stumbled along the path in a southerly direction and came across a lineman's cabin, next to the tracks. We had reached our first attack objective. Dawn was slowly lighting the eastern sky. After a short break to catch our breath I was ordered to fire the agreed signals from a spot approximately 100 meters down the path toward the enemy: white = first attack objective reached; red = fire artillery in front of us; green = we continue the attack. I quickly made my way forward and fired the signals some fifty meters from a barn in a field. Then I noticed a movement, heard the dull bang of a hand grenade, and simultaneously felt a burning pain in my right abdomen. Right away, everything came alive. Our 21 cm mortars opened up, and my comrades raced past me. Just then, the sun was coming up, a layer of haze covered the enemy territory. Soon after, I was sent off from the collection point for the wounded at the lineman's cabin, with several other comrades, in a VW-Kübel of the 'HJ' Division. We raced across the wide-open terrain, under fire from mortars and artillery, to the main dressing station at the edge of Caen. I was operated on immediately.[27]

From the other side, the former sergeant L.R. Gariepy of the 6th Armoured Regiment of the 2nd Canadian Armoured Brigade reported on his observations:

I witnessed a real blood bath among the infantrymen in a field near Carpiquet. The Germans had penetrated the forward positions of the De-La-Chaudière regiment, rough and tough French-Canadians who, at home, started fights during the weekend as entertainment. We were close-by when the alarm was sounded at approximately 04.00 hours. The de-la-Chaudière regiment rushed into the semi-darkness and virtually cut the throats of most of the soldiers they came across, wounded as well as dead. I watched this terrible blood bath directly from the turret of my tank at the first light of day. These boys were obviously crazed with confusion, having been surprised in their sleep. The officers of this regiment had to aim their pistols at their own men to bring them back to sanity. This happened just before the massacre of several Canadian prisoners by the SS. (According to statements by Madame Corbasson-Fleming, a Canadian scouting party had been captured in her house in St. Germain-la Blanche-Herbe, shot to death and buried at a close-by farm.[28]

Forces for a renewed attack, which would have had any hope of success, were not available. Thus, the enemy in Carpiquet was fought with only a limited artillery effort as of 5 July. He did not start his attack in the Carpiquet sector again until his major offensive on 8 July.

The losses of I. Bataillon of SS-Panzergrenadierregiment 26 were very high, in particular if one considers that it had already suffered considerable losses on 26 June. It lost 155 officers, NCOs and men. Among the dead was the chief of 1. Kompanie, Hauptsturmführer Eggert. In detail, the losses were distributed as follows:

Unit	Dead			Wounded			Missing		
	Officers	NCOs	Men	Officers	NCOs	Men	Officers	NCOs	Men
Staff	1	-	-	-	-	1	-	-	-
1.Komp.	2	-	13	-	-	4	-	3	21
2.Komp.	-	1	3	-	-	7	-	-	3
3.Komp.	-	1	8	-	2	16	-	5	43
4.Komp.	-	1	2	-	1	17	-	-	-
Total	3	3	26	-	3	45	-	8	67

The losses amounted to 32 killed, 48 wounded and 75 missing, for a total of 155.[29]

Most of the missing, a large number of whom were probably killed, were members of 1. and 3. Kompanie. All of 3. Kompanie and I. Zug of 1. had been in action near the village of Carpiquet, i.e. north of the airfield. They had been attacked by three infantry battalions and two tank companies. No Panzers were available for direct support, since there was no chance of maneuvering inside the village. With seventy-five casualties, 3. Kompanie was almost annihilated during this day.

The Canadian war history reported on enemy losses:

On 4 July, The North Shore Regiment (New Brunswick) suffered the heaviest losses of the whole campaign, a total of 132, among them 46 killed. The Royal Winnipeg Rifles also had 132 losses, among them 40 killed.

The other infantry units and the tanks which had been involved at Carpiquet suffered the following losses: 10th Armoured Regiment 20, among them 8 killed; The Queen's Own Rifles of Canada 26, among them 4 killed; de-la-Chaudière Regiment 10, among them 3 killed.

The losses amounted to 377, among them 123 killed. No information was found on losses of tanks.[30]

The action by I. Bataillon of SS-Panzergrenadierregiment 26 was beyond any praise. Sturmbannführer Bernhard Krause formed the backbone of the resistance around his command post in the forward line. But, officers, NCOs and men of his Bataillon, left to their own devices, fought with the same determination. Decisive, also, were the actions by the few Panzers of the 9. and then of 4. Kompanie. Despite a shortage of ammunition, the artillery of the Division and the Korps, as well as Werferregiment 83 and the SS-Werfer-abteilung 12 which was assigned to it, provided outstanding support to the infantry. On the request of the "HJ" Division, Oberstleutnant Böhme was later awarded the German Cross in Gold in recognition of his personal valor and the courageous action of his Regiment. Standartenführer Meyer awarded to a forward observer, Stabswachtmeister (sergeant) Grupe of 3. Batterie who had led the fire on the airfield, the Iron Cross I on the battlefield, and spontaneously donated his own Iron Cross.[31] Finally, the comradely action of SS-Panzergrenadierregiment 1, led by Obersturmbannführer Albert Frey, deserves great appreciation.

In relation to the forces put into action, the enemy achieved only a modest success and paid for it dearly. However, the situation of the "HJ" Division in the bridgehead had further worsened. The enemy stood in Carpiquet and all of 1. Regiment of "LAH" was in action in the front lines. The Division prepared for the expected major attack on Caen.

CHAPTER 4.2
Attack on Caen on 8 and 9 July, Withdrawal from the Bridgehead, Attack on Maltot on 10 July 1944

As well as Montgomery, the German leadership, too, endeavored to create and assemble reserves for the coming battles. Already, in the evening of 30 June 1944, the relief of the Panzer-Lehr-Division by 276. Infanteriedivision had begun. During the first days of July, 16. Luftwaffe-Feld-Division was transported from the disembarkation stations near Paris by vehicles of 21. Pz.-Div. whose positions the Luftwaffe division took over. At 19.35 hours on 5 July, General Freiherr von Buttlar of the Wehrmacht operations staff telephoned Supreme Command West and advised that the Führer had emphasized ". . . that, in the framework of the planned replacement operation, 12. SS-Panzerdivision 'HJ' should also be relieved." It was ". . . particularly important that the remnants of the worn-out divisions were really pulled out. As far as it was possible in consideration of the situation, it is recommended to concentrate the available forces in a Kampfgruppe (battalion, etc.) and to make available the other forces, including the supply troops, for re-formation."[1] The planned take-over of the sector of "HJ" Division by 271. Infanteriedivision was not yet possible since it was still on the march forward. The partial Canadian success near Carpiquet made it doubtful whether Caen could be held against an attack by stronger enemy forces for a substantial length of time. The new Supreme Commander of Panzergruppe West, General Eberbach, and Feldmarschall Rommel discussed relief of the Panzerdivisions and their further use, as well as the defense of the Caen Bridgehead, on 5 July. General Speidel attended the meeting and offered an observation. Here follow a few exchanges made during the discussion:

> Generalfeldmarschall Rommel: We must try to get out of the bridgehead with as little damage as possible, meaning we cannot just rigidly hold on. However, the positions at the Orne must be held under all circumstances. In order to bring up the required ammunition, transport must take place even during daylight, in particular during bad weather.
>
> General Speidel: Transport does not help, the stores are empty at this time.
>
> GFM Rommel: Supreme Command West has proposed to assemble the Pz.-Divs. near Vire. (So that they could be put into action in the American as well as the British sector, Author). But this is impossible since the Pz.-Divs. must be located immediately behind the infantry as support and since movement across long distances is no longer possible in case of an enemy breakthrough, in particular because of the enemy air superiority.
>
> . . .
>
> GFM Rommel: The 12. SS-Panzerdivision must be pulled out. It must be replaced by 271. I.D.
>
> General Eberbach: In this context, consideration must be given to the fact that 12. SS-Pz.-Div. will fight significantly better.
>
> . . .
>
> GFM Rommel: Two Panzerdivisions of the Gruppe must be ready to be sent to the north in case of a new invasion, or to the west if a significant enemy breakthrough at AOK 7 takes place.[2]

The "HJ" Division was not informed of these considerations. It prepared for the defense of Caen in its sector. Its border on the right, also the right border of I. SS-Panzerkorps, was the railroad line Caen-Luc sur Mer. Its neighbor on the right was 16. Luftwaffe-Feld-Division, part of LXXXVI.A.K. The border to the south ran along the western edge of Caen and then along the Orne river. It was reasonable to allocate the city of Caen to 16. Lw.-Feld-Div. since a Panzerdivision is less efficient than an infantry division during fighting inside a town. On the other hand it was clear that the combat-inexperienced Luftwaffe-Feld-Division, inadequately equipped with anti-tank weapons, would have great difficulties withstanding an enemy attack supported by tanks. For this reason, one Panzerabteilung of 21. Pz.-Div. was attached to the division. Under these circumstances, it was disadvantageous that the "HJ" Division continued to depend on only one bridge across the Orne, located in the sector of its neighbor. The Orne bridge further south, near St. André-sur-Orne, was inside enemy artillery range and its approach ran only four to five kilometers distant and parallel to the front line on the left wing of the division. The border of the Division on the left ran immediately west of Eterville and was also the left border of I. SS-Panzerkorps.

It was known of the enemy situation that, on both sides of the Divisional border, the 3rd British Infantry Division was in position. To its west was the 3rd Canadian Infantry Division and, adjoining it, the 43rd (Wessex) Infantry Division, extending to the area of Hill 112. It could be assumed with certainty that these troops would be reinforced by further infantry forces and tank brigades, possibly airborne forces, for an attack. Finally, it had to be expected that, after a successful start of an attack on Caen from the north or northwest, the VIII Corps would start another attack from the Odon Bridgehead in the direction of the Orne bridge near St. André-sur-Orne. It was difficult to predict the focal point of the forthcoming battles. The Divisional leadership expected it on the right wing or in the Buron-Gruchy sector. Thus, it moved the Divisional command post to the northern edge of Caen into a section of the abandoned Ancienne Abbaye aux Dames. The reserves were assembled in the area of the Ancienne Abbaye d'Ardenne.

The positions of the reinforced SS-Panzergrenadierregiment 25, led by Obersturmbannführer Karl-Heinz Milius, followed a wide curve from the rail line west of la Bijude-south of Cambes-north of Galmanche-north and west of Buron-northwest of Gruchy-west of Authie-west of Franqueville. The shortest distance between the front line positions was seven kilometers, in reality it was one or two kilometers longer. A gap existed between I. Bataillon on the right wing and II. Bataillon in position on the left. Another gap of several hundred meters separated II. Bataillon from its neighbor on the left, III. Bataillon, whose left wing was located near Gruchy. There, the positions of 14. (Flak) and 16. (Pionier) Kompanie of Regiment 25 connected in the form of strong points. The weak II./26 had taken over the positions of 2. and 3. Batteries (8.8 cm) of Flakabteilung 12 near Franqueville. The 2. Batterie had already been located and fought on 4 July at the road fork at the western exit from St. Germain-la Blanche-Herbe during the Canadian attack on Carpiquet. The 3. Batterie had moved its positions into the area north of St. Germain to fight aircraft and tanks. The 1. Batterie was, as before, in position south of Cussy. The 4. Batterie (3.7 cm) was in position south of the Orne bridge in Caen.[3]

Two Abteilungen of the Artillerieregiment, commanded temporarily by Sturmbannführer Bartling in place of the transferred Obersturmbannführer Schröder, were battle-ready: I. (self-propelled) Abteilung was in position in the bridgehead, its firing positions are not known; III. (heavy) Abteilung, led temporarily by Obersturmführer Harald Etterich, changed positions on 4 July into the area of Faubourg de Vaucelles south of the Orne river. The fear was that, in case of a withdrawal from Caen, the Abteilung would find it difficult to drive through the largely destroyed city. The firing distance was quite sufficient for the established objectives. The Abteilung's observation post and its command post were located in Ardenne. Also in that location was the observation post of III. Abteilung of Werferregiment 83 and of Werferabteilung 12 which were in positions north and west of the city. The post was manned by Oberleutnant Tewes and Wachtmeister Vosloh.[4]

Since Panzerjägerabteilung 12 (tank hunters) was still not battle-ready, the Panzerregiment had to take over the total mobile anti-tank operations in all of the Divisional sector from the rail line Caen-Luc sur Mer to Eterville. On 7 July, the Panzergruppe reported to the Heeresgruppe the number of available Panzers of "HJ" Division: thirty-seven Panzer IVs and twenty-four Panzer Vs.[5] Several Panzers were repaired again prior to 7 July, so that the Regiment could be sent into action as follows: 5. Kompanie with five Panzer IVs, led by Untersturmführer Kändler, at the north and west exit from Buron and with four Panzer IVs under company commander Porsch in ambush position in Gruchy; the re-established 3. Kompanie with seventeen Panthers as battle reserve northeast and west of Ardenne; 6. and 8. Kompanie with approximately twenty-three Panzer IVs as action reserve in the vicinity of the water tower west of Caen, for action in the north west and southwest; 9. Kompanie in ambush position at the eastern edge of the airfield with five Panzer IVs; 1., 2., and 4. Kompanie in ambush positions near Bretteville-sur-Odon and Eterville. The 7. Kompanie had been pulled out to be refitted.

The battle-weary III./26 (armored personnel carrier battalion) and the Divisionsbegleitkompanie (escort company) were available as infantry reserves. III./26 stood ready in the vicinity of the northwestern edge of town. The Begleit-kompanie set up a rear position on 6 and 7 July two kilometers northwest of Caen and thereafter stood ready at the edge of town.

The I./26 was in resting positions south of Caen. The Pionierbataillon was being refitted near Potigny and set up a battle company which was employed at Regiment 25 to place mines. The II. Artillerieabteilung and the Aufklärungs-abteilung had also been pulled out to be refitted and were not ready for action.

The I Corps was tasked with the attack on Caen from the north, Operation "CHARNWOOD". Available for this were three infantry divisions, the 3rd British, the 3rd Canadian, and the 59th Staffordshire Divisions. The latter only arrived in the beachhead immediately before the start of the operation. In addition, there were two tank brigades, the 27th Armoured Brigade and the 2nd Canadian Armoured Brigade, as well as a number of special tanks for mine removal and earth moving, and flame thrower tanks of the 79th Armoured Division. Attached for fire support, or assigned to assist, in addition to the artillery of the three attack divisions were: the divisional artillery of the Guards Armoured Division and of the 51st Infantry Division, two units of army group artillery, 3rd and 4th AGRA. Also, the battleship "Rodney", the monitor "Roberts" as well as the cruisers "Belfast" and "Emerald".[6] This amounted to a total of 656 guns.[7]

General Montgomery had requested from General Eisenhower action by heavy bombers as special support. This had been approved. In order not to endanger his own troops, Air Chief Marshal Sir Arthur Harris demanded a safety distance of 5.5 kilometers to the rear edge of the target sector. Based on this, immediate help for the attacking troops could not be expected. Thus, it was decided that the air attack would take place in the evening before the offensive. It was expected to hit rear positions and approaches so that the defender could not bring any reinforcements forward.[8]

Formation and objectives for the attack forces had been ordered as follows:

a) in the eastern attack sector:

Units: 3rd British Infantry Division with attached units;

Objective: Breakthrough to the positions of 16. Lw.-Feld-Div. and advance via Lebisey to the Orne bridge in Caen.

b) in the central attack sector:

Units: 59th Staffordshire Infantry Division with attached units;

in detail:

1. along the dividing line between 16. Lw.-Feld-Div. and "HJ" Division;
Units: 176th Infantry Brigade, 271st Anti Tank Battery, One platoon 248th Anti Tank Battery, "A" Company Machine Gun Battalion (heavy 7.75 mm), 13/18 Hussars (tanks) with attached mine removal, flame thrower and engineer tanks, and 116th Field Regiment (light artillery).
Objective: 1. la Bijude, 2. Epron, 3. Couvre-Chef, 4. Orne bridge in Caen.

2. Attack sector: the sectors of I./25 and of II./25
Units: 197th Infantry Brigade, 2/6 South Staffords (infantry battalion), 298th Anti Tank Battery, 248th Anti Tank Battery (without one platoon), "C" Company Machine Gun Battalion, East Riding Yeomanry (tank unit) with attached special tanks as above, and 110th Field Regiment (light artillery).

Objectives: 1. Galmanche, 2. Mâlon and St. Contest, 3. Bitot and la Folie, 4. Orne bridge in Caen.
3. Reserves of the 59th Division:
Units: 177th Infantry Brigade (without one battalion), 269th Anti Tank Battery, "B" Company Machine Gun Battalion, and 61st Field Regiment (light artillery).
Objective: Capture of the Orne bridge in Caen and formation of a bridgehead. For this, 72 assault boats were assembled near -Château de Bénouville.
c) in the western attack sector:
Units: 3rd Canadian Infantry Division with attached units;
in detail:
Attack sector: Sector of III./25
1. Units: 9th Canadian Infantry Brigade, 27th Armoured Regiment (tanks).
Objectives: 1. Buron and Gruchy, Château de St. Louet and Authie, 2. Franqueville.
2. Units: 7th Canadian Infantry Brigade.
Objectives: Cussy and Ardenne, Orne bridge in Caen.
3. Units: 8th Canadian Infantry Brigade, 10th Armoured Regiment (tanks).
Objective: Breaking through the German positions at the eastern edge of the Carpiquet airfield, once the 7th Brigade has reached Caen in the advancing attack on the Orne bridge.[10]
Reserve of I. Corps: 33rd Armoured Regiment (tanks) in Basly.

The VIII Corps was to be ready to start an attack from the Odon bridge-head against the upper course of the Orne within twenty-four hours.[11]

Radio silence had been ordered for the involved units for the start time of the attack minus four hours.[12] This was generally carried out so that radio monitoring could hardly gain any information worth mentioning.

Operation "CHARNWOOD" had been expected on the German side, despite the absence of dependable information on the enemy. Scouting parties of Regiment 25 were unable to penetrate the enemy forward lines. Here follow the observations on the enemy as recorded in the war diary of I./25 for the period 3. to 5. July when the diary, regrettably, ended:

3.7.1944: Weak enemy harassing fire. Activity of our own artillery against Cambes and a park north of it. One enemy ammunition vehicle or storage completely destroyed.
4.7.1944: Minor enemy artillery activity, however increased German artillery activity. . . . Our own artillery is firing a large number of duds. In one salvo, eight of ten shells were confirmed to be duds. Brisk traffic by single trucks on the roads leading to Cambes from

the north in the evening hours. Constant noise from tracked vehicles during the night in the northern section of the Cambes park. Only minor enemy air reconnaissance activity during the day. Scouting parties during the last three days have determined that the forward enemy infantry units have been reinforced and are located at the northern edge of Cambes. The enemy is throwing up entrenchments during the night and advances only weak securing forces to the southern edge. Throughout the day, brisk enemy vehicle traffic to and from Cambes on the roads from the north, several trucks with mounted enemy infantry. During the morning, loud shouting, howling and singing can be heard from Cambes. This could be an enemy relief or reinforcement of the troops located in the Cambes sector. Our neighbor to the left (II./25, Author) reports, among others, 44 tracked vehicles, with a large number of tanks among them, on the road leading from the north to Cambes.

5.7.1944: 14.30 to 15.00 hours, heavy enemy artillery and mortar fire on the connecting line to the left of 2. and 7. Kompanie. After one-half hour of preparatory fire, a strong enemy assault unit approaches from Cambes parallel to the main line of defense of 7. Kompanie. The assault unit is fired on in time and has to withdraw under the crossfire of our infantry weapons. Only minor harassing artillery and mortar fire on the Bataillon sector during the day.[13]

In the only surviving documented copy of the morning report of I./25 of 7 July to the Regiment, it is stated:

Between 20.00 and 21.00 hours, rockets were launched at the Epron Hill, 300 meters behind and parallel to the main line of defense, and on the town of la Folie. Subsequently, barrage attacks on la Folie. At 03.00 hours, renewed fire attack on la Folie and Couvre-Chef as well as on a chain of hills 1,500 meters south of Epron. Only weak artillery and mortar harassing fire on the Bataillon sector during the night. Other than that, no special incidents occurred. The scouting parties, sent past Cambes to the west and east and toward Anisy on orders of the Division, have not yet returned. Reconnaissance results will be provided after their return.[14]

Although it does not belong into this context, some information on personnel and weapons strength of I./25, from the daily report of the Bataillon of 6.7.1944, is listed here.

6. Battle-ready weapons:
   Stabskomp.   2 light MGs (machine guns);
   1. Komp.   12 light MGs, 4 heavy MGs, 2 mortars (8 cm);

2. Komp.   11 light MGs, 5 heavy MGs, 2 mortars;
3. Komp.   12 light MGs, 4 heavy MGs, 2 mortars;
4. Komp.   4 light MGs, 6 mortars (8 cm), 2 Pak 40 [7.5 cm, self-propelled];
Zug 13./25.   1 heavy infantry gun [attached Zug heavy infantry guns 15 cm, self-propelled], 1 light Mg.

7. Fighting Strength
    Stab   4:4:35 [4 officers, 4 NCOs, 35 men]
    1./25   2:12:95
    2./25   1:15:83
    3./25   2:14:86
    4./25   1:10:98
    Zug 13./25   1:3:14
    Total   12:58:411[15]

The start of the attack on Caen had been ordered for the early morning hours of 8 July 1944. However, preparatory firing already began in the afternoon of 7 July. The battleship "Rodney" fired twenty-eight salvos from its 34.6 cm guns on Hill 64, 1.5 kilometers north of Caen, where the roads from Epron and Lebisey meet. The English assumed that a German intelligence headquarters was located there. A wide road led from that point into the center of town and to the undamaged bridge across the Orne. The 3rd British and the 59th Staffordshire Divisions had been ordered to capture the road junction. Both were to attempt to be there first.[16]

From 21.50 to 22.30 hours, the bombers of Royal Air Force Bomber Command attacked a narrow and long rectangle at the northern edge of the town of Caen. The troops were first alerted by a steadily increasing and overwhelming humming noise. Then, immense squadrons of four-engined bombers could be seen in the evening sky flying towards the city in formation. They approached at a relatively low altitude, which meant that their target could not be too far away. The commander of I./25, Sturmbannführer Waldmüller, believed that the German positions would be attacked. Thus, he ordered his men out of their foxholes and forward in the direction of the enemy, to take cover there. He assumed that the enemy had abandoned his positions. This was reported by the former Bataillon adjutant, Untersturmführer Willi Klein. Soon after, when the lead aircraft were over the edge of town, a hissing sound could be made out. The operations squad of the Divisional staff heard immense explosions, and terribly thick clouds of smoke rose in front of them. The Flak of the III. Flakkorps regiment, in position there, the 3. and 4. Batterie of Flakabteilung 12 and the four-barrel Flak of the Panzer-regiment at the northwestern edge of town had opened fire. However, enemy artillery fire limited their action somewhat. Still, several aircraft could be observed being hit. They wobbled and pulled out of the formation, trailing smoke. The Flakzug of the Panzerregiment knocked down a four-engined bomber.[17] Altogether, however, the effect of the anti-aircraft fire was minimal. The bombers flew, unless they were hit, straight ahead, unperturbed. It was, at the same time, a frightening and impressive picture.

When the four-engined bombers turned around to fly back, light bombers and fighter-bombers appeared and attacked special point targets. As soon as the squadrons had flown off, the Ia sent orderly officers to the regiments in order to gather reports. He also used the telephone to determine the situation. He learned, reassured, that the front line had not been hit. Instead, the rain of bombs had come down well behind it. Soon, more detailed reports arrived. They indicated that some losses had occurred after all. Two Panzer IVs had been totally destroyed. Several others had been turned over and covered with rubble and dirt. They could be righted and made ready for action again. Losses of personnel were minimal.

The Panzer Flakzug, too, in position between Ardenne and the edge of town, had been hit, without significant losses of personnel or material. The SPW-Bataillon (III./26) (armored cars) lost one killed, five wounded and one missing. Parts of the Divisionsbegleitkompanie had found themselves under the carpet of bombs and suffered a few losses. Unterschar-führer Leo Freund was there and reported:

> After the first bombs had exploded near us, we hurried toward the tunnel in the quarry. In addition to Untersturm-führer Stier and myself, eight more comrades of the rifle platoon had taken cover there. Outside, the hail of bombs continued without abating. In fact, it was getting worse. we could tell from the vibrations that the steamroller of bombs was coming closer all the time. Then, the first bombs dropped directly on our tunnel. Pieces of rock fell from the ceiling and the small room was filled with dust. We were already toying with the idea of leaving this trap when a bomb dropped right outside the entrance. The entrance was blocked off, completely covered by masses of rock. For a few minutes we sat, paralyzed by shock, in total darkness. Then, one of us started to yell something. It was thanks to the level-headedness of Untersturmführer Stier that panic did not break out. In a very reasoned manner he stated that we had been buried. He directed us to lie flat on the ground, not to smoke or to talk in order to conserve oxygen. Further, he ordered the men to take turns digging at the covered entrance, removing rocks. Who knows how long we kept digging in this way for our lives. We had probably all given up hope.
>
> Suddenly, a shrill shout came from the entrance: 'Light!' All of us rushed forward and, in fact, there was a narrow opening. We greedily sucked in the little bit of fresh air. Then, we heard voices outside, loudly shouting our names. It did not take long until the hole was

large enough for a person to crawl through. Helping hands stretched out toward us and pulled us into the open. Laughing and crying, we embraced each other.

The men carrying our food forward had searched for us without success in the quarry during the night and then spotted the blocked tunnel entrance. They had called other comrades to help and then worked feverishly to free us. Regrettably, the joy of our rescue was greatly dampened. None of the mortar squad had survived. The bombing steamroller had moved right over it and dug up the ground. We could only pull our dead comrades from the dirt-filled positions. Their faces were blue; they had suffocated.[18]

The fighting spirit of the troops had not been diminished by this, quite the opposite. They were surprised by the negligible impact of this immense effort. However, the men were disappointed by the insignificant success of the Luftwaffe Flak. The civilian population, regrettably, suffered painful losses although most of them had been evacuated. They were estimated to be 300–400 persons.[19] The enemy had sent 467 bombers into action, dropping 2,562 tons of bombs.[20] Even when one takes into account the encouraging impact on the attacking troops, one must state that this air attack was a total failure. In addition, there were the heavy losses among the French population which, after all, was supposed to be liberated. It would be impossible to maintain that these losses were unavoidable in view of the achieved success.

Immediately after the end of the air attack, the artillery of VIII Corps opened harassing fire on the roads leading to Caen from the south and southwest. Around 23.00 hours, the artillery of I Corps started to individually shell the villages of la Folie, St. Contest, St. Germain and Authie. This lasted throughout the night.[21]

At 04.20 hours on 8 July, the major attack on Caen started with a surprise fire attack by all of the artillery of the 59th Division, the 3rd Canadian Division, the 105th Field Regiment, parts of the 4th AGRA, the 3rd AGRA and of the 107th Heavy Anti-Aircraft Regiment on the la Bijude and Galmanche sectors and, simultaneously, by the artillery of the 3rd British Division on the adjoining sector to the east. The fire on the sector of 16. Lw.-Feld-Division at la Bijude also took in the positions of I./25. The positions of II./25 near Galmanche were the target of the fire there. At the same time, the 6th North Staffords and the 2/6 South Staffords, together with supporting tanks and heavy weapons, crossed the 'starting line' for the attacks on la Bijude and Galmanche, respectively. The capture of la Bijude was reported at 07.30 hours. At 09.30 hours, the last nest of resistance there had been wiped out.[22]

The war diary of the 2/6 South Staffords reported on the battles in the sector of II./25 in terse words:

04.20 hours: artillery preparations started, as the troops cross the 'starting line'.

04.30 hours: Companies are held back by very heavy machine gun and mortar fire. Many losses, including officers and NCOs. Some disorganization.

07.00 hours: Attached tanks report reaching their objective but no sign of infantry. Infantry is half-way to the target.

07.10 hours: 'A' Company has almost reached its target after having previously been thrown back. 'C' Company has reached the line of trees (330 m northeast of Galmanche).[23]

The commander of 7. Kompanie of II./25, Obersturmführer Kurt Havemeister, reported on the course of the battles on 8 July:

We were still feeling pretty good during the artillery fire in the night. Only its substantial duration and increasing violence indicated to us that our main line of defense was covered in its total width. This was finally the real thing. I was glad that we had given up the thinly held trench positions, defenseless against tanks, just in time and moved the platoons under cover inside the building ruins with their safe cellars. . . . Around 05.30 hours, the explosions in front of us suddenly stopped and the artillery fire moved backward. The attack was imminent! Leutnant Kinzig of the Werferbatterie and his radio operators established contact while we could already hear the roar and fire from enemy tanks. All of us crawled out into the open of the remaining positions where we saw innumerable tanks rolling toward us in full width. Our few Panzerfausts could hardly increase our confidence. We felt paralyzed when, like an express train, fire from the Werfers howled unexpectedly above us and slammed into Cambes, only 1,500 meters away and at the same elevation. The forward Werfer observer had tears of joy in his eyes. His 'hit' was supposed to be launched only if a pincer movement attack against us was detected, but it certainly must have helped I. Bataillon. By then, the tanks had approached to within 300 meters, and chunks of dirt from the explosions were flying by our heads. We could already make out enemy foot soldiers, but did not fire yet. Swearing at our own artillery helped somewhat to vent our frustration. They were still firing at les Buissons, not concentrated enough, for our taste. Could we believe our eyes? The tanks on our right had disappeared into the cover of Cambes. The wedge in front of us set out at high speed in the direction of 5. and 6. Kompanie on our left. Their infantry was hardly able to keep up. . . . The tanks rotated on their tracks over the bunkers and positions of the two companies, took them out of action, and rolled over them. Soon after, enemy

infantry arrived. They inspected our empty forward positions under
fire from us, without moving into them. Our rubble fortress was not
attacked, the infantry continued in the same direction as the tanks.
It quickly turned quiet at 5. Kompanie, while the din of fighting
could still be heard at 6. Kompanie further to the left.[24]

In the early morning hours, the impression had been created at I Corps
that the attack of the two divisions in action on the left was making good
progress. Thus, at 06.30 hours it ordered that Phase II be started at 07.30
hours.

It was the mission of the 3rd British Division to clear out the woods in
the sector of 16. Lw.-Feld-Division east of Lebisey which was to have been
taken in Phase I. The division reported the mission accomplished at 08.35
hours.[25]

In Phase II, the 59th Infantry Division, together with the 7th Norfolks
and supported by the tanks of the 13/18 Hussars, was to capture Epron.
With the 2/4 The Lancashire Fusiliers (LF) it was to take Mâlon, and with
the 1/7 Warwicks, both supported by the tanks of the East Riding Yeomanry,
St. Contest. In addition to the artillery of the 59th Division, that of the 51st
Highland Division and of the Guards Armoured Division, the 150th Field
Regiment and parts of the 4th AGRA were available for this attack.[26]

At the same time, the 3rd Canadian Infantry Division had orders to start
the attack and capture the towns of Buron, Gruchy, Château de St. Louet
and Authie.[27]

While the Divisional sector had previously come primarily under harassing fire and only Galmanche had suffered annihilating fire, all of the forward lines of the Division now came under heavy barrages. Apparently, the
barrels of most 656 enemy artillery guns were pointed at this sector. The
ground trembled and the front line was enveloped by smoke and haze to
such an extent that it could no longer be seen by observation posts in the
rear. The German artillery opened fire on confirmed or assumed enemy
assembly areas, but with severely restricted use of ammunition.

One hour after the start of the attack, the 7th Norfolks reported that
they had reached the extreme edge of la Bijude town. At 13.10 hours, they
were still fighting inside the town, supported by the tanks of the 13/18 Hussars.[28]

The 2/5 LF had started their attack on the road la Bijude-Cambes in
order to take Mâlon. An approximately 500 meters long tank trench had
been built in a flat curve north of the village before the start of the invasion.
The positions of I./25 ran north of it in the direction of the western exit
from la Bijude, almost parallel to the direction of the enemy attack. The
early morning artillery fire on the neighbor to the right, to prepare and support the attack on la Bijude, had also partly hit the Bataillon. However,
thanks to the extensive reinforcement of the positions, the impact had been

negligible. The new attack hit the Bataillon with its full force, but then broke down under the defensive fire of light and heavy infantry weapons, artillery and rocket launchers. At 07.55 hours, the 2/6 South Staffords received a report indicating that their neighbor on the left had been thrown back to the railroad station at Cambes.[29] Simultaneously, the war diary of the 59th Division noted: "2/5 LF unable to start the attack on Mâlon."[30]

At 07.35 hours, the 1/7 Warwicks had also started their attack past Galmanche to the west on St. Contest. There, only parts of 11. Kompanie of III./25 were in position at the northern edge of the village, together with some heavy artillery weapons. The battalion attacked with two companies at the point. Another one followed to clear the terrain and the fourth remained in reserve. The company advancing in the east was pinned down by fire from Galmanche. The one attacking to the west of it and the reserve company were pinned down by mortar fire. "A" Company, whose mission it was to clear the terrain, and the tanks of the East Riding Yeomanry supporting it, then went on the attack past the point companies. They reported, at 08.00 hours, that they had reached the town.[31] Shortly thereafter, the tanks were engaged in a fire fight with twelve Panzers which were advancing from Buron in an easterly direction.[32] The attack was repelled and the battalion remained under fire from individual pockets of resistance, manned by infantry and machine gunners. This prevented it from preparing, as planned, for defense. A scouting party sent to Bitot reported the town free of the enemy. St. Contest could only be cleared by nightfall, and the companies then dug in at the southern edge of the village.[33]

The twelve Panzers mentioned in the war diary of the Warwicks, reported to have attacked the tanks of the East Riding Yeomanry from the direction of Buron, were, in reality, the five Panzer IVs of Untersturmführer Willi Kändler. During the barrages of the morning, two of these had been located at the western exit from Buron, the other three at the northern exit. The Panzers guarding in the north had spotted the tank attack on their right flank on St. Contest. Kändler had then assembled his five Panzers and moved them into position in a meadow, bordered by hedges, immediately southeast of Buron. He recalled the battle with the tanks of the East Riding Yeomanry.

> From this spot we could hit the English in their sensitive broadside at an angle of almost 90 degrees. Although the firing distance was between 800 and 1,000 meters, the broadside offered a larger target, as well as thinner armor and greater vulnerability, than the front. Willy Schnittfinke was a quickly reacting gunner, a decisive requirement for our survival. With great calm and accuracy he swiftly followed my directions and target indications on the intercom or through pressure on his left or right shoulder. That indicated swinging the gun in the corresponding direction, a pinch meant: Stop! Then, the target had to be made out immediately. We were able to

watch our hits easily. With our Panzer alone, we knocked out five Sherman tanks there on this day. But we were in action not only against enemy tanks. With our machine guns we forced enemy infantry into the ground and inflicted heavy losses on them. During these hours we fired ten thousand aimed rounds of machine gun ammunition. We confirmed their accuracy by watching the interspersed tracers through our gun sights and binoculars.

Each of our five Panzers landed hit after hit while we suffered no losses. The hedges provided us with good cover. We frequently moved the Panzers small distances to new positions so as to reduce the enemy's chances of accurately targeting our muzzle flashes.[34]

The fighting in Galmanche continued during the attack by the Warwicks on St. Contest. Together with the tanks, the 2/6 South Staffords overcame one pocket of resistance after the other. Since the anti-tank guns had been destroyed by the barrages, tanks could only be attacked using close combat anti-tank weapons. The chief of 6. Kompanie, Hauptsturmführer Dr. Thierey, knocked out three Shermans with Panzerfausts. He was killed during the attempt to knock out a fourth.[35]

Further entries in the war diary of the 2/6 S Staffords follow:

07.30 hours: Phase II starts at 197 Brigade.

07.55 hours: Report: our own troops have been thrown back to the Cambes rail station.

08.10 hours: Troops at the point re-assemble.

08.30 hours: Report: Point troops pushing toward attack objective.

09.30 hours: 1/7 Warwicks re-assemble at attack objective St. Contest. Repeated artillery fire on the area of the battalion command post (northern sector of Cambes).

10.30 hours: Two tank squads support 'C' Company on the right wing as it attempts to penetrate into Galmanche.

12.00 hours: Four prisoners brought back to the battalion. Identified as members of 5. Kompanie Panzer-grenadier-regiment 25 of 12. SS-Panzerdivision.

12.30 hours: 29 prisoners brought back to the battalion. Identified as members of 5. and 6. Kompanie Rgt. 25, some identified as belonging to 8. Kompanie.

13.00 hours: 17 prisoners brought back to the battalion. Identified as members of 5. Kompanie Rgt. 25.

The 9th Canadian Infantry Brigade, too, had been ordered to attack at 07.30 hours. The Stormont, Dundas & Glengarry Highlanders were at the point with two companies, supported by one company of the 27th Canadian

Armoured Regiment, when the attack on Gruchy started. In their war diary it was noted: "The artillery fire is now unbelievable. We have never heard anything like it. The smoke, which is now rising, is so dense that it darkens the sun."

Twenty minutes later, the spearheads of the battalion disappeared into the smoke close to the edge of town. Only then, the German light infantry weapons and heavy machine guns opened fire on the shadowy enemy. An anti-tank gun in position between Gruchy and Buron impeded the advance of the tanks. It was eliminated half-an hour later and the tanks could begin clearing the terrain between the two villages. During this, they came under artillery fire. Mortars and rocket launchers concentrated violent fire on the rear parts of the battalion and on Vieux Cairon, where a command post was located. During such a fire attack, the deputy commander, Major A. M. Hamilton, was wounded. At 09.45 hours, the battalion reported that Gruchy was taken.[36]

Simultaneously with the Stormont, Dundas & Glengarry Highlanders, the Highland Light Infantry of Canada Battalion had started its attack on Buron, also supported by one tank company and heavy weapons. When the two point companies approached the slit trench, they came under fire from there. After violent hand-to-hand combat, these forward positions were taken. They then started the attack on the main line of defense at the edge of town. They ". . . ran under a hail of machine gun fire into the barrages from artillery and rocket launchers . . ." and suffered many losses. "The outside edge of the village was energetically held by a ring of resistance pockets, most of which contained machine guns. They covered our troops with constant and annihilating fire, and it was almost impossible to get through."[37]

Tank support was requested, but they could not come forward because of a mine field on the right wing. "D" Company penetrated into the western sector of town, suffering heavy losses. Only half of the company reached the orchard at the southwestern edge of Buron.

"B" Company, adjoining to the east, initially did not advance at all. First, it had no contact with its tanks. Then, the tanks did not want to advance because of a mine field. Finally, they did move forward, and bitter fighting by infantry and tanks against the well-fortified pockets of resistance set in. These could only be silenced from a close distance. In the meantime, "C" Company had also been moved forward and slotted in between the two point companies. During the fighting which lasted for hours, the Canadians lost track of the situation. Finally, at 11.30 hours, the battalion received a situation report by messenger. "D" Company had only one officer and thirty-eight NCOs and men left. "B" Company was reduced to one officer and a third of its NCOs and men, "C" Company had approximately 50 percent, "A" Company two-thirds of their strength at the start of the attack. The companies had reached their attack objectives, but throughout the village, pockets of resistance were still fighting. The German artillery, mortars, as well as infantry guns, were firing on Buron. "The fire was so incessant and violent that even the slit trenches were not safe." The Canadians suffered so many losses that not enough Jeeps and carriers were available to transport the wounded.[38]

The barrages which launched Phase II of the enemy attack left no doubt at the Division that the offensive had extended to all of the northern sector, i.e. the positions of Regiment 25. Reports on the course of the various battles had not yet been received when fighter-bombers attacked several targets north of Caen between 08.00 and 09.00 hours. A squadron of 6 to 8 two-engined aircraft attacked the Divisional command post directly. The commander and Ia watched as the bombs were released and dropped on them.

They leapt into the ground-level map room and on into the cellar behind. An immense explosion shook the air and made the building tremble. The candles in the cellar died, a thick cloud of dust penetrated into all the rooms and quickly darkened them. Suddenly, a man shouted: "We are buried alive!" The Divisional commander asked, in turn: "Where did you come from, then?"—"From outside", was the surprising answer which caused general mirth. Since no further bombs appeared to be dropping, the "buried" felt their way to the outside. They saw, in the lifting smoke, that a number of bombs had hit the nave and other parts of the church, located barely fifty meters from the entrance to the command post. Rock debris had fallen on the mobile roof under which the radio vehicles had been parked, but no substantial damage had been caused. Telephone connections to the front and the Korps, however, were interrupted for some time. Somewhat later, the radio monitoring Zug intercepted an enemy radio message regarding the supposed destruction of the Divisional command post.[39]

Soon after, the Supreme Commander of Panzergruppe West, General der Panzertruppen Eberbach, arrived at the Divisional command post. He had left his own command post by vehicle at approximately 09.00 hours. At that time, a report from LXXXVI. A.K. was available, indicating that the enemy had opened his attack in the sector of 16. Lw.-Feld-Div. at approximately 6 A.M. after intensive air attacks and heavy barrages. Further, that enemy tanks had penetrated with tanks into Lebisey and were advancing on Calix. The Armee commander had asked the commander of I. SS-Panzerkorps if 12. SS-Panzerdivision could support its neighbor on the right at least with artillery. The Korps had no contact with 12. Division, because of the bombing raid on the command post, but promised to request the Division to support its neighbor, if at all possible, even with Panzers.[40] At that time it was already known at the Division that la Bijude had been taken and the enemy was attacking Epron. During the presence of the Supreme Commander, the first reports on the course of the fighting at Regiment 25 arrived: enemy had penetrated into Galmanche, Gruchy was lost, enemy in Buron and St. Contest. General Eberbach realized immediately that "HJ" Division would need all its forces to hold its own. Thus, supporting the neighbor division was out of the question, except by fire from the units located on the right wing. He ordered action by II. Panzerabteilung of 21. Panzerdivision with 16. Lw.-Feld-Division.

Nothing could be predicted regarding any decisions which this day would later demand. Developments had to be awaited. The Divisional leadership was certain that General Eberbach would not leave it in a lurch, he had fully understood the seriousness of the situation. From the command post of the 12., Eberbach drove on to the neighbor on the right in order to gain a direct picture of the situation.

At 10.15 hours, the chief of Panzergruppe West spoke with the chief of LXXXVI. A.K. He did not yet believe that this fighting was already part of the major enemy offensive, but ordered again to start moving II./Panzerregiment 22 (of 21. Panzerdivision) immediately across the Orne to Caen. This same order had already been issued on the previous day. It could, however, not be carried out since the Abteilung commander, driving ahead, had not found any way of crossing the city after the air attack.[41]

The battles in Buron lasted throughout the morning. The enemy was able to take, with difficulty and under heavy losses, one strong point after the other. At 14.30 hours, the Stormont, Dundas & Glengarry Highlanders started their attack on Château de St. Louet, while the North Nova Scotia Highlanders (NNSH), supported by three companies of the 27th Armoured Regiment, attacked Authie. The NNSH had suffered heavy losses in their assembly area, an orchard south of Buron. These were caused mainly by mortars and 8.8 cm Flak. The war diary of the battalion recorded this:

> Major E. S. Gray, commander of 'Able'-Company, was the first officer lost during this day. The company was then taken over by Captain L. J. Sutherland. Soon after, Major F. C. Kennedy, commander of 'D' Company, lost his right arm and handed over command to Captain S. Byrd who was critically wounded shortly thereafter and lived for only a few hours. Major Kennedy took back command of the company again for two hours. His arm had been hanging only by a small flap of skin, and had been cut off by his squad leader. Captain S. V. Matson of the Support Company took over 'D' Company and the battalion was then ready to advance.

The attack by both battalions advanced fairly speedily. At 14.00 hours, the SD&GH reported having penetrated into the Château de St. Louet. They took "approximately twenty-five prisoners" there, members of 16. (pionier) Kompanie.[42]

The NNSH had pushed into Authie at 15.30 hours, but came under heavy artillery fire there. When the accompanying tanks prepared to advance on Franqueville, they came under fire from the Bogensberger Zug of 3. Panzerkompanie and lost several Shermans. Untersturmführer Bogensberger was awarded the Iron Cross I for this. After Authie had been cleared, the battalion reconnoitered toward Franqueville and was able to dig in there with some weak forces.[43]

The remnants of III./25 were encircled in Buron, but resisted desperately. The Bataillon commander, holder of the Knight's Cross Hauptmann Steger, still had radio contact with the Ardenne abbey and reported the development of the situation. In this extremely critical situation, the Divisional commander drove to the command post of Regiment 25 at Ardenne in order gain a personal understanding of the circumstances on the spot, and to take charge. He reported on this trip through hell:

Erich Holsten had 'saddled his fastest horse'. Our trusty Volkswagen stood ready. Michel, my loyal Cossack, was already sitting in the car when I got in. We all knew that a daring drive was ahead of us. After a few minutes we reached the von Ribbentrop Kompanie. The forward Panzers were engaged in a fire duel with Sherman tanks in position at St. Contest. Ahead of us lay the Ardenne abbey. Its whole site was under artillery fire. The tall towers no longer existed. Accusingly, their stumps stretched into the sky. We were still on the rear slope when doubt suddenly set in. I took the steering wheel myself. There could be no stopping or turning around in this situation. The lane leading to the abbey was ripped apart by explosions from shells, the terrain was covered with bomb craters. We had barely got across the last rise in the terrain when heavy stuff whistled by our ears. The tanks at St. Contest were firing at us. Cold sweat was running from all my pores. The car was virtually flying across the terrain. If only that damned twittering of the enemy machine gun fire would stop! Only a few meters separated us from the ruins. Then we had made it. The direct fire could no longer hit us.

The large orchard of the abbey resembled an inferno. Shell after shell exploded outside the entrance to the Regimental command post. We hesitated for a few seconds before the final leap. Taking advantage of a short pause in the fire, we raced to the building. Killed comrades were lying, crushed, in the vicinity of the command post. Jumping out of the car, I recognized the dead body of the commander of the Stabskompanie, killed by a shell fragment.

We caught our breath as we stumbled into the hallway of the old building. The Regimental commander was wounded and in the process of talking to the commander of III. Bataillon, Hauptmann Steger. The only contact with the battalions was by field phone. The cellar ceiling seemed to move under the incoming fire, despite the fact that the cellar was dug deep into the ground and supported by immense arches. A constant booming penetrated our ears. I spoke with Hauptmann Steger in Buron. He reported that the majority of his Bataillon had been killed and that enemy tanks were sitting just outside the town. He urgently requested help. All available Panzers were sent to Buron to break the encirclement. The attack failed. From the church tower, I watched the armor battle wavering to and fro. Both sides suffered heavy losses.

Enemy tanks were advancing on Ardenne from Authie. The von Ribbentrop Kompanie destroyed these tanks and defended the Regimental command post. The burning tanks were sitting 100 meters west of Ardenne.

More and more wounded dragged themselves into the huge cellars of the abbey. The medics performed superhuman tasks saving the wounded. My old comrade-in-arms, Dr. Erich Gatternig, worked unceasingly to diminish the suffering and pain. The moaning became almost unbearable in the ancient vaults. The stream of wounded never stopped. But we could not break off the battle yet! We had to wait for nightfall, move out our wounded under cover of dark, and give the units at the point a chance to break through.

I sat in the Panther as we rolled forward in the direction of Cussy. It was being defended by the chief of 1. Batterie of SS-Flakabteilung 12, Hauptsturmführer Ritzel. The small village was only a heap of rubble. Three Sherman tanks sat burning in front of the battery position. The losses at the Batterie were high. One gun had been knocked out by artillery fire. Hauptsturmführer Ritzel was standing at the gun, acting as the gunner. He promised me to do everything to hold his position until nightfall, thus enabling the transport of the wounded from Ardenne. A short time later I was back in the abbey.[44]

The previously mentioned attack on Buron, pushing past Cussy on the left, was carried out by I. and II. Zug of 3. Panzerkompanie, led by Obersturmführer von Ribbentrop, at approximately 17.30 hours. Unterscharführer Heinz Freiberg reported:

At high speed we crossed the open terrain to the village wall of Buron. My Panzer was driving as the extreme right vehicle. As we were passing an opening in the wall, there were two sudden explosions. The Panzer of Sepp Trattning and another stood in flames. We immediately fired both MGs at the wall opening. I spotted some movement there and then a further flash. Already, we were hit in the turret mantlet and the armor piercing shell dropped into the fighting compartment. Our gun sight optic was broken, the gunner was wounded in the face and I had a small shrapnel in my left arm. The turret crew bailed out immediately and, because of the heavy machine gun fire, took cover behind the Panzer. The driver and radio operator had not noticed this activity and sat placidly in the Panzer, its engine running quietly. I jumped back up on the 'crate', yelled the order 'Backward, march!' through the throat microphone dangling across the edge of the turret, and we set out toward Ardenne. After a few meters' drive, the pedestal of our antenna, which I had used as a foothold, was shot off. Thus, I lost a heel. After some 500 meters we reached our infantry where our gunner and loader had already arrived."

The Kompanie knocked out several tanks, carriers and anti-tank guns. It lost seven Panthers.[45]

There was no longer any hope of relieving III./25.

At that time, the renewed attack by the 2/5 LF on the position network of I./25 had broken down. The British battalion had already suffered losses from artillery and mortar fire during the march to the assembly area and the assembly. Most losses, however, occurred during the attack, from machine gun and infantry fire. Altogether, the battalion lost 9 officers, 103 NCOs and men. Among them were 3 company commanders, two of whom were dead and one was wounded. The battalion was then pulled out as a reserve of the 197th Brigade.[46]

One hour previously, parts of the 3rd British Infantry Division had already captured Hill 64 from the 16. Lw.-Feld-Div. Scouting parties of the 33rd Armoured Brigade and the 9th Infantry Brigade were sent into westerly, southwesterly and southerly directions. They reported that they had penetrated deeply into Caen and encountered few enemy soldiers. Their advance had been greatly impeded by ruins and rubble.[47] Thus, the enemy stood deep in the flank of I./25 and threatened the Orne crossing. The Waldmüller Bataillon was ordered to deploy one Zug to secure the right flank. The Division reinforced it by attaching one Panzer IV Kompanie.

After the Divisional commander had returned to the command post, he reported his impressions to the commanding general, Obergruppenführer Sepp Dietrich, by telephone. The I. Bataillon was threatened in its deep flank after the defense of the 16. Lw.-Feld-Div. on its left wing had completely collapsed, and enemy reconnaissance forces had penetrated into the eastern, northeastern and northern outskirts of Caen. Remnants of II./25, in action to the left of I./25, were still holding on in Galmanche where they were encircled. The enemy had already pushed past them and penetrated into St. Contest. Remnants of III./25, encircled in Buron by the enemy, fought a desperate fight. Gruchy, Authie, Château de St. Louet and Franqueville had been captured by the enemy. A breakthrough on the left wing to the Orne bridges had to be feared, possibly at the same time as one from Calix. The result would be the encirclement of the remainder of the Division and its annihilation. The commanding general recognized the seriousness of the situation but he recalled that the Heeresgruppe insisted on carrying out the Führer order to hold Caen at all cost. He could not lift this order. The Divisional commander found himself facing a difficult conflict: Did it make any sense to have the Division bleed to death here or could he disregard a Führer order? The senior general staff officer telephoned the chief of staff of I. SS-Panzerkorps. He submitted to him the Division's judgment of the situation in the same way as the commander had done previously with the commanding general. Brigadeführer Kraemer listened to all this quietly and asked about available reserves; there were none. He wanted to know the ammunition stores of the artillery; they had shrunk to a minimum. Finally, he spoke the saving words: "If you are thrown back to the southern banks of the Orne while fighting a superior enemy, it could never be considered to be a withdrawal contrary to orders." The Ia expressed his thanks and stated that the Division would do its utmost. He hung up and reported to the Divisional commander. Standartenführer Kurt Meyer heaved a sigh of relief. The Division immediately issued instructions to the attached units through individual orders. They stated:

Regiment 25 will withdraw its battalions to the edge of Caen after nightfall. Before this, the battle-ready heavy weapons will have moved positions and be ready to fire.

Divisionsbegleitkompanie and III./26 will cover the withdrawal and positioning. The III./26 will expand the rear positions established by the Begleitkompanie through strong points on both sides.

Panzerregiment 12, in cooperation with Regiment 25, will free the cut-off and encircled parts of the Regiment.

Panzergrenadierregiment 1 will establish contact with I. Bataillon on the left wing of III./26 and maintain contact, as previously, with the "Frundsberg" Division.

Together with the units still in action in the bridgehead, the artillery and mortars will change positions to the southern bank of the Orne. They will support, in cooperation with Regiment 25 and I./1 "LAH", by fire attacks, the disengagement from the enemy, and then delay any pursuit through harassing fire.

After nightfall, Flakabteilung 12 will move to the southern bank of the Orne and take up positions so as to defend the Orne bridge from air attacks in cooperation with the Flakregiment of III. Flakkorps.

Aufklärungsabteilung 12 will reconnoitre in the right flank of the Division and will guard the approaches to Caen and to the Orne bridge in Caen.

Pionierbataillon 12 will keep the Orne bridge in Caen open and prepare it to be blown up. This demolition may only take place on orders from the Division.

The Divisional command post will be moved to Caen-South (Faubourg de Vaucelles). Nachrichtenabteilung 12 will prepare communication links to the new location.

Plans for 9 July: Regiment 25 and Regiment 1 will move into new defensive positions during the night 8-9 July on the southern bank of the Orne from the eastern edge of Vaucelles to the bend of the Orne (Regiment 25), from there to the north of Louvigny to the west of Eterville (Regiment 1). The III./26, with attached Divisionsbegleitkompanie, will cover the withdrawal. It will then pull back, in a fighting withdrawal, to the Orne bridge, and be the last to cross the Orne. The artillery will have the same mission as above. It is important to gain time for the move into the new defensive positions.

At 19.15 hours, Feldmarschall Rommel approved the withdrawal of the heavy weapons from Caen and a regrouping in the rear.[48]

In the meantime, at 18.35 hours, two battalions of the 7th Infantry Brigade of the 3rd Canadian Infantry Division had been moved forward to Authie. The First Battalion, The Canadian Scottish Regiment, advanced on Cussy, the Regina Rifle Regiment on Ardenne. A moving wall of artillery fire rolled ahead of the point companies. Behind this, the German artillery and the rocket launchers of Werferregiment 83 aimed curtain-fire which forced the companies following in the second line to dig in. The Canadian Scottish finally penetrated into Cussy. The last survivors of 1. Flakbatterie, under Hauptsturmführer Ritzel, fought to the last man and died at their guns. The battalion then came under fire from Bitot, which was still being defended by weak forces, and from the Ardennes Abbey. The Regina Rifles were stalled at a strong point northwest of Ardenne. They were only able to further advance after the Canadian Scottish had overcome the strong point through a flanking attack with the support of a tank company and heavy machine guns of the Cameron Highlanders. The Reginas finally managed to penetrate into the outer reaches of the abbey. The Canadian Scottish had Cussy firmly in their hands at 21.30 hours. They had lost two officers and thirty-two NCOs and men killed, five officers and sixty-three NCOs and men wounded, and two missing.[49]

The defenders longed for nightfall. Before that, any disengagement was impossible. The enemy had only partially reached his attack objectives and brought his reserves into battle. At 21.00 hours, the 5th South Stafford Regiment was moved forward in order to break, together with tanks of the East Riding Yeomanry, the last resistance in Galmanche, mainly that of 7. Kompanie in its "fortress". The 2/6 South Staffords were pulled out in order to regroup in the Anisy area. The fighting lasted into the falling night.[50]

The I. Corps held some hope that a fast group might be successful in reaching the Orne bridge before it was destroyed. Thus, it ordered a battle group of the reconnaissance unit Inns of Court, with attached parts of the 7th Canadian Reconnaissance Regiment, to advance along Route Nationale No. 13 from Bayeux to Caen. Then, they were to penetrate into the city and to the bridge. They reached St. Germain-la Blanche-Herbe as darkness fell, but were stopped there by a mine obstacle and infantry fire.[51]

And still, I./25 was holding like a breakwater in a tidal wave under the exemplary leadership of Sturmbannführer Hans Waldmüller. The 6th North Staffordshires, pulled out of the reserves and supported by tanks of the 13/18 Hussars, "Crocodile" flame thrower tanks, flail tanks and "Petards", started an attack on this last bastion behind a moving wall of fire at 21.00 hours. A company of the East Ridings supported the attack by fire from Galmanche. The chief of 1. Kompanie, in action on the right wing of the Bataillon, Oberleutnant F., reported on the course of the battles:

> After renewed artillery preparation, the enemy attacked, to my surprise, once again, this time with flame thrower tanks. These caused a shock at first, but the Kompanie remained in its position. I valued this valor very highly from the young soldiers who had only just gone through their first experience of battle. After the first tank was knocked out by tank hunter weapons, the mood improved considerably. This added more encouragement, and several more tanks were knocked out in that manner. The attack stalled and the tanks retreated, partially from our position into which they had penetrated. At approximately that moment I was wounded twice.[52]

Rottenführer (corporal) Eberhard Köpke of 1. Kompanie recalled the close-in anti-tank fighting in a letter to a comrade who was taken prisoner on that day:

> The field of oats, in which we were located, had disappeared without a trace, the trenches were also gone and heavy smoke and the smell of exploded shells covered the field. The earth was completely dug up. I crawled over to the Kompanie command post, and there I saw what was coming at us. Tanks of any number and description. Well, the noble craft of warfare would have to be practiced now. I fired the first Panzerfaust wide, since the chap was still too far away from us. But I had another one handed to me immediately from somewhere, and it was a direct hit. I fetched the third one from the command post. There, Gerold, who had shouted news of my success to the men below, was shot through the neck. But I did not have much time because II. Zug had almost been smoked out by the flamethrower tanks. Two tanks had already made it across the trench. One was knocked out by Schomer with his Ofenrohr (stove pipe), I got the other one. The II. Zug was in terrible shape, almost everything

had been burned. Together with the newly arrived Zug leader and with Grünhagen, their rags nearly burnt off their bodies, we tried to hold what we could. Then, more tanks arrived at the railroad embankment. I crawled over there once more, again pressed on the small head of the Panzerfaust, and was lucky, the thing exploded.[53]

The attack by the tanks and the 6th North Staffordshires collapsed. Both sides had incurred high losses.

The communications connection between 1./25 and the Bataillon had been interrupted. Just as the chief of 1. Kompanie made contact with the leader of the neighbor Kompanie, Obersturmführer Braune, to jointly deliberate on the next moves, he was hit in the hip by a salvo of tracer bullets. The leader of the Granatwerfer (mortar) squad, Unter-scharführer Siegfried Bleich, reported on the further -developments:

> While the two Kompanie chiefs were discussing, a messenger of our Kompanie suddenly appeared. He had been sent to the Bataillon command post. He carried Waldmüller's order: 'Kompanie must try to fight its way to Caen!' Today, it seems like a miracle to me that this man had found his way to the front and survived it. He would have deserved to have his name recorded. Unterscharführer Granzow accepted the responsibility to lead the remnants of the Kompanie, including all the wounded who could be gathered, to the rear. The two of us agreed to meet in the first village behind the front line. Together with a Sturmmann, I searched the terrain for wounded men, but also in the hope of finding Panzerfausts in the abandoned positions.
>
> In the field we found a boy who had dragged himself back this far, despite a wounded foot, but could go no further. I carried him on my back through the haze caused by the phosphorous grenades. I have seldom felt so worn out as I did after this ordeal. Someone had found a wheel barrow and was pushing it ahead of him. Only when I got closer in the falling darkness did I notice that our chief was riding in it. We then told the boys to take cover and wait for stragglers. Suddenly, armor noises were coming closer. Of course, the boys were very excited, until someone hailed us. Waldmüller had sent our Panzers forward to bring us back. At that time we were down to barely thirty men.[54]

This disengagement by I. Bataillon was possible only because I. Zug of 1. Kompanie prevented a further enemy advance on the right flank. Obersturmführer Schümann and most of his men were killed during this action. The last of them were still fighting two days later in a hopeless position. The following details were found in a letter from the staff sergeant of 1. Kompanie, Hauptscharführer Herbert Stengel, written on 15.7.1944 to a wounded fellow Kompanie member:

> I'll give you a few details on our losses now. Oberleutnant F. is wounded, Kretschmar is wounded. Willy Rademacher, Moye, Au, Hillebrecht, Willinger, Scheible, Schall were killed. Of your squad, Stephan and Mandel are still here. Karl Schmidt and Käßmann are dead, all the others are wounded. Hauptmann Steger, Dr. Hermann, Obersturmführer Schümann are also dead. We had twenty-three killed on 8 July. No-one can imagine what the deaths of our comrades mean to us. They bring such obligations for us . . .
>
> But I can report to you that the fighting spirit of the Kompanie is unbroken. The Kompanie fought valiantly. A great number of Panzers were knocked out in close combat: Köpke, Schomer, Radoch, Hollinger. Willy Rademacher was killed around noon on 8. July. 'Tommy' attacked and Willy was standing in the trench, encouraging his men. There, he was hit directly by a tank gun. The greatest hero of the Kompanie must have been Willinger. He had orders to secure the right flank of the Bataillon. It was the most difficult spot in the sector, and he had been ordered to hold it. 'Tommy' broke through three times at his position, and three times he and his squad drove the enemy back. During the third attack he was seriously wounded and could not be rescued. He carried out his orders to the last, and sealed them with his death.[55]

Fortunately, Untersturmführer Hermann Willinger was found wounded by the British and cared for. He survived.

The remnants of 7. Kompanie could not withdraw from Galmanche either without being harassed. Obersturmführer Havemeister wrote about it:

> We intercepted a radio message ordering withdrawal to a new main line of defense outside of Caen. Since our 'Berta' device had long since given up its ghost, our friends, the forward Wehrmacht observers, once again came to our assistance. We had to bury some dead comrades in a section of ditch. Our greatest concern was then the transport of three seriously wounded men.
>
> The enemy left us completely alone. I totally prohibited any firing. From the close-by location of 5. Kompanie we could clearly hear the howling of a victory celebration. They were not even guarding in our direction. With extreme quiet, we carried the seriously wounded on their stretchers to the southeast corner of the park. There, a tall field of grain adjoined the remnants of the park wall. A volunteer messenger was on his way to the Bataillon. It had to assume that we were also wiped out. After a wordless parting, Leutnant Kinzig took

over this squad of wounded. Together with his radio operators, four uninjured carriers, three medics and the walking wounded he set out in the direction of la Folie. Unnoticed by our enemy neighbors, but frequently forced into cover by fighter-bombers, they reached the Bataillon and the vehicles. Together with the approximately forty uninjured men I had with me, I wanted to wait for dusk in our safe position. At the fall of dusk we crawled, split into three squads, through the gap in the rear wall of the park into the grain fields. As it grew darker, we rushed through the fields. By-passing the enemy-occupied towns of St. Contest on our right and la Folie on our left, we reached the road Buron-Caen after some two hours. In small groups we caught rides on vehicles to the new main line of defense.[56]

Some members of III./25 also managed to make their way to Caen during the night, as reported by Rottenführer Paul Hinsberger:

As darkness fell, we assembled for the breakthrough. We were thirty-six men. Ahead of us stood a Canadian vehicle column, the men gathered around fires. In the vicinity of the previous trench of 11. Kompanie, of which no-one was left, we lost five men in an unexplained manner. Along the road Buron-St. Contest, a jeep loaded with Canadians rolled right past us. We reached the rear positions outside Caen with thirty-one men.[57]

Returning members of his Bataillon, who had seen him hit, reported the commander of III. Bataillon, Hauptmann Steger, killed. Weeks after the notice of his death had arrived, Mrs. Steger received a letter from her husband, whom she believed killed, written in a prisoner of war camp. This was a rare, fortunate, event.

The enemy had already gained a foot in the terrain just outside the Ardennes Abbey, some even close to the outer walls. Obersturmbannführer Milius requested artillery fire on the abbey around midnight, in order to gain some breathing space. The Werferabteilung received permission to fire two salvos on Ardenne. The fire was to be directed by the forward observer in the abbey. The hoped-for result was achieved. The enemy withdrew. Supported by the remaining Panthers of 3. Kompanie, all of the garrison of the abbey, including all the wounded, were able to pull back to the outskirts of Caen.

Soon after midnight, the Divisional commander visited. He recalled:

I found the survivors of I./25 in a bunker at the edge of town. These totally worn-out soldiers had fallen into a deep sleep. The officers had taken over guard duties. Stragglers staggered into the bunker, letting themselves drop where ever there was a free spot. What luck that the Canadians and English did not pursue. The soldiers of 12. SS-Panzer-division were at the end of their physical endurance. They had fought at the front line for four weeks without any relief, and suffered the mighty hammer blows of the battle of materiel. They marched into battle with fresh, glowing faces. Today, mud-covered steel helmets threw their sha-dows on sunken faces whose eyes had beheld the beyond all-too-often.[58]

The Division issued orders to leave the assembly areas at dawn, and to take up the new positions at the southern bank of the Orne from the Vaucelles district to the estuary of the Odon into the Orne rivers. The III./26, the Divisionsbegleit-kompanie and a part of II. Abteilung of the Panzerregiment with remnants of 3. Panzerkompanie were ordered to withdraw, offering delaying fighting, across the last Orne crossing. They were to incorporate themselves into the defense after the Pioniers had blown up the bridge.

The enemy had reached the majority of his attack objectives on the wings, although some centers of resistance held out to the west of Epron and in Buron until the fall of darkness. In the central sector, at the 59th Infantry Division, Mâlon, Couvre-Chef, la Folie, Bitot, parts of Galmanche and Ardenne had not been captured, but abandoned by German decision. However, there was no doubt that these positions could not have been held any longer, because of the completely open right flank and also because of the heavy German losses. But, a decisive objective had not been reached, a bridgehead across the Orne near Caen, or in Caen itself.

The war diary of the Highland Light Infantry of Canada, which had fought in Buron, commented on the close of the day:

Night fell upon a quiet and smoking village. It had witnessed one of the most violent battles fought in the history of war. It was the first major battle of the HLI, and 8 July will enter its remembrance as a memorable day. The men were completely worn out. The reorganization showed how much their numbers had been reduced, too few to fight off a nightly counterattack. Although they burrowed into the ground like dogs, they were convinced that their day's labor had not been wasted. And despite being dead tired, they were ready to advance on Caen the next day, should the opportunity arise. Readiness at one-hundred percent level was kept up throughout the night, but the enemy had spent his force during the day. Except for a few infantrymen, cut off behind the lines, everything was quiet and the night passed without incidents.[59]

The losses were heavy on both sides. The 59th British and 3rd Canadian Infantry Divisions had each suffered more than 1,000 casualties. The following, incomplete, accounts which were available, give some detailed indication of the bitterness of the fighting:

197th Infantry Brigade, 8. July 1944 until 14.00 hours:

2/6 South Staffordshire Regiment: 80 losses;

2/5 The Lancashire Fusiliers: 60 losses, 112 until the evening;

1/7 Warwickshire Regiment: 48 losses.

9th Canadian Infantry Brigade:

The Highland Light Infantry of Canada: 262 losses, of which 62 were killed;

attached tank company: 11 of 15 tanks knocked-out;

The North Nova Scotia Highlanders: 201 losses;

1st Canadian Scottish Regiment: 34 killed, 68 wounded, 20 missing.[60]

The "HJ" Division mourned the following losses on 7 and 8 July 1944:

Unit	Dead			Wounded			Missing		
	Officers	NCOs	Men	Officers	NCOs	Men	Officers	NCOs	Men
Div.Begl.	-	1	6	-	-	1	-	-	-
Flak 12	1	1	7	-	1	5	-	3	24
Nachr.	-	-	-	-	1	2	-	-	1
Pz.Rgt.	-	3	10	2	8	24	1	1	9
Rgt.25	5	12	68	2	19	83	2	8	90
III./26	-	-	2	-	1	1	1	-	4
A.R., Werfer	-	-	-	2	5	6	-	-	-
Total	6	17	93	6	35	122	4	12	128

These losses amounted to 116 killed, 163 wounded and 144 missing, for a total of 423.

No accounts of the losses of III./25, in position at one of the focal points, are available. However, one must assume that its losses were similar to those of II./25. If one doubles these, one arrives at a total of 152 killed, 200 wounded and 180 missing, for a revised total of 532.

In the evening, Panzergruppe West issued the following order to LXXXVI. A.K., the I. and II. SS-Panzerkorps, by teletype so that "ULTRA" could not listen in:

The Caen bridgehead is to be cleared, inconspicuously, of the mass of heavy weapons during the night 8 to 9 July.

Sufficiently strong forces, reinforced by Pioniers and numerous forward observers, will remain behind and offer resistance along the line Calix-Point 64 (north of Caen)-northern edge of St. Germain-airfield 300 meters south of the eastern town edge of Carpiquet. Only in the face of a superior enemy attack, withdrawal to a line eastern bank of the Orne-northern edge of Vernoix-northern edge of Bretteville (the line of the forward strong points).[62]

This order from the Panzergruppe approved the measures which the "HJ" Division, looking ahead, had already taken. Even on the following day, Heeresgruppe B and the Supreme Command West, could not bring themselves to issuing a similarly clear order and report to the OKW accordingly.

The I Corps had ordered, for 9 July 1944, that the 59th in the center would capture Couvre-Chef, la Folie, Mâlon and Bitot, and then stop. The two divisions on the wings, the 3rd British Infantry Division to the east and the 3rd Canadian Infantry Division in the west, were ordered to take Caen from the flanks.

During the last hours of the night and the early hours of the morning of 9 July, the worn-out and totally exhausted survivors of Regiment 25 marched through the ruins of Caen and across the only usable Orne bridge to the south bank of the river, there to build up new defensive positions. The heavy weapons which had not been destroyed, were already in position. As well, artillery and rocket launchers were ready for action, even though there was some shortage of ammunition. Between 3 and 4 A.M. the Divisional command post was moved initially to Faubourg de Vaucelles and then to Garcelles.

A British scouting party reported Couvre-Chef to be clear of the enemy at 07.00 hours. Reconnaissance of the 7th South Staffords came under machine gun fire from positions near Mâlon, and under artillery fire, at 10.00 hours. One-half hour later, the 6th N Staffords, supported by tanks and behind a moving wall of fire, again attacked the network of positions. They captured it at 12.45 hours. Very likely, their enemies were individual pockets of resistance which had, regrettably, not received the order to withdraw. Bitot was reported free of the enemy at 13.50 hours, la Folie was occupied at 16.40 hours without resistance being encountered.[63]

At around noon, the spearheads of the 3rd British Division reached the center of Caen. There was only sporadic resistance.[64]

At the 3rd Canadian Division, the Stormont, Dundas & Glengarry Highlanders were ordered to take St. Germain, the North Nova Scotia Highlanders to take Venoix. To achieve this, they first occupied Franqueville and then advanced under heavy mortar fire along the railroad line from Carpiquet to Venoix. Since the road, running parallel, was mined, the vehicles had to be sent back to Carpiquet. The battalion continued its march on foot. All the houses were methodically searched for single riflemen. Any civilians suspected of collaborating with the Germans were thoroughly scrutinized.[65]

At dawn, 3. Flakbatterie (8.8 cm) had pulled out of its position immediately north of St. Germain-la Blanche-Herbe and moved to the southern bank of the Orne. Subsequently, the 2. Batterie (8.8 cm) moved positions at approximately 9 A.M., helped by the tractors of 3. Batterie since its own vehicles were out of service.[66]

The Divisionsbegleitkompanie was attacked by a superior enemy force at 10.00 hours. It withdrew to Caen under delaying fighting. At that time, tanks coming from the north and northwest had already penetrated into Caen. With them, in addition to the Canadian infantry, were many civilians, among them those with the white steel helmets of the French Red Cross. Directed by these civilians, familiar with the location, the enemy advanced with his many tanks from the northwest into the city. The Begleitkompanie, under continued delaying fighting, withdrew further through the city and crossed the railroad bridge in Caen at approximately 16.00 hours. Throughout its withdrawal, the population of the city had remained calm.[67]

At approximately the same time, its neighbor, III./26, came under attack from the Canadians and was pushed back, using delaying fighting, toward the city and the Orne bridge. Just ahead of the last rearguard of the Begleitkompanie, Sturmbannführer Olboeter crossed the Orne bridge with the last parts of his Bataillon. When the first Canadian troops reached the bridge, it had been kept open until then for stragglers, it was blown up by the Pioniers. The gun-equipped armored personnel carrier Zug had set up positions in an orchard on the southern bank. It opened concentrated fire on Canadian tanks and infantry assembling in the Caserne Hamelin. The enemy obviously suffered bad losses. After this fire attack, the armored personnel carriers rapidly changed position. Immediately thereafter, an enemy artillery fire attack churned up the terrain.[68]

The last to face the enemy were the men of the Divisionsbegleitkompanie. A report by Unterscharführer Leo Freund on the last action of this day showed that, despite all the determination with which this bitter fighting was carried out, there was also respect for the brave enemy and human consideration. He wrote:

It was 9 July 1944. The Divisionsbegleitkompanie was in position north of Caen as the last line, securing the withdrawal of the Division. The sector of I. Zug contained a quarry where the Zug command post was located. The 2. Gruppe (squad) of I. Zug, with its leader Werner Richter, had moved into a position on the left wing. Everyone was waiting for the expected English attack on Caen. In this situation, Werner Richter had a premonition that something would soon happen to him. He called me over and told me of his apprehension. He asked me to send his personal effects to his family. This, I promised and asked Werner Richter for the same favor in case anything happened to me, trying to dispel Werner's sad thoughts. We separated then, but not without a joke about who would get it first.

While still on the way from Werner Richter's foxhole to the Zug command post, I was caught by an artillery fire attack. Leaping through the explosions, I made it to the command post. While I was still telling Untersturmführer Erwin Stier about Werner Richter's bleak forebodings, and shells were hammering our positions without pause, the MG gunner 1 of the Richter Gruppe rushed into the command post. He reported that his Gruppe leader had been killed. Without paying any regard to the exploding shells, I ran to the dead friend together with the MG gunner. I found him in his foxhole almost exactly as I had left him, sitting on the edge. However, his upper body had toppled over. Shell shrapnel had penetrated his neck and ripped open his right shoulder. We carried him to the quarry in a tarpaulin. We all knew that, after this fire attack, the English attack would have to start right away. And then they were there! They advanced on our positions in a wide front. We would not be able to withstand this superiority for long. But, Werner Richter was still lying in the quarry. He had still to be buried. Deciding quickly, Erwin Stier, Arthur Schenk and I began digging a grave. The quarry provided good cover, but made the digging all-the-more difficult. Already, there were shouts from all sides that the enemy was immediately outside our positions, when the order came to withdraw to the outskirts of Caen. The soldiers came out of their positions and, in delaying fighting, pulled back. Only the three of us remained in the quarry. We had taken off our weapons and helmets and were desperately working the rocky ground which was to be Werner Richter's last resting place. An icy shock suddenly raced through us. We looked up, and into innumerable rifle muzzles. The British had reached the quarry in the meantime and were standing, weapons at the ready, approximately twenty to thirty meters away, watching the three of us performing our sad effort. After recovering from our first shock, we continued our work. We bedded our dead comrade into the hole, barely half-a meter deep, and gathered rocks so as to build up a mound. Any moment, we expected a fire salvo to put an end to our effort. But, nothing happened. We tied two pieces of wood to form a cross and stuck it between the rocks. Erwin Stier spoke the words of good-bye and a short prayer. Our hands folded, we stood around the mound of rocks and quietly said farewell to our comrade Werner Richter.

But then we were brought back to the grim reality. We had finished our work and the English would no longer hesitate. But still, nothing happened. Furtively, we reached for our helmets and weapons. The behavior of the English soldiers had given us courage again and we wanted to take advantage of the hesitation of the enemy. We walked slowly toward the exit from the quarry, constantly expecting to be brought down by a rifle salvo. But we left their field of fire without being bothered, and our tension lifted. We raced in long jumps to the edge of Caen. We paid sincere tribute to the enemy's fair conduct.[69]

Although 16. Lw.-Feld-Division and the attached Panzergrenadierregiment 1 had only been able to take up the new defensive position behind the Orne and behind the Odon, respectively, in a makeshift manner, the enemy made no serious effort to establish a bridgehead across the river. Very likely, he too was exhausted after the bitter and bloody battles and did not want to take any risk. After the self-sacrificing fighting by the defenders of Caen, such risk would loom large. Thus, the exhausted defenders gained time to reinforce their positions.

Fortunately, the losses of "HJ" Division on 9 July 1944 were minor when compared to the previous day. The men who were fighting from their cut-off strong points during that day, and effectively slowed down the enemy advance, are likely to be found among the missing reported on 8 July. These are the numbers:

	Dead			Wounded			Missing		
Unit	Officers	NCOs	Men	Officers	NCOs	Men	Officers	NCOs	Men
Div. Begl.	-	1	3	-	-	2	-	-	1
Flak 12	-	-	-	-	-	3	-	-	-
Nachr.12	-	-	-	-	-	1	-	-	-
Pz.Rgt.	-	2	2	-	1	5	-	-	8
III./26	-	-	10	-	-	9	1	1	10
A.R., Werf.	-	1	1	-	-	1	-	-	-
Total	-	4	16	-	1	21	1	1	19

The losses amounted to 20 killed, 22 wounded and 21 missing, for a total of 63.[70]

After the section of Caen north of the Orne was occupied, the planned attack from the Odon bridgehead started on 10 July. Its objective was, if possible, to establish bridgeheads across the Orne above Caen, if undamaged bridges were encountered. This operation, led by VIII Corps, carried the code name "Jupiter". Available for the attack were the 43rd Infantry Division with attached 46th Infantry Brigade, the 31st Tank Brigade (less one unit), and the 43rd Armoured Brigade. Artillery support was to be provided by the divisional artillery of the 43rd Division, of the 11th Armoured Division, of the 15th Scottish Infantry Division with the attached 55th Field Regiment, and by the 3rd and 8th AGRA artillery units. Attacks by fighter-bomber were planned for all of the day. The attack was scheduled to start at 05.00 hours.[71]

With regard to the intentions of the 43rd Infantry Division, its war diary stated: "The high terrain between Odon and Orne along a general line Hill 112-St. Martin-Vieux-across from Feuguerolles sur Orne-Maltot is to be captured and held. The bridges across the Orne, if they are found undamaged, must be secured by cover from the western bank." Logically, this included establishing a bridgehead.[72]

Shortly before midnight on 9 July, the 214th Infantry Brigade pushed ahead of the 43rd Infantry Division in order to achieve a more favorable starting position for the attack early on 10 July. By 04.50 hours, it had reached the line Odon bridge in Verson-Fontaine Etoupefour-Gournay without encountering any resistance. The 129th Infantry Brigade secured to the west.[73] After the preparatory fire, which started at 05.00 hours, the troops of the 43rd Division, assembled at the forward line, started the attack. By 08.00 hours they had reached Eterville and the slope of Hill 112. As the attack toward Maltot continued, Eterville was captured and secured. The action-ready parts of Panzerregiment 12, without 2. Kompanie which stood in the area east of Bretteville, had been assembled in the sheltered terrain southeast and east of Maltot during the previous day. Parts of 5. Kompanie were very likely immediately northeast of Maltot. Untersturm-führer Kändler and his Zug had still been battle-ready immediately south of Eterville in the evening of 9 July. Just before dawn on 10 July, he and his Zug had been pulled back to the road Louvigny-Maltot. Untersturmführer Kändler's Zug was then positioned on the road, approximately 500 meters northeast of the crossroads which is located approximately 400 meters northeast of the exit from Maltot in the direction of Louvigny. Columns of German vehicles were coming from Louvigny. Time and again, he had to make room for them and, for that reason, he moved his Panzers into the open field along the road. At approximately 7 or 8 A.M. in the morning, he observed the enemy laying a smoke screen between Eterville and Maltot. He advanced with his Panzer in order to gain an open field of view. After some 200 to 300 meters, Kändler encountered German infantry in their positions. Because of the smoke which also covered their positions, they were somewhat apprehensive. After he had crossed the lane leading from the northeastern exit from Maltot to the Eterville church, he spotted a tracked enemy vehicle racing at full speed along the road from Etoupefour to Maltot. He opened fire, and the first shot by his gunner, Sturmmann Schnittfinke, scored a direct hit on the vehicle which went up in flames. He drove onward to the road fork 1.5 kilometers northeast of Hill 112 and, to his great surprise, spotted a large armor unit rolling diagonally from the north across the eastern slope of Hill 112, apparently in the direction of Feuguerolles and St. Martin. He immediately called the other two Panzers of his Zug, commanders Unter-scharführer Jürgens and Rottenführer Biback, on the radio to come over to his position. Then he reported to his Kompanie chief who cautioned him about engaging in battle. When his three Panzers were assembled, they opened fire. Kändler's Panzer knocked out seven tanks, the number of kills achieved by the other two are not known. When English ambulances drove onto the battlefield to rescue the wounded, firing was stopped. Then, the Panzers came themselves under fire from Eterville. One of them was rendered immobile. Untersturm-führer Kändler took it in tow and withdrew with his three Panzers to his starting position.[74]

In the afternoon, the 7th Hampshires and the 4th Dorsets, supported by tanks, managed to penetrate into a section of Maltot. At 17.00 hours they reported the town in their hands. Toward the evening, SS-Panzerregiment 12 and, to its left, the heavy SS-Panzerabteilung 102 (Tigers) under Sturmbann-führer Hans Weiß, with parts of SS-Panzergrenadierregiment 21, attacked with the objective of recapturing Maltot and Hill 112. The 4th Dorsets suffered heavy losses and withdrew across the positions of the 7th SLI at 20.30 hours. They assembled approximately one kilometer west of Eterville which they had taken in the morning.[75]

Hill 112 was captured by the Panzers. Parts of Panzer-regiment 12 advanced to the square wooded area on the Hill. When the enemy barrages set in again, together with more artificial smoke, the Hill was abandoned again. The Tigers moved into ambush positions immediately south of the Hill. Panzerregiment 12 returned to its starting positions. The top of Hill 112 probably remained no-man's land.[76]

As darkness fell, the forward parts of the 43rd Division and the attached 8th Canadian Infantry Brigade, which had joined the attack in the course of the day, were positioned immediately northwest of the road Bretteville-sur-Odon-Eterville-Esquay. This was, generally, at the rear slope of the range of hills extending from Hill 112 to Louvigny. It was only from the rounded top of Hill 112 that the enemy could observe the hills on the other side of the Orne valley.

At 06.00 hours on 11 July 1944, 1. SS-Panzerdivision Leibstandarte SS "Adolf Hitler" took over command of the previous sector of the "HJ" Division. Artillerieregiment 12 and one Panzergrenadierbataillon remained in action under the command of the "LAH" Division. All the other units assembled in the Sassy-Condé-Garcelles-Potigny-Bons area to be refitted to the extent possible.[77]

On 14 July, the Supreme Commander West, Generalfeld-marschall von Kluge, visited Panzergruppe West and I. SS.-Panzerkorps. Obergruppen-führer Sepp Dietrich gave a briefing on the situation. A note in the war diary of Supreme Command West stated:

The losses were emphasized, as was the outstanding attitude of the 'Hitlerjugend' Division. Its commander, Standartenführer Meyer, personally reported to the Feldmarschall. The discussion centered on relieving the worn-out divisions and the bringing forward of new ones. . . . Losses since the start of the invasion: 12.SS-Pz.Div. "HJ": approximately 5,000 men . . .[78]

CHAPTER 4.3
Final Observations on the Fourth Battle for Caen

With the failure of the attack by the VIII Corps from the Odon bridgehead with the objective of gaining a bridgehead across the Orne above Caen, the fourth battle for Caen had come to an end. It had not achieved the expectations of the enemy. In a letter of 7 July 1944 to General Montgomery, General Eisenhower, the Allied supreme commander, gave his assessment of the situation. He also expressed his expectations on the continuation of the operation. Among others, he wrote:

> On the British side, we are approaching the limits of the available means. Very soon, we will also approach the capacity limits of our present ports to bring forward and supply American troops. Thus, the enemy will be able to increase his relative strength, as he seems to be doing already.
>
> This requires that any possibility of expanding our bridgehead must be explored in order to increase the maneuvering room for our troops before the enemy achieves substantially the same strength, e.g. in infantry, tanks, and artillery. On the left wing we need depth and elbow room and, finally, enough terrain to secure the landing beach of 'SWORD' [west of the mouth of the Orne] against enemy fire. We should use all means to gain suitable airfields . . .
>
> Your plan, to hold fast on the left wing and tie down enemy armor forces, while your right wing pushes down the peninsula (the Cotentin, Author), threatening the rear and the flank of the forces opposite the Second British army, is well known to me . . .
>
> It appears necessary to me that we expand all possible energy for a decisive effort so as to prevent a standstill or the requirement to fight a major defensive battle, considering the limited depth we now have in the bridgehead.

We have not yet attempted a major offensive with all available forces and material on the left wing . . .

I . . . will do anything within my means to provide you with every unit you feel required. If, for instance, you need an American tank division for an attack on your left wing, I would be glad to make it available to you and send it as quickly as is possible.[1]

The commander-in-chief of the air forces of the expeditionary corps, Air Chief Marshal Sir T. L. Leigh-Mallory, had already written on the urgency ". . . to gain terrain south and southeast of Caen . . ." since it was ". . . the most suitable for the establishing of airfields" in a letter of 29 March to General Montgomery.[2] This was emphasized once again by General Eisenhower.

General Montgomery replied to General Eisenhower with a letter on 8 July, when the "CHARNWOOD" operation was already under way. Regarding the Caen area, the following passages are noteworthy:

There are three matters clear in my mind:
1. We must take the Brittany peninsula . . .
2. We do not want to be enclosed in a narrow piece of terrain; we must have room to maneuver, for the rear services, and for airfields.
3. We want to tie down the enemy in battles, so as to exhaust his forces and, generally, to kill Germans. Where, exactly, we do this is unimportant as long as we carry out Points 1 and 2.

Then, it was explained that the primary objective had been the capture of Cherbourg. The, also desirable, capture of Caen had not been possible due to a lack of forces. Since the progress of the 1st US Army had been slower than expected, he had then decided to become active near Caen, so as to

. . . take Caen and gain bridgeheads across the Orne. This action will, indirectly, benefit the fighting on the western wing.

The operations of the Second Army on the eastern flank started today, they are progressing well. They will achieve the capture of Caen and the advance of the eastern wing to the Orne, with bridgeheads across the Orne . . .

It is possible that the best proposal for the Second Army is, to continue its action and push to the south, with its left wing at the Orne. It may also be a good plan to cross the Orne and establish itself firmly along the road to Falaise . . .

The attack on Caen by the Second Army, now under way, is a big 'show' in-as-much as only the I Corps is taking part. The VIII Corps will start the 'race' on Monday morning (10 July). I will throw everything into it.[3]

These letters indicate clearly the high expectations which General Eisenhower as well as General Montgomery had lodged with the "CHARNWOOD" and "JUPITER" operations. Their objective, unquestionably, was the high plain south of Caen. In heavy and bloody battles, the town of Caen, the Orne river to the bend south of the city, and the lower course of the Odon had been captured. The losses of the I Corps amounted to 3,817 men in three days.[4] It is probably correct to assume the majority of these losses occurred in the sector of the "HJ" Division since the 16. Lw.-Feld-Div. had been able to resist for a shorter time and less effectively.

Conversely, the "HJ" Division had lost 595 men. The losses of the neighbor to the right were likely much higher. Still, together with those of 12. Division, they would probably not have approached the total of the British losses. The I. SS-Panzerkorps was located approximately along the line to which General Geyr von Schweppenburg had proposed withdrawal on 30 June, but still north of the line originally approved by Feldmarschall Rommel. The threat to the British "SWORD" landing sector from the German Caen bridgehead had disappeared. The enemy had gained enough space to assemble, unhindered, for the push to the south east of the Orne. If, more quickly than had previously been the case, action-ready infantry and Panzer divisions could have been brought in to relieve the Panzerdivisions still in action, the threat in the Caen area, as well as near Caumont and at the base of the Contentin, could have been fought off. The enemy could not have been sufficiently strong in all three sectors simultaneously.

While the enemy had only achieved a part of his objective, the German side, also, had only a partial defensive success to its credit. However, with the existing ratio of forces, it had to be valued all-the-more highly where the sector of the "HJ" Division was concerned. Facing each other were:

Forces	Germans	Allies
Infantry	3.5 battalions	18 battalions
Panzers/tanks	3 companies	12 companies
	32 Panzer IVs	244 medium tanks
	17 Panzer Vs	44 light tanks and special tanks
Artillery	1 light Abteilung	7 light units
	1 heavy Abteilung	2 heavy units
	2 Werferabteilungen	4 battle ships
	12 light field howitzers	5 light units to form occasional
	12 heavy field howitzers	points of concentration
	4 10 cm guns	
	144 barrels 15 cm launchers	
	90 barrels 21 cm launchers	
		656 barrels, of which $^2/_3$ (436 barrels) were aimed at the "HJ" at all times
	262 barrels	

It had then become important to the "HJ" Division that the required reinforcements arrived on a timely basis so that they could be incorporated before the next action. As well, Panzers and Pak were urgently needed. Since the start of the invasion, forty-four of ninety-eight Panzer IVs, and 21 of 72 Panthers had been totally lost. Seventeen Panthers had been provided by 5.7.1944 for the re-activation of 3. Kompanie. On 11 July, 19 Panzer IVs and twenty-four Panzer Vs were reported ready for action, twenty-seven Panzer IVs and twenty-four Panzer Vs were being repaired within a short time frame, up to the next fourteen days. Of twenty-eight Pak 7.5 cm, four were still ready for action. The Panzerjägerabteilung was still not battle-ready.[5]

SECTION 5

Operation 'GOODWOOD' to the Eve of Operation 'TOTALIZE'

CHAPTER 5.1
Relief and Rest Period in Mid-July 1944

The relief of the Panzerdivisions, in action at the front lines, by Infanteriedivisions, which had to be brought forward, had repeatedly been requested since the end of June. The first such operation started on 30 June when the Panzer-Lehr-Division was relieved by 276. Infanteriedivision. At the beginning of July, the positions of 21. Pz.-Div. had been taken over by 16. Lw.-Feld-Div. The 272. Inf.-Div. was scheduled to take over the sector of "HJ" Division. It had not reached the front line by 11 July so that 1. SS-Pz.-Div. "LAH" had to relieve it from its sector. The 271. Inf.-Div. set out from southern France at the end of June. It only relieved 10. SS-Pz.-Div. "Frundsberg" at the end of July, and can be used as an example to show how the considerable delays occurred.

The circumstances are shown in three studies by the commander of this Division, Generalleutnant Dannhauser, and a comment by General Max Pemsel, the former Chief of Staff of 7. Armee. These were written in 1946 and 1947.

The Division had been established in southern France in early 1944. It was a regular Infanteriedivision 44 with 3 Infanterie regiments of 2 battalions each, a Divisional fusilier battalion, a field reserve battalion, one Artillerieregiment with 3 light and 1 heavy Abteilungen, a Pionier battalion, a Divisional Panzerjägerkompanie, a Nachrichtenabteilung, and the usual rear services.

The commanders and the officer corps were mostly experienced in battle, from the eastern campaign, as were a third of the NCOs and men. A further third consisted of recovered wounded, the last third of recruits from the homeland. The average age of the Division was approximately thirty years. The Divisional commander assessed his troops:

Attitude and morale of all officers, NCOs and men is very good. This soldierly attitude and fighting spirit has been maintained undiminished throughout the difficult action despite the high losses and the enemy materiel superiority. The Division entered the fighting at full battle strength.

Weapons and equipment are fully provided and completely new. The supply of the material was initially significantly delayed. This interrupted the course of the training.

Immediately before the action, Generalleutnant Dannhauser provided the following judgment on the battle-readiness of his Division:

Absolutely prepared for defense. Only limited suitability for offensive action because of known gaps in training.

Even during its training period, the Division was put into action in the Sète-Montpellier sector on the Mediterranean coast. At the end of June, it received orders for transport to the invasion front. It was relieved by 198. Reservedivision.

The reader will expect that the Division would have moved in the most expeditious manner and shortest distance possible in order to relieve one of the worn-out Panzerdivisions, the "HJ" Division or the Panzer-Lehr-Division. Far from it! The Division was given an interim destination of Rouen. It moved by rail from Montpellier via Dijon, Châlons-sur-Marne into the area east of Rouen. The rail transport was significantly delayed by bomb damage to bridges and railroad stations. The last of the missing units arrived in the combat area twenty-one days after the first unit. Air attacks had caused personnel and materiel losses. Some of the transports were unloaded along an open stretch of track and the troops marched on foot to the assembly areas east and northeast of Rouen. General Dannhauser wrote on the plans of the Heeresgruppe:

The reason for the assembly in the area east of the Seine could likely be traced back to the expectations of the supreme command of a second landing at Pas de Calais. This could also be concluded from a verbal briefing by the supreme commander of Heeresgruppe B, Generalfeld-marschall von Kluge, who made the Division available initially to LXXXI. A.K. in Rouen for possible action east of the Seine in a northerly direction.

In mid-July, the Division was assigned to Panzergruppe West, which immediately ordered it into the Caen area without awaiting full completion of assembly and readiness. The units were to be brought forward using any available means of transport and, as they arrived, were to relieve the Panzer units there. The crossing of the Seine started on 15 July. Six ferries, some of them makeshift ferries of the most primitive construction with limited carrying capacity, were available. Because of the tight fuel situation, the troops covered the majority of the 150–200 kilometers distance from the unloading area to the operational area on foot. They marched at night and along secondary roads since supplies were rolling along the main roads during the few hours of darkness. The first advance parts relieved units of 10. SS-Panzerdivision "Frundsberg" on 22 July. During this, the first-arrived Bataillon became engulfed, shortly after the relief, in a strong enemy attack on Maltot and suffered heavy losses. By 2 August, the Division had taken over a six kilometers wide sector from the Orne east of Maltot to east of Hill 113, northeast of Evrécy.

At the end of his study on the action by his Division at the invasion front, on which will be reported later, General Dannhauser offers a revealing conclusion:

> Without any doubt, action three weeks earlier by the fresh, newly equipped and battle-ready Division in the battle for Caen, would have played a remarkable role.[1]

In his comment on the studies regarding the action by 271. Infanteriedivision at the invasion front, Generalleutnant Pemsel remarked, among others:

> The 271 Infanteriedivision was the best of the 270s divisions put into action in the Caen sector. It was the most advanced in training and equipment.
>
> The move of 271. I.D. by order of Heeresgruppe B of 29.6.44 into the area north of the Seine was proof as to how much the Heeresgruppe (Rommel) lived with the thought, at that time as well as later, of a second Allied landing north of the Seine. It is interesting that Rommel's successor, von Kluge, also pointed primarily to deployment of the Division north of the Seine in a direct order to the Divisional commander.
>
> When, in an order of 3 July, the supreme command of the Wehrmacht finally wanted to put the Division into action west of the Seine, it was reported that the Division could not be re-routed for railway-technical reasons of blocking the fuel and munitions trains. This reasoning was not sound since the Division had to be already unloaded in the Paris area because of destruction of railway facilities. Thus, the Division could not be blocking other trains. In addition, the fighting units of the Division arrived, in a staggered fashion, within a period of twenty-one days in the Rouen area.

Because of the totally inadequate capacity of crossing the lower Seine river, the Division then arrived for action west of the Seine from its assembly area near Rouen in a one-unit-at-a-time manner.[2]

Here, one again encounters the false image of the enemy which the general staff of the Heer, Abteilung Fremde Heere West, under Oberst von Roenne and with the collaboration of Major Michel, had provided: "Thirty Divisions too many". One has to agree with the assessment of Generalleutnant Dann-hauser: if the overall situation had been judged correctly, his Division could have been put into action at the front near Caen at the latest at the end of June 1944. To achieve this, an early relief from the quiet Mediterranean front and transport through western France would have been required. However, other divisions were located, inactive, much closer to the invasion front, waiting for a second landing at Pas de Calais.

The "HJ" Division was moved to the Sassy-Condé-Garcelles-Potigny-Bons area. The Artillerieregiment and one Panzergrenadierbataillon under the command of 1. SS-Panzerdivision "LAH" remained in action. The firing positions of III. Abteilung were located east of Fontenay-le Marmion and around Rocquancourt. The Abteilung command post was situated in the quarry north of Fontenay, south of Hill 88. The forward observers were with the infantry in Vaucelles.[3] No firm information can be provided on the attached Bataillon, it was probably I./26. According to a report by Sturmmann Heinrich Bassenauer, it was involved in setting up positions along the Orne near St. André-sur-Orne after Caen was abandoned. The 4. Kompanie secured a bridge near St. André.[4] In the daily report of Panzergruppe West of 1.7.44., the following command posts were listed: Divisional staff in Garcelles (ten kilometers southeast of the Orne bridge Caen); Panzerregiment: three kilometers west of St. Sylvain (16.5 kilometers southeast of the Orne bridge Caen); Regiment 25: two kilometers north of Sassy (twenty-six kilometers southeast of the Orne bridge Caen); Regiment 26: Ouilly (six kilometers west of Sassy).[5]

During the few quiet days, no refitting occurred since neither replacements for the casualties nor the lost Panzers and weapons arrived. The troops were able to rest, service their weapons and vehicles, and evaluate their recent experiences. At the same time, the repair services and the supply troops worked with all available energy on bringing Panzers and vehicles back into battle-ready condition, and to transport ammunition, fuel and provisions forward.

Since, in the short term, no reinforcements could be expected from the reserves, units had to be amalgamated and core groups had to be pulled out for later reinforcement. At the Panzerregiment, 9. Kompanie was reinforced by parts of the 5., and renamed 5. Kompanie. Other parts of 5. Kompanie were reassigned to the 8. The core group of 6. Kompanie was probably pulled out. On 17 July, twenty-one Panzer IVs and eighteen Panthers were ready for action. Obersturmführers Gasch and Gaede were on their way to Linz to pick up thirty-six Panzer IVs. They had not yet returned by that date.

It is probable that the Regimental staff and the remnants of the Regimental units as well as II. Bataillon were pulled out of Panzergrenadierregiment 25, and that I. Bataillon was reinforced with the remnants of the III. As documented in a letter by Unterscharführer Köpke of 6.10. 1946, 1. Kompanie received four NCOs and seventy men. Obersturmführer Alfred Braun took over the Kompanie, Zug commanders were Untersturmführer Zetsche and the Oberscharführers Granzow and Bleich.[7] A Kompanie listing of 3. Kompanie has survived. It indicates two officers, twenty-four NCOs, and 145 men. The information in it on age and profession is revealing.[8]

The core group of II. Bataillon of Panzergrenadierregiment 26 was probably moved for refitting. Some of the men were assigned to I. Bataillon as indicated in the list of losses of 7. Kompanie for the period 21 to 23 July.

Panzeraufklärungsabteilung 12, except for two armored reconnaissance car platoons, was pulled out for refitting. They were moved to their billet area around Rugles, where they had been prior to the start of the invasion. The other core groups, destined for refitting, also returned to their previous billet areas, where parts of the supply troops had been left behind.

The units remaining in the resting area were, despite consolidation and probable addition of reserves from Feldersatzbataillon 12 (field reinforcement battalion) to which they had transferred personnel prior to departure for the front on 6 June, not fully up to strength when their next action loomed. It clearly proved to be a disadvantage, even a mistake, that the required reinforcements could not be provided to the worn-out divisions during the pause in the fighting. These reserves were primarily used to set up new units. Thus, on the situation map, divisions were shown which sometimes were only regimental Kampfgruppen, although that was not clearly indicated. The superior command authorities in the vicinity of the front still had an understanding of the real battle strength of the units which were only shown as tactical markers on the maps. However, the farther a command authority was removed from the front, and the more large units it commanded, the more difficult it was to properly connect the tactical markers to the real fighting strength at the time, despite the daily reports and monthly situation summaries. This could easily lead to false estimations and wrong decisions. In addition, the value in combat of a coordinated and battle-hardened unit, reinforced by reserves, is higher than that of a newly formed unit, after a possibly short training period.

More quickly than had been hoped, the resting period for the "HJ" Division came to an end. For many units, it did not last even one week.

CHAPTER 5.2
Operation 'GOODWOOD'. Breakout by the British from the Bridgehead East of the Orne River. Defensive Fighting near Vimont from 18 July to 4 August 1944

In order to carry out General Montgomery's orders, issued on 30 June in Directive No. M 505, the First US Army started its offensive. The first objective was to reach the line Caumont—Vire—Mortain—Fougères. An attack from Vire to capture Flers (thirty-two kilometers southwest of Falaise) was envisaged. It was further planned, after reaching the base of the Cotentin peninsula near Avranches, to turn one Corps away in order to capture Brittany. The bulk of the Army would swing wide south of the Bocage to the east and take the lines Laval-Mayenne and subsequently Le Mans-Alençon.[1] The attack progressed only slowly. The superior American forces, fourteen divisions facing six German divisions, could not deploy adequately. St. Lô was being stubbornly defended, in the central sector, flooded areas impeded the advance. The attack had to be restricted to a 2.5 kilometers wide strip along both sides of the road Carentan-Périers. On the right flank, the steep hills near the crossroads la Haye-du-Puits faced the American bridgehead. On 10 July, the attack ground to a halt. It now became important for General Montgomery to tie down the German forces in the Caen area so that no significant parts could be pulled out to resist the American offensive. The situation for the Allied landing troops was critical. They still depended on a single man-made harbor and could not yet use the Carpiquet airfield which was located within observation and firing range of the German artillery. Almost no new infantry divisions could be expected as reinforcements in the beachhead. The available American tank divisions could not fully deploy in the Bocage terrain. In his directive No. M 510 of 10 July 1944, General Montgomery had ordered that the Second British Army would attack west of the Orne to the south, with its left wing, along the river. This, in order to capture the line Thury-Harcourt (twenty-three kilometers southwest of the Orne bridge Caen)-Mont Pinçon-le Bény Bocage (twelve kilometers northeast of Vire), and there to establish contact with the left wing of the First US Army. That attack did not come about. Thus, in a note on 15 July, he ordered the Second British Army to conduct an operation from the Caen area with the objective to tie down the German Panzer divisions there and to "write them off" so that they could no longer be useful for other purposes. Attacks by the XII British and the II Canadians Corps on 16 and 17 July were meant to create the impression at the German command that the plan was to cross the river between Caen and Amayé-sur-Orne. The real offensive, Operation

"GOODWOOD", was ordered for 18 July. The VIII Corps would then attack with the three tank divisions, the 11th, the Guards, and the 7th Armoured Divisions, from the bridgehead northeast of Caen to the south and south-east. The objective was to capture the area Bourguebus-Vimont-Bretteville [sur-Laize?], "to engage and destroy the enemy." General Montgomery ordered thrusts by armored reconnaissance units from this area "far to the south toward Falaise in order to shake up the enemy, alarm him and determine his deployment." The II Canadian Corps was ordered to take Vaucelles (Caen-South) during the attack by VIII Corps, and to establish a strong bridgehead across the Orne. The I Corps with the 3rd British Infantry Division was directed to take on the securing of the left flank. After the setting-up of the bridgehead, the VIII Corps was to be given freedom to engage in other operations as the situation required.[2]

On the German side, a major enemy offensive from the bridgehead east of the Orne was expected. In action, in this area and under the command of Panzergruppe West, were:

LXXXVI. A.K. with

711. Inf.-Div. in the coastal sector from the mouth of the Seine to the mouth of the Orne near Franceville-Plage;

346. Inf.-Div. in the sector from Franceville-Plage to north of Touffre-ville;

16. Lw.-Feld-Div. in the sector north of Touffreville to Colombelles, with attached Pz.-Gren.-Rgt. 192 of 21. Pz.-Div. adjoining on the left to the Orne bridge in Caen-South.

I. SS-Pz.-Korps with

272. Inf.-Div. from the Orne bridge in Caen-South to west of Eterville (beginning on 17 July).

Dividing line between LXXXVI. A.K. and I. SS-Panzerkorps: road Falaise-Caen (to I. SS).

During the period from 13 to 17 July, 1. SS-Pz.-Div. "LAH" was relieved by 272. Inf.-Div. Thereafter, it was available to the Korps in the area Ifs-Bully-Bretteville-sur-Laize (excl.)-Cintheau (excl.)-Tilly-la Campagne. The 12. SS-Pz.-Div. "HJ" had moved to the already mentioned area Garcelles-Potigny-Olendon-Sassy-Condé-Fierville for short-term refitting. -Schwere (heavy) SS-Panzer-abteilung 101 was located, with one battle-ready Kompanie, in the area around Grainville-Langannerie. Werferbrigade 7 was assigned to the Korps.

The focal point of the enemy attack was to be expected in the sector of 16. Lw.-Feld-Div. It had suffered severe losses during Operation "CHARN-WOOD", the attack on Caen on 8 and 9 July. Because of these, not only had Pz.-Gren.-Rgt. 192 of 21. Pz.-Div. been attached to it and slotted into the left wing, but the mass of this Division and other units were in readiness in the depth of the main battle field. The forward parts of 16. Lw.-Feld-Div. only formed a thin infantry screen since, based on previous experiences, it could hardly be expected that a heavy deployment of infantry could better with-

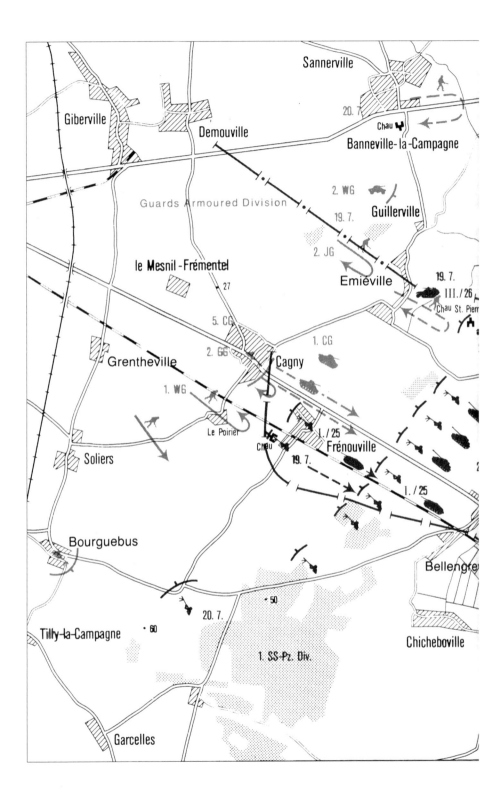

Sannerville

Giberville

Demouville

20. 7.

Chau

Banneville-la-Campagne

Guards Armoured Division

2. WG

19. 7.

Guillerville

2. JG

le Mesnil-Frémentel

Emiéville

19. 7.

III./26

Chau St. Pierr

27

5. CG

1. CG

2. GG

Cagny

Grentheville

1. WG

Le Poirier

I./25

Chau

Frénouville

19. 7.

Soliers

I./25

Bourguebus

Bellengre

50

20. 7.

Tilly-la-Campagne

60

Chicheboville

1. SS-Pz. Div.

Garcelles

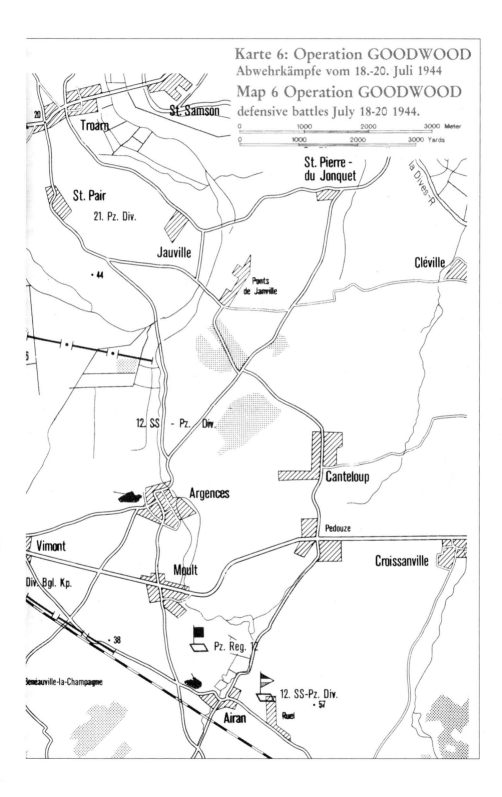

Karte 6: Operation GOODWOOD
Abwehrkämpfe vom 18.-20. Juli 1944
Map 6 Operation GOODWOOD
defensive battles July 18-20 1944.

0   1000   2000   3000 Meter
0   1000   2000   3000 Yards

St. Samson

Troarn

St. Pierre -
du Jonquet

la Dives-R

St. Pair
21. Pz. Div.

Jauville

Cléville

• 44

Ponts
de Janville

12. SS - Pz. Div.

Canteloup

Argences

Pedouze

Vimont

Croissanville

Div. Bgl. Kp.

Moult

• 38

Bénéauville-la-Champagne

Pz. Reg. 12

12. SS-Pz. Div.
• 57

Ruel

Airan

stand the moving wall of fire from the enemy artillery. The von Luck Kampf-gruppe, named after the commander of Pz.-Gren.-Rgt. 125 of 21 Pz.-Div., Oberstleutnant von Luck, was located to the rear in several strong points:

II./Pz.-Gren.-Rgt. 125 in the Touffreville-Emiéville area;

I./Pz.-Gren.-Rgt. 125 in the Cuverville-Giberville-le -Mesnil-Frémentel-Démouville area;

Sturmgeschützabteilung 200 (assault guns) with 1. -Batterie near Démouville, 2. Batterie near Giberville, 3. Batterie near Grentheville, 4. Batterie near le -Mesnil-Frémentel, 5. Batterie near le Prieure (each battery consisted of 6 Pak (7.5 cm long) and 4 howitzers (10.5 cm) on "Hotchkiss" chassis).

It was the mission of the Panzergrenadiers and the assault guns, in close cooperation, to repel the enemy who had broken through the front line in mobile warfare.

In readiness, in the Sannerville—Emiéville area, to support the von Luck Kampfgruppe were: I./Pz.-Rgt. 22 (Panzer IVs) and Heavy Panzerabteilung 503 (Tigers). Assembled further south, on the high ridge near Bourguebus, were: Panzer-Aufklärungs-Abteilung 21 and Panzerpionier-bataillon 220 with directive to secure the firing positions to their rear of the artillery of 16. Lw.-Feld-Div. and 21. Pz.-Div., as well as of the heavy Flak batteries (8.8 cm). Behind the high ridge, in great depth and in addition to the previously men-tioned artillery, a 8.8 cm Panzerjägerabteilung and two heavy Flak Abteilun-gen (8.8 cm) were in position. Werferbrigade 9 was attached to LXXXVI. A.K. All that is known about it is that one Abteilung with 72 barrels had its firing positions around Grentheville.[3]

According to accounts from Oberst Möser, commander of the Flakregi-ment in action in the Troarn-Caen-South sector, seventy-eight Flak 8.8 cm and twelve other heavy Flak stood, deeply staggered, in his sector. As noted in Feldmarschall Rommel's records, 194 artillery guns and 272 rocket launchers with 1632 barrels were in action in this sector.[4] This figure proba-bly included SS-Panzerartillerieregiment 12 which was attached to 272. Inf.-Div. whose own artillery regiment was advancing overland from the Loire river. To that point, it had been transported by rail from Perpignan at the Spanish border. The short summer nights delayed the advance. As of 16 July, only III. Abteilung remained assigned. Sturmbannführer Bartling continued as artillery commander of the mixed unit for several more days.[5]

On 16 July at 19.50 hours, during the preparations for repelling the imminent British-Canadian major offensive, the order from Heeresgruppe B arrived at Panzergruppe West that, instead of 21. Pz.-Div., 12. SS-Panzerdivi-sion was to be pulled out and assigned to AOK 15. The Heeresgruppe ordered the Division at 21.00 hours to leave immediately for the Lisieux-Pont l'Evêque area for attachment to LXXXVI. A.K. (This is obviously an error since LXXXVI. A.K. was subordinate to Panzergruppe West. Its coastal sector between the mouths of the Seine and Orne had belonged to the sector of 15. Armee until a few weeks previously.)[6]

This order caused great surprise. What were its reasons? On 16. July, Generaloberst Jodl, chief of the Wehrmacht operational staff, telephoned the chief of staff of Supreme Command West. He stated that the relief plan of Heeresgruppe B command had been approved. Then, he concluded: "The Führer places particular value on preserving 12. SS-Pz.-Div. 'HJ'" At 15.15 hours, the chief of staff of Supreme Command West informed his Ia about an exchange he had with General Warlimont at the Führer headquarters. Accordingly ". . . the Führer expresses concern for the next few days regarding the sector of 711. I.D., behind which no fast mobile unit is located. Further to the north, as well, attacks could take place. Thus, it had to be considered whether 12. SS-Pz.-Div. 'HJ' could be moved up somewhat, behind the 711. I.D. . . . ." Feldmarschall von Kluge, Supreme Commander West, spoke with General Speidel, chief of staff of Heeresgruppe B, at 16.45 hours. The transcript, as it was recorded, follows:

v.K. (von Kluge): . . . Do you have all of the 12. out now?

Sp. (Speidel): The artillery of 'HJ' is still in.

v.K.: . . . Where is 12. located?

Sp.: Southeast of Caen, that is the 'HJ'

v.K.: How do 12. and 21. compare in strength?

Sp.: 'HJ' is the weaker one.

v.K.: I would recommend the 12. . . Advise the unit that it will possibly be moved. Artillery and anti-tank weapons must be taken along!. . .

Sp.: I will do that.

The Feldmarschall telephoned General Warlimont between 17.08 and 17.12 hours:

v.K.: I would like to ask you, what is the reason for the Führer's pressure to have a unit sent up there? (Lisieux area)

W.: The reason is two-fold. First, the expectation that during the next days, in view of the special weather conditions . . .

v.K.: Well, the usual reports.

W.: . . . and the concern that a new landing is expected still closer to the present beachhead and will then put pressure on our coastal front which is only thinly held.

v.K.: What do they expect the distribution of forces to be opposite the sector where the enemy really attacks now. We cannot be strong enough there.

W.: After the four fast units came out, this is considered to be sufficient.

v.K.: I have much greater problems on the left wing. I very much dislike doing what you say.

W.: I will report your comments to the Führer again.

v.K.: You do not have to tell him anything further. I just wanted to discuss with you again that I consider it most appropriate to leave all forces in their present positions in order to repel the major offensive which must be expected. . . . They want to send something everywhere, but that cannot be done with out present forces. We want to achieve full success, after all. Further, we are facing this whole situation calmly.[7]

Once again, the false picture of the enemy by Fremde Heere West had a negative impact. The consequences would show themselves later.

As ordered, a Kampfgruppe under the command of Obersturmbann-führer Wünsche started out in the evening of 16 July 1944. It consisted of: the staff SS-Panzerregiment 12; one mixed Panzerabteilung, staff I. Abteilung (Sturm-bannführer Jürgensen), eighteen Panzer IVs, thirteen Panzer Vs; one Panzergrenadierbataillon: I./26 (Sturmbannführer Krause); one armored Panzergrenadierbataillon: III./26 (Sturm-bannführer Olboeter); one battery of light self-propelled field howitzers of I.(Sfl.)/SS-Pz. Artillerieregiment 12.

The Kampfgruppe left its billet area after dark on 16 July and arrived, after a night march, in the assembly area on 17 July. The command post was set up in Valsemé (fourteen kilometers northwest of Lisieux). The leader of the motorcycle reconnaissance Zug, Oberscharführer Harry Wontorra, reported on this move:

Our route led via Mézidon to Manerbe. We drove ahead in our Schwimmwagen and marked the route with our 'Wünsche' signs. Our Panzers dragged huge tree branches behind them to wipe out the traces of the Panzer tracks. The night was very dark. At dawn we made camp, in the evening we continued on to Valsemé. Three Lightnings flew low over us in the morning. In quick intervals they returned time and again as if they were searching for us. They constantly flew down the road triangle Valsemé-Malheur-la Haincronchie. Next to us in the yard sat our Flak Zug. I heard the Zug leader request permission to open fire from the commander. His request was denied. If the fire missed, it would have been all over for us. So, the three Lightnings continued to fly overhead. After breakfast, they returned. Our comrades from the Flag Zug were cursing the denial to open fire. Other than that, it was very quiet. We did not hear the roar of guns, only the singing of birds. After lunch we took our clothes off to sunbathe. Life was good! But then, they came back, those three, one after the other. Suddenly, an order was heard: 'Open fire!' With a deafening noise, the Flak hurled its salvos at the enemy. The first, the second, and the third Lightning, as well, were hit and tumbled to the ground, burning. The pilot of the last wanted to save himself with his parachute, but it did not open because of the low altitude. The pilot slammed, head-first, into a meadow 200 meters away from us. As we were, we ran over to him immediately. The pilot's head was smashed, his life vest ripped. One of us secured his documents and took them to the staff. We crawled back into our bushes and waited for what would happen next. Soon, a reconnaissance aircraft approached from the north. It searched and searched. Likely, it did spot the aircraft wreckage but, luckily, not us.[9]

The move of the rest of the Division without the staff of the Artillerieregiment and III. Abteilung into the area north of Lisieux had been ordered for the night of 17–18 July.[10] However, this move did not take place.

Generalfeldmarschall Rommel visited the command post of I. SS-Panzerkorps in Urville, among others, in the afternoon of 17 July 1944. The commander of "HJ" Division had been ordered there to report. The Feldmarschall expressed his appreciation for the efforts of the Division and then requested to be provided with an assessment of the situation. Oberführer Meyer closed with the entreaty: "Herr Feldmarschall, give us air cover, give us our own fighter squadrons. We are not afraid of the enemy ground forces, but we are helpless against the massed action by the Air Force." Agitated, the Feldmarschall replied: "I have written report after report. Even from Africa, I have pointed out the paralyzing effect of the fighter-bombers, but the gentlemen just know everything better. My reports are simply not believed. Something has to happen!" When the Feldmarschall warmly said farewell, Obergruppenführer Sepp Dietrich asked him to be careful and to avoid the major roads. He advised exchanging the big car for a Volkswagen. The Feldmarschall, smiling, waved this off and drove away. A short time later he was seriously wounded near Ste. Foy-de-Montgomery during a fighter-bomber attack on his car.[11]

In the evening of 17 July 1944, Feldmarschall von Kluge had a telephone conversation with Generaloberst Jodl at the Führer headquarters. During it, he offered the opinion that the withdrawal of 12. SS-Panzerdivision was adverse. He needed forces near Caen, available there, since he expected the major thrust in that area. Jodl insisted that the "HJ" remain where it was. von Kluge replied: "Then it can be brought back, if it becomes necessary."[12]

Soon after, the Feldmarschall telephoned the Supreme Commander, Panzergruppe West, General Eberbach. The conversation offers a comprehensive assessment of the enemy situation.

E.(Eberbach): We expect the major offensive near Caen for tomorrow, in three directions of thrust. Two divisions and two tank brigades are standing ready in the bridgehead. In the Caen area are two divisions and two tank brigades. In the area west of Caen between Bretteville and . . . are, in the first line, three divisions and one tank brigade. In the second wave behind, two divisions and two tank brigades stand in readiness.

v.K.: Which area do you mean with the last sector?

E.: The sector opposite II. Korps between Bretteville and Juvigny.

v.K.: Where did you get this information?

E.: From prisoner statements . . . The situation is quite difficult since adequate reserves are not available. Can the 'HJ' not be brought up again?

v.K.: The 'HJ' is out of the question. I have nothing, either.

. . .

v.K.: What can we move to the left into the St. Lô area? What can you give up?

E.: The 'HJ' is the only one.

v.K.: No, that is impossible. I will dispense with a transferral of forces to Hausser. You must hold the line under all circumstances and with all means, and achieve the utmost. For tomorrow, then, everything is clear.[13]

In fact, the expected offensive from the beachhead east of Caen did start in the morning of 18 July 1944. The English and Canadian artillery fire on known and assumed positions of the German Flak set in at 05.25 hours. Soon after, an immense aerial armada approached: 1,595 English Lancaster, Halifax, and American Superfortress-bombers.[14]

The heavy night-bombers dropped a carpet of heavy explosive bombs with delay detonators on the western flank of the attack sector near Colombelles, and another one on the eastern flank from Touffreville to Emiéville and on the Cagny area. The heavy daytime-bombers attacked the areas further south with fragmentation bombs equipped with sensitive impact detonators, making sure that the area remained passable to tanks. Then, 482 medium bombers (Mitchells, Bostons, Mosquitoes) dropped fragmentation bombs on the attack sectors of the tank divisions. Fighter-bombers attacked strong points and gun positions on the flanks.[15]

According to statements from the commanding general of III. Flakkorps, the three Flakregiments put into action to defend against the expected air attack managed to knock down approximately thirty aircraft.[16] Statements by Air Chief Marshal Leigh-Mallory indicate that the RAF lost six bombers.[17] In any case, the tight concentration of Flak was unable to prevent such a large mass of bombers, flying in loose formation, from carrying out their objective and safeguard the German troops.

These air attacks, the heaviest flown in support of ground troops until that time, completely smashed the forward lines of 16 Lw.-Feld-Div. and also hit the Panzer assembly area. Many of the Panzers were put out of action by hits, others were rendered useless for an extended period of time because of sand in their engine compartments and optical mechanisms.

At 07.45, after the medium bombers had turned away, the tanks of the 11th Armoured Division started their attack behind a moving wall of fire from approximately 700 Allied guns. In addition, forty-eight heavy anti-aircraft guns and twenty-one battleship guns fired on various targets.[18]

The tanks overran the positions of 16. Lw.-Feld-Division and the strong points close behind. Those who were not already dead or wounded could no longer think of resistance after the terrible bombardment and the effects of the moving wall of fire. The heavy weapons, in particular the anti-tank guns, were destroyed. The resistance of a few courageous soldiers bounced off without much impact on the immense mass of 200 tanks which rolled over them. At 08.30 hours, the tanks of the 29th Armoured Brigade had reached the rail line Caen-Troarn. To the west of them, the 159th Infantry Brigade of the 11th Armoured Division, supported by the tanks of the 2nd Northamptonshire Yeomanry, attacked in the direction of Cuverville and Démouville. At the same time, the 3rd British Infantry Division had advanced from the Escoville area for an attack in the direction of Troarn—Emiéville, supported by the tanks of the 27th Armoured Brigade. In Touffreville, it encountered fierce resistance by parts of II. Bataillon of Panzer-grenadierregiment 125, supported by an assault gun battery.

In the meantime, at 07.45 hours, the 3rd Canadian Infantry Division had also started an attack with two brigades from the Ranville area. North of Colombelles, in the Colombelles steelworks, and in Giberville, it encountered bitter resistance and advanced only slowly.[19]

At approximately 09.00 hours, the 29th Armoured Brigade started out to continue the attack across the rail embankment of the line Caen-Troarn, with two tank units as spearhead, one following as a reserve. During this, their direction of attack changed from southeast to southwest in the direction of Bourguebus and Hubert-Folie with the objective of capturing the Route Nationale from Caen to Falaise. Soon after crossing the rail line, the tanks came under fire from the three batteries of Sturmgeschützabteilung 200 which had set up positions in le Prieuré, le Mesnil-Frémentel and Grentheville. Another battery was advancing from Giberville to Grentheville. One 8.8 cm battery of the Luftwaffe stood, ready to fire, in Cagny. The carpet bombing had not knocked it out. Oberstleutnant von Luck, whose Kampfgruppe command post was located east of Cagny, organized the defense in this sector. Within a few minutes, 16 Shermans had been knocked out.

The attack by the tanks of the 23rd Hussars ground to a halt at noon west of Frénouville. At the same time, the attack by the tanks of the 2nd Fife and Forfar Yeomanry stalled outside Soliers, those of the 3rd Royal Tank Regiment outside of Hubert-Folie and Bras. In the course of the fighting, the batteries of Sturmgeschützabteilung 200 had moved their positions to le Poirier, Four and Hubert-Folie. The 3. Batterie held its position in Grentheville until 15.00 hours, then moved to Soliers. These assault gun batteries, and the 8.8 cm guns in position near Bras, supported by the artillery of 16.

Lw.-Feld-Division and 21. Panzerdivision as well as the rocket launchers, had stopped the thrust of the tanks. The motorized infantry battalions of the 11th Armoured Division had been left behind, fighting the strong points, past which the tanks had pushed.

Around noon, the armored personnel carrier battalion of 1. SS-Panzer-division arrived on the high ridge of Bourguebus. Soon after, a Panther Abteilung, commanded by Obersturm-bannführer Jochen Peiper pulled up. They rolled toward the tanks of the 2nd Fife and Forfar, advancing south between Soliers and Four. These tanks withdrew to the east of Soliers. The 23rd Hussars were to carry the attack forward, past the stalled tanks of the 2nd Fife and Forfar and the 3rd Royal Tank Regiment, once again via Soliers and Four. They, too, were pushed back, with heavy losses. By the afternoon, the 11th Armoured Division had lost 126 tanks. During a counterattack from the Frénouville-Four area, the enemy was thrown back behind the rail line Caen-Vimont.

The Guards Armoured Division followed behind the 11th Armoured Division. It had assembled west of the Orne before the start of the attack. Its left battle group swung, after crossing the rail line Caen-Troarn, toward Emiéville, while the right advanced in a southerly direction toward Cagny and Frénouville. After the heavy bombing raid which had hit the Panzers of Panzerregiment 22 and the heavy Panzerabteilung 503 (Tigers), assembled for the counterattack, the survivors immediately began to make the Panzers which had not been knocked out, ready for action again. When the 5th Guards Armoured Brigade started an attack from the direction of Démou-ville on Cagny around noon, this small Panzer unit started a counterattack into the flanks of the tanks rolling past. The tank attack began to stall. Unfor-tunately, two Tigers were knocked out at this deciding moment, through the penetration of the frontal armor. That had not yet happened at the invasion front. The Tiger crews feared that they were facing a new anti-tank weapon of an extraordinary effectiveness, and stopped the attack. From le Prieuré, their first attack objective, they would have had an ideal field of fire for their long-range 8.8 cm guns. After the war, on the occasion of a battlefield tour by the members of Camberley Staff College, it was determined that these two Tigers had, erroneously, been identified as enemy tanks by the 8.8 cm Luftwaffe Flak battery in position near Cagny, and knocked out.

The Panzer Kampfgruppe was diverted to Frénouville and incorporated into the defensive line there. The 5th Guards Armoured Brigade captured Cagny at approximately 16.00 hours. The Flak battery, in position there, blew up its guns in accordance with orders, the crews abandoned the town.

The attempt by the Guards Armoured Division to break through from Cagny to its attack objective, Vimont, faltered at the defensive line of assault guns and Panzers near Frénouville and le Poirier. Sixty tanks were lost.[20]

The VIII Corps wanted to re-start the attack which had stalled at the high ridge of Bourguebus at all costs. Thus, it ordered the 7th Armoured Division to advance with its Armoured Brigade via la Hogue to Garcelles-Secqueville. Further, the 11th Armoured Division was ordered to renew its attack in order to capture the road Caen-Falaise west of Bourguebus. Major General Erskine, the commander of the 7th Armoured Division, intentionally delayed the advance of his division through the corridor. Thus, it could only join the fighting around 18.00 hours. However, the attack by the two divisions did not achieve its goals. Still, even if the advance had been an energetic one, the attack would surely have faltered at the completed assembly of the Panzers of 1. SS-Panzerdivision.[21]

The first attack by the Canadian Infantry Brigade on Colombelles had been beaten back in the morning. An air attack on the Château north of Colombelles at 13.30 hours had been unsuccessful since "the bombs had bounced off the hard ground and ricocheted across the Château". A fire attack by all the the artillery available to the Division partially hit their own troops and caused confusion. Soon after 15.00 hours the Château was set on fire by the shelling. The de la Chaudière Regiment then penetrated into the terrain defended by parts of 16. Lw.-Feld-Division. At 18.00 hours, the Canadians started their attack on the steelworks of Colombelles and were able to push their way inside. However, several pockets of resistance continued to fight throughout the night. To the east, the rail line Caen-Troarn was reached at approximately 21.30 hours. At around 24.00 hours, the 9th Canadian Infantry Brigade succeeded, advancing along the low-lying bank of the Orne, in penetrating into the outskirts of Vaucelles.

The II Canadian Corps had ordered the 7th Infantry Brigade of the 3rd Infantry Division in the morning to push reconnaissance ahead across the Orne in Caen. If only minor resistance was encountered, one battalion was to follow. The reconnaissance forces met only weak resistance. At 17.15 hours, under cover from artillery, mortars and machine guns, a battalion went across the river. A few hours later, the central sector of Vaucelles was captured. Several attempts by the 3rd Canadian Infantry Division to bridge the Orne near Hérouville (four kilometers northeast of Caen) failed, with losses. Soon after midnight, engineers of the II Canadian Corps and the 2nd Canadian Infantry Division began bridging in Caen. Within twelve hours, they had completed a bridge usable by tanks at the main street, a ferry usable by tanks just above the city, and two light bridges in the vicinity of the ferry and in the harbor area. With this, the bottleneck of the Ranville crossing, with only two double bridges (across the Orne and the canal) was relieved. It had caused considerable delays during the day to the advance of the Guards Armoured Division and the 7th Armoured Division.[22]

When darkness fell, the attackers had approximately reached a line from north of Emiéville-Cagny-north of le Poirier-north of Four-north of Soliers-northeast of Bras-south of Giberville-Mondeville-Vaucelles. The 11th Armoured Division, having lost 126 tanks, of which forty were total losses, assembled for the night north of the rail line Caen-Vimont. The German troops were holding the villages south of the rail line, past which the tanks had pushed during their attack.

While the heaviest fighting raged east and south of Caen in the morning of 18 July 1944, the "HJ" Division was split into three groups. The Wünsche Kampfgruppe stood in the area northwest of Lisieux, Waldmüller Kampfgruppe (reinforced Panzergrenadier Bataillon of Regiment 25) in the refitting area northeast of Potigny. The Artillerieregiment and Flak Abteilung were in position and action behind the ridge west of Bourguebus in the sector of 272. Infanteriedivision. The Divisional command post was still located in Garcelles-Secqueville.

The move of the rest of the Division, i.e. mainly the Waldmüller Kampfgruppe, which had been ordered for the night 17 to 18 July, had been postponed. The reason was that Panzergruppe West expected the enemy offensive, with certainty, for the morning of 18 July and had ordered an alert for the Division in the evening of 17 July. When a dangerous development became obvious around noon near Cagny, General Eberbach urgently requested from the Heeresgruppe that "HJ" Division be moved up in order to throw back the enemy who had broken through there. This would not be possible without the Division. Two hours later, at 15.00 hours, the OKW released the Division. It was immediately ordered to move forward into the breakthrough area and to take over the sector from the Emiéville church to Frénouville inclusive from 21. Panzerdivision and prepare for the defense there. The neighbor on the right was 21. Panzerdivision, on the left was 1. SS-Panzerdivision.[23]

The "HJ" Division established contact immediately with 21. Panzerdivision and reconnoitered its new operations area. The terrain in which the future battles would likely take place varied greatly. The main thrust until then of the British tank units had been in a generally south-southwesterly direction, lately southwest. The Canadian attack was in a south-southeasterly direction, depending on the course of Route Nationale No. 158 from Caen to Falaise. From this it could be concluded that the enemy was attempting to take the undulating high plateau between Caen and Falaise, which was very favorable for activity by tank units and offered an airfield near Rocquancourt. In order to achieve a breakthrough to the southeast, the ridge of hills had first to be captured. It stretched (starting from the left) from Hill 88-2.3 kilometers west-northwest of Rocquancourt -south of Tilly-la Campagne (eighty meters)-south of la Hogue (sixty meters) to Bellengreville (twenty-five meters), dropping off to the east and north. The German main line of defense ran approximately parallel to this ridge, with strong points in the villages of Bras, Hubert-Folie, Bourguebus, la Hogue, and forward strong points in Soliers and Four.

At noon on 18 July, the Guards Armoured Division attacked Cagny from Démouville in a generally southerly direction. It could be assumed with some certainty that this British tank division which, so far, had not seen action on the mainland, would continue its attack in the direction of Vimont. Between Vimont and la Hogue stretched pastures, approximately three kilometers wide, crossed by creeks barely traversable for tanks. Adjoining to the west was a wooded area, also some three kilometers wide. A creek bed runs from Vimont for two kilometers in a northeasterly direction, ending up in a wide lowland, two kilometers wide, crisscrossed by ditches and rows of trees. The northeastern edge of the lowland is bordered by a creek, the Cours de Janville. The lowland extends for approximately four kilometers, its elevation is six to nine meters above sea level. Behind it, the terrain rises from twenty meters west of Troarn to 44 m southeast of St. Pair and east of the path of the Muance creek, east of le Fresne, to more than forty meters, up to the dominating Hill 80 northeast of Moult. Between the Muance creek and the path of the creek near Vimont, a rise in the terrain reaches an elevation of approximately thirty-eight meters. The towns of Bellengreville, Frénouville and Cagny, with an elevation of twenty meters, are located barely above the lowland. Emiéville sits just above the wet meadows. The important Route Nationale No. 13, leading from Caen via Vimont and Lisieux to Paris, crosses the Laison sector seven kilometers east of Vimont. A further 2.5 kilometers to the east, a lowland of almost nine kilometers width, the Vallée d'Auge, stretches between the Dives and Vie rivers. It is crisscrossed by numerous watercourses, making it impassable for tanks, except on the Route Nationale. Only then does the road reach the high terrain of the Pays d'Auge which offers possibilities for tanks to deploy in the direction of Lisieux. Could this road be seriously considered for a major offensive in the direction of Paris? Not really.

A lesser road branches off the Route nationale in Vimont. It offers the possibility to cross the Dives near Mézidon or St. Pierre-sur-Dives, at the crossroads west of Airan. Close cooperation between the Guards Armoured Division and the British tank units, located just down from the ridge of hills at Bourguebus, would have made this possible. However, it is possible that the enemy put emphasis only on preventing the approach of German reinforcements near Vimont.

In fact, the enemy was aware that 12. SS-Panzerdivision had been moved to the Lisieux area. The enemy situation report of the Guards Armoured Division, finalized on 18 July at 21.00 hours, stated: ". . . 12. SS-Panzerdivision, very weak, is on the march from Lisieux where it had been for refitting. Enemy intentions: 12. SS will probably show up in our left flank, not in any noteworthy strength after its heavy losses."[24]

In the neighbor sector to the right of 21. Panzerdivision ran another Route Nationale, No. 815, from Caen via Troarn to Pont-l'Evêque, an enemy attack axis. Between Banneville and Troarn, only the narrow creek bed of the Cours de Janville offered an obstruction. Behind it, however, the one kilometer wide valley of the Dives and several smaller watercourses provided a serious tank obstacle with an adjoining narrow passage near St. Samson. During 18 July, it was exposed to a number of fierce attacks.

The Division came to the conclusion that the enemy situation and the terrain required that, first of all, a bridgehead had to be held near Bellengreville, and to prevent an outflanking of this position to the south via Chicheboville, Béneauville-la-Campagne and Navarre. A threat could also arise from the right neighboring sector if the enemy took Troarn but could not cross the Dives valley. He could then have, by way of St. Pair, Ponts de Janville, reached the Route Nationale No. 13 south of Canteloup, capturing or blocking the Laison crossing near Croissanville. Thus, contact with the neighbors, securing of one's own deep flanks, and holding in readiness of a reserve, as strong as possible, of Panzers and Panzergrenadiers in armored personnel carriers were required. Panzergrenadiers of the motorized battalions, and the approaching Panzerjägers, had to hold the main line of defense.

The devastating effects of the carpet bombing in the morning of 18 July on the front line positions, at the start of the attack, made it appear reasonable to only establish individual positions forward, i.e. battle front positions, and to set up the main line of defense markedly separate and to the rear. The operational reserves would be held as far as possible to the rear, staggered, but could not be separated from their probable operational areas by bottlenecks.

The relief operation started at 05.30 hours on 19 July.[25]

The Waldmüller Kampfgruppe took over the sector along both sides of the road Cagny-Vimont, its bulk to the left of the road. The Divisionsbegleitkompanie set up a rear position behind the Waldmüller Kampfgruppe south of Vimont at the left boundary of the Division, and prepared for defense. The replacement was completed by noon.

The advance of the Wünsche Kampfgruppe encountered significant difficulties. In the afternoon, Feldmarschall von Kluge inquired by telephone from Panzergruppe West when the arrival of Wünsche could be expected. Here follows the further course of the conversation:

General Eberbach: I cannot predict that since the bridges across the Dives are smashed. 'HJ' must advance, as bridges allow, to Argences. From there it must push to the north.

Feldmarschall von Kluge: Might the 'HJ' not approach via Troarn?

General Eberbach: The bridges near Troarn cannot be repaired. We will try to have the division advance via Hotot.

Feldmarschall von Kluge: When do you expect the 'HJ' to arrive?

General Eberbach: Tomorrow morning at the earliest. The division is assembled, initially along various lesser routes, so that it cannot be smashed by the bombers.

In fact, the Wünsche Kampfgruppe marched, by way of Hotot, Crois-sanville, to Moult and Argences where it arrived around noon on 19 July. The Regimental command post was set up in Ingouville (one kilometer south of Moult), that of I. Abteilung in Moult.[26]

Panzergrenadierbataillon Krause (mixed Bataillon of remnants of I. and II. Bataillons Regiment 26), a part of Kampfgruppe Wünsche, was put into action next to Waldmüller Kampfgruppe on the right. Adjoining was the SPW Bataillon (armored personnel carriers) Olboeter, extending to the right Division boundary near Emiéville. The 8. Panzerkompanie under Obersturmführer Herbert Höfler moved into an ambush position to the right of the road Cagny-Vimont, between the avenue to Château St. Pierre and le Hameau de Franqueville. At the Route Nationale stood I. Zug under Untersturm-führer Willi Kändler, the other two were staggered to the rear and the right.

Together with the Wünsche Kampfgruppe arrived 1. Kompanie of SS-Panzerjägerabteilung 12, still being set up under the command of Ober-sturmführer Georg Hurdelbrink. This Kompanie had just received its new Panzers. They were Jagdpanzer IVs (tank destroyers) with the 7.5 cm Pak 39/L 48. They were only 1.85 meters high, compared to the Panzer IV with 2.65 meters in height. The Kompanie had been moved from the area Nogent-le-Roi (fifteen kilometers southeast of Dreux) and attached to the Wünsche Kampfgruppe on 17 July. The Panzerjägerabteilung had been sorely missed until then, its responsibilities had been taken on by the Panz-erregiment whose Panzer IVs and Panthers were, because of their greater height, less suitable.

The light self-propelled battery (Wespen = wasps), part of the Kampf-gruppe, was the only available artillery there. The bulk of the Artillerieregi-ment and assigned Werferabteilung 12 and Flakabteilung 12, led by Sturmbannführer Bartling and in action with 272. Infanteriedivision, still had to be pulled out and brought in.

The Panthers of the mixed Panzerabteilung were held in readiness as an operational reserve in the Argences-Vimont area. Despite the expected carpet bombing of the main battlefield, they could not be assembled further to the rear since there were only a few crossings of the Muance. They could easily be destroyed and then the Panzers could not have been moved in if necessary.

In the meantime, the replacement Panzers had presumably arrived at the base of II. Abteilung where Sturmbannführer Prinz was waiting for them. Obersturmbannführer Wünsche ordered Untersturmführer Horst Borgs-müller to drive immediately to la Saussaye near Elbeuf and to give Prinz the marching order to the operations area of the Regiment. Borgsmüller reported:

As we left Ingouville, a violent thunderstorm set in. It was difficult to differentiate the thunder from the explosions of the shells. My driver and I were wet to the skin on our sidecar motorcycle. Half-way to our destination, the weather turned better and, immediately, the fighter-bombers showed up. Time and again, we had to look for cover. We only arrived in la Saussaye after dark. We roused Sturm-bann-führer Prinz and his adjutant, Obersturmführer Hartmann, from a deep sleep. He was awake immediately and asked what was going on. Then Prinz woke up, too, and I handed him the order to leave immediately for Vimont with the Panzer IVs. Prince's first reac-tion to this was: 'I won't get out of there again!'[27]

Then Division set up its command post near Airan, at the western edge of Ruel. In the war diary of Panzergruppe West and on the "Frontlage" (front line) maps, the location is given as Argences. That is an error, the command post of 16. Lw.-Feld-Division was situated there. The combat-ready parts of the Aufklärungsabteilung were also located in the vicinity. The mixed Pionierkompanie of Pionierbataillon 12 was put into action through-out the sector of the Division to set up obstructions, mine barriers and con-struct positions.

What, then, was the situation at the enemy opposite the "HJ" Division?

In the evening of 18 July, the Guards Armoured Division, together with the 32nd Guards Brigade (three motorized infantry battalions) had tem-porarily prepared for defense around Cagny. The 5th Guards Armoured Brigade (three tank units and one armored infantry battalion) had moved into positions opposite an "anti-tank umbrella along a general line Emiéville-Frénouville". The 2nd (Armoured) Battalion Grenadier Guards was in Cagny, the 1st (Armoured) Battalion Coldstream Guards on the hill south-west of Cagny. The 2nd (Armoured) Battalion Irish Guards was situated west of Emiéville, the 2nd Armoured Reconnaissance Battalion Welsh Guards secured toward the German positions north of Emiéville from the west. The plan for the next day was to advance to Vimont. On 18 July, the Guards Divi-sion had lost sixty of its authorized strength of 343 tanks.[28]

During the night 18–19 July, the enemy had re-grouped his forces, as had also happened on the German side. Thus, the night passed without noteworthy hostilities. In the morning of 19 July, parts of the 11th Armoured Division attacked the newly occupied positions near Bras and Hubert-Folie at the left wing of the "Leibstandarte". They were repelled, with losses. The 7th Armoured Division attacked Soliers and Four. Soliers was lost, Four was held.

The Guards Armoured Division attacked the towns of Emiéville and Fré-nouville from the area around Cagny. It was repulsed by the Panzer-grenadiers of III./26 and I./25 in action there and the Panzerjägers (tank destroyers) who had, fortunately, just relieved parts of 21. Panzerdivision.

The major offensive of the British tank units only started in the after-noon. After violent barrages, the 11th Armoured Division again attacked Bras and Hubert-Folie with strong forces. After eventful fighting, Bras was abandoned and new positions south of the town were taken up. Toward the evening the enemy attacked Hubert-Folie, completely destroyed by the barrages. Finally, this village, too, had to be given up. The attacker had suffered serious losses. From 17.00 hours on, the barrages were directed on Bourguebus, Four, le Poirier and Frénouville. The 7th Armoured Division attacked Bourguebus and Four, the Guards Armoured Division attacked le Poirier and Frénouville. After bitter fighting, the 1. SS-Panzerdivision gave up Four at approximately 15.00 hours, but la Hogue and Bourguebus were held.

The Waldmüller Kampfgruppe, with the attached Panzerjägers fought off the attack on Frénouville. The Welsh Guards occupied le Poirier in the afternoon. On the right wing of the Division, near Emiéville, III./26 repelled an enemy attack, it lost two killed and six wounded.

In the evening, around 20.00 hours, approximately 24 German fighter aircraft were in action in the Cagny area, as noted in the situation report of the Guards Armoured Division.[29] This air attack was an action by a squadron of heavy fighters (Me 110) which had started from airfields in Holland and Belgium. They crossed the front line at an altitude of about fifty meters, after having dropped their auxiliary tanks. The first wave dropped their bombs on the enemy positions. The second wave dropped short, into the Waldmüller Bataillon positions, but caused no damage. The Bataillon was too widely spaced to offer a favorable target. The Divisional commander and General der Flieger (Luftwaffe) Peltz, who commanded the squadron, were there to observe the action. They, too, were not injured. The third wave bombed the Orne crossings in Caen. The attack was planned to be repeated the next day. The first consideration at the Divisional command post was how to better direct the heavy fighters to their target. A Luftwaffe officer to guide the attack could not be provided. The best solution appeared to be, to have machine guns fire tracers on identified enemy positions from the forward front line as soon as the heavy fighters approached. Indeed, this process proved itself during the following day.

When the tanks attacked in the morning of 20 July, the forward position Frénouville was abandoned. The attack on the positions northwest of Bellengreville and the attack on Château St. Pierre Oursin, southeast of Emiéville, were repelled after the forward position near Emiéville was also given up. Oberscharführer Roy and "Hans" of the newly arrived Panzerjägerkompanie knocked out a tank each on the left of the Route Nationale, setting them on fire.[30]

The neighbor to the right, 21. Panzerdivision, repelled another attack on Troarn two kilometers west of the city. The neighbor on the left, the "LAH", withdrew from the forward position near Bourguebus, but held the positions along the line la Hogue-Tilly-la Campagne.[31]

Torrential rains fell in the afternoon, forcing the fighting to be halted.

In the evening of 20 July 1944, the troops heard on the radio about the attempted assassination of the Supreme Commander of the Wehrmacht,

Adolf Hitler, at the Führer headquarters in Rastenburg. It was incomprehensible that soldiers would attempt a coup against the supreme military leadership while they were, themselves, involved in bitter defensive fighting against the enemy who demanded "Unconditional Surrender", not willing to negotiate a cease-fire or even peace. The commander of 21. Panzerdivision, Generalmajor Feuchtinger, visited the commander of the "HJ" Division at his command post. He affirmed that the battle-proven comradeship was not at all impaired by the assassination attempt by an isolated group of officers of the Heer. That appeared self-evident. Two telephone conversations on 21 July between the Supreme Commander West, Feldmarschall von Kluge and his chief of staff, General der Infanterie Blumentritt, illustrate how the supreme staff in the west reacted.

Telephone conversation Feldmarschall von Kluge—Gen.d.Inf. Blumentritt.

Time: 00.50–01.00 hours.

v.K.: Krancke (commander of the Kriegsmarine Gruppe West, Author) telephoned. Arrests are taking place in Paris.

Bl.: Something has to be done. I have to make contact, regarding Stülpnagel.

v.K.: Then he must be suspended from duty.

Bl.: Zimmermann is sitting opposite me and we have the curious telegrams which arrived in front of us. The first telegram reads: "Signed: Supreme Commander of the Reserve Heer, OKW No. 5000/44 secret." The teletype message took a strange route. Its origin seems to be in Berlin, it arrived here via Châlons s.M.

v.K.: Did the message come from the OKW?

Bl.: The route of the message has been determined by inquiries and investigations by the officers, the chief of the intelligence service, and General Gimmler. It simply arrived as secret, a more than curious manner. Zimmermann said to himself that something was wrong there and put it aside. Through Gen. Gimmler anything further could be stopped. Friedl at the OKW was telephoned and told that something was not right there. Thereafter, a second message arrived from the OKW with the following content:

". . . I would suggest that Herr Feldmarschall, as the supreme commander, send a message of congratulation and loyalty to the Führer." Also, the chief of Supreme Command Southwest (?) suggested that I, as the oldest chief send a message to the Führer on behalf of the general staff officers.

v.K.: Yes, agreed.

Bl.: I will immediately draft such a message and call you, Herr Feldmarschall, again shortly to read it to you.

v.K.: Yes. I am still awake. Follow up the matter with Stülpnagel and Krancke immediately.

Telephone conversation Feldmarschall von Kluge-Gen.d.Inf. Blumentritt.

Time: 01.17–01.25 hours.

Bl.: Admiral Hoffmann just telephoned me.

v.K.: Who is that?

Bl.: He is the chief, at Krancke's. He confirmed the same thing
once more, that patrols of the Heer in Paris have directions to carry
out certain arrests. I believe the security forces are somewhat mislead. I suggest that I take on being military commander for a short
time to bring this matter back to normal.

v.K.: I herewith order you to discuss the matter, bring it to order
and return it to normal status.

Bl.: But I must be given authority to negotiate with the commanders of the security forces.

v.K.: Of course.

Bl.: May I now read to Herr Feldmarschall the Message to the
Führer: 'The attempt on your life, my Führer, carried out by a mur-
derer's foul hand, has failed thanks to a benevolent act of provi-
dence. On behalf, also, of the three military elements under my
command as the Supreme Commander West, I express my congratulations and assure you, my Führer, of our unshakable loyalty, whatever may happen.'

v.K.: Yes, I agree to that.

Bl.: Then, tomorrow morning, subsequently, on behalf of all general staff officers in the west, as the oldest I would like . . . v.K.: Are
you the oldest?

Bl.: Yes, I believe even for the east if Z. is no longer there. May I
read to Herr Feldmarschall: 'On the occasion of the failed attempt
on your life, my Führer, I convey the congratulations and respectful
expressions of loyalty from all of the officers of the general staff in
the west.'

v.K.: Agreed.

Bl.: Then I will be on my way to Paris immediately to put things in
order there.[32]

Regarding the attitude of the command of the Heer on the question of
a military coup, it is surely indicative what General-feldmarschall von Rundstedt testified during the interrogation by the defense counsel of the OKW,
attorney at law Dr. Laternser, at the Nuremberg trials:

Dr. Laternser: Did you, or other supreme commanders, attempt
to have the continuation of the war, recognized as being hopeless,
called to a halt?

Feldmarschall von Rundstedt: Generalfeldmarschall Rommel, as
well as I, has attempted twice with Hitler to bring about a change in

the conduct of the war or an end, in particular a change, meaning withdrawal and removal of the front line to the German border. These proposals, as was to be expected, did not find approval.

Dr. Laternser: If Hitler, then, refused to consider such attempted advice, did you not consider a violent overthrow?

Feldmarschall von Rundstedt: I would never have considered such a thought. That would have been vile, naked treason and would not have changed the facts. The Armee and the population still believed in Hitler at the time. Such an overthrow would not have succeeded. And even if I, possibly with the help of the Allies, would have brought about an overthrow, the fate of the German people, after the famous declaration by the three major powers, would have been exactly the same as it is now, and I would be known as the greatest traitor of my fatherland for all times.[33]

Just what impact the coup attempt had on the military leadership of the other side is shown in a coded message of 23.7.44:

TOPSEC, personally to General Montgomery from General Eisenhower. Thank you for your message. My letter to you was written before receipt of your M 512. We are obviously in full agreement in our conviction that an energetic and determined attack must be carried out by the First and Second Armies. A general attack also appears to be indicated at this time since, obviously, the enemy has to use SS troops to assure battle-readiness of other units. There obviously exists some confusion and doubt among the enemy ranks which we should exploit.[34]

It must be remarked, on this matter, that no Waffen-SS troops were sent into action to restore the situation in Paris, as is also obvious from the discussions between Feldmarschall von Kluge and Generalleutnant Blumentritt. The troops stood at the front where there was only one objective for the Heer and Waffen-SS: to hold the front line, under attack.

The deterioration of the weather conditions in the afternoon of 20 July 1944 caused General Montgomery to break off the "GOODWOOD" offensive. Despite the immense effort by the enemy air force and the concentrated mass of nine tank units, it turned into an Allied defeat. Although it had been possible to enlarge the bridgehead east of the Orne and, above all, to create an Orne crossing in Caen, neither a breakthrough nor a significant territorial gain had been achieved. This partial success had cost extraordinary losses, especially of tanks. The defensive achievements were due in particular to the staggering in the depth of the German defenses with many strong points of Panzergrenadiers and assault guns, or of tank hunters. The assembly of Panzers and Panzergrenadiers of "LAH" Division near at hand had been able to return the situation to the starting position with a counterattack. The effect of the Allied air force must be credited with the fact that the Panzers of Panzerregiment 22 and Tigerabteilung 503, assembled on the eastern flank, did not have an early enough and decisive impact. The progress of the battle confirmed to the defenders, what "EPSOM" had already shown, that only armored and mobile anti-tank weapons could survive carpet bombings and moving walls of fire, and then effectively combat the enemy. Surely, the concentrated German artillery played a significant part in the successful defense, but it lacked the required amounts of ammunition which was available to the enemy. It was surprising, however, how easily the enemy managed to establish a bridgehead across the Orne. Finally, the move of Kampfgruppe Wünsche to Lisieux proved to be a significant drawback since the Kampfgruppe was prevented from joining the action as early as noon on 18 July near Cagny.

It was not only the deteriorating weather which forced General Montgomery to break off the "GOODWOOD" offensive on 20 July. It had been shown that a limited success could only be achieved through massive air force action. The bomber squadrons, however, were needed for the offensive operations of the First US Army on the western wing and were no longer available near Caen. Montgomery noted his further intentions in his Directive M 512 of 21 July. Accordingly, the operations on the eastern wing were to continue until the following line was reached: mouth of the Dives at the Channel-along the Dives to north of Troarn-along the Muance to St. Sylvain-Cauvicourt-Gouvix-Evrécy-Noyers-Caumont. It was decisive, however, that the First US Army now carried out the planned operation. In accordance with this Directive, the First Canadian Army took over the previous sector of I Corps on the eastern wing. It was then the mission of the Second British Army to take the line mentioned above within its limits and then be as active as possible with the forces in action east of the Orne. This was meant to create the impression for the enemy that a major operation in the direction of Falaise and Argentan was planned.[35]

The German leadership did not recognize Montgomery's intention to move the focal point of his operation to the western wing near St. Lô. The war diary of Panzergruppe West of 21 July notes:

> In the course of the day, tank assemblies and those of other enemy forces in the area Cuverville-Colombelles-le Mesnil-Emiéville-Banneville-Soliers-Hubert-Folie-Cormelles were taken under concentrated artillery and mortar fire by the entire artillery of LXXXVI. A.K., the I. and II. SS-Panzerkorps. It is assumed that the enemy has completed his assembly after bringing in approximately 800–1,000 tanks and that a new attack to break through to the south will commence shortly.[36]

The observed enemy movements were the relief of the tank units by infantry divisions. The 5th Guards Armoured Brigade had been withdrawn already on 20 July. The 32nd Guards Brigade was to be relieved by the 51st

Highland Division. This was, initially, made impossible by the bad weather.[37] With the relief, the short encounter between the Guards Armoured Division and the SS-Panzerdivision "Hitlerjugend" ended. It had been a fair battle. A former member of that division, who gladly recalled it for many years after the war, wrote to the Author:

> Two of my comrades of the 3rd Battalion The Irish Guards (part of the 32nd Guards Brigade, Author) were taken prisoner by SS troops. One of them (Sergeant Major) escaped and got back to us. He said that both of them had been treated well by the SS. The other man, Guardsman Trickett, had been seriously wounded, but was given medical care and recovered. Later, he tried to escape but died during the attempt.[38]

After the relief, there were no further enemy attacks in the "HJ" Division's sector. The enemy artillery fired harassing fire and both sides reconnoitered briskly. The situation is illustrated in a letter by Unterscharführer Eberhart Köpke, in position at the edge of the swampy lowland near Bellengreville:

> When the sun rose again over the marsh, the situation turned even less bearable. We were hoping, in vain, for rain. Billions of mosquitoes rose from the ground and, within a few hours, you could hardly recognize anyone from the Kompanie, they all looked so well-nourished. The nose was only a couple of holes in the center of a full moon. Any available curtains were soon desirable objects since we could wind them around our heads. But there was some consolation even now, it did not look any better on the other side. The prisoners we took appeared just as stout as we did. Our cheerful Hansel was especially valuable here through his excellent scouting sorties. He was promoted to Unter-scharführer by the Divisional commander when he handed over some of his prisoners at the Divisional command post. He was also awarded the E.K. II (Iron Cross II) here.[39]

Feldmarschall von Kluge visited troops in the sector of Panzergruppe West on 22 July 1944. During a telephone conversation he informed General Eberbach that he ". . . was particularly impressed by the exemplary attitude of 12. SS-Panzerdivision. In any case, the high morale of the troops must be emphasized."[40] During this visit, the Feldmarschall almost crossed over the forward front line. A similar conversation between the Feldmarschall and General Eberbach is recorded in the appendix to the war diary of Supreme Command West under the date of 24 July, meaning that the drive to the front had taken place on 23 July. The date is not important, but several other pieces of informations are noteworthy:

Eberbach: Today was a relatively quiet day. In the morning we had some shells fired at us. The II. SS-Korps intercepted a radio message in which General Rosh told his men that signi-ficant losses had to be taken in order to mislead the enemy, so that the attack could be carried out, with the element of surprise, at another spot.

von Kluge: This indicates that the main attack will come near Caen and southeast of it. You will have heard by now that I spent all day yesterday with the troops. I can only say one thing, that the men are in relatively good spirits. I was mainly at the 'HJ' Division and took a very good look at it. I also had a look at the English. It was very quiet, we could do anything. I have a special impression of Wünsche, with whom I walked along the positions. He, too, makes a perfect impression.

Eberbach: The 'HJ' Division is good, in morale and training.

von Kluge: I made a mistake, Wünsche is Regimental commander. That was Maier.

Eberbach: They call him 'fast' Maier. A great guy![41]

The intercepted enemy radio message, relayed by General Eberbach, was an invaluable pointer. Regrettably, the Feldmarschall interpreted it wrongly. That an attack would be carried out ". . . at another spot" could not be an indication of the Caen area where a large operation had just been halted after severe losses. It was an indication of the American "COBRA" Operation, the planned attack by strong concentrated forces near St. Lô. Available at 7. Armee were only the worn-out Panzer-Lehr-Division, 2. SS-Panzerdivision "Das Reich" and the weakened 17. SS-Panzergrenadier-division "Götz von Berlichingen", in action—as was the Panzer-Lehr-Division—since the start of the invasion. In comparison, 1.,12.,9., and 10. SS-Panzerdivisions and 21. Panzerdivision were assembled in the Caen area. The 21., 12. and 1. were in action in the front lines. The 10. had already partially been relieved by 271. Infanterie Division and 277. Infanterie Division had taken over the positions of the 9. In addition, Panzergruppe West had available 2. Panzerdivision, relieved by 326. Infanterie Division. The 21. Panzerdivision was on the advance to an assembly area behind "LAH" Division. It arrived seven weeks after the invasion had started from the area north of the Seine. The plan had been to assign it to 7. Armee, but it was stopped at Caen because of the expected major offensive there. Thus, five Panzer divisions were located in the Caen area. Another, newly created, was on the advance. The "HJ" and 21. Panzerdivisions, however, were at only half of their battle strength. Even if General Montgomery had not achieved the objective of his operation, in the respects of terrain gained and enemies worn out, the tying down of the bulk of the German Panzer forces had, nevertheless, been achieved. However, the main cause of his partial success was a mistaken assessment of enemy plans on the German side. A contributing factor to this, no doubt, was the lack of aerial surveillance intelligence, of which there was no shortage on the enemy side.

The American "COBRA" operation started on 24 July 1944, as had "GOODWOOD", with carpet bombing. On the next day, in the framework of Montgomery's diversionary plan and after three hours of massive artillery preparation, the Canadians attacked in the early hours between Bourguebus and the Orne along a width of seven kilometers with infantry and tanks. They were able to gain only little ground in the sector of the "LAH", but they were successful in pushing back the 272. Inf.-Div. despite brave resistance. By late afternoon the breakthrough area, which had a depth of one to three kilometers and a width of five kilometers, had been cut off. Through a counterattack by 272. Inf.-Div. and parts of "Hohenstaufen" Division during the same evening and night, the old main line of defense between Tilly and the Orne was re-established despite the determined resistance of the Canadians. Subsequently, "Hohenstaufen" took over the sector of 272. Inf.-Div. which, in turn, relieved 21. Pz.-Div. during the night 28–29 July, in order to free up this Panzerdivision. The Panzerdivision moved into the area of Fôret de Cinglais, southwest of Bretteville-sur-Laize. The 2. Panzerdivision moved into the previous billet area of "Hohenstaufen". On 29 July, 116. Panzerdivision started marching to AOK 7 where the situation had taken a threatening turn. Still, the bulk of the Panzerdivisions remained in the Caen area since a major offensive continued to be expected there.[42]

During his visit to "HJ" Division on 23 July, Feldmarschall von Kluge had given notice that it would shortly be relieved by an Infanteriedivision so that it would be free for action at trouble spots. This was becoming an urgent need. First, the Wünsche Kampfgruppe was rebuilt. The units belonging to it were pulled out. It consisted of: Staff SS-Panzerregiment 12, I. Abteilung SS-Panzerregiment 12, I. Abteilung SS-Panzerregiment 1, III. Bataillon SS-Panzergrenadierregiment 26 (SPW), and Schwere (heavy) SS-Panzerabteilung 101.

The Kampfgruppe had at its disposal sixty-one Panthers, four Panzer IVs and nineteen Tigers. Its command post, from 31 July on, was in Fierville-la Campagne. It was a reserve of I. SS-Panzerkorps. As well as III./26, the I/26 was also relieved by a battalion of Grenadierregiment 731 of 272. Inf.-Div. and, from 04.00 hours on 2 August onward, was held in readiness as a Divisional reserve. The parts of the Division, outside the Wünsche Kampfgruppe, were denoted as "Kampfgruppe Meyer" in the daily reports. Among others, it had 22 battle-ready Panzer IVs and 27 Jagdpanzer IVs. The Artillerieregiment with Werferabteilung 12 and Flakabteilung 12, which had been in action with 272. Inf.-Div., had returned to the Division on 28 July. During the night of 3–4 August, 272. Inf.-Div. took over the sector of the "HJ" Division. The sector was assigned to LXXXVI. A.K. The Meyer Kampfgruppe was assembled, as an operational reserve of I. SS-Panzerkorps, in the Vieux Fumé-Maizières-St. Sylvain-Bray-la Campagne area, so that it could be sent into action to the northeast and northwest. Simultaneously, the relief of "LAH" Division by 89. Inf.-Div. began. It was to continue unit by unit as troops arrived. The relieved parts were assembled behind the front line of I. SS-Panzerkorps in such a manner that they could march off at short notice for other duties.[43]

For "HJ" Division, a chapter was finished. During the last two days of the British "GOODWOOD" operation it succeeded, despite the organizational and physical separation of its units and after a difficult advance in three groups, in stopping the attack of the Guards Armoured Division approximately one kilometer southeast of the starting positions, preventing the planned breakthrough to Vimont. Fortunately, it did not have serious losses. Later, the artillery fire caused significant casualties. During the period 19 July to 4 August, "HJ" Division lost, in the Vimont Sector, eighteen killed, 114 wounded and two missing, for a total of 134.[44]

The figures of enemy manpower losses, the Guards Armoured Division and later the 49th Infantry Division, are not available. The losses of armor, in view of the force ratio, are illuminating. Neither the parts of the mixed Panzerabteilung, sent into action, nor SS-Panzerjägerabteilung 12, in its first action, suffered any losses of Panzers. It was quite different at the 5th Guards Armoured Brigade:

	battle-ready	not battle-ready more than 24 hrs	less than 24 hrs	total losses
17.7.	235			
18.7.	153	62	1	
19.7.	198	18	15	
20.7.	166	27	5	37 from 18–20 July[45]

Replacing the losses incurred since the start of the invasion from Feldersatzbataillon 12 was possible only in an inadequate extent. Thus, Oberstgruppenführer Sepp Dietrich requested, on 1 August 1944, the provision of 2,000 members of the Ausbildungs-und Ersatzbataillon 12 (training and replacement battalion) in Arnheim. Supreme Command West supported the request. However, only 261 recruits were transferred to "HJ" Division since, in the opinion of the command authorities, the continued existence of the Bataillon would otherwise be threatened.[46] To what extent replacements from the reserve units of the other elements—e.g Panzers, Pioniers—arrived, cannot be determined. The situation there would hardly have been more favorable. Since the start of the invasion, the "HJ" Division had lost 6,164 men, as indicated in a report from the "Panzergruppe" of 20 July.[47]

Since the start of the American offensive in the west, the situation of 7. Armee had deteriorated to an extremely critical state. The next chapter will report on that. Before that, an assessment on the overall situation in the west by Feldmarschall von Kluge should be recorded. He provided it on 21 July in a letter to Adolf Hitler in which he wrote:

Herewith, I submit to you a report from Generalfeldmarschall Rommel which he handed to me before his accident and which he had discussed with me.

I have now been here some fourteen days. Through long consultations with the crucial commanders at the local front lines, in particular also with those of the SS, I have arrived at the conclusion that the Feldmarschall, regrettably, is correct. In particular, yesterday's exchanges with the commanders of the units near Caen, immediately after the recent bitter battles, have provided the sad proof that there is no way, in our present situation—including that of materiel—for us to find an operational method negating the complete domination and the virtually devastating effect of the enemy air force without giving up the battle field. Whole Panzer units, sent out to counterattack, were caught by extremely heavy carpet bombing. Only after a lengthy effort, partially by towing, could they be brought out of the churned up ground. This meant they arrived too late.

The psychological effect of such massive bombing, like an elemental natural force, raining down on the fighting troops, in particular the infantry, is a factor which must be taken especially seriously. In this respect it is irrelevant whether the carpet bombing catches good or poor troops. They are more or less destroyed; in particular, their materiel is smashed. If this occurs several times, the staying power of such troops is put to the most severe test. They remain in position, die. What is left over is no longer the kind of fighter the situation absolutely demands. The troops are facing a force against which there is no defense any more. This will gradually become noticeable to an ever increasing extent.

I came here with the firm determination to carry out your order to hold firm at any cost. However, if one has to experience that the cost is the slow but certain annihilation of the troops—I am thinking here of the most praiseworthy 'Hitlerjugend' Division, concern for the near future of this front is more than justified. Further, one sees that the arriving materiel replacements are totally inadequate in almost all respects and personnel replacements are also less than needed. Weapons, especially artillery and Pak as well as ammunition for them, are, by far, below required level to carry out adequate operations. The focal point of the defensive fighting is, thus, determined by the good will of the gallant troops.

I can report that the front line is being held, until now, thanks to the admirable valor of the troops and the determination of the total leadership, in particular the subordinate one. However, there are almost daily losses of terrain.

Nevertheless, despite the all-out effort, the moment has drawn nearer when this front, already so heavily strained, will break. Once the enemy has reached open terrain, an orderly command conduct will hardly be possible considering the lack of mobility of our troops. As the responsible commander of this front I hold myself responsible to draw your attention, my Führer, to these conclusions in a timely fashion.

My last words during the commanders' briefing south of Caen were: 'We will hold on. If no means to improve our situation fundamentally become available, the alternative is honorable death on the field of battle.'

Supreme Commander West
signed: von Kluge
Generalfeldmarschall[48]

An assessment of the conduct of the German leadership and the situation on the German side, provided by General Bradley, Supreme Commander of the First US Army, since the end of July of Twelfth Army Group, on 29 July 1944 is informative:

The expectation of landings north of the Seine river prevented the enemy from quickly concentrating sufficient forces to withstand the attack in Normandy when it finally came. The Normandy landings have now been identified as the major Allied efforts in the west. The reinforcements by the enemy in this area are nevertheless too little and too late, and his communications and supplies have been too much impeded for a counterattack.[49]

The progress of developments and the information obtained through "ULTRA" had made this clear assessment possible. At that time, General Bradley did not know the reasons for the misjudgments on the German side.

CHAPTER 5.3
Action by Aufklärungsgruppe Olboeter near Chênedollé from 3 to 8 August 1944

While the "HJ" Division was still in defensive action in the Vimont sector, the situation on the left wing of the invasion front had taken a dangerous turn for the worse. Simultaneously with the containment attack by the II Canadian Corps south of Caen, the Americans had started operation "COBRA" west of St. Lô on 25 July 1944. Massive bombing raids preceded the attack by several infantry and tank divisions along a narrow front. They destroyed the majority of the troops in the front lines and the Panzers in position at critical points. In conjunction with this attack, which proceeded in southerly and southwesterly directions during the next few days, the Americans had also started an attack on the western coast of the Cotentin peninsula on 28 July. In the evening of 30 July they had reached Avranches. Counterattacks by 2. and 116. Panzerdivisions, after forced marches from the Orne valley and the area south of Caen, into the left American flank south of St. Lô had only been able to slow down their advance but had not prevented the break-through at the coast.

After breaking off Operation "GOODWOOD" near Caen, Montgomery had pulled his tank divisions out of the area around Caen. He attacked with them east of St. Lô, on both sides of Caumont, on 30 July, in the "BLUE-COAT" operation, toward the south and southeast. A battle group of the 11th Armoured Division had captured le Bény-Bocage (sixteen kilometers south of Caumont) on 1 August. It was threatening Vire in the rear of the troops who were sealing off the eastern flank of the American wedge which had broken through.

During this extremely critical situation, the Heeresgruppe brought in all available Panzer units from the area south of Caen. In this context, a fast group was taken out of the newly formed Wünsche Kampfgruppe. It was given the designation "Aufklärungsgruppe Olboeter" and consisted of 2. Panzer-kompanie under the command of Obersturmführer Gaede with 13 combat-ready Panthers, 9. Kompanie (armored personnel carriers) of Regiment 26, 1. Batterie of Artillerie-regiment 12 (six light self-propelled field howitzers—Wespe) and 2 armored reconnaissance squads (six armored cars, 80 Watt) of 1. Kompanie of Aufklärungsabteilung "LAH". The Aufklärungs-gruppe was attached to II. SS-Panzerkorps on 2 August at 22.25 hours and dispatched into the area east of Vire.[1]

On 1 August, II. SS-Panzerkorps had ordered 10. SS-Panzerdivision to clear out the British penetration near Coulvain (five kilometers southwest of Villers-Bocage) through a counterattack. The 21. Panzerdivision and 9. SS-Panzerdivision were directed to close the gap between Panzergruppe West and 7. Armee and to establish contact at Hill 205 (presumably 207 on map 1 : 25,000) immediately west of le Bény-Bocage.[2]

Here follows a description of the situation on the left wing of II. SS-Panz-erkorps where Aufklärungsgruppe Olboeter was put into action. Parts of 9. SS-Panzerdivision "Hohenstaufen" had already arrived in the morning of 2 August in the area east of le Bény-Bocage, to secure and reconnoiter. During the night 1–2 August, the Schwere SS-Panzerabteilung 102 (Tigers) had also been pulled out of its ambush positions near Hill 112 and brought up together with the rest of the "Hohenstaufen".

Tigerabteilung 102 of Sturmbannführer Weiß encountered the "A"-Squadron of the 23rd Hussars in the evening of 2 August. It knocked out all their Sherman tanks, except four. The Hussars and the 8th Battalion The Rifle Brigade (armored) changed over to defense on the ridge immediately north of le Bas Perrier, 1.5 kilometers north of Chênedollé. To the west, the 2nd Fife and Forfar Yeomanry (Sherman tanks) and the 3rd Battalion The Monmouthshire Regiment prepared for defense after having pulled back from the road Vire-Condé. These battalions, part of the 11th Armoured Division, had faced the "HJ" Division as early as 28 June south of Cheux. The 3rd Battalion The Monmouthshire Regiment was now commanded by Major J. J. How who had, previously, been chief of a company of this battalion.

In the morning of 3 August, the 11th Armoured Division had received orders not to advance any further but to await the arrival of the Guards Armoured Division which was tied down northeast of Arclais by 21. Panzer-division, as well as that of the Americans who were approximately the same distance away to the northwest. The English had been ordered to by-pass Vire since it was located in the American attack sector.[3]

On 3 August, the "Hohenstaufen" Division attempted to smash the furthest advanced British forces through concentric attacks from the east, south and southwest. Because of a lack of forces, it could only achieve a partial success. The Korps-Tigerabteilung and the Panzeraufklärungsabteilung attacked from Vire along the road to Villers-Bocage. After knocking out a number of tanks they captured, as ordered, the hill northwest of la Bistière. Parts swung off to the northwest and established contact with 3. Fallschirmjäger (para-troopers) Division near la Graverie. At the same time, Panzerpionier-bataillon 9 attacked to the right of the Weiß Kampfgruppe in order to capture Burcy and later gain contact with the Weiß Kampfgruppe near la Bistière. The attack, led without Panzer support, initially made good progress but then stalled under the fire of several tanks. A British counterattack forced the Pioniers to pull back and switch over to defense along a line from south of Pavée-south of Burcy.[4]

The Olboeter Aufklärungsgruppe and Heerespionier-bataillon 600 arrived in the combat area in the evening of 3 August. The Pioniers initially set up defenses around Chênedollé. The Panzergrenadiers of Sturmbann-führer Olboeter probably took over the sector les Templeries-la Teinturerie. The Panther-kompanie took up ambush positions on a broad front directly south of the road Vire-Vassy, with its left wing near Viessoix. There was no contact with the Weiß Kampfgruppe. It can be assumed that the attached armored reconnaissance squads were sent into action to determine the situation and secure the gap.

The English reconnoitered against this securing line from the north during 3 August, using armored car squads. They reported la Teinturerie occupied by infantry and mortars, and that they had come under fire from a Panther in the vicinity of the railroad embankment.[5]

Unterscharführer Karl Bassler, Panzer commander in 2. Kompanie, reported that a British reconnaissance vehicle had been knocked out on 3

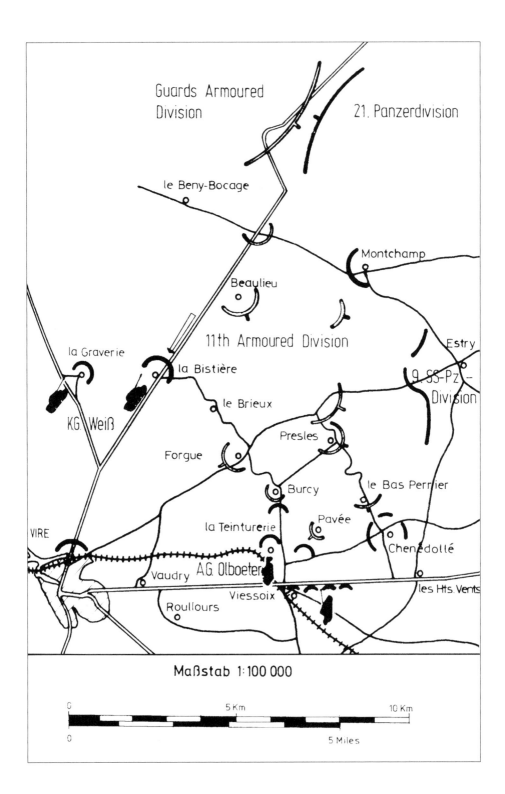

Guards Armoured
Division

21. Panzerdivision

le Beny-Bocage

Montchamp

Beaulieu

11th Armoured Division

la Graverie

Estry

la Bistière

9. SS-Pz.-
Division

le Brieux

Presles

K.G. Weiß

Forgue

le Bas Perrier

Burcy

Pavée

la Teinturerie

VIRE

Chenédollé

Vaudry

A.G. Olboeter

les Hts. Vents

Viessoix

Roullours

Maßstab 1:100 000

0   5 Km   10 Km

0   5 Miles

August, but remained intact except for its windshield. Valuable maps with notes on the enemy positions were found inside the vehicle. The car was then used for some time by the Regimental staff.[6]

In the late evening hours of 3 August, the 11th Armoured Division received infantry reinforcements from three battalions of the 3rd Infantry Division. The 2nd Battalion The Royal Warwickshire Regiment was ordered to relieve the 8th Battalion The Rifle Brigade near le Bas Perrier.[7]

The plan of "Hohenstaufen" Division for the following day was to close the still existing gap along a general line Hill 175 (presumably 173 on map 1 : 25,000) to approximately 600 meters east of la Ferronnière-Beaulieu-la Graverie and to destroy the English forces south thereof.[8]

The attack along the road Chênedollé on the English positions immediately north of le Bas Perrier hit the enemy exactly at the moment when the Warwickshires relieved the 8th Battalion The Rifle Brigade. The attackers succeeded in breaking through to le Bas Perrier and to within 400 m of the English positions to its north. There, the attack came to a standstill under heavy defensive artillery and tank fire. The assault units, belonging to SS-Pionierbataillon 9 and Pionierbataillon 600, were drawn back to the ridge on both sides of Point 243, north of Chênedollé. The Olboeter Aufklärungsgruppe was apparently not involved in this fighting. The Weiß Kampfgruppe fought off several English attacks along the road Vire-Villers-Bocage. In the face of superior enemy forces, it had to withdraw to new positions directly north of Vire after darkness had fallen.[9]

In order to clear up the critical situation in the Chênedollé area and west of it, 10. SS-Panzerdivision disengaged from the operational area Aunay-la Bigne during the night 4/5 August and moved into the area around Vassy. The 2. Tigerkompanie was assigned to Pionierbataillon 600 in Chênedollé.

The 11th Armoured Division had set up all-round defensive positions: among others, the Warwickshires with a Hussars tank company near le Bas Perrier, the Monmouthshire Battalion—relieved during the course of the day by the 1st Battalion The Royal Norfolk Regiment—with a tank company of the Fife and Forfar Yeomanry around Pavée, the 1st Battalion The Herefordshire Regiment with a company of the Fife and Forfars around Forgues.[10]

The Warwicks, together with a company and several tanks of the Hussars, tried to capture the hill north of Chênedollé. They were fought off and pulled back to le Bas Perrier. An attack by Aufklärungsabteilung 9 and the Pionierbataillon "Hohenstaufen" with the Panzergrenadierkompanie of Sturm-bannführer Olboeter, from the area north of Viessoix on Pavée, supported by several Panthers, artillery and mortars, was repulsed. The troops returned to their starting positions. The 9./26 lost four killed who could not be recovered. The English losses amounted to approximately 100 men, mostly to the heavy mortar fire.[11]

In the afternoon of 6 August, 10. SS-Panzerdivision "Frundsberg", together with two Kampfgruppen, started an attack on the English positions near le Bas Perrier and near Pavée. The violent, bloody fighting lasted until nightfall. The English suffered approximately 500 losses, the German losses are not known.[12]

The Olboeter Aufklärungsgruppe was apparently not involved in these attacks.

The American spearheads reached the area north of Vire in the evening. The city was occupied before noon on 7 August. Renewed attacks by "Frundsberg" Division, planned for that day, did not take place. The Division was pulled out for action with 7. Armee and the German main line of defense was moved back to a line Chênedollé-Viessoix-Roullours. Violent English attacks on Chênedollé and the positions northeast of Viessoix were fought off, with the attacker suffering significant losses. Aufklärungsgruppe Olboeter knocked out 6 tanks. Unterscharführer Bassler reported on the role of his Panther, which was located on the left wing and guarded toward the west, on what appeared to be the first combat encounter with the Americans:

> The enemy attacked from the direction of Vire. Panzergrenadiers of the "Frundsberg" had dug in to the west of us. It did not take long before enemy tanks appeared on the western horizon. We opened fire at 2,700 meters and knocked out three tanks. A fourth one was abandoned by its crew without obvious reason. After it had been quiet for some time we drove forward in a passing Kübelwagen and inspected our "handiwork". Dead or wounded enemy soldiers were not found. The contents of the fighting vehicles had already been distributed by the Panzergrenadiers. We received a share of several tasty English (or American) cookies.[13]

The bitterly fought-for town of Chênedollé was given up during the night of 7–8 August and the front line was straightened. The last parts of the "Frundsberg" and Olboeter Aufklärungsgruppe disengaged.

In the afternoon of 8 August, 5. Panzerarmee advised II. SS-Panzerkorps to be prepared to let go of Gruppe Olboeter and Pionierbataillon 600.[14]

The departure was probably ordered toward evening. Despite the comradely welcome at the "Hohenstaufen", the men of "HJ" Division were glad to return to their own "bunch". Bitter battles awaited them there. Fortunately, they could not foresee that.

References

PART I
Chapter 00.1
1) Personal information from the then-Ia of the Kommandoamt (head-quarters) of the Waffen-SS, Standartenführer Joachim Ruoff, to the Author
2) Letter by the chief of the SS-Hauptamt (central office) regarding the creation of the "Hitlerjugend" Division of 18.2.43 to the Reichsführer-SS and the chief of the German police
3) File note by the SS-Hauptamt (central office) of 9.3.43 regarding a discussion between Berger, Möckel, and others, on 8.3.43
4) Letter from the SS-Führungshauptamt (central operations office) of 10.3.43 to the SS-Hauptamt regarding the creation of the SS-Division "Hitlerjugend"

Chapter 00.2
1) Führer order, copy without date, microfilm T 175, roll 108
2) Order by the SS-Führungshauptamt, command office of the Waffen-SS, organization diary No. 784/43, secret command material of 24.6.43
3) Order . . . (see 2 above) diary No. 1660/43, secret command material of 30.10.43
4) Condition report to the chief of staff of the Panzer forces, Federal Archives/Military Archives (F/M), inventory RH10/321
5) As 4)

Chapter 00.3
1) Blohm, Erich: Hitlerjugend—a social action community, author's edition 1977, quoted as in Herbert Taege ". . . Über die Zeiten fort (across time)—the face of a young generation during ascent and ruin", Lindhorst 1978
2) Herbert Taege, see 1), page 88
3) Letter of 6.3.82 from Heinrich Springer to the Author
4) Order from the scientific and administration headquarters of 25.6.43, Federal Archives Koblenz; personal information to the Author from Helmuth Thöle

5) Letter by Elmar Lochbihler of 4.3.81 to the MUNIN Verlag, copy in the hands of the Author
6) As 3)
7) Letter by Paul Kamberger of 3.9.77 to the Author
8) Letter by Harald Zimmermann of 27.3.78 to the Author
9) Report by Georg Isecke to the Author in December 79.
10) " Die 3. Kompanie", association of the 3. Kompanie, SS-Panzerregiment 12, author's edition, 1978, p. 22
11) Report by Karl Kugler to the Author in May 1954
12) Condition reports, loc. cit.

Chapter 00.4
1) Letter from SS-Panz.Gren.Div. "Hitlerjugend", section Ic of 19.9.43, F/M
2) Report by Karl Friedrich Hahn of 23.1.69 to the Author
3) As 2)
4) Special order of the Division of 4.12.43, F/M
5) As 2)
6) As 2)
7) Order from Abteilung IIa of the Divisional staff of 10.11.43, F/M

Chapter 00.5
1) Directive No. 51, F/M, inventory RW4/v. 560
2) War diary AOK 7, Ic, F/M, inventory AOK 7, Box 112/135, 41703/26; 57352/2
3) Situation map Supreme Command West, F/M, inventory Kart RH 2W/199
4) Stacy: "The Victory Campaign", loc. cit., p.60
5) Wilmot, Chester: "Der Kampf um Europa" (the struggle for Europe), Frankfurt/M., Berlin 1954, p. 198
6) British Army of the Rhine Intelligence Review, 4 March 1946, p. 10 and following
7) Irving, David: "Rommel", Hamburg 1978, p. 494
8) As 6)
9) Hubatsch, Walther: "Hitlers Weisungen für die Kriegsführung" (Hitler's directives for the conduct of the war), Frankfurt/M, 1962, p. 238
10) General der Panzertruppen Freiherr Geyr von Schweppenburg, Studie (study) B-258, "Geschichte der Panzer-gruppe West" (history of Panzer group west)
11) Letter by General der Panzertruppen retd. Leo Freiherr Geyr von Schweppenburg to the Author of 20.2.71
12) Letter by Generaloberst retd. Guderian to General retd. von Geyr, quoted from an article by General von Geyr in "Süddeutsche Zeitung"

(newspaper) of July 1960, titled "Legend of war history", comment on the book by Friedrich Ruge "Rommel und die Invasion"

13) War diary Supreme Command West, appendices, F/M, inventory RH19 IV/1

14) War diary Supreme Command West, appendices, F/M, inventory RH19 IV/1

15) As 14) RH19/36

16) As 14) RH19 IV/38

17) "Europäische Wehrkunde" (European defense -intelligence) 2/80, p. 89; concerning: Friedrich Ruge "Rommel und die Invasion", E.W. 10/79

18) War diary Supreme Command West Ia, appendices 1.5.–31.5.44, RH19 IV/41

19) As 18) RH19/41

20) As 19)

21) As 18) RH19 IV/38 (6.5.44)

22) War diary AOK 7, Ia No. 2528/44 secret command material of 13.5.44 "Report on the journey by the Supreme Commander in the region of the LXXXIV. A.K. from 10–12 May 44", F/M

23) War diary Supreme Command West, Ia, appendices 1.6.-30.6.44, F/M RH19 IV/37

24) As 5) p. 195

25) Montgomery, Field Marshal Sir Bernard Law: -"Normandy to the Baltic", London, no date

26) "Report by the Supreme Commander to the Combined Chiefs of Staff on the operations in Europe of the Allied Expeditionary Force, 6 June 1944 to 8 May 1945"; 1946, The Cossac Plan- and as 5), p. 193

27) Dufresne, Michel: "World War II OVERLORD, Directives and Selected Messages", Vimer 1979

28) As 7), p. 467

Chapter 00.6

1) Notes by Paul Baier, copy in the hands of the Author

Chapter 00.7

1) Study by Oberstleutnant von Criegern, chief of staff LXXXIV. A.K., first part "The battles of the LXXXIV. A.K. in Normandy from the Allied landing to 17 June 1944"

2) As 1)

3) Report by Walter Krüger of 10.8.1980 to the Author

4) Report by Hans Lierk of 7.2.1976 to the Author

5) Report by Jochen Leykauff of 5.2.1980 to the Author

6) Report by Karl Kolb of 1954 to the Author

7) List of losses

8) Condition report of 12. SS-Pz.-Div. "HJ" of 1.6.1944, F/M, RH10/321

9) As 5)

PART II
Chapter 0.1
1) Copies of the war diary of Heeresgruppe B, with appendices, 1.6.–15.6.44, in possession of Manfred Rommel

2) War diary Heeresgruppe B, Ia. Evaluation of situation and weekly reports 21.5.–2.7.44

2a) Letter from Service Hydrographique et Océano-graphique de la Marine of 21.9.81 to M.D., copy in the hands of the Author

3) Quoted after Janusz Pielkalkiewicz, "Invasion France 1944", Munich 1979, p. 121

4a-f) War diary Supreme Command West, F/M, RH19 IV/40, pp. 66, 67, 94, 95, 123, 124

5) Irving, David: "Rommel", a biography, Hamburg 1978, p. 493 and following, and war diary of the Kriegs-marine Command West from 1.6.44–30.6.44, p. 6228, F/M, M326, PG37, 580-37589

6) Report by Hans Siegel to the Author of 14.8.80

7) Letter from Willy Schnittfinke of 19.4.1976 to the Author

8) "Die 3. Kompanie", author's edition by the Kompanie association 3./SS-Panzerregiment 12, 1978, p. 34, and verbal report by Willi Kändler to the Author on 7.8.1977

9) As 6) and report by Richard Rudolf to the Author on 11.6.77

10) As 3) and Chester Wilmot "Der Kampf um Europa", Frankfurt/M and Berlin, 1954, p. 233 and following pages

11) War Diary 6th Battalion The Durham Light Infantry, 3–5 June 1944, The Public Record Office, London

12) As 5), p. 490

Chapter 0.2
1) Chester Wilmot "Der Kampf um Europa", loc. cit., p. 252 and 253

2) As 1), pp. 253/254, and "BATTLEFIELD TOUR 6 AB DIV", Staff College Camberley

3) Diary of Unterscharführer August Zinßmeister, copy in the hands of the Author; report by Gerd Freiherr von Reitzenstein of 8.4.1972 to the Author; diary of the Divisionsbegleitkompanie, p. 4

4) Report by Oswald Beck, communications Zug Regiment 26 to the Author on 30.11.1970

5) Study by Generalleutnant Richter, B-621

6) Study by Generalmajor Feuchtinger: The History of the 21. Panzerdivision for the Period from its Creation to the Start of the Invasion, MS-B-441, and the so-far unpublished manuscript by Werner Kortenhaus "Die 21. Panzerdivision im Westen 1943–1945"

7) As 1) Assault from the Sea I and II, and Staff College Camberley, BAT-TLEFIELD TOUR 50 DIV

8) Letter from Otto Günsche to the Author of 2.10.1081

Chapter 0.3

1) War diary Supreme Command West 6.6–30.6.44, appendix 4 Ia No. 5654/44, secret command material of 24.7.44, p. 3 and 4

1a) Report by Peter Hansmann to the Author on 30.6.82

2) Diary of Unterscharführer August Zinßmeister, 1./A.A. 12, copy in the hands of the Author

3) War diary of the I./SS-Panzergrenadierregiment 25 for the period 1.5.-5.7.1944

3a) Report by Peter Hederich to the Author on 1.5.68

4) Report from the adjutant of SS-Flakabteilung 12, Unter-sturmführer Karl Kolb, of 1954 to the Author, and report by Hans Krieg, Albert Herzer, and Paul Baier, 4. Batterie SS-Flakabteilung 12

5) War diary 7. Armee, Ia/war diary draft, long distance telephone calls, etc., loc. cit., p. 11

6) As 3)

7) As 3)

8) War diary Heeresgruppe B, loc. cit., pp. 45 and 51

9) Report by Martin Besel of 17.11.1975 to the Author, manuscript in the hands of the Author

10) Report by Hellmuth Pock to the Author on 20.4.1976

11) War diary of the Divisionsbegleitkompanie, loc. cit., p. 4

12) As 3)

13) Diary of Kurt Pörtner, formerly SS-Panzerpionier-bataillon 12

14) Lists of losses of all regiments, battalions, and independent companies, including the supply troops, submitted to the Wehrmacht information office; German office for the notification of the closest relatives of killed members of the former German Wehrmacht, Berlin

15) As 3)

16) Report by the former adjutant of III. Abteilung SS-Panzerartillerieregi-ment 12, Untersturmführer Kurt Göricke, to the Author on 11.5.1954

Chapter 1.01

1) War diary Heeresgruppe B from 1.6.–15.6.44, from the personal estate of Generalfeldmarschall Erwin Rommel

2) "Die 21. Panzerdivision im Westen 1943–45", manuscript by Werner Kortenhaus

3) War diary AOK 7, Ia, appendix long distance telephone calls and discussions, Supreme Commander-chief-Ia

4) As 2); position map 716. Infanterie Division, appendix 3 to supreme command of Heeresgruppe B Ia No. 3050/44 secret; study MS-B-441

Generalmajor Feuchtinger "History of the 21. Panzerdivision for the Period from its Creation to the Start of the Invasion."
   5) Study by Generalleutnant Richter, MS-B-621
   6) As 2) and Feuchtinger Study, see 4)
   7) As 6)
   8) As 6)
   9) Maps "Battlefield Tour 50th Division, D-Day to D+9" and Stacy, loc. cit.
   10) Chester Wilmot, loc. cit., map after p. 256
   11) Letter from Monsieur P. of 28.12.75 to the Author

Chapter 1.02
   1) Study by SS-Brigadeführer and Generalmajor der Waffen-SS Fritz Kraemer "Das I. SS-Panzerkorps im Westen 1944", MS-C-024
   2) War diary AOK 7, loc. cit.
   3) War diary AOK 7, long distance telephone calls, etc., p. 11
   4) As 2)
   5) As 2) and interview with Brigadeführer Kraemer on 28.4.1948, B-814 interview with Generalleutnant Bayerlein
   6) As 1)
   7) As 2)
   8) As 5)

Chapter 1.1
   1) Panzermeyer: "Grenadiere", Fourth Edition, Munich 1965, p. 211 and following pages, and war diary AOK 7, Ia; 7.6.44 (regarding time of the attack)
   2) As 1) p. 215
   3) Report by Kurt Göricke of 11.5.54 to the Author
   4) Reports by Willy Schnittfinke (5./Pz.Rgt. 12) and Hans Fenn (6./Pz.Rgt. 12) of 15.2.71 to the Author
   5) Scarfe, Norman: "Assault Division, A History of the 3rd Division from the Invasion of Normandy to the Surrender of Germany", 1947, p. 97 and following pages
   6) War Diary 9th British Infantry Brigade
   7) Stacy, C.P.: "The Victory Campaign", Official History of the Canadian Army in the Second World War, Volume III, Ottawa 1966, p. 114 and following pages
   8) As 7) p. 126
   9) As 7) p. 126 and following pages
   10) War Diary The North Nova Scotia Highlanders (NNSH)
   11) War Diaries NNSH and 27th Armoured Regiment
   12) Report by Hans Fenn on 15.2.71 to the Author
   13) Report by Karl Vasold on 2.6.77 to the Author

14) As 7) p. 128
15) Report by Paul Hinsberger to the Author
16) As 14)
17) War Diary 27th Armoured Regiment
18) As 10)
19) Reports by Kurt Havemeister and Franz Xaver Pfeffer of 10.8.80 to the Author
20) Report by Emil Werner of 14.10.1980 to the Author
21) Report by Hans Siegel of 28.2.69 to the Author
22) Report by Helmut Stöcker of 20.7.76 to the Author
22a) As 5), pp. 97/98
23) Letter from H.Y. to the Author
24) Diary: Divisionsbegleitkompanie, pp. 4/5
25) Study by Generalmajor Feuchtinger, loc. cit. p. 25
26) As 7), p. 132
27) As 22)
28) War Diaries NNSH and 27th Armoured Regiment, and as 7)
29) War diary I./25, loc. cit., list of losses II. Panzer-abteilung and information from Schlitz Symposium on 22/23.5.76, lists of losses of the I./25, II./25, III./25

Chapter 1.2
1) Chester, Wilmot: "The Struggle for Europe", German edition, Frankfurt—Berlin, 1954, p. 284 and following pages
2) War diaries 69th Infantry Brigade and 50th Division, map Battlefield Tour, Staff College Camberley 1974
3) War Diary 6th Battalion The Durham Light Infantry, "Route and Dispositions", 6–18 June 1944
4) War diaries 50th Division, 69th Infantry Brigade
5) Diary of Unterscharführer August Zinßmeister, 1./SS-Pz.Aufkl.Abt. 12, copy in the hands of the Author
6) Report by Gerd Freiherr von Reitzenstein of 8.4.72 to the Author, based on diary entries
7) Report by Kurt Fischer of 22.4.1973 to the Author, with addenda
8) As 3)
9) War Diary 6th Battalion The Green Howards, June 1944, sheet 4
10) As 6)
11) Report by Max-Heinrich Martens of 3.12.79 to the Author

Chapter 1.3
1) Personal report by Friedrich Wilhelm Hahn of 25.10.76 to the Author
2) Report by Karl Düwel, the then-chief of the 3./26, of 28.12.76 to the Author

Chapter 1.4

1) War diary Heeresgruppe B, loc. cit., discussions, considerations, decisions, 7.6.44, p. 62
2) As 1), pp. 63/64
3) As 1), p. 64 and following page
4) War diary AOK 7 and appendices, loc. cit., p. 18 and as 1), pp. 70/71
5) As 1), p. 56
6) Copy of the Divisional order, in possession of the Author ("Appendix 112")
7) Study MS-C-024 by Brigadeführer Fritz Kraemer "Das I. SS-Panzerkorps im Westen 1944"

Chapter 1.5

1) War Diary 1st Bn The Regina Rifle Regiment, and Stacy, loc. cit., p. 135
1a) Study by Brigadeführer Fritz Kraemer, MS-C-024, loc. cit.
2) Reports by Karl Friedrich Hahn, Richard Borrmann, Karl Düwel, Heinrich Bassenauer, X. Hoffmann to the Author
3) War Diary 1st Bn The Regina Rifle Regiment
4) Report by Heinz Schmolke of 25.5.1977 to the Author
5) Stacy, loc. cit., p. 135
6) As 4), and Friedrich-Wilhelm Oberlach of 25.2.80
7) Report by Paul Dargel of 31.10.79 to the Author
8) As 5), p. 135
9) War Diary 24th Lancers of 8.6.44
10) As 4)
11) As 7)
12) Report by August Henne of 3.2.1980 to the Author
13) As 5), pp. 135/136
14) As 13)
15) Lists of losses of II./26 for 8.6.44
16) Report by Wilhelm Pallas to the Author
17) Report by Karl Kugler to the Author of May 1954
18) As 17)
19) Report by Hans-Georg Keßlau to the Author of January 1973
20) Reports of 16.2.72 by Helmut Mader and Hans-Georg Keßlau, together with Hermann Asbach
21) Reports on losses of the III./26
22) Ritgen, Helmut: " Die Geschichte der Panzer-Lehr-Division im Westen 1944–1945", Stuttgart 1979
23) 8th Armoured Brigade Operation Order No. 25 of 25 May 1944
24) Petition by lawyer Dr. jur. (LL D) A. Oehlert of 20.11.48 to the supreme military justice authorities

25) War Diary Regiment Inns of Court of 8.6.44

26) War Diary 6th Bn The Durham Light Infantry, 8.6.44

27) As 26)

28) 8th Armoured Brigade, Operation Order No. 25

29) War diary 8th Armoured Brigade, Sherwood Rangers Yeomanry, 24th Lancers, 8.6.44

30) Report by Gerd Freiherr von Reitzenstein of 8.4.72 to the Author

31) Various reports by Kurt Fischer to the Author

32) Lists of losses of Panzeraufklärungsabteilung 12

33) Interview with Brigadeführer Kraemer and General-leutnant Bayerlein, Kraemer B-814, Landsberg 28.4.48

34) Report by Max Wünsche of 13.2.1980 to the Author

35) Report by Hans Kesper of 14.7.77 to the Author

36) Report by Reinhold Fuss of 14.7.77 to the Author

37) Report by Dr. Jürgen Chemnitz of 27.6.76 to the Author

38) Report by Leopold Lengheim of 16.12.79 to the -Author

39) As 37)

40) Diary of Karl Hahn, copied excerpts in the hands of the Author, diary of the Divisionsbegleitkompanie, and report by Leo Freund to the Author

41) As 1)

42) The Victory Campaign, loc. cit., p. 137

43) As 36) and letter of 7.10.80 to the Author

44) Study B-258 by General der Panzertruppen Freiherr Geyr von Schweppenburg "The History of Panzergruppe West"

45) Report by Alois Morawetz of 4.8.76, and supplement of 2.4.80 to the Author

46) "Die 3. Kompanie SS-Panzerregiment 12", 12 SS-Panzer-division "Hitlerjugend", author's publication, Kompanie association, 1978

47) Letter from Rudolf von Ribbentrop of 28.1.77 to the Author

48) Letter from Max Wünsche of 13.2.76 to the Author

49) Lists of losses of I. Panzerabteilung

50) Report by Helmut Pock of 20.4.76 to the Author

51) Report by Paul Dienemann of December 1979 to the Author

52) As 50)

53) As 44), and Panzermeyer: "Grenadiere", loc. cit. p. 229

54) Report by Helmut Schuck of 11.3.76 to the Author

55) Report by Sturmmann Alois Banz of 27.12.69 to the Author

56) Letter from Dr. med. Zistler of 29.4.76

57) Lists of losses of SS-Panzerpionierbataillon 12

58) Diary of Unterscharführer August Zinßmeister, loc. cit.

59) As 29), War Diary 24th Lancers, Ritgen, loc. cit.

60) As 29)

61) Report by Hans-Ulrich Dietrich to the Author on 27.11.79

62) As 29) and Ritgen, loc. cit.

63) As 30)

64) War diary I./25, loc. cit.

65) Report by Hans Siegel to the Author of 28.2.69

66) Scarfe, Norman: "Assault Division", London 1947, p. 98 and following pages

67) As 64)

68) As 64)

69) Report by Kurt Havemeister to the Author on 10.8.76

70) Report by Karl Vasold to the Author on 2.6.77

71) Report of the 7. Panzerkompanie of 26.9.44, copy in the hands of the Author

72) Report: "Die Schwere SS-Korps-Artillerie-Abteilung 101/501" by Heinrich Garbade, and report by Erich Hüttner, handed to the Author on 30.3.81 by Fr.K. Meyer

73) Report by Garbade, as 72); Study by Kraemer MS-C-024; war diary I./25, loc. cit.

74) Ritgen, loc. cit., p. 112

75) War diary AOK 7, telephone conversations and discussions, p. 23

76) War diary Panzergruppe West/Pz. AOK 5, loc. cit., 10.6.44

77) War diary Heeresgruppe B, loc. cit., pp. 115/116

78) As 76)

79) KV 7225, quoted after Bennet, Ralph: "ULTRA in the West", London 1979

80) As 77), pp. 88, 90, 94, 97

Chapter 2.1

1) Report by Gerd Freiherr von Reitzenstein to the Author on 8.4.72

2) Report by Georg Isecke to the Author in December 1979

3) War Diary 69th Infantry Brigade, 4/7 Royal Dragoon Guards, 11.6.44

4) Report by Paul Dienemann to the Author on 3.12.79

5) Report by M. to the Author on 4.5.80

6) War Diary 6th Battalion The Green Howards, 11.6.44

7) As 3), and report of the commander of the 6th Green Howards, Lt.Col. Hastings, MC, during the battlefield tour of the Staff College Camberley, 1974

8) War Diary 4/7 Dragoon Guards of 11.6.44

9) War Diary 69th Infantry Brigade and Ritgen, Helmut: "Die Geschichte (history) der Panzer-Lehr-Division", pp.134/135

10) As 3) and 5)

11) As 1)

Chapter 2.2
1) Stacy, loc. cit., p. 139
2) The History of The First Hussars Regiment, 1856–1945, p. 73 and following pages
3) McKee, Alexander: "Caen, Anvil of Victory, 1966, p. 97
4) As 1) and 2)
5) As 2)
6) Report by Alois Banz to the Author on 27.12.1969
7) Report by Horst Lütgens to the Author on 1.7.1968
8) Report by Ernst Behrens to the Author on 5.4.1968
9) Report by Hans Siegel to the Author on 22.10.1972
10) As 1), p. 140
11) As 1), and Ellis, loc. cit., p. 253
12) Lists of losses
13) As 9)
14) Verbal report by Herbert Wendel, October 1969

Chapter 2.3
1) Reports by Karl Friedrich Hahn of 3.1.1969, Erwin Wohlgemuth of 30.5.1072, and Hans Kesper of 14.7.1977 to the Author
2) Stacy, loc. cit., p. 138
3) Ellis, loc. cit., Appendix IV, p. 539
4) Report by Karl Friedrich Hahn, see 1)
5) Report by Hans Kesper, see 1)
6) War diary of the Divisionsbegleitkompanie
7) As 5), and verbal report of 4.2.73
8) Report by Erwin Wohlgemut, see 1)
9) As 7)
10) McKee, Alexander: "Caen, Anvil of Victory", 1966, pp. 100/101
11) Report by A.P., Caen
12) As 2), p. 139
13) Lists of losses

Chapter 2.4
1) War diary Heeresgruppe B, loc. cit., pp. 91/92—Discussions, etc., p. 94
2) War diary 7. Armee, loc. cit., 11.6.44
3) 22 ARMD BDE OPS, 6–15 Jun 44
4) Chester Wilmot, loc. cit., pp. 323/324, and letter from General Montgomery to "Freddie" of 12.6.44
5) As 3)
6) As 3)
7) Reports by Rolf Möbius of 10.10. and 29.11.79 to the Author
8) As 7)

9) Report by Jürgen Wessel of 4.8.77
10) War diary Panzer-Aufklärungs-Lehrabteilung
11) As 8), 9), and report by Georg Isecke, loc. cit.
12) As 3)
13) Submission for the awarding of the Oak Leaves with Swords to the Knights' Cross by the chief command of I. SS-Panzerkorps "Leibstandarte" of 13 June 1944, copy from the collection of Jost W. Schneider
14) As 8)
15) As 7)
16) As 3)
17) As 3)
18) Report by Gerd Freiherr von Reitzenstein, loc. cit.
19) War diary AOK 7, loc. cit., 12.6.44

Chapter 2.5
1) Letters from Richard Schwarzwälder of 4.1.72 and 25.1.73 to the Author

Chapter 2.6
1) War diary 7. Armee, loc. cit., 14.6.44
2) War diary Panzer-Lehr-Division, appendix 167
3) Diary Divisionsbegleitkompanie, 14.6.44
4) As 3)
5) 49th Division Intelligence Summary No. 3 of 14.6.44
6) As 5), I.S. of 15 June, and 49th Division Operation Order No. 2 of 15.6.44
7) Report by Gerd Freiherr von Reitzenstein, loc. cit.
8) Diary of August Zinßmeister, loc. cit.
9) Letter from the German Heer liaison officer at the Staff College Camberley, Oberstleutnant i.G. Berthold Graf Stauffenberg, of 4.12.75 to the Author
10) 49th Division Operation Order No. 2 of 15.6.44
11) 49th Division I.S. No. 5 of 16.6.44
12) 49th Division O. No. 3, Forecast of Future Operations of 16.6.44
13) 49th Division O.O. No. 3 of 16.6.44
14) 49th Division O.O. No. 5 of 17.6.44, and Operation Instruction No. 4 of 16.6.44, Addendum of 17.6.44
15) Reports by Hermann Asbach, Hans-Georg Keßlau, Karl Kugler, Helmut Mader, Heinz Pochstein to the Author
16) Situation report 12 SS-Panzerdivision "Hitlerjugend" of 18.6.44 for the day of 17.6.44, Ia diary No. 764/44, copy in the appendices to the war diary Heeresgruppe B, F/M, inventory RH19/IX/ 2 and 3
17) War Diary 8th Armoured Brigade Group of 18.6.44
18) Reports by Hans-Georg Keßlau to the Author on 11.12.72

19) Statement from Sturmmann K., copy in the hands of the Author
20) 49th Division I.S. Nos. 6 and 7 of 17. and 18.6.44
21) Lists of losses
22) As 16)
23) War Diary HQ 147th Infantry Brigade Summary June 44
24) 49th Division I.S. No. 8 of 19.6.44, Part II, 6b "Gens"
25) Ritgen, loc. cit., p. 141
26) Report by Hans Siegel to the Author on 12.11.72
27) Report by Rudolf Polzin to the Author of April 1977
28) Diary of Madame Lemaigre-Demesnil, copy in the hands of the Author
29) Letter of Monsieur A.P. of 27.10.68 to the Author

Chapter 2.7
1) Situation report 12. SS-Pz.-Div. "Hitlerjugend", section Ia, of 16.6.44, for 16.6.44, to Heeresgruppe B, Ia, No. 3725/44g.K. (secret command material)
2) Report by Emil Werner to the Author on 14.10.80
3) War diary I./25, loc. cit., 19.6.44
4) Report by Kurt Havemeister to the Author on 18.6.76
5) Report by Franz-Joseph Kneipp to the Author on 31.10.79
6) As 3), list of losses
7) As 3), 12.6.44
8) As 3), 13.6.44
9) War diary 7. Armee, loc. cit., 12.6.44
10) As 9), 13.6.44
11) As 9), 15.5.44
12) As 9), 17.6.44

Chapter 2.8
1) Ritgen, loc. cit., pp. 140/141
2) Diary Divisionsbegleitkompanie, p. 7
3) Report by Leo Freund to the Author on 20.12.72
4) As 2), p. 8
5) Lists of losses

Chapter 2.9
1) Chester Wilmot, loc. cit., p. 332
2) Situation report of the "HJ" Division for 17 and 18 June 1944
3) Situation report, as 2), for 16 June 1944

Chapter 2.10
1) Reports by Siegfried Schneider to the Author on 21.5.79
2) As 1)
3) As 1)

4) Study B-827 by O. Eckstein on the activity by the senior quartermaster west during the period of the preparation to repel the invasion and during the fighting

5) War diary AOK 7, appendix telephone conversations, etc., pp. 36, 39, 47, 50

6) Report "Divisions-Nachschubtruppe 12" (supply troops), Albert Schlüter and comrades to the Author on 12.12.81

7) Report by Emil Maître to the Author on 8.11.71

8) Report by Willi Wagner and comrades to the Author of 13.12.81; report on losses of the Divisionsbegleit-kompanie of 12.6.44 (Missy), and personal report by Dr. med. Karl App (M.D.) to the Author

9) Report by Georg Isecke, loc. cit.

10) Report by Willi Wagner to the Author on 13.12.81

11) Report by Kurt Fischer of 12.6.44

12) Report by Dr. med. Friedrich Zistler to the Author on 2.3.54

13) Report by Walter Schwabe to the Author on 11.5.82

14) Chester Wilmot, loc. cit., p. 336 and following pages

Chapter 3.0

1) War diary Heeresgruppe B, daily reports from 6.6.–31.8.44; assessment of the situation on 11.6.44, Ia No. 3356/44 g.K. of 12.6.44, F/M, inventory RH19/IX 9, part 1

2) As 1), report on the Führer briefing on 17.6., 09.30–12.30 hours, F/M, inventory RH/IX 1

3) Situation map Supreme Command West of 19.6.44, F/M, location Kart RH2W/202, and report from RH2/V 1500

4) War diary 7. Armee, appendices, F/M, inventory RH20-7/135

5) War diary 5. Panzerarmee, F/M, inventory RH21-5/50

6) As 5), 63 181/4, teletype message from Supreme Command West to Panzergruppe West of 21.6.44

7) As 1), operations orders, F/M, inventory RH19/IX 4, pages 23/24. The map mentioned in the letter from the Feldmarschall, and which was to have been attached to it, could not be found in the surviving documents. The map, which was attached to the letter from Panzergruppe West of 26.6.44 to Heeresgruppe B, probably reflects to a large extent Rommel's modified plan

8) War diary Panzergruppe West, appendix 15, page 24 with map, F/M, inventory RH21-5/50

9) War diary Supreme Command West, F/M, inventory RH19TV/48 page 180 and following pages

10) Tac HQ 21 Army Group No. M 502 of 18.6.44

11) As 10), M 504 of 19.6.44

12) War diary 7. Armee, situation of the assembly movement, and Wilhelm Tieke: "Im Feuersturm letzter Kriegsjahre" (inside the fire storm of the last war years), war history of the II. SS-Panzerkorps, Osnabrück 1975
13) War diary 5. Panzerarmee, appendix 12
14) War diary 5. Panzerarmee, 24.6.44 and appendices

Chapter 3.1
1) Reports from I. SS-Panzerkorps of 26.6.44 to Heeresgruppe B, F/M, inventory RH19/IX/3
2) Situation report by 12. SS-Pz.-Div. "HJ", loc. cit., of 24.6.44 and as 1)
3) Operation Orders 49th Infantry Division, 11th -Armoured Division; with reference to Herouvillette, Ellis: "The Battle for Normandy", London 1962, p. 275
4) Situation reports as 2) of 19.6., 20.6., 21.6., 22.6., 23.6., 24.6.44
5) War diary I./25, loc. cit., 22.6.44
6) Letter from Montgomery to "Freddie", Tac HQ 23.6.44, M. Dufresne, loc. cit.
7) Cipher from UNITY DDE/WMR 25 June 1944 to 21st Army Group Supreme Commander. M. Dufresne, loc. cit.

Chapter 3.2
1) 8th Armoured Brigade Group Operation Order No. 26 of 24.6.44— 147th Infantry Brigade O.O. No. 5 of 23.6.44—7th Infantry Brigade Operations Instruction No. 2 of 23.6.44
2) Kamp, T.C.: "A History of the Royal Scots Fusiliers 1919–1959"
3) "Normandy to Arnhem" by Brigadier T. Hart-Dyke
4) As 2)
5) Situation report of the "HJ" Division for 25.6.44, and report by Karl Kugler of May 1954 to the Author
6) Divisional newspaper of the 12. SS-Panzerdivision "Hitlerjugend"— "Panzerpimpfe" (Panzer youths), -series 1 of 9.11.44, copy in the hands of the Author
7) Report by Karl-Heinz Gauch to the Author on 7.11.69
8) Report by Dr. Rolf Jauch to the Author on 6.6.74
9) As 5)
10) War Diary 147th Infantry Brigade
11) Report by Hans Siegel to the Author on 12.11.72
12) As 2)
13) 49th Infantry Division Intelligence Summary No. 12 of 25.6.44
14) As 3)—War Diary 8th Armoured Brigade Group of 25.6.44
15) Lists of losses
16) As 5), and diary of August Zinßmeister, loc. cit.
17) As 5)

18) As 5)

19) War diary AOK 7, Ia, appendices, individual notes, pp. 196/197

20) Supreme Command West, Ia, No. 467/44 g.K. for commanders only of 25.6.44

21) Report by Helmut Schuck to the Author on 11.3.76

Chapter 3.3

1) Martin, H.G.: "History of the 15th Scottish Division 1939–45", Blackwood 1948, p. 29 and following -pages. 11th Armoured Division Operation Order No. 1 of 23.6.1944, War Diary VIII Corps, "EPSOM", p. 2 of 26.6.1944

2) 11th Armoured Division, O.O. No. 2, see above

3) "History of the 15th Scottish Division", see above, p. 32 and following pages

4) Report by Ludwig Ruckdeschel to the Author on 15.11.1973

5) Report by Dr. Rudolf Jauch to the Author on 6.6.1974

6) Panzermeyer: "Grenadiere", loc. cit., pp. 243/244

7) How, J.: "Baptism of Fire", Western Mail, 27.6.1981

8) War Diary 7th Royal Tank Regiment

9) War Diary VIII Corps, p. 4

10) Report By Ernst Behrens to the Author on 6.1.1972

11) Report by Hans Richter, The National Archives of the United States, Microcopy No. T-354, R 154

12) War Diary VIII Corps, p. 3; War Diary 9th Royal Tanks

13) Report by Erwin Wohlgemuth to the Author on 23.2.1975

14) Report by Heinrich Bassenauer to the Author on 23.2.1975

15) Report by Aribert Kalke in April/May 1975 to the Author

16) "Das Schwarze Korps" (the black corps), 9 November 1944

17) Report by Paul Dargel to the Author on 31.10.1979

18) Report by Dr. med. Willi Kändler to the Author on 15.10.1979

19) Report by Max Anger to the Author on 2.7.1975

20) Report by Hans Hartmann to the Author on 28.7.1979

21) War Diary 8th Armoured Brigade of 26.6.1944

22) As 21)

23) Report by Heinz Berner to the Author on 14.1.1980

24) Situation report of 12. SS-Pz.-Div. of 26.6.1944, F/M, loc. cit.

25) War diary AOK 7, appendices, telephone conversations, etc., loc. cit., p. 72 and following pages

26) As 9), p. 4

27) As 9), pp. 4/5; as 3), pp.37/38

28) War Diary 9th Royal Tanks

29) As 24)

30) Diary of Bernhard Georg Meitzel, quoted after a study by H. Meyer, manuscript lost

31) Report by Jochen Leykauff to the Author on 9.9.1979
32) As 3), p. 36; War Diary 6th RSF
33) As 14)
34) As 24)
35) As 21)
36) Report by Hans Siegel of December 1963, copy in the hands of the Author
37) As 11)
38) Report by Hans Richter to the Author on 31.12.1974
38a) Situation report of the 12. SS-Pz.-Div. of 26.6.1944, F/M, loc. cit.
39) Commander report Pz.-Lehr-Div., war diary Heeresgruppe B, appendices, loc. cit.
40) War diary Pz.-Lehr-Div., Ib, appendix 195, appendix 195b, situation report of the 21. Panzerdivision,; otherwise, as 24)
41) Diary Divisionsbegleitkompanie 12, loc. cit.
42) War diary 7. Armee, appendices, telephone conversations, etc., p. 85
43) As 42), pp. 85 and 89
44) As 9), pp. 6/7

Chapter 3.4
1) Letter from Rolf Möbius of 29.11.1976 to the Author
2) War Diary 227th Infantry Brigade from 26.6. to 1.7.1944
3) 49th Division Order No. 8 of 26.6.1944
4) As 2)
5) War Diary 10th Highlanders Light Infantry
6) Report by Hans Siegel of December 1963
7) Ellis, loc. cit., p. 280
8) War Diary 7th Battalion The Royal Tank Regiment
9) 49th Division I.S. No. 14 of 27.6.1944
10) War diary Panzer-Lehr-Division, Ib, appendix 198
11) War Diary 227th Infantry Brigade
12) Diary of August Zinßmeister, copy in the hands of the Author
13) War Diaries of 227th Infantry Brigade and 23rd Hussars
14) Report by Siegfried Schneider, loc. cit., to the Author
15) Report by Dr. Med. Willi Kändler to the Author on 15.10.1979
16) History of the 15th Scottish Division, loc. cit., pp. 40/41
17) As 16)
18) Report by Günther Burdack, Hermann Asbach, Hans-Georg Keßlau, Hans-Werner Bönig, and Strobel of November 1981
19) As 9)
20) Report by Hans-Georg Keßlau of 10.7.1980
21) Divisional order Panzer-Lehr-Division, as 10), appendix 198
22) War diary Heeresgruppe B, daily reports from 6.6. to 31.8.1944, p. 70 and following pages

23) Lists of losses
24) War diary 7. Armee, appendices, p. 242, F/M, RH20-7/135
25) War diary 7. Armee, appendices, telephone conversations, etc. p. 88 and following pages
26) Study by Albert Stückler, P-159
27) As 21)
28) War Diary 8th Armoured Brigade of 27.6.1944
29) As 9), Part II, 3

Chapter 3.5

1) War Diary 23rd Hussars, sheet 2
2) War Diary 2nd Fie & Forfar Yeomanry
3) Report by Dr. med. Willi Kändler to the Author on 15.10.1979
4) Report by Willy Kretzschmar to the Author on 5.11.1979
5) As 3)
6) Report by Heinz Nußbaumer to the Author on 5.7.1976
7) As 3)
8) 11th Armoured Division, Intelligence Summary No. 11, of 28.6.1944, Appendix 3D
9) As 8)
10) As 2)
11) War Diary 20th Armoured Brigade, sheet 9
12) History of the 15th Scottish Division, loc. cit., p. 42 and following pages
13) War Diary VIII Corps, "EPSOM", p. 15
14) As 12)
15) As 12)
16) As 13), p. 18
17) 2nd Battalion The Glasgow Highlanders, France, June–July 1944
18) Taurus Pursuant, History of the 11th Armoured -Division
19) Letters by Mr. J.J. How of 25.10.1976 to the Author, and of 19.2.1976 to Werner Kortenhaus
20) Letters by Albert Frey of 7.7. and 31.10.1976 to the Author, and a personal conversation with Max -Hansen
21) Personal report by Werner Kortenhaus of 11.9.1976
22) History of the 3rd Battalion The Monmouthshire Regiment, J.J. How, pp. 16/17
23) As 21)
24) War Diary 10th Battalion Highland Light Infantry, Intelligence Log
25) As 21)
26) War Diary 4th Armoured Brigade, sheet 17
27) As 26)
28) 49th Division Intelligence Summary No. 15, Part I of 28.6.1944
29) Lists of losses

30) Appendices to the war diary AOK 7, F/M, RH20-7/135, p. 376
31) War diary Panzer AOK 5, former Pz.-Gruppe-West, Ia, part 1, 10.6.–8.8.1944, appendices to supreme command Heeresgruppe B, Ia, No. 4072/44 g.k.
32) As 31), appendix 20
33) War diary 7. Armee, appendices, discussions, etc., pp. 94/95
34) As 33), pp.95 and 98
35) Ellis, loc. cit., p. 281
36) Study by General der Panzertruppen retd. Geyr von Schweppenburg B-258 "Geschichte der Panzergruppe West"

Chapter 3.6
1) War Diary VIII Corps
2) War diary Panzer AOK 5, former Panzer-Gruppe-West, Ia, part 1, 10.6.–8.8.1944; morning report of 29.6.1944
3) As 1)
4) As 1)
5) War Diary 29th Armoured Brigade
6) Report by Willy Kretzschmar to the Author on 5.11.1979
7) As 5), and 11th Armoured Division, Intelligence -Summary No. 12 of 30.6.1944
8) As 2), evening report
9) As 1)
10) Tieke: "Im Feuersturm letzter Kriegsjahre", Osnabrück 1975, loc. cit.
11) 11th Armoured Division, as 7)
12) As 1)
13) As 1)
14) War diary AOK 7, discussions, etc., p. 102
15) As 14), p. 103

Chapter 3.7
1) Report by Dr. med. Willi Kändler to the Author on 15.10.1979
2) Report by Willy Kretzschmar to the Author on 5.11.1979
3) Report by Georg Fugunt of September 1980 to Götz Großjohann, copy in the hands of the Author
4) War Diary VIII Corps and Wilhelm Tieke: "Im Feuersturm letzter Kriegsjahre", loc. cit.
5) War diary Panzer AOK 7, loc. cit., appendix 26
6) War Diary VIII Corps
7) Lists of losses
8) Report by Monsieur P. to the Author on 8.5.1975
9) War diary 7. Armee, appendices, discussions, etc., loc. cit., p. 90
10) "Die Waffen-SS im Wehrmachtsbericht" (Waffen-SS in the Wehrmacht Report), Osnabrück 1971

11) Submission for awarding the Knights' Cross with Oak Leaves to Obersturmbannführer Wünsche of 1.7.1944, copy from the collection of Jost W. Schneider
12) Chester Wilmot: "Der Kampf für Europa", loc. cit., p. 359

Chapter 4.0
1) F/M, RH2/ v. 1500
2) War diary Supreme Command West, appendices, p. 260
3) War diary Heeresgruppe B, Ia operation orders, Ia No. 3960/44 g.k. chiefs only
4) Situation map Supreme Command West of 26.6.1944, F/M Kart RH2 W/203
5) War diary Heeresgruppe B, appendices, Major i.G. Wolfram, report on the journey by Supreme Commander Heeresgruppe B to the briefing at Führer headquarters on 29.6.1944, 18.00 hours
6) War diary Panzergruppe West, appendix 38
7) As 6), appendix 48
8) War diary AOK 7, telephone conversations and discussions, etc., from 6.6. to 30.6.44, p. 105
9) As 3), operation orders from 1.7. to 27.7.1944, p. 107, F/M, RH19 IX/4
10) War diary Panzergruppe West Ia from 10.6. to 8.8.1944

Chapter 4.1
1) Reports by Richard Rudolf and Ernst Haase of 30.1. and 10.3.1977
2) War diary Heeresgruppe B, daily reports from 6.6. to 31.8.1944, F/M, RH19 IX/9
3) Stacy, loc. cit., p. 153
4) McKee, Alexander: "Caen, Anvil of Victory", loc. cit., p. 213
5) As 3)
6) War diary Supreme Command West, appendices, orders and reports from 1.7. to 10.7.1044, as well as daily report of 2.7.1944
7) Report by Heinz Förster to the Author on 3.5.1979
8) Report by Alois Hartung to Heinrich Bassenauer, according to a letter of 20.1.1978 to the Author
9) Report by Gerhard Amler to the Author on 21.6.1979
10) Ellis, loc. cit., p. 309
11) Information from Kurt Göricke to the Author
12) As 3), p. 154
13) As 4), p. 208
14) Report by Karl-Heinz Wambach to the Author on 20.1.1974
15) As 4), p. 212
16) As 3), pp. 154/155
17) As 1)

18) Report by Aribert Kalke to the Author on 1.12.1968
19) Report by Erich Wohlgemut to the Author on 30.5.1972
20) Report by Herbert Kraft to the Author on 16.9.1976
21) Report by Oswald Beck to the Author on 30.11.1970
22) Report by Herbert Engemann to the Author on 21.4.1976
23) As 7)
24) War diary Heeresgruppe West Ia from 10.6. to 8.8.1944
25) As 3), p. 155
26) As 22)
27) Report by Gerhard Franz to the Author on 1.8.1971; it is probable that 1. and 3. Kompanies of SS-Pz.-Gren.Rgt. 1 were temporarily assigned to III. Bataillon, since it was not yet fully assembled
28) As 4), p. 214
29) Lists of losses
30) As 3), p. 155
31) verbal report by Johann Niemeyer to the Author on 20.11.1979

Chapter 4.2
1) War diary Supreme Command West Ia, appendices, orders and reports of 5.7.1944
2) War diary Panzergruppe West Ia, appendix 65
3) Map entries by Dr. Rudolf Fend of 26.8.1977
4) Reports by Kurt Göricke of 6.10.1980 and Johann G. Niemeyer of 20.11.1979 to the Author
5) As 2), appendix 79
6) Ellis, loc. cit., p. 311
7) Stacy, loc. cit., p. 160
8) As 6), pp. 312/313
9) 50th Infantry Division O.O. No. 1 of 6.7.1944
10) As 7)
11) As 6)
12) As 9)
13) War diary I./25, loc. cit., F/M
14) Morning report I./25 of 7.7.1944, individual files, F/M
15) I./25, individual files, F/M
16) As 6)
17) Letter from Hans-Joachim Heinemann of 13.2.1978 to the Author
18) Report by Leo Freund to the Author on 20.12.1972
19) Prof. Henri Containe: "Souvenirs Civils sur la Bataille de Caen", quoted after Stacy, pp. 158 and 160
20) As 7), p. 158
21) As 7), p. 160
22) War Diary 50th Infantry Division, I.S. No. 1 of 8.7.1944, and as 9)
23) War Diary 2/6 South Staffordshire Regiment of 8.7.1944

24) Report by Kurt Havemeister to the Author on 10.8.1980
25) War Diary 59th Infantry Division of 8.7.1944
26) As 9)
27) As 9)
28) As 25)
29) As 23)
30) As 25)
31) War Diary 1/7 Warwickshire Regiment of 8.7.1944
32) As 25)
33) As 31)
34) Report by Dr. Willi Kändler to the Author on 1.1.1980
35) Panzermeyer, loc. cit., p. 261
36) War Diary The Stormont, Dundas and Glengarry Highlanders of 8.7.1944
37) "1st Battalion The Highland Light Infantry of Canada 1940–1945", Ontario 1951
38) War Diary The Highland Light Infantry of Canada of 8.7.1944
39) Among others, a field post letter from Helmut -Schmieding
40) War diary Panzergruppe West Ia of 8.7.1944
41) As 40)
42) As 36)
43) History of 3. Kompanie, SS-Panzerregiment 12, loc. cit.
44) As 35), pp. 265/266
45) As 43)
46) War diary 2/5 LF of 7.8.1944
47) As 25)
48) As 40)
49) War Diary First Battalion The Canadian Scottish -Regiment of 8.7.1944
50) As 25), and War Diary East Riding Yeomanry of 8.7.1944
51) As 7), p. 162
52) Report by F. to the Author on 27.2.1976
53) Report by Erich Köpke
54) Report by Siegfried Bleich to the Author on 8.7.1974
55) Letter from Herbert Stengel of 15.7.1944 to Horst Henze, copy in the hands of the Author
56) As 24)
57) Report by Paul Hinsberger to the Author on 24.10.1975
58) As 35), p. 268
59) As 38)
60) War diaries of the units named, and as 7), p. 161, and as 6), p. 314
61) Lists of losses
62) As 2), appendix 87
63) As 25)

64) "Assault Division" by Norman Scarfe, Collins 1947, p. 113
65) War Diary North Nova Scotia Highlanders of 9.7.1944
66) Report by Dr. Rudolf Fend to the Author
67) War diary of the Divisionsbegleitkompanie, loc. cit., pp. 11/12
68) Report by Hermann Asbach to the Author on 14.11.1975
69) Report by Leo Freund in 67)
70) Lists of Losses
71) War Diary 43rd Infantry Division of 10.7.1944
72) As 71)
73) As 71), and Ellis, loc. cit., p. 317
74) As 34)
75) War Diary 4th Battalion The Dorsetshire Regiment of 10.7.1944
76) Wilhelm Tieke: "Im Feuersturm letzter Kriegsjahre", Osnabrück 1975, p. 153
77) As 1), daily reports of 11. and 12.7.1944
78) As 1), note on the visit to the front by Feldmarschall von Kluge, of 14.7.1944

Chapter 4.3

1) Letter by General Eisenhower to General -Montgomery of 7.7.1944, Public Records Office, London
2) Letter by Air Marshal Sir T.L. Leigh-Mallory to General Montgomery of 29.3.1944, see above
3) Letter by General Montgomery to General -Eisenhower of 8.7.1944, M 508, see above
4) Chester Wilmot, loc. cit., p. 381
5) War diary Panzergruppe West, appendices

Chapter 5.1

1) Studies B-256 and B-528 by Generalleutnant Dann-hauser "Einsatz der 271. Infanteriedivision" (action by the 271. Infanteriedivision) and "Nachtrag zur Studie 256" (supplement to study 256) of 1.10.1946 and 8.5.1947, Research Institute for Military History, Freiburg, Germany, (MH)
2) Comment by Generalleutnant Max Pemsel on the work by Dannhauser, part I, with addendum of 13.5.1947, MH
3) Letter by Kurt Göricke to the Author of 6.10.1980
4) Personal report by Heinrich Bassenauer to the Author on 29.10.1978
5) War diary Panzergruppe West Ia, appendices of 10.6.–8.8.1944, F/M
6) As 5), daily report of 17.7.1944, F/M
7) Letter by Eberhard Köpke to H., copy in the hands of the Author
8) Kompanie list 3./25 of 13.7.1944, individual files I./25, F/M

Chapter 5.2

1) General Montgomery, Directive No. M 505 of 30.6.1944, quoted after Michel Dufresne, loc. cit.
2) Montgomery: Notes on Second Army Operations 16–18 July 1944, Public Records Office, London
3) Draft of the history of the 21. Panzerdivision by Werner Kortenhaus, and notes by Oberst von Luck
4) Chester Wilmot, loc. cit., pp. 374/375
5) Report by Kurt Göricke to the Author on 6.10.80
6) War diary Panzergruppe West. loc. cit., F/M
7) War diary Supreme Command West, appendices -reports and orders from 11.7.–20.7.44, F/M
8) As 6), appendices, addendum to the daily report of 17.7.44, F/M
9) Letter by Harry Wontorra to the Author of 12.11.78
10) As 8)
11) Panzermeyer: "Grenadiere", loc. cit., p. 272
12) As 7)
13) As 7)
14) Terrain Study for Normandy NORTHAG
15) Stacy, loc. cit., p. 169
16) General der Flakinfanterie retd. W. Pickert in: -Wehrkunde (defense science), 3/54, p. 169
17) As 15), pp. 169/170
18) As 15)
19) As 15), p. 171
20) As 3)
21) As 4), pp. 377/378
22) As 15), p. 173
23) As 6)
24) Guards Armoured Division Intelligence Summary No. 10 of 18.7.44
25) As 6)
26) As 7), and map by Wontorra
27) Report by Horst Borgsmüller to the Author on 28.1.80
28) War Diary Guards Armoured Division Sitrep of 19.7.44, and as 4), p. 378
29) As 28), Sitrep of 19.7.44
30) Notes by Helmut Zeiner and report by Dr. Willi -Kändler
31) As 3)
32) War diary Supreme Command West, appendices, etc., of 21.7.44, F/M
33) Statement by Feldmarschall von Rundstedt as a witness for the defense in the case against the OKW 1946/47
34) Topsec Cipher Message D/5/23 of 23.7.44, M. -Dufresne, loc. cit.
35) General Montgomery Directive No. M 512, M. -Dufresne, loc. cit.

36) As 6)
37) As 28), of 21.7.44
38) Letter from A.H. Southam of 16.2.78 to the Author
39) Letter from Eberhard Köpke to "Hermann" of 7.10.46, copy in the hands of the Author
40) As 6) of 23.7.44
41) As 7) from 21.–31.7.44
42) As 41), daily reports from 24.–29.7.44
43) War diary Panzergruppe West, appendix 249, F/M
44) Lists of losses
45) As 3)
46) War diary Supreme Command West, appendices, etc., from 1.–10.8.44, F/M
47) As 43), appendix 158
48) As 32) F/M
49) Twelfth Army Group (US), Letter of Instructions No. 1, Annex 2 of 29.7.44

Chapter 5.3
1) War diary Panzergruppe West Ia, 10.6.–8.8.44, appendices, addendum to the daily report of 2.8.44, according to the list of losses, not 10./26 but 9./26
2) Order by II. SS-Panzerkorps of 1.8.44, after Tieke, loc. cit., p. 205
3) Report by Major J.J. How to the Author on 7.11.77 to the Author; also, see his book: "Normandy: The British Breakout", London 1981
4) Tieke, loc. cit., pp. 216/217
5) As 3)
6) Report by Karl Bassler to the Author on 1.1.76
7) As 3)
8) As 4), daily report 9. SS-Panzerdivision
9) As 3), and 4), pp. 220/221
10) As 3)
11) As 4), p. 223; list of losses III./26; as 3)
12) As 3)
13) As 6)
14) War diary Panzergruppe West Ia, from 10.6. to 8.8.44, 16.45 hours

About Hubert Meyer

Born in 1913 in Berlin.

Graduated from secondary school in 1913, studied chemistry during summer semesters from 1932 until 1934, passed basic exam.

Joined Regiment "Deutschland" of the SS-Verfügungstruppe (Special Disposal Troops) in August 1934.

In 1936-37 attended the third course at the officer cadet school (war school) Bad Tölz, graduated.

Transferred to the position of Zug (platoon) leader in the 10. Kompanie (company) of the Leibstandarte on 1 May 1937.

Participated in the Polish Campaign from 1 to 29 September 1939 as Zug leader in the 10. Kompanie of the Leibstandarte.

Participated in the Western Campaign from 10 May to 24 June 1940 as the adjutant of III. Bataillon of the Leibstandarte.

Participated in the Balkan Campaign in Yugoslavia and Greece from 6 to 30 April 1941 as company chief of the 12. Kompanie of the Leibstandarte. Participated in the Russian Campaign 1941/42 from 2 July to 8 August 1941 as company chief, as previously—wounded for the first time—and from 20 November 1941 to July 1942 as company chief, as previously. Transferred to the artillery regiment of the Leibstandarte for preliminary general staff training.

Participated in the battles for Charkow from 22 January to 9 March 1943 as Hauptmann (captain) at the staff of the 1. Regiment of the Leibstandarte and as leader of the III. Bataillon of the 1. Regiment—wounded for the second time; transferred to the Divisional staff.

Attended the tenth war course at the war academy of the Heer (army) from 15 June to 30 September 1943, achieved qualification for the position of first general staff officer of a Panzer (tank) division.

From 1 October 1943 to 8 May 1945, first general staff officer of the 12. SS-Panzerdivision "Hitlerjugend"—from 7 September to 31 October 1944, simultaneously, acting Divisional commander.

From 8 May 1945 to 8 April 1948, captivity and internment by the Americans.

Index

Index